D1196944

M. C. O'Brien
102 Neff Ave.
Masontown, Pa.

EDUCATIONAL PSYCHOLOGY

Arden N. Frandsen
UTAH STATE UNIVERSITY

EDUCATIONAL PSYCHOLOGY

*The principles
of learning
in teaching*

McGraw-Hill BOOK COMPANY, INC. *1961*

New York Toronto London

EDUCATIONAL PSYCHOLOGY

Library of Congress Catalog Card Number: 61–11387

21798

*This book has been set in Linotype Caledonia,
a contemporary type face designed by W. A. Dwiggins.
Heads are in Gothic No. 20 and italic Caledonia Bold.
The picture editor is Gabriele Wunderlich;
the lithographic drawings are by Irwin Rosenhouse;
and Robin King and Denny McMains made the graphs and charts.*

PREFACE

Teachers in modern schools, whether elementary or secondary, are often amazed at children's eagerness to learn, at their creative problem solving, persistent efforts in self-improvement, and their academic, athletic, and artistic accomplishments. And teachers, being curious and scientifically oriented, often wonder *why* and *how* children learn and under what conditions they might learn even more effectively. They also wonder why some of their pupils do not learn, why they do not want to learn, or why they cannot learn. Although we do not know all the answers to these questions, we do know some of them. We know that certain basic psychological principles underlie the learning process. And we know that if these principles are imaginatively applied in the classroom, laboratory, or shop, on the playground or ball field, or in any learning situation—they will produce positive results.

In this *Educational Psychology,* I have tried to introduce the prospective elementary or high school teacher to these principles of learning and show how they can be applied in effective teaching. To achieve this aim, I have drawn upon two rich sources of information. First there are the reports of hundreds of psychologists who, during the past half century, have done a vast amount of research in the broad field of learning. Then there are the published or firsthand reports of many teachers who have had practical experience in guiding the learning of children and youth.

Without oversimplifying the subject, I have sought to present those insights which teachers need in order to understand the psychological principles of learning and apply them in their teaching. By meaningful organization of the book as a whole and by generous use of pertinent classroom illustrations, I have tried to make these principles easy to master, remember, and apply. The concepts of educational psychology are organized around the major functions of teaching and the conditions that have been found essential to effective learning. Thus organized, these concepts offer an integrated explanation of how we learn and a practical guide for teachers in providing the conditions of effective learning in their classrooms. I hope that this volume may stimulate resourceful teachers to improve their already established teaching methods and encourage them to invent new and more effective procedures.

The first major function of teaching is to set up educational goals. Then we can select and organize an appropriate curriculum in order to meet these goals. In practice, we find that this curriculum must be adapted to the needs of children at varied levels of readiness for learning and with widely different patterns of abilities. After the curriculum is adapted to individual needs, we must still guide the children in their mastery of academic concepts and skills. We must also foster their mental health and social development. Finally, as a check on the effectiveness of all our efforts, we must continuously evaluate the children's progress toward attaining important educational objectives. Prospective teachers will naturally ask how educational psychology can help them to understand and carry out these major functions of teaching. It is the purpose of this book to answer that question.

In Part 1, we have an overview of what children learn in a modern school and how they learn it. The modern school, as we find in Chapter 1, aspires to excellence in the full educational development of children and youth. It does so in the interest of the individual's self-realization and his effectiveness in society. The modern school is concerned with mastery of the significant concepts and skills of our social heritage. It also emphasizes the goals of learning how to learn, initiative and competency in problem solving, and creative productivity. Teachers, in their efforts to lead children toward these goals, are guided by various psychological principles. These principles help them to develop more efficient ways of learning. They help teachers shift emphasis from directive teaching to guiding their pupils in self-discovery learning.

The major theories of learning are considered in Chapter 2. From considering them all, we develop an integrated explanation of how we learn and determine what conditions are essential for effective learning.

Part 2 introduces the children we teach and the marked individual differences among them. In Chapter 3 we learn that appropriate readiness is an essential preliminary condition of effective learning. We learn how to recognize the emerging signs of readiness for beginning or taking a next step in a learning activity. Chapter 4 describes the ways of appraising children's developing abilities and differentiating talents. And in Chapter 5 we discuss ways of teaching in groups a wide range of uniquely different individuals.

In Part 3, comprised of Chapters 6 through 11, we deal directly with the dynamic processes of learning—with motivation, structuring approaches to problems, the trial-and-check process in learning, efficient mastery of concepts and skills, sustained retention—and adaptive applications of them. In harmony with the modern goals of education, we emphasize teacher guidance of children's self-discovery learning, development of efficient modes of attack, cultivation of resourcefulness, and effective and creative problem solving.

Part 4 considers the teacher's role in fostering healthy emotional and social development. These aspects of development are important both for the sake of the children and as essential conditions of learning. In Chapter 12 we shall discuss emotional maladjustment as a factor that frequently impairs intellectual efficiency, and mental health as a factor that facilitates achievement. The several ways in which teachers can guide children toward better mental health are described in Chapter 13. Chapter 14 shows how the interpersonal relations of the classroom may be utilized to foster healthy self- and social development.

Because learning—both academic and social—is a trial-and-check process, effective guidance of children's learning requires continual evaluations of progress. Procedures for appraising progress in personal-social learning are described in appropriate places throughout the book. Part 5 presents the general principles of measurement and a variety of procedures for appraising the attainment of academic objectives. As we shall learn in Chapter 15, periodic evaluations of progress contribute to every other teaching function. By apprising both the pupil and the teacher of current achievement, such periodic evaluations guide and facilitate future learning.

The writing of a scientific professional book is an ambitious project. Fortunately, the task need not be accomplished singlehanded. As the numerous references, graphs, pictures, drawings, and case studies of school children show, hundreds of people and many agencies have contributed significantly to the production of this textbook in educational psychology. For these indispensable contributions, I am deeply grateful. The specific contributions of authors and publishers are acknowledged in bracketed, end-of-book references and the source of each picture is mentioned under it.

The observations of the children and youth in their classrooms—those I have been privileged to make personally and many others generously contributed by my students—are acknowledged only in general. Although I value very highly the enrichment which these case studies give to the principles of learning in teaching, it seems advisable, as an added precaution in keeping the children anonymous, to omit references to the specific contributors of the "studies" as they are presented in the text, with some modifications from the originals. Among many other contributors to my acquaintance with classroom activities, however, I am happy to acknowledge the more substantial contributions of case studies and descriptions of classroom activities of the following teachers and students as a group: Donald Barber, Robert Beede, Genevieve Bylinowski, Genae Ericksen, Phyllis Frandsen, Dollie Gallagher, William T. Gilkey, Ruth Boyd Gustafson, Arlen Hagen, Annette Hansen, Eva C. Honn, Allan Laidlow, James F. Mick, Ivan Pederson, Kenneth E. Robbins, Francine Wiggins, Julia Whitney, and Faye Williams.

Arden N. Frandsen

CONTENTS

Part 1

TEACHING AND LEARNING
IN THE MODERN SCHOOL

Chapter 1

EDUCATIONAL PSYCHOLOGY
IN THE MODERN SCHOOL

Teachers and prospective teachers naturally wish to enhance their understanding of children and youth, and to become more effective in providing pupils with the guidance needed for effective learning. The study of educational psychology can help them do so. The twofold purpose of this science is, in fact, to develop and apply psychological principles in the interests of better teaching.

Educational psychologists have much to offer, because they have extensive resources at their disposal. In their research, they "have access to children of all ages and ability groups in ongoing 'complete' learning situations [18]." In developing their underlying principles of teaching, they draw upon every field of psychology, especially the fields of learning, child and adolescent development, social psychology, individual differences, and mental health. From these fields they have, as we shall see, developed principles that are applicable to all the major functions of teaching.

3

Educational needs and educational theories change with the changes in society. In order to contribute more meaningfully to current needs, educational psychologists must always reexamine their principles and adapt their concepts to the changes that are taking place. Since it is our aim to put psychological concepts to work in the interests of more effective teaching, we should take a look at the needs, objectives, and curricula of the modern school.

First, however, let us look back for a moment at the historical background of present-day social patterns [30]. In the colonial period (1647–1776) of our history, when religious activities were emphasized, the curriculum for school children consisted of reading, writing, spelling, arithmetic, the catechism, prayers, and singing of hymns, plus severe moral discipline. As our society evolved, our needs changed. In the national period (1776–1876), Americans were inspired by political ideals such as those expressed in the Declaration of Independence. These political ideas influenced educational objectives, and the universal development of intelligent and effective citizens became a dominant purpose of our schools. During the period of expansion and reform (1876–1929), when the emphasis was upon efficiency and economic goals, the curriculum was further expanded. Our schools sought to teach as much practical knowledge as possible. From 1929 to the present, the curriculum has come to reflect more closely the contemporary scientific, industrial, and democratic features of our society. Now our pressing concern with international affairs, the development of nuclear energy, the exploration of outer space, and our need for intensified scientific study of all our resources, including man himself, have heightened our interest in education for scientific efficiency [35].

These changes in society have instigated basic changes in educational theory. Some of these latter changes have involved the question of what to teach. It is impossible to construct a curriculum that embraces *all* useful knowledge. We have therefore seen the development of the elective system, wherein high school and college students are permitted to select certain courses from among many alternatives. Today some educators believe that this choosing of some courses and ignoring of others tends to leave "chasms of ignorance between." On the other hand, our last thirty years of experimentation with survey courses covering *all* the "essential" concepts and skills have seemed to lead to "specialization in superficialities [5]." We cannot achieve an "encyclopedic coverage of knowledge," nor can we predict exactly what specific knowledge we shall need in the future. We have thus been forced to reorient our thinking. We are beginning to recognize that learning how to learn and how to solve problems is more important than merely accumulating a store of knowledge. Difficult, novel problems, for which there can be no adequate prepared-in-advance and remembered solutions, present themselves to individuals day by day. For these problems we need backgrounds of information—information that has been functionally organized; but we also need an effective, creative approach to problems [13]. Therefore, in educating our children for citizenship in the new age, we are not trying to prepare them for sharply prescribed roles. We are not attempting to develop the "socially adaptable man, the technically proficient man, or even the scientific man." Our paramount educational aim is to develop man's creative powers for constructive service in society [8, p. 21].

This concept of education, far from blueprinting and stereotyping the education of children and youth, aims at developing independence and versatility. The modern school, rather than aiming only at the mastery of comprehensive arrays of facts, emphasizes learning how to learn, resourcefulness in using the sources of knowledge, ability to do creative problem solving and to function effectively—both personally and socially. As Buswell has remarked, the graduate of such a school might say: "There are many things I do not know and many skills I do not have, but I know how to get them; I know how to learn what needs to be learned [5, p. 180]." Teachers who accept such a theory of education can implement it by giving their students guidance in self-discovery learning, in constructive problem solving, and in exercising their curiosity and creativity.

The challenge: to provide a better education for all children. How do we meet the challenge?

Kindergarten: expanding social horizons

Special classes for deaf—and other handicapped—children

Stimulating classrooms and imaginative teachers

Enriched curricular and extracurricular activities

scientists, scholars—citizens all

*Maximum
intellectual
development—
mathematicians,
engineers . . .*

Prevocational training

In harmony with the goal of developing independence and versatility in children and youth, the teacher's role in the modern school is becoming less stereotyped and more creative. Professional teaching is now conceived as involving continuous growth in the understanding of children, of subject matter, of society itself—and of how to provide the conditions of effective learning in a wide variety of settings. It is more than the routine application of specific "methods" of teaching reading, art, science, or other subjects. In a continuing trial-and-check process, creative teachers develop, try out, and evaluate more promising procedures for guiding children's learning. And educational psychology, as the basic science of education, helps teachers to invent new teaching hypotheses and suggests ways of appraising their effectiveness.

Scientific, psychological studies of education—made mainly during the last half century—have yielded a store of useful facts and principles. There are several ways in which we might organize these concepts, but the most helpful way is to consider them in relation to the major functions of teaching.

THE MAJOR FUNCTIONS OF TEACHING

The six major functions of teaching may be defined as (1) setting educational goals; (2) arranging a curriculum to achieve these goals; (3) adapting the curriculum to children's varied levels of readiness and different patterns of abilities; (4) providing the conditions for effective learning, retention, and application; (5) fostering healthy emotional and social development; and (6) making periodic or continuous evaluations of children's progress toward their educational goals.

From psychological studies of education, we have learned how to define educational objectives that are attainable, and how to relate curriculum content to these objectives. We have discovered the wide range of inter- and intraindividual differences among children; and we have worked out some practical ways of adjusting instructional programs to these differences. We have gained some understanding of how we learn and of the conditions of effective learning. Further, we have found in these studies that mental health and constructive social behavior are necessary, both for the student's academic achievement and for his self-realization and social effectiveness. We have expanded our educational objectives to include these important aspects of development. And, finally, we have learned how to measure growth or changes in children's abilities, knowledge, skills, attitudes, interests, and actions. Thus we are able to measure the readiness of children and youth for "next steps" in learning and their progress toward educational objectives.

Throughout this first chapter, we shall undertake to present a brief overview[1] of the first two functions of teaching; and then in future chapters we shall elaborate the other four more thoroughly. In seeking to establish a working concept of the aims of the school, the teacher asks: "What are the objectives toward which elementary or secondary school children should strive?" Having achieved a tentative answer, or an approach to an evolving answer, the teacher next determines the kinds of learning activities or curriculum experiences by which these objectives can best be attained. Let us consider now the first of these problems.

OBJECTIVES OF THE MODERN SCHOOL

Modern education is concerned with the welfare of both the individual and society. As teachers, we strive to develop the constructive potentialities of every individual as fully as possible. And, at the same time, we aim to preserve and enhance the conditions of constructive living in society. In attaining these objectives, we turn to the accumulated and continually expanding knowledge which makes up our cultural heritage, and we find it rich in curriculum resources. Because of this combination of goal-curriculum factors, the modern school is not exclusively child-centered, community-centered, or subject-matter-centered. It is subject-child-community-centered.

When we seek to formulate the general aims of an education that considers the *individual* in his *society*, we encounter four broad principles:

1. To attain self-realization, the individual should achieve an inquiring mind; skills for effective communication; knowledge for maintaining, protecting, and improving his health and for satisfying intellectual, recreational, and aesthetic interests and skills; and ethical character. (The other parts of the formulation are concerned with both self-realization and social effectiveness.)

2. The individual should achieve comfortable, useful, and happy social relationships in his family, with friends, and with other people at work and play. He should develop respect for humanity in general.

3. He should attain economic efficiency by becoming an intelligent consumer and by preparing for efficient work performance in a field suited to his talents and interests and to the needs of his society.

4. He should develop civic responsibility, which involves a sense of social justice, an understanding of his society, participation as a citizen, tolerance, interest in conservation, and devotion to the ideals of democracy [34].

[1] The aims and curriculum of the modern school are treated extensively in other courses and in separate books devoted especially to them.

In the laboratory-classrooms of the modern elementary school, children acquire the basic learning skills and understanding of their natural and social world. (Science Materials Center, New York; photograph by Wallace Litwin.)

In summarizing the "ultimate goals of education," Findley says that elementary, secondary, and college level schools should "look to the development of a community of individuals enjoying an increasingly satisfying, constructive way of life [15]." This involves, as the above statement also implies, attainment of intellectual proficiency, occupational competency, effective group participation and leadership, satisfying family life, constructive aesthetic and leisure interests, health, and a confident, reassuring concept of personal worth.

These are general orientations to the aims of education. Let us also examine the specific objectives for elementary and secondary school children.

Elementary school objectives. Kearney's report includes nearly two thousand different objectives contributed by specialists in elementary education and child development and evaluated as appropriate by successful classroom teachers and supervisors. Besides being guided by the general goals of elementary education, the specialists tried to formulate objectives which are attainable and observable, and thus can be measured and evaluated.

Kearney has classified these objectives according to nine curriculum areas in which children develop continuously throughout the elementary and junior high school levels [22, p. 40]. These areas are as follows:

1. *Physical development, health, and body care,* including individual health, elementary aspects of public health, safety, physical education, grooming, and understanding of growth.

2. *Individual social and emotional development,* including mental health, emotional stability, growth of personality, and self-understanding and evaluation.

3. *Ethical behavior, standards, and values,* including observance

of moral and civil laws, observance of the customs and mores of the culture, and the development of such characteristics as sportsmanship, kindliness, and helpfulness.

4. *Social relations,* a category which grows out of the preceding two and is "devoted to the individual as a person in his personal-social relations with others with whom he associates in home, community, and place of work."

5. *The social world,* which considers the behavior of the child in relation to the broader social setting of community, state, and nation and includes geography, civics, economics, government, and the traditional American way of life.

6. *The natural environment,* as revealed by the physical and biological sciences, which emphasize learning to think scientifically and the use of scientific methods both as scientists and for solving problems in everyday living.

7. *Aesthetic development,* including both appreciation of the arts and personal participation in art, music, crafts, and other creative activities.

8. *Communication,* including an understanding of the language, effective use of language skills in reading, handwriting, composition, usage, spelling, punctuation, speaking, and listening.

9. *Quantitative relationships,* consisting mainly of arithmetic, including understanding our number system, knowledge of how it is widely used in solving quantitative problems in society, and the development of problem-solving skills.

Within each of these nine broad and interrelated curriculum areas, objectives are further classified as indicative of four "types of behavioral change": (1) *knowledge and understandings,* which would include the objective of learning "how to use the table of contents of a book"; (2) *skills and competencies,* under which we would place such objectives as "skill in attacking unfamiliar words"; (3) *attitudes and interests,* under which we would include "enjoyment of a wide variety of reading materials"; and (4) *action patterns* which "refer to broad generalized ways of behaving, such as ways of responding to problem situations through the union of intelligence with good working habits and scientific methods of thinking."

Although limitations of space prevent our undertaking a more thorough consideration of Kearney's report, teachers of elementary and junior high school pupils will find in the report itself a detailed and comprehensive guide to curriculum planning.

Secondary school objectives. Modern secondary education attempts to prepare all youth for effective citizenship in our increasingly complex society, to provide some of them with the basic skills needed for entering some kind of useful work, and to provide others with the basis for advanced professional training in college and graduate school.

Lists of specific behavioral goals for high school students have been formulated by committees of educators, teachers, curriculum specialists, psychologists, and interested citizens. In a report prepared by French [17], the behavioral goals are set forth in a four-by-three table, which includes four "areas of behavioral competence" and three "directions of growth" involved in achieving maturity (to completion of the twelfth grade). The four areas of competence are (1) maximum intellectual growth; (2) cultural orientation and integration for participation in social, cultural, ethical, and aesthetic experiences; (3) improvement and maintenance of physical and mental health; and (4) economic competence through wise choice of and beginning preparation for work and a disposition to safeguard our natural and human resources.

The three directions of growth are (1) toward self-realization; (2) toward desirable interpersonal relations with family, school friends, and members of community groups; and (3) toward effective membership or leadership in large religious, cultural, social, political, and economic groups.

The twelve area-by-direction cells in the table include the following direction areas [17]:

1.1. Growth toward intellectual self-realization by developing effective study skills, intellectual curiosity and industry, independence in learning, life-time interests in learning, effectiveness and taste in communication of ideas, command of quantitative thinking, artistic and literary tastes and some creative competence, and effectiveness in problem solving.

1.2. Growth toward cultural orientation and integration: by developing the characteristics and understanding of the good citizen, as illustrated by such behavior as "accepts democracy as a form of government and as a way of life"; "a perspective on present-day events, cultures, and conditions"; a scientific orientation toward the physical world—including growth in ability to apply scientific facts and principles; effective application of ethical values to his own decisions and behavior; and aesthetic and artistic appreciations.

1.3 Growth toward personal mental and physical health: by developing self-understanding, emotional stability, and acceptance of health and safety practices.

1.4. Growth toward economic understanding and independence: by beginning an intelligent choice of life work (in terms of understanding of one's talents, interests, and opportunities); preparing for efficient work through some work experience; becoming a more intelligent and economical consumer; and achieving understanding of our national economic life.

2.1. Intellectual growth toward desirable interpersonal relations in small groups: by developing acceptable family membership, friendship relations, effective role participation in small, organized groups—such as "Uses his background of knowledge and understanding of democracy in participating in organized school-group activities (student government, club, and class affairs)."

2.2. Growth toward cultural orientation and integration in small groups: by recognizing the importance of the family and of cultural and intellectual activities within the family; by adopting cultural and social amenities in small-group interpersonal relations; and by effective and democratic junior participation in religious, civic, and political activities.

2.3. Growth toward maintenance of health and safety in small groups: by contributing to physical and mental health and safety in the home, small peer groups, and in school and community—such as "Conforming to the safety and health rules for use of public parks, beaches, playgrounds, and other community recreational facilities [17, p. 162]."

2.4. Growth toward economic competence and independence in small groups: by intelligent cooperation in family financial matters; by becoming a responsible and effective member of work groups; and by "manifesting interest and participation in the economic affairs of the community [17, p. 169]."

3.1. Intellectual growth as a member of large social organizations: by following and studying national and world problems; by identifying —as a "junior member"—with large organizations interested in cultural, social, economic, and political affairs; and by "intelligent appreciation and support of democratic goals and principles of American cultural, social, and political traditions [17, p. 182]."

3.2. Growth toward world cultural orientation and integration: by viewing national and world events in the light of their historic and cultural pasts, by developing a cultural background, and by seeing vocational activities in their cultural settings.

3.3. Growth in recognition of and participation in physical and mental health improvement activities as world problems: by supporting world-wide health organizations; by developing understanding and interested support of the roles of research and political action in solving public health and safety problems; and by developing interest in and support of programs to improve the health of the handicapped.

3.4. Growth toward intelligent economic participation in large political, economic, and industrial organizations by recognizing the "economic interdependence of the peoples of the world"; by supporting organizations designed for conservation of human and natural resources; by understanding the need for government regulatory activities in economic matters; and by sensing the problems of maintaining and expanding our economic system.

These summary statements, as paraphrased above, indicate rather clearly the general goals toward which we must aim, but for guidance in day-to-day curriculum planning, the high school teacher will find much of value in the detailed statement of objectives set forth in French's report.

THE CURRICULUM OF THE MODERN SCHOOL

From our discussion and study of the first function of teaching—the setting of educational goals—we have gained a working concept of the general and specific objectives of the elementary and secondary schools. The teacher's next function is to provide a curriculum for the attainment of these goals. The curriculum includes not only specific subject matter, but *all* the learning experiences from which the desired behavioral goals or understandings, skills, attitudes, interests, and action patterns are to be achieved. The content of such a curriculum is partially implied in the foregoing statements of aims.

Elementary school subjects. Modern educational objectives still justify the study of school subjects that became a part of the curriculum in the colonial period of American education and have since been expanded to suit our current needs. Both for self-realization and for playing his role in democratic society, the child needs training in communication activities—reading, oral and written expression, listening, handwriting, and spelling. He needs arithmetic understanding, computational skills, and problem-solving competency for many personal and social functions. To understand and participate in his social world, he needs to develop some broad and organized concepts about how his world has evolved. He can derive these concepts from the study of history, geography, civics, sociology, economics, vocations, and biography—all of which constitute the social studies curriculum of the elementary school. For effective personal and social adaptation to life, he needs a scientific understanding of his natural environment. He needs functional knowledge of the physical and biological sciences, including knowledge of plants, animals, the earth, astronomy, agriculture, industry, the achievements of science in the enrichment of life, and the scientific method of problem solving. An interest in the arts and an opportunity to express himself in art, sculpture, crafts, music, literature, creative writing, rhythm, and varied recreations contribute to his aesthetic development, to his self-realization, and to his effectiveness in and enjoyment of many other activities. The study of health, physical development, and body care is essential to both self-realization and good citizenship.

Secondary school subjects. The curriculum of the comprehensive high school encompasses "the educational needs of *all* the youth of the community." These needs include general education suited to *all* the future citizens of our increasingly complex democratic society; individualized elective programs for the development of vocational skills; and specialized elective programs for advanced preliminary

*The arts—as well as language, mathematics, science,
and social studies—are a part of the general
education curriculum of the modern high school.*
(North Cache High School, Richmond, Utah.)

training in the intellectual disciplines basic to college and graduate study leading to high-level professional and creative work [10, 16].

The subjects begun in the elementary school are continued as the general education curriculum of the secondary school. The areas usually. included are English, literature, languages, social studies, physical and biological sciences, mathematics, music, art, crafts, physical education, and homemaking. But more differentiated and more penetrating courses are, of course, developed at the higher level. Extending beyond "general science," for example, there are separate courses in the high school in biology and physical science or in the special fields of zoology, botany, physiology, chemistry, physics, geology, and astronomy.

The individualized vocational programs often include sequences of courses which prepare youth for technical, nonprofessional work in industry, business, agriculture, homemaking, and personal-service occupations. Courses in woodwork, stenography, farm machinery, and dental laboratory techniques are examples of the many vocational sequences offered. They often vary from school to school to suit the occupational needs and opportunities of the region.

Many high school students are prospective candidates for advanced professional training, even at the doctoral level. It has been estimated that approximately 3 per cent of the school population are "intellectually gifted" and that from 15 to 20 per cent are "academically talented." For those students who intend to continue their education beyond the high school level, we provide sequences of courses leading to relatively advanced levels of accomplishment in the sciences, English, foreign languages, mathematics, music, art, and other fields. To cite one example, a large comprehensive high school offers to its students who are interested and talented in mathematics the following sequence of courses: Algebra I and II, Geometry I and II, Algebra III, Solid Geometry, Trigonometry, College Algebra, and, for the fourth year, Analytic Geometry and Calculus [2].

The personal-social experiences curriculum. The attainment of personal and social objectives—such as developing a healthy self-concept; establishing secure, constructive, and happy social relations in the classroom and in other peer groups; becoming an effective participant or leader in group problem-solving activities; and developing ethical character and democratic ideals—is not directly related to any particular subject. *All* the child's social experiences—both in his regular school subjects and in nonacademic group projects which involve living with his classmates and teacher—contribute to attaining these objectives. The child achieves self-understanding, self-acceptance, feelings of personal worth and self-confidence from the discovery, development, and creative use of his talents in many different school subjects and projects. From the experience of working under his teacher's guidance and living in accepting, permissive, approving, and encouraging relationships with his classmates and teacher, he becomes a secure, productive, and happy member of his classroom and of other groups. As we shall point out more specifically in Chapter 14, the school, as a "working democracy," is rich in opportunities for guidance in social and ethical development. In group problem-solving activities —both in subject-matter and in extracurricular projects—children learn, under guidance, that sharing, contributing one's part on a team, taking individual responsibility, being a good sport, and making other constructive social contributions constitute satisfying and effective patterns of social behavior.

SELECTION AND ORGANIZATION OF CURRICULUM EXPERIENCES

There are so many important concepts, attitudes, and skills for elementary and secondary school children to learn that the task of learning them all sometimes seems impossible. We need to ask: Which of the wide range of potential curricular experiences—from both subject-matter and social-living experiences in the school, home, and community—are of most value? Which should we include in the school curriculum? In answering these questions, we need to evaluate all promising experiences in the light of their possible usefulness in helping us to attain the educational objectives set forth above. In our attack on these ever-present and never permanently solved problems, we have developed the following principles of curriculum selection and organization:

1. *Functional utilization of the cultural heritage.* Our cultural heritage—represented in the accumulated achievements of previous generations in language, mathematics, science, technology, arts, and literature—constitutes a large and tremendously useful body of knowledge for guidance in effective and satisfying living. The schools, by transmitting this rich and continuously growing background of concepts and techniques, enable each new generation "to ride on the shoulders of previous generations" and eventually to enrich the cultural heritage for succeeding generations [33]. Some educational philosophers believe that "a realistic knowledge of man's cultural heritage is the most reliable guide for future action[1]."

The elementary and especially the secondary school's subject matter is, of course, drawn from the cultural heritage. But our accumulated knowledge is too vast, complicated, and even contradictory for passing on as a whole. Moreover, since our society needs creative problem solvers, it would probably be unwise to pattern school curricula solely on closely drawn, logical classifications of knowledge. The whole superstructure of accumulated knowledge should be, however, a rich resource to which each new generation can turn for aid in the solution of its problems. And for effective use, its logical organization needs to be comprehended. In a curriculum designed to meet the problems of modern society, the systematic textbook presentations of knowledge are, therefore, important. From textbooks, encyclopedias, and other references, children and youth achieve useful understandings of subject-matter areas as organized bodies of knowledge. Such organization gives greater meaning to concepts and makes them easier to remember and apply; an understanding of the classification system makes it possible for a person to locate new information when he needs it.

2. *Meeting society's changing needs.* A curriculum which contributes effectively both to the individual's and to society's welfare must be responsive to contemporary needs. The different emphases on religious, political, and economic content in the selection of the curriculum at different periods of our history reflect the changing needs of society. Present-day emphases on science, industry, democratic living, and international understanding reflect the features of modern society. Current needs toward which the school is expected to contribute include those of national defense, expanded productivity, improved standards of living for more people, and enriched personal lives for all of us [8].

3. *Social utility.* Since we cannot include in the curriculum all of our social heritage, to help us make selections from it we need some guide such as: What knowledge is most useful? Applying the criterion of social utility, we have observed how universally, frequently, or with what crucial importance representative citizens in the country *use* the different concepts and skills in language, arithmetic, social studies, science, and other subjects. Kyte and Neel, for example, selected a core vocabulary in spelling comprised of the words that both children and adults have been found to use most frequently in their writing [25].

The "adult words" were selected from Horn's "A Basic Writing Vocabulary," which contains the 10,000 words most commonly used in adult writing [19]. Twenty-eight hundred of these words account for 97.2 per cent of the words adults write [26, p. 386]. Rinsland's "basic vocabulary of elementary school children," which includes 14,571 different words used three or more times in 6,012,359 running words of children's writing for all elementary grades, supplied the "children's words [31]." Kyte and Neel note that 500 of the most frequently used of these words account for 82 per cent of the running words children write. Mastery of this list of the 500 words of greatest social utility "should assure spelling proficiency in the case of a large per cent of the words written by adults and by children at various grade levels [25]."

The criterion of social utility is undoubtedly an important guide for developing a more useful curriculum. It has resulted in the elimination of much useless and irrelevant content. Used as a sole criterion, however, it would tend to produce a static curriculum comprised only of the things present-day adults do most frequently. Such a curriculum would not meet the needs of a constantly changing society. Furthermore, the present practices of parents are not necessarily ideal models for their children. For example, our children might communicate

better and more enjoyably if they used a greater variety of words in their writing than their parents use.

4. *Transfer of training.* A central and pervasive factor in learning is transfer, which we shall discuss more fully in Chapters 7 to 10. It involves making generalizations—or deriving principles—from specific learning or problem-solving experiences and applying them to new learning situations. Without transfer, the learning of children and youth could not progress stepladder fashion as it does. And the more efficiently we organize sequences of learning activities—so that prior achievements may be applied to subsequent learning—the more efficient the learning will be. Thus, according to this criterion, a good curriculum should emphasize meanings, the interrelationships among concepts, and inductive discovery and wide-scope applications of principles.

Some important aspects of training that may be applied or transferred to all kinds of learning situations are eagerness to learn, learning how to learn, and initiative and effectiveness in creative problem solving. If our children and youth succeed in mastering some practical learning and problem-solving procedures in school, they can leave school with confidence that they will "know how to learn other things as the necessity arises [33, p. 52]." We shall learn in Chapter 7 how we, as teachers, can foster the development of these procedures.

5. *Children's interests and needs.* There is sufficient scientific support, as we shall see in Chapter 6, for us to accept the assumption that children and youth are inherently active, curious, and creative. In taking account of this child characteristic in curriculum planning, many teachers believe that children "should have a part in initiating, planning, carrying out, and evaluating [their curriculum] experiences [21, p. 210]." To assume that children and youth are naturally intellectually active and creative does not, however, minimize the importance of teacher guidance and planning. Functioning interests are not, as Jersild and Tasch have shown, innate. Although potential interests in learning activities are inherent in every child, their development depends upon appropriate experiences.

"According to this concept, we will not simply utilize the interests a child happens to have acquired as a guide to what and how to teach [20, p. 86]." Teachers also guide the interest development of children. As children, under teacher guidance, explore and take part in significant activities, they develop interests, which they satisfy by understanding of subject matter, by mastery of useful skills, and by creative effort. For example, in pursuing such a problem as the "effects of inventions and scientific discoveries upon our living," children turn to subject matter for solutions. They "use it to find out, to verify some point, to gather new information, to enjoy, and to appreciate something [21, p. 334]." The problems of living in their "miniature democracy" also present needs for subject matter, skills, and creative problem solving. Children need a baseball field or a piece of physics laboratory apparatus, so they construct it. They need safety in crossing streets, so they participate in solving their traffic problem.

Such a curriculum, organized around the interests and needs of children and youth, draws upon much traditional subject matter. But it emphasizes child purposes, problem solving, and creative effort as the children meet in miniature the problems of their society.

6. *Resources in the local environment.* School activities are centered in the classroom. But, as we shall see in examples throughout this book, the curriculum is greatly enriched by extending it to include other significant activities within the school as a whole, the home, and the community.

Opportunities for attaining many objectives, both in mastery of subject matter and in personal-social development, are enhanced by experiences in the school library, the science laboratories, the auditorium, on the playground, in the lunchroom and its kitchen, and in other departments of some schools. Moreover, the special talents of individual teachers in art, music, dramatics, science, literature, or government can, on occasion, be utilized to enrich the curricula of all classes in an elementary or secondary school. There are many ways in which the students and teachers in each class can contribute to, and profit from, the enrichment of all classes. For example, unique classroom projects can be shared with the rest of the school through interclass visits or auditorium programs, or projects can be worked on cooperatively by students from various courses.

The different talents and curriculum resources from each child's home can be drawn upon to enrich classroom activities. The home also provides opportunities to apply many school-learned concepts and skills. Along with the school, it supplies important experiences which permit the attainment of such objectives as improved interpersonal relations in the family, better home planning and management, a knowledge of child rearing, and an understanding of the role of the family in society. It should contribute to learning the constructive use of leisure time, to social and moral development, to physical and mental health, and to the development of confidence and pride in oneself [15].

Many concepts in science and social studies, and many social attitudes and aesthetic interests, are learned best from teacher-guided pupil excursions into the community—to a zoo, a park, a museum, a theater, a farm, a factory, a power plant, a city water department and its facilities, and so on. Some modern schools feel that this kind of curriculum enrichment is so important that they maintain school buses, not only for bringing students to school, but for taking them into the community and its environs for educative experiences.

7. *Readiness for learning.* As we shall see in greater detail in Chapter 3, children and youth are both growing and learning as they progress through the elementary and secondary schools. They develop continuously, each child at his own rate, in motor, intellectual, academic, and social competencies. The curriculum of the modern school is adjusted to children's emerging stages of maturity. Each year it attempts to provide rich, full, satisfying experiences suited to each child's particular pattern of abilities, interests, and needs.

In studies of the optimum grade placement for effective mastery of concepts and skills, we have tried to determine the appropriate levels both for beginning and for taking progressively advanced steps in reading, arithmetic, language, and other school subjects. Some comparisons of the progress of American children with that of children of other countries, however, suggest that we may have been more concerned with provisions for delayed readiness than with detecting and making provisions for early readiness.

Wilson has compared the achievement of American and Canadian children in such subjects as reading, arithmetic, and spelling. He reports that British Columbia third grade children, who had earlier spent a "comparatively brief" period in preacademic readiness activities, attained higher levels of achievement than California third grade children who had had a "fairly long" readiness program [36]. Buswell too has discovered that eleven-year-old English school children surpass the achievement in arithmetic of eleven-year-old California children; and that, grade by grade, the placement of concepts in arithmetic is about a year earlier for the English children [6]. Pursuing a similar curriculum of earlier grade placement of corresponding topics, Kramer has found that the pupils in the fifth and sixth grades of schools in The Netherlands surpass in arithmetic the achievement of Iowa fifth and sixth grade pupils [24]. In not every American-European comparison, however, are the American children retarded in school progress. Doremus, for example, reports that sixth grade Glen Park, New Jersey, children excel the achievement of British children in arithmetic [12]. Since the factors causing the differences are complex and not clearly apparent, we must defer interpretation of them until we have more data.[1] At this time, however, they alert us to the possibility of

---

[1] One probable factor is a difference in the relative emphasis given to a subject. K. Kramer, in "Work-study skills in Iowa and The Netherlands," *Elem. School J.*, 1960, 61 (Dec.), 81–85, reports that in the reading of maps, tables, graphs, and references—skills that are given more emphasis and time in America in comparison with Dutch schools—sixth grade American children surpass their counterparts in The Netherlands.

early readiness—especially to signs of earlier-than-usual readiness—in some children.

8. *Adapting the curriculum to individual differences.* Each child is a unique individual. In every classroom, children differ widely in mental maturity, in experience background, and in patterns of abilities and achievements. Children in a first grade classroom, for example, may range in achievement-related mental maturity from mental ages of 4 to 9. As they advance through the grade levels of the elementary and secondary schools, the differences increase rather than diminish. The typical sixth grade class covers a range of approximately eight years in reading comprehension [11, p. 141]. Seventy-one high school seniors recently exhibited a range of grade equivalents in reading of from 4 to 16 [23].

Besides these extensive interindividual differences, there are equally important intraindividual differences. Each child has a pattern of unevenly developed abilities. For example, a child of average intelligence may be below average in reading, average in arithmetic, and distinctly superior in art. Adequate provision for variations in individual children requires a curriculum of broad and diverse activities, guidance in differentiated participation, adjustments in rates of progress, and flexibility in providing for the needs of each child. Several devices for appraising developing abilities and differentiated talents have been developed, and we shall discuss and evaluate them in Chapter 4. The perplexing problem of teaching unique individuals in groups seems to be ever present; in Chapter 5 we shall examine a variety of ways in which it has been tackled.

9. *Organization of the curriculum.* Paralleling the teacher's con-

tinuous interest in and reconsideration of aims and curriculum resources is another problem related to the curriculum—that of organization. Teachers have persistently striven to find the most effective pattern of curriculum organization. Up to about 1930, both the elementary and secondary curricula were largely subject-centered. During the twenties and thirties there was a movement toward the child-centered curriculum, especially in the elementary school [32]. From this concept, there evolved, quite rapidly, the contemporary child-in-society emphasis [21]. In our very recent concern with scholarship in all areas and especially in science, the role of academic subject matter is being reemphasized [10, 35]. Thus the curriculum of the modern school is subject-child-society-centered.

When we consider how to incorporate these general concepts into the actual structure of the curriculum, four types of organization come to mind:

1. The curriculum may be thought of as a list of separate subjects which are not intrinsically organized, but which can be functionally organized by relating them to the child's interests and to society's problems.

2. We may think of correlations within the curriculum, such as combining English and social studies in the core curriculum of the high school, which facilitates a problem-solving approach [7].

3. We may consider fusing certain related subjects into broad fields—language arts (including reading, composition, handwriting, spelling, grammar, punctuation, and speech and listening) or social studies (combining history, geography, civics, economics, and sociology)—which, like correlation, facilitates problem solving.

4. We may consider an integrated curriculum, which draws upon both a wide scope of subject matter and the creative experiences of children for the solution of the community problems in which they become interested.

Although the traditional classification of subjects still predominates, especially in the high school, many contemporary leaders in curriculum planning favor a more integrated organization. In the integrated curriculum, learning and problem-solving units may grow out of a specific need, such as the need for a school-supply store; or they may grow out of a developed interest in such constant social functions as the protection and conservation of life, property, and natural resources; the production and distribution of goods and services; or communication and transportation of goods and people [30, p. 145]. The advantages claimed for the integrated curriculum are that motivation is intrinsic; the organized subject matter and observation, exploration, and experimentation in the immediate environment contribute to solutions; and therefore resourcefulness and creative problem solving are developed.

The specific problem-solving units within any one or combination of these patterns of curriculum organization are so numerous and varied that any description of them would be incomplete. Nevertheless, for an instructive glimpse of the modern curriculum in action, let us turn to a specific illustration.

THE MODERN CURRICULUM IN ACTION, AN EXAMPLE

In a university high school offering the usual variety of separate courses, the faculty has organized the curriculum to achieve more effective mastery of the fundamental concepts and skills in each subject, development of problem-solving techniques, guided practice in cooperative group behavior, and personal-social development. Relying on the assumption that children naturally want to learn, the teachers try to develop a curriculum that appeals to children's natural curiosity, interests, and enthusiasm for learning. As a device for coordinating many of the activities carried on in the separate courses, the day-to-day curriculum is posted on a bulletin board in the main corridor of the school. On it are displayed the current curriculum units for grades 7 through 12 in the areas of language arts, social studies, mathematics, science, foreign languages, home economics, industrial arts, art, music, business education, physical education, and home room. In order to maintain continuity and to avoid undesirable duplication in the selection of units of study, cards on the completed units are placed in a permanent curriculum reference file. The unit card below on Social Studies VI, grade 12, for April 3 to June 5, is typical [3, p. 10].

Problem: How can we preserve both our prosperity and our living standards?

I. The problem confronting America
   A. *U.S.* productive achievement and future potential
   B. Dangers to our economic system from inflation and depression

II. Causes of poverty and depression

III. Possible courses of action
   A. To aid farmers
   B. To improve housing
   C. To improve health conditions
   D. To raise incomes
   E. To prevent inflation
   F. To prevent depressions

IV. Comparative economic systems

Since every instructor keeps his current units posted, all the teachers and students are continually aware of the projects in progress.

Often a unit initiated in one class can be enriched by simultaneous complementary study in other classes. For this reason, teachers and students—informed by the bulletin board of units in progress—are encouraged to join other classes in coordinated studies of problems. Thus, although units are sometimes confined to a single class, they often draw the interest of two or more classes. For example, when a social studies class initiated a unit of city planning and housing, the instructors in science, mathematics, and foreign languages recognized it as an opportunity for coordinated study. Not only could they make unique contributions to the social studies class, but they could enrich their own classes as well. They therefore joined forces with the social studies teacher, and together all planned an enlarged fourfold approach to the study unit [3, pp. 11–12].

For a closer view of such project learning, let us follow a chemistry class in its study of a unit: "The Water Supply in Our Community [3, pp. 44–51]." Since the teacher was alert to the opportunity of relating subject matter both to student interests and to significant community problems, he capitalized on a spontaneous classroom discussion of water to initiate the unit. As he listened to the discussion, he foresaw the possibilities of reviewing the general principles of solubility, ionization, and hydrolysis and of further practice in scientific problem solving. Because the students were apparently interested in the topic, and already had a background of chemistry principles, the instructor decided that they were ready for the unit. The varied approaches suited to the problem—excursions, demonstrations, laboratory experiments, special projects for the gifted students, and a variety of reading materials—would provide differentiated learning activities for students of every level of ability and talent.

A sequence of structuring and trial-and-check attacks on the problem helped the students to increase their knowledge both of the principles of chemistry and of individual and group problem solving. By means of leading questions, the introduction of question-raising materials, explanations and demonstrations, and other modes of teacher guidance of pupils' self-discovery learning, the teacher guided the students in structuring and in developing effective approaches to the problem. For example, the teacher showed the pupils some flasks filled with a colorless liquid and asked: "What do you think is in these flasks?" The students guessed that they might contain acid, lye, alcohol, water, gasoline, kerosene. Upon learning that they all contained water, a student asked: "Is it suitable for drinking?" This led to a formulation of the criteria of potable water. From their previous personal experience and scientific knowledge, the students generalized the criteria: the water should be free of disease-producing agents, of suspended matter, of unpleasant tastes, odors, and colors. Upon discovering that one of the flasks contained Mississippi River water and that another had the odor of hydrogen sulfide, they then asked *how* water is made potable.

The students sought solutions to the problem in a variety of activities which involved practice of fundamental concepts and skills: observation of the teacher's demonstrations of a sand filter, charcoal absorption of color and odor, alum precipitation of suspended and colloidally dispersed solids; tests for the presence of chloride ions in chlorinated tap water; individually and team-conducted supplementary experiments; and the reading of texts and varied supplementary materials. To complete the trial-and-check process of learning, they checked the accuracy of their tentative solutions to the problem against the textbook explanations and against reports of the water department chemists.

In the sequential development of the general problem, such subsidiary questions as the hardness of water were raised. By continued structuring and trial-and-check problem solving, the students defined hardness and learned how to control it. From opinions, personal experience, and textbooks, they generalized: "Hard water produces soapsuds only with difficulty, produces a curdy substance in water when soap is added, and produces scaly deposits [consisting of calcium and magnesium] in kettles and hot-water pipes."

Their decision to compare the hardness of water in Minneapolis and St. Paul led to further practice of the concepts and skills they were studying. Using as a criterion the number of drops of soap required to produce suds lasting one minute, they compared these tap waters with each other and with both distilled and river water. Finding tap water, and especially river water, harder than distilled water, they next asked: "How is water softened?" This led to further structuring of the problem and to tests of the effectiveness of borax, trisodium phosphate, and sodium carbonate on waters hardened by magnesium or calcium—and to generalizing problem solutions.

In all these experiments, the students related their specific findings to the general principles of chemistry, including chlorine reactions in water, nature of colloids, processes of absorption and filtration, the hydrolysis and ionization of aluminum sulfate, and the chemical composition and properties of softening materials. During regularly scheduled practice periods, they studied more systematically the concepts and skills encountered in the project, such as writing equations for the reactions observed. They related these concepts to other problems. And they took a comprehensive test to evaluate their mastery of the concepts studied.

EVALUATING THE MODERN SCHOOL

In order to achieve the two major goals of self-realization and social effectiveness for our children, the modern school has developed, in the last half century, the subject-child-community-centered curriculum. For efficient mastery of the concepts, skills, and attitudes of this curriculum, educational psychologists and teachers have striven to discover and apply the conditions of effective learning. Since we wish to work scientifically and to respond constructively to our critics, we need to make periodic appraisals of the success of our efforts. Because of this and other needs for achievement testing, we have devoted Chapter 15 to the procedures for appraising school achievement. However, let us anticipate that final chapter by referring here to the use of tests in evaluating some of the accomplishments of the modern school.

Criticisms. The increasing complexities of modern civilization have produced demands for more and better education. While our population increased fourfold between 1870 and 1955, high school enrollment increased eight times [35, p. 21]. In this period we assumed increased responsibilities for technological training, for producing informed citizens, and for developing social and mental health. As a consequence, the curriculum expanded greatly in both the number and scope of courses. But our critics claim that during this period of marked increases in school enrollments and of a greatly expanded curriculum, the quality of American education suffered. It is claimed that a lowering of academic standards, an overemphasis on social learning, the addition of unimportant courses and topics to the curriculum, and a neglect of the most talented students prevent us from achieving the high quality of education our society needs [28].

The record of achievement then and now. During this period of ongoing expansion in both enrollment and curriculum, when we have tried to organize the curriculum around children's interests and significant community problems, and when we have also tried to foster social development and mental health, what has actually happened to educational efficiency? A review of the scientific appraisals of the school achievement of children and adolescents in modern schools shows that in the development of academic skills, health, creative problem solving, and social effectiveness (such as self-initiative and cooperativeness), they tend to surpass the attainments of children in the older, traditional schools [27].

In one comparison of "then" and "now," the same test of reading comprehension administered to 148 sixth grade pupils in 1931 and to a comparable group of 198 sixth grade pupils in the same school in 1948 reveals no decline in mastery of reading skills [14]. Another study shows that World War II draftees significantly exceeded World War I draftees in comprehension and rate of reading [29]. On the same spelling test, administered to fifth grade pupils in 1881 and to comparable fifth grade pupils in 1951, 58 per cent of the 1881 pupils and 64 per cent of the 1951 pupils attained scores of 70 or higher. The median score on tests of achievement in English, social studies, natural science, literature, and mathematics of typical *United States* high school seniors tested in 1955 was about five percentile points higher than that of comparable seniors tested in 1943 [4].

Such studies indicate that the schools of today are not less efficient than the schools of yesterday. Furthermore, our world leadership in national product per man-hour—based, as it is, on scientific and technological training—is another indication of the efficiency of today's schools. Despite society's demand that we teach more pupils more concepts and skills, the modern school seems to be gaining in effectiveness.

The challenge. Our not unsatisfactory record does not, of course, justify complacency. Modern life demands an improved education in which each individual achieves more nearly the full realization of his potentialities. We need better informed citizens, more competent people in a wide range of professions, and wiser leadership in our cultural, political, and technological pursuits. Moreover, our evolving, ever more complex society presents a "constant and growing demand for talents of all varieties." Thus, it appears that the society of the future will require increases in "the quality and quantity of talented individuals of all kinds [35, p. 11]."

To meet the educational challenge of our time, we are embarked on "the pursuit of excellence." "Our conception of excellence," however, embraces "many kinds of achievement at many levels." It recognizes that "there is excellence in abstract intellectual activity, in art, in music, in managerial activities, in craftsmanship, in human relations, in technical work [35, p. 16]."[1] We also recognize that excellence is not solely an innate capacity; it is a product of developed ability, motivation, and character. In our efforts to improve educational efficiency, we are also alerted to such possibilities as finding that some of our students are ready earlier than we have suspected for more advanced levels of learning. According to Chase, our young people are as able to master mathematics, science, and language as are the youth of Europe and the Soviet Union and, in meeting the challenges of the twentieth century, we cannot afford to ignore this fact [8, p. 22]. Moreover, the high levels of attainment achieved in some of our schools indicate "the possibility of putting high achievement within the reach of children and young people with a wide range of abilities and interests [8, p. 20]."

SUMMARY

In order to promote more effective teaching, educational psychology seeks to develop and to apply to teaching those psychological principles that underlie the learning process. To achieve this goal, educational psychology must adapt itself to changing educational needs, objectives, curricula, and theories. In the light of these factors, the modern school is abandoning the attempt to achieve an encyclopedic coverage of knowledge. Instead, it emphasizes learning how to learn, to use the sources of knowledge, to do creative problem solving, and to function effectively—both personally and socially. With this general orientation, educational psychology applies its developed principles creatively to the major functions of teaching.

The major functions of teaching—around which this book is organized—are (1) developing a working concept of the aims of the school; (2) selecting and organizing a curriculum for achievement of these aims; (3) providing the conditions for effective learning, retention, and applications of concepts and skills; (4) recognizing and providing for the extensive differences in the levels of maturity and patterns of abilities of children; (5) fostering children's healthy emotional and social development; and (6) appraising children's attainment of educational objectives.

For guidance in achieving the general aims of education—the self-

[1] Copyright, 1958, Rockefeller Brothers Fund, Inc. Reprinted by permission of Doubleday & Company, Inc.

realization and social effectiveness of our children—teachers need to study such specific statements of objectives as Kearney's for the elementary school and French's for the secondary school.

The curriculum of the modern school includes academic subject matter selected from the vast storehouse of our social heritage and teacher guidance in the social experiences which children have as they work together in their "miniature democracy"—the school. Some of the considerations which guide teachers in selecting and organizing the curriculum content are a functional utilization of the social heritage, meeting society's changing needs, social utility, transfer of training, children's interests and needs, the resources of the local environment, the levels of readiness of the learners, individual differences in patterns of abilities, and the need to provide an integrated organization for effective training in problem solving and in social relations.

Despite society's demands that we teach larger numbers of pupils a greater number of concepts and skills, the modern school seems to be doing an increasingly efficient job. The growing complexities of modern life, however, demand even better schools. We are, therefore, embarked on "the pursuit of excellence." Our goal is to develop every individual's potentialities. As its contribution toward this goal, educational psychology enhances our understanding of children and youth and increases our knowledge of how to provide the conditions of effective learning.

GUIDES FOR STUDY, REVIEW, AND APPLICATION[1]

1. For the challenging task of teaching in the modern school, what unique contributions to your professional preparation do you expect of educational psychology?
2. What are the two major purposes of educational psychology? How is the achievement of these purposes related to changes in educational theory?
3. What are the major functions of teaching, around which the concepts of educational psychology are organized?
4. What are the general goals of the modern school, which educational psychology should guide teachers in helping children attain?
5. From observation or reading of an example of a modern elementary or secondary school curriculum unit, point out applications of the nine principles of curriculum selection and organization. Several of these principles are illustrated in the films *Effective Learning in Ele-*

[1] NOTE: These questions at the end of the chapter facilitate the student's mastery and effective application of the concepts developed. Read at the beginning, they provide an overview of the problems to think about as the chapter is studied. Answered at the conclusion of the chapter, either individually or in class discussion, they give guidance in review. The suggested observations and films extend the range of application of the concepts learned.

mentary School (20 minutes) and, at the secondary level, *Teacher and Pupils Planning and Working Together* (19 minutes), McGraw-Hill Text-Film Department.

6. The modern school has both its critics and champions. What is your evaluation of it? Consider both what has been and needs to be accomplished.

Chapter 2

HOW WE LEARN: AN INTEGRATION OF THEORIES

Teachers need to understand how children learn—how they discover
solutions to problems, how they become good problem solvers, and
how they acquire appropriate responses to a large and ever-widening
range of situations. We need especially a practical set of principles
to guide us in providing the conditions of effective learning in all the
academic and personal-social areas of the school curriculum.

Since understanding how individuals learn and discovering the
conditions of learning are major scientific interests of psychologists,
we should expect them to have discovered many facts which would
help us. And, indeed, educational psychology does provide many such
facts and concepts. But in order to apply these concepts effectively,
teachers need a comprehensive theory that will unify them and give
them a wide-scope meaning.

As compared to a mere collection of the facts about learning, an
integrated theory will yield a more thorough understanding of the
whole learning process. It will be easier to master, to remember, and

to apply—in guiding learning, in evaluating methods of teaching, and in analyzing instances of effective or ineffective learning. Moreover, such a theory should enable creative teachers to invent new and better ways of teaching and guiding children. Therefore, we shall explore the major theories of learning which psychologists have developed in more than half a century of intensive study of the problem. We shall search for a theory which will generalize for us our understanding of what is otherwise only a collection of facts.

THE VARIETIES OF SCHOOL LEARNING

Because of the many different kinds of learning activities in which children and youth engage, a practical theory of learning must be broad in scope. A schedule of the activities of a typical sixth grader suggests that even in a single day the variety of a child's learning experiences is very great. The child may listen with interest or with boredom in the news-sharing period. If he should contribute a news item, he may try to express himself more fluently than he did yesterday. Working individually or on a team, he may discover new, exciting facts, and formulate enlightening concepts in a graph, a poster, a craft construction, or in a written report. He may be challenged by the responsibility of being chairman of a committee. Both in relation to projects and in specifically scheduled periods, he will have occasions to practice such skills as reading, spelling, arithmetic, and writing. He is likely to struggle—and to succeed or fail—with the "story" problems in arithmetic. In art, he may try—in several attempts—to create a design in color and line and he will experience either aesthetic satisfaction or discouragement with his product. There may be a new song to learn in the music period. At recess time, he may strive intensely to improve his skills in baseball, volley ball, hopscotch, or marbles.

Since many of these activities are social, the child, as he seeks to master the concepts and skills of the curriculum and the playground, is also learning to feel accepted, loved, and esteemed by his teacher and classmates or, in unfortunate instances, rejected and unworthy. Depending upon his maturity and skill, he may be thrilled or embarrassed with social dancing in the auditorium. If he has the appropriate talent and developed skills, he may become a confident and popular hero on the playground. If he lacks competitive play skills, he may come to feel unwanted and withdraw to the sidelines. In such a routine as the morning health inspection, he may learn self-attitudes which color his behavior for the remainder of the day, or longer. From a deserved compliment, a child may glow with pride and self-respect. With a less fortunate preparation for the day, he may suffer shame, as Alec did when the student health inspector observed: "Your fingernails are dirty again!" A child's self-concept of competence or inferiority is built up around his success or failure in meeting each day's demands. To understand and control this tremendous variety of learning, the teacher needs both specific concepts and unifying principles.

As a guide for differentiation of teaching procedures, we may classify what is learned into five kinds of psychological controls of behavior: differentiated and meaningful *perceptions; knowledge and understandings; skills and competences; attitudes and interests;* and intellectual, verbal, or motor *action patterns.* In acquiring these psychological controls of conduct, children engage in two broad classes of learning behavior: They acquire new responses, and they extend those responses to an increasing range of stimuli. Perceptions, concepts, and skills are acquired by a process of repeated trial-and-error problem solving—of search and discovery. The range of effective stimuli for eliciting innate or acquired responses—especially interests, attitudes, and emotions—is extended by associating them with appropriate new stimuli. What we want to find out—so that we can use and apply the information—is *how* these behavior patterns are learned. First, what are some of the major theories of learning? What do they tell us about how learning takes place?

THEORIES OF LEARNING

A preliminary search for general explanations of learning reveals no dearth of suggestions. Hilgard, in his *Theories of Learning,* reviews no fewer than ten. We cannot expect to discover *the* true theory among all those that have been developed. In fact, as Guthrie has suggested, theories are not true or false; they are simply more or less useful for particular purposes [6, p. 9]. So our difficulty is not in finding *a* theory, but in selecting the *best* one from among several alternatives. Since we are concerned here with finding or formulating a learning theory which will have maximum usefulness as a guide to teaching, we shall examine several of the most promising theories, always keeping this aim in mind.

It may be that, because of the comprehensive variety of learning with which we are concerned, this criterion of maximum usefulness will impose a bias toward choosing the most comprehensive theory. Actually, each theory which we will review, although it attempts to encompass all the pertinent facts known about learning, appears most adequate for explaining a specific kind of learning. But as a composite they yield a comprehensive and practical outline of principles which we may employ in formulating our guide. We shall be eclectic in our consideration of learning theories; but we shall strive to achieve an integration rather than a mere collection of ideas.

Theories of learning classified. Our analysis of learning theories is simplified by the fact that present-day theories are classifiable into three major categories [23]: the stimulus-response contiguity theory, developed and ingeniously applied by Guthrie [4, 5, 6]; the stimulus-response reinforcement theory, both pioneered and extensively applied to education by Thorndike [2, 27] and systematically developed by Hull [11], Spence [25], and Miller and Dollard [17]; and the cognitive insight theory developed by Tolman [28, 29] and applied to teaching by Lewin [14] and by Hartmann [9]. Let us examine these three theories and try to get an understanding of the type of learning which each seems most adequate to explain. Then, with this basis or background, we shall attempt to work out an integration of the three concepts which, in the hands of creative teachers, may be of great practical value.

STIMULUS-RESPONSE CONTIGUITY THEORY

A given stimulus or combination of stimuli will tend to elicit a given response, and, according to Guthrie, learning consists essentially in extending these innate or acquired responses to other or substitute stimuli [5, p. 23]. As the diagram suggests, learning is a process—called conditioning—of shifting responses to new stimuli.

Conditioning illustrated. In an experiment carried out with three-year-old Peter, it was seen that a certain set of stimuli—friendly, reassuring Mrs. Jones and some well-liked food—elicited from Peter the responses of security, confidence, and pleasure. By the process of conditioning, these responses were extended to a new stimulus—a rabbit which had previously elicited fear. Peter's fear of the rabbit had previously been extended to include anything that resembled it—a rat, a fur coat, a feather, cotton, or wool. Now, as he sat secure and confident near Mrs. Jones, eating food of which he was "very fond," the feared rabbit was brought into the room (in a wire cage) and placed at a distance from him. Over a period of several days, and with the same set of favorable stimuli present, the rabbit was brought, step by step, closer and closer to Peter, but never so close as to arouse his fear. Gradually Peter came to extend his response of confidence to the rabbit, and eventually was able to allow it into his playpen and to fondle it affectionately [12, pp. 110–111].

How we learn: an integration of theories   33

Conditioning explained. In the diagram, R_1 represents the *response pattern* to be learned (confidence and pleasure, as conditioned reactions to the rabbit). S_1 represents an already-adequate *stimulus* (friendly, reassuring Mrs. Jones) for eliciting the desired response. S_2 and S_3 are additional conditioned stimuli (the rabbit, rat, etc.) to which the conditioned response is to be extended. When the response originally made only to Mrs. Jones was shifted and extended also to the rabbit, *learning* had taken place. As a simple statement of this comprehensively applied principle of learning, Guthrie writes: "A stimulus pattern that is acting at the time of a response will, if it recurs, tend to produce that response [5, p. 23]."

What causes such learning? For Guthrie, only one factor—contiguity in time of the cue and the response—is essential. Theoretically, repetition is unessential because, according to the theory, an association gains its full strength in one pairing of the stimulus and the response. But there are at least three reasons why repetition is a practical necessity in many areas of learning: The significant stimulus may not be responded to appropriately in every trial; the conditioned response pattern is often comprised of several components—not all occurring in every trial; and if a concept or skill is to be useful, it must be made elicitable in a variety of situations. Neither is reward for correct performance theoretically essential, but it is indirectly helpful because it eliminates the need or occasion for learning other interfering responses to the conditioned stimulus.

Another example illustrates Guthrie's primary reliance on the principle of contiguity. A 10-year-old girl, despite a hundred reminders to pick up her hat and coat and hang them in the closet, persisted in her annoying habit of tossing them on the floor as she entered the house. Application of the principle of contiguity corrected the habit. The appropriate signal for hanging these articles should be entering the house, *not* the delayed reminder to hang them in the closet. When the girl was directed to pick up the garments, put them on, return to the street, and hang them up when she reentered, entering soon became an effective cue to hang her coat and hat in the closet [4, p. 21]. This retraining procedure was effective, according to Guthrie, because *entering the house* and *hanging up the clothing* were associated closely in time.

Experimental support for the theory. The major experimental support for this theory is the observations by Guthrie and Horton of the repetitive behavior patterns that cats exhibited in their escapes from a puzzle box [7]. Entering the box from a door in the rear, a cat would explore the approximately 4-foot-square floor of the box, near the center of which was an upright tippable post. By tipping the post slightly—with his nose, paw, swaying body, or a backing movement—he tripped an electric control which opened a door in the front of the cage through which he then escaped. The experiment showed that whatever pattern of behavior a cat happened to discover for escaping on the first trial, he persisted in using on subsequent trials. If, because of some adventitious change in his mode of entry or some other feature of his behavior, the cat hit upon a different solution, then this newer, more recently practiced habit persisted, until it also might be changed by some new fortuitous circumstance. If the cat escaped from the cage immediately after releasing the latch with some particular movement, then opportunities for learning different responses to the post were eliminated and the first or most recently learned pattern was preserved.

Contiguity in teaching. As a guide in teaching, Guthrie's principle of contiguity is deceptively simple. It is merely this: Induce—by whatever means or circumstances an ingenious teacher can contrive—desired patterns of behavior in the presence of cues or signals intended to elicit them. Subsequently—without special inducements—the conditioned cues will elicit the desired responses, unless in the meantime these same cues have become associated with other responses [5, p. 25]. This, of course, often happens when we are dealing with a classroom full of active youngsters, and so repeated practice in a variety of situations is usually needed for establishing habits.

Peter's changed reaction to the feared rabbit is analogous to what happens in many school situations. For example, when a child first enters school, he may feel timid. It is his first long absence from home and the school is big and strange. But if his teacher is warm, friendly, and reassuring and does not press him too quickly into new or difficult activities, he will probably respond to her with feelings of security and confidence. Very shortly this response to his teacher is extended to all school situations of which she has become a significant part. We can think of other kinds of school learning which resemble the episode of retraining the voluntary habit. For instance, a child may first recognize a printed word only when it is presented in combination with a familiar picture. Later the printed word alone elicits the appropriate response.

STIMULUS-RESPONSE REINFORCEMENT THEORY

Originally set forth by Thorndike, this theory is also called "trial and error" learning. It involves the idea that an individual, as he progresses through school and life, continually meets problems which require the combined application of generalizations from his past experience and creative on-the-spot problem solving.

The very young child, for example, in his attempts to master the language, must discover meaning in numerous auditory and visual symbols and must differentiate and integrate complicated verbal and

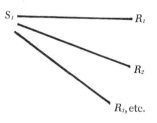

perceptual responses. Later, the school child attempts to master the biological, physical, and social science concepts required for understanding his expanding world. He is then involved in problem-solving search and discovery. The many motor skills needed for participation in school, work, and play activities are also acquired through problem-solving effort. All these concepts and skills are learned by trial-and-error (or trial-and-success) problem solving. The diagram suggests that this kind of learning involves discovering appropriate responses to problem situations. This type of learning is dramatically illustrated in a simple experiment reported by Miller and Dollard.

Trial-and-error learning illustrated. The experimenters have hidden a flat piece of candy under the center book on the lower shelf of a 4-foot-long bookcase containing books of similar color and size. They bring a six-year-old girl into the room and tell her that a piece of candy is hidden under one of the books and that she may have it to eat if she is able to find it. They give the child no directions, but only tell her to return each book to its place after looking under it. Motivated by her appetite for the candy and by the challenging, game-like problem, the child makes several goal-directed trials [17, pp. 14–16]:

First, she looks under a few books on the top shelf. Then she turns around. After a brief pause, she starts taking out the books on the lower shelf, one by one. When she has removed eight of these books without finding the candy, she temporarily leaves the books and starts looking under the magazines on the top shelf. Then she returns to look again on the top shelf under several of the books she has already picked up. After this, she turns toward the experimenter and asks, "Where is the candy?" After a pause, she pulls out a few more books on the bottom shelf, stops, sits down, and looks at the books for about half a minute, turns away from the bookcase, looks under a book on a nearby table, then returns and pulls out more books. Under the thirty-seventh book which she examines, she finds the piece of candy. Uttering an exclamation of delight, she picks it up and eats it. On this trial, it has taken her 210 seconds to find the candy.

She is sent out of the room, candy is hidden under the same book, and she is called back again for another trial. This time she goes directly to the lower shelf of books, taking out each book methodically. She does not stop to sit down, turn away, or ask the experimenter questions. Under the twelfth book, she finds the candy. She has finished in 86 seconds.

On the third trial, she goes almost directly to the right place, finding the candy under the second book picked up. She has taken only 11 seconds.

On the following trial, the girl does not do so well. Either the previous spectacular success has been due partly to chance, or some uncontrolled factor has intervened. This time the girl begins at the far end of the shelf and examines 15 books before finding the candy. She has required 86 seconds.

Thereafter, her scores improve progressively until, on the ninth trial, she picks up the correct book immediately and secures the candy in three seconds. On the tenth trial, she again goes directly to the correct book and gets the candy in two seconds.

Her behavior has changed markedly. Instead of requiring 210 seconds and stopping, asking questions, turning away, looking under magazines, searching in other parts of the room, picking up wrong books, and making other useless responses, she now goes directly to the right book and gets the candy in two seconds. She has learned.

From Miller and Dollard's description of this child's behavior, we note two signs of progress in learning: there were gradual though uneven reductions in the number of books provisionally picked up, and there were similar reductions in the time required to find the candy. It seems safe to infer also that the child's concept of the solution to the problem became clearer and more differentiated, and that she became more confident of her solution.

Often it is helpful to both the pupil and his teacher to see a graph of some phase of the progress made in successive attempts to acquire

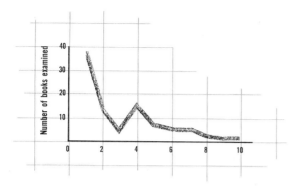

Fig. 2.1. *Learning curve for six-year-old girl's trial-and-error efforts to find candy under a certain book in a bookcase.* (From N. E. Miller and J. Dollard, *Social Learning and Imitation*, Yale Univ. Press, New Haven, Conn., 1941, p. 15.)

new skills. Figure 2.1 portrays the progress of this child in terms of the number of books examined before the correct one was chosen.

Explanations of trial-and-error learning. What explanations can we find for the learning that obviously took place? Thorndike, in over half a century of experimenting and theorizing, has developed a number of explanatory principles which constitute his trial-and-error, or "connectionist," theory of learning [2, 27]. Several of his principles are illustrated in the experiment outlined above:

1. The child, motivated by her desire for the candy and by the challenging task, is in a state of *readiness*, or is mentally set for a certain kind of searching behavior.

2. *A multiple and varied attack* on the problem begins; she tries provisionally book after book and makes other explorations, as well, in her search for the candy.

3. According to the "law of effect," the responses followed by *motive satisfaction* are selected for continued use, and those attended by dissatisfaction are eliminated. In this instance, the obviously unrewarding explorations are quickly eliminated, and eventually only the book covering the candy is picked up.

4. It is also assumed in the theory that with *repeated exercise* of the correct stimulus-response connections, when accompanied by both *belongingness* and motive satisfaction, these connections are strengthened. The learning curve shows that by the ninth trial the S-R connection between perception of the right book and picking it up has been so strengthened that there is no longer any competition from any other book or any exploratory effort.

5. Two supplementary principles are significant, especially from the point of view of teaching activities analogous to this one. First, the correct S-R connection could have been learned more quickly if the significant stimulus cues had been more *identifiable*—if the correct book had been marked distinctively instead of resembling all the other books on the shelf. And second, if this six-year-old child had had readily *available* such a verbal response as "seventh book from the

left on the bottom shelf," she could have mastered the problem more quickly.

6. Another important aspect of the theory is the assumption that, on meeting other situations which have elements in common with this one, the child will respond by *analogy* with a pattern of searching behavior similar to that found successful in this particular problem.

In the attempt to bring out all Thorndike's explanatory concepts as they apply to this experiment, we may have skipped over too quickly the central feature of the theory—the law of effect. Thorndike [2, 27] and other reinforcement theorists [11, 17, 25] explain the law of effect in this way: Of the multiple trial-and-error responses made to a stimulus (S_1 in the diagram), whichever response (R_1, R_2, or R_3) is rewarded or reinforced will automatically be strengthened. According to their theory, habits are established gradually. Each reinforcement of a stimulus-response connection adds an increment of strength to it and raises the probability that it—rather than some other competing response—will be elicited when the same stimulus recurs. For reward to operate in learning, however, other conditions are also necessary. As we shall see when we take up the role of motivation in a later chapter, reward is a very complicated factor.

Miller and Dollard [17] have adapted from Hull's [11] systematic development of this theory four explanatory principles of learning. Since these principles add to our understanding of those developed by Thorndike, they are worth considering here. These four conditions of learning are: drive, cue, response, and reward. Drives—hunger, thirst, activity needs, approval, etc.—impel the individual to respond in some way. Cues—distinctive, discriminated stimuli—signal and guide specific responses. The signaling cues and motivating drives elicit responses. The reward—as motive satisfaction or drive reduction—reinforces and thus strengthens the cue-response connection. As illustrated in the child's learning to find the candy under a particular book, both desire for reward and a challenging task can motivate our searching or problem-solving effort. The cues guiding the child—cues which she had to discover for herself in this instance—were the only slightly distinctive size, color, markings, or position of the book hiding the candy. Going directly to the correct book and picking it up emerged as the learned pattern because only this pattern was reinforced—by finding and eating the candy. Other responses, being unrewarded, were eliminated.

Reinforcement in teaching. An oversimplified rule for teaching, according to reinforcement theory, is: Elicit from the learner—by appropriate motivation, teacher directions, and contrived cue arrangements—desired responses and see that they are promptly rewarded. Skinner, in his application of this principle, has suggested that many skills such as those used in arithmetic, spelling, reading, shorthand, or

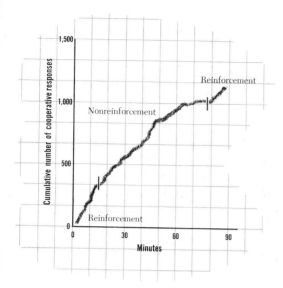

Fig. 2.2. *Cumulative number of cooperative responses emitted by a pair of fast-responding children under conditions of reinforcement, nonreinforcement, and resumed reinforcement.* (After N. H. Azrin and O. R. Lindsley, *J. Abnorm. and Soc. Psychol.*, 1956, vol. 52, p. 101.)

Morse code could be taught effectively by analyzing them into specific S_1–R_1 sequences that could be fed into a mechanical device which would reward the individual promptly for a correct response and fail to reward him for an error [24]. There is, of course, much experimental support for this principle of reinforcement. As an illustration of it, let us examine Azrin and Lindsley's demonstration of how they taught children to cooperate solely by rewarding instances of cooperation [1].

Twenty children, aged seven to twelve, were subdivided into 10 cooperative teams and shown how to put pairs of styli (each child manipulating a stylus) into pairs of three holes at opposite ends of a table divided by a screen. When both children of a team placed their styli in opposite holes within .04 seconds of each other (which joint act was defined as a cooperative response), a red light flashed and a jelly bean fell into a cup accessible to both children. Leaving two children in the room with the apparatus, the experimenter, without other directions, said, "You can play any game you want while I am gone." To test the role of reinforcement in acquiring and maintaining such a response, every cooperative response was reinforced during the first 15 minutes. Then, during a second period, there was no reinforcement. Finally, in a third period, reinforcement was resumed. The results of such controlled reinforcement, for a high-scoring pair of children, are presented in Figure 2.2.

The cumulative curve of emitted cooperative responses tells the story. It reveals that during the initial period of reinforcement, the children learned to respond jointly at a rapid and steady pace. Their cooperative responses continued for a while—but at a slower rate—during the period of nonreinforcement and finally, after several minutes, they ceased altogether. When reinforcement was resumed, the initial rapid rate of responding was immediately restored. In general, the results indicate that by manipulation of reinforcement, cooperation between children can be developed, maintained, or eliminated.

COGNITIVE, INSIGHT THEORY

Both Guthrie—in his contiguity-conditioning theory—and the stimulus-response reinforcement theorists have minimized the role of understanding or insight in the learning process [10]. Contiguity or reinforcement, respectively, is assumed by these theorists to strengthen stimulus-response connections automatically, without the mediation of ideas or thinking. In contrast, the cognitive or insight theorists—and we might add, most teachers—are impressed with the place of understanding and intellectual interpretation in the learning process. Rather than focusing their attention exclusively on stimuli and observable responses, the cognitive or insight theorists seek to explain learning in terms of intervening structuring or conceptualizing processes which serve as guides to learned performance.

For example, there are indications in the data on three-year-old Peter that the change in his response to the rabbit was really produced by his reinterpretation of the situation. He at first interpreted the rabbit as dangerous. This could be inferred from his remark as it was brought in for the second day of training: "Beads [on the table] can't bite me, beads can only look at me." Several days later, toward the end of the training period, another comment, "I like the rabbit," suggests that he has reinterpreted the situation.

The cognitive theorist would explain in a similar fashion the six-year-old's discovery and retention of a pattern of behavior for locating a hidden piece of candy. That is, he would infer that on successive trials the child built a mental schema or cognitive map to guide her performance, such as "bottom shelf, second red book, near the middle."

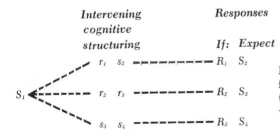

Expectations s_2, s_3, s_4, etc., are confirmed or disconfirmed by perceiving the consequences S_2, S_3, S_4, etc., of provisional responses R_1, R_2, R_3, etc.

As the diagram suggests, such learning is analyzed as trial-and-error problem solving (just as it is for the stimulus-response reinforcement theorists); but, intervening between problem stimuli and to-be-discovered responses, there are significant cognitive or brain processes by which mental maps for guiding performance are constructed. According to the diagramed analysis, an individual on meeting a problem situation, S_1, observes the situation as a whole and constructs a tentative cognitive map of alternative courses of action. The tentative hypothesis, represented by r_1s_2, implies that provisional response R_1 is expected to produce consequence S_2. Hypothesis r_2s_3, if acted on as provisional response R_2, should result in change S_3, and so on. These expectations are to be confirmed or disconfirmed on the basis of *perception of the effects* of provisional responses R_1, R_2, R_3, etc. In order to broaden our understanding of this concept, let us now examine some of the data which Tolman used in developing his version of cognitive theory and some of the ways he applied the theory to explain other instances of learning.

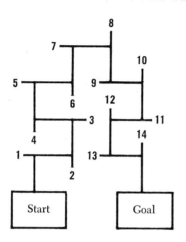

Development of Tolman's cognitive theory. This experiment involves observation of the problem-solving behavior of a hungry rat which is placed at the entrance of a maze such as the one diagramed. The rat wanders about into both true paths and blind alleys until he finally reaches the food box. On repeated trials—usually one every 24 hours—he tends to make fewer errors and to require less and less time to complete a run from start to goal [28, p. 189].

Now in both the contiguity and reinforcement theories, learning is assumed to consist of strengthening stimulus-response connections between "sights, sounds, smells, pressures, etc.," and "walkings, runnings, turnings, retracings, smellings, rearings, and the like [28, p. 189]." Wrong responses are eliminated and correct responses are strengthened because—according to contiguity theory—correct responses occur more frequently or recently; and—according to reinforcement theory—correct responses are rewarded. Tolman accepts neither of these explanations. He believes that the brain, rather than merely connecting specific stimuli with outgoing responses, works them over, elaborates them, and constructs a "tentative cognitive-like map of the environment," which serves as a guide to routes and relationships and thus determines what responses the animal will emit [28, p. 192]. Tolman cites five kinds of data in support of the theory [28, 29]. Again, the experiments are with animals.

1. *Latent learning.* While a daily rewarded group of rats were gradually, during seven days, reducing their errors in a maze, a non-rewarded group exhibited no significant reduction in errors. However, when food reward was introduced to the latter group on the seventh

day, their errors dropped "astoundingly," and in just two days this group equalled the performance of the other. Apparently they "had been building up a 'map'" during the nonrewarded trials which they could use "as soon as they were motivated to do so." Such data suggest that reinforcement is necessary for *performance* of learned behavior, but not for observational learning. However, satisfaction of such motives as curiosity or intrinsic satisfaction in exploratory activity itself may have reinforced the learned orientation which these animals apparently accomplished during the non-food-reward trials.

2. *Vicarious trial and error.* Tolman has observed that when animals have become goal-directed, at critical stages in learning—at choice points—they hesitate and look back and forth at alternatives as though they were establishing a cognitive guide or conceptualizing the task before executing it.

3. *Searching for the significant stimulus.* Animals presented with an electric shock while feeding appeared to look for a significant stimulus to avoid. When the rats could see a distinctive visual pattern near the food cup as they touched it and were shocked, they learned in one trial to avoid touching the cup. However, when the same experiment was tried in the dark, the animals did not learn to avoid the cup as the shock was administered. This behavior is interpreted by Tolman as indicating that cognitive map making is selective of significant aspects of the situation.

4. *Hypotheses as guides to provisional trials.* As further support of his theory, Tolman reports Krech's presentation to rats of four units of two alternative choices in a problem box, with randomized right or left choices at each trial. In this insoluble problem, the rats behaved as though they were testing hypotheses. They demonstrated successions of systematic choices—all right passages for several trials, then all left, or they entered all dark doors.

5. *Spatial orientation.* Instead of learning only the specific paths to the goal on which they were trained, rats developed generalized, flexible orientations so that they could reach goals by alternative approaches. This tendency was demonstrated when rats, trained to follow a right-angled path from starting point to goal, were blocked on the original path and permitted to choose among paths radiating in all directions from the starting position. Their predominantly chosen path was a diagonal one leading more directly toward the goal, rather than the specific right-angled direction on which they had been trained.

Let us now illustrate the application of cognitive, insight theory to Homo sapiens, where the assumption that our subjects think seems less unsubstantiated.

Cognitive explanations of learning. Harter confronted 74 two- to six-year-old children with the *Obstacle Peg Test.* The equipment for this test consists of an 8¾-inch-diameter grooved board (Figure 2.3) containing within the grooved path three unremovable pegs with differently colored tops. Each child was directed: "Slide the red ball [pointing to the red peg top] to the red hole in the center [pointing again] [8]." Since the pegs are not removable, the task can be accomplished only by sliding the otherwise obstructing yellow and green pegs out of the way into grooves at positions 2, 3, 4, or 5.

Of the 74 children tested, 53 succeeded by overt trial-and-error moves in moving the red peg to the red hole within the five minutes allowed. The other 21 children, less mature in both chronological and mental ages than the successful group, were apparently too immature to master this problem. Of 50 children in the successful group who were given a second trial, "thirty-two made no trial-and-error moves." The insight or understanding achieved on the first trial served as a sufficient cognitive guide for clearing the path and moving the red peg without error directly to the center hole.

How do cognitive theorists explain such examples of learning? Emphasizing the role of perception in the learning process, Hartmann would probably say that the children in the *Obstacle Peg Test* situation, as a result of their goal-directed observation and thinking, progressed perceptually "from a relatively undifferentiated, homogeneous stage to a more elaborate and internally differentiated condition [9, p. 202]." That is, the children organized and reorganized perceptual patterns of the significant elements of the situation in relation to the goal. In this way, they achieved insight into the problem. They got "the point of the situation"—and learned how to solve it. According to Lewin's view, learning is a process of differentiating relatively unstructured problem situations. A "previously vague and unstructured area becomes cognitively structured and specific." And the cognitive structures thus created and reconstructed in learning become guides to more adequate action in these situations and in similar ones [14, pp. 224–229]. Since cognitive structures are a guide to action, vague and undifferentiated perceptions of a situation tend to result in halting and restrained behavior. As perception of the situation be-

Fig. 2.3. Obstacle Peg Test, *illustrating trial-and-error and insight learning: "Slide the red peg to the No. 1 hole."* (From G. L. Harter, *J. Genet. Psychol.,* 1930, 38, p. 362.)

comes clearer and more differentiated, behavior becomes more accurate, sure, and economical.

For Tolman also, learning is a process of observation. By perceptually differentiating and organizing the response-guiding cues in his problem situation, the individual constructs a "tentative cognitive-like map" as a guide to provisional solutions. And on the basis of his perception of the effects of provisional trials, he confirms or disconfirms his expectations, and thus reorganizes or structures more surely his developing cognitive guide. As applied to learning in the *Obstacle Peg Test* situation, the cognitive or insight theory assumes that the child first perceives the board as an undifferentiated pattern of pegs and grooves. He observes this vaguely structured situation and, since he is goal-directed to slide the red peg to the center hole, he tentatively structures his perception of it. Mentally, he differentiates a probable clear path from the side paths for the obstructing pegs. Then, guided by this more specifically structured cognitive map, he tries out the pattern of moves he expects will solve the problem. After several provisional moves in the first trial, the correct pattern became clearly differentiated and confirmed, and served to guide the children without error in the second trial.

Since much of what goes on in learning cannot be seen, we can only infer—from observing limited segments of the process—what is taking place in a child's mind as he works out a problem. Sometimes, however, children spontaneously verbalize their problem-solving behavior, and thus provide the psychologist and teacher more intimate glimpses of the problem-solving process. For example, as the psychological examiner demonstrated stringing seven alternately cubical and spherical beads, he directed seven-year-old Bryan to "watch what I do. . . . When I am through, I am going to take this one away and see if you can make one just like it." Perceiving the task only vaguely at first, Bryan verbalized his uncertainty: "I don't know about that." Then, with an insight into it, he declared: "Oh, I see how you are doing it." And before beginning the task—during the five seconds observation permitted—he revealed his cognitively structured map for guiding his approach, by saying: "Square, round, square, round, square, round." That this verbalized conceptualization of the response-guiding cues in the task actually did guide his performance was further suggested by another comment the child made as he was about to string two spherical beads in succession: "Oops, excuse me, it should be a square next."

Similar observations are afforded teachers as they observe children at work on such learning problems as identifying the meanings of words in reading, discovering or achieving understanding of concepts in science and social studies, struggling with a problem in mathematics, achieving a satisfying result in creative art—indeed, in every aspect of the curriculum.

Emotional control in learning. Emotional control—a significant factor affecting learning, however it is explained—has an especially important role in Tolman's theory. The cognitive maps which the learner constructs as guides to understanding or performance in learning situations may be narrow or broad in scope or application. "Narrow-stripped maps" are restricted in application; they serve as guides to appropriate behavior only in situations very similar to the original problem. They prevent one from seeing alternative approaches to problems. Consequently, they impair effective performances in situations that require flexibility and adaptability. Broad cognitive maps, however, are generalized for flexible and adaptable application to a wide variety of only somewhat similar situations. The less effective narrow-strip cognitive maps are induced, according to Tolman, by brain damage, inadequate environmental cues, overrepetition on a restricted variety of practice situations, and by frustrating, anxiety-provoking conditions [28].

Because of frustration and anxiety, children sometimes regress. They then produce narrower, less mature, cognitive guides than they are capable of conceptualizing when undisturbed. For example, after a disturbing interference with their play, a group of pre-school children regressed to a level in play constructiveness 17 months below their usual level [13]. Other anxious, insecure children cling unduly to stereotyped, first-learned patterns of behavior because they fear the risk of failure in mastering more mature procedures. A bright child persisted from grade 3 to grade 6 in reading at the slow rate of 45 words per minute because she could not give up her labored phonetic approach—sounding each letter or syllable and then repeating the synthesized word—in identifying every unfamiliar word she encountered. In still other children, such defenses of their self-concepts as displaced aggression result in restricted cognitive maps which divert them from the real sources of frustration. For example, Pete, feeling his dancing skill inferior to that of his adolescent peers, deprives himself of needed practice by the aggressive rationalization: "I don't have time for such kid stuff [26, p. 24]."

We will take up the matter of emotional control more thoroughly in later chapters dealing with mental health, but a brief mention of it here helps to explain its role in Tolman's theory.

SUMMARY OF EXPLANATORY PRINCIPLES OF LEARNING

Our examination of these three theories yields several widely recognized explanatory principles of learning. Let us see how these principles fit into the various theories.

Contiguity in time between stimulus-response connections is the only essential condition demanded in Guthrie's conditioned-response theory. Contiguity is also implicit as one factor in both the reinforcement and cognitive theories. The more promptly a reinforced response follows the eliciting stimulus, the more likely is the connection to be strengthened. Similarly, for cognitive theory, the more promptly the learner perceives the consequences of provisional, goal-directed trials, the more certainly he can confirm or disconfirm expectations or insight into stimulus-response relationships.

Reinforcement is the fundamental explanation for Thorndike and other reinforcement theorists of how selected responses in trial-and-error problem-solving learning gradually become strengthened. Reinforcement is not theoretically an essential condition of learning in either Guthrie's contiguity or Tolman's cognitive theory; but it is recognized as a practical advantage for learning in both. And if we assume such motives as curiosity, exploratory or self-realization drives (which data presented in Chapter 6 seem to justify), then all learning activity seems intrinsically reinforced.

Cognitive theory emphasizes a number of *intervening mental processes* as fundamental to learning: goal-directed searching; preliminary conceptualizing or structuring of tasks as guides to executing them; and observation or perception, both in searching for response-guiding cues and for checking the consequences of provisional trials. The other theorists recognize thinking as a characteristic, complicated human process; but they prefer to explain learning by simpler concepts, without the assumption of meditating ideas. In their attempt to explain both human and animal learning with the same concepts, they strive to avoid the assumption that the rat at a choice point in a maze is "buried in thought," an assumption which Guthrie attributes to Tolman [6, p. 143].

In their explanations of learning, all the theories employ in some fashion the concepts of *readiness, motivation,* and *transfer of training.* All three theories assume that a sufficient level of maturity and an appropriate pattern of abilities—for discriminating, manipulating, conceptualizing, and integrating—are necessary for learning concepts and skills. As was illustrated in the *Obstacle Peg Test* problem, the level of complexity of the task must be appropriate to the child's level of maturity before he can be expected to succeed with it. Since reinforcement consists of motive satisfaction or drive reduction, motivation is assumed in reinforcement theory to be a response-selecting factor. It is assumed that motive satisfaction and motive dissatisfaction determine the selection and elimination of responses in trial-and-error learning.

In all the theories, motives arouse, direct, sustain, and determine the intensity of learning behavior. And in all three theories, it is observed that responses learned in one situation are generalized for application in related situations. Peter, conditioned to feel confident with the rabbit, transferred this response to other previously feared objects—to cotton, feathers, a fur coat, and a rat. Thorndike noted that responses learned in a specific situation are emitted in analogous situations. Transfer is *emphasized* in cognitive theory: Instead of learning specific stimulus-response connections only, individuals—when emotionally and otherwise unhandicapped—learn broad orientations, general principles, and generalized modes of adjustment applicable in a wide scope of related situations. Let us now try to see how we, as teachers, can utilize these explanatory principles in developing a practical theory of learning for guidance in our work.

AN INTEGRATED THEORY OF LEARNING

What do we mean by "a practical theory of learning"? What would this theory explain about learning? How could it help us to be better teachers? A practical theory of learning for teachers should explain how we acquire multiple behavior patterns. It should explain how responses are shifted to new stimuli, and how appropriate responses to problem situations are discovered and mastered. It should explain the learning of the great variety of concepts, skills, and ideational, verbal, and motor action patterns of the school curriculum. And it should explain the simultaneous acquisition of attitudes, interests, and emotions. As a first step toward an integrated theory, let us consider a two-factor concept.

Concomitant problem solving and conditioning. As we have already seen, a twofold classification of learning helps us to understand how appropriate responses to a problem situation are discovered, and how responses are extended to new stimuli.

Problem-solving learning, from which concepts and skills emerge, involves a motivated individual who, upon meeting a situation to which he cannot adjust adequately, on the basis of either innate or previously acquired behavior patterns, cognitively structures tentative approaches and makes multiple goal-directed provisional tries. Experiencing the effects of these trials, both *perceptually* and as *motive satisfaction* or *dissatisfaction,* he selects—often from several trials—a pattern of behavior which promises to meet the motivating conditions more adequately. When this or a similar situation arises again, the adequate pattern recurs more directly and with less attention and effort.

Conditioning accounts for the shifting of innate or acquired patterns of response to new stimuli. When a rewarded response[1] is elicited by a combination of stimuli (including an already adequate stimulus and associated significant conditioned stimuli), the conditioned stimuli also become effective in eliciting the response. Mowrer believes that conditioning is especially appropriate for explaining the extension of attitudes, interests, likes and dislikes, and such emotions as love, anger, and fear to new stimuli [18]. For example, to develop interest in a new activity according to this formula, we associate the new activity with conditions which already lead to motive satisfactions. As Pressey and Robinson have written: "An interest grows with tropical lushness in the warm sun of success and approval. It withers if not so nourished and stimulated, may even be blighted by only one devastating experience if instead of success and approval it meets ridicule or contempt and failure [22, p. 156]." In many school learnings—reading, science, social studies, literature, music, art, perhaps in every subject—there are significant motivational-emotional components. When the study of concepts and skills in these subjects is made a part of a classroom activity already adequate for leading to satisfying uses—mastery, pleasure, approval, and other gratifications—then these subjects also become effective—as conditioned stimuli—in provoking interest, appreciation, and eagerness for more of such learning.

For learning such motivational-emotional responses—involuntary and mediated largely by the autonomic nervous system—contiguity of stimulus-response associations is the significant determinant, Mowrer believes [18]. What the individual learns to do about his conditioned desires, angers, and fears, however, is a matter of problem solving. Solutions to such problems, the mastery of concepts, and the acquisition of skills involve the discovery, differentiation, and integration of new, voluntary patterns of behavior. Such problem-solving learning—

---

[1] For Guthrie, of course, reward is not theoretically essential; it is only practically advantageous [6, p. 123].

comprising the major emphasis in the school curriculum—is mediated largely by the central nervous system and must be explained by such additional principles of learning as reinforcement and insight.

Concomitant problem solving and conditioning are illustrated in the following case. We will also see that a sequence of significant teacher-guided learning experiences are involved [3]. When Philip's teacher noticed that he had withdrawn to the sidelines to watch his preadolescent classmates play baseball, she asked: "Philip, why aren't you in the game?" Probably, because prior baseball experiences with his classmates had been humiliating, Philip had become conditioned to respond with anxiety to the baseball-with-his-classmates situation. To avoid intensified anxiety, he had learned—by problem solving—to withdraw from the game. Challenged, he now—in further problem solving—elaborated this solution. First, in self-protection from further embarrassment, he rationalized: "They already have the same number on each side." But his teacher persisted: "I am sure there is someone you can pair with to enter the game." To this further challenge, Philip partially gave up his defense, projecting onto his classmates some of the blame for his lowered self-concept: "Ah! They don't want me in the game! They don't think I'm any good!" Let us interrupt our drama for a moment and diagram a two-factor explanation of Philip's learning up to this stage [19].

Conditioning and problem solving are often intertwined in learning sequences. Conditioning initiates problem solving, and problem solving produces desires or fears which elicit further problem solving.

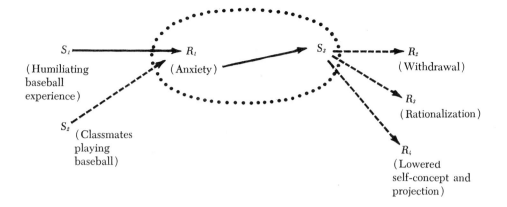

In the diagramed episode of this learning sequence, S_1 (an adequate stimulus for it) elicits anxiety, R_1, and this response is extended to conditioned stimulus S_2 (his classmates playing baseball). But anxiety is at the same time both a response and a painful internal drive, S_3, to which Philip reacted—problem-solving fashion—by R_2, R_3, and R_4. Whichever response or combination of them is most reinforcing (anxiety reducing), will become habitual in this and in related situations. Fortunately for Philip, however, his teacher guided him to a better solution.

She looked for an opportunity to reinforce Philip's still latent need for self-esteem and to condition him to feel more confident with his classmates. The opportunity occurred soon afterward when rain frustrated his classmates' desire for baseball and confined the children indoors. Angered, some of them blamed the weatherman who, they said, had promised a sunny day. At this point the teacher remembered Philip's superior knowledge of weather and raised the question of the cause of rain. Philip was provided an opportunity to explain and to demonstrate—by condensing droplets of water on the outside of a glass filled with water and ice cubes—the cause of rain. As Philip competently answered his classmates' many questions about the weather and observed their absorbed interest in his demonstration, his self-respect mounted. His confidence and self-esteem before his classmates were so strongly reinforced by this dramatic success in problem solving that the next day he was able to join the group in baseball. The renewed confidence extended to baseball play (the previously feared conditioned stimulus) and enhanced the efficiency of his play—which further reinforced his confidence and returning self-esteem.

Intellectual and motivational-emotional learning thus appear to be closely associated. Interests, appreciations, and attitudes of confidence are associated—as conditioned responses—with successful and otherwise satisfying problem solving in science, mathematics, and

literature, or in the mastery of verbal and motor skills. Anxiety and avoidance are associated with failure in these activities. And problem solving often emerges from motivational-emotional conditioning. Interests are satisfied or anxiety reduced by problem solving. In such learning, the principles of contiguity and reinforcement are both applicable. To develop such attitudes as eagerness for learning, interests in science or art, and love and respect for people, teachers should associate these situations or activities with conditions which lead to motive satisfactions and see that the adaptive responses made in these situations are rewarding.

Now that we have discussed the various explanatory concepts, let us encompass *all* of them in a definition of learning.

Definition of learning. It is difficult to formulate a definition that is concise but at the same time comprehensive enough to cover all these learnings. But perhaps a useful definition can be implied in a few statements. Emphasizing our bias for cognitive theory, we may say that learning involves a reorganization or differentiation of an individual's perceptual, cognitive, and motivational-emotional structure which functions as a guide to more adequate and satisfying adjustments (ideational, verbal, motor, emotional) in both the specific situation and in related problems and situations. Guided by both

Melton [16, pp. 667–668] and Munn [21, p. 374], we may define learning as "a change in experience or behavior." The change is produced by purposeful observation, overt activity or thinking, and associated motivational-emotional reactions. It "results in more adequate satisfaction of the motivating conditions." Implied in the phrase "experience or behavior" are combinations of perceptions, cognitions, overt actions, attitudes, and motivational-emotional feelings. For example, in typical learning situations, such as learning to recognize the meanings of words in reading, the child changes in many ways. Vague visual stimulus patterns are differentiated into meaningful concepts. Cognitive guides for the identification of new words are developed. Verbal and visual action patterns are differentiated and connected with appropriate stimulus patterns. And dynamic, motivational-emotional self-attitudes develop simultaneously—by conditioning, in the sense of shifting responses to new stimuli. While the child learns to read by problem solving, he also builds interest or distaste for the activity and confidence or anxiety about himself, depending on such conditioning factors as success and esteem or failure and humiliation. This definition can be elaborated into a practical guide for teaching.

Essential conditions for effective learning. Proceeding from our definition of learning and drawing upon the summary of explanatory principles, we are now able to derive the following conditions as essential for effective learning:

1. *Readiness,* including sufficient mental maturity for the level of learning undertaken, suitable abilities, and an appropriate background of experience.

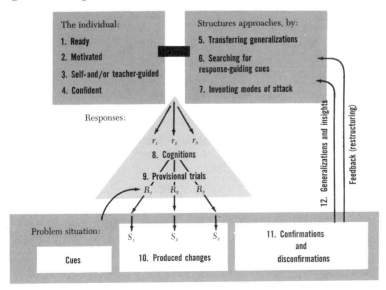

Fig. 2.4. *The complexly interrelated facets of problem-solving learning.*

How we learn: an integration of theories 53

2. *Motivation,* which arouses, sustains, directs, determines the intensity of learning effort and which, in conjunction with perception of the effects, defines and reinforces (as drive reduction) goal-achieving provisional trials.

3. *Opportunities for structuring effective approaches to problems* in which the student, by generalizing from his past experience, by self-discovery or invention, and with teacher guidance finds response-guiding cues and a mode of attack.

4. *Repeated trials,* consisting of goal-directed, provisional trials oriented toward discovery, differentiation, and integration of more effective patterns of behavior.

5. *Prompt perception of the effects* of each tentative trial, with provision for confirming correct solutions and for revising errors in subsequent goal-directed efforts.

6. Provisions for *transfer,* by organizing, generalizing, applying, and extending solutions.

7. Associated conditions favoring *confidence and mental health and preventing anxiety and distorting self-attitudes* which otherwise impair learning efficiency.

Implications of the conditions of learning for teaching. Since according to our analysis these are essential conditions of learning, we should expect to find them provided for in every instance of good teaching. As a preliminary test of this generalization, let us briefly point out applications of the seven conditions of effective learning in the chemistry unit "The Water Supply in Our Community," which we described in the preceding chapter.

The pupils were evidently interested in the topic. This fact and their developed background of chemistry principles led the instructor to assume that they were *ready* for a unit involving applications of the concepts of solubility, ionization, and hydrolysis. In the possibilities for differentiated activities in the project, he saw that he could provide suitable learning experiences for students at different intellectual levels and with varied talents.

As *motivation* to initiate and to sustain their learning efforts, the teacher relied upon the students' spontaneous manifestations of interest in the water supplies of their communities, their natural curiosity in exploration of and need to understand common things, and their joy in constructive, creative use of their developing proficiency in scientific problem solving.

The teacher *structured* a problem-solving approach to the unit by the introduction of question-raising materials (the flasks of liquid), leading questions ("Is the water potable?"), explanations and demonstrations, and guidance of the students' self-discovery observations and experiments. In their attack upon the problem, the students were led to utilize previously achieved generalizations and to discover new response-guiding cues and concepts.

In the goal-directed, trial-and-check process of learning, there were opportunities for both repeated trials and perception of the effects of provisional trials. *Repeated opportunities* for the discovery and improvement of the concepts and skills they were acquiring were provided in excursions, observation of demonstrations, the conducting of experiments, reading of texts and supplementary materials, discussions, and in writing reports. To improve fundamental proficiencies, such as writing equations for the chemical reactions observed, there were systematically scheduled practice periods. The students *checked* the correctness of their tentative solutions to the sequence of problems they attempted against the textbook explanations, against reports of the water department chemists, and by taking a test on the unit and discussing their corrected answers to it. In these ways they confirmed their tentative understanding of some of the concepts they were trying to master and discovered the need for revising their thinking about other concepts.

Transfer was involved in three ways. There were applications in this project of the students' background of previously achieved concepts and skills. Specific, newly learned concepts were generalized and related to the general principles of chemistry. And the students extended their understanding of principles, such as that of the scientific method of problem solving, for application to other projects.

Because of the expert provision of the foregoing conditions of effective learning and of the differentiated activities for children of different abilities, frustration and feelings of helplessness were avoided. On the contrary, the contributions of individual students and the sequence of worthwhile achievements of the group as a whole enhanced each student's *sense of personal worth and confidence in problem-solving learning.*

SUMMARY

Following an analysis of present-day theories on how we learn, we have developed in this chapter a comprehensive, integrated theory of learning to explain, and to guide teachers in directing, the great variety of learning in which children and youth engage. The theory encompasses explanation of how they learn differentiated and meaningful perceptions; knowledge and understandings; skills and competencies; intellectual, verbal, and motor action patterns; and, concomitantly, motivational-emotional attitudes, interests, and appreciations. It explains both the shifting of innate or acquired responses to new stimuli and the discovery of appropriate responses to numerous problem situations.

From a review of the stimulus-response contiguity, stimulus-response reinforcement, and cognitive theories, we have derived a number of explanatory principles: contiguity; reinforcement; motivation; readiness; transfer of training; and such cognitive processes as goal-directed searching, preliminary conceptualizing or structuring of approaches to problems, and perception of the effects of provisional trials.

As a first step toward a practical integration of these concepts, a two-factor theory suggests *problem solving* as the explanation of how concepts and skills are discovered and integrated into effective solutions of problem situations, and *conditioning* as the explanation of the concomitant acquisition of motivational-emotional components of learned behavior patterns.

In terms of these concepts, learning is defined as a reorganization of the individual's perceptual, cognitive, and motivational-emotional structure. The organization, or reorganization, results from purposeful observation, overt activity or thinking, and associated motivational-emotional reactions. And the perceptual-cognitive-motivational pattern achieved functions as a guide to more adequate and satisfying adjustments (ideational, verbal, motor, emotional) in both the specific and related problem situations.

The explanatory concepts, our definition of learning, and the two-factor orientation have helped us to arrive at the following essential conditions of effective learning—conditions which are present in every instance of good teaching:

1. **Readiness.** This condition implies that the child's initial success and his satisfactory progress in a learning activity depend upon his level of maturity, pattern of abilities, and an appropriate background of generalizations from his previous experience.

2. **Motivation.** This is a necessary condition of learning because motivational processes arouse, sustain, direct, determine the intensity of learning effort and, in conjunction with perception of the effects, define and evaluate the consequences of provisional trials. There are many ways to motivate pupil learning, but, as we shall suggest in Chapter 6, perhaps the best way is to provide for the child's natural desire for constructive and creative use of his talents. Related to reliance on such "activity motivation" are appeals to interest, provision for constructive use of the concepts and skills learned, arrangement of opportunities for mastery of worthwhile tasks, and knowledge of progress.

3. **Structuring approaches to problems.** The child profits from teacher guidance in directing his attention to goal-directing hypotheses, response-guiding cues, efficient modes of attack, and new

stages or steps in learning sequences. Such teacher guidance on how to approach a problem is accomplished by explaining, demonstrating, correcting the pupil's provisional trials, and by arrangement of learning sequences and leading questions which encourage pupil self-discoveries.

4. Repeated trials. This requisite for learning consists of active provisional trials or of goal-directed self-activity oriented toward discovery, differentiation, and integration of more effective patterns of behavior.

5. Perception of effects. Since problem-solving learning is a trial-and-check process in which improvement depends upon discovery of better response patterns, perception of the effects of each goal-directed trial is essential for effective learning. Perception of the effects of provisional trials makes it possible to check their correctness and adequacy. By scanning the consequences of his problem-solving efforts, the learner confirms his correct responses and is guided in correcting his mistakes.

6. Transfer. Efficient learning depends upon the individual's full utilization in new problems of his previously mastered generalizations and skills, upon his finding the unifying principles in otherwise complex and multiple-element tasks, and upon developing generalizations for subsequent application.

7. Mental health. As a final condition of effective learning, the individual should feel secure, accepted by his teacher and classmates, and confident of his learning abilities. Otherwise defenses motivated by anxiety may prevent or impair the learning process.

Our analysis of teaching in the unit on chemistry suggests that the essential conditions of learning constitute an inventory of the significant features of any learning activity. It is thus a useful guide in the teacher's task of selecting, evaluating, or creating practical methods of teaching. In this chapter, however, we have merely outlined the necessary conditions of learning. Here we have left unexplored many important subsidiary facets of which we need a much more thorough and detailed understanding. This is to be achieved in the following chapters—where the experimental support for each condition, the interrelationships of the conditions, and the possibilities of varied applications of them are fully developed.

GUIDES FOR STUDY, REVIEW, AND APPLICATION

1. Some critics of modern teacher training believe that theoretical training in the psychology of learning is unnecessary for the practical job of teaching. What are the advantages you see for teachers in achieving a comprehensive understanding of how we learn?

2. As children learn academic concepts and skills, they also acquire feel-

ings of confidence and interest or of anxiety and dislike in some or even all school subjects. How can we explain such multiple learning?

3. Explain in terms of stimulus-response reinforcement theory how a child acquires a particular concept or skill—such as division by a fraction or sustained visual fixation on the copy rather than the machine in typewriting.

4. What are the similarities and differences in the stimulus-response-reinforcement and the cognitive-insight explanations of such problem-solving learning as how to identify unfamiliar words in reading or to use the slide rule?

5. Explain according to the two-factor theory of learning an instance in which responses were *both* extended to new stimuli (by conditioning) and discovered (by problem solving). How children learn both academic skills and confidence are well illustrated in the film *We Go to School* (11 minutes), Coronet Instructional Films.

6. Describe an interesting example of especially good or poor teaching. Point out effective or ineffective applications of the seven conditions of effective learning.

Part 2

THE CHILDREN WE TEACH

Chapter 3

READINESS FOR LEARNING: ADJUSTING LEARNING TO MATURITY AND DEVELOPMENT

Our children enter and advance through the grades of the elementary and secondary school at approximately the same ages, but are they equally ready for the academic tasks they meet? Studies of two children —typical of those we as teachers are likely to encounter—illustrate our answer to this question.

Nine-year-old Tom came to the child guidance clinic with his third grade teacher and his mother for help with his reading problem. Although Tom was beginning his third year in school, he still did not read. His mother explained that for the latter half of his first year at school and all during the second year she had supplemented his teacher's persistent efforts with almost nightly sessions at helping him with his reading—all without success. Both his teacher and mother were baffled and worried. Tom, however, had become less anxious and perplexed since he had discovered the "cause" of his inability to learn to read. When the clinician handed him a primer-level book

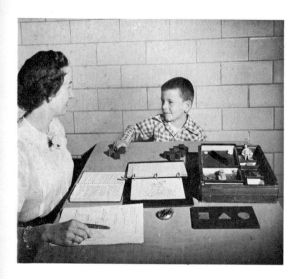

Individual intelligence examinations yield important indexes of readiness for beginning or taking next steps in learning. Besides yielding mental ages and IQs, they reveal children's problem-solving methods, their zest in or fear of challenging tasks, their confidence or insecurity in social situations, and their specific proficiencies. (Edith Bowen Laboratory School, Utah State University, Logan, Utah.)

and asked him to try to read a selection, Tom demonstrated why he could not read. The book jiggled in his hands. He explained: "That's why I can't read, books always jiggle." But nothing else jiggled for him—only books.

Since mental immaturity is sometimes a cause of reading retardation, the psychologist decided to test Tom's mental ability. On the Stanford-Binet intelligence scale, he earned a mental age of 7–3 and an IQ of 80. The minimum mental age generally accepted as necessary for success in first grade reading is about 6–5 years [82], therefore Tom should, during the last year, have been able to make some progress. But if we consider that when he first attempted reading in the first grade his mental age was probably about 4–10 (MA = IQ/100 × CA), we begin to see Tom's problem in a different light. No child with this mental age succeeded with reading in Morphett and Washburne's investigation of children's reading abilities.

Although it is possible that Tom started out in first grade with wholehearted effort and confidence, he was almost certain to experience failure, frustration, confusion, and, with pressure from teacher and parents, tension. In this state, Tom observed that the book jiggled, and his frustrating situation thus became less baffling. It was more comfortable to think that reading was impossible for him because books jiggled than to think that he was unable to learn, as he had begun to believe. Having found what he considered a rational justification for his problem, he could stop trying. Consequently, his practice sessions were at best perfunctory. When he finally developed sufficient mental maturity for beginning reading, at about eight years of age, his distorted attitude persisted and interfered with the effort and confidence required for success in learning to read.

Caroline, at age 5–7, presented a contrast in respect to readiness for beginning reading. Since age 4, she had shown an insatiable interest in stories read aloud to her. On her own initiative, she had learned to recognize many story titles and the single-word captions of pictures in her books. Because of her maturity-suggesting interests and other manifestations of appropriate maturity, her parents thought that she might be ready for the first grade despite the fact that she was one month short of meeting the usual chronological age requirement. They accordingly requested that Caroline be accepted into the first grade. The psychologist's report—to the school to which they had applied—includes the following appraisal of her readiness:

The IQ of 122 classifies Caroline as "superior" in general mental ability, at the 91st percentile of children her age, according to Terman's norms. When school begins in September, her mental age will probably be about 7 years, 2 months, which will probably place her in mental maturity a little above the average of first grade children, and above the minimum mental age set by Morphett and Washburne's experiment for satisfactory progress in first grade reading.

Several other traits revealed in the testing are indicative of probable good adjustment to school. Her vocabulary is at the eight year level. Her articulation is mature. Her sentence structure and verbal formulations are distinctively advanced for her age. For example, she defined "envelope" as "something you put a letter in." And "scorch" was defined as "something an iron does—it browns it if you get it on cloth." (The average sentence length of six-year-olds is five words.) She is confident enough with a strange psychologist to participate spontaneously in conversation with him. Her approach to problems indicates that she should be a good learner: she listens intently and grasps directions promptly; she persists in trying varied attacks on a problem; and she profits immediately from her learning experiences. For example, after two failures, on a *third* trial (with new digits each trial), she succeeded in repeating correctly five digits. Although she didn't succeed in copying a diamond, she made improvements in three successive trials. She is able to remember and to repeat the ideas of a story read to her as well as average eight-year-old children. Both precise auditory perception and attentiveness are indicated by her promptness and accuracy in following directions. Adequate visual perceptual discrimination is suggested by her success in discriminating the one slightly different form from four other identical forms in Test VI:5. Her number concepts are also probably beyond the six-year level, as she demonstrated by counting

One step . . . ㅤ ㅤ *follows another . . .* ㅤ ㅤ *as children mature and learn*

*Readiness depends on physical,
motor, intellectual, and social
development*

Getting ready for reading

*Developing self-assurance,
social ease, leadership*

Developing basic motor skills

Fine muscle control

*Peak proficiency
reached in
adolescence*

out blocks in *groups* rather than singly (as is usual at this level). She seems confident of her abilities, and the absence of timidity in her relations with the psychologist suggests that she will likely also be socially secure with her teacher and classmates.

Tom and Caroline are not average children. They deviate from the norm in many ways—in intelligence, in their attitudes toward themselves and others, in their needs. But each is typical of many children, and in order to be able to develop their potentialities, they require our special attention.

THE ROLE OF READINESS IN LEARNING

Each child is a unique individual, but in appearance one six-year-old child is very much like another six-year-old. Because of the many ways in which children of the same age are alike, we have set up rather rigid age-grade levels in our schools. Our question now is: What if a particular child is *not* very much like his coevals? What happens to this child if we fail to adjust his learning tasks to his ability? And, equally important, what are the consequences if we do try to adjust them? What happens if the education *does* fit the child?

Sufficient maturity for initial success in learning produces several desirable outcomes. Children who, like Caroline, have adequate maturity for their curriculum progress efficiently. Because of their satisfying accomplishments, such children develop interests in learning. Also, because of their successes, they become self-confident as learners and problem solvers, and learn to approach an ever-widening array of activities with greater effectiveness. As was suggested in Chapter 1, postponing academic learning for early-maturing children, or having them mark time may prevent their achieving the educational progress of which they are capable.

On the other hand, if children such as Tom are pressed to attempt learning tasks beyond their maturation levels, they are denied these achievements and health-promoting advantages, and several undesirable consequences may ensue. Besides making no progress—or, at most, progress that is painfully slow—they are likely to lose interest in learning. They may become rebellious against and resistant to teacher guidance or overdependent on it. Like Tom, they may develop self-defensive attitudes which will continue to interfere with effective use of their abilities, even when they have become sufficiently mature for the task.

Beginning reading for Tom should have been delayed. But *overdelay* is also a failure to adjust learning activities to a child's maturity and has its unhappy effects. Early interests—in music, art, crafts, science, dancing, tennis, etc.—often grow and persist into adulthood. Having attained some skills in these areas, the child develops a self-concept of his potentialities which motivates sustained efforts to improve them. Lacking such skills, he is likely to build up a self-concept of incompetence. If he is behind his peers in verbal, motor, or social skills, a child should—with advanced maturity—quickly catch up with them. But if he is embarrassed about his limitations, he may avoid situations requiring these skills and thus never acquire them [55].

Mastery of reading, spelling, arithmetic, and, indeed, of every intellectual subject is facilitated by adjusting the curriculum to the mental maturity of the learners. Conversely, we may say that appropriate maturity facilitates general achievement. In Figure 3.1, Carter reports the mean scores on the *Metropolitan Achievement Tests* for grades 2 through 6 of 25 boys of "normal" chronological and mental age for their grade levels and of 25 boys of "below normal" maturity for their grade levels, in these respects. For these two groups, equated for IQ, the more mature children begin with an advantage which they maintain throughout the elementary school grades.

The scope of readiness. Readiness for learning is a comprehensive concept. It includes (among other aspects of personality) the physical, motor, intellectual, and social aspects of development, and it applies at every stage of growth—from birth to maturity. As teachers, we must recognize that children and youth are both learning and growing as they progress through school. Year by year they are growing in size, changing in bodily proportions, and developing more differentiated nervous systems, which make possible more complex and effective problem solving. Their gradual attainment of both subject-matter and personal-social-development objectives is a product of both their growing (or maturation) and learning experiences. Moreover, as children grow through the stages of maturity—at varying rates—each child develops his own unique pattern of abilities. As

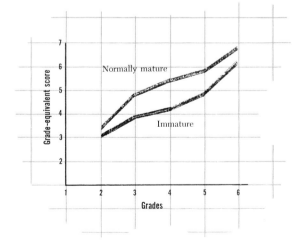

Fig. 3.1. *School achievement of 25 boys of normal chronological and mental age for grade and of 25 boys immature in chronological and mental age for grade, but equated for IQ.* (Adapted from L. B. Carter, *J. Educ. Res.*, 1956, vol. 50, p. 97.)

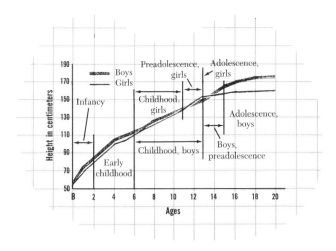

Fig. 3.2. *Growth in height of boys and girls from birth to maturity.* (From L. Cole and J. B. Morgan, *Psychology of Childhood and Adolescence,* Rinehart, New York, 1947, p. 4. 1 cm. = 0.4 inch.)

a condition of effective learning, it is highly important that—in every phase of the curriculum—learning tasks and activities be adjusted to each child's level of maturity and pattern of abilities [103].

TYPICAL SEQUENCES OF GROWTH AND DEVELOPMENT

As a guide in adjusting school curricula to each child's level of maturity and pattern of abilities, teachers need a thorough understanding of child and adolescent development. Effective teaching requires alertness to emerging new abilities and to enhanced capacities for learning, which appear as children mature and learn. Here only an outline of conspicuous trends in physical, motor, social, and intellectual development is sketched.[1]

Physical growth. The general trend of growth in body size is indicated in Figure 3.2, which shows the average growth in height from birth to maturity. Cole's comparable figure of average growth in weight is similar to the one for height, except that the spurt of growth in weight in preadolescence is accentuated [21].

The period of most rapid growth comes during infancy. Especially during the first year, but at only a slightly slower rate during the second and third years, the child grows rapidly in both height and weight. In later early childhood—from ages 4 to 6—the child makes average annual gains of only 2 or 3 inches in height and 5 or 6 pounds in weight. This slow, steady rate of growth continues throughout childhood to approximately age 11 for girls and to age 13 for boys. Then, after a short period of almost no change, another stage of rapid growth begins with preadolescence. It reaches its

[1] For an interesting and thorough presentation, see Gladys G. Jenkins, Helen Shacter, and W. W. Bauer, *These Are Your Children,* Expanded Ed. Chicago: Scott, Foresman and Company, 1953.

peak rate at about age 12½ for girls and 14½ for boys. At these ages, average gains in height are only slightly accelerated; the average increments in weight, however, jump to 10 or 11 pounds per year [11, p. 93].

Afterwards, the rate of growth falls rapidly, until growth in height ceases completely at maturity—at ages 18 to 20. By age 16 the average adolescent girl is about 64.4 inches tall and has almost attained her mature height. And by age 18, the average boy is about 67.5 inches tall and has likewise almost reached his full height. Increases in weight, however, continue—especially for boys. The vertical lines in Figure 3.2, arbitrarily marking the onset of adolescence, also indicate the approximate ages for attainment of puberty (sexual maturity)—about 13 for girls and 15 for boys.

Paralleling growth in height and weight, there are typical changes in body proportions. The 4- to 5-year-old—although still relatively long in torso and short in limbs—has lost most of the soft, round contours of babyhood. During the years of slow, steady growth, from ages 6 to 9, the body gains are not evenly distributed. Arms, and especially legs, become relatively longer; hands and feet become noticeably larger; while the head—which had attained 90 per cent of its adult length at age 5—comprises a smaller proportion of the entire body length. By age 9, the typical child entering the fourth grade is slim, although sturdily built, and he is definitely nearer to adult than to baby proportions. This pattern continues on the average to about age 11 for girls and 13 for boys.

The unevenness in rates of growth of different parts of the body sometimes produces striking disproportions during the spurt of growth in preadolescence and in early adolescence. First, very rapid growth of limbs may give the preadolescent a gangling appearance. Later, large gains in weight may make some children look unduly fat. Dif-

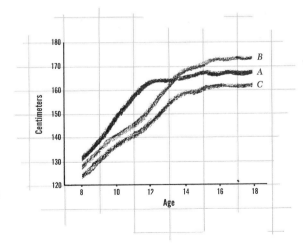

Fig. 3.3. *Curves of growth in height of three girls illustrate the uniqueness of the growth pattern of each individual.* (From Nancy Bayley, *Child Developm.*, 1956, vol. 27, p. 73.)

ferential rates of growth of the nose, jaw, or ears may temporarily distort the facial features. As maturity is approached in adolescence, the typical characteristics differentiating the sexes appear. The girl's straight legs become curved, hips widen while shoulders remain relatively narrow, and the breasts develop. In the adolescent boy, the hips remain narrow, the shoulders broaden, and athletic muscular development emerges.

Probably we can all think of specific children who deviate widely from this generalized trend. Actually, children are alike only in that they *all* pass through these stages of growth; in doing so, each child follows his own unique pattern of timing and organization. Figure 3.3, showing the growth in height of three girls from age 8 to 18, illustrates the uniqueness of individual growth patterns. At every age, children differ from their age mates in size, in body form, and in degree of maturity. Even in the middle of the period of steady growth (age 8), where the average height of boys is 51 inches, 10 per cent of them are likely to be under 48.5 inches and another 10 per cent over 54 inches tall [11, p. 93].

Individual differences are most marked in the preadolescent stage. A child who begins the preadolescent growth spurt as early as 9 years of age, may suddenly shoot ahead of his classmates. Or, if the growth spurt is

delayed until age 14—when most of his classmates are well advanced into adolescence—he may fall behind them in size. Similarly, the age at which the adolescent growth cycle is completed varies (from ages 15 to 19) according to the time (from 4 to 7 years) different children require to go through this stage [77]. Although growth is continuous, the rate of growth for each child is not constant. In a given year, one 10- to 15-year-old child may gain as much as 20 or 30 pounds and 4 or 5 inches in height; during the same year, another 10- to 15-year-old may grow inappreciably.

Such variations in timing and in rates of growth produce problems of readiness for both motor (especially athletic) and social activities. For example, high school boys vary greatly in their readiness for such strength- and coordination-demanding activities as football. Among the boys who came out for football in one high school freshman class, there were three distinct types: John, who was physically mature, 6 feet 1 inch tall, and weighed 175 pounds; 14½-year-old Henry, of average height (5 feet 6 inches) but skinny (weighing only 100 pounds); and Isaac, who was 5 feet 3 inches tall and weighed 100 pounds. All three boys aspired to places on the varsity team. Only John earned a varsity letter for three years. Henry, who grew 4 inches in height and gained 40 pounds before his junior year, earned varsity letters in his junior and senior years. Because of his slow physical development, Isaac failed to win a letter. During the year after graduation, however, he gained 30 pounds and grew 2 inches in height. These examples indicate that high school coaches and other teachers, of course, need to provide interesting activities suited to children who are at various stages of readiness and who span a wide range of physical maturation.

Despite these inconstancies or irregularities of growth patterns, growth in size is predictable. Relatively tall (or short) children tend to become relatively tall (or short) adults. Correlations with mature height (at age 18) from measurements made at ages 6 to 10 are about .75. From measurements at age 16½, the correlation with mature height is .85. Correlations between measurements made in preadolescence, however, and height at maturity drop to .60 to .65 [93].

Development of motor skills. During the whole growth process, from birth to maturity, children make continuous gains in motor skills. Before reaching age 5, children learn such basic motor skills as running, jumping, climbing, swinging, throwing a ball (awkwardly), riding a tricycle, dressing themselves (almost completely), and many goal-directed manipulatory activities such as building with blocks and drawing crude forms with crayons. The 5-year-old can also skip and dance, and sometimes he can even ride a small bicycle. He can dress himself, except for tying laces, and he can use a fork and spoon fairly skillfully. He builds crude bridges, boats, and houses of blocks, boards, and boxes. And he is learning to catch and throw a baseball or basketball and to roller-skate.

In the elementary school years (from ages 6 to 12), the child takes great strides in motor development. At 6, he usually learns to ride a bicycle. He learns manuscript writing and he is able to paste, cut, paint, and draw. During the next couple of years—with developing motor coordination—he improves these and other motor skills. His bicycle riding becomes expert. He becomes skillful in manuscript writing, and by 8 he is ready for cursive writing. He learns to throw, catch, and bat a ball with greater control, and he employs these skills more effectively and confidently in organized games. He becomes more skillful in using craft tools, and he uses them creatively.

From ages 9 to 12, while the child is continuing to develop large-muscle strength, he is also improving in fine-muscle control and coordination. He becomes an effective participant in such skill-demanding motor activities as Little League baseball. The 12-year-old develops near-adult precision in manipulatory control of shoulder, arm, wrist, and fingers in writing, drawing, and in playing musical instruments and using craft tools. Capacity for well-integrated body control, as in swimming and diving, becomes almost mature.

In adolescence, further development of strength, speed, control, and endurance takes place. Depending on individual talents and interests, peak levels of proficiency are often reached in the motor skills employed in typewriting or crafts, in music, and in such sports as football, tennis, swimming, or track.

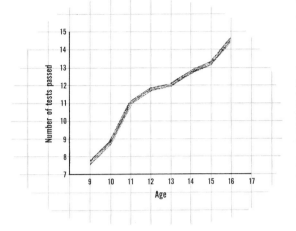

Fig. 3.4. *Motor abilities continue to emerge during later childhood and adolescence, as is indicated by the increasing number of Brace tests passed from ages nine to sixteen.* (Adapted from D. K. Brace, *Measuring-motor Ability: A Scale of Motor Ability Tests*, A. S. Barnes, New York, 1930, p. 129.)

For a view of more precisely measured motor development, let us examine the psychological studies of emergence of motor abilities, of improvement in motor skills, and of the organization of motor abilities.

Emergence of motor abilities. New motor abilities emerge as a child matures. At about age 4 a child can manipulate blunt-pointed scissors. He can copy a square accurately at age 5. At 6, he can ride a bicycle. At 7, he can copy forms of such complexity as a diamond. At 8, he can maintain the continuous fine-motor control required in cursive handwriting. Figure 3.4 reveals the gradual emergence of a variety of complex motor abilities.

Brace tested several hundred boys and girls from ages 9 to 12 on 20 different "stunts" (including hopping through a loop formed by grasping a toe with the opposite hand; kicking the right foot up to the shoulder while standing on the left foot). As the figure shows, an increasing number of tests (failed at younger ages) are mastered as the children mature.

Improvement of motor skills. The ability to throw a ball forward (though without good control) emerges at 3 or 4 years of age. As a result of maturation and learning, children gradually become able to throw the ball greater distances. On the average, at age 5, boys can throw a baseball 24 feet, 33 feet at age 6, and 41 feet at age 7 [54, p. 28]. Improvements are similar in catching a ball, running, jumping, and hopping. Accuracy in catching a carefully thrown tennis ball was found to be 66 per cent (of 10 catches) for 7-year-old boys, 84 per cent for 8-year-olds, and 90 per cent for 9-year-olds [91, p. 251]. In these age groups, boys tend to surpass girls in all these motor skills except hopping [54, p. 28]. On strength-demanding tests, such as gripping the hand dynamometer, boys are superior to girls at every age, but especially in adolescence [12, p. 162]. On simple,

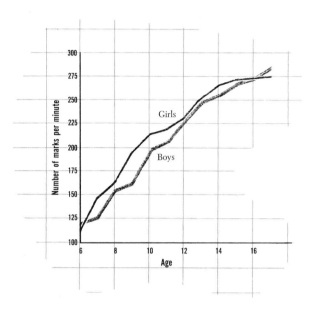

Fig. 3.5. *Having emerged in early childhood, such motor skills as speed of making straight marks with a pencil improve throughout childhood and adolescence.* (Adapted from R. J. Clinton, *J. Educ. Psychol.*, 1930, vol. 21, p. 226.)

fine-motor skills, such as finger-reaction time to a light signal [41] or speed of making short, straight marks [20], the improvement curves of boys and girls are more nearly equal. The curve shown in Figure 3.5 is typical of the maturation-learning curves of many motor functions.

Organization of motor abilities. The development of motor skills depends on many relatively independent motor abilities rather than on a single, all-round motor ability.

Guilford has classified motor abilities (of trunk, limbs, hands, fingers, and body as a whole) into seven types and suggested the activities in which they are used [45]:

Motor Ability	*Activity*
Strength	Shot put, push ups, and chinning
Impulsion	Reaction time, jumping, and bar vaulting
Speed	Two-plate tapping, looping string around a succession of pegs, marking crosses in squares
Static precision	Walking heel to toe on a 1-inch board, keeping a stylus balanced in a hole at arm's length, threading a cord through eyes in a row of pegs
Dynamic precision	Jumping and clicking heels together while in the air, arm aiming, hand aiming (dotting circles moving in an irregular order)
Coordination	Jumping rope, manipulating complex controls with feet, two-hand nut-and-bolt assembly

Flexibility	Bending over backwards with hands on wall, vaulting over a table with hands on it, and squatting slowly on one leg

Correlations between test scores on pairs of these abilities and activities range from many near zero to a few fairly high. Goodenough tested 80 five-year-old children on walking speed, walking errors, finger tapping, needle threading, holding stylus steady in hole, reaction time, and stylus tapping [42]. Correlations ranged from zero (for walking errors and walking speed or for stylus tapping and needle threading) to .38 (for needle threading and holding stylus steady in hole). In an investigation which involved pairs of athletic skills (such as basketball dribble, football passing, baseball throw, 50-yard dash, broad jump, and shot put), Ragsdale and Breckenfeld [85] found atypically high correlations ranging from .28 to .82 for 155 boys varying in age from 11 to 17.[1] The high correlation of .82 was for throwing distances—for passing a football and throwing a baseball. The common factors of throwing and of strength in both skills account for the high relationship. The common factor of strength probably also accounts for the fairly high correlations between baseball throwing and shot put (.77), between broad jumping and shot put (.68), and between baseball throwing and broad jumping (.72). Accuracy of football passing, however, correlates only .28 with the 50-yard dash and .38 with broad jumping. Between accuracy in football passing and in basketball dribbling the correlation is also relatively low (.38).

Seashore used a greater variety of motor tests (of both gross and fine motor abilities) in testing college students, and has reported several zero-to-very-low correlations [90]. For example, between football punting and chinning, the correlation was .06; between accuracy of keeping a stylus on a moving target and standing broad jump, the correlation was .08; and between the 440-yard run and distance of throwing a baseball, the correlation was .22.

The fact that children and youth have differentiated patterns of motor abilities should be taken into consideration by curriculum planners. They should seek to give each individual the opportunity to explore a wide variety of play, craft, and athletic activities, so that each can find the joy of successfully expressing his unique pattern of motor talents.

Intellectual development. The child's and adolescent's intellectual growth parallels his motor development, as a relatively independent dimension of personality. As the child grows, he assimilates a wealth of information and knowledge. He learns to differentiate one object

[1] These correlations are spuriously high because of the influence of age on these developing skills. For groups more restricted in age, the correlations would very probably be lower.

from another and one class of objects from another class. He learns the meaning of abstract terms and learns to deal abstractly with verbal, numerical, and spatial symbols. The individual's capacity to learn and to reason attains maturity in his early twenties, but his intellectual development continues throughout life as he acquires additional knowledge and new or expanded insights. The intellectual development of the child and adolescent is many-faceted. We can only give a suggestion of it here by brief comments on the development of intelligence, language, conceptualization and portrayal of things and events in drawings, and ability to reason.

Development of intelligence. Repeated measurements of intelligence—the general capacity to learn and to solve problems—are perhaps the best index of growing intellectual abilities. Bayley has produced the graph of mental growth presented in Figure 3.6. Using the Stanford-Binet scale, the Wechsler-Bellevue scales, and the Terman group test of mental ability for testing different age levels, Bayley converted the scores into comparable units. For purposes of comparison, the curve for growth in height is also shown in the figure.

The two curves are similar in that both show a long period of steady gains in childhood and a leveling off during adolescence. There are, however, significant differences. At every age, a child's relative physical maturity is ahead of his relative mental maturity. In infancy and preadolescence, sharp gains characterize the curve for physical growth but are absent in the growth curve for intelligence. Mental growth continues at least until age 20 whereas physical growth is completed at about 18. The figure also shows that girls have an accelerated rate of physical growth as compared to boys but that this acceleration is not characteristic of their growth in intelligence.

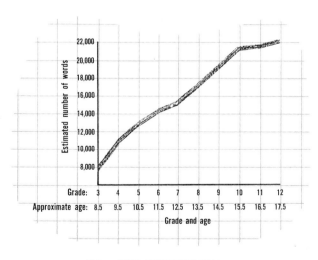

Fig. **3.6.** *Growth from birth to maturity of intelligence and of stature, both expressed as fractions of maturity status (percentage of status at age twenty-one).* (From Nancy Bayley, *Child Developm.,* 1956, vol. 27, p. 70.)

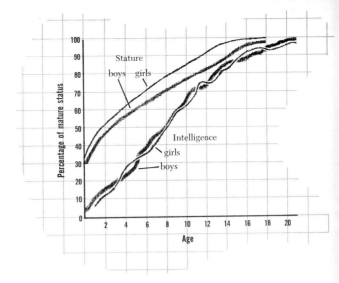

Fig. 3.7. *Estimated number of different words in the recognition vocabularies of children and adolescents. (As indexes of total recognition vocabulary, these estimates are far too small* [73].*)* (After N. B. Cuff, *J. Educ. Psychol.,* 1930, vol. 21, p. 216.)

Development of language. Language pervades nearly every aspect of the individual's intellectual life. The child's growing understanding and conceptualization of his expanding world of things and events is largely grasped and symbolized in words. The extent of an individual's vocabulary, the correctness of his articulation, and the length and differentiation of his sentences are commonly employed as indexes of language development during childhood and youth [73].

Before he is a year old, the infant communicates his feelings and needs by crying, by undifferentiated sounds, and by gestures. When he is about one year old, his first real word emerges. During his second year, the average child adds nearly 300 words to his vocabulary. The first grade child is likely to recognize the meanings of as many as 20,000 words (including both basic words and derivatives); the twelfth grade adolescent, about 80,000 words; and the college student, about 150,000 words [73, p. 529]. As an indication of the *rate* of vocabulary growth during the elementary and secondary school years, Cuff's estimates of the number of different words in the recognition vocabularies of children in grades 3 through 12 are presented in Figure 3.7.

A child's ability to articulate words improves progressively throughout early childhood: when he is two years old, only about one third of his speaking vocabulary is correctly articulated; by the time he is six, his articulation is about 90 per cent correct [73, p. 537].

Development of language skill in children is also characterized by increasing length and complexity of sentence structure. The two-year-old child's average sentence contains two words; the nine-year-old's, about six or seven; and the sentence length continues to increase into adolescence. Whereas the two-year-old uses only simple sentences, the proportion of compound and complex sentences increases with age, from early childhood to maturity [73, pp. 546–550,

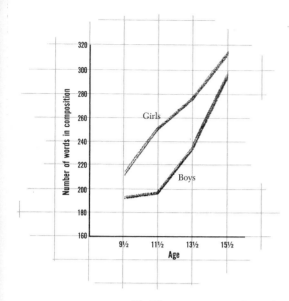

Fig. 3.8. *Integrated use of language improves during childhood and adolescence, as is indicated by increases in mean length of written compositions of boys and girls from 9½ to 15½. (From L. E. Harrell, Jr., Monogr. Soc. Res. in Child Developm., 1957, vol. 22, serial no. 66, no. 3, p. 29.)*

556]. Using as an index of sentence complexity the ratio of number of subordinate clauses to total number of clauses in oral stories, Harrell [47] found that the ratio increases from 11.6 at 9½ years of age to 18.6 at 15½. In order to indicate progress in an integrated use of the language, Harrell reported the increases in the length of children's written compositions, from age 9 to 15. His data are shown in Figure 3.8.

Intellectual development expressed in drawings. Drawing is like a second language. With crayons or easel paints, the school child grasps and expresses his concepts of the world about him. Two studies indicate that as children mature from early childhood to adolescence, their perception, conceptualization, and artistic portrayal of objects and events in their environment become increasingly more representa-

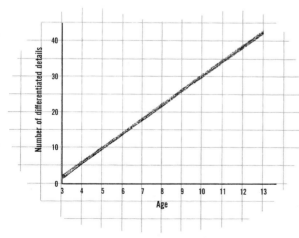

Fig. 3.9. *The conceptualization and portrayal in drawing of such objects as a man become increasingly differentiated from ages three to thirteen. (After Florence L. Goodenough, Measurement of Intelligence by Drawings, World, 1926, p. 39.)*

Fig. 3.10. *Drawings of a man by children at three levels of maturity illustrate increasing differentiation of details with greater maturity.* (From Florence L. Goodenough, *Measurement of Intelligence by Drawings*, World, 1926, pp. 116, 126, 140.)

CA, 5-7; IQ, 90   CA, 11-4; IQ, 100   CA, 12-0; IQ, 108
Score = 8   Score = 38   Score = 41

tive, differentiated, complex, and integrated. Lantz rated children's easel drawings on four points: form, differentiated details, meaningfulness, and interrelations of the parts [70]. Total scores increase slowly from age 4–0 to age 5–6 and then more rapidly to age 8–6 (the highest age studied). Goodenough found, as is shown in Figure 3.9, that from ages 3 to 13, children exhibited an increasing differentiation of details in their drawings of a man [40]. Typical drawings for ages 5, 11, and 12 are reproduced in Figure 3.10.

Development of reasoning abilities. Since independent creative thinking is a highly prized educational attainment, teachers are eager to begin cultivating children's problem-solving and reasoning skills. "With the help of skilled, artistic teachers, who know when to ask a leading question and when to withhold comment," Almy believes that children just beginning school "will work out tentative solutions, encounter new problems or see the old ones in a new light, revise answers, build concepts, and acquire the skills of effective thinking [1, p. 151]." In support of her belief, she cites five-year-old Tommy's problem-solving experience in building a garage for his collection of toy autos [1, p. 148]:

"I need a ramp," Tommy announced. Rather than construct the ramp for him, his teacher facilitated his problem-solving orientation by suggesting that he might find some blocks with which to build it. Fifteen minutes later, Tommy exhibited his independently achieved solution: "See I put three flat ones here, and a slopey one on top, then two flats and a slopey, then one flat and a slopey, and then just a slopey."

Such faith in young children's reasoning abilities is justified by psychological studies of their development. Roberts [87] tested forty-three 2- to 5-year-old children on their ability to discover a principle and apply it in new, different situations (a definition of reasoning). Although the 2-year-olds failed, the 3- to 5-year-olds succeeded. Moreover, from ages 3 to 5, the children were able to master the principle more effectively. Other experimenters have shown that preschool children transfer self-discovered generalizations [94] and make inferences

Readiness for learning   77

from prior experiences for applications to new problems [67]. These experiments support the conclusion that even 3-year-old children are ready for reasoning when the complexity of the problem is adjusted to their level of maturity. Heidbreder [48], for example, tested children from 3 to 10 for mastery of the same choice-guiding principle applied to three problems graduated in complexity. Only the 10-year-olds solved the third (most complex) problem; the 4-year-olds mastered the first and second problems; but the 3-year-olds failed on all three. Other experiments demonstrate that with increasing age, the effectiveness of reasoning improves.

To determine the relation of age to effectiveness of reasoning in learning, Gellerman conducted a maze experiment with 38 children, aged 3 to 13. He directed the children to enter the maze (diagramed)

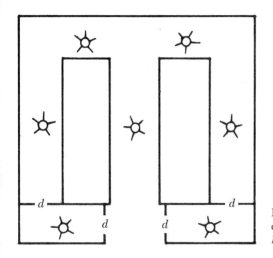

Double alternation problem: appropriate doors (d) open (permitting passage) only when the sequence RRLL is followed.

to "look around," and "to keep moving." The children were left to discover for themselves how to get through the door-obstructed passages and to continue moving freely through the maze. No particular path could be learned as correct because a path discovered as correct for one trial might be confirmed on a second trial, but disconfirmed on a third trial. Only the principle—to take two successive left-hand turns around the left rectangle and then two successive right-hand turns around the right rectangle—was found to be effective as a guide to behavior in the maze. A 12-year-old's explanation of how she learned the solution suggests the insight-discovery process: "It's a lot of walking. First, I didn't know what to do. I thought the doors opened by electricity in a certain way—twice around to the right of it, and twice around to the left of it . . . When I finally decided to get

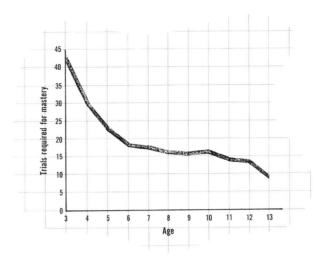

Fig. 3.11. *Ability to learn the principle of the double-alternation problem improves rapidly in early childhood and more slowly throughout childhood.* (After L. W. Gellerman, *J. Genet. Psychol.*, 1931, vol. 39, pp. 197–226.)

the knack of it, I took four or five trials, and told by which doors were closed which way I should go [39]."

Figure 3.11, showing the average number of trials required to master the principle (demonstrated by three perfect trials in succession), indicates that the problem is especially difficult for 3- and 4-year-olds, and that effectiveness in such reasoning increases with age.

On another maze problem, Maier [75] found that from ages 4 to 8, children improved in ability to generalize from two different prior experiences the solution to a third problem. Burt tested children from ages 7 to 14 on 50 miscellaneous reasoning problems, graduated in degree of complexity, and found that the total number of problems mastered increased with age. The average number solved by a 7-year-old was 6; by an 8-year-old, 12; by a 9-year-old, 18, and so on until at age 14, the average was 48 [17].

Testing a larger range of ages, Moore determined the relations to age of successful reasoning both on verbal syllogisms (such as, "If all horse-chestnuts grow buck-eyes and my neighbor is going to plant a horse-chestnut tree in his yard, can I be sure it will grow buck-eyes?") and in detecting autistic fallacies (such as, "If one washes, he cleanses himself from dirt. If one sins, he is dirty. If one washes himself, he cleanses himself from sin.").

Figure 3.12, presenting the percentage of correct explanations of such problems for 6 years to adulthood, shows that for certain kinds of reasoning considerable maturity is required. Verbal reasoning on the uncomplicated syllogisms improves gradually from age 6 to 12, but there is also marked improvement on into adolescence. Children under 12, however, are apparently not ready for dealing with such verbal abstractions as the autistic fallacies. It is not until adolescence that they are able to comprehend such complex concepts.

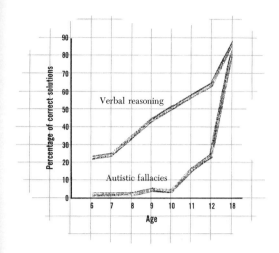

Fig. 3.12. *Ability for mastery of simple syllogisms improves during childhood; more complicated syllogisms require the maturity of adolescence.* (After T. V. Moore, *Stud. Psychol. and Psychiat.*, Cath. Univ. of Amer., 1929, vol. 2, no. 2.)

School accomplishment. The intellectual development indicated by the curves of growth in intelligence, language, drawing, and reasoning is also expressed in increased capacity for and progress in school learning. From grade to grade, children gradually improve in oral and written communication, in reading and arithmetic, and in their ability to understand concepts in social studies, science, literature, and other subjects. Figure 3.13, which shows the curve of growth in knowledge of science from grade 2 through grade 11, is typical of many aspects of school accomplishment. The achievement reflected in such curves is a product indirectly of maturation and directly of school learning experiences.

Self- and social development. Growth in size, in motor skills, and in intellectual abilities and accomplishments all contribute to the

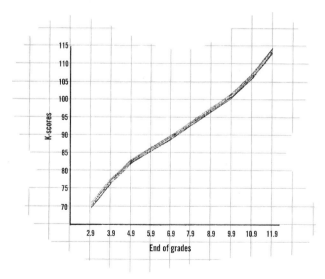

Fig. 3.13. *Growth in understanding of science, from end of grade 2 to end of grade 11. Approximately comparable K-scores for knowledge of science (including understanding of plants and animals; of the earth, weather, and atmosphere; conservation; physiological and health concepts; and elementary principles of physics and chemistry).* (Adapted from T. L. Kelley and associates, *Stanford Achievement Test Manual*, Yonkers-on-Hudson, N. Y., World, 1953, p. 21.)

child's social development. As the child matures in these respects, he becomes more independent, self-directing, and effective in playing his various social roles. He becomes both a participating and contributing member of family, school, play, and other peer groups. His social development involves a number of changes in behavior: (1) He learns to participate in groups of increasing size and complexity of interaction; (2) he extends his social attachments from mother and other family members to peer friendships and to gang and other organized peer groups; (3) he responds increasingly to social motives; (4) he achieves an enriched understanding and differentiation of his role in the interpersonal relationships of family, play, work, and other social groups; (5) he gains greater self-direction and increasing responsibility, consideration, and love for other people [3]. Emerging social maturity is also manifested in the accomplishment of personal-social achievements characteristic of each stage of development—of infancy and early childhood, childhood, and adolescence [22].

The five-year-old, who has accomplished the developmental tasks of infancy and early childhood, has already achieved "a well-formed picture of himself [11]." He recognizes his own role and the differentiated roles of mother, father, siblings, and of some other familiar persons in his neighborhood. He has a sense of belonging in his family and in small peer groups—where he receives and gives affection, expresses his feelings, and strives for approval. His social interactions are already beginning to take on some complexity. He has become competitive in play activities and in his claims of achievements [44]. Although he does not yet cooperate very well, he does—with supervision—participate constructively in informal groups of three or four and in larger formal groups. He conforms to authority and leadership and is learning to respect some rights of others; generally he takes turns and does not snatch. He has achieved considerable independence in self-care—in dressing, feeding, toileting, and in self-occupied play. Although boys and girls play well together, they are becoming aware of sex differences—that girls play with dolls and that boys play with trucks and guns [13].

From about six to twelve years of age, children take great strides in social growth. During these years of childhood, the individual becomes more of an individual. He develops a self-concept, establishes a role for himself in his peer group, and weans himself away from close dependence on adults. He develops a well-differentiated sex role and achieves the motor, communication, and intellectual skills needed for greater personal and social effectiveness [22].

During the early school years, social attachments are extended from family to peers. While the six-year-old is parent- and teacher-oriented, the eight-year-old is becoming peer-oriented [11]. The six-year-old establishes peer friendships, which shift frequently, but by the time the child is eight, friendships have become more stable "best-friend" relationships. The child now begins to form gangs or clubs or finds scouting appealing. In school projects and organized games, he learns cooperation, how to follow rules, and he extends such regulations to his informally organized gangs. With enhanced pride, he grows in self-direction and in his capacity for taking responsibilities. At six, he likes to set the table or erase the blackboards. After a year of self-confidence-building experiences in the first grade, he learns to assert his "rights" on the playground or in the classroom. He is sensitive to peer approval, however. He wants to succeed, to do what is right, and to be fair. He enjoys the independence and trust of having a weekly allowance. He is also becoming more self-critical; he compares himself with his peers, and is beginning to recognize that he has both talents and weaknesses. He develops admiration and sympathy for other children. Sex roles are becoming more clearly understood, and by the time boys and girls are eight, they are definitely cognizant of sex differences [53, p. 153].

The report by Anderson and his associates [4] of the mean self-ratings on "work habits" and "social responsibility" of over 3,000 children at ages 9 to 17 gives us a quantitative sampling of growth on these indexes of social maturing. As is shown in Figure 3.14, the development of independence and ability to share responsibilities continues during later childhood and adolescence. The curves show that with increasing maturity and social experience, children accept more home duties and other social responsibilities.

In the intermediate school years these developmental trends continue. The 9- to 12-year-old child wants to do things especially well:

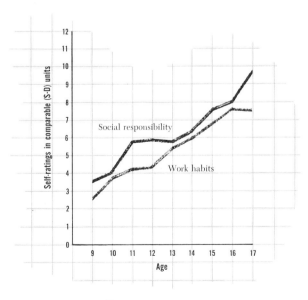

Fig. 3.14. *Social maturing in later childhood and adolescence involves, as the curves show, more self-acceptance of home duties and other social responsibilities.* (After J. E. Anderson and others, *A Survey of Children's Adjustment over Time,* Inst. of Child Developm. and Welf., Univ. of Minn., 1959, pp. 11–12.)

"He wants to be a good ball player, to know how to pitch and catch well. He wants to learn how to swim; he is no longer content just to splash around [53, p. 168]." Although he is fond of parents and teacher, he is also becoming critical. "Signs of growing independence, such as rebelliousness, disobedience, backtalk, discourtesy are common [11, p. 49]." Peer-group influence is strong with respect to dress, play, possessions, and behavior. For fear of being different from his fellows, the child becomes an all-out conformist. Because of his growing intellectual abilities, however, he is open to reasoning, to talking things over. He participates effectively in group planning, takes responsibilities, can be loyal and sympathetic, and he likes to be considered fair and trustworthy. Although boys and girls participate together in supervised activities, their play and gangs are organized on sex lines. In preadolescence, however, boys and girls again take an interest in each other—teasing, taking one another's possessions, and making other awkward gestures toward association. At ages 12 to 14, both boys and girls enjoy mixed parties [11].

During adolescence the child is becoming an adult. He has difficult personal-social adjustments to make. The important developmental tasks of the adolescent are (1) to achieve a comfortable acceptance of his rapidly developing body; (2) to become confident and happy in new social relationships with age mates of both sexes; (3) to achieve self-directing independence from parents—without loss of mutual affection and respect; (4) to make plans and preparation for adult economic and social status; (5) to achieve confidence in respect to more sharply identified self-roles; (6) to build a system of values to which he can wholeheartedly commit himself [22].

None of these developmental tasks is easy for adolescents. Instead of accepting their rapidly changing bodies as normal, for example, 30 to 40 per cent of adolescents are disturbed. Boys are disturbed about being too small, too thin, or too fat, being weakly built, or about suddenly changed facial features. Girls are disturbed about being too tall, too fat, or having either under- or over-developed breasts [98]. In their desire to reassure themselves about their bodies and personalities, to learn effective group participation, to become more independent of their parents, and to feel themselves full-fledged members of a society of equals, adolescents turn to their peers for guidance and security. They need greater areas of freedom in which to make their own decisions, but at the same time they still need parental security and support. They are striving toward adulthood, and they begin to develop confidence and pride in mature responsibilities—in doing an adult job.

In early adolescence, the differentiated sex groups of preadolescence are abandoned. By 14—although without wholehearted interest on the part of the boys—both boys and girls are dating. In later adolescence, both sexes become absorbed in dating and going steady. The adolescent crowd is replaced by twosomes or foursomes. And crowd-dominated behavior gives way to more independence in making decisions and in setting personal and social standards [11].

Adolescents take significant steps toward the achievement of social maturity. They earn money for independent selection and purchase of clothing and for personal expenses. They "go out" on their own responsibility. They drive and sometimes own cars. Some adolescents take full-time jobs. Many continue their education and vocational preparation in college. Nearly all begin courtships looking toward marriage.

The Vineland Social Maturity Scale lists the following indexes of attainment of social maturity (at age 20 to 25 on the average): "assumes personal responsibility, assumes responsibilities beyond own needs, contributes to social welfare, and provides for the future [28]."

Patterns of physical, motor, mental, and social development. Although growth is continuous during childhood and youth in every dimension of personality, the interrelationships of different traits are complex. There are not only significant relationships between traits, but there are also important areas of independence. Children typically develop variegated patterns of physical, motor, intellectual, and social traits. The case of 10-year-old James, who is about to complete the fourth grade, illustrates this uneven development.

James is of average size, sturdily built and well proportioned. He plays baseball moderately well, rides his bicycle expertly, and skates awkwardly. His mental age is a little above average for his chronological age group, but he does better in the abstract-spatial than in the verbal parts of the intelligence test. His arithmetic work in school is good. He also does well in using the science and social studies information he gains from sources other than reading. He is alert and curious, and reasons through problems well. In reading and spelling, however, James performs at about the beginning of the second grade level. Socially, he is independent in self-care (rides his bicycle over a mile to and from school) and he gets along well in work and play with other children. He has some close friends and belongs to a gang. He is embarrassed, however, and sometimes cries, when he tells his mother about the comments other children make about his poor reading. His greatest handicap in overcoming his reading disability is his own concept of himself as "unable to learn to read." Because of this self-concept he cannot apply to his reading the wholehearted, confident effort it requires.

There are a number of studies of the relationships among different dimensions of personality which provide a scientific basis for helping us to understand such instances of uneven development. We have noted earlier in this chapter the relative independence of some of the motor abilities. In several measures of physical ability and measures of mechanical and intellectual abilities of 100 junior high school boys, Paterson and his co-workers discovered zero or very low intercorrelations [84]. Intelligence itself—as we shall see more clearly in the next chapter—is not a unitary trait. Between tests of verbal, numerical, spatial, and mechanical reasoning, interrelations range only from .40 to .60 [7]. Between measures of physique (such as height and weight) and of intelligence, the correlations are near zero [25], and intelligence and athletic abilities are relatively unrelated [64]. Measures of height and weight of children (for single age groups) are also unrelated to achievement in reading and other academic subjects both in the early [65] and the later stages of growth [25].

As an illustration of more significant relationships between different aspects of development, let us examine the relation of physical and motor growth to social development. Mussen and Jones have compared the projective stories of early- and later-maturing 17-year-old boys [83]. From their analysis, these investigators infer that the early maturers accomplish the developmental tasks of adolescence more effectively than the late maturers. The physically accelerated boys tended to appear self-confident, independent, and mature in interpersonal relations, whereas the physically retarded boys seemed to feel inadequate, rejected, dominated, and either overdependent on their families or rebellious toward them. A study of the personality inventories of young adults who had been physically accelerated in adolescence showed that they tended to score higher in self-esteem, socialization, dominance, and self-control than those who had been physically retarded [62]. Jones also found that superior muscular strength in adolescence is related both to favorable self-appraisal on personality inventories and to adult-judged popularity with peers [61]. Two cases reported by Jones suggest the possible relationship of accelerated or retarded physical and motor development to social adjustment.

Reed was about a year ahead of the average of his classmates in physical development. He was taller and heavier than the majority; he was well proportioned, and an outstanding athlete. On the dynamometer tests of strength and on other athletic abilities, he scored consistently above the 90th percentile. He was popular, a recognized leader, and president of his class in the senior year. His relations with his family (of superior socioeconomic status) were "unusually harmonious." Of superior intelligence, "he was rated by his teachers as having a 'capable' and 'original' mind, high in scholastic interest and achievement." At 15 years of age, Reed was well-adjusted, free of worries, "although sometimes ill at ease among girls." Later ratings continued to be favorable: "As usual, Reed appears poised, assured, friendly but unconcerned about the impression he makes on others . . ." On an inventory of personal-social adjustment, he presented a self-picture "of a well-integrated, secure, tolerant individual, dependably successful in the things that he wanted to do [61, p. 289]."

Lonnie was a late maturer. Small in stature although "fairly" well proportioned, he was "deficient in muscular development," low in strength, slightly below average "in other aspects of motor performance," but relatively quick and agile. Of superior intelligence (85th percentile), he was "quick-witted," "tended to dominate social situations by repartee and general activity," and in the ninth grade he "reached a relatively high position of popularity and general prestige." In senior high school, however, he became frustrated by his dropping status in the social life of his peers and reacted with "increased aggressiveness, talkativeness and attention-seeking [61, p. 293]." He was judged "unpopular" by his peers. When Lonnie was age 16–8, an observer wrote: "His short stature has so interfered with his athletic achievement that he is at a loss to know what to do when other boys begin to play baseball. . . . When anyone is watching, he assumes the role of a swaggering, arrogant somebody. . . . He is sensitive to criticism and shows his discomfort when Bob heckles him." In his senior year, he became interested in girls and in dances, but "the larger girls in his own grade treat him like a pet Teddy bear. . . . He would not dance as he was too small for the girls [61, p. 294]." His family gave him little aid or support in dealing with his conflict. On the self-inventory of personal-social adjustment, "he reported many indications of personal inferiority and resulting ego injury." His recurrent daydream epitomizes his self-concept: "I seem to be in a room which is awfully big, and keeps getting bigger and bigger, and I am very, very small [61, p. 295]."

These two studies—and others—illustrate that an adolescent's social adjustment sometimes depends on his physical development. But other cases show just as clearly that social adjustment is not inevitably related to physical development. Jones has described another adolescent who, like Lonnie, was physically retarded and socially maladjusted at about age 15, but who, by the age of 18, had achieved a fairly good social adjustment [60].

Like Lonnie, Reed, and James, the poor reader whom we described above, every child is a unique individual. Therefore, our presentation here of developmental norms of physical, motor, intellectual, and social development should not be regarded as a guide of what to expect of every child at each stage of development. These norms are, rather, a set of criteria for interpreting each child's unique pattern, sequence, and rate of development.

In our discussion of developmental trends, we have assumed that readiness for learning at each new stage of school progress is a product of both maturation (growth) and prior learning. In real-life situations these factors are complexly blended. But some experiments have been designed to bring out the distinctive influences of maturation and of prior pertinent experience on readiness for learning.

MATURATION AND READINESS FOR LEARNING

In order to determine the role of either maturation or learning as a separate factor affecting readiness, the other factor must be controlled. The effect of maturation on readiness has been determined by observing whether or not development occurs in the absence of (or with restrictions of) opportunity for learning, and by comparing the gains from the same training given at different stages of maturity.

Development of motor skills. Dennis [26] found that Hopi Indian children whose locomotion was restricted by confinement on a "cradle board" walked as early as other Hopi children left free to crawl, stand, or try walking. He concluded that walking depends mainly on maturation. In an experiment which confirmed this conclusion, McGraw [74] found that untrained Jimmy began walking (at 14 months) on the same day as his extensively trained twin brother. Apparently training cannot hasten the age of walking [27]. When children are ready, not before, they very quickly learn to walk, and this readiness seems to involve only maturation. The skill of ball throwing, however, is a different matter. By giving the same training in throwing a ball to children of different ages in early childhood, Dusenbury found that both maturation and learning affect the development of this skill. As is shown in Figure 3.15, the three weeks of training given the trained groups produced more development than occurred in the same time for the untrained (control) groups. The role of maturation in the development of this particular skill is indicated by the higher initial scores and the more rapid rate of progress achieved by the older children.

The relative influences of maturation and training on development of motor skills varies with the complexity of tasks. Mattson [76] found that training was no advantage over maturation alone in helping kindergarten children develop skill in manipulating a simple rolling-ball maze. However, on a maze of intermediate complexity and especially on one of greater complexity, training added significantly to gains achieved. Training, however, cannot make up for deficiencies in

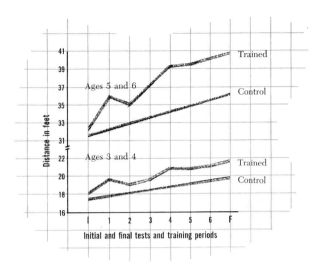

Fig. 3.15. *Role of maturity in learning is indicated by average distances a ball is thrown by boys in trained and in control groups, ages three to four and five to six.* (From Lois Dusenberry, *Res. Quart. Amer. Ass. Hlth. Phys. Educ. Rec.,* 1952, vol. 23, p. 13.)

maturity. If the task is too complex for the maturity level of the learners, neither trained nor control groups make progress [37, 50].

For effective participation in competitive athletic activities and for achieving adolescent social status, early physical maturation is an advantage. Jones and Bayley report that adolescent boys who matured early (as compared with those maturing late) tended to be taller, more athletic and masculine in build, and more attractive physically [63]. Hale has observed that out of 60,000 Little League baseball players in 1955, of the 112 boys who participated in the "World Series," 92 were in the 12-year (oldest) age group [46]. They approximated average 14-year-olds in size. And those in the crucial positions on the teams (such as pitcher or fourth order in batting) were either pubescent or postpubescent in physical maturity.

Verbal learning. Several experiments demonstrate that the effectiveness of verbal learning is dependent upon chronological and/or mental maturity. One such experiment involved a study of twins, who were given daily training in learning the names of common objects [99]. Each of the children was given one hour of daily practice for a period of five weeks. Twin A, whose training began when he was 89 weeks of age, progressed more rapidly than did twin B, whose training period began at 84 weeks. Apparently twin A learned more rapidly because of greater mental maturity and/or because of the age differential at the time of training.

Choosing mental age as a better index of capacity for verbal learning than chronological age, Foster compared the ability of children ranging in mental age from 3 to 5 to memorize stories read to them. To 22 children of chronological ages 2–7 to 4–9 (each child taken separately), she read and reread 10 times eight different stories,

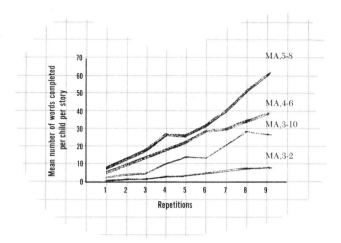

Fig. 3.16. *Verbal memory for stories reread 10 times improves in maturing from mental age three to five.* (From J. C. Foster, *J. Genet. Psychol.*, 1928, vol. 35, p. 34.)

such as "The Dog and the Kitty Cats." On each reading, the experimenter paused at a certain place in the story and asked the child to complete it as far as he could. The child was rewarded with approval for his successes, and the experimenter reread the uncompleted or incorrectly recalled parts. Figure 3.16 shows the average number of words completed per story for four different mental age groups, and demonstrates clearly that readiness for such learning is a product of mental maturity. Children with mental ages as low as 3–2 are too immature for such learning. And each increase in mental maturity from mental ages 3–10 to 5–8 is accompanied by improved capacity for memorization.

Morphett and Washburne conducted an experiment to find at what mental age children are sufficiently mature for beginning read-

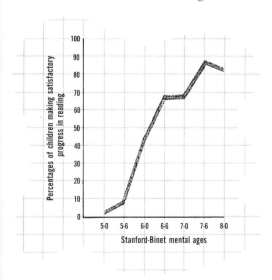

Fig. 3.17. *Sufficient mental maturity is a condition of "satisfactory" progress in first grade reading.* (Adapted from Mabel V. Morphett and C. Washburne, *Elem. Sch. J.*, 1931, vol. 31, p. 498.)

ing. They determined the percentage of children at each half year of mental age from 5 to 8 who had attained, after a semester of instruction, a certain criterion of satisfactory reading achievement. Their results are graphed in Figure 3.17.

This maturation curve indicates that no child with a mental age as low as 5–0 and only a very few at 5–6 succeeded in reading. Even at mental age 6–0, less than half the children mastered beginning reading. At mental age 6–6, however, over 70 per cent of the children made satisfactory progress. On the basis of these and other similar data, teachers generally agree that a mental age of about 6–6 is the approximate minimum for success with first grade reading—as it is usually taught. Since some children did not succeed even at mental ages of 7 or 8, it is apparent that other factors of readiness are also important [89]. Mental age, however, is an important factor determining readiness for reading at every level of school progress. Brighter children not only learn to read at younger ages, but attain higher levels of proficiency throughout their school careers [2].

Maturation also affects the mastery of concepts. Robinowitz found that the inductive discovery of the meaning of the concept of "opposite" (in classifying words and in giving opposites of other words) related to mental maturity [88]. Ausubel and Schiff found that the ability to learn and to apply mechanical-causation principles (such as the fact that the longer side of a teeter-totter will fall when both sides are released from their supports) increases from ages 5 to 11—especially from 8 to 11 [5].

Another experiment indicated that for a wide range of both chronological and mental age, the ability to memorize poetry improves with added maturity. Stroud and Maul conducted a study to determine the average number of lines that could be memorized in 15 minutes by 172 school children and 28 college freshmen—ranging in

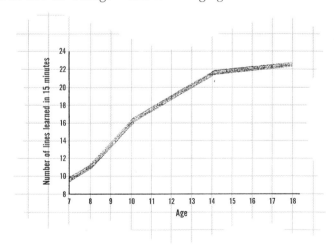

Fig. 3.18. *Skill in memorization of poetry improves rapidly through childhood and more slowly in adolescence.* (Adapted from J. B. Stroud and Ruth Maul, *J. Genet. Psychol.*, 1933, vol. 42, p. 245.)

age from 7 to 18 [100]. The results, presented in Figure 3.18, show that memorizing ability increases rapidly up to age 14 and very slowly after that age.

Two other studies also suggest that maturity beyond early adolescence contributes little to learning efficiency. Finch and Floyd [33] used as their subjects 147 students in French classes. They found that the correlation between age (from 11 to 19) and achievement in vocabulary was only .10, and between age and grammar, only .12. College students, who are even more mature, show no appreciable difference in level of achievement whether they take such verbal-concept courses as general psychology as freshmen (age 18) or as sophomores (age 19), provided the experience factor is equal for the two ages [34].

Social learning. Effective social learning depends upon a complex combination of physical, motor, and intellectual factors of readiness. Two experiments indicate that the young child's ability to cooperate increases with age. Wolfle and Wolfle observed that the cooperative behavior of two- to five-year-old children depends on the growth in language skills characteristic of this age [105]. The more fluent older children were more effective in a task requiring cooperation than the two- to three-year-olds who "could not talk well." Greenberg provided two- to seven-year-old children building blocks and asked, "Which is prettier?" or said, "I would like to see who can build prettier this time." Figure 3.19 shows that instances of competitive behavior (such

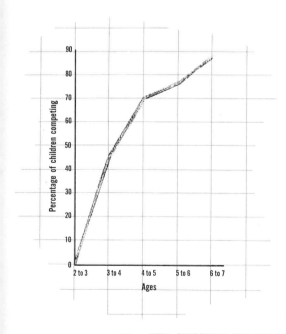

Fig. 3.19. *Competitive social interaction emerges with increasing frequency from ages two to seven.* (Adapted from Pearl Greenberg, *Amer. J. Psychol.*, 1932, vol. 44, pp. 221–248.)

as block grabbing) and remarks (such as "Mine is bigger") increased rapidly from ages two to five and then more slowly up to age seven.

As we have already seen, accelerated physical maturation in adolescence facilitates the accomplishment of developmental tasks, appropriate socialization, and the growth of healthy self-esteem and self-confidence.

PRIOR EXPERIENCE AND READINESS FOR LEARNING

In reviewing the experiments dealing with the role of maturation in determining readiness for learning, we have observed that the effect of prior experience was usually controlled but not excluded. Similarly we shall find that experiments to demonstrate the distinctive role of prior learning in determining readiness for subsequent learning have not completely eliminated the influence of maturation.

Motor skills and experience. An individual's prior experience in motor skills determines to a great extent his readiness to learn advanced and more complex skills. High school and college coaches always consider prior training as well as physical maturity and talent in selecting promising players. An experiment by Carpenter [18] suggests indirectly the importance of experience in development of motor skills. Among her tests of the motor educability of six- to nine-year-old boys and girls, she included a number of complex-pattern hopping tests. Although boys are usually superior to girls in such motor skills as running, jumping, kicking, and ball throwing [54, 93], Carpenter found that on the hopping tests, the girls surpassed the boys at every age. Since games such as hopscotch and jump rope are usually considered girls' games, it may be that the superiority of the girls in this particular motor skill is due to their much more extensive practice in hopping.

Intellectual accomplishments. Many observations and several experiments indicate that pertinent prior experience or special readiness instruction facilitates subsequent learning in school subjects.

Some skills can be developed at surprisingly early ages by giving children appropriately guided experience. Dubin [29] reports that two- to four-year-olds whose attention was called to possibilities just beyond their present stages in easel painting made more progress in drawing than did children who were not given such guided experience. Jersild and Bienstock [57, 58] have shown that preschool and kindergarten children who are given appropriate training can acquire skill in singing simple songs with a range of two octaves. The singing range of four- and five-year-old children who have not had such training is about one octave.

We have already observed that language development occurs

during the early years of childhood as a result of maturation. Several studies indicate that it also occurs as a result of guidance and experience. Sommer [95] reports articulation tests and retests (after 12 weeks) of equated groups of two- to six-year-old children. An uninstructed group improved 28 per cent—from maturation alone. However, the group given 12 weeks of corrective guidance in articulation improved 57 per cent. As a related indication of the role of guidance in readiness for learning, Fast [31] found that children who had been given a year of prereading instruction in kindergarten made better progress in first grade reading than children (of comparable mental age and IQ) who entered the first grade without kindergarten experience. In another experiment involving kindergarten children, Herr reports that Spanish-speaking children, because of their language handicap in speaking English, are usually retarded in reading during the primary grades. However, when given a year of instruction in a prereading language-improvement curriculum prior to the usual age for entering the first grade, they did better in reading than "other Spanish-speaking" children not given such readiness instruction [49].

Although it has frequently been found that girls are more advanced in language and reading than are boys, McCarthy questions the idea that the difference is based on sex. Rather, she attributes it to variations in language readiness experiences [72].

Readiness for first grade arithmetic is enhanced by appropriate, meaningful experiences with numbers and quantitative relationships in the kindergarten [14, 69]. Of equated groups of kindergarten children, Koenker found that the group given guided experience in counting, grouping, comparing, and measuring in connection with games and stories, in keeping records of attendance and height and weight, and in reading the clock and calendar was more ready for first grade arithmetic than a group not given such experience [69].

Readiness experience is important at every level of learning. At the high school and college levels, certain prerequisites must be fulfilled before a student is admitted to advanced courses in many fields. A minimum of prior achievement is important, even in readiness for remedial instruction in reading. A high school student who has attained a third grade reading level—a sight vocabulary and some word-identification skills—can make good progress from remedial reading instruction, but students below this level profit much less from similar instruction [92]. College freshmen and sophomores, who are not ready for chemistry because of deficiencies in understanding arithmetic, can improve their achievement in chemistry by remedial study in arithmetic [68]. And in such a subject as geography, a college student "with extensive travel experience" tends to do "higher quality work than the student with limited travel experience [78, p. 220]."

Social development. Like other aspects of personality, social behavior is a product of both maturation and learning. Increasing maturity brings increases in capacity for learning, but self-direction and ability to participate effectively in complex social interactions require learning. A good example of this is the acceleration of social development which occurs when children first leave the relatively simple social situations of their homes to meet the greater social demands of the school. From interviews with mothers of first grade children, before the children entered school and again three months later, Stendler and Young found that 75 to 85 per cent of the children had improved in independence and in social responsibility. The children became more independent in dressing, beginning work, entertaining friends, running errands, and in staying alone. They demonstrated improved social responsibility by helping in more activities, by being more self-controlled, and in general by acting more mature [97].

DETERMINING READINESS FOR LEARNING

Readiness for each new stage of learning is a product of both maturation and prior experience. For simple skills and in the years of infancy and early childhood, perhaps maturation is the more important factor of readiness. For more complex performances, however, and in later childhood and adolescence, prior pertinent experience becomes relatively more important. Readiness for increasingly differentiated curricula also depends on each individual's unique pattern of abilities. How to appraise each child's intellectual abilities and differentiated talents and to adjust curricula to them are the topics of the next two chapters. In concluding this chapter, we shall summarize the signs of *developmental* readiness—readiness as a product of growth and background experience.

As useful indexes of readiness for learning, the teacher has at hand some chronological and mental age norms, developmental sequences, readiness aptitude tests, manifestations of interest, and combinations of these signs.

Chronological and mental age norms. Since children enter school at an average age of 6½, and generally advance at the rate of one grade per year, curriculum specialists and teachers have been able to determine—mainly on the basis of experience—the curriculum content which is approximately appropriate for children at each age from 6½ to 18½ (for grades 1 through 12). Reading, for example, is appropriate for the 6½-year-old and is begun in grade 1. Cursive writing is usually introduced at the beginning of grade 3. Algebra is introduced at the beginning of grade 8. The age trends reviewed earlier of physical, motor, intellectual, and social development partially constitute a normative guide for such grade placement of curriculum content.

Experimental studies of the optimum ages for learning varied concepts and skills is another guide. Among such studies, we are reminded of the findings that kindergarten children profit from training in language articulation and can learn to sing a range of two octaves; that certain concepts of mechanics are grasped more readily by 11-year-olds than by 5- to 8-year-olds; that 11-year-olds can master French vocabulary and grammar almost as easily as 17-year-olds; and that such courses as general psychology are learned equally well by college freshmen and sophomores.

For grade placement of the intellectual content of the curriculum, however, it has been determined that the mental age at which the particular content can be assimilated is a much sharper criterion of readiness than chronological age. Growth of vocabulary [101], of abstract reasoning ability [52], and academic accomplishment (which we shall take up in Chapter 4) are all more closely related to mental than to chronological age. As an example of such norms, a mental age of approximately 6–6 has already been mentioned as an important sign of readiness for first grade reading. Another illustration is the mental age placement of arithmetic processes outlined in Table 3.1.

Table 3.1. *Tentative recommendations of the Committee of Seven (on placement of arithmetic concepts in relation to mental age)*

Optimum MA	Arithmetic item
6–7	Informal activities with concrete numbers and space relations; addition of sums under 10; begin easy subtraction.
8–9	Difficult subtraction facts (3-digit subtraction); easy multiplication (products under 20, and 5 x 5); simplest forms of square measure and comparisons of areas; learn minutes, hours, days as measures of time; learn to read calendar and clock to quarter hour.
9–10	Column addition of digits 3 high and 3 wide; multiplication of products over 20; easy division facts (dividends under 20); meaning of ½, ⅓, ¼, ¾, etc., of whole objects; learn inches in yards; learn areas of rectangles.
11–12	Mastery of all multiplication facts; multiplication with multipliers as high as 3 digits and multiplicands as high as 4 digits; division facts; short division (1-place divisor); long division; fractional and decimal equivalents; division and multiplication with decimals; learn square measure in feet or inches.

SOURCE: Washburne, C. (chm.). *Child Development and the Curriculum,* Thirty-eighth Yearbook Nat. Soc. Study of Educ., part I, pp. 309–314, Chicago, 1939. Distributed by the Univ. of Chicago Press.

From the results of teaching each computational process in arithmetic over a range of three grade levels in 300 school systems, a committee determined for each concept the mental age level at which 75 per cent of the children could attain 80 per cent accuracy [102]. Useful as they are, however, these norms are not static and as improved ways of teaching are discovered, it will be necessary to revise them.

Another limitation of both chronological and mental age norms is that they are inapplicable to the grade group as a unit because of the wide range of mental maturity of children in every grade. Fortunately, there are supplementary procedures which teachers may follow in adapting the curriculum to individual differences.

Developmental sequences. We observed earlier that all children go through approximately the same stages of development—though not at the same rate. Such developmental sequences—in reading, language, mathematics, science, art, music, and probably in every aspect of the curriculum—provide another sign of readiness for learning. For example, at any "stage" in a curriculum sequence, the best answer to the question about a particular child's readiness for the next step is evidence that he is about to complete the preceding one.

As an illustration of developmental sequences, consider the successive steps of progress in reading comprehension. The first step is comprised of the prereading activities of the kindergarten and the forepart of the first grade. When the child meets the intellectual and social standards of the six-year-old, and when he enjoys listening to stories or looking at picture books, can describe a picture or relate an experience in four-or-more-word sentences without infantile mispronunciations and can repeat a sentence of six or eight words, then he is ready to begin to read [80].

Taking the second developmental step in learning to read, the child begins to recognize some sight words. With teacher guidance and on his own initiative, he learns to recognize his name on his locker and art-materials compartment, the names of animals under their pictures on the wall or in picture books, and some of the words the teacher uses to write stories and experiences told by the children in the class. At this stage, written words are usually recognized only by their general contour, distinctive details, or context. For example, the word "rabbit" has two "ears" in the middle, while "dog" is a "small" word.

When enough sight words are recognized for effective use of context in simple sentences or paragraphs, the child is ready to take the third step, that of learning independent methods of identifying unfamiliar words. In combination with the context—which is constantly employed—he learns to use word-form clues, phonetic analysis, and structural analysis in identifying unfamiliar words.

When some workable understanding of these techniques has been acquired, the young reader is ready for the fourth developmental step. He learns—from extensive practice on easy material—to use the techniques skillfully, confidently, and in efficient hierarchical order. By the time he has accomplished this fourth step, the child has become quite rapid and proficient in reading comprehension.

He is now ready for the fifth step, learning techniques suited to different purposes—skimming, following a narrative for general understanding, reading for organization of details, following directions, outlining, evaluating critically, and selecting or rejecting ideas for the purpose at hand. At the completion of this stage, the child is almost a mature reader.

In the sixth stage, however, the high school student attains higher levels of comprehension—in more effective inferential use of context, in extended and more differentiated vocabulary development, in advanced structural analysis of words, and in more effective interpretation of punctuation clues.

In any single grade, different children will be found at several different stages of reading comprehension. In the third grade, for example, Joe may be able to recognize words only by their general contour. He is probably ready for the third stage—learning how to identify words independently—a step which is usually begun late in the first grade and continued intensively during the second grade. Jane, however, also in the third grade, may already be using all the techniques of word identification rapidly and efficiently, even in relatively difficult material. She is, of course, ready to take the fifth step—suiting techniques to different purposes—a step not usually undertaken until the fifth grade.

Tests of readiness aptitude. A skilled teacher can tell a great deal about her pupils' readiness simply by observation, but there are also a variety of tests which are effective in helping us to determine whether a child is ready to begin or to advance a step in a learning sequence. The general purpose of readiness tests is to inventory the specific abilities which analysis has revealed are desirable or necessary for mastering the next learning task.

For example, before a child is ready to progress from prereading activities to initial attempts to read, his oral-language comprehension and expression should at least equal the level of the "experience reading" and primers in which he will begin to read. His experience and information background should include the concepts about which he will read and which he will hear read to him. He should be able to make rather precise perceptual discriminations, differentiating both auditorily and visually between such sound and visual symbols as "big" and "pig." His articulation should not be distinctly immature. He should be able to learn from his experience—to understand and to remember, for example, the parts of a story read to him. He needs sufficient social poise and self-confidence to be able to exert himself in problem solving with systematic effort and assurance. And his mental age should approximate 6½ years.

As the illustration cited in the introduction to this chapter shows, the Stanford-Binet individual intelligence test can yield information on many of these indexes of a child's readiness for reading.

Another gauge of some of these abilities is the *Monroe Reading Aptitude Tests* [79], including measures of language comprehension, expression in sentences, and articulation; tests of visual and auditory perception; and a motor test of the child's ability to follow with a pencil a pattern of dots and lines. The *Gates Reading Readiness Tests* [38] measure ability to grasp and execute directions; familiarity with printed words and ability to discriminate between them; ability to learn new words; auditory discrimination; and ability to read the letters of the alphabet and the numbers from 0 to 9. The *Metropolitan Readiness Tests* [51], intended to measure "total readiness" for the first grade, include tests of comprehension vocabulary; understanding of sentences; range of information; visual-perceptual discrimination of animals, objects, figures, letters, and words; and knowledge of numbers. They also include a copying test intended to measure visual perception and motor control like that required in learning to write.

In addition to special readiness tests, aptitude and achievement tests are helpful in appraising readiness for learning at various stages of progress. The insight into pupil readiness which such tests afford is suggested in Figure 3.20. This figure presents the IQs and achievement profiles of two pupils beginning the fourth grade. Pupil A, mentally immature and retarded in school progress, is not ready for the regular fourth grade curriculum. To give him needed opportunity for

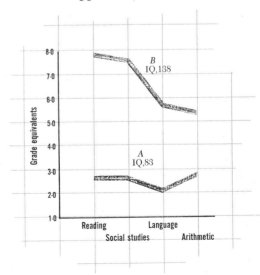

Fig. 3.20. *Variation in test-demonstrated readiness of two pupils in the fourth grade* (CMM IQs and *Iowa Every-pupil Tests of Basic Skills* achievement profiles).

successful accomplishment, his teacher will have to adjust the levels of his curriculum—vocabulary, abstractness of concepts, and assumed experience background—to the average second to third grade levels. Pupil B is more than ready for the usual fourth grade curriculum. To give B an equally needed opportunity for effective use of his talents, it will be necessary either to accelerate him to the next grade or to provide him with a greatly enriched fourth grade curriculum.

Teacher-made or specialist-prepared *diagnostic* tests are used to find out specifically the extent to which each pupil in a class possesses the essential ancillary concepts and skills for taking a next step in a learning sequence. For example, pupils about to begin the study of division with two-figure divisors were first tested for mastery of nine such subskills as understanding the place value of three-digit numbers, multiplication of a two-figure number by a one-figure number in the form of quotient-times-divisor, operation of one-figure divisors with dividends of two to four figures, and mental multiplication of a two-figure number by a one-figure number [16]. On such a test, fifth grade pupils vary from no item to every item correct. Since there is a definite correlation ($r = .46$) between the readiness test scores and final achievement with two-figure division, the test serves as a guide to economy of learning. It indicates which children need remedial teaching and exactly where they need it before taking the new step. Souder has found that pupils make greater progress when they have such specific knowledge of their individual levels of readiness [96].

Interests as signs of readiness. In addition to chronological and mental age norms, developmental sequences, and readiness tests,

teachers have discovered that children's emerging interests are signs of readiness for learning. The child who spontaneously chooses to occupy himself with picture books, who asks his mother to read him the caption under a picture, or who writes wordlike arrangements of letters and asks, "What does it say?" is probably ready to learn to read. In an experiment illustrating the significance of readiness at a more mature level, high school students of only average intelligence who especially enjoyed reading and expressing themselves in writing proved to be unusually creative and productive in a "stiff, concentrated reading and writing course [71]." Teachers at every level can cite illustrations of the fact that high interest is an important factor in successful learning.

Five-year-old Jill, after hours of self-initiated and uninstructed piano practice, had learned to play some pieces by ear. Now she wanted to take lessons as her older sister did. Although piano lessons are not usually begun until children are more mature, Jill was accepted for instruction because of her unusual interest. Half a year later, her teacher said: "Jill knows how to read simple music and has memorized many simple pieces which she recalls with ease. She will start the first grade next year advanced in music development because

she has had guidance suited to her earlier-than-usual readiness for piano instruction."

Here is another case where interest played an important part in readiness. Bill, despite only average intelligence and against the advice of his counselor, insisted on taking eleventh grade physics. He was a member of the school's model-builders' club, and was especially interested in gas engine–driven model airplanes. Although his final achievement test score in the course was below average, the report on his independent project was exceptional: "He not only described how gas engine–driven model airplanes are built but brought out construction features and related them to leverage in the unit on mechanics. He disassembled the model airplane's engine and pointed out and described the workings of each part. He described how the engine was a modification of the four-cycle internal combustion engine the class had studied recently."

Interest, however, does not make up for deficiencies of mental maturity. As a high school freshman, Laura was baffled in first year algebra. "Hardly a day went by during the semester that Laura did not stop in during her teacher's free period for help with her homework." But, in spite of conscientious, individualized teaching, extra help, her own sincere and persistent efforts, and her success (with help) in completing daily assignments, Laura was unable to master the concepts of algebra. Her teacher concluded: "Laura's main obstacle to satisfactory achievement in algebra is insufficient mental maturity, as indicated by an IQ of 85."

Both abilities and interests develop as children grow. Some students of child psychology believe that, as new abilities emerge, children spontaneously express them in appropriate activities and find high satisfaction in doing so. With respect to this view of the child's development, Jersild writes: "As his capacities for doing, thinking, and feeling emerge in the process of growth, he has an impulse to put them to use [56, p. 24]." Thus it is thought that a child's interest in an activity may be indicative of his ability for effective participation in it. According to this theory, accelerated intellectual maturing should be accompanied by an earlier-than-usual emergence of intellectual interests. Some findings support the theory. Intellectually gifted children, for example, often learn to read without systematic instruction before entering school. And while eight-year-old children of average intelligence choose to read from 8 to 10 books a year, some intellectually superior children read as many as 150 books a year [24].

The theory would also seem to predict that as differentiated patterns of aptitudes develop, corresponding interests emerge. But data on aptitude-interest relationships show only a tendency in this direction [43]. Among 156 college students, for example, Wesley, Corey, and Stewart [104] found the following correlations between aptitudes and corresponding interests: .44 between mechanical interest and understanding of mechanical principles; .24 between interest and skill in computational work; .33 between interest and knowledge of science; .29 between artistic interest and artistic judgment; and .21 between interest and talent in music. The average of several such correlations was .30. Although these correlations show some relationship, they are so low that many instances of discrepancy should be expected. Despite a child's talent in some area, a corresponding interest may fail to develop because of lack of experience or because of unfortunate experiences. Moreover, the relationships may change. A current indifference to an activity may be transformed into enthusiasm after a highly satisfying experience in it.

As indications of readiness for specific activities, however, manifest interests are useful supplementary clues. And in guiding children's learning activities, teachers should be alert to their appearance. Children reveal their interests by their contributions to regular class activities and projects, by things and ideas they bring to class for "sharing," by their choice of reading or other activities in "free" periods, and by self-initiated learning projects. Interests can also be discovered in teacher-pupil interviews, by asking children to rank in order of preference different activities and courses engaged in recently, and by interest inventories which we shall describe in Chapter 6.

Combination signs of readiness. In actual classrooms, children are likely to exhibit varied combinations of the signs of readiness for learning. As an illustration of this concept, let us note the signs of readiness which a teacher observed in two students who had not yet entered his course in high school chemistry. These sophomore boys first attracted the teacher's attention by visiting the laboratory and asking questions while the teacher made before-class preparations. Upon learning that the worn brushes of a static machine prevented its working, they wanted to repair it. They received permission to work on it, and in about three weeks had it going like new. After this they built electric motors, repaired an electrolytic apparatus and other electric appliances in the laboratory. Later in the year, on their own initiative but with teacher guidance, they prepared an exhibit of ethyl alcohol which they had made by fermentation of sugar with yeast used as an enzyme.

As signs of readiness for chemistry, these self-initiated activities indicated both unusual interest and talent. The teacher-judged high level of intelligence of these boys was confirmed by checking the personnel records, which revealed IQs of 135 and 128. When they joined the chemistry class the following year, the teacher considered them not only ready but a challenge: "Their great curiosity and ability to grasp concepts rapidly made some curricular adjustments necessary. They could finish the regular experiments very soon. Instead of giving them extra regular high school laboratory experiments to do—which would not satisfy their desire for creative achievement—I had them begin working on some advanced organic experiments. They made aspirin tablets, did some glass blowing, prepared ether, and made some perfumes which they gave to their girl friends."

SUMMARY

Readiness as an essential condition of effective learning is a comprehensive concept. It may be said to possess longitudinal and horizontal dimensions, and to embrace the dynamic processes of development. Readiness emerges longitudinally as children and youth develop from birth to maturity; we note that from year to year they become ready for learning more difficult concepts and skills. The horizontal dimension encompasses the wide scope of personality features which are significant in successful mastery of the elementary and secondary school curricula. As important aspects of readiness for such learning, we have sketched in this chapter the emergence and improved functioning of certain physical, motor, intellectual, and social traits, and the development of uniquely different patterns of abilities and other traits. Readiness for increasingly complex learning tasks is a product of the dynamic processes of maturation (growing) and learning (pertinent prior experience).

Both specific instances of children's successes and failures in learning and especially designed experiments demonstrate that appropriate readiness is an essential condition of effective learning. When they are ready for an initial or an advanced step in learning, children progress efficiently, develop interest in the activity, and become self-confident as learners and problem solvers. When they attempt learning tasks beyond their levels of maturity or unsuited to their patterns of abilities, children make little or no progress, become discouraged rather than interested, and develop attitudes and self-concepts which impair effective use of their developing abilities. Overdelay, however, is both wasteful and hazardous. Children with advanced maturity can sometimes master delayed tasks more quickly than they could have at younger ages, but if they delay mastery of significant developmental tasks, they sometimes build up self-concepts and defensive attitudes which divert them from ever attacking those tasks with wholehearted effort and confidence.

Guides which teachers may use in adjusting curricula to the developmental readiness of their pupils include chronological and mental age norms, the child's position in developmental sequences of learning activities, tests of readiness aptitudes, manifestations of interest in learning new concepts and skills, and varied combinations of these guides.

In the next chapter, we shall explore further, as a factor of readiness for learning, the appraisal of unique patterns of intellectual abilities.

GUIDES FOR STUDY, REVIEW, AND APPLICATION

1. We have been careful in American schools not to press children into reading or other academic learning until they are mature enough to succeed. Our critics, however, sometimes accuse us of unnecessary delay in beginning and in making progress in academic subjects. Cite examples of the consequences for both academic and personal-social learning of appropriate, immature, and overmature readiness.
2. Modern elementary and secondary schools provide a wide variety of play, craft, and athletic activities. What scientific data on the development and organization of motor abilities justify such diversity in the curriculum?
3. How is progress in school accomplishment related to intellectual development—of intelligence, language, perception, and reasoning?
4. How is social development—from infancy through adolescence—related to the physical, motor, intellectual, and motivational-emotional development of children? An interesting answer to this question is implicit in the film *Social Development* (20 minutes), McGraw-Hill Text-Film Department.
5. Illustrate the interrelations between the physical, motor, mental, and

social aspects of personality by using these concepts in describing a child or adolescent you know.

6. Readiness for the sequences of motor, mental, and social learning of the elementary and secondary school is a product of *both* maturation and learning. Cite experiments and observations which demonstrate the role of each of these factors.

7. Using the criteria of readiness for learning, appraise a child's readiness for beginning or taking a next step in an elementary or secondary school subject.

Chapter 4

APPRAISING ABILITIES

Our scientific achievements are opening up the possibilities of attaining a rich life in the modern world. We can take advantage of these possibilities only by making full use of our human resources. And the greatest source of joy for every individual is the self-realization of his potential talents. Yet, despite the great need of both society and the individual for the development of each citizen's constructive and creative talents, these talents sometimes remain unidentified or underdeveloped. For example, of the top 30 per cent in academic ability of high school students, less than 60 per cent continue into college the further development of their diverse talents [121]. Besides our urgent need for professionally trained talent—in mathematics, physical and biological sciences, engineering, teaching, social and political sciences, languages, and the creative arts—we also need many other technically trained and skilled persons for the thousands of jobs required in doing the diverse work of the world. If the needed individual abilities are to be fully developed—for the good of society and the happiness of the individual—they must first be recognized and properly appraised.

Teachers, of course, are not alone responsible for discovering and developing the talents of their pupils. Parents—and the children and young people themselves—share this responsibility. Teachers, however, because of their training and the specially devised tools available to them, are peculiarly well equipped to fulfill their share of this responsibility. As a first step in providing curricula and guidance suited to each child's potentialities and needs, teachers should become sensitive to the wide range and varied patterns of children's learning abilities. The task is not easy. It requires a multiple approach because, as we shall see, unchecked assumptions about intellectual abilities are subject to error.

RECOGNIZING INTELLECTUAL ABILITIES

Before examining psychological tests of abilities, let us consider some *untrained* estimates of intelligence. Later on we shall seek to define intelligence and to identify the manifestations of intelligence at various levels of the child's development.

Untrained estimates. In 1898, before the invention of reliable intelligence tests, a little boy named Mayo was placed in an institution for the mentally retarded. Mayo's mother and a physician decided that he was "lacking in many ways." Although he was not "foolish," he rolled his eyes, made peculiar noises, and would not protect himself from other children. In 1957, when he was 67 years of age, Mayo was given an intelligence test. It was discovered that his IQ was 120. No one in charge of Mayo's supervision had recognized his intellectual superiority, but during his years in the institution, Mayo had learned to read, to write letters, to manage fractions and long division, to draw well, to sing, to conduct a 30-voice choir, and to play the violin, piccolo, clarinet, bass horn, cornet, and saxophone [1].

It is unlikely that such gross oversight of an intellectually superior child could occur today. But consider another case of a more recent date.

Rulon was considered by all his teachers to be a child of "average general intelligence." At the beginning of the fourth grade, he was slightly advanced in reading, and almost up to average in arithmetic; in language and social studies, he was retarded about one year. Since he required constant prodding to accomplish ordinary assignments and often made excuses for not completing tasks begun in school, his teacher wondered whether he really lacked ability or was just lazy. Although she had begun to suspect the latter, she was greatly surprised when he earned an IQ of 152 on the *California Test of Mental Maturity.* Upon discovering his underdeveloped potentialities, she began to take a special interest in him, to guide his learning more carefully, to enrich the fourth grade curriculum for him, and to encourage his creative efforts. By the end of the sixth grade, his achievement matched his very high ability. In reading, language, social studies, and science, he now achieved at seventh to eleventh grade levels.

Even among the mentally retarded, it is highly desirable—and often possible—to discover socially useful and personally satisfying talents. Consider, for example, 16-year-old Perry, whose Stanford-Binet IQ was 68. This youth first came to the attention of the psychologist when he inquired: "When are you going to test my brain again? I think it is getting worse." Perry had found that helping the librarian in the state training school, where he had been committed as mentally retarded, could be very confusing. This perplexity plus his learning difficulties in school could, of course, worry him about the state of his brain. Perry's self-attitude changed, however, when his special talent in mechanical assembly was discovered and put to use. He was found to be among that 10 per cent of a hundred boys of his age and intelligence who scored above average on the *Minnesota Mechanical Assembly Test* [29]. On the basis of his very high score (96th percentile) on this aptitude test, he was assigned as helper to a supervisor in charge of keeping the institution's sewing machines in repair. Two weeks later, Perry's supervisor enthusiastically reported that he was a "whiz" in the job; that he could oil, adjust, or replace a worn part in a machine as well as any normally intelligent boy he had formerly had as an assistant. With such satisfying self-expression and approval, Perry was no longer worried about his brain.

As these examples suggest, human abilities are varied, unevenly developed, and complexly organized. Fortunately, the procedures being devised for appraising them are increasing in variety, in scope of coverage or depth, and in reliability. Let us now consider how scientific appraisals of general intelligence are made.

Manifestations of intelligence. The wide range of differences in intelligence in a classroom of school children is manifested in several ways—by variations in level and quality of performance on intelligence tests, in school-curriculum activities, in self-initiated creative projects, and in other personal and social activities. Intellectually superior children and youth solve problems more accurately and more rapidly than do children of average or below-average ability. They grasp concepts more quickly and understand more complex ideas. They perceive finer differentiations in situations and concepts. They pose problems and ask questions more readily and answer them more effectively. Both in school and out, their activities are characterized by greater independence, originality, and inventiveness. They use language and other symbols more appropriately, precisely, and effectively. They learn more rapidly and can comprehend more complex concepts; therefore they know more. Their knowledge is functionally organized for more effective application to new problems; their modes of approach in problem solving are more integrated, flexible, adaptive, efficient, and creative. In summarizing the manifestations of intelligence, Stoddard says that "intelligence is the ability to undertake activities that are characterized by (1) difficulty, (2) complexity, (3) abstractness, (4) economy, (5) adaptiveness to a goal, (6) social value, and (7) the emergence of originals . . . [99, p. 255]."

Intelligence defined. Such a classification may add concrete meaning to the concept of intelligence, because teachers can actually observe their pupils exhibiting some of these manifestations. However, if it is to be a workable concept, which teachers and school psychologists can *use*, it needs to be defined more sharply and expanded in scope.

If we think of intelligence as a trait determining individual differences in school achievement, we can define it as the general intellectual capacity for learning and problem solving. Garrett says that "intelligence . . . includes . . . abilities demanded in solution of problems which require comprehension and use of symbols," such as words, numbers, diagrams, equations, and formulas which represent ideas and relationships [36, p. 372]. This definition relates the functioning of intelligence to the tests which psychologists use to measure it.

The variety of symbols mentioned in Garrett's definition is more

than matched by the variety of intellectual tasks found in the school curriculum. The learning tasks which confront children in language, social studies, science, music, art, mechanics, and in other parts of the curriculum are not all alike, and pupils typically perform them with uneven efficiency. An expanded "new conception of intelligence" proposed by Thurstone helps to account for this differentiation in pupils' levels of achievement [110]. This new concept assumes not only that individuals have a general capacity for learning and problem solving, but also that they have different patterns of more specific capacities for various kinds of learning.

These capacities, however, are not measured directly. Only intellectual efficiency is directly appraised; capacities for learning and problem solving are inferred from that appraisal. An individual's intellectual efficiency depends on his basic capacities, his background of experience, the quality of his learning and problem-solving methods, the intensity of his motivation and concentration, and his degree of emotional control. The intelligence test is an attempt to measure potential ability while differences due to these other factors are at least partially controlled.

Psychologists attempt to control variations in prior learning opportunities by devising intelligence-test items which are (1) novel problems unrelated to prior experience (especially school content), or (2) measures of knowledge for which opportunities for acquisition have been ample, unrestricted (except by capacity) as to level capable of being attained, and approximately equal.[1] On the basis of the relative amount of an individual's accumulated knowledge which meets these criteria, we *infer* his capacity for learning.

A bright child's range of information and understanding of concepts is greater than the average child's, not because he has had better opportunities for learning them, but because, it is assumed, he has more capacity for learning. Variations in work methods are partially controlled by the directions for the test, to which the trained examiner adheres very carefully. Motivation is controlled by keeping it high throughout the test—both by the intrinsic challenge and interest appeal of the test items and by the rewarding approval of the examiner in the individual test. Anxiety and other emotional disturbances are reduced to a minimum by building up the child's confidence. This is accomplished by beginning the test with items on which the indi-

[1] In present-day tests, these criteria are, of course, only partially satisfied.

vidual can surely succeed and by giving warm, friendly encouragement of his efforts as the items become more difficult. When testing emotionally maladjusted children, whose intellectual efficiency is sometimes impaired by uncontrollable emotional disturbances, the well-trained and experienced psychologist can make allowances for this factor in estimating basic capacity.

The first intelligence test was devised in 1905. Today, tests of general intelligence, differential abilities, and "practical" aptitudes are used almost universally as guides in adjusting curricula to both elementary and secondary school children's abilities. For a more intimate understanding of these abilities and how they are appraised, let us examine some of the tests which psychologists use to measure them.

INDIVIDUAL TESTS OF GENERAL INTELLIGENCE

At least two hours are usually required for a psychologist to administer and interpret an individual intelligence test, and for this reason individual testing is expensive. However, for very young children and for those who are educationally retarded or emotionally handicapped and who present complicated guidance problems, individual testing is well justified. Such testing permits better control of factors—other than capacities—which affect intellectual efficiency. And, as was shown in Chapter 3, where we discussed the use of the intelligence test in appraising readiness for first grade reading, individual testing yields much more than merely objective measures of abilities. The psychologist is able to observe the quality of a child's problem-solving methods, to note his confidence and interest or anxiety and defensive adjustments when confronted with challenging tasks. He is able to infer—from a child's verbal responses to a variety of practical problems and questions—something about his self-concept and other significant attitudes.

For appraising the abilities of children and adolescents, and for observing other important characteristics, psychologists have a variety of individual tests from which to choose [21].

The Stanford-Binet intelligence scale. Since 1916, when Terman revised Binet and Simon's test of general intelligence (the first valid one), the *Stanford-Binet Intelligence Scale* has been the leading individual test of "the general ability to do abstract or conceptual thinking [68]." The 1960 *Stanford-Binet Intelligence Scale* is designed to measure "intelligence at work"—in complex mental tasks which reflect both prior learning and goal-directed, adaptive problem solving [107]. The 142 items in the scale are arranged in a developmental sequence of 20 mental age levels, with six tests plus an alternate at each level.[1]

[1] The eight tests plus an alternate at the average adult level is an exception.

The mental age levels range from two years up through average mental maturity to superior adult levels I, II, and III.

A 45-word vocabulary test and other items, such as making change or naming the days of the week, reflect the extent of an individual's prior learning. However, it is assumed that opportunities for learning words and similar concepts which are appraised in the test have been ample, unrestricted, and approximately comparable for all the children for whom the scale is suitable. Therefore, the extent of a given child's knowledge of such items is taken as an index of his capacity for such learning. For example, if a 10-year-old child defined 15 of the 45 words on the vocabulary test, it would be inferred that he has superior capacity for such learning, since this is the average score found for the norm group of representative 12-year-olds [107].

The following examples are typical of the many novel problem-solving items in the scale:

Age of child	*Test item*
Five	Assemble a cut card.
Seven	Give opposite analogies such as "Wolves are wild; dogs are_____."
Nine	Make a drawing showing how a folded and cut paper would look if it were unfolded.
Twelve	Find the absurdity in a picture in which a man's shadow is wrong with respect to the sun.
Fourteen	Tests of deductive verbal reasoning.
Average adult level	Tests of arithmetical reasoning.

Although the items in the S-B scale include tasks requiring perception, memory, interpretation, imaginative manipulations, and reasoning with verbal, numerical, and spatial symbols, the scale as a whole is heavily weighted with verbal content [71, 107]. It samples mainly verbal-abstract learning and problem-solving abilities. Since the verbal-abstract abilities appraised by the S-B test are also employed in learning language, science, social studies, mathematics, and other abstract subjects, we shall not be surprised to find (in the section of this chapter on validity) significant correlations between S-B scores and academic achievement.

In the selection of items for the scale, Terman and Merrill were guided by three criteria. (1) The item must measure a complex, verbal-abstract intellectual function. (2) It must discriminate between successive age levels, as is indicated by the larger percentages of children passing the item at each higher age. (3) It must correlate well (the average is .66) with the total score, and thus contribute to the internal consistency and homogeneity of the scale [107].

The items are distributed over the age levels of the scale where the percentages of individuals passing the six tests at each level yield mean mental ages equalling mean chronological ages. The mental age, as the interpretive unit of measurement in this developmental scale, is a derived score based on the highest levels an individual reaches on the scale. The goal in conducting a test is to match an individual's best performance against the levels of the scale. Therefore, the psychologist begins with some exploratory testing near the level on the scale corresponding to the individual's age. He tries to find a basal age (the highest level at which all six tests are passed). From the basal age, he proceeds up the scale to the level at which all six tests are failed. By adding to the basal age the appropriate number of months of mental age for the items passed beyond this level, he determines the individual's placement on the scale (his mental age). For example, if a mentally accelerated 10-year-old attains the level on the scale of representative 12-year-old children, he is assigned a mental age of 12–0. Should our 10-year-old be retarded in rate of mental growth and fail to go beyond the average performance on the scale of representative 8-year-olds, he would be assigned a mental age of 8–0.

The mental age—which increases continuously from birth to maturity—is an index of intellectual maturity, of readiness for the kinds of verbal-abstract tasks with which representative children of the corresponding chronological age succeed. Mental ages are convertible to intelligence quotients (IQs), which indicate both the child's relative brightness among his age mates and his *rate* of mental growth. This rate, as we shall see in greater detail later on in this chapter, remains relatively constant. In the 1916 and 1937 revisions of the S-B scale, the IQ was determined by dividing an individual's mental age (MA) by his chronological age (CA), and multiplying by 100, according to the formula: $IQ = MA/CA \times 100$. Because of the uneven difficulty of the items at different levels of the scale, however, these ratio IQs fluctuated more than was desirable. To achieve greater constancy of IQs, the mental ages of the 1960 S-B scale are converted to *deviation* IQs, based on norm groups with established means of 100 and standard deviations of 16 at each age. For the above hypothetical examples, these deviation IQs would be 116 and 78, respectively. The ratio IQs depart slightly from these values. At most ages, however, the discrepancies between ratio and deviation Stanford-Binet IQs are very small [107].

The Wechsler intelligence scales. Wechsler conceives intelligence to be an "aggregate" of capacities for effective intellectual functioning. He has constructed two tests—each comprised of 10 or 11 interrelated subtests classified into verbal and performance scales—in separate batteries for children [114] and for adults [116]. The *Wechsler Intelligence Scale for Children* (WISC) is intended for ages five through fifteen. *The Wechsler Adult Intelligence Scale* (*WAIS*) appraises intellectual growth in adolescence and young adulthood, in later adulthood, and in old age. Examples of items from comparable subtests of both scales suggest the nature of the abilities which they measure.

Information. Each scale has 29 items, such as "Why does oil float on water?" (*WISC*) and "Who wrote *Hamlet?*" (*WAIS*) This subtest samples the individual's range of scientific, social studies, literary, and miscellaneous information. Besides being an excellent measure of general learning ability, it measures verbal comprehension and ability to profit from school experience.

Comprehension. In each scale, 14 questions such as "Why is it better to build a house of brick than of wood?" (*WISC*) appraise the utilization of practical information in formulating comprehensive and generalized solutions to personal-social problems. The subtest is a good measure both of general verbal reasoning and of verbal comprehension.

Arithmetic. Intellectual efficiency in arithmetic reasoning is measured in *WISC* by 16 items and in *WAIS* by 14 items. A typical item is: "A man with $18 spends $7.50. How much does he have left?" (This test item is found in *WAIS*.) The subtest is a good measure both of general reasoning with numerical symbols and of attention and concentration.

Similarities. The 16 items in *WISC* and 13 items in *WAIS* of this subtest measure the ability to conceptualize and to formulate generalized answers to such questions as "In what way are a piano and a violin alike?" (*WISC*) It is a good measure of general reasoning with verbal symbols and of verbal comprehension.

Vocabulary. This subtest calls for oral definitions of such words as "bicycle" and "microscope" (*WISC*), and "winter" and "travesty" (*WAIS*); the individual goes as far as he can in a list of 40 words arranged in order of difficulty. As a sample of the individual's understanding of words, the subtest is an excellent measure of general learning ability and of verbal comprehension.

Picture completion. Drawing on his background of familiar concepts and exercising perceptual-conceptual discrimination, the individual points out the "most important thing missing" in pictures of objects or events, such as the picture of a man and a dog walking in the snow, with tracks shown only for the man (*WAIS*). The 20 pictures in *WISC* and 21 in *WAIS* are good measures both of general abstract reasoning and of "perceptual organization."

Picture arrangement. The individual is shown three to six irregularly arranged, separate cartoon-like pictures (in seven sets in *WISC* and in eight sets in *WAIS*) and asked to originate, plan, and formulate a "sensible story" as a guide to arranging the pictures in an appropriate sequence. As an example, ready for rearrangement there

 are pictures of a man (1) eating, (2) hauling, (3) cultivating, and (4) sowing corn (*WISC*). The subtest is a good measure of both general reasoning with meaningful, pictorial symbols and perceptual organization.

Block designs. This subtest involves the use of four or nine identically shaped blocks with differently colored faces (red, white, and red-white in *WAIS*). The individual is expected to analyze pictured designs, such as the one shown here, and to reproduce them with the blocks. The subtest is a good measure of general abstract reasoning and an excellent measure of perceptual organization.

Object assembly. From perception of a miscellaneous array of five to seven jigsaw-like pieces, the individual is expected to conceptualize and construct a familiar configuration, such as of an automobile (*WISC*) or of a hand (*WAIS*). In both *WISC* and *WAIS*, the four items of this subtest are a fair test of general reasoning with pictorial symbols and a good measure of perceptual organization.

Digit symbol. Guided by a model giving a different nonsense symbol for each of the nine digits (such as "⌣" for "1," "⊢" for "4," and "v" for "6"), the subject writes as many as he can of the symbols for miscellaneously ordered numbers—in 120 seconds in *WISC*, and in 90 seconds in *WAIS*. The subtest measures general learning ability, speed of perceptual discrimination, and intensity of motivation.

On both *WISC* and *WAIS*, the 10 or 11 subtests are made comparable by converting the varied raw scores into comparable standard scores. In addition to yielding profiles of several subtests, the batteries yield verbal, performance, and full-scale IQs. These are deviation IQs, derived by converting the sums of verbal, performance, and full-scale standard scores into IQ distributions at each age, with means of 100 and standard deviations of 15. The scales do not provide mental ages directly. Wechsler, however, has provided a table of score-age equivalents from which MAs can be derived for *WISC* scores [115, p. 382].

The correlations between the verbal and performance scales and among the subtests indicate that they are measuring, at all ages, both common and differentiated mental functions. At the 10-year level, for example, the correlation between the verbal and performance scales is approximately .70. And between different pairs of subtests, the correlations range from .20 (between *Picture Completion* and *Digit Symbol*) to .75 (between *Vocabulary* and *Information*) [114].

Using the WISC in teaching. Its use in the study of an underachieving ninth grade boy illustrates the kind of information that *WISC* can yield. Ellis's junior high school marks were almost uniformly D's. In nine courses in the seventh grade, he earned five D's and four C's—the C's being in Social Studies, Physical Education, Shop, and Health. In the eighth grade, he earned six D's, two C's—in Shop and in Science—and one B—in Physical Education. Now in the ninth grade, all his marks are D's, except for a C in Industrial Arts and a B in Physical Education. Despite his poor record, his teachers suspected that Ellis might have undeveloped potentialities for higher achievement. To check this hypothesis, the school psychologist's help was enlisted.

Examination of the cumulative record revealed that both his learning difficulties and some signs of greater potentiality were manifest early in his school career. His second grade teacher had observed that "he is capable of doing much better work; but he wastes too much time, works too slowly, and lacks self-confidence." Adding to the record, his third grade teacher noted that although "he does average work, he could do better." But he is "too easily distracted, his attention wanders, he is dissatisfied with school, and seems to resent the responsibility of work." The comments were not all negative. On the favorable side, there are such comments as this: "He has a good attitude toward his classmates and participates well with them." By the sixth grade, his scores on the *Iowa Tests of Basic Skills* showed that he was retarded from one to two years in reading, language, arithmetic, and work-study skills. As we see in Table 4.1, Ellis's *WISC* subtest scores and the IQs based on them confirm the teachers' impression of potential abilities beyond his meager achievements.

The performance IQ of 136 indicates that Ellis is superior in ability to reason with abstract and pictorial symbols—on problems independent of prior school experience. However, the relatively low verbal IQ of 86—based on the more schoollike, verbal subtests—suggests that he has failed to use his good abstract learning and problem-solving abilities in profiting from school experience.

Table 4.1. *Standard scores of educationally retarded and personally maladjusted Ellis, a ninth grade boy, age 15–1*

Verbal subtests	Standard score*	Performance subtests	Standard score
Information	7	Picture completion	16
Comprehension	9	Picture arrangement	11
Arithmetic	5	Block designs	15
Similarities	10	Object assembly	19
Vocabulary	6	Digit symbol	15
Digit span	7		
Verbal IQ	84	Performance IQ	136

* In the norm group the mean is 10 and the standard deviation is 3.

Observations on the specific subtest performances elaborate the impression of intellectual inefficiency. His vocabulary and range of information are meager and unprecise. For example, he defined "nonsense" as "somebody that does something wrong." Rather than to strive for precise concepts, he has become satisfied with remotely related associations and with "making up." The Fourth of July, he says, "is celebrated as the dedication of the United States" and "c.o.d. has something to do with the mail." Asked what the stomach does, he said: "It mixes your food." His relatively poor performance in arithmetic reasoning and in reciting digits read to him suggests deficiencies in attention and concentration. His own comment on the difficulty he experienced with the arithmetic problems suggests that he is distracted by anxiety-motivated impulses: "I can't think. Makes me nervous. I wonder if I will do them right."

The able underachiever is a puzzling paradox. He challenges us to understand and to learn to prevent or correct his intellectual inefficiency. At this point we merely remind ourselves that effective learning depends not upon only one but upon seven conditions. But we shall not simply drop the problem with which Ellis has challenged us. We shall return to his problem in subsequent chapters—especially in those on motivation and mental health.

GROUP TESTS OF GENERAL INTELLIGENCE

As a guide to teachers in adjusting each child's curriculum to his level of maturity, a group test of intelligence is both economical and, for most children, otherwise satisfactory. Such a test can usually be administered to an entire class within an hour; in another three or four hours all the tests can be scored. Several group intelligence tests are available for elementary and secondary school children [21]. Like the individual tests which we have just discussed, they sample pupils' learning and problem-solving abilities. Let us examine a few of them in order to get an understanding of both their general characteristics and some of their distinctive features.

The Otis quick-scoring mental ability tests. The series includes three forms: *Alpha,* for grades 1 to 4; *Beta,* for grades 4 to 9; and *Gamma,* for high school and college students [81].

Alpha consists of 45 sets of four pictures or diagrams as shown here.

First, in a nonverbal test of ability to generalize and to discriminate, the child is required to mark with a horizontal line the one picture or diagram in each set of four which is different from the others. Then, for a measure of verbal comprehension, the child is required to execute for each of the 45 items a specific orally presented direction. For the example above, the direction is: "Mark the lines that appear to run most nearly in the direction of telegraph wires."

Both *Beta* and *Gamma* are comprised of a variety of items. In addition to novel measures of verbal, abstract, and numerical reasoning, schoollike vocabulary and arithmetic items are included. The following are typical of the 80 multiple-choice questions in both *Beta* and *Gamma*:

> The opposite of weak is (1) poor, (2) sick, (3) tall, (4) strong, (5) young. (*Beta*)
> The first drawing below is related to the second as the third is related to (which) one of the remaining four? (*Gamma*)

> A race must always have (1) spectators, (2) a circular track, (3) a starting gun, (4) contestants, (5) victory. (*Gamma*)
> One number is wrong in the following series. What should that number be?
> 1 3 9 27 36 243–(1) 2, (2) 81, (3) 5, (4) 15, (5) 45. (*Gamma*)
> If grapefruit are 4 for a quarter, how much will two dozen cost? (1) 23¢, (2) 60¢, (3) 96¢, (4) $1.50, (5) $1.00. (*Beta*)

Tables of average scores for ages 5 to 12 for *Alpha* and for ages 7 to 19 for *Beta* provide bases for converting raw scores into mental ages. For *Alpha*, a child's IQ is computed conventionally, by dividing his derived mental age by his chronological age at the time of testing and multiplying by 100. Both *Beta* and *Gamma* IQs, however, are computed by adding to 100 the deviation of an individual's score from the mean score of his age group. For example, since the mean score of 12-year-olds on *Beta* is 35, if a 12-year-old child should earn a score of 45, his Beta IQ would be 110—that is, $100 + (45 - 35)$.

The Davis-Eells test. The *Davis-Eells Test of General Intelligence or Problem-solving Ability* [22] was designed to yield an index of problem-solving ability (*IPSA*). The test is prepared for three levels (first grade, 30 items; second grade, 47 items; and third to sixth grades, 62 items) and is "composed of mental problems of a kind found in most of the basic areas of children's lives: school, home, play, stories, work." All the items are pictorially presented (requiring no reading) and are intended to be free of influence from specific training at home, at school, or in play relationships. In this way, the authors have tried to minimize the effect of variations in prior learning experiences. Despite the use of pictorial content, the oral directions and the verbal symbols employed in reasoning through the problems make the test "highly verbal."

Of the 62 items in the *Elementary Form* (for grades 3 to 6) 20 items require interpretations of relatively complex situations, such as that shown in Figure 4.1. The child organizes the pictures into a meaningful pattern and chooses the most probable one among three statements:

> 1. The man fell down and hit his head.
> 2. A ball came through the window and hit his head.
> 3. The picture does not show how the man got the bump on his head.

The next eight items require the child to discriminate among, and to evaluate, alternative ways of selecting a certain sum from a variety of coins. A typical problem involves choosing the best among three pictorially presented ways of beginning to take 40 cents from a quarter, two dimes, five nickels, and four pennies.

In each of another 19 items, the child is expected to interpret

Fig. 4.1. *A problem-solving item from the* Davis-Eells Test of General Intelligence, *requiring an interpretation ("What happened?") of the situation.* (Yonkers-on-Hudson: World Book Company, 1953.)

Fig. 4.2. *A problem-solving item from the* Davis-Eells Test of General Intelligence, *for which the child decides, "Which boy is starting the best way to get over the gate?"* (Yonkers-on-Hudson: World Book Company, 1953.)

three pictured actions and, with foresight of their probable consequences, to select the best solution to the suggested problem. For Figure 4.2, he decides "which boy is starting the best way to get over the gate."

The test is concluded with 15 pictorial analogies which measure associative learning or reasoning. For example, a picture shows a human foot near a boy, and a horse's hoof near a horse, a dog, and a cat. The child is presented the problem: "The foot helps the boy walk. This animal foot does the same thing for what?"

Distributions of scores of representative children at each six-month age level are equated (in a table) to deviation IQs or "indexes of problem solving," for which the mean is set at 100 and the standard deviation at 16. Thus a child who happened to earn an *IPSA* of 116 would be 1 standard deviation above the average of his age mates on this test.

The Kuhlmann-Finch tests. These tests are comprised of five interrelated kinds of problems which appear to require, for solution, reasoning and mental manipulations of verbal, pictorial-diagrammatic, and numerical symbols [58]. Like the Otis and Davis-Eells tests, however, they yield a single measure of general intelligence. In a typical item, shown below, a child, at the fourth grade level, is directed to "see how the first three pictures go together with one other picture," and then to find (among the five alternatives) the missing picture.

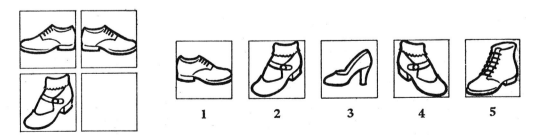

In constructing the test the authors were guided by four principles:

1. In order to provide a maximum number of items of appropriate difficulty at each level, they provide separate test booklets for each grade from 1 through 6 and for junior and senior school levels.

2. To achieve maximum freedom from effects of specific training and to avoid cultural bias, they made the vocabulary simple; it excludes schoollike content, and expresses symbol relationships only in terms of the universal concepts of form, position, size, number, and familiar words.

3. In order to achieve a measure of mental development which discriminates significantly between age levels, the authors selected only those items on which children "become more proficient each year as they progress toward mental maturity [58]."

4. To avoid the undue influence of any single high or low subscore, the median of the five subtests is taken as the index of an individual's general intelligence.

As norms, the distributions of scores of representative children at each age level are converted to standard deviation IQs, for which the mean is 100 and the standard deviation is 16. When mental ages are desired, they are computed by the formula: $MA = IQ/100 \times CA$.

The Terman-McNemar test of mental ability. This test, intended for grades 6 to 12, is a measure of general verbal intelligence [105]. Its seven types of multiple-choice verbal items include three which reflect prior learning and four which measure verbal reasoning. Those reflecting prior learning include such items as "Larceny is a term used in (1) forestry, (2) medicine, (3) theology, (4) pedagogy, (5) law." Verbal reasoning is involved in such items as "Night *always* has (1) stillness, (2) moon, (3) clouds, (4) ghosts, (5) hours."

The average correlation of .53 between passing or failing each item and the total score indicates that the 162 items of the test constitute a fairly homogeneous measure of verbal intelligence. And the fact that the items were selected to discriminate well between age levels makes it also a measure of mental growth, which continues through adolescence on this scale. Mental ages can be determined from a table giving the average standard score (based on deviations from the median of 14-year-olds) for each age. As indexes of relative brightness, both standard deviation IQs and percentiles corresponding to IQs are provided in the manual [105, pp. 8–9].

The Lorge-Thorndike intelligence tests. These tests are arranged in five levels, from kindergarten through grade 12; they measure verbal and nonverbal factors of abstract intelligence by a variety of subtests. The subtests were constructed to measure general conceptual reasoning, flexibility, and facility in organizing concepts and symbols into new relationships [67].

Level 5 (for grades 10 through 12), for example, is comprised of five interrelated verbal and three interrelated nonverbal subtests. The verbal series includes subtests of word knowledge, ability to complete sentences sensibly, arithmetic reasoning, formation of concepts for classifying words, and verbal analogies. The verbal reasoning required in these tests is illustrated by a *Verbal Classification* item: "Think in what way the words (lawyer, nurse, engineer, accountant) go together and then select a word among (1. merchant, 2. butcher, 3. carpenter, 4. teacher, 5. clerk) that belongs with them."

Tests of the nonverbal series require reasoning with pictorial, diagrammatic, or numerical symbols, and include as subtests formation of concepts for classifying figures, discovery of principles determining construction of number series, and insight into figure analogies. The abstract quality of the reasoning required in the non-verbal tests is suggested by a *Figure-analogies* item: "Choose the figure among the five alternatives which is related to the third in the same way that the second is related to the first."

Although each of these subtests measures to some extent a different mental function, they are also all interrelated as measures of general intelligence [67]. Between pairs of verbal tests, correlations on fifth grade children range from .56 to .79. Between pairs of non-verbal tests, the correlations range from .54 to .60. The correlation between totals of verbal and nonverbal scores is .66.

The California test of mental maturity. This is another bifactor test of intelligence [101]. It is prepared for five levels (for kindergarten to grade 1, grades 1 to 3, grades 4 to 8, grades 7 to 10, and grade 9 to adulthood). Like *WISC*, *WAIS*, and the *Lorge-Thorndike Intelligence Tests*, it yields verbal, nonlanguage, and total scores from which mental ages, IQs, and percentiles can be derived. It also provides a profile of mental ages and percentile scores on five much less reliably measured subfactors: memory, spatial relations, logical reasoning, numerical reasoning, and verbal concepts. Since only 3 of the 13 subtests are directly dependent on previously acquired vocabulary or arithmetic knowledge, the test as a whole appraises ability to use verbal, numerical, pictorial, and spatial symbols in solving problems.

The content is suggested by sample items for measuring the five subfactors. As measured in the *Elementary Series*, for grades 4 to 8, the memory factor includes measures of both immediate (paired associates) and delayed recall (recalling items from a story after 30 minutes). The spatial factor includes tests of perception and imaginal manipulation of diagramed figures, such as is required in identifying the first pattern from among the other four:

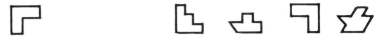

Logical reasoning is measured by both verbal and pictorial items. For example, the child looks at three pictured objects (a suit coat, a dress, and a pair of pants) and generalizes that they are all articles of clothing. Then, guided by his derived concept, he must indicate which one among the next four objects (a clock, a sweater, a teacup, and a bird) is like the first three. The numerical-reasoning factor includes items on deducing the principles in number series, on making change, and on arithmetic reasoning problems. Finally, the verbal-concepts factor is covered by a 50-word vocabulary test.

To a considerable extent both the major bifactors and the sub-factors of the *CMMT* are measures of general mental ability. The fairly high correlation of .75 between the verbal and nonlanguage scores indicates that these two parts measure largely the same mental functions. They probably measure reasoning, but with different symbols—one verbal, the other pictorial and spatial. More differentiation of the functions measured by the five subfactors is suggested by the lower correlations among them, ranging from .25 to .60. The high correlation of .80 between the vocabulary subtest and the total test score indicates that the test as a whole is mainly a measure of verbal reasoning.

TESTS OF DIFFERENTIAL ABILITIES

As the variety of items used to measure it suggests, intelligence is not a single, unitary ability; it is a constellation of abilities. Individual differences in the capacity to learn and to solve problems are therefore dependent upon each individual's unique *pattern of abilities,* rather than upon differences on a single dimension of intellectual ability.

Factors in intelligence. As a logical basis for proposing this "new conception of intelligence" Thurstone [110] reported the results of his attempts to discover the ability or abilities underlying the performance of 240 college students on 56 tests of seemingly different mental processes. He first found the correlation between each of these tests and every other; and discovered, upon examining the resulting table of 1,540 correlation coefficients, that there were several significant clusters of interrelated tests. Between pairs of tests from different clusters, the correlations seemed low. But when he applied a statistical procedure called "factor analysis" to the table of intercorrelations, he was able to determine precisely the clusters of interrelated tests and their degrees of independence from other clusters. Thurstone found that the interrelations of the 56 different tests could be accounted for by seven factors: number facility, word fluency, memory, perceptual speed, inductive reasoning (with abstract symbols), verbal reasoning, and spatial visualization.

As a further illustration of the concept that capacity to learn and to solve problems depends upon a pattern of abilities, let us examine the results of a factorial study of *WAIS*. Cohen has found that four factors seem to account for most of the correlations among the 11 subtests. All the subtests, but especially *Vocabulary* and *Information*, contribute to measurement of the most general factor—general intellectual ability. A second factor—measured by *Vocabulary Comprehension, Information,* and *Similarities*—Cohen called "verbal comprehension." A third factor—to which *Object Assembly, Block Designs,* and *Picture Arrangement* contribute significantly—he named "perceptual organization." *Arithmetic* and *Digit Span* contribute to measurement of a fourth factor, "memory," which involves attention, concentration, and freedom from distractability [16, 17].

Such specific studies have not yet revealed all of man's differentiated intellectual abilities. Guilford has estimated that measures of over a hundred factors may be required to account for all of them [40]. Some psychologists are still pursuing their isolation and measurement. In the meantime, other psychologists are doing some very practical research work on the most frequently found factors. Their work is oriented toward the problem of educational and vocational guidance, and they have constructed useful tests of differential abilities. Let us take a look at one of them.

The differential aptitude tests. The *DAT* is an integrated battery of tests for appraising seven abilities considered indicative of differentiated potential achievement in several areas of the curriculum of junior and senior high school students. The battery, in two equivalent forms, includes the following tests [9, 10]:

1. *Verbal Reasoning*—which measures ability to understand, to generalize, and to "think constructively" with words from varied content areas.

2. *Numerical Ability*—which tests the individual's understanding of number concepts and relationships and computational facility.

3. *Abstract Reasoning*—which measures perceiving, conceptualizing, and generalizing with abstract symbols independently of specific verbal, numerical, or other cultural experience.

4. *Space Relations*—which measures imaginative visualization and manipulation of spatial elements into tridimensional patterns.

5. *Mechanical Reasoning*—which tests the subject's understanding and application of mechanical principles in the solution of varied pictured and mechanical problems.

6. *Clerical Speed and Accuracy*—which evaluates speed of precise perception of similarities and differences among letter combinations.

7. *Language Usage*—which measures recognition of the correctness of spelling, grammatical construction, punctuation, and word usage.

A typical item from each *DAT* subtest suggests how these abilities are measured.

The *Verbal Reasoning* test includes 50 items, each like the following: Make a "true" and "sensible" sentence from ". . . is to night as breakfast is to . . ." by selecting a beginning word from "1. flow, 2. gentle, 3. supper, 4. door" and an ending word from "a. include, b. morning, c. enjoy, d. corner" (Example Z)

The *Numerical Ability* test requires the subject to choose the correct answers to 40 such problems as the following "$\sqrt{16/25} \times 4/49$ = a. 8/35, b. 64/1225, c. 7 21/25, d. 19 9/64, e. none of these" (Number 21, *Form* B)

The *Abstract Reasoning* test has 50 items in which the subject selects from five alternatives the item which should come next in the first, logically developed series:

The *Space Relations* test asks which tridimensional figure or figures can be made from the two-dimensional pattern. It contains 40 such items as:

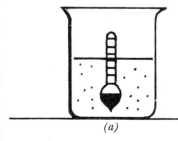

The *Mechanical Reasoning* test, in 68 items, presents such problems as "In which jar is the liquid lighter?"

[If equal, mark (c).]

(a)   (b)   (c)

The *Clerical Speed and Accuracy* test, comprised of 200 items like the one below, asks the subject to underline in the second set the same letter and/or digit combination as is underlined in the first:

3A   3B   3̲3̲   B3   BB   BB   3B   B3   3A   33   (Example Z)

The *Language Usage* test, in two parts, requires recognition of (1) spelling errors and (2) grammatical, punctuation, and usage errors in sentences.

That the subtests tend to measure differentiated abilities rather than general mental ability is indicated by the relatively low correlations among them. For separate age groups, the average intercorrelations range from .06 (for Mechanical Reasoning and Clerical Speed and Accuracy) to .62 (for Verbal Reasoning and Language Usage). The median intercorrelation of pairs of subtests is .425 [9].

Percentile and standard T-score norms for the test are based on the distributions of scores of over 47,000 representative boys and girls in grades 8 through 12 from over 100 school systems in 26 states [10]. As is illustrated in Figure 4.3, when scores are interpreted according to appropriate norms, the battery yields a profile of comparable derived scores on seven differential abilities.

As an illustration of *DAT* profile interpretation [8], let us examine the test scores and other data on the tenth grade boy whose profile is presented in Figure 4.3. The boy was registered in a college preparatory curriculum, and he was failing in English, history, and Latin. In the light of his below-average score on *Verbal Reasoning* and his especially low scores on the tests of language learning ability, his failures are not surprising. The poor prognosis for him in a strictly academic curriculum was confirmed by his Otis IQ of 104, and his 35th percentile score in reading comprehension. Encouraged, however, by the discovery of relatively high scores in mechanical, spatial, and abstract reasoning, he decided to "explore his interests in mechanical and technical work." The shift in educational goals proved

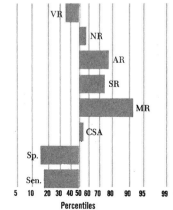

Fig. 4.3. DAT *profile of a tenth grade boy about to transfer from a college-preparatory to a mechanical-technical curriculum.* (From G. K. Bennett, H. G. Seashore, and A. G. Wesman, *Counseling from Profiles, a Casebook for the Differential Aptitude Tests,* The Psychological Corp., New York, 1951, p. 61.)

wise: both his achievement and interests in learning improved. With test- and experience-based confidence of success, he now plans to "enter a technical training institute in a two-year college [8, p. 60]."

Besides the *DAT*, several other batteries are available to the school counselor who wishes to appraise differential abilities [102]. The *Holzinger-Crowder Unifactor Tests*, designed for grades 7 through 12, measure four abilities considered especially significant in predicting academic achievement: verbal, spatial, numerical, and reasoning abilities [45].

Also intended for educational guidance of secondary school students, the *Segel-Raskin Multiple Aptitude Tests* [91, 93] use more schoollike content in testing grades 7 through 12. These tests yield a profile of comparable scores on nine specific aptitudes (such as word meaning, reading comprehension, language usage, arithmetic reasoning, and applied science and mechanics) and on four basic factors (verbal comprehension, perceptual speed, numerical reasoning, and spatial visualization).

Thurstone's ideas about differential abilities are applied to school testing in the *SRA Tests of Primary Mental Abilities* [112]. The tests cover three levels (ages 5 to 7; 7 to 11; and 11 to 17) and include measures of five or six factors: verbal comprehension, word fluency, number facility, spatial visualization, reasoning, and perceptual speed.

The *Flanagan Aptitude Classification Tests* are designed primarily for the vocational guidance of high school students, and yield percentile scores on 19 "job tasks [27]." Different combinations of three to eight scores on the Flanagan tests indicate the student's probable success or failure in 37 specific, professional and skilled occupations and many other analogous areas.

TESTS OF SPECIFIC PRACTICAL APTITUDES

The purpose of tests of factored differential abilities, such as those we have just described, and of tests of specific "practical" aptitudes is to predict educational and vocational achievement, but the directions of approach are different. The former begin by analyzing the individual, the latter by analyzing the subject or occupation. Constructors of aptitude tests are concerned first with the mental processes which analysis indicates are required in learning a particular subject or occupation. The test items consist of direct samples of performance in the subject or occupation, samples of performance in analogous activities, or separate measures of the specific processes into which the performance has been analyzed. Although there are many such tests, we shall confine ourselves here to illustrations of some typical tests for predicting relative success in learning art, music, and mechanics.

Art aptitudes. According to Meier's analysis, artistic aptitude is a combination of such interworking factors as "perceptual facility," "creative imagination," "pride in doing things well," "initiative," "sustained planning," "assiduous effort," art-craft abilities, and "aesthetic judgment [73, p. 4–5]." Our first two illustrations are tests of artistic performance.

The *Knauber Art-Ability Test,* intended for junior and senior high school and college students, samples the students' drawing abilities by rating their performance on 17 drawing problems [53, 54]. The problems include such tasks as drawing a picture of Santa Claus, a cup and saucer, a "little church at the foot of mountains" (giving a "spiritual quality to the church"); completing several designs, such as filling in appropriate light-dark values and detecting "mistakes" (such as in the size of an object or the correctness of a shadow) in several drawings.

The *Lewerenz Tests in Fundamental Abilities of Visual Art* [51] are based on a subjective analysis of artistic performance. They are designed to measure such abilities as recognition of aesthetic proportion, originality of line drawings, perception of light and shade, visual memory, and color recognition.

As examples of tests which measure artistic judgment or appreciation, let us examine somewhat more closely the *Meier Art Judgment* and the *Graves Design Judgment* tests.

The *Meier Art Judgment Test* [73] is based on the assumption that both present-day art and the art of the old masters involve applications of such "universal principles" as proportion, balance, "sequence in arrangement of values," rhythm in arrangement of lines, and unity of composition. Furthermore, the ability to discern the functioning of these qualities in art situations is believed to be indicative of artistic judgment, and as such is prognostic of emerging art talent. Constructed according to these principles, the test consists

Fig. 4.4. *One of the hundred experimental items in the* Meier Art Judgment Test, *requiring the subject to choose the picture with the more artistic arrangement.* (Iowa City, Iowa: Bur. Educ. Res. and Serv., Univ. of Iowa, 1940.)

of 100 pairs of adapted pictures of classic and contemporary artists. The subject is directed to choose the more pleasing and artistic picture of each set (see Figure 4.4). The correct picture always exemplifies some aesthetic quality, which is depicted inartistically in the opposite picture. Since the "correct" picture was originally an artist's expression of art principles and was accepted as better by 25 art experts in the validation of the test, an individual's total score indicates how well his own judgment matches the artistic judgment of artists and art experts. Individual scores are interpreted from percentile norms on approximately one thousand "persons interested in art" at each of the levels: junior high, senior high, and college.

Like the *Meier Art Judgment Test,* the *Graves Design Judgment Test* [38] was constructed to measure perception and application of such basic aesthetic principles as unity, dominance, variety, balance, continuity, symmetry, proportion, and rhythm. However, it is comprised of abstract rather than representational pictures. From each pair (or triad) of abstract designs (see Figure 4.5), the subject is directed to choose the design he prefers. The "correct" member of the pair (or triad) was drawn to conform to the above art principles, and the "wrong" member or members violate one or more of them. The 90 items of the test were selected on the basis of three criteria: (1) agreement among art teachers in selection of the "correct" design; (2) discrimination between art and nonart students in frequency of selection of the "correct" design; and (3) internal consistency— greater frequency of choice of the preferred design by students scoring highest on the test as a whole. Total scores thus indicate how well students' aesthetic judgments agree with artists' intended application of art principles and with the judgments of art students and teachers. Individual scores are interpreted against percentile norms for high school and college art and nonart groups.

Seashore measures of musical talents. In analyzing the capacity of individuals to learn music, Seashore isolated six specific abilities as fundamental "in hearing, appreciating, and performing of music

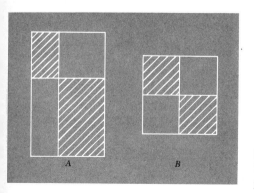

Fig. 4.5. *An item from the* Graves Design Judgment Test, *directing the subject to choose the design he prefers.* (New York: The Psychological Corp., 1946.)

[90, p. 3]." The tests, which are recorded for phonograph, are designed to measure these abilities. Four measure the perception of differences in pitch, loudness, duration, and timbre of a series of pairs of tones. A fifth requires judgment of similarity or difference in rhythmic patterns. And the sixth test, of tonal memory, requires the subject to detect which note is changed in a repeated series of tones.

The tests are designed for upper elementary school, secondary school, and college students, for whom percentile norms make it possible to construct profiles of comparable scores. Used in combination with case histories of music study, auditions, and other indexes of potential success in music, such profiles are intended to aid in the guidance of students interested in music.

Minnesota mechanical ability tests. From a tryout of several tests which appeared to measure processes analogous to those needed in secondary school shop work, three tests (*Mechanical Assembly, Spatial Relations,* and *Paper Form Board*) were found to predict the quality of shop work or products the students would produce [82, p. 219].

In the *Minnesota Mechanical Assembly Test,* the subject is required to assemble a number of mechanical gadgets, such as a bicycle bell, a Corbin rim lock, a spark plug, an inside caliper, and a petcock. He is guided by his understanding of the relationships among spatial clues (the parts of the gadgets) and by the results of his trial manipulations of the parts.

The *Spatial Relations* test is a perceptual-motor task requiring the subject to replace in the appropriate holes of form boards a large assortment of wood pieces of varied sizes and shapes. Efficient performance requires accurate perceptual discrimination, rapid hand-arm manipulation, and planned economy of movements.

The *Paper Form Board* test requires the perception and mental manipulation of pictured parts of geometrical figures to determine which among five geometrical figures they would make when correctly assembled.

Percentile norms, from ages 11 to 20, are provided for scores on each test, for boys and girls separately. As is indicated by intercorrelations of the three tests in the battery, ranging from .49 to .63, they measure to some extent both general and specific, although interrelated, mechanical abilities.

Uniqueness of specific aptitudes. As was suggested in the previous chapter, individuals typically possess differentiated patterns of abilities. Further confirmation of this concept is provided by data showing the relative independence from verbal-abstract intelligence of the measures of mechanical, musical, and art abilities just described.

Correlations between Otis IQs and *Mechanical Assembly* of .06 and between Otis IQs and *Spatial Relations* of .18 indicate that the abilities measured by these aptitude tests are independent of verbal-abstract intelligence. The *Paper Form Board,* however, involving mental manipulations and discriminations of spatial patterns, has a rather definite relation to the Otis IQ, the correlation between them being .53 [82, p. 204]. Similarly, low correlations are often, though not always, reported between verbal-abstract intelligence and art ability and appreciation. Scores on the *Seashore Measures of Musical Talent* are unrelated to Otis IQs [28]. The relatively low correlations between general intelligence and these art, music, and mechanical aptitude tests should not, of course, imply that high general intelligence is unimportant for advanced achievement in these areas. For success in many occupations in these fields, both specific talent and high general intelligence are needed. The low relationships do indicate, however, that for some occupations requiring these talents, a certain minimum of general (or abstract-verbal) intelligence may be sufficient for successful performance.

As aids to teachers and school counselors in determining readiness for learning and as guides for educational and vocational directors, all tests of intellectual abilities should meet certain standards of trustworthiness, utility, and effectiveness. Tests should be reliable, they should reflect both status and (in repeated applications) development, and they should be valid predictors of achievement.

RELIABILITIES OF TESTS OF ABILITIES

A trustworthy measure of ability must be reliable; that is, it should be accurate and self-consistent in repeated applications, unless, of course, the ability measured has changed in the meantime. The case of a third grade child who was tested and retested because of his apparent inability to learn to read illustrates the meaning of test reliability. The child's teacher persisted in her efforts to teach him, but eventually she began to doubt the accuracy of the S-B IQ of 115, which had been reported for him. When he earned an IQ of 120 on the alternate form of the same test, however, the teacher concluded that his intelligence had been reliably measured and that other faulty conditions of learning accounted for his failure. The discrepancy of five IQ points between two equivalent forms of the same intelligence test is within the range of tolerance of a reliable test—a topic which we shall discuss more fully in a moment.

How reliability is determined. The reliability of a test is usually determined by administering it—or alternate forms of it—twice to a large, representative group of individuals at a single age level. Or a test may be divided into two parts for scoring—the answers on odd and even items may be scored separately. The reliability of the test is indicated by the correlations between the pairs of scores thus obtained.

If a trait is being reliably measured, the scores on alternate forms, or on the odd and even items of the same test, will be approximately equal, except for relatively small errors of measurement. And the approximate rank order of the individuals from the first to the second administration of two forms or halves of the same test will be maintained. Such approximately maintained ranks would produce a high correlation between the pairs of scores. From the correlation between the pairs of scores for a test and the standard deviation of the distribution of scores on a representative population, we compute the standard error of measurement (σ meas.).[1] This meaningful indication of a test's reliability, when subtracted from and added to the obtained score, shows the expected range of fluctuations in scores on the middle two-thirds of a large number of retests.

Typical reliability of tests of abilities. Let us now illustrate these concepts in evaluating the reliability of our typical tests of intelligence, differential abilities, and practical aptitudes.

When Terman and Merrill correlated *Forms L* and *M* of the 1937

Table 4.2. *Representative reliability indexes of IQs on typical tests of intelligence*

Test	Procedure	r	Approx. σ meas.
Stanford-Binet [106]*	Alternate forms, median r	.91	5.0
Wechsler Intell. Scale for Children [114]	Split-half, age 10	.95	3.4
Wechsler Adult Intell. Scale [116]	Split-half, age 18–19	.97	2.6
Otis Quick-scoring Mental Ability, Beta [81]	Alternate forms, grade 6	.83	
Davis-Eells Test [22]	Split-half, grade 4	.83	6.5
Kuhlmann-Finch Tests [58]	Split-half, age 9 and 12	.88	5.4
Terman-McNemar Test of Mental Ability [105]	Alternate forms, grades 7 and 9	.95	3.5
Calif. Test of Mental Maturity [101]:	Split-half, grades 4–6	.95	3.5
Verbal IQ		.94	3.9
Nonverbal IQ		.92	4.5
Lorge-Thorndike Intelligence Tests [67]:			
Verbal IQ	Alternate forms, level 3	.90	4.7
Nonverbal IQ	Alternate forms, level 3	.81	5.6

* Numbers in brackets refer to bibliographic references for the chapter.

[1] The computation and meaning of the standard error of measurement are taken up in Chap. 15.

Stanford-Binet test, and computed the reliability coefficients separately for 21 age groups, they reported test-retest correlations for the S-B ranging from .85 to .95, with a median correlation of .91 [106]. Reliabilities tended to be higher for school-age than for preschool children and for duller than for brighter children. With a reliability coefficient of .91 and a standard deviation of 16 (see Chapter 15), the standard error of measurement of the S-B is approximately 5 IQ points. Applying this concept to the S-B IQ of 115, which was obtained as the initial score of the third grade child mentioned above, we may say that two-thirds of the IQs obtained in a large number of retests of this child could be expected to fluctuate between 115 ± 5, or approximately from 110 to 120. In other words, according to the normal curve of probabilities, the chances are 2 in 3 that his "true" S-B IQ lies between 110 and 120. There is still 1 chance in 3, of course, that some retests might show greater "error" fluctuations—as much as 10 or even 15 or more IQ points.

In Table 4.2, we have assembled similar typical reliability coefficients for other intelligence tests. The reliability of a test depends on a number of factors—the age and brightness of the subjects, the skill of the examiner, the suitability of the testing situation—and we have tried to report studies based on properly tested, single-age, and otherwise representative groups. As the table shows, the reliability coefficients of these typical intelligence tests range from .83 to .97.

Trustworthy interpretation of a profile of differential abilities, such as from the *Differential Aptitude Tests*, depends on the reliabilities of the separate subtests. There are reported in Table 4.3, for the *DAT* subtest scores, both indexes of internal consistency (split-half reliability) and of stability (test-retest correlations between ninth grade and end-of-twelfth-grade scores).

The split-half correlations of the *DAT* subtests, ranging from .86 to .94, indicate that these tests are as reliable for their purposes as

Table 4.3. *Representative reliability indexes of subtest scores on the DAT*

Measure of reliability	VR	NR	AR	SR	MR	CSA	Spell.	Sent.
Split-half r, 186 10th grade boys*	.90	.89	.90	.94	.86	.93	.92	.88
σ meas. of scores	3.0	2.9	3.4	6.5	4.9	3.1	7.1	5.1
Test-retest r in 9th and 12th grades, for 71 boys*	.87	.75	.62	.59	.73	.68	.77	.75

* The reliability coefficients are similar for girls.
SOURCE: Bennett, G. K., Seashore, H. G., and Wesman, A. G. *A Manual for the Differential Aptitude Tests.* New York: The Psychological Corp., 1952.

Table 4.4. *Representative reliability indexes of specific, "practical" aptitude tests*

Test	Procedure	r
Knauber Art Ability Test [54]	Split-half, students in various grades	.95
Lewerenz Fundamental Abilities of Visual Art [51]	Test-retest, 100 pupils in grades 3 to 9	.87
Meier Art Judgment Test [73]	Split-half, 100 h. s. students	.81
Graves Design Judgment Test [38]	Split-half, 246 art students	.85
Seashore Measures of Musical Talent [90]	Test-retest, grades 6, 7, 8	.51 to .87
Minnesota Mechanical Assembly [82]	Split-half, 217 7th, 8th, grade boys	.94
Minnesota Spatial Relations [82]	Split-half, 217 7th, 8th, grade boys	.84
Minnesota Paper Form Board [82]	Split-half, 217 7th, 8th, grade boys	.94

are good intelligence tests. The test-retest correlations, ranging from .62 to .87, indicate that, although many adolescents' profiles are likely to change in some respects, they remain sufficiently stable to justify using the *DAT* as a tentative guide in educational planning.

Typical reliability indexes for the practical, specific aptitude tests mentioned above are reported in Table 4.4. Except for the less reliable parts of the *Seashore Measures of Musical Talent*, these aptitude tests are also apparently as reliable as the tests of general intelligence.

PATTERNS OF DEVELOPMENT OF ABILITIES

Given appropriate cultural opportunities, wise guidance, and ample encouragement, the individual's capacities for learning and problem solving continue to grow from birth to adulthood. The pattern of growth of general intelligence, as measured by the S-B and the *WAIS*, is indicated in Figure 4.6. As the figure shows, S-B scores (converted to mental age units) continue to increase through 18 years of age. The standard scores on *WAIS*, which has more ceiling for top scores, show further increases in intelligence from age 16 to the 20- to 24-year age group. With one exception[1] *all* the tests of general intelligence described here reveal similar patterns of mental growth. The rate of

[1] In selecting items for the *Davis-Eells Test of Problem-solving Abilities*, which is not necessarily intended as a scholastic aptitude test, discrimination between age levels was minimized.

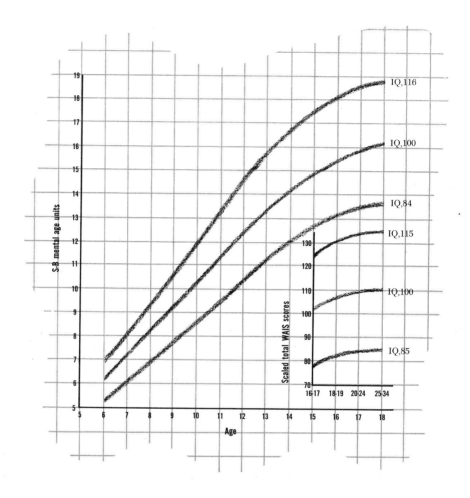

Fig. 4.6. *Average mental growth curves through childhood and adolescence to mental maturity of individuals approximating IQs of 84, 100, and 116 on the S-B and on WAIS.* (Adapted from P. McNemar, *The Revision of the Stanford-Binet Scale*, Houghton Mifflin, Boston, 1942, and from D. Wechsler, *Wechsler Adult Intelligence Scale* [*Manual*], The Psychological Corp., New York, 1955.)

increase tends to be sharp during childhood and to decline during adolescence. On the basis of these and other data, Nancy Bayley has concluded that for intellectually stimulated individuals, mental growth continues at least through 21 years of age [7, p. 15].

As is suggested in Figure 4.6, the score on a general intelligence test (interpreted either in mental age or standard deviation units) shows the individual's level of mental maturity at the time of the test. The IQ indicates his relative brightness, his rate of mental growth, and the potential level of ability he is likely to reach at mental maturity. On the S-B, for example, a child of average intelligence is likely to level off at maturity with a mental age of approximately 16. An individual with an S-B IQ of 116 is likely to attain a theoretical mental age of approximately 19, and he may attain an even higher level on WAIS or on the Terman-McNemar or Lorge-Thorndike group tests [67, 105]. The mental growth of a child with an S-B IQ of 84 is slower, and is likely to cease at a lower level—at about a mental age of 14, according to Figure 4.6.

As growth in general intelligence proceeds, the child also develops differential abilities and specific aptitudes. Garrett [36] and others [48, 112] have cited some variations in test intercorrelations at different ages which suggest that in the young child intelligence is global and somewhat generalized; as he matures, patterns of less closely inter-related differential abilities emerge. Thurstone, for example, says that the degree of correlation among the primary mental abilities (verbal meaning, spatial visualization, reasoning, perceptual speed, number ability, and memory) declines with age [112]. The median correlation among pairs of these tests for grade 1 is .62; for ages 7 to 11, it is .37; and for grade 10, it is .22. Notwithstanding the incomplete confirmation of Garrett's developmental theory of intelligence, we can agree with him that, although single-factor tests of intelligence are appropriate for the elementary school, tests of differential abilities are more helpful at the secondary level because of the increasing need for differential guidance at this level.

FACTORS AFFECTING THE RATE OF MENTAL DEVELOPMENT

Because of errors of measurement, retest IQs obtained after only short intervals of time tend to fluctuate. They fluctuate—as we have learned —about five points in either direction for approximately two-thirds of the retests and somewhat more than this for another third. However, as several studies over longer time intervals show, the general trend of mental growth is relatively constant.

Constancy of the IQ. In one investigation of 58 children of ages 2 to 5 in which retests were given 6 months after the initial tests, 59 per cent of the S-B IQs changed from 0 to 5 points; 24 per cent changed from 6 to 10 points; and 17 per cent changed from 11 to 15 points [31]. Bradway has reported S-B IQ changes in children who were tested at ages 4 and 5, and retested 10 years later [12]. One-third of them changed less than 5 IQ points, three-fifths of them changed less than 10 points, and three-fourths of them changed less than 15 points. A group of elementary school children, with IQs ranging from 46 to 90, were tested and retested after a median interval of 17 months. It was found that the WISC IQs fluctuated 5 or fewer points for 50 per cent of the children; 10 or fewer points for 76 per cent; 15 or fewer points for 90 per cent; and 20 or fewer points for 97 per cent of the children [118].

As concrete examples of such test-retest variations in IQ, let us examine Woodworth's retest records of a few specific children [122]. The S-B IQ of child A at age 6–8 was 83; at age 7–1, it was 75; at age 8–2, it was 84; at age 8–7, it was 81; and at age 12–10, it was 77. Child B at age 6–6 earned an IQ of 105; at age 7–2, it was 95; at age 8–3, it was 107; at age 9–6, it was 101; and at age 12–8, it was 103. A gifted child, tested first at age 5–3, earned an IQ of 176; at age 6–2, he earned 153; and at age 11–5, he earned 143. The last-obtained IQ is still in the highest 1 per cent of Terman's standardization group, but it is lower by 33 points than the initial IQ. Such drops, however, are not characteristic of gifted children [42, 60, 108]. Testing high initially, they tend to maintain their high rates of mental growth—a fact which is clearly indicated in Figure 4.7. This figure presents graphically the S-B IQs obtained from repeated testing over a 6-year period of three gifted children and of one child of average ability [43].

Studies of IQ constancy have disclosed three general trends:

1. Correlations between test-retest scores tend to decrease (that is, IQ fluctuations increase) as the time interval between tests is lengthened. For example, on 50 superior children, the correlation between IQs obtained at ages 10 and 12 is .88; at ages 7 and 12, it is .67; and at ages 3 and 12, it is .46 [96].

2. With equal intervals between test and retest, correlations tend to become higher (IQ fluctuations decrease) as children become older. For example, on the same 50 children, at ages 6 and 7, the correlation is .83; at ages 10 and 11, the correlation is .91.

3. Since IQ increases for some children tend to be balanced by decreases for other children, the average IQs on retests of groups of

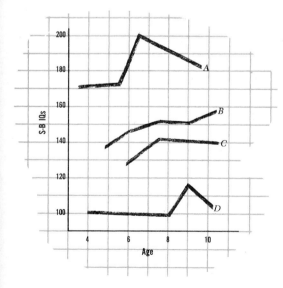

Fig. 4.7. *S-B IQs tend to remain relatively constant, as is shown by the records of repeated tests from ages four to eleven for three gifted children (A, B, C) and one child of average intelligence (D).* (From G. Hildreth, *J. Genet. Psychol.*, 1954, vol. 85, p. 243.)

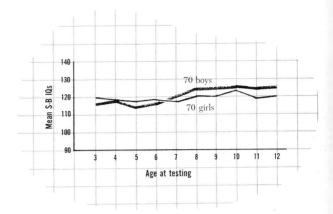

Fig. 4.8. *Means of IQs tend to remain constant, as is shown by the mean S-B IQs of 140 children retested at birthdays from three to twelve.* (After L. W. Sontag, C. T. Baker, and Virginia L. Nelson, *Amer. J. Ortho-psychiat.,* 1955, vol. 25, p. 557.)

children tend to remain relatively constant, except for small gains of two or three IQ points attributable to practice. This tendency for the mean IQ to remain relatively constant is shown in Figure 4.8 [95].

It is not surprising, of course, to find that IQs, especially of *groups* of children, tend to remain constant. Intelligence tests are constructed to produce constancy of IQs in representative populations, that is, to produce mean IQs of 100 and, usually, similar variability of scores throughout the age range for which a test is appropriate. But the IQs of some children do increase, and the IQs of others decrease. Therefore it is· pertinent to ask: What factors account for these individual variations? Are there practical ways to accelerate the rate of mental growth, to increase children's IQs?

Personality and IQ change. It seems probable that those children whose IQs increase are highly motivated—both to do well in tests and to profit from their opportunities to learn. They therefore accumulate more functional knowledge and become more effective in learning and problem solving. This hypothesis is supported by a comparison of personality traits of 35 children whose rate of mental growth was most accelerated and 35 whose rate was most decelerated. Figure 4.9 presents the average changes in IQ from ages 3 to 12 for these two groups.

From personality studies of these children, Sontag, Baker, and Nelson discovered that the group of boys and girls who gained from 4 to 24 points surpassed those who lost from 3 to 13 points in several desirable personality traits [96]. Those who gained in IQ excelled in such traits as independence and self-confidence; they exhibited more interest in self-initiated hobby and science activities; they were more effective and more persistent and achieved greater intrinsic satisfaction in solving problems; they worked harder and were more ambitious in school; and they were more competitive in academic, sport, and social activities. It is probable that those children discovered early in life the rewards of such approaches to problems and learning tasks.

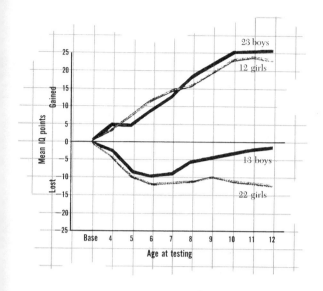

Fig. 4.9. *Individual children gain or lose in IQ, as is shown by the mean IQ points gained by the most ascending and lost by the most descending children of a group of 140 retested on the S-B at birthdays from ages four to twelve. (From L. W. Sontag, C. T. Baker, and Virginia L. Nelson, Monogr. Soc. for Res. in Child Developm., 1958, vol. 23, serial no. 68, no. 2, p. 38.)*

Since these responses were reinforced both by intrinsic satisfactions and by encouragement and approval of parents, teachers, and peers, the children were able to master intellectual concepts and skills more rapidly. Thus they became more effective in learning and problem solving.

Educational opportunity and mental growth. In devising tests of innate capacity for learning and problem solving, psychologists have tried to avoid school content or to select items on which learning opportunities for all children are approximately comparable. They have not, of course, succeeded completely in attaining this goal. Otis, however, justifies some schoollike content (especially vocabulary and arithmetic items) on the assumption that all the children for whom his test is intended have had the same educational opportunities [81]. Under this condition, he believes it is "reasonable to assume" that differences in school accomplishment are indicative of differences in capacity to learn. Let us note, however, some studies of the effect of unequal educational opportunities.

Eleven pairs of orphanage preschool and kindergarten children were chosen for study. Over a period of 92 days one child of each pair was given 50 hours of training (stories, discussions of pictures, excursions, and conversations) in order to improve his understanding of frequently used words. The trained group gained 14 IQ points, whereas the other members of the equated pairs of children, those who had not received such intellectual stimulation, sustained a loss of 2 IQ points. Such motivation and training, Dawe believes, brought these underprivileged children nearer to a full utilization of their intellectual capacities [23, p. 209]. Her conclusion is supported by

Wheeler's study of the effect on the rate of intellectual growth of a more general environmental improvement [119].

Using the *Dearborn Intelligence Tests*, Wheeler tested 946 children in 21 different underprivileged mountain schools of Tennessee in 1930; in 1940, he tested a comparable group of 3,252 children from the same schools and families. During the 10-year interval he notes: "There has been definite improvement in the economic, social, and education status of this mountain area [119, p. 333]." As is shown in Figure 4.10, children at every age, from 6 to 16, earned higher intelligence scores in 1940 than in 1930. Wheeler attributes the improved performance to increased attendance in better-taught, supervised, and equipped schools and to a general enrichment of cultural stimulation.

In another study, which involved the testing of adults, Lorge used the *Otis Mental Ability Tests*, with their schoollike content [66]. He found that variations in the scores of 131 men, 34 years of age, were related to differences in the extent of their schooling beyond the eighth grade. First, he classified the men according to their estimated abstract intelligence at age 14. In this way, he was able to divide them into nearly homogeneous groups. Within each group, Lorge found that those who had continued their schooling longest (from grades 8 to 16) attained higher scores on the intelligence test given at age 34. Attempts to accelerate the rate of mental growth of children already experiencing "normal" educational and general cultural stimulation, however, have produced no or only minimal gains on tests like the S-B which contain non-schoollike content.

Lamson found that 141 children, transferred from a traditional elementary school curriculum to a "rich and vital," individualized, child-interest-centered curriculum, did not achieve higher IQs. Entering the new school with S-B IQs averaging about 110, the children

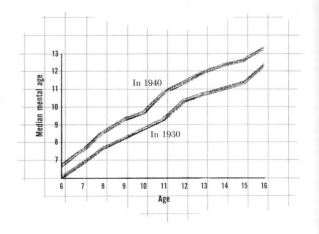

Fig. 4.10. *For children of underprivileged mountain schools, mental growth is apparently accelerated by improvement between 1930 and 1940 in the education and socioeconomic status of the region.* (Adapted from L. R. Wheeler, *J. Educ. Psychol.*, 1942, vol. 33, p. 328.)

maintained that same rating after one to three years in the enriched curriculum [61].

Although preschool and kindergarten attendance helps children to achieve desirable intellectual, social, and personality objectives, it apparently does not significantly increase the rate of mental growth. Of the 58 preschool children mentioned above who were tested and then retested six months later, 30 attended an intellectually stimulating college nursery school. The remaining 28 were similarly treated and equally able children, but they did not attend nursery school. The former group gained, on the average, 3.34 S-B IQ points, whereas the latter, the control group, had a mean gain of .53 points [31]. Larger gains have been reported [117]; but this relatively small advantage of 2.81 points is fairly typical [98]. Moreover, similar or slightly larger gains associated with kindergarten attendance are more likely to result from more efficient test behavior (acquired in making the initial adjustment to a school situation) than from "actual growth in intelligence [70, p. 32]."

Despite certain claims of phenomenal increases in IQ when mentally retarded children are transferred from regular classes (where they are often not ready for the instruction given them) to special classes, the results of more carefully conducted research on IQ gains of such children is not reassuring [44, 52, 83]. Hill found no average gain in IQ among 107 mentally retarded children (ages 11 to 18 and with IQs from 50 to 81) who had spent a mean of three years and nine months in a special class planned to meet their particular needs [44]. Although test-retest fluctuations of individual children ranged from 22 to –22, three-fourths of them fluctuated only from 0 to 7 points. But the net mean change was –.33 IQ points. Similarly, for 111 elementary school slow learners (whose S-B IQs ranged from 75 to 90, with a mean of 85), Pritchard, Horan, and Hollingworth found that individualized instruction in a curriculum especially adapted to the needs, interests, and experiences of the children produced—after a minimum interval of two years—a net gain in IQ of only 1.11 [83]. These investigators would agree with Hill's conclusion that, although a "well-planned special education program" may facilitate achievement and the personal-social adjustment of children, it does not seem to accelerate their rate of mental growth.

Socioeconomic status and intelligence. That the intelligence of children is related to the socioeconomic status of their parents is indicated in several studies. For example, when Byrns and Henmon classified 100,820 Wisconsin high school seniors according to the occupational status of their fathers, they found the median percentile scores on group intelligence tests to rise with parents' position in the occupational hierarchy—from 45.8 for unskilled laborers to 68.5 for professional workers [15]. Comparing Illinois high school students in the highest and lowest quarters of the distribution of combined verbal and abstract reasoning scores on the *DAT*, Monhandessi and Runkel found higher scores associated with such socioeconomic factors as living nearer to or in larger communities, attending larger schools, and the value of farm products sold in the county [78]. Terman and Merrill report a similar relationship of S-B IQs of children to the occupational status of their parents [106, p. 48].

Although the intelligence–socioeconomic-status relationship is well established, the *degree* of the relationship should not be over-emphasized. In the Wisconsin study [15], the correlation between child intelligence and rank of parental occupation was found to be only .18. Looking at the low positive relationship in another way, we note that children covering the entire range of intelligence (from mental retardation to intellectually gifted) are produced by parents in every occupational category. Moreover, the cause-effect direction of the relationship is uncertain. Such studies as Wheeler's suggest that favorable socioeconomic factors foster development of intelligence. On the other hand, it should be observed that the differences in intelligence corresponding to socioeconomic status appear in children as young as 2 to 5½ years of age [106, p. 48]. It should also be noted that such differences do not increase with living a longer time in such different homes. These facts suggest, as an alternative interpretation, that biologically intelligent families may select or create intellectually stimulating communities. In the development of general intelligence, these factors seem to operate reciprocally.

Institutionalization versus foster home placement and IQ. Several studies indicate that children in institutions for the feeble-minded tend to decline slightly in IQ as they mature. For example, Sloan and Harmon [94] report that among 1,446 inmates of the Lincoln State School, the mean S-B IQ dropped from 50 at age 14.8 to 46 at age 20.8. Apparently such institutions—which rightly emphasize practical, nonverbal training—restrict children slightly in learning how to manage the items in intelligence tests intended for children in a more verbal environment. When children at the borderline of mental deficiency (with IQs near 70) are placed in orphanages (where the average levels both of intelligence and of intellectual stimulation are higher) no decline in IQ seems to occur [20].

Orphanages, however, provide only limited intellectual stimulation. They do not build up warm, security- and confidence-giving personal relationships or promote individual development. When normal or near-normal children are transferred from their own inadequate homes to good foster homes rather than to orphanages, not only is a loss in IQ averted, but the IQ is sometimes raised. Among 75 children placed in "average" or "better than average" foster homes at a median age of three years, Schott found that the median S-B IQ rose from 93.5 to 99.3, after a median interval of 13 months [89]. Of several studies of foster home placement, Freeman has reported the largest S-B IQ gain [35]. He found that 41 children, eight years of age, placed in homes of average quality, had gained an estimated 5 points during four years of placement, and that 33 children placed in better foster homes had gained an estimated 10 points.

It seems plausible to assume that children living in inadequate homes have feelings of anxiety and acquire defensive reactions to unhealthy parent-child relationships which depress their rate of mental growth. After being placed in good foster homes, which provide opportunities for healthy emotional adjustments, such children earn higher IQs because they then are free to develop their intellectual capacities more fully.

Medical treatment for acceleration of mental growth. Both indirect and direct medical treatments have been considered as a means of accelerating mental growth. As an example of the indirect approach, let us examine Roger's study of the effect of removing diseased tonsils [86]. Testing 28 boys of average intelligence before tonsillectomies and again six months later, he found a mean gain of 2.25 S-B IQ points. This small, statistically insignificant gain was matched by a similar gain among a control group of children whose diseased tonsils were not removed.

As an example of the direct approach, two well-designed studies of the effect of feeding glutamic acid to feeble-minded children are of interest. In these studies, the S-B IQs of both experimental and control subjects remained practically constant. For Quinn and Durling's subjects, the initial mean S-B IQ of the experimental group was 53.2. After six months of standard glutamic acid feedings, the final mean IQ was 55.3. Among the control group, treated in the same way except for the absence of glutamic acid feedings, the initial and final mean IQs were 49.4 and 51.3, respectively. McCullock obtained similar results in his study [69]. He would agree with the conclusion of Quinn and Durling that "the present experiment does not furnish support for the proposition that the administration of glutamic acid to mentally deficient subjects results in improved ratings [85, p. 229]."

Biological determinants of intelligence. An analysis of the factors determining the development of intelligence indicates that it is a product of complexly interacting hereditary and environmental factors. The importance of biological determinants is suggested by two kinds of studies:

1. *Efforts to accelerate the rate of mental growth through changes in the environment.* The limited success of experiments of this kind

suggests that abilities cannot be developed beyond the limits of biological potentiality.[1] On the other hand, the fact that gains *are* achieved by some children—by better motivated and intellectually stimulated children and especially by those for whom environmental handicaps are removed—indicates that full intellectual development requires rich and emotionally healthy environmental stimulation.

2. *Studies on the hereditary transmission of intelligence.* The first of the two studies which we shall cite deals with pairs of individuals having varying degrees of biological relationship. The findings in the study indicate that there is a parallel between degrees of biological relationship and mental development. For example, the correlation was found to be .00 between pairs of IQs of biologically unrelated orphans who were reared together for one-fourth of their lives. For individuals with closer degrees of biological relationship, however, the correlations between pairs of IQs increase correspondingly: for siblings reared together, it is .50; for identical twins reared together, it is .90 [120].

Terman has provided us a striking illustration of the tendency of children to resemble their parents in intelligence. The mean IQ of children of unselected parents is 100; and the IQs of children of intellectually superior and of intellectually inferior parents deviate significantly upward and downward, respectively, from the mean of 100. In 1920, Terman selected for a long-range study 1,000 gifted individuals, ranging in age from 3 to 19 and in IQ from 135 to 200. In 1959, he and Oden reported the mean IQ of the offspring of these individuals. It was not 100, as would be expected if intelligence were unaffected by heredity; the mean IQ of 1,528 children of these intellectually superior parents was found to be 132.7 [108, p. 146].

It is, of course, conceivable that the parents of these children provided greater than usual intellectual stimulation for them, and that this enriched environment produced their relatively high IQs. To account for their superiority according to such an environmental hypothesis, however, we should have to assume that their environment alone raised the mean IQ from 100 to 132.7. Such a large environmentally stimulated gain seems very unlikely in the light of our review of attempts to accelerate the rate of mental growth. The intellectual superiority of these children is probably an interaction product of both superior genetic and superior environmental factors.

The extent to which each of these general factors contributes to mental development is difficult to ascertain, although we may assume that their influence varies for different abilities. Burt has given us one possible answer to this question. In considering the evidence for

---

[1] Actually, of course, we probably rarely develop human capacities to their potential limits.

the innateness of general intelligence, he estimates that "at least 75 percent of the measurable variance in intelligence is attributable to differences in genotype [13, p. 177]."

Accepting such a view as a tentative working hypothesis, teachers usually try to provide a curriculum suited to each child's mental maturity and pattern of abilities; they do not often attempt to change the intellectual capacities of their pupils. Their goal for every child is the discovery and full development of his potential capacities and the cultivation of his intellectual efficiency to the highest possible level.

PUPIL VARIATIONS IN INTELLIGENCE AND IN SCHOOL ACHIEVEMENT

We know that in any typical elementary or secondary classroom, children differ in their performance on tests of both intelligence and school achievement. To grasp the scope of the teaching problem which this situation presents, let us examine the extent of individual differences among pupils.

Individual differences in intelligence. As an example of the complete range of IQs which may be expected in an unselected school population, the standardization sample for the S-B is perhaps the

Table 4.5. *IQ distribution and classification of 2,904 children, ages 2 to 18*

IQ	N	Percentage	Classification
160–169	1	0.03	Very superior; at 9 years may equal aca-
150–159	6	0.2	demic achievement of average 12-year-old
140–149	32	1.1	
130–139	89	3.1	Superior; needs enriched curriculum
120–129	239	8.2	
110–119	524	18.1	Bright; should succeed well in average curriculum
100–109	685	23.5	Average
90–99	667	23.0	
80–89	422	14.5	Below average; needs adjusted curriculum
70–79	164	5.6	Slow learner; may achieve 5th or 6th grade level by age 16
60–69	57	2.0	Mentally retarded; needs special class
50–59	12	0.4	
40–49	6	0.2	Mentally retarded; usually unable to learn
30–39	1	0.03	to read

SOURCE: Adapted from Merrill, M. A. *J. Educ. Psychol.*, 1938, 29, 650.

most representative. The distribution of S-B IQs of the 2,904 representative children, ranging in age from 2 to 18, is presented in Table 4.5.

We see in the table that approximately 46 per cent of these children—those whose IQs range from 90 to 109—are considered to be of "average" intelligence. With decreasing frequency, as they deviate above and below this average, they range in IQ from as low as 30 to as high as 169, or from seriously "mentally retarded" to "very superior." Assuming that this distribution is representative of school children in general, we can predict the expected range of IQs in a typical classroom. For example, in a group of 35 to 40 pupils, there would be, possibly, 1 mentally retarded child, 2 slow-learning children, and 4 children below average in capacity for academic learning. These 7 children might experience considerable frustration unless the regular curriculum were adapted to their limited mental maturity and differential patterns of abilities. There would be about 16 children in the middle range of intelligence; 6 or 7 would be considered bright; and there would be about 4 intellectually superior children who would need an enriched curriculum. There might be 1 extraordinarily gifted child who would need a radically enriched or accelerated curriculum to match his distinctively high learning capacities.

As an index of capacity for learning in the elementary school grades, the mental age is more meaningful than the IQ. Generally, a child whose mental age is about 6–6 is ready for learning at the first grade level. At a mental age of 8–6, he is ready for the third grade level of reading and other school activities. At a mental age of 12–0, he should be making average progress at the sixth grade level. Just as children vary in IQ at every age or grade level, they also vary considerably in mental age. For example, in a typical sixth grade, for which the average mental age on the *California Test of Mental Maturity* is 12.4, the range of mental ages extends from 7 to 15.[1] The sixth grade child whose mental age is only 7 approximates the average mental maturity of second grade children. The top sixth grade child, with a mental age of 15, equals the mental maturity of average tenth grade students.

Variations in achievement. Individual differences in school accomplishment are fully as extensive as those in intellectual ability. Cornell, for example, found the range of achievement (a composite of reading, language, arithmetic, social studies, and science) of 585 ten-year-old pupils to spread from second grade to ninth grade performance. The levels of achievement of the middle 80 per cent of these pupils was found to extend from grade 3 to grade 6 [19].

In this study, the range of over-all school achievement of children from ages seven to twelve in a New York community was

[1] Data obtained from Logan, Utah, city schools.

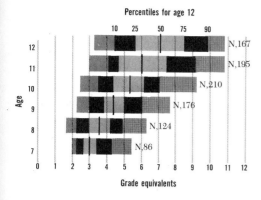

Fig. 4.11. Stanford Achievement *grade equivalents for children ages seven to twelve from 14 New York rural districts combined.* (From E. L. Cornell, *Educ. Res. Studies, No. 1,* Univ. of the State of N. Y. Bull., 1937, Albany, N. Y., p. 26.)

computed. In Figure 4.11 the scores which these children earned on the total *Stanford Achievement Test* have been converted to grade equivalents. In the standardization of the test, the grade equivalent was established by equating the mean score earned at each grade with the corresponding grade level. A grade equivalent of 6.5, for example, would be assigned to every score which equaled the average score of pupils from the standardization population in the fifth month of the sixth grade. Thus interpreted, the figure shows that eight-year-olds range in performance from below the average of second grade pupils to the average of sixth grade pupils. For every age represented, the range of achievement is very wide. Since the range of individual differences increases with grade progress, the range of differences in achievement is even greater among high school students. As Figure 4.11 also shows, there is extensive overlapping in achievement from age to age. Some pupils at seven years of age, for example, equal the achievement of some twelve-year-olds.

Tests of intelligence are designed to measure capacities for learning and problem solving; thus it would seem logical to expect that individual differences in intelligence are related to variations in achievement. This logical expectation is reinforced by the further observation that effective performance both on typical intelligence tests and in academic school subjects involves the comprehension and mental manipulation of verbal, numerical, pictorial, and abstract symbols. In studying this relationship, we shall examine, for different tests and different populations of school children, the correlation between measures of intelligence and achievement.

VALIDITY OF INTELLIGENCE TESTS IN PREDICTING SCHOOL ACHIEVEMENT

How valid are tests of general intelligence, of differential abilities, and of practical aptitudes in predicting school achievement?

Validity of general intelligence tests. Tests are designed for different purposes, and they differ in validity for their purposes. To be valid for predicting school achievement, tests should demonstrate significant correlations with acceptable criteria of school accomplishment. Table 4.6 indicates the typical relationship (as well as some atypical relationships) between general intelligence and school achievement at the elementary school level. The scatter diagram shows the correlation between S-B IQs of 50 fourth grade children and their composite achievement scores in reading, language, arithmetic, social studies, and science. This diagram, in which corresponding IQs and grade equivalents of achievement scores are plotted for each child, indicates a definite tendency for pupils of lower IQs to earn relatively low grade equivalents and for pupils of higher IQs to earn relatively high grade equivalents.

The coefficient of correlation for this table is .63. Using the coefficient of determination (r^2) to interpret it, we can see that the correlation indicates that 40 per cent of the variation in achievement of these pupils is related to (possibly caused by) variations in intelligence. The other 60 per cent of the variation in achievement is probably related to differences in motivation, efficiency of work methods, nature of previous school and home experience, emotional control, patterns of aptitudes other than general intelligence, and errors of measurement.

Examining the diagram closely, we note some intelligence-achievement discrepancies. Pupil A, whose IQ is only average (from 100 to 104), attains a grade equivalent of 6.0 to 6.2; intellectually

Table 4.6. *Correlation between S–B IQs and school achievement for 50 fourth grade children*

IQs	Stanford achievement grade equivalents											f
	3.0	3.3	3.6	3.9	4.2	4.5	4.8	5.1	5.4	5.7	6.0	
135							I					1
130										I	I	2
125						I						1
120			IB				I	II	I	I		6
115					I		II	I	I			5
110		I		II	I	I		II				7
105					I			I	I			3
100				IIII	I						IA	6
95		I	I	II	I		I					6
90	I	II		I		I	I					6
85			I		III							4
80	I		I	I								3
f	2	4	4	4	10	5	7	7	3	2	2	50

SOURCE: Adams School, Logan, Utah.

Table 4.7. *Representative validity coefficients for predicting composite school achievement of tests of general intelligence*

Test and reference	Group, N, and Criterion	r with achievement
Stanford-Binet Scale [33]	4th grade, 50; Stanford Achievement Test	.63
Wechsler Intelligence Scale for Children [100]	Single Elem. grade; Iowa Tests of Basic Skills	.66
Wechsler Adult Intelligence Scale [30]	H. S. seniors, 83; grades in H. S.	.69°
Otis Quick-scoring Mental Ability, Alpha [4]	4th grade, 276; Stanford Achievement Test	.57
Davis-Eells Test [32]	5th grade, 56; Iowa Tests of Basic Skills	.44
Kuhlmann-Finch Tests [32]	5th grade, 56; Iowa Tests of Basic Skills	.61
Terman-McNemar Test of Mental Ability [63]	11th grade, 300; Essential High School Content Battery	.62
Calif. Test of Mental Maturity [3]	3rd grade, 100; Progressive Achievement Test	.66

° For the 83 high school seniors, the other factors affecting achievement were especially well controlled. In a more typical group of 50 tenth grade students, $r = .56$.

superior pupil B, whose IQ is between 120 and 124, attains a grade equivalent of only 3.6 to 3.8. It is probable that for pupil A, the factors other than intelligence have been especially favorable. For pupil B, they have presumably been unfavorable. Except for these two marked discrepancies, however, the table shows a definite correlation between IQ and achievement. Similar correlations have also been reported at the high school and college levels.

The "representative" validity coefficients of the intelligence tests described in this chapter are presented in Table 4.7. As can be seen, the validity of the Wechsler tests and some group tests of intelligence equals that of the S-B in predicting composite school achievement. Except for the Davis-Eells test, which is probably the least valid in predicting school achievement since it fails to discriminate well between age levels, the correlations range from .57 to .69. For these same tests, the correlations between intelligence and achievement in separate school subjects vary from .34 (for *Otis Alpha* and spelling) to .77 (for *Otis Beta* and reading), and the median correlation is .55.

From our selection of what we believe are representative studies of the validities of typical tests, we conclude that reliable developmental measures of intelligence are valid—as one factor—in predicting academic achievement. Often a teacher's prediction of school achievement is sharpened beyond the possibilities indicated by these coefficients because the teacher may have knowledge of some of the other factors affecting achievement. For example, if it is known that a child —in addition to having an IQ of 125—is well motivated, emotionally healthy, being given expert teacher guidance, and has ample opportunity for efficient practice, his school achievement is very likely to be high. On the other hand, if all or some of these other significant factors affecting achievement are unfavorable, it is unlikely that his achievement will match his superior intellectual capacity.

Intelligence and nonacademic achievement. Abstract-verbal intelligence is not equally related to every school accomplishment. In addition to developing academic skills, the school is also concerned with developing motor and mechanical skills, art and music talents, social adjustment, and mental health. Between measures of abstract-verbal intelligence and achievement in these nonacademic areas, low correlations have often been reported.

For example, among 100 junior high school boys, Otis IQs were found to correlate .21 with the quality of their shop work and .24 with their proficiency in gymnasium activities [82, pp. 205, 239]. As is indicated in Figure 4.12, athletic achievement is also independent of intelligence. The IQs of 80 high school athletes (those who won athletic awards) are neither all high nor all low; they are distributed about the average—from very low to very high—in approximately the same way as are the IQs of 493 nonathletes [50].

Although advanced academic progress in art and music are as closely related to intelligence as are other academic accomplishments, initial progress in these areas is not nearly so dependent on general intelligence (beyond a needed minimum) as it is on specific talents. Barrett reports a correlation of .21 between the IQs of ninth grade students and the quality of their classroom art work [5]. Among a group of high school students just beginning practice on brass, wood, and string instruments, Lamp and Keys found correlations of from .20 to .33 between the *Terman Test of Mental Ability* and achievement [59].

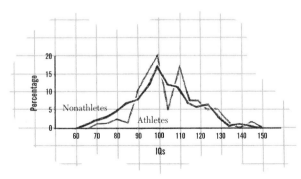

Fig. 4.12. *Both athletes and nonathletes are distributed over the entire range of intelligence.* (From R. H. Jones, *Sch. and Soc.*, 1935, vol. 42, p. 416.)

The relation of intelligence to social adjustment is complex and it varies for different aspects of social adjustment. There is a slight correlation between superior school achievement, which is dependent on superior intelligence, and a child's social acceptance by his peers [14]. Moreover, adolescents' self-ratings on such traits as "self-assurance" and quality of "socialization" are related to their verbal-abstract abilities [65, p. 146]. As a determinant of delinquency, intelligence is only a minor indirect factor. The distribution of IQs of 500 juvenile delinquents (with court records) resembles that of unselected children [75]. The delinquents' mean IQ, however, is 8 to 10 points lower and there are relatively more low and relatively fewer high IQs among them. But delinquents cover the entire range of intelligence—from mentally retarded to intellectually gifted.

Among the factors contributing to mental health, level of general intelligence does not seem to be especially significant. The correlation between IQs of high school students and their scores on a self-inventory of mental health symptoms is zero [26]. Moreover, individuals who develop serious mental illnesses are not confined to any particular category of intelligence. The distribution of intelligence scores of 510 psychiatric patients is indistinguishable from the distribution of a very large group of normal individuals [72]. For both groups, the distributions look very much like those of the athletes or nonathletes in Figure 4.12.

Validity of tests of differential abilities. The constructors of these tests intended them to be measures of capacity for varied kinds of learning. They did not expect each test to predict general academic achievement. They did, however, expect that certain combinations of

Table 4.8. *Correlations indicative of the validity of the DAT (given in the ninth grade) for predicting achievement on the Iowa High School Content Battery in the twelfth grade, for 106 boys*

Achievement	DAT subtests							
	VR	NA	AR	SR	MR	CSA	Spell.	Sent.
Mathematics	.65	.66	.46	.40	.40	.33	.40	.52
Science	.65	.46	.55	.36	.43	.09	.42	.51
Social studies	.57	.38	.46	.25	.23	.01	.34	.35
English	.65	.57	.38	.27	.32	.29	.62	.64
Composite achievement	.75	.63	.51	.36	.38	.25	.59	.63

SOURCE: Bennett, G. K., Seashore, H. G., and Wesman, A. G. *A Manual for the Differential Aptitude Tests.* New York: The Psychological Corp., 1952.

abilities—such as verbal, abstract, and numerical reasoning—would predict academic achievement just as well as do tests of general intelligence. And they expected measures of other differential abilities—such as spatial visualization, mechanical reasoning, or speed of perceptual discrimination to be especially effective in predicting achievement in pertinent specialized activities. To see how well the tests fulfill these expectations, we shall select—from a mass of data on the *DAT*—what seem to be representative studies [9].

The validity of the *DAT* subtests in predicting high school academic achievement is indicated in Table 4.8. The correlations in this table are between *DAT* scores earned by 106 ninth grade boys[1] and their scores on the *Essential High School Content Battery* in the twelfth grade. These correlations show that, when achievement is reliably measured (as it is by the *High School Content Battery*), certain *DAT* subtests (especially *Verbal Reasoning* and *Numerical Ability*) predict academic achievement as well as or better than do tests of general intelligence. Other subtests (especially the *Clerical Speed and Accuracy* test and the *Space Relations* test) seem to be invalid as predictors of academic achievement.

The differential predictiveness of the *DAT* tests is not distinctive. *Verbal Reasoning* is the single most valid subtest in predicting academic achievement, and it predicts about equally well for every academic subject. *Number Ability* is almost as valid in predicting achievement in English as in mathematics. The language usage tests, however, are better at predicting achievement in English than in other subjects.

Turning to predictions of a less reliable criterion, let us examine in Table 4.9 some representative correlations between the *DAT* and grades earned in several different high school courses, one to seven semesters after administration of the *DAT*.

As the table shows, grades in English, mathematics, social studies, modern languages, and physics are predicted best by *Verbal Reasoning, Number Ability,* and the language usage tests. The *Space Relations, Clerical Speed* and *Accuracy,* and *Mechanical Reasoning* tests are almost uniformly poor predictors of achievement in these academic courses, but some differential predictive validity is suggested. For example, mechanical drawing is predicted best by *Space Relations, Verbal Reasoning, Number Ability,* and *Sentences.* Shorthand is predicted best by *Spelling, Sentences,* and *Verbal Reasoning.* And physics is predicted best by *Number Ability, Verbal Reasoning,* and *Mechanical Reasoning.* As a comparison of Tables 4.8 and 4.9 indicates, however, the *DAT* is less valid in predicting grades than in predicting test-measured achievement.

[1] The correlations are similar for girls.

Table 4.9. *Representative correlations between the DAT and boys' high school grades*

DAT tests	English	Math.	Soc. stud.	Modern lang.	Art	Mech. draw.	Wood-work	Physics	Short-hand[*]
VR	.55	.40	.55	.41	.27	.54	.23	.59	.40
NA	.55	.45	.45	.46	.41	.49	.41	.60	.34
AR	.35	.30	.35	.29	.21	.28	.06	.38	.25
SR	.25	.25	.25	.13	.34	.57	.07	.15	.18
MR	<.19	<.19	.25	.21	.24	.30	.30	.47	.19
CSA	<.19	<.19	<.19	.28	.32	.30	.00	.22	.25
Spell.	.45	.25	.35	.35	.08	.33	.09	.22	.68
Sent.	.55	.35	.45	.52	.11	.49	.19	.34	.57

[*] Girls.

SOURCE: Bennett, G. K., Seashore, H. G., and Wesman, A. G. *A Manual for the Differential Aptitude Tests.* New York: The Psychological Corp., 1952.

Validity of tests of "practical" aptitudes. Although the practical aptitude tests are not new, evaluations of their empirical validity in the school situation is incomplete.

As would be expected, the art aptitude tests discriminate between groups of nonart students, art students, and art teachers. Correlating the grades of ninth grade art students with their scores on art aptitude tests, Barrett [5] has reported correlations of .76 with the *Knauber Art Ability Test*, .71 with the *Lewerenz Test in Fundamental Abilities in Art,* and .35 with the *Meier Art Judgment Test.* Another investigator, however, has reported a correlation of only .40 between the art grades of high school art students and their scores on the Lewerenz test [51, p. 46].

Several studies [59, 62, 79, 97, 103] of the validity of the *Seashore Measures of Musical Talent* in predicting high school and college achievement in music have not confirmed the initial promise of these tests. Of the six measures, those of pitch and tonal memory have proved most valid. For these two measures, correlations with music grades or teachers' ratings on proficiency have ranged from about .30 to .45.

Correlations between composite scores on the *Minnesota Mechanical Assembly, Spatial Relations,* and *Paper Form Board* tests, and the quality of the shop work (in metal, wood, electric, and mechanical drawing work) of junior high school students ranged from .55 to .73. Correlations between scores on the separate tests and the quality of shop work ranged from .52 (for *Paper Form Board*) to .55 (for *Mechanical Assembly*) [82, pp. 204, 219].

In addition to tests of general intelligence, differential abilities, and practical aptitudes, teachers and counselors employ other procedures for estimating a child's capacity for learning. Teachers often judge a child's intelligence by observing his performance in the classroom and in individual creative projects, by the things he creates, by his performance on school achievement tests. Since tests of talent are limited in scope and not always valid, it is highly desirable to supplement them with other procedures, although these, too, have limitations.

Teacher estimates of intelligence. We have already suggested the virtues as well as the weaknesses of teacher estimates of children's intelligence. Let us preface a more scientific study of this subject, however, by mentioning additional illustrations.

Loretta, a fifth grade pupil in a mixed fifth-sixth grade classroom, is being considered for a special promotion to the sixth grade. Her teacher describes her as "a very apt student" who is "doing work equal to and often above the sixth grade students in the classroom." She is "creative in illustrating her social studies reports." And, in addition to her assigned schoolwork, "she reads on her own initiative more library books than any other student in the classroom." Asked to estimate Loretta's IQ, the teacher said: "It might be as high as 120." Actually, her *WISC* full-scale IQ was discovered to be 142, which places her in the category of "intellectually gifted children."

Tom, although in the fourth grade, is described by his teacher as "having trouble with the basic sounds in reading. He has difficulty remembering words he has learned previously. He is slow in all areas of learning. The individual help in reading which both his mother and I have given him seems not to help. He seems very immature. Perhaps he belongs in the special class for mentally retarded children. But I am not sure—he sometimes seems alert and he does fairly well in sports." Although Tom's S-B IQ, found to be 94, is a little below average, his achievement is below that of typical children of his intelligence. Serious retardation in reading and lack of self-confidence make him appear less intelligent than he is.

In both of these instances, the tests disclosed that the children possessed intellectual resources beyond either their own or their teachers' expectations. Let us turn now to more comprehensive studies of the extent to which teachers' estimates of abilities coincide with test appraisals.

If teachers were to estimate the intelligence of their pupils on the basis of peculiar personal characteristics or merely from their appearance—of face, eyes, forehead, or mouth—their judgments would be worthless. As Gurnee has demonstrated, the correlation between such

estimates and tested intelligence is zero [41]. But teachers (acquainted with the manifestations of intelligence) have better bases than appearance or unusual peculiarities of behavior for estimating intelligence. They have many opportunities for comparing and evaluating pupils' performance in intellectual activities involving comprehension and mental manipulation of symbols. They vary, however, in the accuracy with which they judge intelligence.

Alexander reports that when 35 experienced teachers were asked to list in order their five most and five least intelligent pupils, intelligence tests confirmed only 57.3 per cent of their choices as "most intelligent" and only 57.8 per cent of their choices as "least intelligent [2]." In a similar study, Lewis found that the children whom elementary teachers selected as "mentally retarded" and as "geniuses" tended to score somewhat below and above the average, respectively, on intelligence tests. However, the group selected as mentally retarded included a few with IQs as high as 120, and the group selected as geniuses included a few with IQs as low as 70 [64]. In judging intelligence, these teachers followed criteria of doubtful validity. They used terms such as "ambitious," "artistic," and "dependable" as characteristic of the geniuses, and "day-dreaming," "disinterested," and "slovenly" as characteristic of the mentally retarded. It is likely that such irrelevant characteristics as these led Oliver Goldsmith's teacher, in appraising this genius's scholastic ability, to say: "Never was so dull a boy [104]."

Other teachers have apparently learned to estimate intelligence more objectively and with more valid criteria. Olander [80], for example, found a correlation of .74 between the average of four teachers' estimates of 55 ninth grade students' IQs and their test-determined IQs. Gronlund and Whitney report a median corre-lation of .73 between elementary teachers' ranks of their pupils' intelligence and their composite *Primary Mental Abilities Test* scores [39]. A recent study suggests that teachers who have had opportunities to check their estimates against the recorded IQs of their pupils and who have increased their understanding of the manifestations of intelli-gence have been able to improve the accuracy of their judgments [46].

Besides the discrepancies which sometimes occur between teacher-judged and test-determined IQs, Gibbons has observed a constant error in teacher judgments of intelligence [37]. Superior students, though often rated above average, tend to be underrated. And dull pupils, though often rated below average, tend to be overrated. Ap-parently when teachers judge intelligence without the use of intelli-gence tests, they fail to recognize the enormous range of individual differences in the abilities of students.

Tested achievement as a sign of intelligence. Tests of achieve-ment in academic areas—in reading, mathematics, language, social studies and science—measure mental processes similar to those meas-ured by such group intelligence tests as the Otis *Beta* or *Gamma* [18]. Such measures of prior achievement, as direct samples of students' capacities for learning, equal and often surpass tests of intelligence as predictors of subsequent achievement.

For example, variations in the achievement of 172 pupils com-pleting the sixth grade were predicted very well by their earlier (fourth grade) performance on the *Iowa Tests of Basic Skills*. The correlations were as follows: for reading, .78; for social studies skills, .71; for language skills, .57; and for arithmetic, .66.[1] When these same tests were given to approximately 250 students in the seventh grade, the median of correlations with their social studies and science achievement in the ninth grade was .66, and in the eleventh grade it was .62. In corresponding specific areas, the relationships were higher. The correlation for language usage, appraised in seventh grade and again in the eleventh grade, was .77; and for mathematics it was .75 [56].

Of four measures obtained in the ninth grade on 102 to 217

[1] Personal data.

students [25], the best predictor of their eleventh and twelfth grade achievement in biology, chemistry, and physics proved to be their grades in general science (median r = .66). Mathematics grades proved next most valid as predictors (median r = .57). And grades in English were almost as valid (median r = .52). A group intelligence test was least effective (median r = .49). Junior high [11] and senior high [34] school grades are also effective predictors of college grades. They are often more valid than intelligence tests. The combination of high school grades and a test of intelligence, however, is more effective than either used alone [34]. Survey tests of high school achievement—in vocabulary, language usage, mathematics, social studies, and science —are also valid predictors of grades earned in college [24, 47]. One university has found an English test (covering vocabulary, reading comprehension, and mechanics and effectiveness of expression) "to be among the most efficient predictors" of freshman grades [49].

SUMMARY

Our complex and abundantly productive civilization needs the constructive and creative talents of all its citizens. The happiness of every individual depends upon the self-realization of his potential talents. For these reasons, it is important to identify and to develop to their fullest degree the talents of every child and youth in our schools. Because of the scope of the task and the limitations of any single procedure, a multiple approach seems desirable. Procedures which teachers and school counselors may use to appraise developing and differentiating abilities include (1) opportunities to observe the manifestations of general intelligence and special talents of their students both in academic areas of the curriculum and in special creative projects; (2) tests of achievement from which capacities for subsequent learning can be inferred; (3) individual and group tests of intelligence; (4) tests of differential abilities; and (5) practical tests of specific aptitudes in such fields as art, music, and mechanics.

All of these procedures should meet certain standards if they are to be effective aids in adjusting the curriculum to pupils' readiness and in guiding pupils into differentiated curricula suited to their unique patterns of abilities. They should be reliable; they should reflect both present status and potential development; and they should be valid in predicting achievement in the areas for which each is intended. Several procedures and a variety of devices meet these standards well enough to justify teachers and counselors in using them. Each procedure, however, has both merits and limitations. Combinations of them are likely to be most effective.

The most universally applicable procedure is observation—by pupils themselves and by teachers—as pupils try out their talents and compare them with those of other children in a great variety of both routine and creative curriculum activities. Used alone, however, self-discovered and teacher-observed manifestations of general intellectual ability and differential talents lack reliability. They need to be checked and supplemented by other procedures.

Besides being evaluations of the accomplishment of school objectives, survey tests of school achievement are good indexes of capacity for subsequent achievement. Profiles of relative achievement in different subjects are also good guides to the area of most probable success among differential curricula. Achievement tests may fail, however, to reveal the potentiality of educationally retarded children. For such children, tests not so dependent on school experience are needed.

Group tests of intelligence are economical, reliable, and valid predictors of general academic achievement in most cases. The bifactor tests, which include measures of both verbal and nonverbal abilities, may reveal unsuspected potentialities, even in educationally retarded children. However, for children who are educationally retarded, or who have scored low on a group intelligence test, or who are emotionally maladjusted, an individual test is likely to give a more reliable and valid appraisal of potential capacity for learning and problem solving. For children who are inefficient in following brief oral or written directions or who lack self-confidence, the individual test can sometimes detect capacities unrevealed by group tests.

Although single-factor or bifactor tests of intelligence are appropriate at the elementary school level, profiles of differential abilities are more helpful for guidance into differentiated curricula and for vocational planning at the secondary school level. Such tests—including measures of verbal, numerical, and abstract reasoning; of spatial visualization; of speed of perceptual discrimination; of facility in language; and of mechanical reasoning—are suitable as survey tests for every student. Profiles of differential abilities, as well as of differential achievement, are needed for the guidance of students. In certain individual problems of guidance, such uniform testing may need to be supplemented by tests of specific practical aptitudes in art, music, mechanics, and in other specialized fields of study and work.

In the next chapter, we shall see how the procedures for appraising abilities are used in providing suitable curricula and in adapting methods of teaching to the different patterns of abilities of elementary and secondary school children.

GUIDES FOR STUDY, REVIEW, AND APPLICATION

1. To achieve our educational aims of self-realization and social effectiveness, we need to identify and develop the talents of every child and adolescent. What understandings, tools, and professional services are needed to accomplish these goals?

2. To what extent are the unrecognized talents of children and youth being wasted? How do psychological tests help us to reveal human resources which might otherwise be undetected?

3. From your examination of representative items from individual and group intelligence tests, would you agree that our general and precise definitions of intelligence fit what the items seem to measure? Why should such items be indicative of academic school achievement?

4. As devices for self-exploration and as aids to high school students in making educational and vocational choices, describe and evaluate the tests of differential abilities and of specific, practical aptitudes. For sample items, interpretation of profiles, and suggested applications of the tests of differential abilities, see the filmstrip *You and Your Mental Abilities,* Science Research Associates.

5. How accurate is a measure of intellectual ability? The test-retest correlations for most modern tests of abilities range from .85 to .95. How is this degree of reliability achieved in the construction of tests? Referring to the discussion of the standard error of measurement both in this chapter and in Chapter 15, explain how this index of unreliability is applied in the interpretation of a test score.

6. Describe the typical patterns of mental growth, both for individuals and for groups. What factors have been found to affect the rates and levels of mental growth attained?

7. Evaluate tests of general intelligence (both individual and group), of differential abilities, of practical aptitudes, and of prior achievement as predictors of both general academic achievement and achievement in the different areas of the curriculum. Considering the role in learning of *all* the essential conditions of learning, why should we not expect the validity correlations to exceed .60 to .70?

Chapter 5

TEACHING INDIVIDUALS IN GROUPS

Our goal of providing equal educational opportunities for the optimum development of all our children presents a challenging problem. Because of their differences in general intelligence and their diverse patterns of abilities, children's needs vary. Equal opportunity for all cannot be provided by identical curricula and methods of teaching.

THE PROBLEM

Since children whose IQs are 140 and over are able to complete the elementary school curriculum in just half the time usually allotted, they are likely to waste years of precious time in idleness or in busy-work, unless they are accelerated or unless their curriculum is enriched [64]. On the other hand, there are children at the other end of the distribution of intelligence who may spend the first three years of their schooling in futile and frustrating attempts to master the typical first grade curriculum. While intellectually superior children are able

Each child is indeed unique

Intraclass grouping . . .

individual instruction

The teacher's problem: equal opportunity for every child in the classroom

Materials, activities, and teacher guidance . . .

*adapted to pupils
of varied
interests . . .*

*varied talents,
needs, and
personalities*

to attain seventh grade norms in reading, arithmetic, social studies, and science during the first three years of school, children with IQs of 70 or lower are, during the same period, only slowly becoming ready for first grade reading and other academic subjects. According to Cook: "When a random group of six-year-olds enters the first grade, two percent of them will be below average four-year-olds in general mental development, and two per cent will be above average eight-year-olds [25, p. 141]."

The problems related to the task of teaching unique individuals in groups do not diminish as children advance from one grade to the next. In fact, the range of individual differences increases with equal amounts of instruction. Any grade above the primary level includes children covering "the complete range of elementary-school ability [25, p. 141]." For example, the grade-equivalent scores of 307 seventh grade pupils in the rural and urban communities of Illinois were found to range on the *Stanford Achievement Tests* from 2.9 to 12.9 in spelling, from 3.6 to 12.1 in arithmetic computation, from 3.4 to 12.0 in arithmetic problem solving, and from 3.2 to 12.0 in reading comprehension [60]. The trend of these differences is indicated more specifically in Figure 5.1 where the distribution of 307 grade equivalents in arithmetic reasoning is presented. The range of differences persists, of course, at secondary school and college levels. For example, it has been found that some students just completing their high school training have already acquired more knowledge of natural science than have some college seniors who, as prospective teachers of science, have majored in the field [125, p. 227].

Besides these extensive interindividual differences, there are intra-individual differences which complicate the problem and at the same time facilitate its solution. As is suggested in Figure 4.3, page 127, individuals typically possess unique patterns of differential abilities.

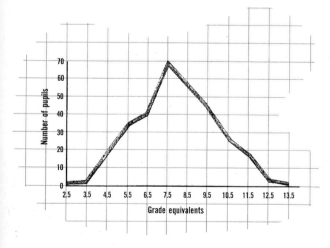

Fig. 5.1. *Grade-equivalent scores of 307 seventh grade pupils in arithmetic reasoning on the* Stanford Achievement Test. (Adapted from H. W. Hightower, *Educ. Adm. and Superv.*, 1955, vol. 41, pp. 459-461.)

Intellectually superior children, for example, are not always high in every ability. In art, music, or mechanical aptitudes, they may range from low, through average, to high [135]. Some mentally retarded children may have special talents in these or other fields. Indeed, the variations within a single person tend to be almost as extensive as the interindividual differences in a group of children [3].

In addition to interindividual and intraindividual differences in abilities, children and youth also differ in interests, personality traits, prior learning experiences, and in family and peer relationships which affect their behavior and development. At every level of ability, some children are found to have particular interests in art, music, mathematics, science, or social studies. In other cases only the unusual sensitivity of teachers makes it possible to discover or to develop *any* interests related to school activities. At each level, some children are confident, socially secure, and efficient in using their abilities. Others, because of anxiety and the development of rebellious or self-inhibiting modes of adjustment, are intellectually inefficient. With respect to parent-child relationships, some children feel accepted, secure, loved, and esteemed; and because of these satisfactions, they are able to apply their talents freely in constructive and creative efforts. On the other hand, children who lack adequate satisfaction of these basic needs or who feel outright parental rejection function far below their potentialities. Wide ranges of parental differences in economic, social, and educational status are also related to the intellectual efficiency and educational aspirations of children. All these factors significantly affect the school progress and patterns of achievement of children and youth.

Because of these individual differences, in general intelligence, patterns of aptitudes, backgrounds of achievement, interests, emotional health, quality of homes, and other factors affecting development, each individual is indeed a unique personality. How can we effectively teach such individuals in groups?

PROPOSED SOLUTIONS

Although the extensive differences among the pupils in a typical classroom complicate the problem of providing individualized teaching and guidance, each child needs a curriculum in which he can efficiently develop his useful talents to optimum levels. Each child needs to experience daily successes in learning tasks in which he is interested and which he considers worthwhile. He needs to be able to work and play with children who accept and esteem each other and who give each other affection. He needs opportunities to make constructive and creative contributions to the group. He needs to belong to a group of children with whom he can advance intellectually, socially, and in mental health. There are several ways in which our schools seek to provide for these needs.

The most common procedure is to permit pupils to progress through the grade levels of the elementary and secondary schools with their age mates. Since grouping pupils by age leaves them very heterogeneous in other respects, however, teachers try to adjust individual differences within classrooms by intraclass grouping, individualized instruction, and differentiation of curriculum content. Some schools, hoping to make it possible to follow a more uniform curriculum, group pupils into different sections of each grade level on the basis of IQ. At the high school level, children are guided to some extent into differentiated curricula suited to their individual interests and patterns of abilities. Other schools—employing retardation, acceleration, or flexible rates of progress—adjust pupil progress to individual rates of intellectual maturation. For the extreme intellectual deviates —the mentally retarded and the gifted—special classes and curriculum adaptations are sometimes offered. And for the intelligent underachievers, diagnostic and remedial teaching may be provided. Perhaps no one of these procedures is best for every pupil in every situation. We need to determine under what conditions and for which pupils each, or a combination of them, is best. Let us therefore study the merits and limitations of each procedure.

HETEROGENEOUS GROUPING

Many observers believe that it is best for the social development and mental health of most children and youth to permit them to advance through the school grades with their age mates. This kind of grouping involves many curricular and instructional difficulties for the teacher. In such groups—as we have learned—children begin at widely different levels of mental maturity and achievement; they advance in mastery of concepts and skills at varying rates; and they have a variety of both common and differentiated experiences. But "If the children have got along fairly well together and can work and play as a team," Washburne believes that the teacher should have "no hesitancy about letting them continue their group experiences together next year, knowing that his successor will carry each child on from where he left off in that fraction of the curriculum where common mastery is necessary [131, p. 147]."

For such a group of children—alike only in age—effective curricula cannot be uniform. In every grade, reading and other materials will have to span several grade levels. Materials, activities, and teacher guidance must be adapted to pupils of varied interests, talents, social needs, and personality characteristics. Let us take a closer look at a few of the individual children we can expect to find in such a classroom [51].

A heterogeneous group of fifth grade children includes Randy, who, despite good intellectual ability, avoids reading because he finds his fifth grade texts too difficult. It includes Raymond, who is effective as a baseball captain but uninterested in schoolwork and even aggressively destructive in classroom projects. There is Kathy, who—in adjusting to her fourth new school in the last five years—is shy and hesitates to participate in classroom activities. There is also Philip—first mentioned in Chapter 2—who, although unusually competent in science, feels awkward, unconfident, and unwanted on the baseball field. And there is Edna, an intellectually gifted child with special interest and talent in music. Imagine 25 other uniquely different children, and you have a picture of a typical classroom of heterogeneously grouped pupils.

In a classroom like this, teachers find that such procedures as *intraclass grouping* and *individualized instruction* are helpful in providing the conditions for effective learning.

Randy's teacher, for example, tries to find a way to support his self-esteem and to remotivate his efforts in reading. When she discovers that he has a talent for building model airplanes, she knows that a book on this subject in a third grade vocabulary will prove both interesting and confidence building for him. Because of Raymond's intense need for status, his teacher decides that he should be given more constructive leadership roles in the classroom. Two teacher-contrived arrangements help Kathy. She is given the responsibility of asking each of her classmates when he will be ready to give his book report, which raises her self-confidence. In addition, an invitation from two of her classmates to join the Girl Scouts helps her to feel that she belongs and is wanted.

When rain interferes with outdoor play during a recess period, Philip is given an opportunity to conduct a scientific demonstration of the cause of rain. This experience so enhances his general self-confidence and his standing among his classmates that he is able to try baseball again—and, because of his increased confidence, he plays with greater success.

Since Edna is able to accomplish the usual classroom work quickly and thoroughly, the teacher enriches her curriculum. In connection with a class unit on pioneer life, Edna is given an opportunity to read library books and to listen to phonograph records of pioneer songs and dances. The unusual knowledge she acquires and the music she selects for illustrating her report to the class add zest to the project both for Edna and her classmates.

Intraclass grouping. Like a miniature democratic community, a heterogeneous group can be flexibly structured and frequently restructured for effective achievement of individual and group goals—both academic and social. A rich variety of curriculum materials covering a range of five or six grade levels can be substituted for strictly uniform grade standards. In this way each child is provided opportunities (in small groups) to progress at his own rate in mastering basic concepts and skills and to contribute in social projects according to his talents, interests, and needs. In the same classroom, curricula and teacher guidance are adjusted to the needs of slow learners, intellectually gifted children, children at intermediate levels of intelligence, and children with a variety of special talents. Let us observe such a classroom in action with Hittinger, whom we paraphrase [63]:

> As a group of fourth grade children enter their classroom before the nine o'clock bell rings, each child finds something interesting to do. David works at the rock collection. Frances feeds the fish. Two boys examine seashells under the magnifying glass. The children report to each other such exciting events as, "My dog had four babies last night."
>
> At the bell, the chairman for the week checks attendance and collects the lunch orders; then he calls on his classmates to contribute their "sharing experiences."
>
> With the teacher's guidance, they plan the morning's work on the class project, "Early California Mission Days." In an orderly, efficient manner several small groups begin their separate tasks: three children lay bricks for the adobe mission; two work on a relief map; seven work on a mural in which they express their knowledge of the era; two children are writing down questions about their community's history which they plan to use when they interview an especially well informed local citizen; five weave baskets, six mold clay utensils; three are consulting reference books in order to prepare a report on water and irrigation; and one child reads a pamphlet on the history of the area. These children are not just having another "history lesson." Rather, the teacher is using the project to increase their understanding of social studies concepts and to develop related reading, writing, arithmetic, art, and craft skills. Moving about the room, she gives each group the specific guidance and encouragement it needs.

Miller and Dresden suggest that intraclass grouping is also effective in adjusting individual differences in high school [98]. In a physics class, the subject "Evaporation and humidity" was broken down into subtopics; the students were assigned to committees (according to talents, interests, and resources) to study and report to the entire class on each subtopic. The teacher helped each small group to formulate their particular problem and to find source materials—in the library, in the audio-visual room, in their homes, and in the community. As the students read, experimented, discussed problems, drew graphs and charts, and prepared their reports, the teacher gave guidance whenever it was needed.

The composition of intraclass groups is determined by a number of criteria. The subgroups may be involved in different subjects or they may work at different levels of abstraction. The children in a group may have similar or complementary abilities. In informally grouped classes, each child may select whichever group he wishes to join; in other classes, children are assigned to groups according to systematically applied criteria. As was suggested earlier, social as well as academic needs are often considered in arranging subgroups.

Differentiating the curriculum according to the ability of his ninth grade students, a general science teacher assigned his three most able students the task of constructing an electric circuit board—to demonstrate parallel and series wiring, short circuits, and other features. The students followed a circuit diagram and, with guidance from both their science and shop teachers, they constructed a circuit board with which they could demonstrate "electricity in action." Two less able boys in the same classroom, interested in auto mechanics, collected several parts of an automobile motor which they exhibited during a discussion of how an automobile motor works.

It is also possible for children of different ability to study the same topic, but with variations in scope, depth of understanding, and levels of abstractness. The slow learner may attain only a superficial understanding of a concept, master only the simpler skills related to it, become aware of only the more immediate applications, and he may rely more heavily on the use of concrete materials. The superior pupil, on the other hand, will achieve a deeper, more generalized understanding of concepts, master more complex skills, see a wider range of applications, and utilize abstract symbols more effectively [132].

Variations in the abstractness of approach may be illustrated in the different ways third grade children solve the following problem: "Frank has 17 cents. How many 3-cent stamps can he buy?" Some children—using concrete objects as counters—may divide the 17 counters into piles of 3 and find that they have 5 piles and 2 counters left over. Other children—using a semiconcrete-symbolic approach—may draw 17 marks, encircle them in groups of 3 each, and count the groups, thus: ||| ||| ||| ||| ||| ||. Still other, more able children may use number symbols and, counting backward from 17 to 1, make a mark for every 3 numbers. At a still higher level, children may subtract 3 successively from 17. Perhaps the most able children—using division abstractly—will divide 17 by 3 [119].

The same variations in approach occur, of course, at the high school level. For example, some students often make measurements of figures to prove geometrical theorems. Other students need to rely on intuitive judgments. More able students may derive and demonstrate theorems deductively. And still more gifted students invent new theorems and make creative applications of them. On the basis of the level of abstractness at which they are able to work, children can select or be assigned to appropriate intraclass groups.

Children with different talents—verbal-academic, artistic, mechanical, musical, organizational-leadership—sometimes complement each other effectively and enjoy working together on the diverse jobs of science and social studies projects. Charles, about to complete the fourth grade at age 11–2, but with a *WISC* mental age of only 9–0, is seriously retarded in reading. He recognizes only about as many words as a second grade child—including such words as *dog, woods, wanted, home, cannot,* and *would*—and he is almost completely lacking in both skill and confidence in the independent identification of words. For example, he read *had* as *went, ran* as *are, without* as *with, then* as *when,* and *began* as *went.* These misidentifications indicate that he readily abandons a systematic word-identification approach for "making up." He has given up learning to read as a mysterious, perplexing process. He needs, of course, specialized guidance in remedial reading.

Because of his teacher's and classmates' discovery and recognition of his special talent in drawing, however, Charles does not feel completely inadequate and unworthy. He draws so well that other children are very pleased to have him on a committee project requiring art illustrations; and as the wall murals in his classroom reveal, Charles's illustrations have often made conspicuous contributions to group projects. He and another child who reads and writes unusually well have together just completed a project on "Hiawatha" in social studies. A half dozen of Charles's creative drawings contributed richly to an interesting report which Charles and his partner made to the entire class.

The intraclass groupings we have just described were flexible and informally arranged. In order to ensure systematic practice of skills at appropriate maturity levels, teachers can structure the groups more systematically, according to measured abilities. For example, using the *Detroit Word Recognition Test,* Lampman classified second grade children for reading instruction into "slow-," "middle-" and "fast-moving" intraclass groups [88]. As is indicated in Figure 5.2, monthly retests of reading accomplishment revealed that the fast-moving group more than doubled the progress of the slow-moving group. Not until the ninth month was the slow-moving group ready for learning skills already achieved by the fast-moving group at the beginning of the testing period.

Children are, of course, regrouped for each particular subject. Johnson explained how a sixth grade class, ranging in arithmetic ages

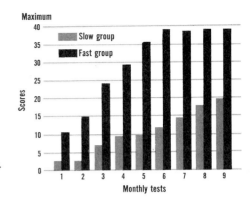

Fig. 5.2. *Illustrating different rates of progress in reading of "slow" and "fast" groups of a second grade class, subdivided into three groups for reading.* (Adapted from P. Lampman, *Elem. Sch. J.,* 1944, vol. 44, pp. 358–360.)

from 8–3 to 14–2, was subdivided into three subgroups for appropriate adaptations of the curriculum and instruction in arithmetic [69]. Group A included children ranging in arithmetic age from 8–3 to 10–9; group B, from 10–5 to 12–10; and group C, from 12–5 to 14–2. The groups were treated alike only in respect to having equal amounts of the teacher's time. The daily 45-minute arithmetic periods were scheduled in this way:

Time	Group A	Group B	Group C
9:00 to 9:15	Teacher guidance	Study	Study
9:15 to 9:30	Study	Teacher guidance	Study
9:30 to 9:45	Study	Study	Teacher guidance

In such programs, each child begins at the level for which he is ready and is guided and encouraged to achieve *his* maximum of growth. Johnson has reported that some sixth grade children reach third or fourth grade levels, whereas others attain eighth, ninth, or tenth grade levels.

Individualized instruction. Although intraclass grouping simplifies the problem of teaching heterogeneous groups of individuals, it does not meet all the needs of each unique personality. Some degree of individualized teaching is also necessary. Such teaching is an attempt to adjust curricula and teacher guidance to each child's level of maturity, pattern of abilities, interests, and needs. In addition to providing differentiated content suited to individual progress in mastering the basic concepts and skills, it encourages children to play cooperative roles in social projects in which each child contributes according to his unique talents, interests, and needs. To find time for individualized guidance of children, teachers must cultivate independence and resourcefulness in their pupils. They can do this by providing devices for efficient individualized practice of skills and by encouraging pupils to initiate their own individual creative projects. In order to master such basic skills as reading, language, spelling, arithmetic, and other systematically arranged subjects, each child begins where he is ready and, with self-instruction materials and individualized guidance, he advances at his own rate in each different subject [131].

Comprehensive and unified projects, however, must be arranged so that teacher and pupils together may plan, study, discuss, engage in constructive and creative activities, share, and evaluate. As Smith points out, children of widely different reading abilities can all participate and contribute in study and discussion within a common interest unit and yet read different materials suited to their various reading levels [117]. For example, in studying how children and their families live in different lands, one fifth grade child may read Louise Ranklin's *Daughter of the Mountains;* another may read something as easy as *Pepper Moon* or *Kintu, the Congo Boy;* and an intellectually superior child may read *Heidi* or *The Good Master.* Similarly, at either the elementary or secondary level, on a social studies problem such as "The importance of water resources in the West," assignments or self-selected topics could be differentiated with respect to content, depth of insight, mode of approach, and method of reporting to the class [108].

The teacher can further individualize and enrich the curriculum by encouraging original and creative projects. Bray [17] mentions a number of such projects undertaken by high school physics students —biographical sketches of famous physicists, descriptions and explanations of interesting industrial equipment, machine drawing illustrations of mechanical principles, and construction of cutaway models of machines. An exhibit of the most interesting projects of former students, he says, motivates new students to undertake similar ones. The National Science Fair has called to our attention such projects as that of a 17-year-old girl who, over a two-year period of independent study, collected and arranged a display of eight cases of insects. She classified the insects correctly and gave full particulars of where—on the family farm—and when each one was found [93].

Gearing each child's opportunities for learning to his level of readiness and to his talents, interests, and needs should be an efficient mode of attacking the problem with which we are concerned in this chapter; and several experiments indicate that it is [75, 85, 140]. Moreover, when pupil initiative and self-selection of appropriate activities and materials are encouraged, pupil interest, self-understanding, and economy of learning all seem to be facilitated. For example, in a fifth grade reading program each child was permitted to choose—from a generous supply of books on science, biography, history, travel, nature, and fiction—all those books which he intended to read completely. It was found that children of average intelligence made seven months' gain in reading age in five months' time [105].

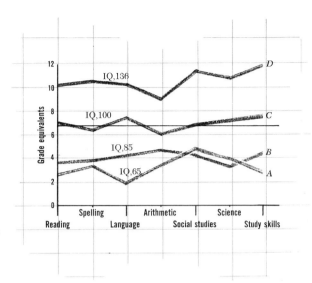

Fig. 5.3. Stanford Achievement *profiles for the lowest-, a low-, the median, and the highest-achieving pupil in a sixth grade class of 25 pupils.*

HOMOGENEOUS GROUPING

The difficulties met in teaching heterogeneous groups of children have led some teachers to prefer more homogeneous groups. Figure 5.3, which presents the achievement profiles of children in a sixth grade classroom who achieved at various levels, suggests the typical extent of these difficulties. The teacher of this class reported:

A, who at age 13–6 is a year retarded and who has an Otis *Beta* IQ of only 65, is doing as well as can be expected of a child of his limited intellectual ability. His relatively high scores in social studies and science, however, probably resulted from lucky guesses, since I am sure he could not read many of the questions. He is unable to participate in any of the regular academic activities of the class. And since he realizes that he does not know as much as the other children, he is very ill at ease in the classroom.

Pupil B, whose Otis *Beta* IQ is 85, with a chronological age of 12–4, has a mental age of 10–5. At this level of mental maturity, his achievement should equal that of children about to begin the fifth grade. Since his median achievement equals only that of children in the second month of the fourth grade, he is not achieving even up to his somewhat limited capacity.

About D, whose age is average for the class and whose Otis *Beta* IQ is 136, her teacher says: "I feel guilty when I realize how little I have done to challenge her and other high ability students to do really top-notch work. She probably could have profited from acceleration. She is a large girl, one of the tallest in the room. Being well-developed physically and skillful in motor activities, she plays ball so well that the boys are glad to have her play with them."

Teaching individuals in groups 171

C, and the other pupils of about average ability, find the sixth grade curriculum in language, arithmetic, social studies, and science challenging; but if they work efficiently, they are able to master most of the expected concepts and skills.

In a relatively large school (having 75 or more pupils per grade), these children and others of similar intelligence and age could be grouped (according to IQ) into three sixth grade sections of equal size. Pupils A and B would be with a group ranging in IQ from 60 through 92. Pupil C would be placed in the average-ability section, ranging in IQ from 93 to 107. Pupil D, of course, would be in the highest section, with pupils ranging in IQ from 108 to 140 or higher. For these three sections of each grade, now more homogeneous with respect to IQ, curricula and methods of teaching should be differentiated. For the middle group, an approximation of the present grade-level curriculum might be satisfactory. For the highest group, the curriculum would need to be enriched, and the goals of achievement extended. And for the lowest group, the curriculum should consist of the minimum essentials, and academic goals should be more limited. Methods of teaching should also be differentiated. On the lowest level, there should probably be more concrete experience and greater practice of concepts and skills, and on the highest level, there should be opportunities for children to proceed more directly to abstract generalizations and to extended applications of concepts.

Initiated early in the history of intelligence testing, homogeneous grouping promised easier and more effective management of uniform assignments, collection and preparation of learning materials, and teacher guidance of the class as a whole. It is claimed that, for both the slow learners and the more capable students, homogeneous grouping is likely to provide more appropriate learning experiences, enhance interest, encourage more satisfying peer identifications and interrelationships, and provide more opportunities for leadership [48]. On the other hand, such grouping has sometimes been considered undemocratic and likely to embarrass children in the lowest group. The research support of these claims is very limited. In general, research has revealed "slightly superior achievement and better personal adjustment" for homogeneous than for heterogeneous groups [120]. For example, Barthelmess and Boyer found that among equated groups of fourth grade pupils selected from homogeneous and heterogeneous classes, those from the homogeneous classes achieved a gain of 12.8 months during a school year while the others gained only 10.4 months [8]. But the evaluative results are not consistent. In at least one comparison [38], the gain in reading achievement for fifth and sixth grade pupils was slightly greater for a wider IQ range (41 points) than for a more narrow-range (29 points) group. Such diversity of experimental results suggests that achievement depends more upon other factors, such as quality of teaching and how well it is adapted to the make-up of the group, than it does upon the degree of intellectual homogeneity of the group.

For data on the question of the possible threat of homogeneous grouping to pupil self-esteem, Luchins and Luchins asked 190 homogeneously grouped fourth to sixth grade children which section they would prefer if they were permitted a choice. From 75 to 96 per cent of the pupils in sections for "dull," "average," and "bright" expressed a preference for the highest section. Only 4 per cent of the bright and 25 per cent of the dull children would voluntarily choose the lowest section [95].

Actually, the extent to which homogeneous grouping on the basis of intelligence achieves homogeneity of the various factors affecting school accomplishment is easily overestimated. Assuming the typical correlation between intelligence and school achievement to be .60, we find that the coefficient of determination (r^2) of this correlation indicates that only 36 per cent of the variation in achievement of pupils is related to variations in intelligence. The remaining 64 per cent of variation in achievement is unrelated to differences in intelligence. Since individuals also differ in such significant factors as motivation, pattern of differential abilities, efficiency of study methods, previous preparation, and emotional control, it is estimated that a threefold classification according to intelligence would reduce the heterogeneity of achievement of a typical class by only about 15 to 20 per cent (28).

This fact is concretely illustrated in Table 5.1, where the grade-equivalent scores in achievement of selected fourth grade pupils from three different narrow-range levels of intelligence are presented. The three intellectually superior pupils exhibit three levels of achievement: R.K., below average for fourth grade; S.C., average; and L.C., dis-

Table 5.1. *Variations in achievement of children with similar IQs beginning grade 4 at three different levels*

Level	Child	IQ	Grade equivalent			
			Reading	Soc. studies	Language	Arithmetic
High	L.C.	138	7–8	7–5	5–6	5–3
	S.C.	134	5–4	4–3	3–9	4–4
	R.K.	152	4–8 (11–2)	3–1 (10–5)	2–5 (7–8)	3–8 (7–6)
Average	B.N.	107	5–0	4–1	3–8	4–8
	D.B.	108	4–1	3–7	3–8	3–8
	C.B.	101	2–0	1–5	2–1	3–2
Low	C.J.	79	3–0	3–4	2–1	3–0
	S.H.	82	2–6	2–6	2–0	2–7
	P.H.	83	1–8	1–2	1–0	3–2

tinctly superior. One of the pupils in the average category for IQ (B.N.) exceeds the achievement of one of the intellectually superior pupils (R.K.) and equals the achievement of another (S.C.). Similarly, the pupil whose IQ is only 79 (C.J.) exceeds in achievement the pupil whose IQ is 101 (C.B.). Moreover, there is a variation in the pattern of achievement for each pupil. For example, the pupil (P.H.) at the low level of ability whose achievements in reading, social studies, and language are all at the level of grade 1 approaches the average of his grade in arithmetic.

Further, despite significant correlations between early and later achievement, the relative achievement status of many pupils changes. An especially marked change occurs for R.K. At the beginning of the fourth grade, his achievement, when compared to his very superior intelligence, is very low. By the end of the sixth grade, however, when his achievement matches his superior capacity, his grade equivalents are reading, 11–2; social studies, 10–5; language, 7–8; and arithmetic, 7–6. Such observations as these suggest that grouping should be flexible and should be arranged separately for each subject or activity.

Homogeneous grouping and differentiated high school curricula. With the aid of a greater variety of tests—of intelligence, differential abilities, practical aptitudes, achievement, and interests—high school teachers and administrators frequently employ a modified type of homogeneous grouping. In large high schools, courses taken by all students—such as English, social studies, science, and mathematics— are sometimes differentiated into three levels of general academic ability [26]. Pupils enrolled in a nonacademic curriculum often take courses in English or mathematics reduced to the practical essentials. The students of average and superior ability, looking toward college entrance, take a more academic curriculum. The intellectually superior students take enriched courses in these and in other elective areas. Sequences of elective courses, which lead to relatively high levels of proficiency in business, art, music, industrial arts, foreign languages, mathematics, science, or homemaking, provide for further differential grouping. Guided by test profiles and other sources of self-knowledge, adolescents choose differentiated sequences in these areas according to their particular talents and interests [128].

ADJUSTING GRADE PROGRESS TO RATE OF MENTAL MATURATION

Another way to allow for individual differences in schoolwork is to adjust the rates of grade progress. Slow-learning children are sometimes expected to repeat a grade; superior children may skip a grade, or part of it; and in some schools—especially at the primary level— flexible, individual rates of progress are permitted. For example, of the four children whose IQs and achievement profiles are presented in Figure 5.3, A and B might have been retarded and D accelerated. Although all four pupils have advanced at the usual rate of one grade per year and are in the sixth grade, the achievement of A and B approximates, respectively, the third and fourth grade levels, and D attains the tenth grade level. Let us consider now some of the merits and limitations of retardation, acceleration, and flexibility.

Retardation. Since intellectually inferior children are unable to keep up with their more able classmates, it is sometimes proposed that their rate of grade progress be more nearly equivalent to their rate of achievement. For example, although Forey, at age 13–7 is in the seventh grade, his mental maturity approximates that of children about to begin the fifth grade. With an S-B IQ of 78, he has a mental age of 10–5. His achievement, however, is far below his potential capacity. In seven years of regular grade progress, he has not learned to read. Like another child described earlier in this chapter, he recognizes a few sight words such as *boy* and *dog*, but he has no skill in independent identification of words. He misread *ran* as *went, woods* as *house*, and *home* as *out*. Reading is a baffling process which he has given up all hope of mastering. When Forey entered school at nearly seven years of age, he was not ready for first grade reading. Although he attained sufficient mental maturity to begin reading during the second or third year in school, he failed to master the initial steps.

Many children do accomplish these tasks in later grades, but there is the hazard that some will not. Teachers of third or fourth grade children, occupied as they are with many other activities, sometimes think they lack time and competency for teaching beginning reading. For children who are not ready to tackle reading and other academic tasks at the ages usually considered normal for such success, delayed entrance into school and/or repetition of some grades is sometimes suggested. For example, entrance to kindergarten of a child of Forey's intelligence might be delayed until he is at least six years of age. He might then remain in either the kindergarten or first grade for two years so that when he becomes eight years of age and attains a mental age of 6–6, he will be ready to participate with a first grade group in learning to read. If such a child happens to be physically small and socially immature, it is assumed that he might also adjust well socially to younger classmates. These hypotheses, although plausible, are not supported by research findings.

On the basis of his review, Goodlad concludes that "studies into the achievement of repeaters indicate that these children do no better than children of like ability who are promoted [47, p. 150]." Moreover, several studies suggest that retarded children tend to become emotionally and socially maladjusted. Sandin, using observation, interview, teacher rating, and sociometric techniques, found that 139 pupils who had failed at least once to be promoted in grades 1 to 8 tended to choose companions above their grade levels, were regarded less favorably as companions or seat mates, were rated less favorably on personality traits, wished more often to quit school, and felt discouraged or unfairly treated more often than their regularly promoted classmates [113]. Bedoian discovered that overage sixth grade pupils are chosen less often in sociometric tests as a team captain, as the president of the class, or as someone to help with school work than either at-age or underage pupils [10]. And in these sociometric tests, the overage pupils earned from their classmates "significantly higher rejective scores." Other studies employing self-inventories of self-esteem and feelings of personal worth show that repeaters or overage children tend to rate themselves less favorably than either nonrepeaters or at-age children [5, 9, 129].

In none of these studies, however, did retardation always have unfavorable effects. Some children adjust well to repeating a grade. At the conclusion of the first year in school, Evan was the smallest child in the room and had not learned to read. He was overdependent on the teacher for security and guidance. In trying to read a primer, he needed his teacher's help "with all the words." Later, when he reread the same material to a student teacher, "she had to help him with nearly every word and had to keep drawing him back to the task." At the middle of the second year in the first grade, he has now begun to learn to read. In fact, although he is still fearful of guessing at a word of which he is not sure, he reads better than the average of his younger classmates. To minimize Evan's possible embarrassment at not being promoted, his teacher has utilized his previous year of experience in the first grade to enhance his feeling of status. For example, when the storekeeping unit was introduced to the new first grade pupils, Evan was given leadership roles in making arrangements for it. In McElwee's study, it was found that retarded pupils were *on the average* less well adjusted than either accelerated or normal-progress pupils, but 61 per cent of them were rated by their teachers as "gets along well with others"; 52 per cent as "interested in school work"; and 40 per cent as "making a good effort in school [96]."

In order to use retardation as a constructive educational device, we need better-designed studies of how to manage it; of its consequences; and of when and for which pupils it may be helpful or detrimental. In the meantime, the present data seem to indicate that learning efficiency of retarded children is not, on the average, improved and that the frequency of social and emotional maladjustment is greater among them than among nonrepeaters.

Acceleration. Some children develop their talents at very early ages. Mozart, for example, was an accomplished musician before the usual age for beginning school; at age 10, Sonja Henie was the figure-skating champion of Norway; Bobby Jones was a state golf champion at age 14. By 16 years of age, John Stuart Mill was publishing studies in the field of political economy; and at age 17, Wagner conducted one of his own compositions [107].

With or without actual grade acceleration, intellectually gifted children often advance rapidly through the grade levels. According to Terman and Oden, "It is a conservative estimate that more than half of the children with IQs of 135 or above have already mastered the school curriculum to a point two full grades beyond the one in which they were enrolled, and some of them as much as three or four grades beyond [126, p. 28]."

Vera is such a child. Her chronological age of 11–6 equals the average of children beginning the sixth grade. But with an IQ of 136, she has a mental age of 15–8. She is large for her age, socially advanced, and her school achievement ranges from the eighth to the tenth grade. She is being advanced to the seventh grade on the basis of the following criteria of readiness for acceleration: (1) Having an IQ of 135 or higher; (2) having achieved grade equivalents a grade higher than present grade placement; (3) being physically above age mates; (4) being advanced a year in social maturity; (5) being interested in learning; (6) being emotionally stable; and (7) being approved for acceleration by both parents and teacher [99].

All or some of these criteria are usually considered in deciding whether or not to accelerate a child. There are, of course, several ways to accelerate school progress. Children are sometimes permitted to enter school younger than the usual age. Grades at any level— elementary, junior or senior high school, or college—are sometimes skipped. A specific course in a sequence (such as in English or mathematics) may be skipped in high school or college. And in some schools, the rate of progress through a grade or unit of the school

system is accelerated [72, 139]. Evaluations of these plans, according to several criteria, are uniformly favorable.

Accelerated elementary school children were rated more frequently by their teachers as interested, socially adjusted, and emotionally stable than were either normal-progress or retarded children [96]. Intellectually superior students who completed junior high school work in two rather than three years surpassed their equally able normal-progress classmates in rate of academic learning [77] and equaled them in social adjustment [76].

Two investigators have found superior academic and social adjustment for high school students who had been accelerated in the elementary grades. Keys found that 113 previously accelerated high school boys and girls were superior to an equated group of nonaccelerated students in scholarship, study habits, and personal and social adjustment [79, 80]. And Wilkins found that students who, because of elementary school acceleration, graduated from high school at ages 15–5 to 16–11, were superior in achievement and well-adjusted socially [133]. In high school the majority of these accelerated students expressed a preference for academic subjects (mathematics, science, English, foreign languages) and for playmates of their own age or (slightly more often) older. The typical accelerated high school student is not a narrow intellectual hermit. Besides enjoying such intellectual activities as reading, he is socially interested. He likes strenuous play, parties, dances, and the company of friends [134].

At the college level, students who have been accelerated continue to succeed—academically and socially [106]. Of the gifted children studied by Terman, those who were accelerated achieved higher grades in college, continued more often in graduate study, and matched the equally intelligent, nonaccelerated in social adjustment [125]. The youngest 1 or 2 per cent of students at Harvard (who entered the university four months or more before the seventeenth birthday) "can be characterized as an overachieving academically superior group," appearing to have no more "adjustmental problems than is characteristic of the college as a whole [84, p. 135]." In a dozen other colleges, 400 gifted students who entered college between the ages of about 15½ and 16½ surpassed their older classmates in scholarship, participated in as many extracurricular activities, and were equally well-adjusted socially [18].

Students can also skip the first part of a sequence of courses without handicapping their subsequent progress. Since scores on an English usage test correlated fairly high with achievement in college freshman English, students scoring above the 90th percentile on the test were given the option of skipping English 1 and going directly into English 2. Superior students who elected to skip English 1 did just as well in English 2 as equally competent students who took

English 1. In both groups approximately 80 per cent of the students earned A or B grades in English 2 [53].

Since acceleration of grade progress seems advantageous, it is surprising that so few children have been accelerated. Although experimental evaluations of retardation and acceleration favor the latter and not the former, actually more children have been retarded than accelerated, until recently. For example, among Los Angeles County tenth grade students, only 2.9 per cent were accelerated one year and only .1 per cent, two or more years. Twenty-two per cent, however, were retarded a year or more [42].

Flexible rates of progress. To avoid the problem of promotion, retardation, or acceleration as a crucial annual event, some schools provide for flexible rates of progress within groups of wider age range. For example, Delong and Anderson propose—as a substitute for grades 1 and 2 or grades 1, 2, and 3—a single primary unit [4, 32]. Delong suggests that this unit be a sequence of six reading levels— from prereading to fairly rapid and skillful independent reading— through which each child moves at his own rate. A child enters at age six and moves along through the curriculum of this unit as fast as he can. Most children complete the primary curriculum in the traditional three years, and are ready to enter the fourth grade at about 9½ years of age. Some children (the 5 or 6 per cent who mature more slowly) need to spend four years in the primary unit before they are ready for the fourth grade. But such children continue in the fourth year to participate in some areas of study with children with whom they have previously associated in intraclass groups. Other children (those of sufficient mental, social, and physical maturity) become ready for the fourth grade after only two years in the primary unit.

Recently an adaptation of this plan, extended over all the elementary grades, has been tried and informally evaluated by elementary schools in several states. These schools usually group together children covering a span of three years in age, and arrange the teaching programs so that each group of children will remain with the same teacher for two years.

Without citing objective data, the several authors who have reported on this plan for flexible progress in wider age-range groups say that it is an effective way of meeting the problem of individual differences in mental maturity [12]. The children make "satisfactory" progress, are interested, achieve good emotional and social adjustment, and learn to recognize and to accept the individual differences they observe among themselves. Teachers become better acquainted with the children and come to understand their individual and group needs more fully. Because the plan incorporates a modified application of the principles of acceleration and retardation, teachers find

that fewer different reading groups are required. Thus the plan also simplifies intraclass grouping.

There has been at least one objective study on the possible effect on achievement of wider age-range grouping. Adams compared fifth grade pupils grouped separately with fifth grade pupils who were grouped together with fourth grade pupils, and discovered no significant differences in rate of achievement [2].

SPECIAL EDUCATION FOR EXCEPTIONAL CHILDREN

We have described several procedures for meeting the problem of teaching unique individuals in groups—intraclass grouping and individualized teaching of heterogeneous groups, homogeneous grouping, and adjusting the rate of school progress to individual rates of maturation. Each procedure has merit for some individuals. By using these procedures imaginatively and appropriately, teachers are able to adjust the curriculum and methods of teaching to the individual characteristics and needs of most school children. Exceptional children —the intellectually gifted, the mentally retarded, and the educationally retarded—need additional adaptations of curricula and methods of teaching.

Intellectually gifted children. As an introduction to what we mean by the term "gifted children," let us note a few characteristics of over 1,000 high school seniors who scored high enough on achievement-aptitude tests to qualify as candidates for awards in the Seventeenth Annual Science Talent Search. These talented students—besides pursuing their interest in science—are also enthusiastic about other activities such as reading, music, sports, photography, creative writing, and student government organizations. For example, one 17-year-old future scientist wrote his prize-winning paper on "The fourth dimension in geometry." The same boy served as editor and activity photographer for the high school yearbook. He was a member of his school's top debating team. He plays the saxophone in a high school dance band and the oboe in the high school orchestra. In addition to all these activities, he has a part-time job and, like many other adolescents, he has a steady girl friend. All of the 40 award winners aspire to scientific careers—14 in physics, 6 in engineering, 5 in biochemistry, 5 in mathematics, 3 in chemistry, 2 in medicine, 1 in astronomy, 1 in biology, 1 in psychiatry, 1 in zoology, and one in a still-to-be-decided area of science [101]. These intellectually gifted students have already demonstrated capacity for creative scientific work. For example, a 17-year-old gifted girl studied the color effects of dyes produced from 50 sources, including lichens, sumac berries, cypress roots, nut hulls, tree barks, lily of the valley leaves, and petals from dahlias, zinnias, salvia, marigolds, and chrysanthemums. She tested the effects of adding alum, chrome, tin, copper, and iron to the natural dyes; the effects of variations in temperature; and the effects of dyes on different fabrics [33].

The interests and talents of intellectually gifted children are not, of course, confined to the field of science; they also find expression in the social studies, in the arts, and in every field of intellectual endeavor. Although no two intellectually gifted children are exactly alike, they do have some characteristics and needs in common. In our review of the psychological and educational studies of these children, we shall note their characteristics; the need for identifying them and ways of doing so; and the appropriate educational goals, curricula, and methods of instruction for them.

Characteristics. Intellectually gifted children are distinguished for their alertness, keenness in observing, effectiveness in abstract reasoning, insight into complex relationships, curiosity, and creative productivity. According to the criterion of *general* capacity for learning and problem solving, they include the highest 1 or 2 per cent of the intelligence distribution. In IQ, they equal or exceed 130 or 140, depending upon the specific standard applied in a given selection. They often enter school with advanced intellectual accomplishments. Moreover, they maintain their intellectual and achievement superiority throughout their school careers, and relatively high proportions of them attain graduate or professional degrees. As adults, they are remarkably productive and creative in scientific, literary, and artistic fields. At 40 years of age, 800 of the men who had been selected by Terman as intellectually gifted at ages 9 to 10 had published 67 books, 1,400 scientific or technical articles, 200 short stories and plays, 236 miscellaneous articles, and had patented 150 inventions [125, p. 224].

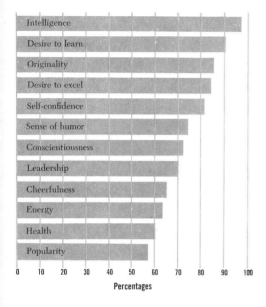

Intelligence

Desire to learn

Originality

Desire to excel

Self-confidence

Sense of humor

Conscientiousness

Leadership

Cheerfulness

Energy

Health

Popularity

0   10   20   30   40   50   60   70   80   90   100

Percentages

Fig. 5.4. *Percentages of intellectually gifted children rated by their teachers as surpassing average-ability children in intellectual and personality traits.* (After L. M. Terman and Melita H. Oden, *Genetic Studies of Genius,* vol. IV, *The Gifted Child Grows Up,* Stanford Univ. Press, Stanford, Calif., 1947, p. 52.)

Gifted children tend, as is indicated in Figure 5.4, to be superior to average-ability children in many desirable traits. From their study of over 1,000 gifted children, Terman and Oden have characterized them as (1) slightly above average in size and health; (2) relatively mature in play interests; (3) equal to the norm in physical-activity interests and superior in intellectual and social interests; (4) normally active in such social organizations as scouting, Sunday school, and group athletics, and in both indoor and outdoor recreation; and (5) superior both in mental health and ethical character [126].

Although gifted children have intense intellectual interests which they pursue avidly, they also have diversified interests—they enjoy sports, collecting, music, arts, crafts, gardening. They tend to be popular among their classmates; they make friends and enjoy them [44]. They often develop efficient study skills, set themselves high standards of workmanship, and take pride in doing the best they can [127]. On the other hand, since they are able to accomplish the usual curriculum in half the time required of average-ability children and "to earn high 'marks' without effort," there is the hazard that some of them may "waste one-half or more of their time during the school day either in idleness or in performance of routine tasks [22]."

The *typical* gifted child is, of course, an abstraction. Studies of individual differences among them remind us that gifted children are not all of one type. On such traits as achievement, contributions to class activities, creativity, leadership, persistence, sociability, and emotional stability, they vary greatly. Gallagher and Crowder report that the teachers of 35 intellectually gifted elementary school children, taught in classes with other unselected children, observed a wide range of individual differences among them. Although the teachers tended to rate the gifted children above average in these traits, the ratings of individual children covered the entire range— from lowest to highest. For example, on achievement, 21 gifted children performed "as well as ability allows"; 12 did "well but below capacity"; and 2 performed "well below capacity." On creativity, 9 gifted children "spontaneously" developed new ideas and applications; 15 were "creative on occasion or in certain areas"; and in 11 cases creativity was "not a strong point [45]."

Intellectually gifted children also differ in special abilities. They tend to be above average in art, music, mechanical, and science aptitudes; but, like other children, they have patterns of differential abilities, with marked inter- and intraindividual differences. In a group of 11-year-old children with S-B IQs of 140 or higher, Wilson found that scores ranged from 59 to 107 in art judgment, from 1 to 221 in a musical ability test, from 16 to 55 in a perceptual-motor-coordination test of mechanical ability, and from 12 to 37 in a science-knowledge test [135].

The criteria for selecting gifted children are often extended beyond superiority in *general* intelligence. According to a broader concept, gifted children include those exhibiting special talents in specific areas, such as art, music, crafts, mechanics, science, social relations, leadership, and organizing ability [136]. When these broader criteria are applied, the number of gifted children is, of course, greatly increased.

Needs for developed talents. In order to meet the demands of our society, to fulfill the individual's desire for happiness, and to attain democratic and cooperative living, our goal must be the full development of each individual's constructive and creative talents. Whether we think of society's needs on a world-wide basis or in terms of our local community, we can understand the importance of this high objective. If we do not strive to develop the abilities of our gifted students, we are not only being unwise but, indeed, profligate in the use of one of our greatest sources of strength. We can also understand what this means in terms of the individual because, as May has said, and we certainly agree, man's most profound joy comes from fulfilling his potentialities. Moreover, in our interdependent, democratic society, we need the complementary interaction of diverse talents. These urgencies require that society make good use of the developed abilities of its most superior members in every field of work [94, 111].

Identification and development. Since superior original capacity develops into genius only under favorable nurturing, gifted children are more likely to become productive if they are recognized, encouraged, and properly guided by their parents and teachers in childhood. The development of potential talent is fostered by favorable home, school, and community environments; by expert teacher guidance; by frequent and developmentally arranged opportunities for practice and use; and by the encouragement of successful and approved performance [107].

Mozart's talent, for example, was richly nurtured. Born into a musical family, he was given early guidance and expert instruction by his father. He was encouraged and admired by his family and friends. From early childhood, he lived with musicians with whom he played, cooperated, and competed, and from whom he received criticism and encouragement. He had opportunities for real accomplishment, and the successes which he achieved provided frequent reward and continually enhanced his aspirations [107, p. 124].

Terman's study of 730 men, all with IQs of 140 or higher, also suggests the role of nurture in developing high innate capacities. The 150 men who were rated highest in achievement, educational attainment, and productivity differed from the 150 rated lowest, in several significant personality traits. The former were also rated higher in motivation and integrated effort to achieve their goals; in self-confidence, strength of character, freedom from feelings of inferiority; and in both social leadership and social acceptance [125, p. 229]. It is probable that early training and nurture were very important in the development of these achievement-enhancing personality traits.

The full development of high talent requires time and individual effort, both of which are apparently favored by beginning early when the time and the greater enthusiasm and energy of childhood and youth are available [107]. Fortunately, the typical characteristics of the intellectually gifted are revealed early in life. At five years of age, children of superior intelligence already exhibit well-developed signs of their abilities. Hildreth, in a study of five-year-olds, administered the S-B test to 50 children whose IQs ranged from 130 to 168 and to 50 average-ability children. She observed that the gifted were superior in quality of language, range of information, judgment and effectiveness of reasoning, willingness to attack challenging problems, the spontaneous relating of experiences, initiative and self-assurance, and in zest for problem solving [61]. And Terman identified, among children aged three to thirteen with S-B IQs of 135 or higher, individuals who later became renowned for their contributions to the sciences and arts. One became the director of a great atomic energy laboratory; one, a historian who directed the research of a hundred social scientists; another is a famous physiologist; another, a distinguished psychiatrist; and so on [126].

Parents and teachers can sometimes identify gifted children simply through observation, although psychological tests are a more reliable procedure. The signs of intellectual superiority noted by teachers—as they observe pupils in such creative activities as art— are sustained interest, extended periods of intense and concentrated work, great sensitivity to and perceptual differentiation of their environment, organization of a large number of elements in their artistic creations, and greater ability to use past experiences in solving problems [87]. Parents report such indications of intellectual superiority as quick understanding of new concepts, insatiable curiosity, extensive information, large vocabulary, unusual and wide interests, retentive memory, and early self-initiated learning projects. As we learned in the preceding chapter, however, such observations are fallible. Only 15.7 per cent of the children nominated by 6,000 teachers as the "most intelligent" in their classes were found—on an intelligence test—to belong to the gifted group [136]. For reliable and valid identification of intellectually gifted children, psychological tests—of intelligence, differential abilities, practical aptitudes, and achievement—are indispensable.

Goals. The major educational goal for every child is the fullest possible development of his talents. For the gifted child this means especially the cultivation of his distinctive capacities for initiative, originality, and creative productivity, and the orientation of his ambitions toward planning, discovering, and inventing for society's welfare and advancement [49]. Poorly trained or inadequately trained youth cannot be expected to make significant contributions to our complex society. Therefore we must encourage those who are gifted to seek advanced training in graduate and professional schools [57].

Besides achieving high degrees of specialization in the fields of their major talents, gifted children should develop many-sided and well-rounded interests. In school they should be given experiences which will develop skill in individual and group problem solving, in discussing problems critically and constructively, and in leadership and cooperative roles with associates of varied levels and patterns of abilities. They need to learn to go deeply into ideas and projects; to acquire efficient habits of study and work; to become effective teachers of themselves; and to take pride in superior workmanship, constructive achievement, and creative contributions [62].

Curriculum. To attain these educational goals for gifted children, a carefully planned and enriched curriculum is necessary. Enrichment should provide especially for development of creative abilities; besides providing for well-rounded development, it should provide for early and unusually high degrees of specialization in a variety of fields. It should offer opportunities for both social and independent projects. It should be, for every child, worthwhile and challenging. Since they require only half the usual time allowed average-ability children for mastery of the basic concepts and skills, gifted children have ample time for an enriched curriculum. Enrichment experiences should, nonetheless, be carefully selected.

Hollingworth, the pioneer thinker about an appropriately enriched curriculum for gifted children, proposed that it should utilize and foster their superior creative abilities and orient them toward thinking about society's need for creative contributions and services [64]. To improve their initiative, originality, and constructive endeavor, gifted children, she suggested, should study (1) the evolution of culture—how man has slowly progressed in his understanding of and use of food resources, shelter, energy, clothing, transportation, sanitation and health, timekeeping, illumination, tools and implements, communication, law, government, education, labor, recreation, and warfare; (2) biographies of creative persons; (3) foreign languages; (4) sciences; and (5) music, art, crafts, and intellectual games. Other writers agree in general with Hollingworth's proposals, but they would provide a curriculum of more diversified experiences, including mathematics, English and literature, and additional phases of the social studies. They have also suggested some specific procedures and devices for enriching the curriculum:

1. Making thorough, firsthand explorations of the local environment — studying trees, animals, and flowers, visiting zoological and botanical gardens, industrial plants, museums, legislatures, and places of historical interest [19, 22, 78, 127].

2. Experimenting and exploring in science—conducting both cooperative and independent research projects, constructing models to illustrate the evolution of common things, collecting and organizing materials and data, and writing comprehensive research reports [6, 19, 22].

3. Encouraging intensive creative work in special fields of interest and talent—writing, crafts, art, music, science, literature, social leadership, etc. [115, 127].

4. Guiding and encouraging extensive and intensive reading according to each child's interests, both in differentiated assignments for class projects and as independent study [19, 21, 127].

5. Developing skills which would be helpful in various school activities—skill in handling equipment, such as projectors, record players, mimeograph machines; in preparing materials for the classroom laboratories; in working on such school projects as the newspaper, yearbook, operetta, plays; in helping a teacher, principal, or school nurse in some worthwhile task [19, 78].

6. Encouraging hobbies and participation in clubs related to children's special interests—crafts, photography, collections, music, art, dramatics, creative writing, science, dancing, athletics, etc. [54, 127].

In addition, gifted children need and want a substantial academic curriculum. At the high school level, students should be encouraged to do advanced work in science, mathematics, language, music, art, and other areas—according to their particular talents and interests. When asked to evaluate their high school experiences, intellectually gifted children say that English, mathematics, history, and science are their most valuable subjects. But they would like these courses to be more thorough, stimulating, challenging, and inspiring [36].

Methods. The emphasis in teaching gifted children should be on self-discovery learning,[1] on deeper penetration into concepts, and on more initiative in original and extended applications of concepts. Because of their superior abilities, these children often need less drill or practice to master skills or to generalize concepts. Instead of being held responsible for every routine practice exercise in their arithmetic book, for example, superior children should be encouraged to carry their already mastered principles into new and creative applications. The time saved from routine exercises can be used profitably in extensive reading, in creative writing and discussion, in research projects, and in more advanced, complex, and abstract use of the basic concepts and skills already mastered. As for learning and problem-solving methods, gifted children should be taught to emphasize meanings, achieve comprehensive views of problems, develop short cuts and efficient modes of approach, and be independent in trial-and-discovery methods. They especially need to be taught scientific methods of solving problems, how to write research reports, and the techniques of effective leadership.

These suggestions, of course, are not limited to a few specific subjects [104]; creative teachers will be able to extend their application to every area of the curriculum. As a generalization, we might say that there should be less teacher telling and demonstrating and more encouragement of pupil self-discoveries. If they are to make really

[1] See Chap. 7.

creative contributions to society, gifted children should eventually become their own best teachers.

Organizational procedures. We have reviewed the characteristics of intellectually gifted children, their own and society's need for ways of identifying them and developing their potentialities, and appropriate educational goals, curricula, and methods. In the light of these observations, it seems that a flexible and multiple approach is the best organizational plan for developing their unusual talents. Each of the procedures outlined for meeting the problem of teaching unique individuals in groups is also applicable to the teaching of some gifted children.

Intellectually superior children of appropriate physical and social maturity should be accelerated one, two, or three years during the elementary and high school grades. In fact, some observers believe that "nearly all children of 135 IQ or higher" should be ready to enter college by age 16 or 17 [107, 127].

Curriculum enrichment is almost universally considered appropriate for gifted children and, as a phase of individualized instruction and intraclass grouping in heterogeneous groups, it can be especially effective. Other writers believe that the best all-round development of the gifted child is most likely in the special class. Experimental evaluations of special class education by Gray and Hollingworth and by Nelson and Carlson have failed to reveal advantages in tested achievement; but these writers believe that it furnishes a richer background and greater intellectual stimulation. In studying with their intellectual peers, gifted children "probe more deeply into subject matter," learn "to use a many-faceted approach," develop greater "intellectual enthusiasm," and become more proficient in research techniques [50, 102].

These procedures are suitable at both the elementary and secondary levels. At the secondary level, however, homogeneous grouping on the basis of aptitudes is appropriate, and guidance into differentiated curricula is especially important. Students talented in music, art, mathematics, science, or language need the opportunity, in high school, to pursue their special interests to relatively advanced levels of proficiency. Such early specialization means reducing the number of required courses or permitting gifted students either to complete them at an accelerated pace or to skip them on the basis of test-demonstrated proficiency. It also means not massive but differentiated curriculum enrichment. If every high school teacher extends the assignments for gifted children, they are left with insufficient time for pursuit of specialized interests. The time gained from their rapid learning should earn gifted children—to some extent, at least—simply more free time to pursue their special interests.

Mentally retarded children. School curricula in which most children attain some degree of success and which interest and challenge bright and superior children frustrate the mentally retarded. The approximately 2½ per cent of children at the lower end of the intelligence distribution whose IQs range from 50 to 70 are, however, able to profit from suitable training in reading, writing, arithmetic, and unskilled or semiskilled occupations. But they are so limited in self-direction, learn so slowly and with such difficulty, and have such inferior problem-solving and generalizing abilities that they require special curricula and educational guidance if they are to achieve up to their potentialities. The approximately ½ per cent of children below 50 in IQ, although trainable, are usually so limited in intellectual resources that they are unable to master reading and other academic subjects. They require care and supervision throughout their lives. Another 5 per cent of school children, the slow learners with IQs from 70 to 80, may adjust to regular classes, but they also find the usual academic curriculum too difficult and require considerable individualized help [83].

Characteristics of the educable mentally retarded. The educable mentally retarded are alike in having IQs ranging from approximately 50 to 70 or 75 and in their need for a special kind of education. In other ways, each is a unique personality. Let us look at the word portraits of some of these children and see what their school experiences have done for them.

Kurt, at age 9–9, is in the fourth grade, has an S-B IQ of 61, and a mental age of 5–11. Kurt completed the man and reproduced the diamond shown in Figure 5.5. When asked to place 7 blocks on a paper near the examiner, he placed 11 on the paper but counted them as 8.

Lack of confidence and emotional and social maladjustment are often associated with intellectual limitations. Harta, who is 9–5 years of age and in the third grade, has an S-B IQ of 58 and a mental age of 5–5. She feels unaccepted by her classmates, parents, and teacher —to whom she reacts alternately with aggression, withdrawal, and impulsive gestures of affection. Anxious, restless, fearful, and resistant of learning tasks, she tends to avoid them either by remaining mute or saying, "I can't." She also sometimes simply free-associates. When

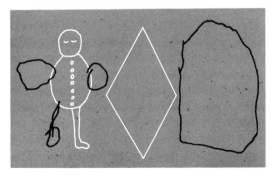

Fig. 5.5. *Because his perceptual analysis of things is undifferentiated, Kurt, at age 9–9, with a mental age of 5–11 and an S-B IQ of 61, completes the man and reproduces the diamond at the maturity level of a five-year-old.*

asked the question: "What is a dress made of?" she said, "Hang up in the closet."

Children who are below average in mental ability require extra time to achieve readiness for academic learning. For example, Carl, in the third grade at age 9–1, with an S-B IQ of 64 and a mental age of 5–10, had only just begun to learn to read after 2½ years of instruction. Trying to read the sentence "A boy had a dog," he could recognize only "A" and "boy." However, by age 12–0 and in grade 5, he had learned to read and had mastered other parts of the curriculum up to his level of mental maturity. Having a WISC IQ of 61 and a mental age of 7–4, he had reached the grade equivalent of 2–7 in reading and 3–1 in arithmetic.

Mentally retarded children are not all alike in intellectual efficiency. Selma, at age 11–10 and in the fifth grade, has an S-B IQ of 60 and a mental age of 7–0. She has greatly exceeded what would be expected of children of her mental maturity. With a mental age approximating that of children about to begin the second grade, her grade equivalent score in reading is 3–7. Although she reads orally with almost perfect phonetic accuracy, her comprehension is nearer to her vocabulary age of 7–10. In defining words, she often gives such free associations as "Haste means don't haste nobody," and "Juggler is like a juggler of water." Despite her phonetic skill, she fails to use context effectively in identifying words because of her limited comprehension. For example, she read *reason* as *roastin*, *appear* as *apple*, and *industrious* as *interesting*.

Selma's intellectual efficiency is unusual. A frequent hazard for the mentally retarded is that—following failure to learn in the first couple of grades because of insufficient mental maturity—both the child and his teacher will give up trying. When the child does later attain sufficient mental maturity to succeed, he fails to learn because hope for him has already been abandoned. Ernie, at age 12–11, is two grades retarded in school. Now in the fifth grade, he sits at a desk separated from his classmates, where he is least likely to disturb them. With an IQ of 57 and a mental age of 7–4, he is now (and has been for the past two or three years) mentally mature enough to learn to read. He is completely unable to read, however, and his teacher doesn't expect him to participate in any class activities. One day when the school psychologist visited the class, he asked the teacher about Ernie's birth date. Not having the information in her roll book, the teacher turned not to Ernie but to his classmates and asked: "Class, when is Ernie's birthday?" Ernie was not expected to know anything.

As the descriptions of these children suggest, mentally retarded children are deficient in their understanding and use of language; their reasoning is superficial, scattered, and not well integrated; and they are limited in judgment and in creative imagination. Therefore, they

learn slowly, make many mistakes, miscomprehend complex situations, frequently fail to grasp cause-effect relationships, and often behave impulsively without due regard for the consequences of their actions [114].

Mentally retarded children in heterogeneous classes. We have observed the problems, the hazards, and some instances of both success and failure in teaching educable mentally retarded children in regular classes. Kirk and Johnson believe that most teachers of regular classes lack understanding of such children and their curricular needs [83]. Moreover, in large classes teachers have insufficient time and professional skill to give the individualized instruction required. Year after year, these children may continue their schooling under this same combination of unfortunate circumstances. Therefore, frustrated in their first attempts to master a curriculum for which they are not ready and subsequently neglected, mentally retarded children often come to feel confused, inferior, anxious, and rejected by their teachers, parents, and classmates.

Studying heterogeneous groups of children in grades 1 through 5 in a school which included one or more mentally retarded children in each grade, Johnson found that the handicapped children were often isolated or rejected and were considered by their normal peers as prone to bullying or fighting [70]. Handicapped at the outset by their inability to attain normal school achievement, the mentally retarded face the additional hazard of developing defensive reactions which will interfere with the efficient use of the limited abilities they do have [11].

As the studies of Carl and Selma illustrate, however, children who receive fortunate guidance may be able to make good adjustments in regular classes. Some writers believe that rural schools with small enrollments can—by intraclass grouping, individualized instruction, and effective use of their school and community resources—provide adequately for the mentally retarded in regular classrooms [121].

The special class. Since mentally retarded children often fail to achieve even up to their limited capacities and also frequently become socially maladjusted in regular classes, experts believe that their educational needs can be met more adequately by specially trained teachers in special classrooms [66, 82]. In order not to completely isolate retarded children from the others, however, these classrooms should be part of a regular public school.

Special classes for the educable mentally retarded (children ranging in IQ from 50 to 70 or 75) usually provide for at least three levels of maturity. From ages 6 to 8 or 10, the children are enrolled in a primary level, preacademic program. At ages 8 to 10, when they become ready for reading, they enter an intermediate academic curriculum, in which, by ages 13 or 14, they should attain second to fourth grade levels of achievement in such subjects as reading, writing, and arithmetic [83]. At 13 or 14, the junior high school age, these children then need to continue part of each day in their special academic curriculum—which replaces for them the usual junior and senior high school classes in English, mathematics, social studies, and science, but they should participate, according to their differentiated talents and interests, with normal adolescents in several such practical or vocational high school courses as shop work, art, music, athletics, and home economics [14].

Because children in special classes require individualized teaching, enrollment in such classes is usually limited to 12 to 15 children. Let us note some of the characteristics of a specific class reported by Kirk and Johnson. As an intermediate level classroom, it includes 14 children, ranging in age from 9–4 to 13–6. The IQs of the children range from 56 to 76, and the mental ages from 6–2 to 8–11. Their levels of achievement range from grade equivalents of 1.0 to 3.3 in reading and from 1.4 to 3.7 in arithmetic. Their median chronological age of 11–5 approximates the average age of normal children about to begin the sixth grade. Their median mental age, however, is nearer the average of unselected children beginning the second grade. When we compare the actual achievements of these children with that expected of normal children of their mental ages, it appears that they are achieving up to their capacities [83].

Identification. Mentally retarded children are usually noticed by their teachers when they persistently fail in school tasks on which their age mates succeed. As we have already learned, however, teachers are often mistaken in their judgments of intelligence. When a number of teachers were asked to select from among their 45,000 fourth to eighth grade pupils those who seemed mentally retarded, they named 3,285 pupils. Intelligence tests, however, classified only 11.6 per cent of these 3,285 children as below 70 in IQ. The remaining 2,904 ranged in IQ from 70 to over 120 [91]. The confidence-demanding and school-task-resembling group intelligence test also often underestimates the intelligence of mentally retarded children. Only an individual test such as the S-B test or WISC, in the hands of a well-trained examiner, is reliable and valid enough for use as an aid in identifying them. Such testing, however, should be only part of a comprehensive case study. To provide the information needed for appropriate curriculum selection and individualized teaching, the intelligence test should be supplemented by appraisals of the achievement, the specific learning difficulties and resources, the special aptitudes and interests, and the social and emotional adjustment of each child. Moreover, as the children progress through the levels of the special class, psychological examinations should be repeated and extended [74, 114].

Educational goals. The aims of education for the mentally retarded—like those for other children—are self-realization and the development of potentialities for contributing to society. Their education should help them to meet the specific personal, social, and economic needs of their daily activities within the family and the community. Physical and emotional health—including specific health habits, independence, self-confidence, and emotional security—should be emphasized. Wholesome leisure and recreational attitudes, habits, and skills should be developed [66, 83].

In a curriculum reduced to the essentials in reading, spelling, manuscript writing, and arithmetic and taught from the viewpoint of practical usefulness, mentally retarded children should be able to attain levels of proficiency suitable for their needs [41]. The basic skills curriculum should be continued into the high school or vocational school level—until the child reaches 14 to 18 years of age. But at this point, mentally retarded adolescents should be trained in unskilled or semiskilled occupations, selected according to each individual's talents. They need to develop pride and satisfaction in working efficiently, in being dependable, and in getting along happily with their fellow workers in whatever job they have. As preparation for their work, they should learn something about the roles of various workers in society; they should be given information about suitable jobs, how to find jobs, preemployment experience, placements; and they should be given follow-up guidance to help them improve their efficiency at work and their social adjustments [14, 83].

Curriculum and methods. The usual academic texts in literature, arithmetic, social studies, and science offer mentally retarded children nothing but frustration. Although systematic practice of basic skills should not be neglected, practice should be meaningful and concrete. In a school-created miniature society, the children should learn to develop and apply the concepts and skills they are expected to use. Classroom projects should grow out of useful home and community activities. They might include a visit to the food market, selecting and preparing foods, caring for children, decorating a room, making a garden, nature explorations, or studies of jobs which different workmen do. Project activities should provide for participation in groups— each child according to his interests, abilities, and needs. One child may contribute information which he learned from his simplified reader. Another may express himself in art media. Another who is skilled in crafts supplies a needed construction. And still another child may report what he has learned from an exploration of the community. All of them need warm approval and encouragement of their efforts and contributions.

In connection with such projects and in routinely scheduled periods, the children should be instructed in the basic academic skills. Oral language is cultivated at all levels of the special class. By the time they reach nine or ten years of age, they are probably ready to begin reading and writing, and should eventually reach third to fifth grade levels of proficiency [83]. In arithmetic, they begin with counting, assembling, and manipulating concrete objects, and eventually "learn to count and to compute up to the level of simple addition, subtraction, and multiplication. Some of them can learn to divide by one-place numbers and to multiply by such common fractions as half, third, and quarter. They can learn to handle decimals well enough to manage simple money problems [41]."

The curriculum of the special class also includes the social studies and science concepts needed to understand the immediate environment. It includes time for recreation, such as music, dramatics, dancing, drawing, and crafts. As children mature, simple manual, craft, household, and vocational skills are emphasized [110]. Social adjustment and mental health are cultivated as aspects of every activity. Special efforts are made to help the children feel comfortable, wanted, secure, approved, and successful.

At the primary level, emphasis is on social adjustment and participation, habits of health and safety, building self-confidence, language facility, manual coordination, and achievement of readiness for the basic academic skills [83].

For the intermediate or academic level, Kirk and Johnson propose two major areas of study: the basic academic skills up to the third to fifth grade levels; and experience units in everyday activities [83]. The experience units should aid the child in (1) understanding his physical environment—home, school, police department, fire department, businesses, industries, farms, neighborhood, community, transportation, etc.; (2) adjusting to his social environment—working with others and being tolerant, honest, friendly, and constructive in various life activities; and (3) developing healthy personal habits—of cleanliness, posture, dress, care of body, exercise, preparation of foods, safety, etc.

At the adolescent level, the curriculum includes continued training in basic academic skills, further social training, and preparation for work. Mentally retarded youth should be prepared for unskilled or slightly skilled work in agriculture, industry, or in trades and services [14, 41]. Combining training in especially equipped classrooms with actual work experience, some of them learn to become "cafeteria and supply room helpers, projectionists, office messengers, janitorial assistants, and so forth." Others prepare for "domestic services, farming, gardener's assistants, filling station assistants, and stockroom work [14]." And other youth learn laundry work, shoe repairing, shopwork, machine tending, or kitchen service [41].

Limited especially in abstract-verbal abilities, the mentally retarded learn more effectively from concrete, nonverbal, and uncomplicated approaches [39]. They need more practice in varied contexts and in the specific situations where applications are expected. As Featherstone has suggested, what they learn "takes a great deal more seeing, hearing, touching, tasting, and smelling" than normal individuals require [41]. Learning to read or remember a multiplication combination, for example, may take 10 to 20 times as many repetitions in varied contexts as for the child of average verbal ability. In teaching family, community, health, and occupational concepts, reading should be supplemented and often replaced by pictorial and auditory presentations and by firsthand experiences. In social studies projects, pictures, films, exhibits, excursions, and dramatized role playing should supplement firsthand experiences.

Results of special class education. Evaluations of the results of special education indicate that the limited intellectual, social, and economic goals set for the mentally retarded are often attained. For example, an adolescent girl with an IQ of 69, in completing her special class education, took a six-weeks on-the-job course in clearing tables and cleaning food counters. She was employed by the cafeteria which cooperated in training her, and after a year's time, she still holds the same job [103].

Many studies indicate that educable mentally retarded children often attain their potential levels in the basic academic skills. Janes reports that when children with IQs ranging from 50 to 80 were transferred from regular to special classes where they had a curriculum suited to their levels of maturity and appropriate adaptations in methods of teaching, they quickly attained reading achievement levels commensurate with their mental ages [67].

In a study of mentally retarded adults with a mean IQ of 67 who had completed a special education curriculum 12 years earlier, Bobroff found a mean grade equivalent in reading of 4.2 and a range of from 2.0 to 5.0. The achievement levels in arithmetic were slightly higher. At ages 28 to 30, approximately 90 per cent of these adults were employed—mainly in unskilled and semiskilled occupations. Although about 40 per cent had at some time received unemployment compensation, only 4 per cent of them had received social welfare aid [15].

Other studies confirm the possibility of the mentally retarded making relatively good social and economic adjustments. Baller [7] and Charles [23] both report satisfactory social and economic adjustments of individuals with a mean S-B IQ of 60 who had, as children, been judged mentally retarded. Now in their forties, 83 per cent of them work as laborers or in semiskilled occupations. Wolfson reports that 61 per cent of 59 males, with IQs ranging from 41 to 79, and 73 per cent of 99 females, with IQs ranging from 41 to 81, have made "a continuous satisfactory social and economic adjustment in the community," seven or eight years after institutional training [138].

Able children with learning difficulties. This third group of exceptional children includes those who have normal intelligence but who fail to achieve up to their potentialities. The underachiever often has such serious learning difficulties that he needs expert guidance. A professionally trained teacher may be assigned to small classes to give special diagnostic and remedial teaching to such children for part of each day [20]. For example, Warren (in the fifth grade) earned a

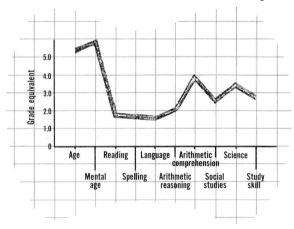

Fig. 5.6. *The achievement profile of an educationally retarded child of "normal" ability who, at age 10-9, has a mental age of 11-2 and an S-B IQ of 104 in the fifth grade.*

grade-equivalent score on *Gray's Oral Reading Paragraphs* of only 1.6. Because of his serious reading handicap, he is also retarded, as is indicated in Figure 5.6, in other basic academic skills and subjects. Warren could be mistaken for a mentally retarded child; however, he has normal intelligence. At age 10–9, he earned an S-B IQ of 104 and a mental age of 11–2, which is equal to the average mental maturity of his fifth grade classmates. Like many other underachievers—at the elementary, secondary, and college levels—Warren's potentiality for school accomplishments is impaired by learning difficulties unrelated to intelligence. To help him overcome his weaknesses and learn to use his abilities more efficiently, he needs diagnostic and remedial teaching and possibly mental health therapy.

Observation of his approach as he read the *Oral Reading Paragraphs* yielded some clues of both his limitations and resources. He recognizes a few sight words, such as *boy, dog, pig,* and *home.* His identification of *pen* as *pighouse,* in a sentence about a pig, suggests that he utilizes both the context and initial consonants in trying to identify unfamiliar words. But since he does not analyze words completely enough and recognizes so few words, Warren makes many such mistakes as reading *give* as *good, lived* as *likes,* and *wanted* as *walked.* In consequence, he is completely baffled by his fifth grade texts. To improve his reading skill, Warren needs to develop such additional aids as word-form clues and phonetic and structural analysis of words. In the meantime, he needs practice and the satisfaction of reading easy materials which are of interest to him [122].

Diagnostic and remedial teaching. Teaching based on test-discovered strengths, weaknesses, and needs has proved especially effective both for normal-progress and educationally retarded children in several areas at every school level. The following case study illustrates the gains sometimes achieved from such teaching [65]. Albert was of normal size and health for his 12–8 years of age; he had a mental age of 13–2 and an S-B IQ of 104. His reading age on a test measuring comprehension and retention of details in multiple-fact paragraphs, however, was only 8–8. In the seventh grade, Albert read at the third grade level. After 15 months of individualized instruction based on test-discovered needs and with practice material adjusted to his level of readiness, he was able to overcome his reading deficiency completely. Gains are often more modest than Albert's, however, and not every child can overcome his learning difficulties. Bond and Fay report that five months of diagnostic and remedial teaching produced a mean gain of six months in reading among a group of 23 children who had formerly gained only two months in reading age per year [16]. In Fogler's group, only 3 out of 17 children failed to improve during three months of remedial teaching [43].

The generally favorable results reported for diagnostic and remedial teaching should not mislead us into assuming that it is a panacea for all learning difficulties. Warren, now in the fifth grade and reading no better than a first grade child, has experienced three or four years of failure in his attempts to learn to read. He may feel inferior and guilty or rebellious, and it may be difficult to motivate him to whole-hearted effort again. He is likely to be confused about modes of attack, and his practice has perhaps been perfunctory. We have already observed that fifth grade reading materials are far beyond his present level of maturity. How can we help such children maximize their intellectual potentialities? Our answer is that we should attempt a more effective application of what we know about the seven conditions of learning outlined in Chapter 2. Let us consider how each of these conditions is important in a case like Warren's.

a. Readiness. Individual tests of intelligence or aptitude are needed to determine a child's potentialities for achievement beyond his retarded status. Observation of his progress and examination of his performance on achievement tests can point out the next step for which he is ready. Warren, for example, was ready to extend his word-identification skills and to read material at the first grade level. The teacher could prepare reading material of appropriate difficulty based on his own experiences or on his dictated stories. Fortunately, however, many books of low-level vocabulary and more mature interest levels have been written specifically for remedial reading purposes [118, 122]. Because of the relatively advanced mental maturity of able but educationally retarded children, deficiencies in learning are sometimes made up very rapidly when the other conditions of effective learning are provided.

b. Motivation. After a long period of unrewarding learning efforts, educationally retarded children frequently become pessimistic about the outcome of another attempt. They tend to avoid opportunities for study. Since this attitude often becomes strongly established, Harris believes that successful remedial teaching is mainly a problem of rearousing and sustaining motivation. In order to correct his expectations of failure, the child who begins remedial instruction must succeed at the outset and, as he continues, his progress should be made clearly apparent to him. The instructional materials should be highly interesting, and the skills mastered should be put to worthwhile use in activities important to him. The child should feel that his teacher thoroughly accepts him, that she enjoys his successes, and that she is tolerant of his difficulties [55].

c. Structuring approaches. Since the remedial teacher knows the most effective processes for learning reading, arithmetic, or other skills, she guides the child step by step toward more effective procedures. For Warren, the diagnosed need was for more complete word analysis—including sensitivity to the total configuration of words; to roots, prefixes, and suffixes; and to vowels and syllables.

Lehman and Cole's success in improving the handwriting of fourth grade children illustrates the role in teacher guidance of the test-discovered needs of individual pupils. Guided by a list of the 27 most-frequent writing illegibilities, such as writing *d* like *cl, n* like *u,* or *h* like *li,* they diagnosed each child's handwriting. Then, by showing each child how to correct his illegibilities and by requiring continual practice and rechecking for improvement, they succeeded in improving the quality and speed of writing of 23 illegible writers. The study reveals that in a period of nine weeks, while the diagnostic-test-guided group achieved a mean gain of 14 points in quality on the *Ayres Handwriting Scale,* a group without such guidance improved only 9 points [89].

d. Provisional trials. In diagnostic and remedial teaching, practice is an economical, goal-directed, trial-and-check process. It is directed toward learning the specific concepts and skills which tests

indicate the learner needs and can master. Warren, for example, with some review of consonant and vowel sounds, would try again to read the sentence: "They *lived* in the *same* house." Before, he had read *lived* as *liked* and *same* as *some*. This time, however, when he met an unfamiliar word, he would be guided to look beyond the initial consonant and to analyze the word more completely. Self-checking against the context for a sensible meaning, or with the teacher's help, he would continue the trial-and-check process of alternatives until he could correctly and confidently identify these words in varied sentences.

Since it takes vigorous effort and a great deal of time to establish new concepts and habits and to become comfortable with them, the time allowance for practice in remedial learning should be generous. Remedial instruction should be continued long enough to habituate the pupil to the improved techniques. It should not be an extra activity which deprives the child of recess play or requires him to remain in school after other children have left. Remedial instruction should be arranged as an important part of the regular school program. It should involve both individual and group assignments, including projects, library visits, independent study, teacher-guided study, and check-up activities. It is especially important in remedial teaching to arrange practice periods so that the child does not become fatigued and anxious. Several short periods in which specific goals are accomplished are better than long ones.

e. Perception of the effects. Checking the results of one's efforts is especially effective in diagnostic and remedial teaching. It is a testing-teaching-retesting procedure. Testing, along with pupil and teacher observation of the correctness of pupil responses, confirms correct responses and guides the learner in revising incorrect responses. Thus, in diagnostic and remedial teaching, the learner works economically at what he needs to learn. For example, during a period of 23 weeks, while test-guided pupils gained 27.3 per cent in computational arithmetic, an equated group, studying without such specific knowledge of weaknesses and needs, gained only 19.3 per cent [52].

f. Transfer. Having discovered a pupil's specific errors and learning needs, the corrective teaching should be generalized. Warren needs not only to avoid reading *give* as *good* and *lived* as *like*; he needs also to learn to analyze *all* unfamiliar words more completely. Or, when a child makes an error in arithmetic such as $90 \times 32 = 272$, and explains that $2 \times 0 = 2$ and that 27, as the product of 3×9, is written next to the 2, he needs to learn the general principles of multiplication by zero and the place value of numbers [56]. Proceeding from specific errors to corrective principles enhances the efficiency of learning. In mastering new concepts, transfer utilizes those generalizations which have already been acquired, and it reduces multiple-element tasks to the application of a few principles.

g. *Emotional control.* The previous failures of children who need remedial instruction often lead to anxiety, feelings of inferiority, and guilt [30]. To these painful feelings and the learning situations which arouse them, children often develop defenses of avoidance, rebellion, overdependence, or denial which divert them from wholehearted learning effort. Warren, for example, rationalized his reading retardation and excused his perfunctory effort to improve with this comment: "My first grade teacher didn't teach me how to read the little words." Such maladjustive modes of defense impair the intellectual efficiency of the otherwise intelligent underachiever [90]. These unhealthy feelings and self-concepts must be replaced by feelings of security, self-respect, and confidence. Dolch suggests that this is accomplished by cultivating a friendly, happy pupil-teacher relationship; by substituting systematic for confused modes of approach; by beginning at a place where the child already feels confident; and by utilizing in each new step previously established areas of confidence [35]. For example, in helping Warren, it is important to recognize that he has already learned to use context and initial consonant clues in word identification and that he now needs to extend his approach to include other techniques.

SUMMARY

Teaching children and youth who differ in intelligence and who have diverse patterns of talents presents a challenging problem. Uniform curricula, constant rates of grade progress, and identical methods of teaching are not effective ways of providing equal opportunities for the optimum educational development of all children. In our search for more effective ways of meeting the problem of teaching uniquely different individuals in groups, we have examined several helpful procedures.

Intraclass grouping and individualized instruction facilitate the teaching of children who are of similar age but heterogeneous with respect to intelligence, aptitudes, interests, achievement, and personality. Homogeneous grouping according to pupils' intelligence reduces only slightly the number of factors affecting achievement, and its advantages are uncertain. At the high school level, however, homogeneous grouping and guidance into differentiated curricula on the basis of abilities and interests seem to be effective adjustments to individual differences in the goals and needs of pupils. Both acceleration and flexible rates of grade progress are advantageous in adapting the curriculum to differences in rates of mental maturation. Retardation of grade progress, however, does not seem to facilitate achievement, and in some instances it may contribute to social disturbances. To meet the needs of exceptional children, several adjustments are desirable. Gifted children profit from early identification and guidance, acceleration, curriculum enrichment, and methods of teaching which foster initiative, originality, and creative organization and applications of concepts. Mentally retarded children need special education which focuses on helping them to meet independently the specific personal, social, and economic needs of their everyday activities. Able but educationally retarded children need diagnostic and remedial teaching.

In this and the two preceding chapters, we have elaborated the concept of readiness as a condition of effective learning. We have discussed the development of readiness for learning at advancing levels of maturity, how to appraise both general and special abilities, and how to use such appraisals in adjusting the curriculum and methods of teaching to marked individual differences among children. As a second condition of effective learning, children should *want* to learn. In order to get a better understanding of this dynamic factor in learning, we turn in Chapter 6 to the problem of motivation.

GUIDES FOR STUDY, REVIEW, AND APPLICATION

1. Nearly every teacher finds in his classroom children for whom the concepts he is expected to teach are too difficult, too easy, or otherwise inappropriate. Summarize the scientific data presented in this and in the preceding chapter which define the extent and nature of the problem of teaching uniquely different individuals in groups.

2. In any kind of grouping proposed or other solutions to the problem of individual differences among school children, what general criteria or objectives should be achieved?

3. Describe classroom illustrations of sensitivity and good provisions for the talents, interests, and needs of individual children. There is an excellent illustration in the film *Guiding the Growth of Children* (20 minutes), McGraw-Hill Text-Film Department.

4. Evaluate (in terms of both research and practical experience) the following ways of providing for individual differences among elementary and secondary school children: (*a*) Heterogeneous grouping—with intraclass grouping and individualized instruction; (*b*) homogeneous grouping—both on the basis of general intelligence and according to specific talents and interests; (*c*) adjusting pupil grade progress to rate of mental maturation—including retardation, acceleration, and flexible rates of progress; and (*d*) special provisions for exceptional children—such as curriculum enrichment for gifted children and special classes for mentally retarded, educationally retarded, and gifted children.

5. Explain and illustrate adapted applications of the seven conditions of effective learning in the diagnostic and remedial teaching of able educationally retarded children. As an example of diagnostic and remedial teaching see the film *Why Jimmy Can't Read* (20 minutes), Syracuse University.

Part 3

THE LEARNING PROCESS

Chapter 6

MOTIVATION AND LEARNING

We have referred to motivation as a problem. In our approach to this problem, let us raise some solution-orienting questions. Must teachers coerce or entice their pupils to learn, or do children learn because of their natural curiosity or an inborn desire to understand their world? How shall we define motivation? What is its role in learning? What are the practical ways in which teachers initiate and sustain children's learning efforts? Which ways are most effective? Is there a general theory of motivation which gives meaning to the observational and experimental facts about it? How can such a theory guide teachers in managing motivation as an essential condition of learning? Let us begin our search for answers to these questions by pointing out the motivation-defining features of a school learning activity.

In her second grade science class, Miss Hopkinson displayed a milkweed caterpillar to the children [43]. It immediately excited their curiosity. "What is it?" "Where did it come from?" "I think it's a worm." "No, it's a caterpillar." "It looks like the picture of a caterpillar in this book."

Joy in creating, manipulating, exploring

Specific help when needed

**Efficient learning
depends
on effective
motivation**

*The need
to understand*

Something new to learn

An urge to achieve

Individually learned interests

An excursion: visiting a museum

With such questions and tentative solutions, the children approached the problem of the caterpillar. Several prior explorations of their environment had proved rewarding and their problem-solving interests had thus been reinforced. They now listened intently and with sustained interest to the story of the caterpillar's metamorphosis as the teacher read from Friskey's *Johnny and the Monarch*. Spontaneously, they were moved to ask: "Will that happen to our caterpillar?" And the teacher's reply was: "Let's watch and see."

This expanding interest and the intrinsic satisfaction in problem solving sustained and directed their learning activities for several days. They discovered that their caterpillar would eat only milkweed leaves. They observed it fasten itself upside down on a twig, change into a "green chrysalis with gold dots," eventually become blue-black in color, and finally emerge as a "beautiful monarch butterfly clinging to the split chrysalis." But children's interest in their world and their spontaneous joy in problem solving are never satiated. "Where will the butterfly go?" asked Susie. And when Barbara brought some fat, green, ugly tomato caterpillars to school, the children were stimulated to ask further questions and to extend and test the generalizations which they had reached in their experience with the milkweed caterpillar.

WHAT MOTIVATION IS

This example illustrates how motives, as internal conditions, arouse, sustain, direct, and determine the intensity of learning effort, and also how they define the satisfying or unsatisfying consequences of goal-directed efforts. Motives are based—as we shall learn—on inherent characteristics of individuals; they are, however, modified by learning. Curiosity about one's environment and satisfaction in problem solving are potential in every human being, but when they are reinforced by such experiences as that just described they activate goal-directed behavior. An infant's motives lack direction and specific association with environmental objects. Hunger, for example, at first merely arouses the infant to activity, but upon experiencing (and learning) the consequences of motivated activity, the child becomes goal-directed. The hungry infant soon learns to direct his behavior toward the breast or bottle which he has discovered satisfies his need. Motives thus acquire direction and attachments to goals. When internal motives become attached to goals, they become motive-incentive conditions. Incentives are the rewarding objects, situations, and events which the child has learned will satisfy his internal motives. Thus, as basic motives are differentiated in experience, it appears that motives initiate goal-seeking, discovered goals give direction to behavior, and incentives satisfy motives and selectively reinforce behavior.

Teachers usually provide incentives which appeal to children's motives and which may be attained as a result of learning effort. Both teaching experience and experiments have shown that passive, perfunctory practice does not produce improvement; efficient learning requires high and sustained effort. This is not always so easily achieved as our caterpillar illustration would seem to suggest. O'Brien, in her remarks on the difficulty of motivating high school students, says that we have "little conception of the contortions—psychological, physical, dramatic, artistic, linguistic—that a high school teacher goes through in the process of exciting the interest of his students in solving problems [73, p. 80]." As a first approach to understanding how to motivate children and youth in our schools, try to recall your own experiences. Think of the best-motivated learning activity you have ever experienced, taught, observed, or read about. Are your examples like these described here?

CLASSROOM ILLUSTRATIONS OF "GOOD" MOTIVATION

Since casual surveys had shown that typically only 40 to 60 per cent of high school students prepare their daily assignments, a principal—substituting for an ill teacher—was surprised to find 93 per cent of the students in a citizenship course fully prepared. Asked what motivated them to do their assignments, the students gave the following reasons [29, pp. 338–339]:

> Assignments of appropriate length and difficulty make it possible for us to master them.
> There is always something new to learn.
> The subject is up to date and it deals with our own present-day problems.
> We begin the preparation before leaving the classroom, and we know what we're supposed to do to complete it.

Our teacher is always certain to check on us.

He recognizes our achievements, and our grades are determined fairly.

These students were effectively motivated by a combination of motives—mastery, curiosity, use, approval, and security. Other students and prospective teachers when asked to describe the best-motivated learning activity of their experience, have contributed illustrations of a great variety of motivating procedures.

One student teacher remembered Latin as his best-motivated course. He discovered that his growing knowledge of Latin was useful in understanding English. Frequent tests revealed his progress. His teacher was friendly, gave specific help when it was needed, rewarded him with ample praise and encouragement, was flexible in adjusting to such student emergencies as the need for a make-up test, and spiced his lectures with bits of humor.

A first grade teacher relies for effective motivation on a rich, meaningful, continually changing classroom environment and his children's natural curiosity and joy in creativity. The interest-stimulating things in his classroom include rabbits, guinea pigs, parakeets, pigeons, hamsters, a turtle, goldfish, plants; a store in which children take turns selling—for pennies—midmorning snacks; a post office where letters are exchanged with classmates; a book center, puppets and a puppet stage, a playhouse, a flannel board, a sand table, a workbench and tools, an easel and art media; charts on which the children read greetings, assignments of classroom chores, news items about the new pigeon egg or baby hamsters, and a continuous stream of stories which the children dictate to the teacher. This stimulating atmosphere produces a hive of busy activities. Paul discovers that the pigeons need a roost. A committee of children decide, with teacher guidance, how to construct it and proudly announce it—not only in the oral sharing period, but as a news item, and in a water color. The reading chart on this incident reads: "Paul made a roost for the pigeons. He said, 'I think they will get used to it in a little while.'"

In this classroom, children are intrinsically motivated to practice in order to improve their speaking, reading, writing, use of numbers, social relations, art, and their understanding of themselves and their environment.

On the theory that a stimulating environment appeals to natural human motives, many teachers arrange excursions—to a farm, a park, a factory, a museum, a science fair, a legislative assembly, and to many other worthwhile places.

Many teachers suggest that school learning associated with seasonal and other exciting events provides effective motivation. For example, after Christmas the teacher of a fifth grade observed that several children had received presents of electrical toys—John, an electric train; Bill, a robot; Nancy, an electric iron and washing machine. Capitalizing on the children's already developed interest, the teacher raised such questions as "What is electricity?" "How does it make your toys move?" "What causes a shock?" To answer these and other questions, the teacher introduced the science unit on electricity, which included demonstrations of magnets, construction of electric motors, and reading assignments.

Finding or creating situations that afford significant uses for what is studied is often mentioned as a means of arousing and sustaining interest. One teacher finds that "one of the best ways to motivate writing practice is to give children real jobs that need to be done, such as writing letters, notices for the school bulletin board, or publishing a classroom or school newspaper." Another suggests that a high school operetta motivates many students—in orchestra, dramatics, art, chorus, music appreciation, and in associated social roles—to strive for a performance which will please their audience.

Long-range individual interests can motivate many useful projects. Following his interest in science, Reinier, a 17-year-old future physicist, won a Talent Search prize for his construction of a home-sized cyclotron for use in atomic research. Jane, another Science Talent Search winner, wants very much "to have a part in the epoch-making step into space." As her project, she calculated the orbit of Sputnik I from her own amateur astronomical observations [97, p. 166].

The search for solutions to problems often motivates children in self- or teacher-guided experimentation. For example, when Johnny observed on Monday morning that "someone has used our paints—we just mixed them on Friday and the jars are not as full as they were," he stimulated some well-motivated problem solving. One child suggested that "maybe the jars have holes in the bottom." Their teacher explained that some of the water had evaporated, and they were led

ANIMALS
What they are
What they are used for
How they reproduce
from then to now

Children are inherently motivated to explore, understand, and create. (Edith Bowen Laboratory School, Utah State University, Logan, Utah; photograph by Ivan Pederson.)

to think of other instances of evaporation—the drying of wet blackboards, pictures, sand, paste, clothes, and grass after a rain. Then they experimented by hanging washed doll clothes in different places—in the sun, in the shade, in a windy place, and in a sheltered one—and learned that things dry faster in windy and warm places. Johnny's satisfaction in his self-achieved generalization is suggested by his spontaneous extension of it: "The clothes dried faster in the wind. I'll make some wind by fanning my picture to make it dry [78]."

A student teacher, believing that love for their teacher inspires some children, cites Judge Irving Ben Cooper's story [13]. Cooper writes that at 13 years of age he felt isolated, a misfit, and unloved. "I slipped into the classroom, and a tall woman came forward, put her arm around me, smiled and said in the kindest voice I ever heard, 'You're Ben Cooper. Well, I'm glad you are going to be one of us. I know you will like it here at Central and I know we are going to like you.'" This warm, frequently reinforced "message of faith" inspired him to achieve high goals and to reciprocate love for people generally.

Identification with self-enhancing roles often sustains our efforts to achieve long-range goals. One student believes she was motivated to practice the piano so that she could be like the famous pianists whom she heard or read about. Still another student says that he studied physiology intensely and took pride in his growing knowledge, well-prepared journal notes, and enduring interest in the subject because he admires his teacher's "profound knowledge of his field, his well-groomed appearance," and also because he enjoys his confidence-inspiring praise, encouragement, and friendly humor.

Another student believes that giving children responsible social roles motivates them to live up to these roles. He illustrates the concept by reporting his observations of a second grade class. Without prompting, the child chairman for the day made the necessary room-keeping assignments (postman, editor, caretaker of rabbit, pigeon, fish, etc.), initiated discussions on the problems which had arisen, and conducted the Show and Tell period. Two boys gave the weather forecast, and their report—which the teacher recorded—became the basis for later practice in reading. Activities, leaders, and participant roles were changed frequently. Every child seemed to take pride in the responsible independent roles he was given. Sometimes teachers dramatize fictional roles—by using puppets, for example, for the characters in "Red Riding Hood" and other stories—and this has been found to motivate practice in reading and speaking.

Superior achievement itself is motivating. In high school English, high standards and helpful teacher guidance brought out the best in each student. Making a choice among five or six alternative composition topics was always challenging. "At first," writes one student, "I couldn't think of anything I could say about any of them. Then Mrs. Ray, drawing on her thorough knowledge and wide experience, would discuss each topic. Before leaving the class I had so many ideas that I couldn't use them all. I had my theme outlined in my mind and I couldn't wait to begin working on it." Another high school student resisted reading and memorizing plays and poetry in her dramatics class until she won a prize for a reading from *Romeo and Juliet*, a play which she had greatly enjoyed as a moving picture. This experience, she said, changed her entire attitude toward the class activities.

The list of motives and incentives which students and teachers consider effective is—we see—extensive. In addition to the illustrations presented, it includes giving children knowledge of their progress, initiating competitive activities, embodying curriculum content in games, and even capitalizing on fears—such as intensifying effort in order to avoid failure in school or learning to swim in order to avoid another near-drowning. For more precise understanding of how individuals are motivated to learn, however, we now turn to some scientific studies of the problem.

THE ROLE OF MOTIVATION IN LEARNING

According to our definition of motivation, learning behavior is aroused, sustained, directed, and selectively reinforced by the individual's motives and incentives. This concept implies that efficient learning and performance are dependent upon effective motivation. Classroom experience, as we have suggested, and many other life experiences support this implication. Mickey Mantle, for example, has observed that it required the extremely high incentives of the World Series baseball games to bring out Don Larson's remarkable potentialities as a pitcher. It was in the 1956 World Series that Larson pitched a perfect game—putting down 27 batters in succession and allowing no one a hit. In nonseries games, in which Mantle believes that Larson did not try as hard, he never achieved this high level of performance [66]. Several experiments indicate that individual differences in school achievement are related to corresponding differences in the intensity of motivation to achieve.

The need to achieve and school accomplishment. Probably as a combination of several motives—which vary from person to person—children and youth develop to different degrees of intensity a general urge to achieve which significantly affects their school accomplishment.

Gough asked students to rate themselves on a questionnaire devised to indicate differences in achievement motivation. He found a significant correlation between these self-ratings and variations in general academic scholarship. The median correlation between need to achieve and scholarship for five different high school classes was .52. High self-ratings on achievement motivation were based on the total number of favorable true-or-false responses to 64 items such as—

> (T) I have a very strong desire to be a success in the world.
> (F) I usually go to the movies more than once a week.
> (T) I always try to do at least a little better than what is expected of me.

The high achievers gave answers which indicated self-confidence, diligent application, seriousness of purpose, conformity and reasonableness in interpersonal relations, and a sense of accomplishment [30].

Studies by Turney [99] and Frandsen and Darke employed high school teachers' ratings of motivation; these also reveal a significant relationship between intensity of motivation and achievement. In the latter study, teachers appraised their students' "industriousness" on a scale of five degrees—from (1) "Needs much prodding in doing ordinary assignments," to (5) "Seeks and sets for himself additional tasks." The correlation between ratings in high school and achievement in college for 353 freshmen was found to be .47. These correlations, approximating .50 on both self and teacher ratings of motivation, indicate that differences in achievement motivation are as important as differences in intelligence in determining school achievement [24].

A third approach to the problem confirms the significant relationship between the strength of the need to achieve and the effectiveness of learning. Since success and doing one's best in school, at work, in social affairs, and in competitive play activities are often rewarded, many individuals become preoccupied with achievement both in actual striving and in fantasy. Although everyone in our culture has some desire to achieve, the diverse factors which determine individual development also cause variations in the concern for achievement.

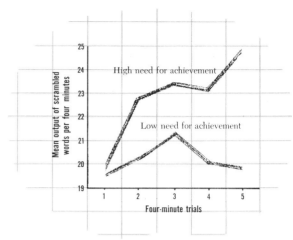

Fig. 6.1. *Average output of scrambled words per four-minute periods for college students with high (N 19) and low (N 21) scores on need for achievement.* (From D. McClelland, J. W. Atkinson, R. A. Clark, and E. L. Lowell, *The Achievement Motive,* Appleton-Century-Crofts, New York, 1953, p. 231.)

The extent of preoccupation with this need in fantasy can be measured by a projective test in which individuals are directed to make up stories about vaguely structured pictures, such as a boy seated before a table looking at a violin. Such a statement as "He is dreaming of the day when he will become a great musician," is considered indicative of the need to achieve. "He is angry at his mother because she makes him practice while he'd rather be outside playing," suggests hostility rather than desire for achievement [50]. Other responses (to other pictures) indicative of the need to achieve are "The boy is studiously and carefully preparing his homework," and "The men are both happy due to the new discovery [62]."

Lowell compared the efficiency of two groups of college students selected by the projective test as high and low, respectively, in the need to achieve. The efficiency-measuring test required the students to construct common words from scrambled letters, such as *west* from *w, t, s,* and *e.* Figure 6.1 shows the performance of 19 students who scored above average and of 21 who scored below average on need to achieve [61].

As the figure illustrates, students who are relatively high in need to achieve are sustained in making continual progress in this learning task. Students with little desire to achieve make no appreciable progress. They may drop in level of performance when extrinsic rewards are withdrawn. Other studies indicate that high school and college students highly motivated by the need to achieve often require no extrinsic motivation for effective learning [18, 44].

Complex influences of motivation. Besides affecting performance efficiency, individual differences in motivation also determine to some extent both how individuals view problems and their selective reinforcement of responses. In complex situations, we tend to perceive

Motivation and learning 213

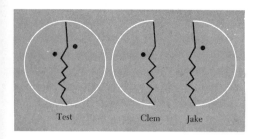

Fig. 6.2. *Between ambiguous alternatives, individuals tend to favor previously rewarded perceptions.* (From C. M. Solley and R. Sommer, *J. Gen. Psychol.*, 1957, vol. 56, p 5.)

what is rewarding and interesting and to avoid what is unrewarding and anxiety provoking [39].

The tendency of individuals to structure problems in accordance with their predominant interests is illustrated by the following experiment. Judson and Cofer directed college students to select the unrelated word in such groups as *prayer, temple, cathedral, skyscraper.* Religious students (as determined by their greater frequency of church attendance) tended to choose *skyscraper,* employing a religious concept to classify the other three items. Less religious students more often chose *prayer,* thinking of the three remaining words in an architectural sense [52].

Such tendencies to prefer one or another of alternative interpretations of perceived objects reflects learning from prior reinforcement of the preferred interpretation. Solley and Sommer demonstrated such learning with five- to seven-year-old children who, in divided groups, were presented in random order ten ⅕-second exposures of the pair of profiles shown in Figure 6.2, representing *Clem* and *Jake.* Half of the children were rewarded with three nickels every time Clem appeared and half of them were similarly rewarded every time Jake appeared. Then, again in ⅕-second exposures, the combined profiles were presented, and the children were asked which face they saw. Each group tended to see the profile which had been rewarded.

Because individuals, as they mature, usually have many dissimilar rewarding experiences, they develop different values. As a result of their diverse experiences, individuals come to value differently, for example, theoretical, economic, aesthetic, social, political, or religious pursuits. Havron and Cofer have shown that it is easier for an individual to learn new associations which are congruent with his developed predominant values than associations which are inconsistent with them [38]. It is also easier for students to proceed from lack of information to correct concepts than it is for them to change biased misconceptions [17]. However, when ulterior conditions or goals make it worthwhile to do so, subjects can readily learn material contrary to their biases [51]. As we shall learn in connection with self-enhancement motivation, when long-range adjustment so requires, even unpleasant learning tasks can be managed efficiently.

For easier comprehension of the diverse multiform motives and incentives operating in human learning and performance, let us classify them as basic internal motives and school motive-incentive conditions.

Basic motives. Human behavior is aroused, intensified, sustained, directed, and reinforced by four basic kinds of motive:

1. Innate physiological drives, including hunger, appetite, thirst, elimination, sex, rest, release from anxiety and other disturbing emotional states, escape from pain, and equilibrium of various other homeostatic needs [91].

2. Innate needs for perceptual, manipulatory, and intellectual activity, which find their highest satisfaction in culture-guided exploration and creative self-realization of potentialities.

3. Learned social motives universal to the individual's culture, including need for recognition by and the presence of other people, love and affection, approval and blame avoidance, security, mastery, self-enhancement, ascendancy in competition, and other satisfactions.

4. Learned individual interests, ideals, and identifications.

The innate physiological drives develop as functions of well-identified body structures and conditions, but they are modified in expression as the individual grows and learns [8]. Perceptual-motor-intellectual activities are also assumed to be intrinsically motivated by innate physiological mechanisms—as yet unidentified, but probably with controls in the brain and glandular system [70]. Both the universal social motives and the individually acquired interests are learned by conditioning wherein gratifications are derived from an extending range of stimuli. For example, the infant at first experiences pleasure mainly from satisfaction of body needs or physiological drives, by being fed. But part of the stimulus which the infant associates with eating is the presence of the mother or another person. Thus, according to the formula for conditioning which we learned in Chapter 2, the general self-satisfaction experienced in the eating situation is extended to the presence of another person. Individual interests are acquired in the same way. To a person interested in art, for example, art media become conditioned stimuli for pleasure. If art media are associated with smoothly going activity, mastery, and approval, the art media in themselves come to elicit interest or anticipation of pleasure.

Conditioning, however, is only half the story of the development of motives. Although eating is probably the infant's major satisfaction, he also enjoys looking, hearing, and wriggling. When growth and problem-solving learning make walking, talking, manipulating, and exploring possible, he discovers many new intrinsically satisfying activities. As talents emerge and are developed, the individual obtains his greatest joy in the constructive expression of them. Thus, the development and elaboration of motives is a product of innate body structures, maturation, and learning—both by conditioning and problem solving.

The individually learned motives, plus differences in the organization of the innate and universally learned motives, give each individual a distinctive and unique *pattern of motives.* In different children and youth the relative importance of such motives as security, sex, mastery of challenging tasks, or esteem varies. Some motives also wax and wane in relative importance as individuals mature.

Despite the necessity of considering these differences in the motivation of individual children, a study of the general principles of motivation will provide a basis for understanding this condition of effective learning.

School motives and incentives. As a result of learning, we associate basic motive satisfactions with numerous incentives—goal objects and events. Combinations of motive satisfactions—and the combinations vary in different individuals—constitute the general need to achieve. An inventory of motive-incentive appeals will suggest more specific ways of motivating children and youth in our schools. Such an inventory includes the following:

1. *Curiosity and desire to understand* one's world and oneself—through science, social studies, literature, and many other observational and problem-solving experiences.

2. *Intrinsic satisfaction in creative, constructive activity*—stimulated by rich, varied learning environments.

3. *Individual or group pursuit of interest-satisfying knowledge, understanding, and skills*—as in self-selected reading, uniquely suitable roles in projects, or creative self-expression in art.

4. *Using what is learned*—in achieving specific long-range goals and purposes by studying electronics to make a radio or English usage in order to write better reports of experiments.

5. *Mastery*—achieved by adjusting learning tasks in every curriculum area to the individual's level of maturity and pattern of abilities.

6. *Knowledge of progress*—revealed by a progress-curve graph of vocabulary, by checking the correctness of combinations in arithmetic, or by comparing compositions written in early and later periods of an English course.

7. *A sense of self-enhancement* of one's potentialities or talents for constructive self-expression and social contributions. Self-enhancement is, of course, dependent on knowledge of progress in specific activities. But from such knowledge and from identification with more mature and responsible social roles, the individual generalizes implications for enhanced evaluation of the self.

8. *Love and affection* of the teacher, *identification* with loved and admired persons, and a sense of belonging—of being accepted and valued by one's classmates, a committee, or other peer groups.

9. *Praise or approval* by teacher, classmates, or parents for meritorious learning effort or achievement.

10. *Blame and criticism,* as a corrective for mistakes, lack of effort, and undesirable behavior, and as a means of promoting future blame-avoidant behavior.

11. *Rivalry for ascendancy* in individual and group competition —in spelling matches, athletic contests, debate tournaments, and science talent contests.

12. *Cooperation and social facilitation* in achieving group goals —such as working out a project in social studies, participating in a school operetta or a classroom panel discussion—wherein each individual contributes according to his interests and talents.

13. *Opportunity to win special privileges*—such as going to the library for "free reading," becoming the concertmaster of the school orchestra, or winning a scholarship.

14. *Sympathy* from teacher and classmates for one's limitations and shortcomings.

15. *Feelings of security* about one's status with respect to achievement, grade promotion, and social and affectional relationships.

16. *Threat of insecurity*—such as the possibility of failing a test unless one studies with effort and succeeds, of not being promoted, or of being disliked and rejected by teacher or classmates for not meeting their standards.

17. *Punishment*—including personal criticism, sarcastic comments, scolding, isolation from the classroom, expulsion, and corporal punishment.

EVALUATION OF MOTIVE-INCENTIVE CONDITIONS

From the point of view of learning efficiency and attaining the general aims of education, which one of—or which combination from—this long list of ways of motivating school learning and behavior is, in general, most effective? In evaluating them, let us consider both classroom experience and experiments in educational psychology.

Security versus threat and punishment. Early in the history of education, teachers resorted to scolding, ridiculing, threats, and other kinds of punishment to motivate children's learning effort and conformity to strict standards of discipline. But these appeals to negative motives have been almost completely abandoned, with developing emphasis on such aims as democratic, self-reliant citizenship, emotional health, happy and cooperative interpersonal relationships among children and adults, and with growing scientific understanding of motivation. The changed attitude of teachers is implied in the results of a study by Briggs, who asked high school principals and teachers whether, as children, various positive and negative incentives had "made them work better, the same, or worse." These principals and teachers believe that "commendation, praise, and encouragement are superior to censure, ridicule, threats, and punishment [5]." Experiments support their opinions, as we shall see in the following reports.

For equated groups of both second and fifth grade children, Otto compared the gains made on the *Stanford Achievement Test* of one group periodically threatened with nonpromotion if achievement were not satisfactory and of another group reassured that they need feel no concern about being promoted. In both grades, the gains of the nonthreatened group exceeded slightly those of the threatened group [74]. In another experiment at the high school level, Janis and Feshbach found that the least fear-arousing of three degrees of negative motivation affected health practices most favorably [48]. Apparently it is not necessary to arouse anxiety in order to motivate learning. In fact, as Symonds concludes from a review of the literature, "censures, criticism, condemnations" are likely to damage children's personalities and to impair their learning efficiency. Anxiety stemming from repeated punishments causes the child "to inhibit or withdraw from situations where otherwise he might approach, explore, and learn [94, p. 460]."

Competition and cooperation. When high school and college students were asked to recall ways in which their elementary school teachers had successfully motivated them, they listed most frequently competitions for prizes and other rewards [76]. It is true that this type of motivation is often effective. Vaughn and Diseren remark that "competition has been used as a motivating influence during the entire history of pedagogy [100, p. 81]." From their reveiw of many learning experiments in both general and educational psychology, they conclude that "competitive conditions of one sort or another generally increase efficiency of work and facilitate learning." In some cases, however, they note that when "the competitive spirit" is aroused in situations where failure is anticipated, it may "disrupt the individual or result in a change in the direction of competitive effort."

The role of competition in energizing school learning (or performance) is illustrated in these experiments: Chapman and Feder directed two equated groups of fifth grade children in 10 daily 10-minute practice sessions in addition. The noncompetitive group was motivated only by "interest" and "conditions of serious school work." The competitive group, in addition to having these incentives, was competing for status on the list of daily scores and for stars for being in the upper 50 per cent of their class. The average performances under these two conditions of motivation are graphed in Figure 6.3.

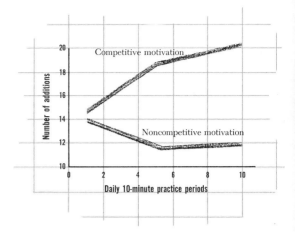

Fig. **6.3.** *Competitive motivation energizes performance of simple additions.* (Adapted from J. C. Chapman and R. B. Feder, *J. Educ. Psychol.,* 1917, vol. 8, pp. 469–474.)

As the graph clearly shows, the children competing for individual rewards surpassed those in the noncompeting group. In similar experiments with other age groups, Hurlock has confirmed the effect of individual competition on such simple learning tasks [46].

Maller, also using addition problems as the learning task for 814 pupils in grades 5 to 8, compared the effects of (1) no special motivation, (2) individual competition for a personal prize, and (3) group competition (with cooperation within groups) for a class prize. Average scores for sums completed were as follows: for no special motivation, 41.4; for group competition, 43.9; and for individual competition, 46.6. Both individual and group competition produced better performance than did no special motivation. Moreover, working for an individual prize was preferred over working for a group prize. Preference for individual versus group competition depends, however, upon the nature of the group. When given opportunities for working individually or in groups as teams, partnerships, teacher-divided groups, or the class as a whole, the children chose more frequently in each instance to work individually. The only instance in which these preadolescent children chose more often to work as a group was when boys were pitted against girls [65].

In more intricate tasks, as Mintz has demonstrated, competition can impair effectiveness. Mintz prepared a complicated apparatus for this experiment. As can be seen from the illustration, he placed a number of cones (with a string attached to each one) in a bottle which was so constructed that water flowed in at the bottom and

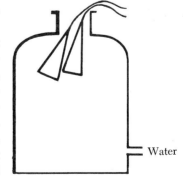

Water

gradually rose upward toward the cones. The task was to remove the cones before they got wet. Competitive groups of adults were individually rewarded with 10 to 25 cents for each dry cone withdrawn; they were penalized 1 penny for cones one-third to two-thirds wet; and they were neither rewarded nor penalized for cones less than one-third wet. Cooperative groups—without rewards or penalties—were asked only to demonstrate their ability to cooperate in removing the cones. In this task, which required orderly cooperation, success-impeding "traffic jams" often occurred for the individually rewarded and fined subjects. Under competitive conditions, only one group pulled out any cones; and this single group extracted only 2 of 19 cones in 40 seconds. Groups working only to demonstrate their co-operativeness avoided the interferences which trapped the competitors. Three cooperating groups pulled out *all* the cones in from 19 to 23 seconds [69, p. 155].

Two experiments indicate that *competitive* and *cooperative* motivation produce different kinds of behavior. Stendler, Damrin, and Haines demonstrated this in comparing the social behavior of seven-year-old children painting a classroom mural when they worked with the possibility of winning an individual prize and when they worked cooperatively to create a mural which might earn a prize for every child in the group. The observers noted relatively more friendly conversation, sharing of material, and mutual help among the children during cooperative activity. They noted relatively more hostile conversation, self-appropriation of material, and obstruction or domination of the work of another child during individually competitive work [90]. In a comparison of competitive and cooperative motivation of college women, Grossack showed that students who were promised group-shared rather than individual rewards worked more cohesively, contributed more positive suggestions to each other, and were less antagonistic [32].

Apparently competition produces complex effects. For many individuals it energizes performance. But those who discover that they are rarely, if ever, likely to win often quit trying, and sometimes feel inferior [19]. When winning becomes highly important but difficult or impossible to achieve, some (not all) children resort to cheating [31, 36]. Coombs believes that competition diverts some individuals from greater intrinsic satisfaction in creative social contributions, inhibits the full use of their unique talents, and encourages aggression, deception, and acceptance of pseudo values. Training in competitive behavior is inappropriate preparation, he believes, for the cooperative, interdependent work upon which our society depends [12]. Therefore, when teachers motivate children by appeals to competition, they should be aware of both its positive and negative results.

Praise and reproof. In their day-to-day experiences in the class-room, some children and youth are often commended—for superior achievement, for constructive contributions to class discussions and projects, for courteous, friendly, and cooperative social behavior, for leadership, or for attractive appearance. In contrast, others are scolded and otherwise disapproved of for inferior achievement, misconduct, and failure to complete assignments or to cooperate in group projects [16]. Although both praise and reproof sometimes motivate children to better achievement and conduct, some research suggests that the relative effectiveness of these techniques depends on individual differences in personality [21, 96]. When motivation is already high—because of intrinsic interest and other incentives—neither praise nor reproof is likely to enhance performance [83]. However, on the basis of his review of the literature on incentives for learning and discipline, Symonds concludes that praise is much more effective and beneficial to the healthy development of personality than is reproof. Symonds and other writers believe that, in addition to other incentives, individuals need to feel accepted and esteemed [55, 91].

These general conclusions are supported by Elizabeth Hurlock's famous experiment in which she evaluated the effects of praise and reproof on 106 fourth and fifth grade children. For 15 minutes on each of five days, Hurlock had her subjects practice a series of addition tests of equal difficulty. According to their scores on the first exercise, the children were divided into four groups: (1) a *control* group, placed in a separate room and given no special motivation; (2) a *praised* group, commended on each succeeding day for the excellence of the preceding day's work; (3) a *reproved* group, scolded for poor work, careless mistakes, and failure to improve, regardless of performance; and (4) an *ignored* group, in which members heard

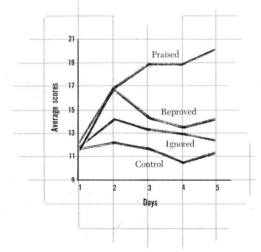

Fig. 6.4. *Effects of different incentives—being praised, reproved, ignored, and "control"—on average scores made on arithmetic tests for four groups on five successive days.* (Adapted from Elizabeth B. Hurlock, *J. Educ. Psychol.*, 1925, vol. 16, p. 149.)

the commendations and scoldings of the praised and reproved groups, but were not mentioned themselves.

As is indicated in Figure 6.4, both reproof and praise motivated children to greater effort and resultant improvement on the second day. On succeeding days the praised group continued to gain. But the reproved group, after a spurt of effort on the second day which was only followed by another scolding, declined in effort and performance on succeeding days.

Effective as praise is, however, it may, like competition, produce undesirable results unless it is applied sincerely and with discrimination. It may divert the learner from activities which otherwise would be pursued for intrinsic interest. When teachers and parents praise only excellent performance, children may set up self-imposed standards of perfection which can be maintained only at the cost of constant anxiety. Some children may be inhibited from experimenting—from testing themselves in new ventures—because they cannot bear the risk of failure. And praise for achievement may only make some children defensive about their actual limitations. Despite these qualifications, praise is an important factor in motivation when used at the right time and place. According to Taft, "a respectful, sincere appreciation based on objective understanding of what the other has tried to do, or a spontaneous joy in a given result, a sharing in the happiness of the creator is educationally sound and the truest encouragement which can be offered [95, p. 150]."

Success and failure. Many teachers have observed that successful learning experiences tend to motivate further learning. Mastery of worthwhile concepts and skills leads the individual, by conditioning, to feel confident, worthy, and eager for new ventures in learning. Frequent failure, on the other hand, produces anxiety, feelings of inferiority, disinterest, and self-defensive avoidance of learning activities—all of which impair learning. Both Lantz [57], using nine-year-olds as subjects, and Rhine [79], working with college students, tested intellectual efficiency before and after specially contrived success and failure experiences. They discovered that success tends to enhance learning efficiency and that, even more significantly, failure impairs efficiency. Lantz also found that success raises and failure depresses ratings of children on such traits as self-confidence and eagerness for further problem solving. The relative attractiveness of different activities is also affected by an individual's success or failure with them. Gebhard found that college students—after experimentally manipulated success and failure experiences with nine intellectual tasks, such as verbal arithmetic, code learning, sentence completing, symbol transposing, and algebraic reasoning—tend to prefer the particular activities on which they have been successful and may expect further success [27].

Especially important in the development of motivation is the influence which success and failure have on the individual's aspirations. Normal children usually aspire to do better next time in a series of equally difficult learning tasks. Working with fourth to sixth grade children, Sears found that children who in the past have consistently experienced success—subjectively in their day-to-day schoolwork and objectively in tests and school marks—continue to set aspiration levels (next-expected achievements) just beyond their past achievements. Because such aspirations are continually reinforced by success, they become self-perpetuating. However, when children have been continually frustrated in their day-to-day learning efforts and disappointed in their marks, they set unrealistic aspiration levels—either too high or too low. Gruen has observed corresponding realistic and compensatory self-protective aspiration levels in both well-adjusted and maladjusted adolescents. Success-frustrated and consequently often maladjusted, some individuals set their goals unrealistically high and enjoy temporary, fantasied social approval for their good intentions. Other maladjusted individuals, overly fearful of failure, set goals unjustifiably low and derive a naïve satisfaction from overreaching them [33, 85, 86].

Inasmuch as success or failure affect so significantly an individual's learning efficiency, interests, and aspirations, it is obvious that every child and youth needs a curriculum in which he can succeed. He needs to succeed with sufficient frequency to reinforce his feelings of self-esteem, confidence, and pleasure in learning [41, 42]. This conclusion does not imply, however, that problem-solving tasks should not be challenging or that children should never experience failure. Besides needing ample opportunities for success, children also need to learn to meet obstacles constructively.

Keister and Updegraff's experiment suggests a variation in motivation which can help children to develop persistence and an effective problem-solving approach. From 81 preschool children, they chose for special training the 12 who were most immature in their approach to perplexing problems. These children ordinarily gave up quickly, were overdependent and destructive; they rationalized, whined, sulked, cried, or yelled in anger when faced with a new and puzzling situation. They were trained, over a six-week period, by means of a series of problems graduated in difficulty (picture puzzle, assembly, and block building). Instead of calling attention to the child's success or failure, the teacher commended only his *mode of attack*. She would make such appropriate comments as "You kept right on trying until you found a way to do it, didn't you?" Before- and after-training tests showed that the group advanced in interest and independent problem solving and greatly reduced or eliminated immature approaches [53]. Such a shift in emphasis from outcome to process is healthy; normal individuals find life's greatest satisfactions not alone in end results but also in the conscientious use of their talents—in planning, building, and putting the finishing touches on a project.

Knowledge of progress. In many school activities—reading, language, spelling, handwriting, arithmetic, shorthand, typewriting, athletic performances and other skills requiring long-continued practice —it is possible, by repeating comparable tests and ratings, to give the learner specific knowledge of his progress at each stage of mastery. Figure 6.5 reveals a high school student's progress over several weeks in typewriting and illustrates such student-constructed records.

Experiments indicate that clear knowledge of progress often, though not always, motivates students to greater learning effort. Brown has reported the following experiment. Using as learning material a review drill on arithmetic combinations in grade 5 and fractions and decimals in grade 7, he divided 138 children into equated groups and had them practice 10 minutes per day for 20 days. Each day the teacher scored the papers for both groups. Only the children in the experimental group, however, were informed of their progress and given their scores for graphing. Brown found that the group with daily knowledge of individual progress "made more continuous gains" than did the group lacking such knowledge. Then the groups were reversed with respect to having and not having knowledge of progress. "Each section when knowing its results made higher scores and more consistent gain than when ignorant of results [6, p. 551]."

Panlasigui and Knight found, among fourth grade pupils who practiced mixed fundamentals over a period of 20 weeks, a "clear

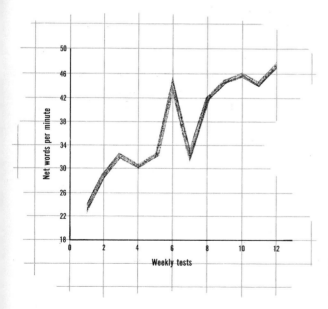

Fig. 6.5. *A's record of progress for the first 12 weeks of a second-semester high school typewriting course.*

advantage from the use of individual and class progress charts [75, p. 619]." The motivating advantage, however, was confined to those children who made substantial progress. As might be expected from the studies on success and failure, knowledge of slight or no gain did not always intensify effort or improve performance. Since multiple motives affect performance, and since motivation beyond optimal limits is unproductive, it is not surprising to find that particular incentives are sometimes ineffective [20, 82].

Self-enhancement. One aspect of every experience or activity is our judgment of its value. According to hierarchically arranged standards of value which we derived subjectively from past experience, we evaluate each new experience in such terms as "joyous," "worthwhile," "satisfying," "indifferent," "unpleasant," "bitter," and so on. Children take increasing satisfaction in the higher levels of accomplishment which their emerging abilities and developing skills make possible. Moreover, their society rewards them for attaining the goals it defines as worthwhile. As a beginner in school, for example, a child reads only with teacher help. Then he masters limited techniques for identifying words independently. Finally he acquires such skill that he feels confident he can read anything. In each step, the child's self-esteem is enhanced. School curricula in music, art, science, mathematics, athletics, and perhaps in every other area provide opportunities for increasingly valued individual and social expression of talents. These self-enhancing opportunities continue through adulthood in increasingly responsible occupational, family, social, and political roles. As Cantril suggests, we come to value more highly those experiences which we share with others, which employ our talents in socially constructive ways, and which give some order and direction to our lives [9, p. 27].

Striving is continually rewarded as individuals grow and learn and find expanding social roles. Thus they become justified in the constant expectation of enhanced values, especially from creative and constructive efforts. Each new experience is potentially better than any prior experience. But as higher values are experienced, individuals reconstruct their standards of value. As Cantril explains, "What is experienced as an increment of value today becomes a part of the (accumulated) value standard tomorrow [9, p. 30]." And, as compared to the new standard, still higher values are sought. Thus "the ultimate, the most generalized goal of man is what can be called the *enhancement of the value attribute of experience.* . . . It is the capacity man has to *sense added value* in his experience that accounts for his ceaseless striving, his search for a direction to his activities, for his characteristic unwillingness to have things remain as they are [9, p. 28; italics supplied]."

Such motivation explains the thrill in creative effort. It explains

the eagerness of children and youth for increased responsibilities and for opportunities to make greater contributions to their social groups. It is not surprising, according to this concept of motivation, that children find a special satisfaction in creative and constructive participation, each according to his talents, in purposeful, social, useful curriculum projects. Such motivation is effective in long-range learning projects because long-range goals can be symbolized, and well-justified anticipations of attaining them make the striving itself intrinsically satisfying. Moreover, since "we fit our specific actions into larger patterns of purpose," we can tolerate temporary frustrations, while we enjoy—in imagination—the enhanced value of the deferred goal.

Another source of motivation from imagined value is the enhancement of the self-concept which children and youth achieve by identifying with the more mature roles they see exemplified by loved and admired parents, teachers, peers, and other ideal characters, whether real or fictional. As an illustration of an ideal motivated by self-enhancement, we may recall the case of Judge Irving Ben Cooper, mentioned above. The love which Judge Cooper, as an adolescent, enjoyed and admired in his teacher he now expresses in his own attitude toward other people [13].

The school provides many instances of self-enhancement motivation. For example, behind the reading interests of young adolescents, Carlson suggests there is the need for identification with characters of status, strength, and courage. Thus, in animal stories, they identify with savage, intelligent, courageous, and noble beasts. In hero stories—in novels, mystery, science fiction, and in biographies—they identify with men of physical strength, intelligence, courage, and moral virtue who effectively meet and solve the problems of life. In stories about people like themselves, they explore in vicarious roles problems of sex, vocational choice, and social adjustments. And in slapstick comedy, the adolescent enhances his self-concept by per-

ceiving himself superior to the ludicrous characters who get themselves into stupid situations [10].

Interests. From an increasing variety of explorations in learning, as children and youth mature, their interests develop and become more and more differentiated. Although the relationship is not high, patterns of individual interests and aptitudes tend to be correlated [101]. Each individual tends to develop interests in academic, work, and play activities in which, because of his particular talents, he is most successful.

One child's first noticeably intense interest was in children's literature. Although her parents read many stories to her each week during her preschool years, they could never read enough to satiate her interest; she always demanded more. When she learned to read independently, she read hundreds of books—animal and nature stories, biographies, and science fiction. Now in high school, she continues her avid reading, including more science and creative literature. Meanwhile, competing interests have been growing simultaneously. As early as six years of age, she became absorbed in drawing. Over the years, her talent has developed and she has produced a stream of artistic creations and illustrations. During later elementary school years, she began writing and illustrating articles and reports on such topics as "Myths," "Greece," "Coral Reefs," "Japanese Architecture," and "Denmark." In junior high school, she elected to take journalism and made frequent contributions to the school paper. She became interested in the inventive aspects of mechanics and electricity and demonstrated such famous experiments as Faraday's generation of an electric current by turning a copper coil between the arms of a magnet. She built crystal, vacuum tube, and transistor radio sets. Her interest in science has expanded to include biology, in which she has also experimented—in animal learning (using white rats) and on rates of growth of the different parts of a plant. Still another parallel interest—music—has been slower in maturing. She began to take piano lessons when she was eight years of age, but never displayed much interest in that instrument. Then, at 11, she shifted to the violin, in which she developed such interest and proficiency that she now plays in an adult community orchestra. In the meantime, she has also taken up the cello, which she plays in the high school orchestra.

Now, at 15 years of age and in the tenth grade, it would be difficult for this girl to make a choice among three major interests—science, art, music—and one minor interest—literature. She says that if she had to choose her college major today, it would be physics, but that she would continue to enjoy art and music.

How can an adolescent who has a variety of strong and competing interests decide which one to concentrate on? How can teachers and parents help? Are there procedures for evaluating such competing interests more objectively and precisely?

Measuring interests. As interest-appraising procedures, teachers observe the degree of interest which children manifest in a variety of curricular and extracurricular activities. They employ cumulative records of interest shown in school subjects, work, and hobbies, and they have at their disposal a number of interest inventories. The adolescent described above took the *Kuder Preference Record, Form C* in order to appraise more precisely her relative interests in several competing areas [56]. The profile of her scores—converted to percentiles according to norms for high school girls—are presented in Figure 6.6.

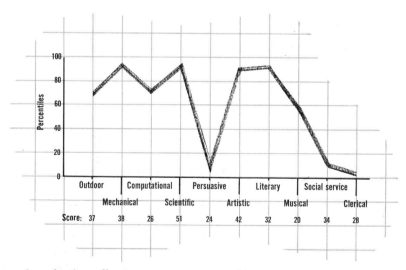

Fig. 6.6. *Tenth grade A's profile of interests as inventoried by the* Kuder Preference Record, Form C, *and interpreted against the norms of 4,466 high school girls.* (*Examiner's Manual for the Kuder Preference Record,* Science Research, Chicago, 1953, p. 20.)

The scores in the 10 areas of interest in the profile are based on the subject's response to a list of 504 specific activities grouped into triads. From each triad, the subject chooses the activity he likes most and the one he likes least. A typical group of three activities is: (a) Build bird houses. (b) Write articles about birds. (c) Draw sketches of birds. A subject who chose (c) as most liked and (a) as least liked would earn two points for interest in art and one point for interest in literary activities. In this way, the 168 triads of items in the various areas are scored. The 10 areas of interest and the liked-most items in each are:

Area of interest	Most-liked items
Outdoor	Farming, traveling, forestry
Mechanical	Operation, repair, construction of machines and appliances
Computational	Mathematics, computing, accounting, in a variety of situations
Science	Research and study in physical, biological, and social sciences
Persuasive	Selling a variety of things, and otherwise persuading people
Artistic	Creative and other work in art
Literary	Mainly writing in a variety of media
Musical	Work in a variety of musical situations
Social Service	Social, medical and teaching services to people
Clerical	Record making and keeping, and secretarial work

As the profile in Figure 6.6 shows, there are marked intraindividual differences in a student's pattern of interests. This adolescent, as we were led to expect from other appraisals of her interests, is relatively high in mechanical, science, art, and literary interests. She is above average (but lower than was expected) in musical interest, and she is above average in outdoor and computational interests. She is distinctly below average in persuasive, social service, and clerical areas. Since she is especially low in selling and social service interests, and since choices on the musical key included being a radio commentator, selling musical instruments, managing a music store, and teaching music, it may be that she was diverted from expressing her "true" interest in this area.

There are also distinctive interindividual differences in interests. Each individual's profile of interests is unique. And on any dimension of interest, a typical population of students exhibits a very wide range. For example, the range of scores in science interest of the 4,466 high school girls with whom the student in Figure 6.6 is compared is from

4 to 66. Scores on the Kuder and other self-inventories of interests are almost as reliable as are measures of abilities. Interest patterns tend to remain fairly stable over the high school years and to remain even more stable during the college and vocational years of life. Appraisals by different procedures tend to be interconsistent. Differentiated patterns of interests are logically related to students' choices of subject-matter majors, extracurricular activities, and occupations. In this chapter, however, we are primarily concerned with the effectiveness of interests in motivating school achievement [4, 28, 60, 64, 77].

Interest and school achievement. Although interests often motivate school learning, it is difficult to demonstrate the relationship. Correlations between degree of interest and teacher marks in a single course are typically very low [22]. This paradox results from the masking influence of other motives and of individual differences in aptitude. For example, a student of high aptitude and low interest in physical science may, because of his high aptitude and *general* high need to achieve, earn an A grade in a required course in chemistry. Another student may, despite a high interest in science, earn only a C grade because of his relatively low aptitude. Such discrepancies reduce an otherwise potentially higher correlation between interest and achievement. In experiments designed to control both individual differences in aptitudes and the masking influence of other motives, significant correlations between interest and achievement in corresponding fields of study have emerged [23, 25, 88]. And in the classroom, interest often seems to be an important determinant of learning.

Lazarus's report suggests that—given the requisite minimum of intelligence—vigorous interest, and probably some corresponding specific talent, can be more significant in determining creative achievement than superior intelligence alone. High school students who especially enjoyed reading and writing were invited to enroll in a "stiff, concentrated reading and writing course." Their achievement was compared with that of 20 intellectually superior students who were guided into a parallel course, but who lacked special interest or specific talent in these subjects. This "high-IQ group just did not do so well on the end-of-semester achievement tests and did not produce the creative writing in quantity and quality as did the high interest group [58, p. 39]." The high-interest group, with a mean Otis IQ of 107, read and reviewed an average of 20.7 books and wrote an average of 14.8 papers. The high-IQ group, with a mean Otis IQ of 120, read and reviewed an average of only 5.5 books and wrote an average of only 8.2 papers.

Spontaneous activity. As a result of differentially rewarded experience, individuals become attracted to multiple incentives—security, ascendancy, praise, success, knowledge of progress, and to various marks of self-enhancement. They also, as they mature and learn, become motivated by a generalized need to achieve and by differentiated interests. But underlying this variety of motive-incentive conditions is man's instinctive tendency to function—to explore, to manipulate, to think, and to create—as fully and complexly as he is able. White sees these varied functions as a unit; he says that human beings have a generalized instinctive tendency to master the environment, a general urge "to do and to learn how to do" [102, p. 307]. We see it manifested in children in such directed, persistent, and integrated activities as learning to grasp objects, to locomote, and to perceive things, in exploring objects and places, in manipulating, exploiting, and effecting changes in the environment, and in achieving ever-higher levels of proficiency [102, p. 317].

Inherent, function-demanding structures characterize man, apes, monkeys, dogs, sheep, mice, probably all animals [71, p. 129]. According to Leuba's review of research on "activity striving," rats left in darkness learn to press a bar which increases the illumination. Sheep ignore food in the goal compartment of a maze in order to rerun the maze. Monkeys solve mechanical problems—rewarded only by their own manipulatory activities. And children learn many things for intrinsic satisfaction in the activities themselves [59, p. 27]. As an example of these studies of spontaneous activity, let us examine in detail Harlow's experiment:

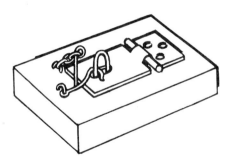

On 12 successive days, the experimenter placed hasps like that shown in the individual cages of eight rhesus monkeys. For experimental purposes the monkeys were divided into two matched groups. Those in Group A were given assembled hasps which required for disassembly (1) pulling the pin, (2) turning the hook, and (3) lifting the hasp. Those in Group B were given unassembled hasps, and no monkey, it happens, ever assembled one. During the 12-day period, monkeys in Group A disassembled the hasps many times, but never did a solution "lead to food, water, or sex gratification [35, p. 232]." Then on the thirteenth and fourteenth days, each animal was observed for five 5-minute periods one hour apart in a test cage, with the hasp assembled in all cases. In these test trials, the four monkeys in Group A disassembled it 31 times, 22 of the solutions requiring less than 60 seconds each. The monkeys in Group B, who had always in the past found the hasp already disassembled, achieved only 4 solutions, none within 60 seconds. Motivated only by intrinsic satisfaction in the manipulatory problem solving itself, the monkeys who had the opportunity to do so learned and maintained this skill.

Another feature of this experiment, however, reminds us of the multiplicity of motives affecting behavior and indicates how competing motives can sometimes divert individuals from the intrinsic satisfaction of problem solving. In a second test—this time with food reward—each animal in Group A watched the experimenter put a raisin under the hasp. Efficient solutions were now disrupted and errors multiplied. Diverted by the food incentive from the three-step, systematic solution, the monkeys tended to attack the hasp directly.

Similar experiments have not been conducted with human beings. Our free observations, however, afford ample evidence of our tendencies to activity. Children are characteristically active. Without urging, even against restraints, they locomote, manipulate, explore, search for problems to solve, and construct all sorts of things. An art supervisor summarized her observations of children's activities in this way: "They put inordinate amounts of energy and persistence into a continual stream of art creations, not because they have to but because it is fun [34]." Even in healthy old age, people find joy in creative activity. Seventy-five-year-old Henry J. Kaiser, for example, "after a restless life of building roads, dams, pipelines, factories, ships, cars, bridges, and homes," still enjoys a creative, busy, 18-hour day. Of life's pleasures, he says ". . . while there is nothing more relaxing than a sail on one of these giant boats, to me the joy of achievement is relaxation. How can I retire? [40, p. 88]"

Generalizing from the experiments on animals and from observations of children, Arnold concludes: "The desire to know and learn is inherently active in all children and does not have to be aroused by some (more) bona fide biological drive [3, p. 221]."[1]

Summary evaluation of school motives. Some significant generalizations emerge from our evaluation of school motive-incentive conditions.

Although individuals are inherently self-motivating, they become sensitive to many incentives both from shared and from individual learning experiences. Among these incentives, security, praise, and success are more effective in motivating school learning and discipline than are punishment, reproof, and failure.

Incentives seldom operate singly and their effects are usually complex. Both praise and reproof may temporarily spur learning effort, but the results vary for different personalities. For long-range motivation, praise is almost universally effective, while reproof loses its

[1] Reprinted from Vol. 77, 1956, of *Education*, used by special permission of The Bobbs-Merrill Co., Inc., Indianapolis, Indiana.

influence, or may divert the learner from exploration and confident problem solving. But praise must be applied with discrimination and always with sincerity. Competition usually facilitates simple performances, especially for individuals who have learned that they have some prospect of winning. But under some conditions it may impede the performance of intricate tasks. As by-products, competition may elicit hostile, selfish, and obstructive behavior, while cooperative arrangements are more likely to evoke sharing, mutual help, and friendliness. Success tends to promote efficient learning, interest, confidence, and realistic aspirations. Repeated failure tends to produce disinterest, avoidance of problem solving, feelings of inferiority, and unrealistic aspirations. Individuals, however, can and do learn to meet obstacles effectively—to find intrinsic satisfaction in doing their best, not in end results alone.

The motives and incentives which provide the greatest intrinsic satisfaction are knowledge of progress, self-enhancement, and pursuit of group and individual interests. Knowledge of progress usually facilitates effective learning, especially when students make appreciable gains. Self-enhancement—based on experiencing increments of value both from personal achievement and from identifying with loved and admired persons—motivates persistent effort to attain long-range goals. Individual interest, as one among multiple motives, is often masked as a factor affecting achievement in a single course. But for some individuals, enduring, differentiated patterns of interest are related to long-range achievement in corresponding subjects. In some instances, intense interest, coupled with specific talent, may produce outstanding achievement. For other, probably less happy individuals, extrinsic incentives and an overpowering need to achieve dominate learning efforts.

Perhaps the most generally effective way to motivate children and youth is to provide them opportunities for creative and constructive participation in purposeful social projects which are valued by both the individual and the community. Comprehensive projects offer scope for spontaneous activity, mastery of skills, self-enhancement, social esteem, expression of talents and interests, cooperation, and perhaps, as combinations of these and other motives, the general urge to achieve.

Let us now try to formulate a more unified concept of motivation. Such a concept will help the teacher to be more systematic and confident in her management of this condition of learning.

A theory of motivation which recognizes all the data just reviewed should take into account both the many motives determining behavior and the central role among them of man's positive creative striving. Maslow has given us the outline for such a theory and several other writers have contributed to it.

Maslow's theory. According to Maslow, man's motives become hierarchically arranged, as follows: (1) physiological drives; (2) needs for safety, security, and freedom from anxiety; (3) love and acceptance in interpersonal relations; (4) self- and social esteem; and (5) self-actualization [67]. In this hierarchy, from lower- to higher-level motives, man's greatest satisfaction is in self-actualization;[1] his most "profound joy," as May puts it, is in the development and constructive expression of his talents [68, p. 96]. The lower-order needs, however, are more demanding; and until they are reasonably well satisfied, higher motives have little effect on behavior. An individual's capacities and energies are mobilized in the interest of any strong motivational need. Thus a hungry, insecure, or unloved individual whose confidence has been undermined by failures or who feels disapproved would not, according to Maslow's theory, be expected to reach the level of self-actualization. Like Harlow's monkeys, who were diverted by their hunger from the intrinsic pleasure of manipulatory problem solving, such an individual would devote all his efforts to allaying hunger, relieving anxiety, or winning love and esteem. He would have no energy left for constructive and creative work.

Many individuals are denied self-actualization and intrinsic joy in learning and work. Maladjusted children and youth, frustrated in their needs for security, love, and esteem, are often ineffectual and unhappy in school. A study by Schoeppe, Haggard, and Havighurst indicates that when adolescents are deprived of these basic satisfactions, they become retarded in social maturing. Martha and Ned, for example, starved for affection, "exert all their energies toward seeking the love of which they have been deprived." Martha, by passive submission, strives compulsively to avoid condemnation. Ned, who is openly rejected and also stronger, expends his energies in compulsive hostility. Both are self-defeating in their efforts to win the friendship they crave [84, pp. 50–51].

But when motives lower in the hierarchy *are* satisfied, then latent higher motives activate appropriate behavior. The individual can then find high intrinsic satisfaction in constructive problem solving. Because of man's innate capacities to learn, to experience increments of value,

[1] "Self-actualization" is Maslow's interpretation of what we have called "spontaneous activity" and what White has called the "instinct to master the environment."

and to symbolize future higher values, the healthy individual is motivated toward self-actualization [1, 2]. In this respect, Herbert and Ann were more fortunate and more healthy than Martha and Ned. They grew up in homes where they were secure, accepted, loved, and "made to feel that they counted as individuals." They learned both the need for and the satisfaction of working, and they enjoyed identification with their parents' social roles. "On this foundation the youngsters began school, and because they were well-socialized, the school eagerly accepted them and they worked to further their socialization. Each new successful accomplishment made the next one easier for Ann and Herb [84, p. 50]."

The constructive, social direction of man's inherent tendencies to activity and self-actualization which—experienced counselors such as Rogers note—comes from the circumstance that individuals achieve motive satisfaction only by interacting with other people and things. Only with culture guidance are individuals able to develop fully their potentialities for complex, intricately coordinated performance. Moreover, man's society rewards his constructive, socialized effort.

Implications for teaching. According to Maslow's theory, when a child's lower-level needs are reasonably satisfied, he does not have to be *pressed* into constructive and creative study and work. The opportunity for self-actualization offers its own intrinsic reward. When a child is uninterested in school, rebels against or otherwise resists study and schoolwork, the teacher should assume that his energies are all bound up in a frustrating attempt to satisfy lower-order needs or that he is not being given suitable learning opportunities. In either case, the teacher should not attempt to *drive* or *press* the pupil into constructive effort. He should try to adapt the curriculum to the child's interests, abilities, and needs. By helping the child in every possible way to satisfy amply the lower-level needs—for safety, love, and esteem—he would *release* the child's energies for constructive work.

This theory of motivation is consistent with the assumption that children need security, praise, and success. It recognizes the importance of developing children's interests, of providing children knowledge of their progress and opportunities for self-enhancement, and of promoting a healthy, but not overanxious need to achieve.

The theory specifically illustrated. For an application of Maslow's theory of motivation in learning, let us resume the incompleted study of Ellis, which was begun in Chapter 4. It will be remembered that despite his almost uniform record of D grades in junior high school, Ellis's teachers suspected that he might have potentially higher academic abilities than his grades had indicated. At the end of the ninth grade, they also wondered what to do about him. For example, should he be promoted to the tenth grade?

The cumulative record, it will be recalled, revealed that although

Ellis sometimes did average work, his learning difficulties had begun early and had persisted. Teachers from grades 2 through 6 had observed his dallying over assignments, inattention, lack of confidence, and unwillingness to accept responsibilities. By the sixth grade, he was retarded one to two years in reading, language, arithmetic, and social studies. As both the elementary and secondary teachers had suspected, however, not lack of capacity but inefficient use of his abilities was the more probable explanation of his inferior school accomplishment.

The school psychologist's individual administration of *WISC* not only confirmed the teachers' hunches, but revealed in Ellis surprisingly superior abilities in abstract reasoning and problem solving. Contrasting with the performance IQ of 136, however, the verbal IQ of only 86 and observations of his performance on the verbal, more schoollike subtests suggested anxiety-disturbed and otherwise impaired intellectual efficiency. We now return to the question of how to account for such a striking discrepancy between potentiality and accomplishment.

In interviews with his parents, it was learned that Ellis's indolence extended to home responsibilities as well. His father said that unless he was checked on continually, he left an array of unfinished jobs. There was, however, one exception to the report of consistent irresponsibility. In the previous summer, in working with his father as a carpenter, Ellis had demonstrated competence, interest, and responsibility. It was also learned from the parents that in contrast to Ellis's irresponsibility, his younger brother does both his schoolwork and home chores admirably.

Ellis—a handsome, well-proportioned 15-year-old—is pleasant in conversation. Facing the prospect of nonpromotion from his junior high school, he admits his shortcomings and blames no one for them except himself. He would like to do better, he says, and is perplexed himself about his lack of diligence. About his future plans, he wrote in a questionnaire: "I plan on finishing my school career, and then I would like to be either a carbonder [carpenter], mechanic, or a jet pilot." In the

interview—during the testing—he added an improbable alternative to his vocational aspirations. He said: "I would like to be an engineer, but I don't even know the times tables." In the same questionnaire, about the help he feels he needs from his teachers, he said: "They should make me do my work." Apparently both Ellis and his teachers are aware of his weak and unreliable urge to achieve. But neither of them understands what diverts him from attaining the aspirations of which he is capable.

Projective testing—a process to be explained in Chapter 13—was added to the diagnostic study. It was expected that Ellis might give the characters, in the stories he was asked to tell about pictures, some of his own otherwise hidden motives, fears, and attitudes. They did provide important clues. His stories about 10 pictures consistently indicate that he feels insecure, guilty, helpless, and dependent, but without strong parental or other support. His insecurity is suggested by his story characters' repeated avoidance of danger—of the hazard of using a gun, of possible injury on a fishing trip, and of an air-raid from which a boy escapes potential harm by "hiding in a safe place." Guilt is suggested by repeated punishments ("being sent to prison for all of his life"), accidentally shooting a brother, and a father's hospitalization and eventual death. Ellis's helplessness, inferiority, and lack of self-confidence are suggested by such phrases as "wondering how to play the violin," "getting there too late" to put out a fire, and by a "boy not knowing what to do." Frequently, the characters rely on their mother; but in one story about a boy who is ill, the mother "doesn't know what to do." The father is not mentioned in any story as a source of support or identification.

We know, however, that Ellis does consciously identify with his father, who is a carpenter. And yet he says he is unhappy, however, about their relationship. He feels that his father is indifferent to his interests, perhaps even rejective, and overcritical. Frequent arguments lead to some avoidance of his father and overreliance on his mother. A slightly younger brother—who does much better both in school and with home chores—may be the rival with whom Ellis, who feels so inadequate, avoids competing by unconsciously resisting work at school and at home.

From the point of view of Maslow's theory, Ellis is ineffectively motivated because his needs for safety, love, and esteem are seriously frustrated. His defense from further loss of esteem is manifested in a passive resistance to entering into competitive school and home tasks in which he believes—because of his often-reinforced and now well-established feelings of incompetence—he would only fail. Before Ellis can enjoy the intrinsic satisfaction of the full use of his talents in constructive schoolwork, he needs to be *released* from his self-defeating efforts to avoid insecurity, loss of love, and esteem. He needs full satisfaction of these needs. And he needs to taste success more frequently.

His father can help to provide these satisfactions by resuming with more appreciation and encouragement the work project in which Ellis was interested last summer, and which does not involve competition with his younger brother. Because of Ellis's interest and test-suggested talent for effective problem solving with spatial patterns, he should do especially well as a carpenter or a mechanic. With guidance toward higher levels of proficiency, knowledge of and appreciation for his specific achievements, and the general feeling of self-enhancement which should come from progress toward long-range goals, Ellis should begin to satisfy more completely his needs for security, love, and esteem. Freed from excessive, though ineffective, striving to satisfy lower-level needs, he should begin to experience the intrinsic joy of constructive work.

Rather than threaten him with the danger of nonpromotion, his teachers can motivate his efforts to complete graduation requirements during the remainder of the semester. By individualizing their instruction, they can help him to avoid uncompleted assignments, and thus lead him to expect success instead of failure. This will probably require helping him to make correct starts, giving him encouragement and specific aid as he works with assignments, and checking his work before study periods are over to make sure that he is able to complete them. His efforts, accomplishments, and expected growing initiative should be warmly approved.

As this help by parents and teachers proceeds, individual counseling should also help Ellis to revise his self-concept—from one of guilt and inferiority to one of self-respect and confidence. These several gains should lead him to the self-actualization level of motivation, on which level he should become independently self-motivated.

SUMMARY

Human behavior is aroused, intensified, sustained, directed, and reinforced by four basic kinds of motives: (1) innate physiological drives; (2) equally inherent needs for perceptual, manipulatory, and intellectual activity; (3) culture-determined social motives; and (4) individually learned interests and identifications. Through learning—by both conditioning and problem solving—these motives become associated with numerous incentives which learners and teachers manipulate in a variety of combinations to motivate school learning and discipline.

The general need to achieve—a combination of motive-incentive conditions which varies in different individuals both as to its components and its intensity—is an important determinant of school accomplishment. Other more specific, effective incentives are security, praise,

success, competitive and cooperative social facilitation, knowledge of progress, opportunities for self-enhancement, and pursuit of individual interests. For healthy children and youth, however, extrinsic incentives are frequently unnecessary. Creative, constructive participation in appropriate curricular activities offers its own high intrinsic satisfaction.

Imaginative and ingenious teachers have discovered many ways of appealing to these motive-incentive conditions. Perhaps the most generally effective procedure is to provide children and youth opportunities for creative and constructive participation—each according to his talents and interests—in purposeful, social, personally and community-valued projects.

Maslow's hierarchical theory of motivation is a unifying concept. Maslow assumes that healthy individuals—whose lower-order needs for physical health, safety, love, and esteem are reasonably satisfied—strive continually and with high intrinsic reward for self-actualization. When the needs for security, love, and esteem are frustrated, however, individuals are diverted from constructive work, and all their energies are mobilized in the anxious, often self-defensive, pursuit of lower-order needs. Such individuals need to be *released* from this anxiety—by ample provisions for security, love, and esteem. Thus freed and with an appropriate curriculum, their inherent, potential desire to learn and to create impels them toward self-actualization.

As students progress through the elementary and secondary curriculum, they continually master new learning tasks or revise their understanding or performance of partially mastered concepts and skills. Being *ready* and *motivated* to begin or to take the next step in a learning task, they face the question: How shall I go about it? Although children are sometimes able in trial-and-error efforts to discover solutions by themselves, they often need teacher guidance in structuring effective approaches to learning tasks. The nature of teacher guidance and how it can be given effectively are the problems which we will take up in the next chapter.

GUIDES FOR STUDY, REVIEW, AND APPLICATION

1. Like ourselves, children and youth are naturally curious. They like to explore new places, things, and ideas, and they enjoy constructing , things. Despite these positive urges, teachers often complain of the difficulties in motivating them to study the academic concepts and skills of the school curriculum. Why? Some answers are suggested in the films *Importance of Goals* (19 minutes) and *Problem of Pupil Adjustment*: Part 1 *The Drop-out, a Case Study* (19 minutes), McGraw-Hill Text-Film Department.

2. As an individual or class project in collecting illustrations of good classroom motivation, extend the following list: the museum-like classroom, the study of electrical toys, doing real jobs, situation-stimulated questions, teacher kindness, giving children responsibilities, constructing, experimenting, and seeing and achieving excellence. Using the categories "basic motives" or "school motives and incentives," classify your list of illustrations.

3. Explain and illustrate the specific roles of motivation in learning.

4. Describe and evaluate (in terms of both experiments and practical experience) the following motive-incentive conditions: security versus insecurity, competition and cooperation, success and failure, knowledge of progress, self-enhancement, interests, and spontaneous activity.

5. Although recognizing man's multiple motives, what are the arguments for (or against) considering his innate urge to do and to learn how to do as the most important motive for school learning? How can teachers provide for the operation of this motive?

6. Is Maslow's theory an adequate interpretation of the facts on motivation summarized in this chapter?

Chapter 7

STRUCTURING APPROACHES TO PROBLEMS

Each individual has a tremendous amount of learning to do before he is ready to play an effective role in society or enjoy his own potential talents and interests. His duties as a citizen; his responsibilities for moral behavior; his needs for satisfying and useful participation in social relationships—in his home, community, nation, and world; his preparation for work; his enjoyment of play; and his acquisition of the fundamental skills of reading, speaking, writing, and computing which are associated with these activities—all require him to master a great deal of knowledge and solve a myriad of problems. Difficult new problems both in school and out of school present themselves day by day. For these novel problems there can be no adequate, prepared-in-advance solutions—only an effective problem-solving approach. Fortunately, society provides teachers to guide each new generation in selecting what is worth learning and in learning how to learn and how to solve problems. The quality of all this learning—especially in childhood and youth—depends most importantly upon skillful teaching.

And among the major functions of teaching, that of guiding learners in structuring approaches to problems is especially significant.

COGNITIVE GUIDANCE OF LEARNING

For the newborn infant, the world of stimuli is probably unstructured and relatively undifferentiated. William James has remarked that the infant probably perceives the world as a big, blooming, buzzing confusion. Except for an innate organizing process within the nervous system for primitive perception of segregated objects, forms, and colors [77, p. 293], the individual's perception and interpretation of the world of things and events depend upon his accumulated experience and—in subtle ways—upon his needs.

In a stimulating learning environment, the child continually meets new and challenging problems to which he reacts with a problem-solving approach. When he meets a word he does not recognize, or a concept in science, for example, which he does not grasp readily, or a play in basketball which he cannot execute skillfully, he will probably emit multiple, varied responses. But even without teacher guidance, his behavior will not be random; it will be purposeful, goal-directed, and cognitively structured (that is, guided by thinking).

Purposeful approaches in problem solving. Such cognitive structuring of a response pattern—as a guide to executing it—is illustrated by an eleven-year-old child's partial verbalization of his approach to the *Object Assembly* items of the *Wechsler Intelligence Test for Children.* Not knowing the object to be assembled from the jigsaw pieces and being unwilling to proceed blindly toward an unknown goal, the child indicated his need for structuring an approach by asking: "What is it?" His provisional effort to structure the task—in which he probably tried out alternative hypotheses—is suggested by another comment that he made when he found a promising lead: "This piece looks like it has something to do with a head." From that point—having achieved an adequate guiding interpretation—he proceeded quickly and with apparent sureness to assemble the pieces into a face. In fitting pieces together to make an automobile—another object which the task required him to identify and assemble—he first tried a variety of tentative arrangements, as though searching for a plausible interpretation. After 30 seconds, he observed: "It's a car." Then he quickly assembled it, adding: "When I looked at the door [a distinctive piece], I knew it was a car."

Sometimes, however, a child's problem-solving behavior does not appear to be so purposeful. Superficial examination of several arithmetic problems collected by Tilton from fourth grade children suggests, at first sight, random guessing. Two of his examples are presented [73].

$$(a) \quad \begin{array}{r} 7 \\ + 14 \\ \hline 12 \end{array} \qquad (b) \quad \begin{array}{r} 32 \\ \times 49 \\ \hline 88 \end{array}$$

As a phase of diagnostic and remedial teaching for these children, who were obviously having difficulty with arithmetic, each child was asked to think out loud as he attempted to solve a problem. In this interviewing process, the cognitive structuring and purposive nature of his problem solving were revealed. For problem (a), a child said: "Seven and four are eleven and one more is twelve." And for problem (b), another child explained: "Multiply nine times two, write down eight, and carry the one. Then add one, three, and four." Lacking understanding of the place value of numbers, both children did the best they could with the concepts available to them. From prior experience in adding digits in single columns, the first child assumed that the same process would work with two-digit numbers. Consequently, he misinterpreted the 10 in 14 as 1. Similarly, in the second example, not comprehending either place values or two-digit multiplication, the child applied—at least provisionally—his already established assumptions about single-digit multiplication and adding after carrying.

Correctly solved problems, as well as such groping responses as these, indicate, when examined thoroughly, that problem solving is always purposeful, although often highly tentative and provisional and sometimes faulty. As Cantril has explained the process, cognitive structuring as an approach to problem situations "involves taking into account many, many factors of past experience, weighing or evaluating them on the basis of the probability that a certain reaction to a certain set of circumstances will be a good bet and then acting accordingly [8, p. 39]."

When the problem situation is unfamiliar and the individual encounters difficulty in structuring it meaningfully on the basis of his past experience, he is likely to *create* solutions by extending already-achieved generalizations. These creative extensions of generalizations sometimes lead to constructive, creative achievements and sometimes to motive-biased perception and solutions of problems.

Extended interpretations. "Creative" extensions of generalizations are suggested in the approaches of the children in Tilton's study. They applied to two-digit numbers the processes they had learned for dealing with single-digit numbers. Other examples of extended generalizations which teachers frequently observe include spelling errors, such as writing *newduls* for *noodles,* or the use of personally invented shorthand expressions such as +*ing* for adding and −*ing* for subtracting. They also occur in nonacademic learning. Leeper cites an illustration of the role of motivation and the child's self-concept in extending perceptions and interpretations of social situations. A young

child was scolded by his mother when, in imitation of her, he picked up a restaurant menu. "Put that back," she said. "Don't be bothering things. You can't read it, anyway." As Leeper observes, the child may extend the interpretation to "I'm not able to do the things that big people can do, and I've got to depend on others [44, pp. 32, 38]."

Biased interpretations. Two types of motivationally biased and self-protective interpretations are cited in the following studies. Cantril illustrates his concept of perception as a process of achieving more effective or satisfying adjustments [9]. Reporting from Bagby, he records the interpretations Mexican and American school teachers gave of pictures of a bullfighter and of a baseball player which were presented simultaneously in opposite lenses of a stereoscope. The interpretations of both groups of teachers appeared to be influenced by their backgrounds of experience and motivational bias. The fused picture they perceived was not a combination of the two separate images. The Mexican teachers tended to see the bullfighter, and the American teachers tended to see the baseball player—but in both instances the figure perceived was more handsome than the men in the separate pictures. Perception, although influenced, is not dominated by individual motives. Even in this ambiguous situation *both* groups of women saw men. In most situations, we tend to agree in our perceptions of common things and events [42, p. 99].

As another kind of distortion in structuring, Hildreth has pointed out that children who need to maintain self-esteem by succeeding with problems beyond their abilities sometimes simplify them by naïvely restructuring them [34]. Charles, with an S-B IQ of 70, at age 6–10 was directed to copy a diamond ◇, a task slightly beyond his level of maturity. He reproduced it, however, as a rectangle ▭, saying, as

Children try out various approaches . . .

**With teacher guidance,
pupils learn how
to solve problems**

and find the correct solution . . .

through a trial-and-check process

*Children discover principles, make
generalizations*

*Each discovery
facilitates new
applications*

he worked, "I twy." Another child, using the same simplifying process, read *organize* as *orange*. Still another simplified her definition of *haste* by giving a rhyme: "It means to hate." And when the question "Who discovered the North Pole?" temporarily baffled a child who needed to avoid failure, he paused and then resolved his dilemma by saying: "Oh yes, who discovered America? Why, Columbus." Simplifying does not always, of course, lead to error, as was demonstrated by a first grade child who simplified the task of writing the number eight by writing two zeros—one on top of the other—8.

THE NEED FOR TEACHER GUIDANCE

In most learning tasks and for the majority of pupils, some kind and amount of teacher guidance facilitate efficient learning. The necessity for teacher guidance, however, appears to vary with the complexity and novelty of the concepts or skills to be learned and with the resourcefulness and self-teaching talents of individuals.

As we have already indicated, some children structure approaches independently and invent solutions to new problems. Johnny, for example, contrived the following graphic solution for subtracting 15 from 30: ++++++++++++//////////////. Making 30 vertical strokes, he counted 15 of them and drew a horizontal line through them; then he counted the remaining unmarked strokes and arrived at his answer [65, p. 96].

Other children require only a minimum of teacher guidance in structuring a problem-solving approach. Jane, temporarily blocked in a problem requiring multiplication of 20 × 30, was helped by a leading question, "What are you studying about?" With this slight orientation, she identified the difficulty and answered: "I am studying 20 × 30, but I don't know how to multiply when both numbers end in zero." Then, beginning to write thirties in a column, she said: "I will just have to add ten thirties. I know that two times that will be the answer [65, p. 97]."

These invented procedures are not efficient, of course, but, as initial approaches, they have the merit of being independent and successful.

Some children reveal, in their confused approaches to problems, the need for more explicit teacher guidance. This need was manifested in pupil reaction to the problem: "After John was 15 years old, he received $60 each year in equal monthly payments for spending money. How much did he receive each month?" Some pupils "divided 60 by 4, because there are four weeks in a month. Other pupils multiplied by 15, because 15 was given in the problem. Still other pupils divided 60 by 30, because there are only thirty days in a month [65, pp. 97–98]." These approaches are, of course, naïve. But they are goal-directed, as is indicated by the determinant use of "because." There was "purpose in the madness" of these pupils.

Persistence of inefficient modes of attack. Experience in diagnostic and remedial teaching has revealed that intelligent students at all levels—elementary, secondary, and college—often function far below their potential capacity.

Bond and Fay, for example, found that faulty word identification and other ineffective reading techniques impaired the reading proficiency of 22 out of 23 children referred to the Minnesota Reading Clinic [4]. Without proper guidance, these children had for a long time made little or no progress. When taught more efficient approaches in reading, and when given an opportunity to build up their self-confidence, they made relatively rapid gains.

Brownell has shown that unless inefficient modes of attack are corrected, they are likely to persist. Practice alone is likely to result only in greater speed and accuracy in using the inefficient methods. He demonstrated that as third grade children practice additions [6] and as fifth grade children practice multiplication combinations [7], they tend to make progress in both accuracy and speed, but not in efficiency of procedures. Individual diagnostic interviewing showed that without teacher guidance they continued to use inferior work methods. In adding, for example, instead of learning to arrive at sums by confident, immediate recall, many children continue to add by counting, by guessing, or by going about the problem indirectly (for $3 + 4 = ?$, they took two steps: $3 + 3 = 6$ and $6 + 1 = 7$). Satisfied with moderate degrees of efficiency, they continue to use methods which are less efficient than those which they might have learned with better teacher guidance.

IMPROVEMENTS IN LEARNING FROM TEACHER GUIDANCE

Several experiments—with children and adults in varied learning activities—indicate that teacher guidance facilitates effective learning.

In the following study, Thompson demonstrated the value of teacher guidance at the preschool level [70]. Nineteen 4-year-old nursery school children were divided into two equated groups. Group A was given little teacher guidance; the teacher initiated a minimum of contacts with the children, permitted them to plan and execute many school activities, and gave them assistance only as requested. Group B was given much more teacher guidance; the teacher volunteered information, gave more specific help and general instruction. She included more structuring suggestions such as "You could look in some of these books and see how they [airplanes] are made," and more leading questions such as "How can we fix it so that we can reach it?" The Group B teacher made more overt, friendly gestures, and gave more general stimulation to the children's thinking. On observational rating scales, Thompson found that the group given more teacher guidance excelled in ascendant behavior, in social participation, in leadership, and in constructiveness when faced with a possible failure.

Keston has shown that teacher guidance aids students in acquiring understanding and appreciation of classical music [39]. He found that high school seniors who had guidance in identifying and comprehending classical pieces gained more in recognition and appreciation of superior music from a year of instruction than a comparable group who only listened to the music.

With respect to learning motor skills, Anderson has shown that teacher guidance aids high school girls—at least in the initial stages—in mastery of basketball shooting [1]. A teacher-guided group of 66 tenth and eleventh grade girls practiced bank shots; they were instructed to hit the backboard lightly, to aim at and to keep their eyes fixed on spots marked appropriately on the backboard to guide their shots from several positions. Compared with a similar group of girls who practiced but received no guidance, the instructed group made greater progress.

At the college level, Davies has demonstrated very clearly the effectiveness of teacher guidance in learning another complex motor skill [14]. Two matched groups of 20 students each practiced archery for two 50-minute periods a week for three months, one group with teacher guidance and the other group without instruction. During each practice period, the guided group was given teacher demonstrations, analyses of procedures used, descriptions of correct methods and improved modes of attack, suggestions on how to eliminate faulty techniques, and explanations leading to insights.

The superior progress made by the teacher-guided group is clearly revealed in Figure 7.1. Both groups started the practice with equal proficiency; but the guided group made better progress from the outset and maintained a steadier and faster rate of gain throughout the learning period. The uninstructed group, in addition to showing slower initial progress, reached a plateau at the eighth session and made practically no improvement for nearly half the three-month period. From these data, Davies concludes that "apparently it takes teaching to prevent the learner from early falling into a set pattern far below his potentialities, yet bringing some measure of success."

Three different experimenters, working with abstract materials, have indicated that *some* guidance in orienting learners toward self-discovery of principles aids them in problem solving. Using a variation of Katona's match task, diagramed below, Corman directed high school students to reduce the five squares to four by changing the position of no more than three matches [11]. Groups instructed to "avoid using

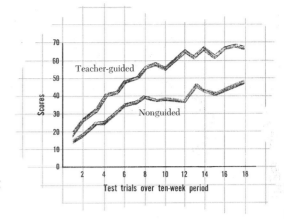

Fig. 7.1. *Teacher guidance facilitates learning archery.* (From D. R. Davies, *J. Educ. Psychol.*, 1945, vol. 36, p. 356.)

a single match as a side of two squares" and given suggestions on how to apply the principle were more successful than groups given no guidance.

The degree of teacher guidance which is most effective in facilitating discovery of principles in verbal contexts was studied by Craig and by Kittel. Craig compared the effectiveness of four degrees of teacher guidance: (1) none; (2) grouping together for study of varied instances of the same principle; (3) grouping, plus a general direction to search for a principle; and (4) grouping *and* the general direction, plus a specific statement of each appropriate principle. Both in original learning of principles and in posttests of transfer of an effective problem-solving approach to similar new items, it was found that gains consistently favored the students who were given greater degrees of teacher guidance—especially on the more difficult items. Craig concludes from these results that guidance toward discovery of principles —short of eliminating the learner's self-discovery, exploratory responses—can profitably be ample. The teacher can facilitate learning and transfer by organizing content for easier discovery of principles, by suggesting the search for principles, and by giving some illustrations of the applications of such principles [12]. However, using similar material and sixth grade pupils as his subjects, Kittel found that an intermediate amount of teacher guidance was most effective in facilitating the original mastery of concepts, their retention, their application to new problems, and the discovery of new principles [41].

KINDS OF TEACHER GUIDANCE

Teachers have developed a variety of procedures for guiding children's learning activities. They sometimes explain or demonstrate a process, give general or specific procedural directions, or suggest that

Structuring approaches to problems   249

*Systematic teacher direction of learning,
although it limits self-discoveries, facilitates
rapid early progress and the attainment of
high levels of proficiency in complex skills.*
(Adams School, Logan, Utah.)

the learner search for general concepts or principles. They may guide
him in structuring and in discovering solutions to problems by asking
insight-suggesting questions. Or they may facilitate self-discoveries
by presenting learning experiences in organized arrangements and in
developmental sequences. They may correct the learner's provisional
problem-solving attempts. And they may simply motivate pupils to
structure and solve problems independently. These procedures cover
a whole range of possibilities. On a continuum which represents the
entire range, a threefold classification would place such patterns as
explicit, systematic teacher direction at one extreme, *teacher guidance
of pupils' self-discovery learning* in the center, and *self-guided learning* at the other extreme.

Systematic teacher direction. There are many skills in which
efficient techniques and good form facilitate the attainment of high
levels of proficiency—in motor skills such as typewriting, tennis, golf,
or figure-skating; in spelling or arithmetic; or in reading, where a
flexible hierarchy of techniques of word identification contributes to
efficiency. Systematic teacher direction in such learning activities often
limits the scope of exploratory trials and self-discoveries. But it also
often produces more rapid and satisfying progress; it may enhance the
learner's pride in mastering the experts' techniques; and it may ensure
a more confident approach because at the outset the child may feel,
"I know how to do it."

As an example of systematic teacher direction, consider the comprehensive, step-by-step approach many children are taught to employ
in learning to spell. Learning to spell a word, they are instructed,
should include knowing its meaning, perceiving it analytically, gen-

eralizing about its relation to other words and to spelling principles, writing it without the model, checking it for correctness, repeating it or trying again to overcome errors, and reviewing.

In addition to the experiments already mentioned—especially those of Anderson [1], Davies [14], Keston [39], and Thompson [70]—several other studies indicate the effectiveness of systematic teacher guidance. Systematic instruction on whole-to-differentiated perception and analysis of words and on word-identification techniques has improved reading efficiency at both elementary and secondary levels [3, 21, 52]. Parker found superior achievement in geometry among high school students who were taught an inductive approach to problem solving, including the following steps: (1) recognizing a difficulty, (2) locating and defining it, (3) searching for possible solutions, (4) working out the implications of solutions, and (5) testing the validity of solutions by further observation and experimentation [57]. The group of students who were taught this problem-solving approach not only excelled in achievement a comparable group left to develop their own methods of solution; they also became better problem solvers—they persisted longer in the face of initial obstacles and they tried more varied attacks on problems.

For three small groups of four-year-olds, Goodenough and Brian compared the effectiveness of systematic teacher guidance with less explicit guidance, as the children learned to toss rings onto a 6-inch peg approximately 5 feet away [22]. Group A, consisting of 10 children, "was given no instruction whatsoever as to manner of throwing," except the direction to try to throw the rings over the post from a position inside a line marking the base. Group B, including 6 children, was given Group A's direction plus demonstration, explanation, and error correction, such as "Not quite so far next time," or "A little bit

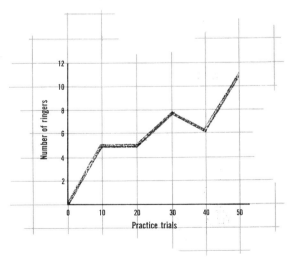

Fig. 7.2. *Resourceful, self-guided child A_{10} makes excellent progress in ring tossing.* (From Florence L. Goodenough and C. R. Brian, *J. Exp. Psychol.,* 1929, vol. 12, p. 132.)

higher so it won't hit the post." Each child was allowed, however, to work out and to use any method or methods he chose. Group C, comprised of 4 children, was given the same general directions as Group B. But, unlike Group B, the children of Group C were required to adhere to a prescribed constant method, ". . . to grasp the ring at the point of juncture, to hold it in a horizontal position, and after swinging the arm back and forth a few times, to pitch the ring forward and upward toward the post." There were frequent demonstrations of the procedure and departures from it were promptly corrected. The median gains in the number of ringers achieved in the second 25 days as compared with those made in the first 25 days were as follows: for Group A, 11.5; for Group B, 17.5; and for Group C, 20.5. Although the median gains favored the groups given more systematic guidance, there were marked intragroup differences. Some children learned well without guidance.

Self-guided learning. Among Goodenough and Brian's ring-tossing subjects in the noninstructed group, there were *some* resourceful, self-guided learners. Child A_{10}, for example, whose excellent progress is graphed in Figure 7.2, began with no ringers in the first day's practice of 20 tosses, but succeeded in mastering the task so well that he pitched 11 ringers in 20 trials on the fifteenth day! From independent trial-and-error efforts, during the first week he discovered an effective mode of attack and continued throughout the experimental period to improve his use of it.

An observation of a more mature child illustrates the application of previously achieved generalizations to a new learning problem. Janet, age 13, was given—for the first time in her experience—a toy flute with six holes. In a surprisingly short time she learned without instruction to play a simple tune. Asked how she accomplished it so quickly, she said: "From science I learned that the shorter the air chambers in a series of glasses, the higher the pitch of the tones that are produced on them. I assumed immediately that by stopping all the

holes, and releasing them one-by-one from the bottom to the top of the series, that I could get a scale of six tones. I tried that and it worked. It took several trials, however, to discover that with all the holes stopped and none of them opened, I could get the other tone at the bottom of the scale. I also found by further experimenting that I could shift the scale an octave higher by tensing my lips and blowing harder at the same time." Since this child knew how to play the piano and read music, she had two other sources of gen-

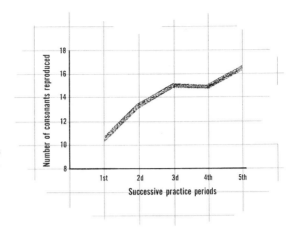

Fig. 7.3. *That children learn how to learn is shown by their improvement in memorizing successive sets of consonants, originally of equal difficulty.* (Data assembled from W. H. Winch, *Br. J. Psychol.,* 1906–08, vol. 2, pp. 52–57.)

eralization for application to the problem of learning to play the flute.

From innumerable experiences in problem solving, children—in addition to achieving solutions to specific problems—learn how to learn. In meeting new problems, they apply concepts and techniques generalized from their past experience with analogous problems. They invent and try out promising hunches. Or, as in solving a perplexing mechanical puzzle, they manipulate and interrelate the components of the problem in every conceivable way, noting what happens on each provisional trial. In this way, resourceful children often become effective self-teachers.

As a more formal demonstration of the validity of the principle of learning how to learn from self-guided experiences, let us review some data adapted from Winch's early experiment on memorizing [75]. Winch asked 36 children, 6 of each age from seven to thirteen (omitting age twelve) to try to memorize from two verbal presentations as many as they could of different sets of 12 consonants (such as *y p j t, c t b s, h r g w*). After hearing each list twice, the children wrote down as much of it as they could remember. Ten lists were presented in each of five weekly practice periods. Since the lists were of approximately equal difficulty (each containing 12 randomly arranged consonants), improvements in later practice periods may be interpreted as improvements in memorizing proficiency. The results, showing an improvement in the average of all 36 children at each succeeding practice session, are presented in Figure 7.3.

In response to questioning, some of the children revealed that their improved proficiency in memorizing resulted from discovering better ways of "how to set about the work." As examples of the self-discovered modes of attack, *s n r d* was memorized as *sin* and *red, p n* was thought of as *pen,* and *l q* was associated with *lick.*

It is clear from the examples and experiments that even without teacher direction, many children learn effective learning and problem-solving procedures. However, without teacher guidance—as has also been shown—children do not always learn the most efficient modes of attack. After acquiring a minimum measure of proficiency, many children are unlikely to develop further proficiency without teacher guidance. Despite these limitations, learning how to learn from self-guided experience is so important as an educational objective that every possible opportunity should be utilized to encourage and reward children's independent learning efforts.

Teacher guidance of pupils' self-discovery learning. To guide children in self-discovery learning, teachers arrange discovery-rich opportunities, ask leading, stimulating, and insight-provoking questions, and do less telling, demonstrating, and explaining. These procedures are well illustrated in a report by Luchins and Luchins of how a teacher led his sixth grade pupils to discover for themselves how to find the areas of geometric figures and to generalize their findings into formulas for efficient application to other areas [48].

The teacher first called the pupils' attention to a 15- by 5-inch rectangle drawn on the blackboard. A pupil who was invited to determine its area used a 1-inch cardboard square. He "laid off the square along the larger base 15 times, repeated this procedure to obtain a parallel row, and was about to start on a third row when he said, 'I don't have to do it again. It will always go 15 times this way and it goes 5 times the other way, so it's 15 times 5 squares.' He computed the area as 75 square inches [48, p. 529]."

Each pupil was then given a scissors, ruler, yellow paper, and various-sized paper rectangles. For different applications of the principle just discovered by one pupil, they were directed to cut out a 1-inch square from the yellow paper, and to use it to determine the areas of several rectangles. As they worked at their task, they were asked whether it was necessary to use the 1-inch square. Some of them generalized that it was necessary only "to find out how many squares fit each way." Using the rule, they could measure the base and the height and then multiply.

When a 10- by 4-inch parallelogram was presented, however, the pupils were baffled. Asked why they couldn't readily determine its area, they replied that the figure was "crooked," the sides were "slanted." Encouraged to try, they objected: "It's no good. The squares stick out on this side and they don't fill up the other side." However, after pondering the possibilities in the scissors, ruler, yellow paper, and the paper parallelogram, one child "cut off the two ends to make the figure straight."

Asked what she planned to do with the two ends, "she hesitated, toyed with them, put them together to form a rectangle, placed it alongside the larger rectangle, thus forming a new rectangle, and triumphantly exclaimed, 'Now nothing's wasted.'" Other pupils followed her lead. Then by asking appropriate questions, the teacher guided them to the generalization that they could convert a parallelogram into a rectangle by cutting off one slanted end and using it to fill the gap at the other end. By asking further guiding questions and by building on their prior experiences with rectangles, the teacher led them to the more explicitly verbalized generalization that the area of a parallelogram can be determined by measuring its base and height and multiplying these two dimensions together.

Merits of self-discovery learning. Although progress is sometimes slower in the initial stages, teacher-guided self-discovery learning facilitates efficient learning in many activities. It has other merits as well [38, 46, 69]. It is fun. Motivation is high because it provides the satisfactions of mastery, esteem, and enhanced evaluation of self from achieving exciting self-discoveries. Full participation in the learning activities results in greater understanding and insight. Retention is better, and if a generalization *is* forgotten, it can always be rediscovered. Because of these advantages, appropriate applications of learned concepts and skills are more likely. And perhaps most important, such teacher-guided self-discovery experiences contribute to the development of independence, resourcefulness, and ingenuity—to a problem-solving approach to life's problems. Various experiments designed to test the validity of some of these claims for teacher-guided self-discovery learning have been conducted.

Experiments on self-discovery teaching. Dawson and Ruddell, using as subjects six pairs of equated fourth grade classes, compared teacher-guided self-discovery with systematic teacher direction in learning division [16]. In the first group, the teacher—by providing visual and manipulative experiences with counting discs, spool boards, and place-value charts—led the children "to discover mathematical principles and concepts." The teachers of the systematically directed classes began each class period with an explanation of the process to be learned and then directed the pupils' work on problems illustrating it. Dawson and Ruddell found that the pupils who devoted more of their time to development of meaning and generalizations with the manipulative and visualization procedures learned more, demonstrated better retention, and transferred concepts more effectively in working new examples.

Two experimenters, Hirschi and Sobel, have compared these two general procedures in teaching algebra to several comparable pairs of ninth and tenth grade classes. Teacher-directed classes followed the text closely and were given systematic explanations of the abstract principles. The self-discovery classes participated in a concrete, inductive approach in which the teacher guided them to self-discovery and generalizations of concepts. In general, both experimenters found the two procedures equally effective, with two exceptions. On one specially devised test, Hirschi's self-discovery classes surpassed the teacher-directed classes [35]. And for pupils of higher intelligence, Sobel found the differences on both immediate and delayed-retention tests favored the inductive, self-discovery method [64]. In a number of related experiments, additional data favorable to self-discovery learning have been contributed [24, 25, 51, 53]. Because of the several variables determining the relative effectiveness of these methods, however, comprehensive evaluation of them will require more and better-designed experiments in other curriculum areas.

In the meantime, it seems prudent to assume that all three methods—systematic teacher direction, self-guided learning, and teacher guidance of pupils' self-discovery learning—have an appropriate place in every curriculum area. We need to learn to use them all more effectively. For more appropriate and effective application of the teacher-guided self-discovery method, we need a deeper understanding of the process of problem solving.

PROBLEM SOLVING ANALYZED

As we consider how problems are solved, let us recall our observations on the problem-solving behavior of the children who discovered how to find the areas of a rectangle and a parallelogram, and of the quick mastery by the thirteen-year-old child of the toy flute. Let us remember also instances of our own problem-solving activities. Such observations and several psychological studies indicate that problem solving is a multiple-aspect process. It involves a motivated, goal-directed individual who, being temporarily impeded in his attempts to attain his goal, successively restructures the problem situation and produces and applies provisionally to it varied, integrated patterns of percepts, concepts, and generalizations.

Guided both by his background of already-achieved generalizations and by cues in the problem situation itself, the individual approaches a problem in a tentative, try-and-see attitude. Structuring the problem situation perceptually and conceptually in a certain way, he produces—from past experience and invention—a solution which he tries provisionally, because—in a tentative hierarchy of possibilities— it promises to solve the problem. Perceiving the effects of his goal-directed tries, the individual confirms or disconfirms his tentative expectations. Failure to achieve a satisfying solution leads to restructuring of the problem situation and to the production of different solutions. The solutions—as responses to difficulties—are often recombinations of products of the individual's past experience. But for resourceful individuals they are also, in varying degree, creative inventions. The multiple-response approach is continued until a fitting and satisfying solution is reached. This approach is one of grouping, segregating, and centering of components in the problem situation and the perception of fitting and nonfitting relationships [74]. The solution involves a reorganization of the individual's cognitive and motivational structure, which becomes a guide to more adequate adjustments both to the original and to related problem situations. Analysis of this general problem-solving process—guided especially by Duncker [18] and following Thorndike's outline [71]—yields the following abstracted features, although not in this logical order.

1. *Sensitivity to problems.* Secure and confident children—inherently curious and continually rewarded by their growing understanding—find numerous problems as they explore, raise questions, and experiment in educationally stimulating home and school environments. For example, alert to the differences in their sounds, second grade children asked: "Why do some bells go 'tinkle, tinkle,' and others go 'ding, dong'?" Their teacher, sensing the opportunity for significant self-discovery learning, guided their problem solving—including experiments with rubber bands, tuning forks, water glasses, and musical instruments—to the discovery and generalization of the relation between pitch difference and vibration frequencies [55].

At the secondary school level, an adolescent's observation, curiosity, and questions led to "real life" problem solving in the chemistry laboratory: "The copper connection on the battery cable of our car," he said, "came loose yesterday. We found that it was covered with some bluish material and was completely eaten through in one place. What did that—the fumes from the battery, the heat from the motor, the electric current passing through it, a leak in the battery allowing acid to get on it, or what? [61, p. 606]" Having recognized a problem and produced some tentative hypotheses, this adolescent and very probably his by then well-motivated classmates were ready for the next step in problem solving.

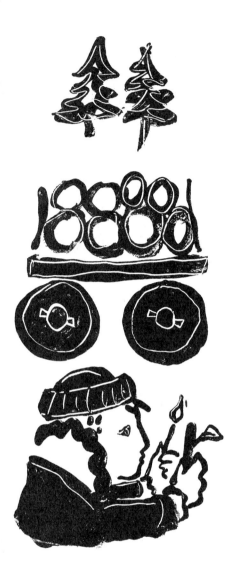

2. Structuring. As a problem is faced, accepted, and examined, a situation which is first vaguely structured becomes more differentiated, often in a succession of closer and closer approximations [28, 30]. The goal, the conditions of the problem, the materials for its solution, and the difficulties which emerge are all perceived and conceptualized from the point of view of the individual's functionally organized background of assumptions and generalizations. From this orientation, the problem is gradually clarified and defined. The difficulties—the gaps to be bridged—are identified. The parallelogram, for example, whose area was wanted, initially appeared to the sixth grade children perplexingly new and undifferentiated. As a first approach, it was perceived as analogous to the familiar rectangle—like the latter, it had width and length (which are factors in area). But the discriminated differences presented difficulties. The ends were "slanted" and the figure was "crooked." The gap to be bridged which emerged—only vaguely at first—became how to convert the unfamiliar parallelogram into a familiar and manageable rectangle.

Similarly, by leading questions, the teacher could guide the chemistry students to a more differentiated structuring of the problem of the loosened battery cable: "Do batteries exude fumes? Does the battery become hot from the motor? How long have copper wires conducted electric current without deterioration? And how could the effect of battery acid on a copper wire be determined? [61]" The questions themselves suggest solutions.

3. Production of provisional solutions. As bridges of the gap in the defined problem situation, solutions seem to emerge spontaneously as interpretations and tentative ways of overcoming the difficulty. They often stem—by transfer—from general, prior, functional solutions of similar problems. The 13-year-old child was able to master the toy flute quickly because she had functionally available from past experience the concept of the relation of the air-chamber length to pitch, knowledge of the musical scale, and well-practiced skill in representing the pattern of a tune symbolically in music notation. The utility of such prior experience in problem solving depends upon its extent, variety, functional organization, and upon the individual's sagacity and flexibility in restructuring it pertinently in relation to his goal [32]. The effective problem solver, however, does not simply ask himself: "What do I already know that I can use in this problem?" Instead, he focuses his attention on the probable gaps and on the potential resources for bridging them, in the problem situation itself [74]. For example, the succession of holes in the bore of the flute suggested themselves to the flute novice as meeting her need for a musical scale. And in the opposite slanted ends of the parallelogram, the geometry students discovered both a relevant gap and the resources for bridging it. For novel problems especially, the solutions constitute both cognitive restructurings of the problem solver's pertinent past experience and creative inventions.

As the problem is clarified and defined, the problem solver constructs a search model as a general guide to discovering a general, functional solution. From the achieved functional solution, specific solutions meeting particular conditions of the problem situation emerge. For example, as a solitary homesteader in a mountainous wilderness of British Columbia, 300 miles north of Vancouver, Ralph Edwards needed a trolley to transport logs for his home. He constructed wheels of well-rounded logs with smooth birch surfacings for rims. But what to do for bearings, with neither metal nor forge, perplexed him. Structuring the problem, his search model became "some tough shapeable material." This functional solution led him to a unique, specific solution. He had noticed and now remembered that partially burned wood was hard to cut—even with a sharp ax. Although he had never heard of such a thing being used, scorched birch, he thought, could be shaped, polished, and fitted into his wheels and shaft, and, greased with bear fat, they might be tough enough [66].

The search model guiding the children in determining the area of the parallelogram was an attempt to analyze the unfamiliar parallelogram into a more familiar figure for which a formula for finding the area was already known. At least two specific solutions are possible. Generalizing from functionally organized experience with rectangles, the children imaginatively restructured their perception of the parallelogram to form a rectangle

for which the area was recognized as $A = bh$. Guided by the concept of triangles in restructuring the parallelogram, however, it might also have been imaginatively analyzed into two congruent triangles

for which the area is recognized as $A = 2\dfrac{bh}{2}$ [71].

For the problem of the loosened battery cable, the search model or guiding functional solution was "something which caused the wire to deteriorate." The questions raised suggested specific possibilities to be tested—fumes, heat, wear, and battery acid. New, inventive solutions, such as Ralph Edwards' bearings, result from radical reformulations of functional solutions. And sometimes the discovery of a new specific solution may lead to a whole family of solutions, classifiable under a new general functional solution. Since the invention of rayon, for example, a great variety of synthetic fibers has been created.

4. Evaluating implications of provisional solutions. As tentative solutions of the difficulty-as-perceived are produced, they are imaginatively evaluated against the symbolically conceived goal and the conditions of the problem. Before carving the toughened burnt-birch bearings, Ralph Edwards imagined their carrying the weight of his heavy logs. Before actually cutting a slanted end off the parallelogram, the children conceptualized it as filling the slanting gap at the opposite end to form a rectangle. And implications of some of the hypotheses on causes of the battery cable deterioration could be tentatively evaluated from remembered experiences of the interested students. In bringing such experience to bear on the problem, their teacher might ask or they might ask themselves: "Have you ever observed fumes exuding from a battery? Is motor heat on the battery sufficient to burn a copper wire? How long have copper wires been known to carry an electric current without deterioration? [61]"

5. Testing plausible solutions. As plausible hypotheses survive the tentative evaluations, they are tested—for consistency with all the conditions of the problem, by appeals to superior sources of knowledge (such as experts, books, or teachers), or by experimental tests. Testing his burnt-birch bearings in his trolley loaded with logs, Ralph Edwards found that they worked. By conducting tests, the students could determine the effects of sulfuric acid on copper wire. And the children could check the possibility of converting the parallelogram into a rectangle by actually reconstructing the figure—placing a cut-off end of the parallelogram at the opposite end to form a rectangle whose area could then be measured by successive applications of the 1-inch square.

6. Generalizing, formulating a conclusion. Working solutions to problems apparently sometimes emerge unverbalized. Hendrix, for example, has reported that students directed to add continually increased successions of the first n odd numbers—first, $1 + 3$; second, $1 + 3 + 5$; then $1 + 3 + 5 + 7$, and so on—discovered and applied effectively the rule that "the sum of the first n odd numbers equals n^2," without verbalizing it [33]. Sometimes explicit and precise verbalizations of solutions develop gradually following vague functional operation of a concept. For example, Heidbreder's subjects first thought that the nonsense word *mank* in her experiment represented "symmetry," then "many small objects," and finally they perceived its precise meaning, "six of anything [28, p. 187]." Often, however, grasping a principle leads spontaneously to verbalizing it. Seven-year-old Karren was directed to discover and to point out on a card, showing five objects, the one object that was different. She paused at the third card in a series of such test items and spontaneously verbalized the guiding principle: "That's a kitten [pointing]. They're all dogs [pointing to the other four objects]."

Such self-initiated or teacher-guided verbalization of solutions ensures more effective applications. Thus it was desirable for the children to formulate verbally their solutions to the problem of determining the areas of the geometric figures in words such as these: "The area of a parallelogram equals the base times the altitude." As will be demonstrated in Chapter 9, verbalization of inductively learned principles facilitates the attainment of an explicit understanding of them. It also facilitates the retention of these principles and their application to varied, new problem situations.

7. Extending implications of generalizations. Problem solving does not end with a solution. It is a continuing process—each solution leading to new applications and implications for further problem-solving activities. Beauchamp has contributed a good illustration of this aspect of problem solving in connection with teaching students to discover and to generalize the requirements for burning [2]. He suggests that pupils may be asked to recall their experiences with burning —in building fires, tending them, and putting them out. Then questions are raised which require explanations of the process. "What kinds of material burn? Why do small pieces of wood catch fire more quickly than larger pieces?" Answers to these and other questions lead to a search for more knowledge or to experimentation, as a result of which the requirements for burning are formulated. To make the generalization functional, however, the pupils are now guided beyond solutions to the problems already presented. They are led to the observation that the generalization formulated should explain *all* situations where burning does or does not occur. New questions are encouraged: "Why is it necessary to strike a match? Why do you blow on a fire to make it burn and blow on a match to put it out?" From consideration of such implications, students are led both to extended applications and —if they are sensitive—to further challenging problems which should yield to the problem-solving procedures here analyzed.

A practical question remains concerning the role of problem solving in teacher-guided self-discovery learning: By what kinds of guidance can teachers develop in children and youth interest and effectiveness in independent problem solving?

TEACHER GUIDANCE IN SELF-DISCOVERY LEARNING

Our analysis of problem solving suggests the following strategic places and ways for effective guidance of self-discovery learning:

1. *Be alert to opportunities for encouraging and rewarding problem-solving effort.* Being aware of the characteristics of problem-solving behavior just described, teachers are alerted to opportunities for guiding and rewarding various manifestations of it in their students. By rewarding children's initiative in problem solving, teachers can encourage continued and extended applications of it.

The effectiveness of rewarding problem-solving effort is well illustrated by an incident observed in a high school class in social studies. The students were waiting expectantly to see a film. When the switches of the projector were turned on, however, nothing happened. With an angry remark about the inefficiency of the audio-visual aids department, the teacher announced that they would have to forego the film. To John, however, the difficulty was a *problem,* not an insurmountable obstacle. His first reaction was "Maybe we can fix it." Then, examining the light in the projector, the threading of the film, and the cord carrying the current from a wall outlet, he discovered that the supplementary cord and the cord from the projector were not joined securely. When this was adjusted, the class and their teacher enjoyed the film. They also appreciated John's problem-solving attitude. There were many subsequent occasions when similar problems were encountered. On these occasions the teacher took advantage of the opportunity not only to reward John but to encourage a similar problem-solving attitude among his classmates, with such approval as "Remember how John's problem solving with the projector saved us from giving up too soon?"

2. *Give guidance only as needed.* When approaching a new problem, children are likely to hesitate, to fumble, to structure it ineffectively, and to produce some unpromising solutions. In the usual temporary period of uncertainty, the child needs time, freedom to make mistakes, and patience from his teacher as he orients himself and produces tentative solutions. Since too much guidance results in overdependent learners, the child needs the opportunity to utilize his own resources—information, skills, generalizations, and inventive capacity. First, a minimum of group guidance should be given to aid pupils in structuring a new problem; then, as children work through a problem, guidance should be given individually as needed. Although teacher guidance should be minimized, it should not be withheld; persistent failure to reach a solution or long-continued floundering does not foster problem-solving interest or confidence [15, 59].

3. *Promote a confident approach.* Some children do not distinguish between *problems* and *questions* for which they have already learned answers. They do not realize that problems require a creative problem-solving attack. If they do not immediately see a solution, they are baffled, give up without trying, or overdependently expect more teacher guidance than they require. They should be made aware of the process of problem solving and they should be encouraged to make problem-solving efforts. Henderson and Pingry suggest explaining, "John, you are not supposed to *know* how to work that problem. You are supposed to *figure out* a way to work it [32, pp. 248–249]." Suggesting to the student that he clarify the problem by rereading it, that he relate it to similar problems already solved, diagram it, plan and estimate a solution, and other such hints should help to initiate a problem-solving approach [20, 32, 46, 56].

For developing confidence in problem solving, students also need a free, problem-solving climate in which they feel at liberty to contribute provisional solutions, to ask questions, and to develop ideas—both their own and those of other children. Teachers can contribute to such an atmosphere by demonstrating their willingness to accept uncertain and even unpromising hunches as provisional trials. Learning from mistakes what *won't* work is, after all, progress toward what *will* work. Teachers also create a problem-solving climate by providing individual and cooperative problem-solving opportunities which lead to satisfying results and by giving students rewarding approval for their efforts.

4. *Organize concepts functionally for varied applications.* Children often approach complex problems with anxiety and bewilderment because, as they say, "We never know what to do. They don't tell us if we should add or subtract . . . [or] use all the numbers [76, p. 125]." Developing a functional organization of concepts helps to avoid such confusion. For example, with effective teacher guidance of pupils' self-discovery learning in arithmetic, the experiences first and second grade children have in counting objects and in combining and separating them prepare them for understanding addition as a way of putting things together and subtraction as a way of taking things apart. Such

a developing functional organization of concepts led a resourceful second grade child to announce, as he paused to reflect on his discovery, "When I learned that $3 + 2 = 5$, I really learned four things: that $3 + 2 = 5$, that $2 + 3 = 5$, that $5 - 3 = 2$, and that $5 - 2 = 3$." Subsequently in the third grade, these self-discovery-led children are set for the discovery that multiplication—as an extension of addition—is a way of combining equal groups, and that division—as an extension of subtraction—is a way of taking apart or separating equal groups. Such learning produces generalizations which have wide application.

When children discover, for example, that three groups of four each equal twelve, and that twelve can be separated into such equal groups as 2 sixes, 3 fours, 4 threes, or 6 twos, they are ready to learn the relationship between multiplication and division. Learning to think of 3 and 4 or 2 and 6 as factors of the product 12, they generalize the equation: $N_1 \times N_2 = N_3$. Given the factors, they multiply to determine the product $(3 \times 4 = N_3)$. Given one of the factors and the product, they divide the product by the known factor to determine the unknown factor $(N_1 \times 4 = 12$ or $3 \times N_2 = 12)$. As these children progress through the elementary and high school grades, they discover many applications of this important principle of problem solving. They find it applicable to such grouping and separating problems as "How many 4-cent stamps can you buy for 28¢?" In the equation they see that $N_1 \times 4 = 28$ [72, p. 323].

Later they find that it applies in the measurement of areas. For example, upon discovering that length times width equals area, the student uses the equation to solve such a problem as this: "A floor containing 180 square feet is 12 feet wide. How long is it?" In the equation, $N_1 \times 12 = 180$ [72, p. 323]. This type of thinking is found equally applicable to problems of percentage, interest, gain and loss, insurance, rate and distance, and, in high school, to varied algebraic uses of the equation.

Such interrelating of concepts, the functional organization of them, and expansions of them with each new insight lead to enriched understanding and extended applications. This principle of effective learning—as we shall discover in Chapter 10—is the heart of transfer of learning.

5. *Provide concrete working materials which facilitate discovery of concepts.* As an illustration of how concrete materials can lead to discovery of concepts, Mulholland describes how fifth grade children discovered that they could compute with fractions by manipulating colored paper discs cut into halves, fourths, eighths, thirds, sixths, and twelfths. For example, using brown discs cut into eight equal parts, Roy announced: "Eight eighths equal a whole." Jane observed: "Two of my eighths are the same as a fourth." And Elsie explained: "Six of the eighths and one fourth make a whole [54]."

6. Provide sequences of problems so that preceding problems contribute functional solutions or "hints" for application to succeeding problems. The child's mastery of the toy flute as a product of an appropriate background of science and music experience illustrates this principle. Schafer-Simmern finds that preliminary experience in molding animals and other objects from plaster of Paris is effective in learning how to shade two-dimensional drawings to give them depth and body. Another illustration shows that understanding of the abstract expressions of factoring, products of monomials and binomials, and of other algebraic expressions can be achieved from a developmental sequence of experiences. The figures shown will help us to explain this sequence. First, students are directed to find the areas of parts 1, 2, 3, 4, and the whole—using

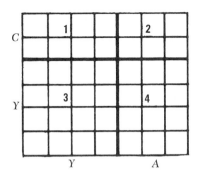

the lined spaces which permit counting the units of space. Second, they are asked to identify the factors for each area, as C and Y for 1. Third, they are directed to find the areas of the unlined figures. Fourth, they are guided to discover the meanings of such algebraic expressions as $Y(Y+C)$, $Y(Y+A)$, and $(Y+C)(Y+A)$. Generalizations developed from these experiences should then be extended in application to such problems as "What is the product of $(X+A)$ and $(X-A)$? [45]"

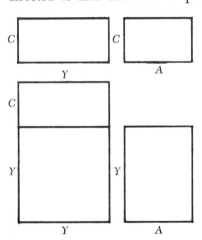

7. Encourage flexibility in restructuring the problem. In attempting to assemble the parts of a caliper, an adolescent boy failed after a long trial because he persisted in his first assumption that it was (when assembled) an instrument for measuring *outside* diameters of objects. He returned the next day, however, for another trial. Then, freer to restructure the problem, he quickly assembled a caliper for measuring the *inside* diameters of cylinders. After a thorough trial of one search model, it is often effective to perceive the problem in a new way—to find a different difficulty or other possible solutions. A suggestion to try solving a related problem first—one more general, or more specific, or a part of the original problem—may suggest clues. Sometimes—as in the example mentioned—restructuring a problem situation is more readily achieved by leaving it temporarily [13, 19, 32]. Maier has demonstrated the effectiveness of such suggestions in improving the problem-solving efficiency of college students. He found that their approach to problems requiring novel mechanical constructions was facilitated by an explanation of the nature of problem solving and such hints as this: "Search for a difficulty and try to overcome it. Don't persist in unpromising approaches. Keep your mind open for new interpretations and possible solutions [49]."

There is a hazard that systematically taught procedures of problem solving in such subjects as mathematics or science may handicap students. They may become stereotyped in their approach. When they meet problems requiring a modification of the initially learned procedure or situations where an alternative approach would be more efficient, they may be unadaptable [47]. To promote flexibility of approach, teachers should encourage children to consider alternative approaches to a problem; they should give the pupils occasions for *varied* applications of the concepts and principles they learn. Teacher-guided self-discovery learning may also facilitate flexibility in problem solving.

8. Stimulate production of relevant hypotheses. As the problem solver focuses on his goal and tries to comprehend all the conditions and materials of the problem in relation to it, hypotheses usually occur. Sometimes, however, a catalyst is needed. Wishing to draw a cowboy riding a horse, a seven-year-old sat immobilized because, he said, "I don't know how." Only a hint was required, however ("Could you use ovals for the body, legs, neck, etc.?"), to initiate creative productivity. Leading questions and a suggestion that the pupil ask himself such questions as the following may stimulate productive thinking: "Have you seen this problem before? Can you restate the problem more functionally and concisely? What in the data could help you solve the problem? [32, p. 257]" Sometimes the suggestion to start with the goal and work back to the conditions given is effective [13, 18, 32].

At other times, supplemental resources may provide ideas. In writing a short story, a high school girl sought a word giving just the right connotation to this sentence: "The boy————the snake." The words "looked at" did not imply the examination of the coloring and markings which she intended. "Examined" implied to her a close examination and manipulation as though the snake were held in the hand, but the boy was really viewing it from a distance. "Watched" was rejected because it attributed movement to the snake, and it was perfectly quiet. "What other possible words are there?" she asked. A suggestion by the teacher that she consult Webster's *Unabridged Dictionary* and Roget's *Thesaurus of English Words and Phrases* for synonyms of the words she had considered produced several additional possibilities and facilitated this stage of her problem solving.

Kogan—from his experience as an engineer—considers the search for an analogous problem and its functional solution as a major strategy in the production of relevant hypotheses. As an approach, he suggests guiding students to a related previously met specific problem—to the difficulty to be surmounted in it, or to the general class of such problems, and to the general functional solution of them. From the general way of solving such problems, it is often possible to derive a specific solution which fits the conditions of a particular problem [43]. Connor and Hawkins suggest that this approach be used in self-discovery learning when a pupil is baffled in structuring or in producing solutions for a problem. Instead of explaining or demonstrating that particular problem, the teacher might give the student another simpler problem illustrating the same principle. In teaching understanding and appreciation of Linnaeus's system of biological classification, a science teacher first has his students sort a variety of objects according to certain basic characteristics: (1) Is the object black or white? (2) Is it made of paper, cloth, or plastic? (3) Is it triangular, circular, square, or rectangular? (4) Is it marked with a dot, hole, plus sign, letter, or number? After working with simple, analogous problems, pupils are often able to transfer the common pertinent principle to the successful solution of more complex problems [10, p. 25]. From such an approach they learn not only the solution of a particular problem but how to solve problems.

9. *Learn to check provisional solutions independently.* Problem solving, as a trial-and-check process, involves perceiving the effects of provisional solutions as a basis for confirming correct hypotheses and for motivating a search for alternative approaches when needed. Procedures and criteria for checking independently the adequacy of provisional trials is especially important in self-discovery learning. Checking specific solutions against approximate estimates is one way to develop independence and ingenuity in self-discovery learning. In checking his solutions of the problem, $8\frac{3}{4} \div 2\frac{7}{8} = 3\frac{1}{23}$, Sam says: "$8\frac{3}{4}$ is about 9; $2\frac{7}{8}$ is about 3. $9 \div 3 = 3$ . . . My exact answer . . . [of] $3\frac{1}{23}$ . . . is a sensible answer when compared with my estimate [62, p. 35]." Self-checking can also be achieved by semiconcrete procedures. For example, $\frac{1}{2} \times \frac{1}{3} = \frac{1}{6}$ can be checked by the diagramed solution [58].

10. Provide experience in solving comprehensible "real life" problems. Only challenging, complex problems in which children are genuinely interested provide integrated experience in all aspects of problem solving. Recognition and formulation of the problem, collection and organization of data, structuring approaches and testing provisional solutions, and formulating and extending the implications of generalizations are possible in real life problems such as that of the battery cable's deterioration or the unit "The Water Supply in Our Community," which we described in Chapter 1 and analyzed in Chapter 2.

SUMMARY

As children work to master the concepts and skills of the elementary and secondary school curriculum, they also—under appropriate teacher guidance—learn how to learn and how to solve problems. Efficient learning of subject matter and the concomitant improvement of problem-solving skills are important and reciprocally related educational objectives. Effective teacher guidance facilitates the attainment of both.

Three general types of guidance and learning are distinguishable: systematic teacher direction, self-guided learning, and teacher guidance of pupils' self-discovery learning. Each probably has an appropriate place in every area of the curriculum. However, since teacher guidance of pupils' self-discovery learning is most likely to develop independent problem-solving attitudes and skills, it deserves extensive application.

Effective teacher guidance of pupils' self-discovery learning depends on an understanding of problem solving. Seven phases of problem-solving behavior are identified: recognizing a problem, structuring an approach to it, producing provisional solutions, evaluating the implications of provisional solutions, testing plausible solutions, generalizing, and extending the implications of generalizations.

To facilitate effective teacher guidance of self-discovery learning, a number of practical suggestions are offered:

Be alert to opportunities for encouraging and rewarding problem-solving effort.
Give guidance only as needed.
Promote confidence and a free problem-solving climate.
Develop functional organizations of concepts.
Provide experiences which facilitate discovery of concepts.
Arrange problem solving in effective developmental sequences.
Encourage flexibility.
Stimulate production of relevant hypotheses.

Guide learners to become independent in checking their solutions. And provide for experience with real-life problems.

Teacher guidance—especially of children's self-discovery learning and problem solving—is intimately related to the other conditions of effective learning. As we discovered in the preceding chapter, opportunities for "real-life," creative problem solving and curiosity-satisfying excursions into the by-paths prompted by student interests release high, intrinsic motivation. Thus the teacher, as a good guide in problem-solving learning is also a good motivator. As we have learned in this chapter and as we shall elaborate further in the chapter on transfer, generalizing is important both in structuring approaches and in finding solutions to problems. At its nucleus, problem-solving learning is a goal-directed, trial-and-check process.

GUIDES FOR STUDY, REVIEW, AND APPLICATION

1. Assuming that you are motivated to master Russian, fly-fishing, or the principles of learning in teaching, how would you approach the task? How would you begin your learning efforts?
2. Cite illustrations which show that children's learning and problem solving are purposeful and guided by cognitive "maps."
3. Are teachers really necessary? Cite experiments and examples which show that some teacher guidance is likely to help learners of all ages in mastering skills, concepts, and general principles.
4. What do you think of the suggestion that teaching should consist of less telling and showing how and more of arrangement for pupil self-discovery? Describe and evaluate teacher guidance of pupils' self-discovery learning and cite illustrations of it.
5. Using the outline of the process and features of problem solving, analyze experienced or observed specific examples of problem solving.
6. Read or observe what seems to be an example of effective teacher guidance of pupil self-discovery learning (The film *Learning Is Searching*, New York University Film Library, is an excellent example). How many of our suggestions for facilitating such learning can you find illustrated?

Chapter 8

THE TRIAL-AND-CHECK PROCESS IN LEARNING

Structuring an approach is only the initial step in many learning tasks. In mastering language, computational, musical, or other complex skills, both *repeated trials* and *checking their consequences* are equally important and long-continued steps. When we analyzed the seven essential conditions of learning, we separated these two closely articulated conditions and designated them "repeated trials" and "perception of effects." Actually, in the goal-directed trial-and-check process of learning, they are complementary and often occur almost simultaneously. In this chapter, therefore, we shall discuss them together, but we shall define the distinctive role which each has. Although "practice" sometimes implies repeated trials only, we often give the term a broader connotation to include both the making and checking of provisional trials. As an introduction to a systematic analysis of these conditions of learning, let us observe their operation in a rehearsal of such a typical complex skill as madrigal singing.

During regularly scheduled practice periods and in repeated

trials, the singers strive for improvement in ensemble attack and release, blend and balance, suitability of dynamics, and musical discrimination. To check the correctness of their goal-directed trials, the
members and director of the group ask themselves after each performance (sometimes recorded): "Are the attacks clean? Are the
releases exact? Were the soft and loud passages contrasting and appropriate so as to produce the desired musical effect?" In the evaluation of provisional trials, correct procedures are confirmed as a basis
for more confident performance next time. And the faulty passages
to be remedied in a subsequent rehearsal are marked on the score.

From this description, we can see the intimate relationship between provisional trials and checking results. But let us also try to
see the unique role of each factor.

THE ROLE OF REPEATED TRIALS IN LEARNING

Experience has taught us well that long-continued practice extended
over several years is necessary to attain high levels of proficiency in
any subject or skill—language, mathematics, science, music, art, or
sports. To attain virtuoso skill on the violin, for example, may take
ten or twelve years of three to five hours of daily practice. The
archery scores shown in Figure 8.1 typify the gradual improvement
which results from such practice.

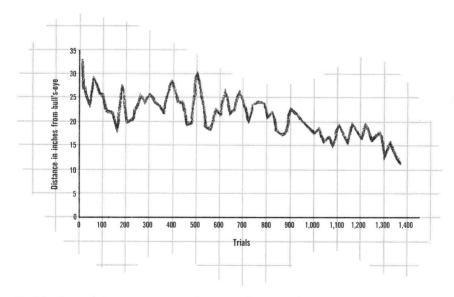

Fig. 8.1. *Progress from practice in archery for subject C, who achieved the best
final score of several subjects, in over 1,300 shots. (Championship scores at the
time were 8 to 11 inches from the bull's-eye.)* (After K. S. Lashley, *Papers from
the Dept. of Marine Biol.,* Carnegie Inst. of Washington, 1915, vol. 7, p. 117.)

Seeing the results of practice

Language student hears her accent

Warm-up practice helps skiers (or you) . . .

Routine drill is often meaningless

to get a good start

*Practice plays
a complex role in learning:
it may improve, leave unaffected,
or even impair proficiency*

The young adult whose record is reproduced in this figure used a 6-foot bow which required a pull of 44 pounds. His arrows were 28 inches long, and his 48-inch target had a 10-inch bull's-eye. The target was set at a distance of 40 yards and had a 14-foot square of muslin screen around it to permit registering outside shots. Because of his talent and his opportunity to study and observe other learners for two weeks prior to beginning his own overt practice, this individual's initial score is much better than that of the usual beginner. Despite these advantages, however, he is still—after more than 1,300 shots (12 per day)—far from championship performance. In the trial-and-check process, which constituted his practice (in the broad sense) and produced the fluctuating but gradually improving scores, he tried out different methods in successive trials. He eliminated interfering habits, achieved insights into better methods, and improved adjustments in aiming and loosing arrows [39].

The mastery of many school tasks requires similar amounts of practice. For example, a record of a five-year-old child's progress in reading shows that he gradually advanced from recognition of no word on the first day to recognition of 43 different words on the thirty-fifth day. Words were presented to him on separate cards and it was found that several presentations of each word were required before he could recognize the word immediately and confidently. *School*, for example, required 18 exposures [26]. Among a group of third grade children, it was found that the discovery and memorization of the correct products for 39 multiplication combinations (3×7 to 9×9) required an average of 19.2 repetitions per combination [71, p. 113].

Sometimes, however, a concept is mastered in a single trial, as was demonstrated by the third grade child whose introduction to borrowing in subtraction followed his mastery of carrying in addition. He immediately grasped the significant generalization and announced: "Why, it's just the opposite of carrying." In other instances, despite large amounts of practice, improvement does not occur. From the sixth to the fifteenth week of practice in archery, for example, Davies's uninstructed college students failed to make appreciable gains (see page 249).

In other learning activities, practice seems to impair proficiency. Seashore and Bavelas report an instance of deterioration rather than improvement from practice. In a succession of 15 trials, the experimenters coaxed 18 children to "draw another man; this time a better one." Bored with the repetitions and receiving no approval for their efforts, the children—with two exceptions—tended to draw more hurriedly and to produce poorer drawings [58]. One subject's deteriorating performance is graphed in Figure 8.2.

These illustrations indicate that practice plays a complex role in

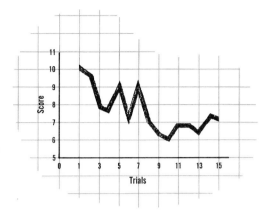

Fig. 8.2. *Bored repetitions of drawing a man produce deterioration of a child's performance, as is indicated by a tendency to include fewer differentiated features.* (Adapted from H. G. Seashore and A. Bavelas, *J. Genet. Psychol.*, 1942, vol. 61, pp. 279–314.)

the learning process. They show that practice may improve, leave unaffected, or even impair proficiency. Although experience demonstrates that practice *is* an essential condition of learning, its effectiveness apparently depends upon the nature of the practice, as well as upon the simultaneous operation of the other conditions of learning.

WHAT PRACTICE IS

An industrial arts supervisor was perplexed to observe an adolescent boy melting solder into the joint of two pieces of metal. Apparently the boy had no effective goal-directing idea since he was not checking the consequences of his efforts. To the supervisor's query on what he was doing, the boy answered: "I am practicing welding." The supervisor responded: "But you are not making any improvement. You're just pouring the solder on in a way it can't possibly hold the pieces together." The boy replied: "That's why I'm practicing, my welds haven't held. But if I practice, I'll get better, won't I?" As we shall see, such confidence in sheer repetition is most naïve.

Practice as repetition. Several experiments demonstrate that a mechanical repetition of concepts or skills does not produce improvement in them. In one of these experiments, Thorndike read and reread to his adult subjects sentences like the following [63, p. 19]:

> Jackson Craig and his son struggled often.
> Charlotte Dean and her friend studied easily.
> Mary Borah and her companion complained dully.
> Norman Foster and his mother bought much.

After 10 repetitions of the 10-sentence selection from which these sample sentences are taken, he asked his subjects such questions as—

> What word came next after "and his son struggled often"?
> What word came next after "Norman Foster and his mother"?

The trial-and-check process in learning   273

Although the facts needed for answering these two types of questions had been repeated an equal number of times, the percentages of correct answers for them were distinctly different. For the first question, in which "struggled often" had been followed 10 times by the beginning of the next sentence, only 2 per cent of the answers were correct. The 10 repetitions yielded practically no learning. For the second question, calling for the predicate of the sentence beginning "Norman Foster and his mother," 81 per cent of the answers were correct. In this instance the 10 repetitions produced a relatively high degree of mastery of the sequence. On the basis of these results and similar data from other experiments, Thorndike concludes that "repetition of a connection in the sense of mere sequence of the two things in time has then very, very little power, perhaps none, as a cause of learning [63, p. 28]." He explained the advantage of the second type of sequence by his principle of "belonging." It is fitting to complete "Norman Foster and his mother" with "bought much." But as a sequel to "and his son struggled often," "Charlotte Dean" does not belong.

It is also possible, however, to explain the memorization of the sequence "Norman Foster and his mother" and "bought much" in terms of our seven conditions of effective learning. Besides repetition, several other conditions were present which facilitated learning. Supplying a predicate for a subject is a product of *transfer* from much prior experience with sentences. It is *perceived* (checked) as making sense. And completing a logical sequence—resolving an unfinished problem—is *motivationally satisfying* or reinforcing.

Experiments with school subject matter also bring out the relative ineffectiveness of repetition alone in learning. Symonds has shown that "pure repetition of correct form" alone is insufficient for mastery of correct language usage [60]. From such practice, sixth grade pupils made no appreciable gains in correction of usage errors. Only when the teaching incorporated the learning of general grammatical principles, when there was teacher guidance in applying rules for choosing correct constructions, and when both correct and incorrect forms were presented and perceived as right or wrong—only then did appreciable gains occur.

Other experiments show that degree of mastery is not directly proportionate to frequency of repetition of concepts. In teaching 26 concepts in fractions and denominate numbers to fifth grade children, Harap and Mapes found no relationship between extent of mastery of these concepts and the frequency of their repetition in arithmetic projects. In functional study units which involved making candy and conducting a candy sale, the children learned and used the concepts as they had need for them. For example, concept No. 2 (multiplying an integer by a common fraction) was used 51 times, while concept

No. 10 (dividing a common fraction by a common fraction) occurred only once. Yet the percentage of mastery for both concepts was 94. The rank order correlation between frequency of repetition (ranging from 0 to 112 times) of all the concepts and the percentage of mastery of them was found by the writer to be zero. In this project, where the understanding of fractions and the meaningful use of them were emphasized, differences in the number of repetitions proved relatively unimportant [23].

Such experiments as these indicate that repetition alone is insufficient for learning; that its effectiveness depends on the simultaneous operation of other conditions of learning; and that, because of the greater importance of these other conditions, degree of mastery of a concept is sometimes unrelated to frequency of repetition.

Practice as opportunity for discovery. Observation of instances of effective learning reveals that practice rarely consists of mechanical, unchanged repetition of responses. What is repeated is the *attempt* to achieve goals—better goals and by more efficient procedures. Practice affords an opportunity to discover or to try out an idea and to test its correctness and value.

As an example of the role of discovery in practice, let us observe a high school student's attempts to illustrate in a drawing the concept of a child's interest in science. Beginning with an imprecisely structured goal and with only a vague idea of how to achieve it, she took 12 practice trials before achieving a satisfying picture! In trial 1, she drew a boy kneeling to examine a flower. Then another idea occurred; trial 2 and, with some refinement of the same idea, trial 3 depicted the kneeling boy examining an insect under a reading glass. In trial 4, still another idea emerged; the boy, seated before a telescope, was making notes as he looked at the moon and a star. By trial 5, the concept changed again; and the boy was drawn standing with a long-handled butterfly net in his hand. In trial 6, the figure of the boy was improved and a sketch of a butterfly was added. Trial 7 consisted only of sketchy, rough outlines to suggest motion. Having created a satisfactory subject, the student developed the concept of the boy in action about to capture a butterfly in his net. In trials 8 to 12, the proportions, lines, and details were improved; in trial 11, only the boy's posture and head details were changed; and in trial 12, improvements were achieved in the positions of the boy, net, and butterfly. Finally, in drawing 13, with the elimination of all trial sketching, the accepted product was carefully reproduced in ink.

Practice in a goal-directed, trial-and-check process. In the preceding chapter on structuring approaches to problems, it was suggested that the learner meets a problem by drawing upon his background of experience or creative abilities for plausible hypotheses —assumptions of what will probably work. As a provisional trial, he may say, "I'll try this to see if it is correct [35, p. 222]." Perceiving the effect of a trial, he confirms or disconfirms his hunch. If he fails to achieve his goal or achieves it imperfectly, he tries again. At first he may think of no solutions at all or of only a few. Or many alternatives may appear plausible. But with experience—perception of the effects—the number of irrelevant hypotheses is reduced and more appropriate ones are discovered. Action without a hypothesis is useless, random movement. It rarely occurs. Even apparently irrelevant trial-and-error explorations are usually guided, at least gropingly, by hypotheses [15]. And once the correct solution has been completely discovered and confirmed, further repetition of it without variation is unnecessary. From practicing a response in several varied situations, however, the individual learns further where the response is appropriate and where it is inappropriate.

If practice is to be effective it must, according to Jensen, be accompanied by *all* the other conditions of learning. Effective practice is well motivated, goal-directed, and exploratory. It yields knowledge of results of each provisional trial, is frequent enough for remembering discovered correct and incorrect solutions, and is varied to facilitate learning appropriate generalizations and discriminations. It is organized in sequences and interrelations to facilitate transfer and retention [35]. Among these conditions of effective practice, *a plan for checking provisional trials* is especially important.

THE ROLE OF PERCEPTION OF EFFECTS IN LEARNING

The crucial problem-solving process that produces the changes in experience and behavior which constitute learning is one of "approximation and correction," of "trial and check," of reacting to a "feedback" of information by correcting provisional solutions in the light of their perceived consequences [29, pp. 470–471].

In guiding effective learning, coaches, teachers, and learning theorists all become aware of the importance of checking provisional trials. Experts in such skills as bowling, golf, and baseball direct players to observe the results of each goal-directed trial—both their successes and failures—as a basis for improving subsequent trials. Shellenbach, the trainer of pitchers for the San Francisco Giants, says: "The biggest thing in learning control [the most important thing in pitching] is to keep track of how you do. It's like target practice. First you throw 10 or 12 fast balls and keep track of where they go. How many are strikes? Four or five maybe. Then you throw some curves and keep track of how many would be called strikes . . . If you do it regularly, keeping track of exactly what you're doing, you have to get better [3]." Student nurses are directed to practice in pairs while learning to take accurate TPRs (temperature, pulse, and respiration records). Both nurses take TPRs independently on the same patients and compare their records. If there is a discrepancy, they repeat the process. If they agree, their accuracy is confirmed. Both experience and experiments support the importance in learning of such checking of provisional trials.

The waste of repeated trials without checking. Imagine that you were one of Lashley's archery subjects. If your first arrow had struck the target on the outermost left edge, you would probably have tried to correct the error by shifting your aim toward the right in the next trial. In each successive trial, your approach would have been guided by your perception of the effects of preceding trials. But suppose you were blindfolded—that you had no information at all on the results of any trial. Would you—even from over a thousand trials—make any improvement? For an answer to our question, let us examine some experiments designed to test the hypothesis that perception of the effects of goal-directed trials is essential for learning.

In one such experiment which covered a period of 12 days [63], subject T drew 2,203 lines, each intended to be 4 inches long, without ever seeing any of them. The tabulation of the lengths of the lines revealed no appreciable progress toward a precise 4-inch line. The 175 lines drawn on the first day ranged from 4.5 to 6.1 inches, the median length being 5.23 inches. On each of the 12 practice days the 171 to 200 lines drawn showed similar variation, with no closer approximation to a 4-inch line. The 192 lines drawn on the last day ranged from 4.1 to 5.7 inches, with a median of 4.96 [63]. In a different but similar experiment, Thorndike instructed

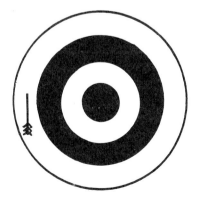

seven blindfolded adults to draw 4-inch lines. He gave them no information about their accuracy or improvement on repeated trials. Their errors averaged almost an inch at the beginning of the practice and, after 400 such trials, the extent of error remained practically the same [62].

Thorndike interprets these results as demonstrating that repetition alone is not a sufficient condition for learning. Perception of the effects is also necessary, as is implied by the statement: *"Had I opened my eyes* after each shove of the pencil during the second and later sittings, and *measured the lines* and *been desirous of accuracy in the task,* the connections leading to 3.8, 3.9, 4.0, 4.1 and 4.2 would have become more frequent until I reached my limit of skill in the task [63, p. 13; italics supplied]."* Other experiments confirm Thorndike's results and his prediction.

Elwell and Grindley presented their ten 18- to 22-year-old subjects a complex coordination task requiring each subject to learn to guide bimanually (by manipulating levers) a spot of light from the outer edge to the center of a target marked by 10 concentric circles. Possible scores ranged from 0 (off the target) to 10 (in the center circle). The light was never visible while being moved. However, during the first 10 days of 20 trials per day, the learner observed the light in starting position and again (after manipulations) in the position to which he had moved it. Thus he was permitted to check how nearly he had come to the aimed-at bull's-eye. Then the subjects continued their 20 trials per day for an additional 5 days; but during this period no subject saw the outcome of his efforts. As Figure 8.3 shows, with opportunity to perceive the result of each goal-directed trial, the subjects gradually learned to improve their accuracy in this motor coordination task. However, when the opportunity for check-

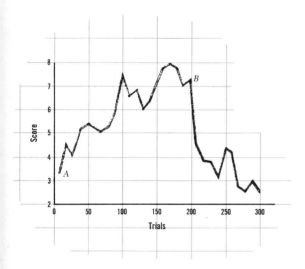

Fig. 8.3. *Average performance of 10 adults on a bimanual coordination task, A with and B without perception of the effects of each provisional trial.* (From J. L. Ewell and G. C. Grindley, *Br. J. Psychol.,* 1938, vol 29, p. 45.)

ing the results of their goal-directed trials was withheld, their accuracy dropped almost immediately to the pretraining level.

Perception of the results of our efforts enables us to confirm the success of our approach or, in the event of failure, to restructure our approach. This fact is suggested by the spontaneous remarks of some of the subjects in the preceding experiment. Perceiving that he had achieved a bull's-eye, one subject said: "I must try to do exactly that movement again." After a failure, he said: "That means that I must pull farther with the left hand [17, p. 48]."

Experiments involving other kinds of tasks also confirm the need for checking in the trial-and-check process. Using the Seashore pitch-discrimination test, which requires the subject to tell whether the second of a pair of tones is higher or lower than the first, Wyatt had 24 college students make 500 such discriminations—100 per day for five successive days. Uninformed of the correctness or incorrectness of their judgments, these students made no appreciable improvement in the five days of practice. When, however, opportunities are provided for checking the correctness of each discrimination, both Wyatt and Connette have demonstrated that college students *are* able to achieve significant improvements in pitch discrimination [10, 75].

These experiments demonstrate that practice produces improvement only when accompanied by provisions for checking the consequences of goal-directed trials. Let us now see how this checking may be done most effectively.

The advantage of precise checking. In attempting to draw 4-inch lines, Thorndike's blindfolded subjects were not entirely without some knowledge of results. From their past experience, they had built up at least a vague concept of a 4-inch line. And they had, as they drew each line, some subjective, kinesthetic, nonvisual perception of their performance. From this admittedly inadequate feedback, however, they could make some slight improvement. Although subject T did not, as Thorndike reported, come any nearer to drawing a 4-inch line in 2,203 trials, his drawings *did* tend to approximate *slightly* more closely his own average of 5.01 inches [57]. Other experimenters have shown that the effectiveness of knowledge of results depends upon its preciseness.

Comparing three degrees of completeness of feedback information, Trowbridge and Cason directed different groups of college students (15 students in each group) to draw, while blindfolded, one hundred 3-inch lines. Group I, like Thorndike's subjects, were given no information as to their accuracy. For Group II, the experimenter said, "Right," for every line drawn within one-eighth of an inch of a 3-inch line. This information, however, was provided infrequently because the subjects, especially in the early trials, rarely came within one-eighth of an inch of being correct. In Group III, the subject was informed precisely on each trial how many eighths of an inch his line was too long or too short. The average percentages of correctly drawn lines were as follows: for no information, 13.6; for the occasional confirmation of "right" responses, 22.6; and for precise information on the correctness of each trial, 54.8 [67, p. 250].

Reed, also using college students as his subjects, has verified the importance of precise perception of effects. His blindfolded subjects made no appreciable progress in drawing lines, rectangles, and circles of prescribed dimensions. With their eyes open and with the standard figures before them, they made *some* progress but soon reached their limits of accuracy. When permitted to measure every fifth figure drawn, however, the subjects, besides improving rapidly in the initial trials, continued to improve in later trials. The precise measurements of trial drawings yielded knowledge of otherwise imperceptible errors and provided guidance for correcting them [54].

The need for prompt checking. Several experiments indicate that contiguity between trials and checking enhances the effectiveness of practice. For 48 adult subjects who practiced throwing small balls back over their shoulders at an invisible target of four concentric rings, Lorge and Thorndike provided information on the results of each throw—with delays of from zero up to six seconds. With the shorter delays, learning was more efficient [42].

In the trial-and-error discovery and mastery of complex clues for guiding multiple-choice selections among geometric patterns differing in color, form, number, size, orientation, and position, Bourne found that for 162 college students, concept mastery is directly related to the promptness of information on the correctness of each response [6]. In still another experiment, Greenspoon and Foreman [22] varied the delay in supplying information on correctness of response as five groups of eight blindfolded college students practiced drawing fifty

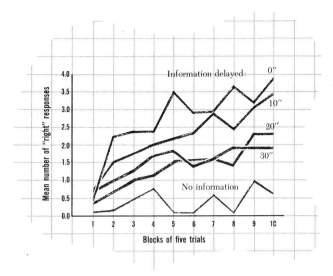

Fig. 8.4. *Promptness of feedback information facilitates learning to draw 3-inch lines. Performance with immediate feedback is compared with delays of from 10 to 30 seconds and with no information.* (From J. Greenspoon and Salley Foreman, *J. Exp. Psychol.*, 1956, vol. 51, p. 227.)

3-inch lines. One group was given no information. Other groups— after no delay and after delays of 10, 20, and 30 seconds—were in- formed as to whether each line drawn was "short," "long," or "correct" (for lines between 2¾ and 3¼ inches). The results, which are typical for these experiments, are graphed in Figure 8.4.

Figure 8.4 reveals that without clear perception of the conse- quences of goal-directed trials, practice yields little or no improve- ment. With information, *immediate* feedback produces the most efficient learning. For this particular task, 10 seconds of delay between the response and perception of its effect reduces slightly the efficiency of learning. When the delays go up to 20 or 30 seconds, the learning is much less efficient.

Other studies indicate that the general implications of these ex- periments are applicable to learning such subjects as chemistry and psychology. Little compared the final test achievement in educational psychology of three groups of students who, during the school year, were given various opportunities to check the correctness of the con- cepts they were learning. Group I saw only the results of beginning and midterm tests. Groups II and III took 12 additional tests. For Group II, these tests were returned and discussed in class. For Group III, a special testing device permitted the student to discover im- mediately—by pressing from one to five keys—the correct answer for each item as he proceeded through each test. Both Groups II and III exceeded the achievement of Group I. And Group III, which experi- enced prompt feedback on each item of the tests, surpassed Group II, whose members learned only later the correctness of their response to the tests as a whole [41].

Learning from mistakes. Since we have found that repetition

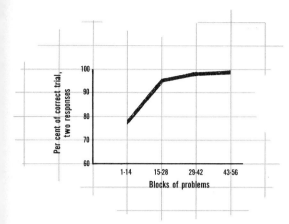

Fig. 8.5. *Perceiving that the first choice on a discrimination problem is wrong, two- to five-year-old children learn to reverse their choices on a second trial. Percentages of reversals on trial 2 of nine children, after solving varying numbers of reversal problems.* (From H. F. Harlow, *Psychol. Rev.*, 1949, vol. 56, p. 59.)

alone is not an effective determinant of learning, it seems safe to assume that unrewarded errors are unlikely to become habitual. Unrewarded mistakes may, in fact, lead to alternative responses—and sometimes to the correct solution of a problem. On this possibility, Dr. Von Braun, head of the U.S. Army's scientific ballistic-missile team, speaking proudly of his team's accomplishments, remarked: "We have already made more mistakes than other people have [56, p. 10]."

Children and even monkeys learn early to be guided by their mistakes. Harlow has shown that both monkeys and two- to five-year-old children, who make an error in a two-choice discrimination problem learn to infer that the alternate choice will be correct. Moreover, as is shown in Figure 8.5, young children learn, from increasing amounts of problem-solving experience, to use the trial-and-check process more effectively.

School children also learn from their mistakes. Sixth grade children do as well in mastering subtraction of fractions from detecting and correcting mistakes as they do from teacher guidance which minimizes experience with errors [1, p. 129]. Junior high school pupils who detect and correct language usage errors equal the achievement of students who do not see wrong forms but, with teacher guidance, practice completing sentences in correct form only. Spelling, however, was found to be improved more effectively by recognizing and correctly rewriting misspelled words than by merely recognizing correctly spelled words [43]. Apparently, children can learn correct responses when either their errors or their right responses are signaled. However, as Holodnack discovered, in comparing signaling either correct or incorrect responses to six- to ten-year-old children who were learning a punchboard maze, young children learn more effectively "if the correct responses rather than the incorrect ones are pointed out and emphasized [32, p. 353]."

Perception of the effects and motivational reinforcement of provisional trials are sometimes confused. Since they have different functions in learning, they need to be differentiated.

Information versus affect in guiding learning. Both informational feedback and motivational reinforcement function in the selection and elimination of correct and incorrect responses. Hitting the bull's-eye, for example, is both perceived as correct and experienced as satisfying. Because of these effects, the learner tries to repeat such performances. When he misses his target, the learner experiences dissatisfaction and also *perceives* that his arrow has struck, say, 20 inches to the left of the bull's-eye. In the next trial, he usually tries to avoid the dissatisfaction of another miss. The dissatisfaction alone does not, however, provide the needed *guidance* for better performance, except to indicate that something different is needed. It is his *perception* of the arrow 20 inches to the left of the bull's-eye which guides him in the next trial to aim much more toward the right. From observation of the effects of goal-directed provisional trials, the learner is informed of the consequences of alternative responses. Such information is crucial as a guide to better performance. Whether the learner uses such knowledge depends upon his motives. Typically, his behavior moves in the direction of greater motive satisfaction; that is, maximally reinforced trials tend to be repeated.

Reed has demonstrated that the pleasant or unpleasant effects of responses do not affect learning, except as they serve as clues for guiding the learner to his goal. He directed each of 78 college students to learn "as quickly and accurately as possible" a multiple T-maze by moving a finger along a wire threaded over a board on which the subjects could be electrically shocked at any given point. He advised them: "Should you experience an unpleasant feeling, you must decide what to do about it without further questioning [53, p. 696]." Despite the different effects for right and wrong responses provided for the different groups, all of them mastered the problem and with approximately equal efficiency. Group I, shocked for each error on the maze, required 7.18 trials. Group II, shocked for each correct response, required 6.82 trials. Group III, hearing "right" for errors, required 7.10 trials. Group IV, hearing "right" for correct responses, required 5.91 trials. And Group V, given neither "reward" nor "punishment," required 7.00 trials. Inappreciably influenced by variations in the verbal or electric reinforcements, each subject apparently discovered for himself kinesthetic clues indicative of the correct and incorrect pathways of the maze. Since the variations in pleasant or unpleasant effects did not affect the efficiency of learning significantly, Reed concluded that learning is "the result of the *interpretation* of these qualities [53, p. 699]." It is the *knowledge* of success or failure (however it is signaled) which enables the learner "to make up his mind what to do in the next trial to make a better performance [53, p. 700]."

Adjustment of performance to expected reinforcement. As every fly-fisherman knows, a strike or hooked fish now and then is sufficient reinforcement to sustain his interest over hundreds or thousands of unrewarded casts. Experiments indicate that, although continuous reinforcement is better for learning, intermittent reinforcement is more effective in sustaining many learned behavior patterns over long periods of nonreinforcement. As one test of this hypothesis, Grant, Hake, and Hornseth [21] directed 185 college students (individually) to guess, for 60 learning and 30 extinction trials, whether or not fol-

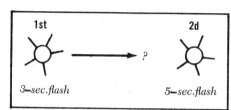

1st 2d

3-sec.flash   5-sec.flash

lowing a 3-second flash of the first light the second light on a board would flash. For five different groups (17 in each group), he provided positive reinforcement (second light flashes) on 0, 25, 50, 75, and 100 per cent of 60 randomly arranged trials. Then on 30 extinction trials, reinforcement was completely stopped for *all* groups. For the five groups on different reinforcement schedules, the average percentage of guesses that the second light would flash are graphed in Figure 8.6.

As the figure shows, *all* the groups began responding positively (predicting that the second light would flash) on approximately 45 to 65 per cent of the trials. Gradually, however, each group adjusted its proportion of positive responses to the actual proportion of light flashes it experienced. The students adjusted their expectations to their checked experience. Guided by perception of the effects of their provisional trials, subjects in each group learned to expect the actual number of flashes given and to emit an approximately matched number of positive responses.

But what happens during extinction, when the second light ceases completely to flash? If each reinforcement added an increment of strength to a response, the group reinforced on 100 per cent of the learning trials should persist more tenaciously in guessing that the second light would continue to flash. Actually, as Figure 8.6 shows, the intermittently (less frequently) reinforced groups persisted longer.

Although this paradox presents difficulties for the stimulus-response reinforcement theory, there is a plausible cognitive theory interpretation of it. In the 30 extinction trials, the change from 100 per cent to 0 per cent, being the most distinctive change, was most easily discriminated. Because of the sharp contrast in feedback, this group learned (inferred) from a single block of five trials not to

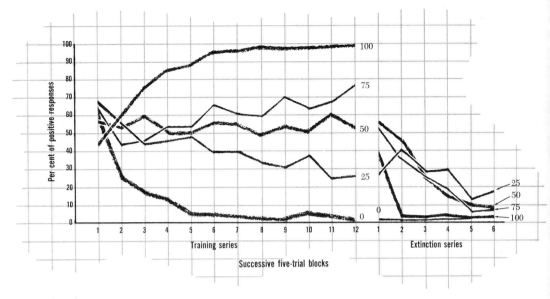

Fig. 8.6. *College students adjust their estimates that "a second light will flash" to frequency of reinforcement, but they cease responding most quickly after 100 per cent reinforcement.* (From D. A. Grant, H. W. Hake, and J. P. Hornseth, *J. Exp. Psychol.,* 1951, vol. 42, p. 2.)

expect a second flash. And, guided by this insight, they immediately adjusted their performance to it. Because it required more trials to discriminate between the less sharply contrasting *intermittent* and *no* reinforcement conditions, the intermittently reinforced group took more trials to give up the expectation of eventual reinforcement.

In a similar experiment with fourth and fifth grade children, Rosenblum has indicated that the development and maintenance of such traits as self-confidence is also affected by reinforcement schedules. Children continually praised for their efforts in copying geometrical designs become more sure of their proficiency in the task than children praised only intermittently. However, when approval ceased for both groups, the self-ratings on "confidence of succeeding" of the theretofore continuously approved group dropped below those of the intermittently reinforced group [55, p. 104].

PROVIDING FOR PERCEPTION OF EFFECTS IN LEARNING

In the trial-and-check process of learning, effective checking of goal-directed provisional trials is essential for efficient learning.

Self-checking. Fortunately, checking is an inherent feature of many learning activities. The correct solution to a problem is often identifiable immediately—because it works. In assembling a jigsaw puzzle, for example, when the correct solution is achieved, the blocks

fit. For alternative patterns, they don't. Similarly, when a child who reads for meaning identifies an unfamiliar word by phonetic analysis and the word as identified fits the meaning, he usually knows he is right. If the word does not make sense, he tries and checks again. When the computed answer to an arithmetic problem matches approximately the estimated answer, a tentative assumption of its correctness is justified. The pitch of a note sung is recognized as right because it sounds right. After many unsuccessful attempts at drawing a bird in flight, an effective technique is finally discovered—because the bird now appears to be flying. In many other learning activities, whether or not a solution fits or works is a pragmatic test of its correctness. Such self-checking, however, is insufficient. For example, the pupil does not always recognize when he is singing off pitch.

Teacher guidance in checking. Teacher guidance in checking provisional trials is needed. Guidance, however, does not always mean telling students correct answers when they make mistakes. Guidance which motivates pupils to search for correct solutions and teaches them how to discover them is often more effective. But whether the teacher guidance is directive or pupil self-discovery—oriented, checking needs to be improved—in the information it gives, in its frequency, preciseness, and promptness.

The common procedure of returning a student's homework composition, exercises in mathematics, or research report in social studies or science several days after it was handed in and marking it only with a letter grade provides him little guidance on how to improve his next effort. Such inadequate teacher checking is unlikely to produce changes in subsequent assignments. On the contrary, it is likely

As a feature of teacher guidance of pupil self-discovery learning, visual models permit children to check the correctness of their provisionally achieved concepts. (Text-Film Department, McGraw-Hill Book Company, Inc., New York.)

Table 8.1. *Long-division errors and symbols for marking them*

Symbol	Error	Symbol	Error
z–om	Zero omitted	s	Error in subtraction
w–q	Wrong quotient	p	Error in placement
w–c	Wrong carrying	bd	Error in number brought down
m	Error in multiplication	r	Error in remainder

SOURCE: Holland, H. *Elem. Sch. J.*, 1941–42, 42, 585–596. Reprinted by permission of the Univ. of Chicago Press.

to make pupil practice sheer repetition. Fortunately, as the several illustrations which follow suggest, there are better methods.

Holland suggests an informative way of checking arithmetic papers [30]. From a list of the errors most frequently made in long division, Table 8.1 is prepared and placed on the blackboard to call attention to the errors children are most likely to make and should try to avoid. The abbreviated symbol for each type of error provides the teacher a convenient device for marking specifically and informatively each child's exercises. For example, when a child sees on his problem No. 2 the symbol *z-om* and on problem No. 7 the symbol *w-c*, he is informed that he has made mistakes by omitting zero in a quotient and in carrying. He is thus guided to restudy these particular concepts. This device has general application in many phases of arithmetic, in language, handwriting, spelling, and in other subjects for which lists of commonly made errors have been inventoried or can be inventoried by a teacher for a particular purpose.

For checking high school and college students' compositions more informatively and precisely, Hook suggests using *Ideaform*. The student's composition paper provides spaces both for specific teacher comment and for checking ("Good," "Fair," or "Poor") on attainment of such objectives as "organization, development, sincerity of purpose and expression, sentence structure and punctuation, paraphrasing, usage, choice of words, spelling . . . and general appearance." Such teacher evaluations—especially when they are summarized for a succession of themes—guide the student toward needed improvement. Comments such as the following provide more specific suggestions: "Would *because* be a better word?" "By the details, you made me feel that I was climbing the mountain with you." Or, "Would this be better if you told us more about the Wright brothers themselves? [33, pp. 33, 34]"

Teachers can provide for informative, precise, and prompt feedback of the results of provisional trials in a variety of ways. Elementary school children listen to tape recordings of their oral language— to check on pronunciation, voice quality, and effectiveness of composition. Then they try again and listen for improvements. In learning to speak a foreign language, students try to imitate, on certain segments of the tape, recordings of model speech interspersed on other segments. Then—to evaluate the quality of their efforts—they and their classmates listen to the playback of both the model's and the students' speech [19]. Keller has found that students learn Morse code more effectively when they have the opportunity to confirm or disconfirm their reactions to each signal as it is made instead of waiting to check the correctness of an entire set of signals at the conclusion of a practice session [36].

Skinner has suggested that by effective application of this principle we can improve the teaching of arithmetic, spelling, reading, and many other learning tasks which can be analyzed into S–R sequences. He proposes that such sequences of problems be fed into machines which register the student's tentative solutions and then indicate to him immediately whether his responses are right or wrong [59].

Special provisions for checking. When the usual provision for perceiving the effects of learning is not possible, the crucial importance of checking is brought more convincingly to our attention. This is illustrated by the great difficulty a deaf child has in learning to articulate words. Deprived of hearing—the usual cue for noting the correctness or incorrectness of our attempts to articulate words—the deaf child must find some other way of checking his speech efforts. The photograph on page 289 presents a device, reported in *Life,* which shows a deaf child immediately and precisely how nearly his own provisional trial matches or approximates the teacher model or oral concept he is striving to reproduce. The teacher has said, "Shoe," into a microphone, and the sound is represented on a grid as a certain pattern of colored lights. As the child says, "Shoe," into another microphone, she can tell, by comparing the pattern of lights she produces with the pattern produced by the teacher, how near or how far away she is from the correct articulation. This precise and prompt feedback on the

The teaching machine provides the learner with informative, precise, and prompt feedback of the results of his provisional trials. (Foringer & Company, Inc.)

As this pupil from the Tennessee School for the Deaf says "shoe" into the microphone, the device translates her sounds into patterns of colored lights which, when compared to a model, tell her precisely how nearly correctly she is pronouncing the word. (*Life*, Sept. 22, 1952, p. 73. Courtesy, Life Magazine © Time, Inc.)

correctness of each goal-directed trial guides her toward improvement in each subsequent trial.

In some activities, normal individuals also need supplementary devices for checking the correctness of their learning efforts. Young children, for example, often have difficulty checking their speech. Since we do not hear our own voices very accurately and do not, of course, see our lip movements, a mirror and a sound recorder are excellent aids in approximating more closely the visual and auditory models of correct speech. Practicing before the mirror often aids the young violinist in matching the visualized, teacher-demonstrated good form for holding and bowing his violin.

In such loosely structured activities as participation in class discussion, self-observation needs some supplementation. Children like to think of themselves as contributing, but they often do not know how well they succeed. To improve their self-checking, a sixth grade class prepared the self-rating scale presented below [7]. Such ratings made immediately after discussions—sometimes in conference with the teacher or another pupil—are more accurate than unaided impressions. Other more precise devices are described in Chapter 15.

The trial-and-check process in learning   289

In a group, I:	(4) Always	(3) Most of the time	(2) Half of the time	(1) Hardly ever	(0) Never
_____ take turns					
_____ stick to the subject					
_____ ask good questions					
_____ pay attention					

Tests as effective checks of mastery. By a parallel teach-and-test process, teachers can facilitate the trial-and-check process required of pupils in mastering the sequences of the curriculum. Well-constructed tests—covering the objectives intended—are useful both in summarizing and in evaluating achievement in a unit of learning. As diagnostic appraisals of objectives already accomplished and of concepts or skills still to be mastered, tests indicate readiness and need for the next step in a sequence of learning activities. Such tests are effective learning devices. They should be used not only as midterm and final examinations but as checks on degree of mastery of each unit in a course. In preparation for a test, the learner practices his skills, and organizes principles for applying them. The test—at the appropriate time—affords an opportunity for checking his understanding and mastery of the skills and concepts. It yields the pupil information which confirms some of his provisionally tried hypotheses and disconfirms others—or indicates the need for revising them. The pupil must, however, see and use his corrected examination papers promptly.

The value of informing pupils on the correctness or incorrectness of their responses to examination questions has been demonstrated by Plowman and Stroud. These investigators had tenth and eleventh grade students, divided into two matched groups of 125 each, study textbook material on the history of bookmaking for 15 minutes. Both groups were then given a 30-item multiple-choice test on the material read. Afterward, one group was allowed to inspect the corrected test for five minutes—a learning opportunity not permitted the other group. After six days, without intervening warning, both groups took another test on the same content. Of these originally matched groups, the students given the learning opportunity of confirming or disconfirming their answers on the first test made significantly higher scores on the second test [50].

Our separate analyses of these two aspects of practice—provisional trials and perception of the effects of these goal-directed trials—confirm the initially described close articulation of these essential conditions of learning. Oriented by this broad concept of practice—as a goal-directed trial-and-check process—let us explore it thoroughly in terms of children's needs.

The amount and kind of practice needed to acquire the numerous concepts and skills taught in the elementary and secondary school curriculum varies. While some concepts are mastered in a single trial, other concepts and most skills require a great many trials. Achieving a pleasing tone with vibrato on the violin, for example, may take thousands of trials. One obvious reason why such skills as reading, language, arithmetic, or musical performance require a great many practice sessions is that they are comprised of thousands of separate, though interrelated, subconcepts and subskills. Moreover, these numerous subconcepts and subskills must be differentiated and organized for appropriate functioning in many different situations.

As an illustration of a multiple-component skill, consider the major phases of computation arithmetic—adding, subtracting, multiplying, and dividing of integers, common fractions, and decimal numbers. Each of these processes is comprised of numerous variations. Division of decimals, for example, consists of 61 such variations as $4/\overline{8}$, $.7/\overline{.49}$, and $103/\overline{6.375}$ [14]. Similarly, in art, the child learns to use variations of line, space, shape, texture, color, and lightness-darkness in composing a drawing. As these concepts and skills are mastered, they are applied, with refinements in skill, to numerous art designs. In science, the truth of such a concept as the interdependence of animal life may be verified by observing that woodpeckers eat insects, bears eat fish, owls eat rats, snakes eat frogs, etc. From such varied experiences, concepts are generalized.

Following Tilton's outline [65], we may classify the multiple-element concepts and skills which children and youth learn according to several types of learning which require practice:

1. *Generalizing responses to multiple cues.* The situations in which concepts and skills are needed are often different from the situations in which they were originally learned. Unless responses are generalized to multiple cues, they may fail in certain new situations. For example, it is said of John Locke, who had practiced waltzing by dancing around a trunk in his room, that when he tried his skill on the dance floor, he was unable to execute the steps he had practiced. The trunk was not there! Like John Locke, students often fail to apply in appropriate new situations those concepts on which they have had only narrow-range practice. The remedy, of course, is practice of varied applications in different situations. A football team, for example, is not easily caught unprepared by its opponents' surprise plays if its own plays are well executed and are the product of many different, adaptive rehearsals of them.

The inductive discovery of variations of the same concept or skill also produces generalized principles. For example, in reading such different words as *beat* and *laid* or *made* and *ride,* a child discovers (with teacher guidance) that the second vowel is always silent and determines the long sound of the first. He then applies the generalization in reading other words such as *straight* and *late.*

2. Making discriminative responses. While the individual is developing generalized responses to multiple cues, he also discovers the hazards of overgeneralizing. Mastery of such skills as reading, language, spelling, or mathematics requires discriminations between many competing responses. The same cue often requires a different response in only slightly different contexts. The child learns, for example, to double the *e* in *proceed* but not in *procedure.* If the beginning reader relies mainly on the initial consonant for identifying unfamiliar words, he reads *wanted* as *went, then* as *there,* and *several* as *seven.* He needs, of course, to learn to respond differently when there are variations in the remainder of the word. Overcoming such faulty generalizations and learning to make such discriminations accurately and confidently requires practice.

The greater the number of competing alternatives among the associations to be learned, the greater will be the number of trials required to master the correct ones. As Beecroft has experimentally demonstrated, it is easier to associate (in respective pairs) 10 such words as *yearly, jolly,* and *fragrant* with 10 such different words as *gigantic, drowsy,* and *remote* than it is to associate them with 10 synonyms, such as *gigantic, massive,* and *immense* [4].

3. Automatization of responses. The individual performs such frequently practiced skills as bicycling, piano playing, or rapid reading without conscious attention to the details of signals or processes. Such automatization of skills is achieved by learning to respond to reduced response-guiding cues. Woodworth has observed that when the inexperienced fielder is moving into position to catch a fly ball, he follows the ball's complete path of flight. The expert, however, is guided to the right position by seeing only the beginning of its trajectory [73].

In the initial stages of learning, the deaf child requires the visual representation of his speech for almost every sound, and the violin student needs a mirror to guide him in maintaining good form in holding and bowing his instrument. But as practice of such skills continues, fewer cues are needed. In a sequence of responses, each response becomes the conditioned cue for the next response in the chain.

As a classroom example of cue reduction, consider the automatization of skillful reading. In the early stages, the child attends both to the context and to a careful visual or phonetic analysis of words— their beginnings, roots and suffixes or prefixes, or each syllable. However, as a result of practice, the learner comes to require fewer and fewer cues. Finally, when he has become a mature reader, he grasps the meaning of a passage from perceiving only parts of some words. In a familiar context, he achieves meaning by merely scanning a page. Many skills are automatized by such reductions in the cues needed to guide performance.

4. *Organizing patterns of responses.* Mastery of complex behavior patterns—such as memorizing prose, poetry, a violin concerto, or assembling a complicated machine such as a carburetor or a watch—requires the sequential or integrated organization of several segments or components. Since all the associations and differentiated insights into the interrelations of segments or components are not achieved in one trial, a smooth performance requires practice. For example, in the early stages of memorizing a poem, the learner grasps the general scheme and some dominant details—with considerable inferred construction of how it "ought to go." At first, segments are correctly associated with adjacent segments or incorrectly associated with competing remote forward and backward segments [51]. After a few trial-and-check practices, the components are better articulated, more appropriate details are differentiated, and misconstructions are eliminated. Finally, a literal reproduction is possible because each segment of the poem is differentially cued both to the central meaning and to the appropriate preceding part [48].

Variations of these processes also characterize the memorization and use of the facts in such subjects as mathematics, language, spelling, science, or social studies. The functional organization of these facts into various patterns for flexible, adaptive application requires practice in dealing with them in a variety of situations.

5. *Refining skills.* The initial performance of a skill often involves helpful ancillary processes which, as practice continues, can be deleted in the interest of efficiency. For example, in achieving "meaningful habituation" in adding $26 + 7$, a child may first count 26 objects and then count 7 more. With a little practice, he finds he can start with 26 and count only the 7 additional objects. Discovering a still more abstract level of functioning, to 26 he adds 4 and 3 (into which he has divided the 7). Finally, from such insight-yielding and confidence-building practice, he immediately recognizes that $26 + 7 = 33$ [8]. Or a football player may learn to tackle in a series of steps, such as approach, contact, and follow through. He may at first verbalize the steps. After some practice, however, he eliminates the word guides and telescopes the steps into an integrated, smoothly functioning pattern. Many skills of the elementary and secondary curricula are refined by eliminating unnecessary elements, by telescoping segments, and by coordinating the parts into more efficient patterns. By such refinements, achieved through effective practice, skills are executed more rapidly, accurately, smoothly, comfortably, and confidently.

6. *Imitating complex patterns.* To improve their performance of complicated behavior patterns, children and youth often try to imitate a more expert classmate, the teacher, a motion-picture film or a sound recording. Successful imitation—of a serve in tennis, a new figure in skating, a chemistry laboratory test, the correct pronunciation of a French word, or a better-organized class report—often requires several trials because the complex model may be incompletely perceived in one trial. In observing the demonstration of the tennis serve, for example, the learner may not at first note every feature. The stance, the grip on the racket, the height to which the ball is tossed, the speed, or the attempt to curve the ball may escape him. In each repeated demonstration, a new aspect of the total performance may be grasped. Certain features may be very elusive, and may not be perceived until they are also explicitly verbalized or demonstrated in slow motion. In other cases—for example, in learning to pronounce a French word—provisional trials must be checked against the model before the learner can reproduce the pattern correctly. Learning from imitation usually requires several trials because the observed pattern must always be translated into independent self-activity.

7. *Discovering solutions.* In such problem-solving activities as mathematics, science, social studies, creative writing, or art, where several alternative approaches or solutions may appear plausible, correct or satisfying solutions can often be reached only by several provisional self-discovery trials. The search for a solution is a process of repeated trial-and-check. We have all experienced this process in trying to solve a baffling problem.

When seven-year-old James was asked to name a flower that rhymes with "nose," he considered: "Not daffodil, not snapdragon, not snowball, not tulip, not pansy." Then, restructuring the problem by slowly repronouncing "nose," he suddenly shouted "Rose!" A chemistry student was at the point of giving up after repeated failures in her effort to learn the laboratory technique of drawing fluid to a particular level in a glass tube by means of suction. In another hour of homework practice on the task, however, she finally succeeded. She discovered that she had been trying too hard. As she said, "I hadn't realized before that you should go lightly." The route to the correct solution of a problem is often the roundabout one of first finding many ways that will not work. Each systematic trial-and-check practice, however, carries the learner nearer to his goal.

Because there is so much to learn and because so many of the concepts and skills elementary and secondary school children need require extensive amounts of practice, we need to use the practice time available to us efficiently. Therefore, in concluding this chapter, and in a more comprehensive study of the question in the next chapter, we shall look for guiding principles.

EFFICIENT USE OF PRACTICE OPPORTUNITIES

Children encounter the academic and personal-social concepts and skills which they need to learn not only in the classroom but in the school as a whole, at home, and in excursions into the community. We must ask, however, whether such opportunities for learning provide sufficient practice for the mastery of concepts or skills, at what stage drill should be introduced. What should be the length and distribution of practice sessions? What is the role of a warm-up in practice? Is implicit practice effective? Answers to these questions can help us to use practice time more efficiently.

Both functional and systematic practice. Such projects as "The Water Supply in Our Community," described in Chapter 1, and the more comprehensive projects of the elementary school provide functional practice of a variety of concepts and skills. For example, in conducting a store which sold children the supplies needed in their schoolwork, elementary school children—besides studying such economic concepts as wholesale, retail, and profit and loss—practiced arithmetic, language, writing, and spelling. Such school chores and social responsibilities as participating in lunch-menu making, writing letters of request and thanks, producing

plays and operettas, and conducting pupil self-government provide additional opportunities for functional practice of curriculum concepts and skills. The practice connected with these activities is not confined to incidental use of the skills; it is also directed toward improvement of them.

The functional practice conducted in connection with a fifth grade experiment in nutrition illustrates the procedure. The children were required to write daily reports on the rats used in the experiment. When it proved difficult to read their daily observations—because they failed to capitalize and punctuate correctly—it became apparent to the children that they needed to improve their skill in writing. The scheduled language lessons of the week were therefore coordinated with the nutrition experiment and devoted to the improvement of the needed writing skills. As the first lesson, the teacher wrote his own previous day's observation of the rats on the blackboard, leaving out the capitalization and punctuation. The children and teacher together correctly capitalized and punctuated his paragraph. From this problem-solving study—including both class discussion and textbook reading—they generalized the principles of capitalization and punctuation needed at their level of writing. Following this general exercise, the children corrected their own reports—with the teacher checking their efforts and guiding them individually when necessary. As in other instances of functional practice, the need for a skill grows out of an interest-motivated project; the skill is improved in teacher-guided practice sessions; and it is fed back into the original and other ongoing projects—with increased competency and satisfaction on the part of the children.

Several advantages are claimed for such functional practice. Child interest is high. The real problems make the study meaningful. The concepts are organized for effective application in problem solving. It provides varied opportunities for each child to participate in group problem solving according to his talents and interests. Because of these advantages, it is believed that such learning is easier, more permanent, and more likely to be ap-

Appropriately equipped classrooms enhance the efficiency of practice in every subject. (Educational Testing Service, Aspen High School, Aspen, Colorado; photograph by Eugene Cook.)

plied in out-of-school situations than learning which takes place in isolated practice activities [28].

It would be difficult and unnecessary, however, to contrive arrangements for functional practice of *all* the concepts and skills which children need to develop to high levels of proficiency. Although projects and school activities provide valuable opportunities for practicing the skills of reading, language, writing, typewriting, spelling, arithmetic, drawing, crafts, and others, they need to be supplemented with systematically scheduled and teacher-guided practice. Otherwise the child fails to achieve the degree of proficiency he needs

The trial-and-check process in learning 297

[20]. Moreover, systematic, continued practice of a skill without immediate significant application is not necessarily poorly motivated. Knowledge of progress in language, science, or mathematical understandings or in academic, craft, art, or music skills is self-enhancing and thus intrinsically well motivated.

The timing of drills for speed and accuracy. Practice for refining skills, for automatizing responses, for increasing speed and accuracy should *follow* rather than *precede* the achievement of understanding and the discovery of efficient modes of attack. For children who still rely on inefficient or immature procedures, such as "counting" or indirect solutions in adding, drills produce gains only in speed and accuracy. From such drill, children do not discover more mature or efficient modes of attack; they merely learn to use more rapidly and accurately whatever procedures they have already found will work [9].

In the early stages of practice on skills—such as reading, arithmetic computation, typewriting, or tennis—teacher direction or guidance of self-discovery learning should emphasize understanding, discovery of efficient modes of attack, and cultivation of good form. When the timing of speed drills is adjusted to the accomplishment of these objectives, the long-range rate of progress and the ultimate level of efficiency attained are greater.

Distribution of practice time. How shall we answer the adolescent's questions about the most efficient distribution of time for practice and for lessons in violin playing or in other complex skills? Should he take a single one-hour lesson or two half-hour lessons per week? And should he spend his seven hours of practice per week in seven hourly practice periods, in twice that number of half-hour sessions, or in a couple of long periods on the weekends? For efficient learning of both verbal and motor skills, research results tend to favor several short practice periods rather than one or a few long ones.

In order to achieve a criterion of mastery of 100 successive catches in juggling, Knapp and Dixon compared the distributions of practice time for two equated groups of 35 college physical education students—both of which were taught the same systematic pattern of juggling [37]. The group given 5 minutes of practice daily required an average total time of 70 minutes to master the skill. The group practicing 15 minutes on each of alternate days required, on the average, 126 minutes. For this particular motor skill, 14 shorter periods proved more efficient than 8 longer periods. Other experiments have confirmed the advantage of shorter practice periods for high school students [38].

Reed found that college students gained more proficiency in addition from either three daily 20-minute periods or six daily 10-minute periods than from an hour of continuous practice [52]. Oseas and Underwood, using very short intervals between practice periods, found that college students identified and remembered abstract concept associations more efficiently when practice trials were distributed rather than massed [49]. Also using college students as subjects, Harmon and Miller obtained data on learning a complex perceptual-motor task (billiard set shots), which suggests that spacing practice periods with increasingly longer intervals between them is economical of the total practice time required [25].

Such experiments do not, of course, provide precise guidance on the most effective distribution of practice time for every school subject. They do, however, suggest that certain principles exist, and that efficient learners and teachers should try to discover optimum distributions of practice for the varied learning activities in which students engage.

Long practice periods on repetitive activities—studying spelling or language usage; memorizing arithmetic combinations, factual details in social studies, science, or a music composition; and practicing such skills as typewriting or free throws in basketball—lead to waning motivation, inattention to goal-directing ideas, fatigue, and to interference between the several only partially learned, competing responses. For such activities, shorter practice periods with rest intervals of an hour or a day between are likely to be more effective. The intervals between practice periods provide opportunities for implicit rehearsals, for achieving perspectives unencumbered with irrelevant

details which tend to be forgotten between practice periods, and sometimes for freeing oneself from interfering mental sets.

For problem solving in science, social studies, or creative pursuits involving integration of many components, however, long practice periods are often needed. Relatively long periods are needed for the varied alternative approaches required to discover solutions to complex problems and for evaluating them before they are forgotten. In such projects, short practice periods would require the student to repeat preliminary preparations; they would interrupt his line of thought just at the moment when he had organized his work (such as his notes for writing a social studies or science report) and was ready to go on to the next step. Long periods would provide time for preparation, organizing, and carrying work through to a satisfying stage of completion. For the systematic practice of the skills related to such projects, however, distributed practice is more effective.

The role of warm-up in practice. Virtuoso-level performers—such as musicians, dancers, athletes—expect to attain perfection only if they are in practice. And like reserve baseball pitchers, who warm up in the bull pen before trying to meet the crucial demands on the mound, they warm up on some preliminary exercises just before a performance. Several experiments have confirmed the validity of the assumption that there is a need for warming up before expecting high level proficiency.

In a sequence of equally difficult learning tasks, 60 college students learned to associate fifteen 10-item lists of pairs of unrelated adjectives [64]. In four-second presentations of each pair, a subject was shown the stimulus adjective for two seconds; during the next two seconds, he was expected to say the associated adjective—after which time it was presented for checking. Learning three different lists per day in immediate succession, each subject was given 10 trials on each of the 15 lists. The average number of correct anticipations on the first trials of each list is graphed in Figure 8.7.

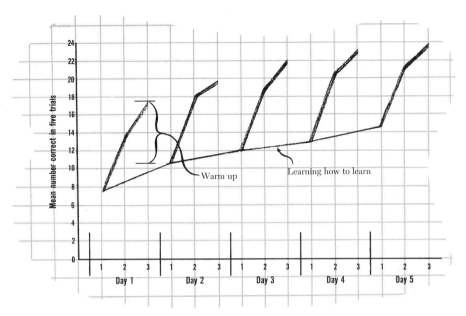

Fig. 8.7. *College students, in learning 15 equally difficult 10-item lists of unrelated paired-associate adjectives, demonstrated both "warm-up" and "learning-how-to-learn."* (From L. E. Thune, *J. Exp. Psychol.*, 1951, vol. 42, p. 252.)

A stable learning-how-to-learn effect is demonstrated in the gradual attainment of higher levels of memorization skill on the initial list for each day, which is marked by the dash line connecting these initial list scores for each of the five days. The warm-up effect is indicated by the sharper increases in memorizing efficiency from the first to second lists on each day of practice. For example, after making only 8 correct anticipations on the first list of the first day, the subjects achieve mean scores of approximately 14 and 18, respectively, on equally difficult second and third lists. The relatively small increments in score from the second to the third lists, as compared to the larger gains from the first to the second, indicate that the warm-up in this particular task is accomplished mainly in the first trial. The warm-up gain is temporary, as is indicated in the drops in score from the third list of one day's practice to the first list of the next day. It takes a warm-up practice on the first list of each day to reestablish the proficiency attained on the last trial of the preceding day.

Implicit and explicit practice. One explanation of the advantage of distributed practice is the claimed added learning which accrues from mulling over or thinking about a task between periods of *actual* practice. Is such implicit practice actually helpful? According to cognitive-learning theory, it should aid in structuring approaches to problems—by formation of cognitive maps to be applied subsequently

in actual practice. With some qualifications, experiments confirm the theory.

Handwriting is a perceptual-motor skill involving both perception of letter forms and their execution in patterns of motor behavior. These two aspects of handwriting are ordinarily learned simultaneously, as interrelated processes; the movement patterns are dependent on perception of form, and feedback from executed movements leads to more precisely differentiated perception of letter forms. To 15 junior high school pupils who were retarded in letter formation skill and in the general quality of handwriting, Leggitt gave training only in analysis and identification of letter formation—without actual writing [40]. From 10 practice periods in visually matching handwriting strokes with the letters, before- and after-practice tests revealed significant gains in both correctness of letter formation and general quality of handwriting. Two better-designed experiments clarify further the role of implicit practice.

For 19 days between pretests and end-tests of skill in feathered-dart throwing and in basketball free throw, Vandell, Davis, and Clugston had three different groups of high school and college students engage in (1) no practice, (2) actual motor practice, and (3) "doing mentally that which they had actually done" on the pretest. While the no-practice group made no gain, both the explicit and implicit practice groups achieved significant and approximately equal improvement. At least in the initial stages of practice, it seems that merely imagining better modes of attack can produce improvement in such motor skills [69].

Eventually, however, gains from mental practice should diminish, since there is no effective feedback of the results of merely imagined provisional trials. This predicted outcome of implicit practice is confirmed by Twining's experiment. In 20 days between pretests and end-tests of skill in tossing 6-inch rings over a peg 10 feet away, a group of 12 college students without any practice improved only 4.3 per cent. From twenty 15-minute daily practices of "mentally throwing rope rings at imaginary targets," a similar group improved 36.2 per cent. Another comparable group, who—in the same number of practice periods—actually tossed rings, improved 137.3 per cent [68]. Implicit practice is effective in structuring approaches to problems. In the long range, however, efficient practice requires the full trial-and-check process in which—as guides to improvement—each goal-directed, provisional trial can be confirmed or disconfirmed in the light of perception of its effects.

SUMMARY

Although repeated trials are necessary, they alone are not sufficient for mastering complex concepts or skills. Both repeated trials and perception of their effects (plus other conditions of learning) are required. Broadly interpreted, practice implies both making and checking provisional trials. It is more a matter of discovery than of repetition. Practice is a goal-directed trial-and-check process in which the learner tries out tentative hypotheses. On the basis of his perception of their effects, he confirms and consolidates responses or disconfirms and revises provisional trials.

In the trial-and-check process, perception of the effects of provisional trials is crucial. For effective learning, it should be pertinently informative, precise, and prompt. Moreover, it is important to distinguish between motivational reinforcement and *perception* of the effects of provisional trials. Both affect the selection and elimination of trial-and-error responses. However, it is perceived informational feedback which guides the learner in confirming or disconfirming responses and in revising subsequent efforts. According to cognitive theory, perception guides learning; motivational reinforcement determines performance.

Many learning activities provide inherent self-checking feedbacks; correct responses fit or work, incorrect ones do not. However, effective teaching—either as teacher direction or guidance of self-discovery learning—provides additional informative, frequent, precise, and prompt checking of pupils' goal-directed trials.

A classification of the various types of learning which require practice helps us to understand why the numerous concepts and skills which elementary and secondary children learn require extensive practice:

1. They often need to generalize responses to multiple cues.

2. The same cue in different situations should elicit discriminative responses.

3. The automatization of responses requires learning to respond to reduced cues.

4. Effective performance often requires the organization of numerous specific responses into patterns of behavior.

5. The refinement of skills requires the elimination of unessential components and the integration of only the essential components into smoothly functioning patterns.

6. The successful imitation of complex models often requires multiple provisional trials.

7. A number of provisional trials are often needed to discover the solution to a problem.

Several principles determine the effective use of practice opportunities. There should be appropriate combinations of both functional and systematically guided and scheduled practice. The scope of effective practice opportunities extends beyond its center—a well-equipped classroom. It includes school-wide activities, homework, and the educational resources of the entire community. Drills for speed and accuracy should not be instituted until *after* the students have achieved an understanding of the skill or concept and have discovered efficient modes of attack. For different kinds of learning tasks, the teacher and students should try to discover the optimum length and distribution of practice periods. Before expecting top-level proficiency in the performance of complex skills, the need for a warm-up exercise should be recognized. Both implicit and explicit practice are effective —each in its place. In structuring approaches, preliminary, imaginary practice is sometimes helpful. However, in more advanced stages of learning and for checking goal-directed trials, actual practice is necessary.

Besides facilitating the mastery of concepts and skills, the thousands of practice activities in which children and youth engage should also produce more efficient learners. But this desired outcome is not automatic. In this chapter we have therefore considered some guides to the efficient use of practice opportunities. We shall continue this interest in the next chapter, where we shall consider the contribution which educational psychology has made and is making to the cultivation of *efficient modes of attack* in learning.

GUIDES FOR STUDY, REVIEW, AND APPLICATION

1. Look back over your learning efforts in reaching a high level of proficiency in some complex system of concepts or skill—such as chess, the periodic table in chemistry, or bowling. Could you describe such learning as a goal-directed, trial-and-check process? For illustration of the trial-and-check process in mastering art skills see either of the films *Design for Growing* (33 minutes), United World, or *Your Child a Genius* (14 minutes), David Robbin Productions.

2. What is the specific role of practice—as provisional trials—in this process?

3. What is practice? Explain why degree of mastery of concepts or skills is *sometimes* unrelated to the number of times they have been repeated —a fact illustrated in Harap and Mapes' experiment.

4. Explain this statement: Practice is necessary but not sufficient for effective learning.

5. Cite experiments and examples to show that checking the correctness of responses is essential for learning, and that the effectiveness of learning depends on how informatively, precisely, and promptly provisional trials are checked.

6. From self-observation in mastering such a skill as typewriting, piano playing, or tennis, find as many examples as you can of the specific kinds of learning requiring practice.
7. In addition to the functional practice which grows out of projects and classroom activities, why is a considerable amount of systematically scheduled classroom and homework practice also needed by elementary and secondary school children? How can it be managed most efficiently?

Chapter 9

EFFICIENT MODES OF ATTACK IN LEARNING

The great amount of academic learning required of individuals living in modern, civilized societies has already been suggested. To accomplish their learning goals, Americans devote 20 to 30 per cent of their lifetimes to full-time education, and many of them continue throughout their lives to spend part of their time in further study. All this effort, however, appears to fall short of satisfying our need for knowledge and skill. Each of us is reminded almost daily that he could function more effectively and with greater joy in his work, recreation, and social activities if he knew more or had more skill. In addition to our individually sensed need for more personal effectiveness, we have, as a nation, become acutely aware of our need for more and better-trained personnel in many strategically important occupations. Indeed, it has been said that one of the ten top scientific events of the last year was the awakening in America of "the necessity of better and more widespread training of scientists [68]." The question is: How can we meet these needs more fully?

There are several approaches to our goal of achieving greater knowledge and skill. One way is to improve the efficiency of our learning efforts. This approach, fortunately, has been a major concern of the science of educational psychology for the past half century.

The importance of the work which educational psychologists have done was amply demonstrated during the emergency period of World War II. When the war came, America suddenly found herself without adequate preparation. The situation required the rapid training of tremendous numbers of men and women for new military and civilian-defense occupations. In accomplishing this great task, psychologists contributed very significantly. On the basis of a survey of their activities, Wolfe says that "the important stock in trade of the psychologist working on military training problems consisted of his knowledge of the principles of learning. The judicious application of these principles helped speed the training of a victorious army and navy [74]."

There is still, of course, much to be learned about how to learn efficiently, but a comprehensive survey of this area of educational psychology yields many practical suggestions—many more, in fact, than most teachers usually apply.

As will be recalled from our discussion in Chapter 7, the teacher has a twofold goal in applying the principles of learning: guiding pupils in their mastery of specific concepts and skills; and teaching them *how* to learn and to solve problems efficiently. Without effective teacher guidance in learning how to learn after the early grades, students do not make significant improvement in study skills from all their practice in studying. With appropriate teacher guidance, however, students who are learning the concepts and skills of any subject-matter area may acquire more effective learning methods also.

In testing this assumption, Leggitt studied the effects of teacher-guided practice in the application of certain study skills, in reading, interpretation of graphs and tables, summarizing, and outlining. During an 18-week semester of a course in American government, 42 pairs of ninth grade students served as experimental and control groups. The effectiveness of teacher guidance is indicated in Figure 9.1. As the graph shows, the group given guided practice improved steadily in study skills. The nonguided group made no appreciable improvement.

Whether the general teaching procedure is systematic teacher direction or teacher guidance of pupils' self-discovery learning, good teachers in every subject try to facilitate effective mastery of specific concepts and skills and at the same time try to guide pupils in becoming more efficient learners. An understanding of the following general

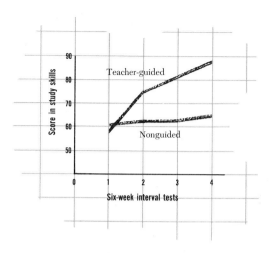

Fig. 9.1. *Teacher guidance in study skills results in improvement as ninth grade students study American government.* (Adapted from Dorothy Leggitt, *Sch. Rev.*, 1934, vol. 42, p. 684.)

principles of efficient learning and appropriate application of them should aid teachers in accomplishing these goals.

ACTIVE "SELF-RECITING" LEARNING

Effective learning is not a process of absorption, of passive reception of impressions—it is more a process of active striving and searching, of creative construction of integrated response patterns to meet problem situations. Gates first demonstrated this principle in an historically important experiment on memorizing, the general results of which have been confirmed in several areas of learning. As they memorized short biographies, different groups of children from grades 3 to 8 were directed to use self-recitation for different proportions of the total time allotted. One group spent the entire practice period reading and rereading a biography. Five other comparable groups spent, respectively, the last 20, 40, 60, 80, and 90 per cent of the time in self-recitation—that is, in actively trying to recite a selection without reading from the copy, but glancing at it only when necessary to prompt themselves. The relative effectiveness of each amount of self-recitation is shown in Figure 9.2. The number of ideas recalled for each condition is expressed as a percentage of the average number recalled for all conditions.

As the figure reveals, spending any proportion of the study time in active self-recitation is superior to devoting all of it to passive reading and rereading. The appropriate proportion of time to spend in self-recitation will, of course, vary with the nature of the content and the mode of attack employed in reading it. For Gates's particular selections, the optimum proportion proved to be about 60 per cent. For longer passages, greater proportions of time will probably be required for reading [55]. It is possible (and desirable) to use the equivalent of self-recitation in the reading itself. If the student employs a question-raising and self-answering mode of attack in studying science, social studies, or literature, little extra time as such may be needed for self-recitation.

Active self-recitation is a general principle of efficient learning. Forlano has reported that self-reciting methods improve efficiency of learning spelling, English vocabulary, and arithmetic combinations [20]. In teaching handwriting, Hertzberg found that a copying method, which required the equivalent of active self-recitation, produced 40 per cent greater gains than did any of four different tracing methods which demanded of the children little or no initiative or active conceptualization of the task [30]. Several studies show that such applications of the principle of self-recitation as outlining, summarizing, and reading to answer questions improve understanding and retention of prose content in social studies and science. Active participation in class discussions of problems also facilitates learning. On this factor, Carpenter and Fort found correlations between frequency of pupil-volunteered contributions to discussions and achievement—in social studies, English, and mathematics—ranging from .43 to .84, for grades 4 to 11 [8, p. 52].

VISUALIZING SIGNIFICANT, RESPONSE-GUIDING CUES

Self-constructed mental maps or conceptualized schema guide the learner in executing anticipated action patterns. According to cognitive learning theory, the more readily the individual can identify the response-guiding cues, the more quickly he should be able to learn appropriate responses to them. Two experiments indicate that children are able to solve experimentally contrived discrimination problems

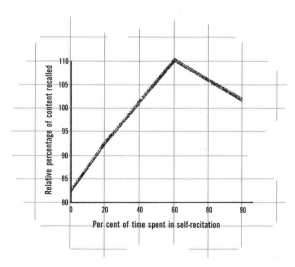

Fig. 9.2. *Self-recitation facilitates memorizing.* (Adapted from A. I. Gates, *Arch. Psychol.,* 1917, vol. 6, no. 40, p. 41.)

more effectively when the guiding cues are presented distinctly than when they are either embedded in a total configuration or require discrimination between remembered cues [5, 54].

Outlines, diagrams, pictures, and motion-picture films are some of the media employed by teachers for making relevant features of problem situations more identifiable. As an illustration of these procedures, both Hall and Erickson have suggested that teachers use chalk of different colors to identify more sharply the significant features of problem-solving demonstrations [15, 27]. And Hanna has indicated that a graphical analysis—which brings out the relevant components of a problem—is superior to a verbal analysis, for teaching fourth and seventh grade pupils arithmetic problem solving. His "graphical dependencies" method is illustrated by a diagramed representation of the problem: "Sam had 12 marbles. He found 3 more and then gave 6 to George. How many did Sam have left? [28]"

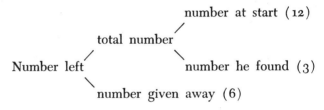

When a complex, sequential pattern of action is to be learned, slow-motion films are often helpful in identifying the significant features of the response to be imitated. For example, when films demonstrating engine-lathe operation were carefully integrated with other modes of instruction on this process, adults given this supplementary visual guidance mastered the skill rather quickly. Other adults, whose instruction was confined to the "conventional lecture-demonstration method," required more time [70]. In teaching 13 equated pairs of tenth grade boys the high jump, Priebe and Burton compared the results of giving explanations and demonstrations only with the results obtained from using these same procedures *plus* slow-motion films of the performances of champion jumpers and of the boys themselves— as they progressed in acquisition of the skill. Good form, defects, and specific coördinations were visualized and analyzed in slow motion

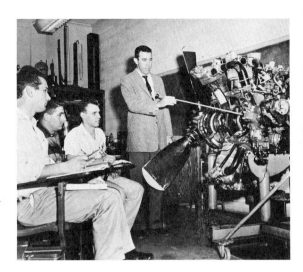

Complex concepts are grasped more readily when the teacher both demonstrates and explains the response-guiding cues. (Utah State University, Logan, Utah; photograph by Arlen Hansen.)

and sometimes in stopped frames. In order to maximize their usefulness, the films were run, discussed, and then rerun. Over a six-week period, weekly tests revealed superior progress for the group whose instruction was supplemented by the films [58].

VERBAL CONCEPTUALIZING AND GENERALIZING

In the experiments described above, the films themselves were accompanied by verbal explanations. Such explanations often enhance the effectiveness of demonstrations. For example, Thompson found that demonstration *plus* teacher-guided verbalization of the steps in assembling a mechanical puzzle reduced the number of trials required for mastering it to half the number required when silent demonstrations only were employed [66]. Words are the human being's most useful tool for designating, discriminating, differentiating, classifying, organizing, generalizing, and operating perceptually and symbolically with things and activities. As such, they are meaningful symbols for conceptualizing approaches and solutions to problems, for remember-

ing, and for generalizing applications to new situations [10]. According to cognitive learning theory, verbalizing facilitates learning because words are effective tools in the cognitive map making which guides performance.

Words in motor learning. The caller for square dancing is not superfluous: his rhythmic verbalizations guide the dancers through the intricate patterns of the dance. Several experiments indicate that both self-guided and teacher-guided verbalizations facilitate discover-

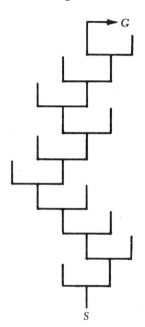

ing and memorizing solutions to perceptual motor problems. Both Warden [71] and Husband [35] directed blindfolded students to learn multiple-U high-relief finger mazes, such as the one diagramed. Upon reaching the criterion of mastery—3 out of 4 trials without error—each subject was asked about his method. The procedure most frequently employed was to verbalize the discovered pattern as a guide to memorizing it, that is, to say to oneself, "Two turns right, two left, one right," and so on. Some subjects, however, constructed visual images of the unseen pattern. Still others said they developed motor-kinesthetic "feelings" for the pattern. In both studies, verbalizing the pattern proved to be the best approach—it required fewer trials and less time to master the mazes than either of the other two procedures. Moreover, when the students in Warden's study were asked to draw the maze as they had imaginatively constructed it, the verbalizers were much the most accurate. Apparently, verbalizing a task aids students in creating a more accurate cognitive guide for learning it. Teacher direction to verbalize such procedures is also effective. The general suggestion to "verbalize what [you are] thinking and doing" aided fourth grade pupils in mastering a complicated design problem which required them to arrange the several parts of a design in layers in a particular order [26]. More explicit verbal instructions to college students on how to learn a maze [44] and how to solve a disk-transfer problem [16] also facilitated mastery.

Labeling in remembering. Two investigations indicate that naming objects they see helps children to remember them and to deal with them more effectively in problem situations. In one experiment, Pyles hid a toy always under the same one of five different nonsense-shaped molds (randomly arranged in each different trial), and directed comparable groups of two- to seven-year-old children to discover and remember in subsequent trials which mold the toy was hidden under. Using counterbalanced orders of groups and conditions to control possible differential practice effects, she varied the extent and kind of verbalization. For condition A, the children were told: "One of these shapes has a

toy under it; see if you can find the shape which has the toy." For condition B, the directions were the same, except that when the toy was found, the mold was given an unfamiliar name, such as *Mobie*, and the children were directed to repeat the name. (The names of the other molds were *Kolo, Tito, Gamie, Bokie*.) For condition C, the directions were similar to those for B, except that the identifying words were already familiar (*cat, dog, rabbit, bear, monkey*). For conditions B and C, in which the objects to be discriminated were named, fewer trials were required to reach the criterion of mastery—four successive correct choices—than for condition A where labeling was not employed [59]. In their experiment, Kurtz and Hovland [42] found that when a group of elementary school children both encircled *and* read aloud the names of 16 familiar objects, they remembered more of them a week later than did a comparable group who had merely encircled them.

Words mediate generalizations. Most of the studies already reviewed could be interpreted to indicate that verbalizing facilitates learning either by designating sharper discriminations or by mediating generalizations. As an example of how a word mediates a generalization, consider the common meaning of the word "balance" in several applications such as balanced scales, equation, diet, account, or art composition. The word "balance" connotes the same *general* kind of operation to achieve equilibrium of components or forces in each of these different situations. Having learned the concept in one situation, the word for it mediates generalizations to other situations. Two studies demonstrate especially well the function of verbalization in generalizing.

Using as subjects 59 preschool children divided into experimental and control groups, Shepard first trained both groups to press a button at the signal of a red light and *not* to press it for a blue light, reinforcing them by saying "Right" and "Wrong" for correct and incorrect responses, respectively [61]. Then, after testing both groups for generalizing—in a test to be described—the investigator trained the experimental group to call red, red-orange, orange, and yellow lights

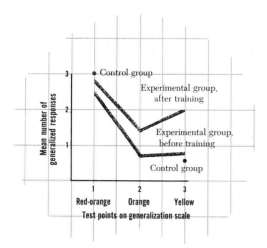

Fig. 9.3. *Preschool children, trained to press a button to red lights only, generalize the response —after verbal training—and tend to press the button to all lights called "Mo."* (From Winifred O. Shepard, *Child Developm.*, 1956, vol. 27, p. 314.)

Mo, and to call the blue light *Lee*. To determine the effect of the verbal training given only to the experimental group, she tested both groups on a generalization test both *before* and *after* the verbal training. The generalization test consisted of a presentation of *all* the lights with the request to press the button at the appropriate signals. Would the experimental group of children, who had been trained to press the button only for a red light, now generalize the response and press the button for all lights called *Mo*? The average number of generalized responses of the two groups both before and after verbal training are graphed in Figure 9.3.

As the graph shows, *after* the verbal training, the experimental group made more generalized responses to lights other than red which also had been called *Mo*. That this increase in generalizing was caused by the verbal training is further indicated by the fact that the control group—without the intervening verbal training—did not generalize responses except for the very similar red-orange light.

In another study it has been shown that children who have already in their vocabulary appropriate terms for labeling concepts—such as the term "triangle" for varied triangular figures—discover such concepts in new situations more readily than do students who lack names for the concepts [62].

Factors affecting effective verbalizing. Whether verbalizing facilitates learning or not depends upon several factors: the student's understanding of the words employed, the degree of clarity or distinctiveness with which the words discriminate between concepts, the learner's maturity and proficiency in verbalizing, and the extent of teacher guidance or of the learner's resourcefulness in labeling.

Meaningfulness. It will be recalled that Pyles found that both nonsense terms and familiar names aided children in discovering under which nonsense-shaped mold a toy had been hidden. Familiar names, however, were more helpful than nonsense names. In concept-guided sorting, Carey and Goss also found familiar names more helpful than nonsense labels [6]. The limitation of meaningless terms becomes more apparent, however, in more complex situations.

Sometimes school children's verbalizations are unrelated to meaningful, concrete experience; consequently, they reflect only a superficial understanding of the concepts discussed. As an illustration, we have Hughes's report of some eighth grade students' definitions of the phrase "cooperate with others." It means, they said: "Do what you are told." "Don't whisper." "Agree with the teacher." A contrasting illustration was provided by a group of kindergarten children. When their teacher observed that they had put their floor blocks away quickly and neatly, she asked them how they had done such a good job. They replied: "Everyone helped. Stacked them right—big ones on the bottom. Nobody got in a fight. It didn't take too long. We weren't forever putting away blocks [34, p. 458]." Such a verbalization of their concrete experience in discovering how to work together efficiently probably enhanced their understanding of the process. The components of the task became both more clearly differentiated and better integrated into an organized pattern. When a process is thus clearly conceptualized, it is more likely to be remembered and applied in other situations as a generalized pattern of effective teamwork.

Distinctiveness. Dietze found for preschool children that distinctively different labels (such as *jod, daf,* and *meep*) are more effective verbal guides in discriminating and classifying forms than similar or rhyming labels (such as *beem, meem,* and *peem*) [12].

Maturity. The factor of individual differences—in maturity and in proficiency of verbalizing—has been found related to effectiveness of verbalizing in learning both abstract concepts [37, 41] and in arithmetic problem solving [18]. Other aspects of this factor were taken up in Chapter 3 when we discussed the role of maturation in terms of readiness for learning.

Guidance. Children learn to employ verbalization both from teacher guidance and from self-guided experience. Norcross and Spiker showed that the effect of guidance in naming specific stimuli is extended to naming other stimuli, with consequent facilitation in learning discriminations [53]. Pyles noted that 13 children, without any guidance, discovered the usefulness of verbalizing in finding under which mold a toy was hidden. Spontaneously calling the nonsense-shaped molds "the cup," "Old Mother Shoe," "the slide," "the smoothed one," and so on, these resourceful children required only 11.9 trials to master the problem, while the uninstructed group as a whole required 47.1 trials.

Summarizing our review, we find that appropriate verbalization helps students to structure and solve problems, memorize and retain concepts, and apply the generalized products of learning to related situations. Words, as labels, classify similar things and events and thus facilitate generalized responses to them. Words also function in designating discriminated differences, and thus they guide appropriately differentiated responses in innumerable situations. As symbols for things and events experienced in the past, the present, and imaginatively anticipated in the future, words make possible complicated, integrated responses to stimulus situations extended in time and place. They—with other less precise and differentiated symbols—make it possible to reason, to substitute imagined provisional trials for more awkward or impossible overt action. And because they also function in communication between individuals, they contribute to cooperative problem solving.

MEANINGFULNESS OF CONTENT AND APPROACH

Social studies, science, literature, mathematics, and other areas of the school curriculum are sometimes approached as a collection of isolated facts to be memorized. Such a procedure, however, is needlessly inefficient. Original mastery, retention, and generalized applications are all more efficient when such concepts are studied as organized, interrelated systems of ideas, and when the learner searches for or creates generalized principles of wide-scope application.

Meaningful content. Several experiments have shown that meaningfulness of content is a determinant of efficient learning. Lyon—acting as his own subject—memorized in one reading per day 200 units each of four kinds of material, varying in meaning. Meaningless nonsense syllables required 93 minutes; almost as meaningless digits required 85 minutes; meaningful prose required only 24 minutes; and both meaningful and otherwise well-structured poetry was memorized in only 10 minutes [47].

A more precise illustration of the close relationship of meaningfulness of content to efficiency of learning has been demonstrated by Noble in a series of experiments [50, 51, 52]. He first constructed a scale of words ranked in order of meaningfulness—determined by the average number of response associations which could be made to each word in one minute. Lowest in the scale is the artificial word *gogey* which produced only .99 association. A word of medium meaningfulness, *rostrum*, elicited 2.73 associations. *Kitchen,* the most meaningful in his scale of 96 words, stimulated his subjects to respond with an average of 9.61 associations [50]. From this scale of words, Noble constructed three 12-word lists—containing, respectively, words of low, medium, and high degrees of meaningfulness. The rates of acquisition and the total number of trials required by 72 college students to mem-

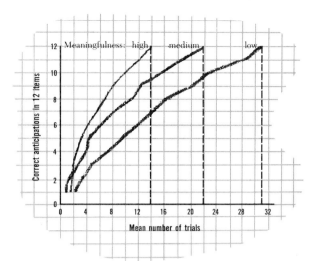

Fig. 9.4. *Rate of learning and total trials, required for mastery vary for lists of words of low, medium, and high degree of meaningfulness.* (After C. E. Noble, *J. Exp. Psychol.*, 1952, vol. 43, p. 440.)

orize each of the three lists—by the serial anticipation method—are shown in Figure 9.4.

As is clearly shown in the figure and in other data [52], efficiency of learning is closely related to the meaningfulness of the material learned. In this instance, the progress curve is steepest for the most meaningful material; it requires less than half as many repetitions for mastery than does the least meaningful list.

Meaningful approach. Efficiency of learning also varies with the meaningfulness of the approach. For example, one may establish—with sufficient repetitions—any number of arbitrary associations between the nonsense word *bep* and each of the following groups of words: *club, picnic, reaches, beet; potato, careful, pasture, raised;* and *crawl, turnip, pleasant, closet.* Reed found that directing college students to search for meaningful concepts governing these and other similar paired associations aided them in learning the associations. In this instance, the common feature connecting *bep* with each group of four words is that each group contains the name of a vegetable. Once this concept is discovered, it can be applied—without further specific practice—in associating *bep* with other word groups containing names of vegetables [60].

This type of generalization—which meaningful material and meaningful approaches make possible—is probably the "secret" of efficient learning. Such learning takes advantage of the learner's background of prior learning. In Reed's experiment, only individuals who had already learned the concept of vegetables as a class of things could, of course, identify the common feature connecting *bep* with the word groups including *beet, potato,* and *turnip.* Another economy which a

Efficient modes of attack in learning 317

meaningful approach to learning affords is that multiple-element tasks can often be reduced to multiple applications of a single general principle. In this case, *bep*—as a generalized concept—designated *any* group of words containing a vegetable name. These advantages of a meaningful approach to learning, as we shall see in the next chapter, are also explainable as products of transfer of learning.

Experiments with school content also indicate the advantage of a meaningful approach to learning. In teaching third grade children borrowing in subtraction, Brownell and Moser compared meaningful and "mechanical" procedures. Using the following example to illustrate a meaningful approach,

$$\begin{array}{r} {}^{5}\!\!\not{6}\ {}^{1}5 \\ -\ 2\ 8 \\ \hline 3\ 7 \end{array}$$

the teacher explained: "I can't take 8 from 5, so I borrow 10 from 6 tens. I cross out 6 and write a little 5 to show that I borrowed a 10. I write a little 1 in front of 5 to show I now have 15 instead of 5." The comparable mechanical explanation was this: "I can't take 8 from 5, so I think 5 as 15. Then I think 8 from 15 is 7, and I write 7. Since I thought of 5 as 15, I must think 6 as 5. Then I think 2 from 5 is 3 and write 3." When the children were tested to measure their accuracy, their retention (after a six-week period), their ability to transfer the approach to untaught three-digit numbers (such as 539 − 242), and their rated degree of understanding, it was found that those children taught meaningfully surpassed those taught mechanically. Furthermore, this experiment suggests that relatively meaningless procedures frustrate the individual's natural need to understand. Children taught mechanically indicate this frustration by asking such questions as: "But where did you get the 1 to make the 5 a 15 . . .? [4]"

In memorizing passages of prose or poetry, it is often effective to read the selection thoughtfully, thinking of the central meaning and constructively organizing the component ideas around it. For example, Cofer found that college students who were learning folk tales required fewer trials to reach comparable levels of mastery when they reproduced ideas in organized sequences than when they attempted to reproduce the tales verbatim [9].

The construction of the miniature, protective palisade aides these children in reviewing a pioneer period of our history. (Trenton School, Trenton, Utah; photograph by Arlen Hansen.)

School learning also affords many practical illustrations of the advantages of a meaningful approach. In the previous chapters we have cited several examples of how children—working with concrete and semiconcrete materials—discovered, generalized, and effectively applied concepts in self-discovery projects. Reading for meaning provides context as a very effective cue in identifying unfamiliar words. Spelling a word such as "appointment" is facilitated by identifying the familiar root, the recognized suffix, and by generalizing from experience with other instances of doubled consonants, as in "appear" or "apply." First grade children are aided in learning manuscript writing by noticing that *all* 26 letters in the alphabet are represented by simple circles and straight or curved lines. Geometry is mastered more effectively by trying to understand and apply creatively its system of theorems than by attempting verbatim memorization of them. And social studies, science, mathematics, and other such subjects are comprehended more effectively as systems of interrelated functional concepts than as collections of isolated facts. Without the integration of basic ideas or principles, collections of facts are useless. For example, students who study mathematics as a collection of rules and techniques are often confused in deciding which rule or technique to apply in a particular problem. The problem $7/8 - 2/3 = ?$ was given to one such student. He decided to use the rule: Invert the divisor and multiply [45, p. 408].

A PRELIMINARY OVERVIEW

The separate parts of an integrated activity or learning project take on meaning as their interrelationships in the whole are perceived. Just as a map-guided exploration of a new city yields more understanding than street-by-street meanderings, so an initially projected comprehensive outline of a topic in social studies or science contributes to efficient mastery of the subtopics.

An overview enhances children's understanding of a complex process. (Edith Bowen Laboratory School, Utah State University, Logan, Utah; photograph by Ivan Pederson.)

There are many illustrations of the application of this principle. The high school band or orchestra conductor, for example, may give his students an overview of a new piece by playing a recording of it. Then, before working on troublesome parts, the ensemble will play through the entire piece. In memorizing a poem, a speech, or a musical composition, the first step should be a complete reading and a self-reciting review. The unifying pattern or thread of meaning in the piece as a whole provides generalized cues for remembering the parts or segments. In learning a complex motor skill such as swimming, we should initially practice the skill as a whole before concentrating on such aspects as kicking, arm movements, or breathing. The comprehensive grasp of the skill makes the practice on the minor features more meaningful and therefore more effective. Knapp and Dixon found that among groups of college students who were learning to juggle three paddle-tennis balls, those who began practice with first one, then two, and finally three balls mastered the skill less quickly than those who tried to juggle all three from the beginning. Those who used only one or two balls failed to attain the speed and to grasp the complexity of performance demanded in three-ball juggling [38].

Another experiment suggests the effectiveness of an overview in problem-solving learning. Hildreth presented three jigsaw picture puzzles (of a train, a steam shovel, and a ferryboat) to 100 children, aged seven to ten, who were subdivided into groups for two different modes of presentation. The picture puzzle to be assembled was presented to one group without explanation or prior opportunity to see it. A preliminary overview was given to the other group. As an aid in organizing the parts, the teacher, prior to the assembly task, showed the latter group the completed picture puzzle and named and pointed

out its various features. A comparison of the results of the two procedures revealed that "puzzle solving proved easier and quicker" when
preceded by a preliminary overview. The educational implication is
that "school problem solving will be more successful to the extent that
the pupils can be given an overview of the whole, some knowledge
of the central meaning of the problem, and some meaningful clues to
aid solution [31, p. 604]."

Whole versus part methods of memorizing. The whole approach
has the advantage of giving greater meaning to a skill or concept to
be learned, but there are materials on which part-by-part memorization is more efficient for some individuals [36]. If the selection is long,
it is sometimes effective to memorize small, meaningful segments separately after a preliminary study of the whole. Relatively immediate,
clear knowledge of progress as subgoals are attained is better motivation than the long-deferred or more vague evidence of progress which
is characteristic of the whole method. Moreover, memorization by the
whole method often entails overpractice on some parts (usually the
beginning and end of a piece are learned first), whereas in the part
method, the amount of practice can be adjusted economically to the
needs of each part. Notwithstanding these merits of the part method,

*Classification reinforces the understanding, retention, and application of concepts
learned.* (Ellis School, Logan, Utah; photograph by Arlen Hansen.)

Efficient modes of attack in learning   321

the whole method is generally more efficient for mature individuals, for children of superior intelligence, and for individuals who have learned to employ it skillfully [63]. Hovland writes, in his summary of the literature, that "the best advice seems to be to learn by using the largest units that are meaningful and within the individual's capacity [32]."

Often a combination of whole and part methods is effective. Given the task of memorizing a five-verse poem, for example, the individual might first achieve an overview and general understanding by thoughtfully reading the entire poem. Then, employing the principle of self-recitation, he might verbalize the main ideas or think through the poem in his own words. After a second reading, he would try to recite it verbatim. This attempt would reveal the verse on which the learner experiences most difficulty. He would then, studying it separately, master this most difficult verse. Then, returning to restudy of the whole, he would repeat the whole-to-part sequence. This alternation between whole and part methods takes advantage of the meaningfulness of the whole, of the enhanced motivation in clear knowledge of progress, and of the economy of adjusting the amount of practice to the needs of each verse. It also employs the principles of self-recitation and perception of the effects.

ORGANIZATION

Organization—as a factor facilitating learning—is another variation of the more general principle of meaningfulness. The thousands of facts and skills which students learn in school can be mastered more efficiently if appropriate techniques and principles are utilized for grouping and classifying them, if they are integrated into expanding developmental systems, and if inductive generalizations can be drawn from them.

Classification. Even from the study of relatively few facts, we can often achieve, through appropriate classification, both meaning-enhancing generalizations and criteria for making fine discriminations. To try to understand, for example, the world of hundreds of thousands of different animals as an unclassified collection would be an impossible undertaking. However, from experience with relatively few animals

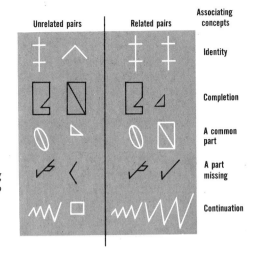

Fig. 9.5. *Already established concepts for classifying pairs of related nonsense figures make them easier to associate than pairs of unrelated nonsense figures.* (After W. C. H. Prentice and S. E. Asch, *Amer. J. Psychol.*, 1958, vol. 71, pp. 247–354.)

and Linnaeus's scheme for classifying them, many children achieve functional understanding of the great variety of animal life. To illustrate: one may never have heard of a dingo, but if he knows that the genus-species name is *Canis dingo*, he immediately infers that it is a doglike animal, since it belongs to the same genus as *Canis familiaris*. Or, one may temporarily confuse the porcupine with the common European hedgehog—both having spiny coverings. However, in Linnaeus's classification, they are discriminated. The porcupine, with its well-developed incisors for eating foliage and bark, belongs to the order *rodentia*. The insect-eating hedgehog belongs to the order *insectivora*.

Many other schemes for classifying concepts and skills provide similar economies in learning. Sentences may be analyzed into subjects and predicates, into parts of speech, and other structural components. There are the times tables—or better, a single 10-by-10 or 12-by-12 table of products—in multiplication. In spelling, we may classify many words according to certain common features; we may observe, for example, that *back, lack, sack,* and *tack* are similar, except for the initial consonant. Such multiple-element bodies of facts can be taught more efficiently if they are organized logically or grouped to bring out common features or principles than if presented as heterogeneously mixed lists [43, 75].

Prentice and Asch have demonstrated experimentally the effectiveness of "logical organization" as a factor facilitating learning and recall of associated abstract concepts. To 32 college students they presented, for associating together, two different series of 16 related and unrelated pairs of figures. In the related pairs, as is shown in Figure 9.5, the second member of a pair is an identity, completion, common part, missing part, or a continuation of the first. Four

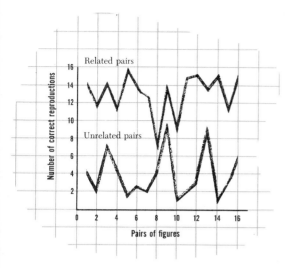

Fig. 9.6. *Correct reproductions of second member of twice-rehearsed pairs of logically related figures is better than for twice-rehearsed unrelated pairs of figures. (From W. C. H. Prentice and S. E. Asch,* Amer. J. Psychol., *1958, vol. 71, p. 250.)*

minutes after the memorization presentations, the first member of each pair in both series was again presented. In these test presentations, the subjects were asked, upon seeing the first member of each pair, to recall and to draw the second member. The average number of correct reproductions of both logically associated and nonassociated forms are presented in Figure 9.6.

As the figure clearly shows, fitting or logical organization greatly facilitates such learning. In two presentations of each series, over three times as many logical associations as unrelated associations were learned.

Sequential integration. Organization can also contribute to efficiency of learning the sequences of topics which comprise many school curricula, such as the series of topics in social studies, science, or mathematics. When each new topic in a sequence is related to or developed as an extension of the organized accumulation or meaningful integration of preceding topics, the efficiency of learning is increased. Such facilitation is more probable when concepts learned are functionally classified or catalogued and hierarchically organized as broad general concepts, subconcepts, and specific illustrations. Then the related new concepts reactivate and mobilize "relevant subsuming concepts in the individual's existing cognitive structure" and enhance the meaning of them [1, p. 335].

Inductive generalizations. In studying a sequence of topics, retention and extension of meaning are also facilitated by searching the accumulating facts or data for organizing principles. Guilford exposed sequences of digits through an aperture and directed students to memorize such sequences as the following: 8-7-9-6-10-5-11-4-12-3-13-2-14-1-15 and 7-12-1-5-11-14-2-8-6-10-3-9-4. Discovering that the first sequence could be conceptualized as a progression of arithmetic differences alternating in sign, or simply as two alternating series, one ascending and the other descending, Guilford's subjects quickly memorized it. For some subjects, the pattern emerged in the first trial; other subjects required several trials or a hint to look for some schema before a helpful pattern of organization occurred. The second series—determined by no particular system—was memorized with greater difficulty [25].

PROCEEDING FROM THE FAMILIAR AND CONCRETE
TO THE NEW AND ABSTRACT

As we have already observed, verbalized concepts or cognitive guides to skilled performances often facilitate learning. But the verbalizations are effective only when they are based on adequate concrete experience. Therefore, concrete experience—actual or recalled—should be the first step in approaching an understanding of abstract concepts. This concrete experience is provided—as the illustrations which follow show—by visual and manipulatable materials in the classroom, by laboratory activities, by excursions into the community, and by drawing on the composite of children's background of experience.

For example, ample visual and manipulatory experience with appropriate objects facilitates understanding such abstract processes as adding, subtracting, multiplying, dividing, and the applications of these processes in problem solving. To provide such experience in the classroom, arithmetic corners include such materials as boxes, play

Problems are more easily understood by proceeding from the concrete to the abstract. (Adams School, Logan, Utah; photograph by Arlen Hansen.)

money, jars of different sorts of beans, rulers, paper of various colors, boxes of small sticks, elastic-tied bundles of sticks or tickets, an abacus and other counting and computing devices. Fernald describes a child's concrete approach to a problem which at an abstract level was too difficult for him: "If there are three brothers and their father gives them each two cents, how much do they have altogether?" Taking up a box of pennies and finding two kinds of beans, he placed on his desk a big red bean for the father, three white beans to represent the sons. Then he gave each white bean two pennies. After counting the pennies he announced his answer: "Six [17, p. 254]." As children acquire understanding and confidence, they learn to express and to solve such problems abstractly—in this instance, as $2 \times 3 = 6$.

The teacher-guided recall of out-of-classroom experiences of children can also be utilized to enrich the meaning of many abstract concepts in science and social studies. The composite extent of such classroom experiences is surprising [2]. Often an analogy can be a bridge for stepping from the already familiar to the new and puzzling. For example, a child orchestra encountered difficulty in learning the rhythm of a dotted quarter followed by an eighth note. When their teacher called attention to the same notation pattern in the familiar songs "America" and "America, the Beautiful," they readily achieved the rhythm in the new instrumental piece.

JOB ANALYSES OF LEARNING TASKS

There are usually several approaches to complex tasks, but often they are not equally efficient. Glancing back and forth, for example, from copy to typewriter results in less efficient typewriting than keeping one's eyes continuously on the copy. And employing all 10 fingers systematically with either of these procedures is more efficient than using the forefingers only. Without teacher or pupil analyses to determine the most efficient mode of attack in learning skills, varied tech-

niques—less effective than potentially possible—are often acquired.

Variations in efficiency of self-discovered approaches. For adding such columns of digits as that below,

$$
\begin{array}{r}
7 \\
6 \\
9 \\
3 \\
5 \\
\hline
\end{array}
$$

the most efficient procedure is to think the cumulative sums consecutively: 13, 22, 25, 30. Mature elementary education students, however, sometimes rearrange the numbers into easier combinations to avoid higher-decade additions. For example, one prospective teacher said: "I added 7 and 3; then I added 5, making 15. Next I added 5 instead of 6. This made 20. Finally, I added 10 to 20, because the other 1 from 6, when added to 9, made 10. The 10 added to 20 made 30 [19, p. 204]."

Flourney observed many similarly inefficient procedures in 48 third grade children whom she directed to think out loud as they solved problems. One child, adding 28 + 6, said: "I took 2 from 6 and then added it to 28. Then I had 30. I added 4 more to 30. Then I had 34 [19, p. 207]." In adding such single- and two-digit numbers, 23 of these children added the units and carried to the tens column. In higher-decade column addition, 11 of them *counted*, but they did not do so in noncolumn addition. And 4 skipped around to find easier combinations. For the same type of problem, 11 of the children employed a variety of procedures. All of these procedures are satisfactory, of course, as initial approaches. But, as the children progress in understanding and confidence, they should be directed or led to discover more efficient procedures. Otherwise immature procedures may persist.

Left-handers—abandoned by their right-handed teachers to instruct themselves in handwriting, sewing, and other manual skills—discover and acquire a variety of awkward modes of attack. In writing, for example, left-handed individuals often twist the wrist into a cramped position above the line being written so that they can see and avoid smearing what they are writing. One child found he could accomplish these purposes by writing backwards, from right to left. He wrote •ℓ for *go.*

Systematic teacher direction for learning efficiently. On the basis of a job analysis of the task, Cole proposes the following adaptations as guides for learning efficient left-handed writing:

1. The position of the paper should be such that the lower edge is at right angles to the arm being used—just the opposite of the position for the right-handed child.

2. The pencil or pen should be grasped at least 1 to 1½ inch from the point. This will avoid the child's covering or smearing with his fingers what he has just written.

3. The hand should slide along on the ends of the two smallest fingers, far enough below the line being written to miss the longest loops.

4. "Any slant between vertical and 45 degrees to the left of the base line is entirely satisfactory." The usual right slant from the base line would require of the left-handed child too great a proportion of push rather than pull movements, and the latter are easier to execute without pricking the paper.

5. As a further aid to avoid pricking the paper, the point of the pen should have a rounded nib.

6. As with the right-handed pupil, either an arm movement or wrist-and-hand movement may be used.

7. "The proportions of the letters are, of course, the same no matter which hand is used," except that the slant is reversed or vertical [11].

Improvements in study methods. Such job analyses to discover efficient modes of attack are applicable to all learning tasks. Guides

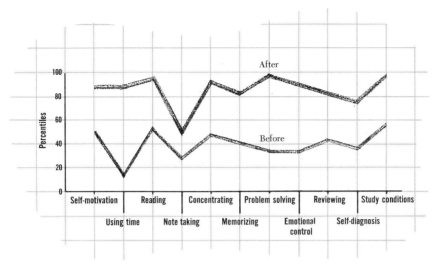

Fig. 9.7. *College student's profile of study skills indicating status before and after guided effort to improve studying procedures.*

to secondary school and college students on how to study are general applications of this principle. The results of self-inventories of study skills, such as those presented in Figure 9.7, can aid the student both in directing his attention to needed improvements in study skills and in evaluating his progress in learning them.

The percentile ranks of the college student represented in Figure 9.7 are based on his self-ratings—before and after a semester of guided effort to improve his study skills—on such items as the following:[1]

Do you try to improve the efficiency of your reading by converting the topical headings of the text into questions and then reading the passage to answer them for yourself?

Do you make good use of notes, by trying to make a question-outline or a topical outline of class notes, and by re-writing in outline form those parts which you could not outline during a class discussion or lecture?

Do you review and prepare for examinations effectively, by working out individual illustrations of general principles?

A threefold approach to improving the study skills of students produced significant improvement; the threefold approach included individual diagnosis, knowledge of effective methods, and specific applications by each student to his own study tasks [57].

Guidance toward more efficient modes of attack in learning can be systematic (as in the handwriting illustration) or it can be accomplished by teacher guidance of pupils' self-discovery experiences. The latter procedure is illustrated in children's self-discovery of how to

[1] From Utah State University Diagnostic Inventory of Study Skills, containing 55 items, 5 under each of the categories in Fig. 9.7.

Efficient modes of attack in learning 329

subtract in problems requiring borrowing, in such examples as 42¢ − 25¢. Using play money to explore the possibilities, Betty—beginning with 4 dimes and 2 pennies—changed all 4 dimes to pennies, then counted the remainder after counting out 25 pennies. Paul changed 1 dime to 2 nickels, and counted the remainder after removing 2 dimes and 1 nickel. Ann changed 1 dime to pennies, and then subtracted by taking away 5 pennies and 2 dimes. Since the teacher was concerned with developing pupil independence and initiative, she led the children to make their own job analysis. She asked them: "Which procedure demonstrated by the three children is most efficient, both when the money is manipulated and also when the problem is expressed in writing? [29]"

THE DEVELOPMENTAL ATTAINMENT OF EFFICIENT MODES OF ATTACK

High levels of efficiency are often finally attained even though the initial approach or intermediate stages are not efficient from the points of view of time and motion. Sometimes auxiliary aspects of performance—ultimately superfluous—are very helpful in the initial stages of learning a complex performance. And when they are no longer needed, they are dropped, either voluntarily or at the teacher's suggestion that the task can be performed more efficiently by eliminating them.

As initial self-discovery processes, a child might add 2 + 5 by making two and five marks (// + /////) and then counting them [48]. Knowing the double 3 + 3 = 6, he may add 3 + 4 by thinking 3 + 3 and 1 more = 7 [64]. He may solve the problem 33 − 17 by representing 33 as three bunches of 10 sticks each and 3 single sticks, and then by removing one bunch and 7 sticks of another [73]. These and other aids often make learning easier, more meaningful, and independent [39]. As the child grows in understanding and confidence, such crutches are abandoned in favor of more efficient modes of attack.

Despite our observation that children voluntarily give up many of these immature habits, some teachers object to the use of crutches on the assumption that practice of the ultimately unnecessary processes tends to fix them as permanent habits. Brownell, however, has demonstrated that most children readily give up such crutches when they are no longer needed.

He found that third grade children who used

$$8 \, {}^{5}\!\!\not{6} \, {}^{1}1$$
$$\underline{5 \quad 4 \quad 9}$$
$$\overline{3 \quad 1 \quad 2}$$

the crutch illustrated to guide them through the

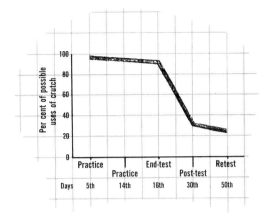

Fig. 9.8. *Crutches, when no longer needed, are abandoned for satisfying short cuts, as is indicated by decreasing use of a crutch for borrowing in subtraction.* (From W. A. Brownell and H. E. Moser, *Duke Univ. Res. Studies in Educ.*, No. 8, Duke Univ. Press, Durham, N.C., 1949.)

ancillary process of borrowing in subtraction achieved greater understanding and accuracy [3]. During 15 days of instruction and for the end-of-instruction test on the sixteenth day, the children were directed to use the crutch to remind themselves that, in borrowing a ten, the 6 tens in the minuend (in this particular example) have been reduced to 5 and that the one unit has been increased to eleven. After the end-test, they were encouraged to perform the operations more efficiently without using the crutch. As is revealed in Figure 9.8, their use of the crutch declined rapidly. In a post-test on the thirtieth day and on the delayed-retention test on the fiftieth day, there were many instances in which the children could have used the crutch. However, Brownell found that on both tests, they used it in only 29 and 22 per cent of these instances, respectively. Even during the instructional period—when its use was advised—some pupils voluntarily began to abandon it. Children returned to the crutch, however, when it was needed—after a lapse of time in use of the skill or with difficult problems, and when it could be employed in learning the new process of long division [4].

As was demonstrated in the preceding chapter, practice does not bind us to habits. Thorndike has shown how initially frequent responses are abandoned when responses providing greater motive satisfaction are discovered. Subject C, asked to write word completions for the beginning syllable *el-*, wrote *evate, ephant, ephant, evate, ephant, ephant, ephant, f, f, f, f, f, f, f, f.* Despite the initial frequency advantage for *elephant*, it was finally abandoned for *el-f*. The general tendency of Thorndike's subjects was to abandon longer completions for shorter ones, because they are easier [67, p. 14].

Generalizing from these results, we may conclude that when a crutch or learning aid clarifies or simplifies the initial approach to a learning task, it should be used without fear that it will become habitual and thus encumber the ultimate mode of attack with unnecessary processes. Inefficient processes are, however, sometimes continued beyond the stage of their effective use because they are comfortable and they permit us to delay exerting the additional effort it would require to master a more efficient procedure. Insecure and unconfident children continue with the old procedures because they fear the possibility of failing in a new learning venture. In all such instances, it is motive satisfaction, however—not repetition—which binds individuals to familiar habits.

SUMMARY

One way in which we can help our children and youth achieve greater knowledge and skill is to teach them how to learn more efficiently. As they learn specific concepts and skills in every area of the curriculum, they can, with appropriate guidance, also become more proficient as learners. In such guidance, both systematic teacher direction and teacher guidance of pupils' self-discovery experiences are effective. Our review of some of the scientifically established factors affecting the efficiency of learning suggests the following generalized principles of teacher guidance:

1. Leading an individual passively through a verbal or motor performance is an inefficient way of helping him to learn it. An active, self-reciting procedure results in more effective mastery and retention of the organized sequences of concepts and skills in many areas of the curriculum.

2. Outlines, diagrams, pictures, and slow-motion films—which aid in visually identifying the relevant features of problem situations and solutions—facilitate the pupil's attempts to structure approaches and execute appropriate patterns of response.

3. When the verbalization is based on adequate concrete experience, appropriate verbal conceptualizing of learning tasks aids in structuring and solving problems, in memorizing and retaining discovered solutions, and in applying generalizations. Words—as symbols for things and events—facilitate discriminating, generalizing, and reasoning.

4. Meaningfulness—both of content and approach—is a general determinant of efficient learning.

5. One way to make learning more meaningful—and therefore more efficient—is to take a comprehensive overview before attempting to master the subparts and details.

6. Organization—as classifications, as integrated developmental sequences, and as generalizations—also facilitates learning by providing a more meaningful approach.

7. Proceeding from the familiar and concrete to the new and

abstract is another meaningful approach which enhances understanding and increases the efficiency of learning, especially when complex concepts are involved.

8. The student without teacher guidance does not always discover the most efficient modes of attack. Therefore, systematic direction or guidance in making job analyses of learning performances often result in the attainment of higher levels of proficiency.

9. The student may ultimately attain high levels of proficiency, even though he does not from the outset use the most efficient approach. When crutches aid the immature learner in the initial stages of comprehending and executing complex performances, they should be utilized. When they are no longer needed, children give them up for more efficient procedures.

Perhaps a student's most important asset in developing efficient modes of attack in learning is the ability to generalize. Since generalizing is so essential a factor in learning, we have already discussed it in several preceding chapters. The development of generalized modes of problem solving was introduced as an important educational objective in Chapter 1. Since the learner utilizes his past experiences, simplifies multiple-element tasks, and anticipates future problems by generalizing, it was defined as an essential condition of learning in Chapter 2. Its significant roles in structuring approaches to problems, in the trial-and-check process of learning, and in meaningful and other efficient modes of attack in learning were brought out in Chapters 7 through 9. In the next chapter, we shall summarize, extend, and systematize our understanding of the role of generalizing in learning.

GUIDES FOR STUDY, REVIEW, AND APPLICATION

1. From all the studying they do, why do not elementary and secondary school students automatically improve their learning and problem-solving methods? How can the efficiency of their learning be improved? For one suggestion, see the film *Successful Scholarship* (11 minutes), McGraw-Hill Text-Film Department.
2. Suggest new applications of the principle of self-recitation.
3. Why do outlines, diagrams, and slow-motion films enhance the efficiency of learning?
4. Explain in terms of cognitive theory why the appropriate use of words enhances learning efficiency in a variety of ways.
5. Explain and cite illustrations of the roles in effective learning of meaning, overviews, and organization.
6. How is understanding of abstract concepts facilitated by supplying or reminding children of appropriate concrete experiences?
7. Of the varied ways in which a problem can be solved or a skill executed, how can children be guided to learn the most effective ways?

8. From observation of what appears to be an especially effective classroom learning activity, point out applications of as many of these efficient modes of attack as you can find. Most of them are illustrated in the film *Helping Children Discover Arithmetic,* College of Education, Wayne University.

Chapter 10

TRANSFER: GENERALIZING IN LEARNING

It is fortunate that children and youth are not required to learn as specific, unrelated responses all the thousands of concepts and skills they need. Such an undertaking would be exceedingly difficult, if not impossible. The task of education is facilitated, however, for both learners and teachers, because they can apply to new learning problems their store of already mastered, pertinent generalizations. They can, furthermore, employ unifying principles to simplify multiple-element learning tasks or to generate mastery of many facts and responses without specific practice of them.

Mastery of reading and writing in the Chinese language is said to be very difficult because the lack of an alphabet makes it necessary that the symbol for each word be committed to memory as a separate task. Memorizing the approximately fifty thousand characters of the language is a formidable job. As we should expect, however, Chinese, like other languages, is constructed on the basis of a few general

Transfer: applying concepts and skills
learned in one situation
to other situations

What principles developed here . . .   *might be applied here?*

Applying a theory;
drawing conclusions

What elements of this learning...

might be transferred to this?

principles. An understanding of these principles makes mastery of the language easier. For example, since *above* is written ⊥ (old form), it is easy to infer, according to the *indicative* principle, that the character ⊤ means *below*. Similarly, knowing that 𝇈 is the symbol for *woman*, it is not too surprising, according to the principle of *suggestive compound*, to learn that 𝇈𝇈 stands for *gossip* [30]. Such unifying principles greatly reduce the number of separate components to be learned in any multiple-element learning task.

The following episode illustrates how a resourceful high school student generalized an earlier-acquired concept and applied it to a new learning situation. Asked what he had learned from studying triangle *ABC*, a student said: "I started out knowing that angle *A* and angle *B* were equal and I have found out that whenever that is so, line *AC* must be equal to line *BC*." His teacher observed that although the student's statement was correct, its usefulness was limited. She suggested that he generalize his discovery beyond the particular triangle studied. When another student in an English class was asked the point of *Silas Marner*, he replied: "Silas was accused of taking some money which he really had not stolen so he ran away. It didn't do him any good though." Then a classmate who had also been in the geometry class remarked: "That is true enough, but it isn't very useful. If you want to make use of that same idea again in another situation, you ought to generalize it. You might say something like this: 'When one is accused of a crime which he has not committed, it is quite useless to try to escape by running away' [45, p. 226]." By generating numerous appropriate specific responses, such general concepts enhance the individual's efficiency.

THE ROLE OF TRANSFER IN SCHOOL LEARNING

Such instances of transfer—both as applications of already achieved generalizations and as inductive derivations and applications of unifying principles—pervade all school learning. For example, as a child's reading vocabulary increases, the effectiveness of context as a clue for identifying unfamiliar words in his reading is multiplied. Using phonetic analysis as a mode of attack in spelling certain words leads to the mastery of certain other words as a by-product, without the necessity of specific practice on them. A few art principles and techniques, once mastered, can be applied in unique creative expression whenever the need occurs. When effective command of mathematics, as a system of interrelated concepts and skills, is developed and generalized from the study of many problems, it is applicable to numerous other quantitative problems in scientific, social, and personal situations. Often transfer interrelations are far-reaching. For example, dramatics, art design, music appreciation, and knowledge of anatomy and physiology all contribute to the ballet dancer's training; and ballet training contributes to good posture and graceful movement, generalized dancing skills, body tone and health, and to interests in literature, art, music, and history.

Indeed, since no two problems or practice sessions are ever exactly alike, progressive development in any curriculum area depends on continual transfer from earlier to later learning activities. Thus transfer is an essential condition of all learning; and the efficiency of learning depends significantly upon how well pupils master general principles which can be applied to other learning situations. Transfer of learning should occur frequently between parts of a school subject (as between functional grammar and correctness of language expression), between different subjects (as between mathematics and science or social studies courses), and between school and out-of-school activities.

But transfer of learning does not always occur where it might logically be expected. Because of this fact, the history of modern education reveals that trust in the efficacy of transfer theories has varied [56, pp. 522–538]. In the early days of American education, teachers relied on a few difficult subjects to discipline the mind so that people would—with strengthened ability to reason—manage all sorts of activities effectively. At about the beginning of the present century, however, Thorndike and Woodworth—on the basis of research yielding only meager evidence of transfer [53, 54, 55]—proposed that "the mind . . . on its dynamic side is a machine for making particular reactions to particular situations [53, p. 249]." Gradual acceptance of this opinion discouraged reliance on transfer. It was assumed that each fact, skill, concept, or ideal needed by individuals in specific situations must be learned as a specific stimulus-response connection. But further and differently planned experimentation on this important concept continued, with such generally positive results that the validity of transfer has become firmly established and the conditions producing transfer have come to be more clearly understood.

Orata, in reviewing 167 experiments on transfer, reports that in 76 per cent of these studies either "considerable" or "appreciable" positive (favorable) transfer occurred [36]. It did not, however, always occur; sometimes there was no influence from activity A to activity B, and sometimes there was interference. In a subsequent further review of research on transfer, Orata listed some of the general factors upon which the extent of transfer depends [37]. Effective transfer is more likely with greater maturity; higher intelligence; recency and stability of the learned patterns to be transferred; favorable attitudes toward learning and its applications; efficient methods of study which emphasize meaning, generalizing, and applications; and the sequential and functional organization of the concepts and skills to be learned.

Since learning depends significantly on positive transfer we are interested in finding out how to control transfer. As a first step toward this objective, let us examine some typical instances of considerable, negative, and inappreciable transfer.

Positive transfer. Knight's experiment demonstrates effective positive transfer from certain taught to untaught examples in the addition of fractions. Two groups of children, of equal ability and equal readiness for the topic, were given the same amount of instruction in adding fractions. Group A practiced adding fractions which had as denominators 2, 3, 4, 5, 6, 7, 8, 9, 10, 12, 14, 15, 16, 18, 21, 24, 28, and 30. Group B practiced on fractions having as denominators only 2, 4, 6, 8, 12, and 24 and depended on transfer of this limited training for mastery of the untaught fractions. The crucial test for transfer was comprised of fractions with denominators of 3, 5, 7, 9, 14, 15, 18, 21, 28, and 30, which were taught to Group A but not to Group B. On this test, Group A scored 14.5 and Group B, 13.25. From practice with only six different numbers as denominators, the children were able to transfer the general principles which they had learned to fractions having other numbers as a denominator. Their ability to handle the other fractions was almost equal to that of the children who had practiced on them. In this instance, of course, both groups of children had already learned how to add, subtract, multiply, and divide *all* the digits as integers. These skills were available for application in fraction combinations [29].

Negative transfer. Negative and positive transfer are alike in that both involve applying earlier-achieved generalizations to new learning problems. They differ only in *accuracy* of principle and outcome. In transfer, faulty or erroneous generalizations produce erroneous results. Asked how he made the error in finding the product for this example

$$\begin{array}{r} 45 \\ \times\ 5 \\ \hline 305 \end{array}$$

David explained: "Well, 5 times 5 is 25. There is 2 to carry; 4 and 2 are 6, and 5 times 6 is 30. So the answer is 305 [17, p. 440]." Not understanding place values, David did not recognize 45 as 40 + 5. Application of his own faulty assumptions led to his error. In their tentative, uncertain approaches to ever higher levels of performance, children often produce such illustrations of negative transfer. In another instance, Archer observed that for words like *create* and *separate*, which drop the final *e* when the suffix *ing* is added, study of such forms as *create, creates,* and *created* sometimes yielded such misgeneralizations as *createing* [1].

Inappreciable transfer. Transfer is not automatic. Sometimes it fails to occur even in successive learning tasks where it might logically be expected.

This fact is illustrated in Buswell and Kersh's report of how superior college students solved a sequence of related problems, two of which are reproduced [8].

1. Find the sums of N consecutive odd numbers.

$$
\begin{array}{ccccc}
1 & 1 & 1 & 1 & 1 \text{ etc.} \\
\underline{3} & 3 & 3 & 3 & 3 \\
& \underline{5} & 5 & 5 & 5 \\
& & \underline{7} & 7 & 7 \\
& & & \underline{9} & 9 \\
& & & & \underline{11}
\end{array}
$$

2. How many x's are in the pyramid?

$$
\begin{array}{c}
x \\
x\ x\ x \\
x\ x\ x\ x\ x \\
x\ x\ x\ x\ x\ x\ x \\
x\ x\ x\ x\ x\ x\ x\ x\ x \\
x\ x\ x\ x\ x\ x\ x\ x\ x\ x\ x
\end{array}
$$

From experience in adding four or five columns of problem (1), the student should discover (inductively generalize) that the sum is always N^2. Having achieved this generalization, its application to problem (2) should quickly produce the total sum of x's in the pyramid, without the need for counting all of them. The student need only count and square the number of rows, since the sums of x's in the rows consist of consecutive odd numbers—beginning with the single x at the apex.

Transfer: generalizing in learning   339

Of 23 students who without hints achieved a correct generalization for problem (1), only 13 applied it to problem (2). And of the 60 students who *with* hints reached a correct solution for problem (1), only 23 transferred the generalization to problem (2).

Grossnickle reports another surprising instance of inappreciable transfer. To 1,075 pupils in grades 5 to 15, he administered a test of 50 multiplication facts followed by a division test requiring the use of these same 50 multiplication facts. On these incompletely mastered processes, over twice as many errors occurred in division as in multiplication (67.5 per cent in division, and 32.7 per cent in multiplication). The results indicate that a child in command of correct operations in multiplication often failed to apply his knowledge when the same multiplication facts were needed in division [18].

Even prospective teachers sometimes fail to apply their knowledge effectively. For 300 students in educational psychology, Horrocks found correlations of only .29 to .40 between their knowledge of facts and principles of adolescent development and their effectiveness in applying these facts to the diagnosis and remedial treatment of adolescent academic, social, and emotional problems—as described in case studies [25].

How can we account for these instances of positive, negative, and unexpected failure of transfer?

EXPLANATIONS OF TRANSFER

As explanations of transfer phenomena, two major theories have been proposed.

Theory of identical elements. According to Thorndike, improvement in one mental function produces improvement in another "only in so far as the two functions have as factors identical elements." For example, some transfer should occur from activity A_{12345} to activity B_{45678} because these activities have elements 4 and 5 in common. The elements which are present in both the originally learned activity and the activities to which it is transferred may be common facts ("such as length, color, number which are repeated again and again in differing combinations"), work methods, general principles, or attitudes [51, pp. 358–359].

Thorndike based his theory originally on the data obtained from some now-famous experiments which he and Woodworth carried out in 1901 [53, 54, 55]. Adult subjects were tested on several functions both before and after receiving training on functions which were similar to, but somewhat different from, those tested. In different experiments, four to six subjects were trained to a "high degree of proficiency" in estimating areas of rectangles, lengths of lines, and weights of objects, and in marking in selections of prose those words which contained *e* and *s* or which were certain parts of speech. Both before and after this training, the subjects were tested in estimating *other* areas, which in some instances were similar to the rectangles and in other instances were markedly different from them in both size and shape. They were also tested in estimating *different* weights and lengths of lines, and in marking words containing *other* both similar and different pairs of letters.

Comparisons of before and after status on both training and transfer tests yielded two general results:

1. Gains from transfer were almost always less than gains from direct training. For example, the average reduction in error from direct training in estimating the areas of certain rectangles was 86.3 per cent. The average reduction in error from before to after on the transfer tests, requiring estimates of areas of *other* geometrical figures, was only 21.2 per cent [53, p. 253]. Gains from transfer, however, *were* appreciable. Garrett observes that the gains from transfer ranged from "little or no improvement" on some functions to as much as 44 per cent on others of the gains directly due to practice [14].

2. The extent of transfer from trained-on to other functions was found to be related to the degree of similarity between them. For example, training in estimating the areas of rectangles varying in size from 10 to 100 square cm produced a reduction in error of 61 per cent in estimating the areas of other 20 to 100 square cm rectangles. Tested before and after on *triangles* with areas from 200 to 240 square cm, the reduction in error was only 14 per cent [54]. In general, it was found that the more the transfer tests differed from the training material, the less effective transfer became. "The spread of practice occurs only where identical elements are concerned in the influencing and influenced function [53, p. 250]." In these judging experiments, Thorndike and Woodworth suggested that the elements carried over from training to transfer tests were learning the relationship of inches to centimeters, skills acquired in estimating the often-used standard areas of 1, 10, 50, and 100 square cm; correction of constant errors in estimating; and mastery of better techniques of judging [54, p. 395].

Let us now see how the theory of identical elements accounts for some of the experimental findings reviewed above.

Identical-elements theory applied. Both Knight, in interpreting the marked transfer in learning fractions, and Grossnickle, in accounting for the failure to transfer multiplication facts to division problems relied implicitly on the then-popular theory of identical elements. Knight explained that "transfer is possible to the extent that skills exist to transfer [29, p. 787]." When the elements to be transferred "have all been practiced in simple skills [with integers] they can be trusted to operate later in higher more involved skills [in fractions]." Grossnickle explained that multiplication facts were not applied without error in division because "multiplication involved in division is a specialized ability and not a generalized reaction to multiplication facts [18, p. 681]." Since the processes are not identical, each requires specific learning. But even in Buswell and Kersh's experiment, where an identical formula is applicable to both problems, many students failed to apply in the second problem the rule learned in the first. Apparently the theory of identical elements is insufficient to account for *all* the phenomena of transfer.

Theory of transfer by generalizing. Thorndike's theory, as we have noted, focuses attention on the *elements* which the influencing and influenced learning activities have in common. In contrast to this emphasis upon *specific* components, Judd's generalization theory assumes that what is learned in A transfers to B because in studying A the learner develops a *general principle* which applies in part or completely to both A and B. According to this theory, generalizations of broad scope, because of their potential widespread transfer, are of paramount importance in teaching.

For an appreciation of the historical origin of Judd's theory and for a clearer understanding of it, let us turn to his 1908 experiment on transfer. The experiment involved two equated groups of fifth and sixth grade boys who were directed to throw darts at an underwater target [27, p. 37].

> In this experiment one group of boys was given a full theoretical explanation of refraction. The other group of boys was left to work out experience without theoretical training. These two groups began practice [throwing darts] with the target under twelve inches of water. It is a very striking fact that in the first series of trials the boys who knew the theory of refraction and those who did not gave about the same results. That is, theory seemed to be of no value in the first tests. All of the boys had to learn to use the dart, and theory proved to be no substitute for practice. At this point the conditions were changed. The twelve inches of water were reduced to four. The difference between the groups of boys now came out very strikingly. The boys without theory were very much confused. The practice gained with

twelve inches of water did not help them with four inches. Their errors were large and persistent. On the other hand the boys who had the theory fitted themselves to the new condition of four inches very rapidly. Theory evidently helped them to see the reason why they must not apply the twelve-inch habit to four inches of water.

Other experimenters, with more precise statistical treatment of their data, have at least partly confirmed Judd's results. Hendrickson and Schroeder, using three equated groups of eighth grade boys as subjects, directed them to practice shooting BB shots at targets first placed 6 inches and then 2 inches under water, until three successive bull's-eye hits were attained. One experimental group was given an explanation of the theory of refraction; another studied the explanation of refraction and was also explicitly warned that changing the depth of water in the second test would change the amount of refraction. Following Judd's experimental design, the principle of refraction was withheld from a third group, the control group. The amounts of transfer of skill from the 6-inch depth to the 2-inch depth, as measured by reduction in number of trials required to attain the bull's-eye criterion, were 34.1 per cent for the control group, 36.5 per cent for the group given an explanation of refraction, and 40.3 per cent for the group given the explanation plus a more specific statement of how it would apply with the changed conditions [21].

Only the principle of refraction *plus* the suggestion to use it produced a significant advantage. Like Buswell and Kersh's college students, some of whom failed to apply the learned generalization for determining quickly the number of *x*'s in a pyramid, some of Hendrickson and Schroeder's eighth grade students probably failed to apply the principle of light refraction[1] to the problem of aiming at submerged targets. Apparently generalizations do not transfer automatically even to pertinent applications.

Judd himself recognized that dynamic, functional generalizations are products of specific ways of learning and teaching [28, pp. 412–413]:

> The first and most striking fact which is to be drawn from school experience is that one and the same subject matter may be employed with one and the same teacher with wholly different effects, according to the mode of presentation. If a lesson is presented in one fashion, it will produce very large transfer; whereas if it is presented in entirely different fashion, it will be utterly barren of results for other phases of mental life.

[1] It is also possible that the experimental and control groups differed so little because, from a background of the science taught in modern junior high schools, the boys in the control group discovered for themselves in the experience at the first depth the equivalent of the principle explicitly taught the experimental groups.

As an elaboration of the generalization theory of transfer, Bayles suggests some of the dynamics of effective transfer. He says that transfer depends upon (1) learning generalizations, (2) opportunity for varied applications of the generalizations, and (3) developing a mental set to be interested in and alert to further applications of the generalizations or principles [4]. Let us re-examine some of the experiments presented earlier in the light of this theory.

Generalization theory applied. According to the generalization theory, the pupils in Group B of Knight's experiment learned not only how to manipulate 2, 4, 6, 8, 12, and 24 as denominators of fractions, but they also inductively generalized from these varied experiences a numerator-over-denominator relationship (N/D). They learned that both the denominator, indicating the size of the fractional parts, and the numerator, designating the number of them, can be represented by any number. They also learned, of course, that in adding or subtracting fractions, the denominators must be converted to common units, and that this can be accomplished—without changing the value of the fractions—by multiplying both numerators and denominators by the same number. As Knight pointed out, the basic skills of operation with *all* integers had already been acquired. Thus the pupils could readily infer that since 2, 4, 6, 8, 12, and 24 could be denominators of fractions, any other integer (including specifically the untaught ones) could also be a denominator (or a numerator) of a fraction, and that the same principles of operation would apply to *all* such fractions. Therefore, in this experiment, transfer worked effectively because all the conditions of transfer were applied—generalizing, varied applications, and a developed set for further uses.

In Grossnickle's and in Buswell and Kersh's experiments, these conditions were less completely applied. In Grossnickle's experiment, the relationship between multiplication and division—as reciprocal processes for putting together and taking apart equal-sized parts—was not emphasized. Thus effective generalizations covering *both* processes were not developed. Such varied forms of multiplication as $6 \times 7 = N$ and $6 \times N = 42$, presented in the equation form suggested in Chapter 7, could have suggested applications of multiplication to division. Moreover, as is explained later, the relatively low degree of mastery achieved in multiplication could have limited the transfer to division.

In Buswell and Kersh's experiment, although the generalization was mastered, *varied applications* of the principle that the sum of N consecutive odd integers is equal to N^2 were not suggested. Transfer of the generalization to the pyramid problem would probably have occurred more often had this problem been preceded by applications of the principle to other problems such as the following: "Suppose that in a two-ball tossing task John makes only one catch [before an error] on the first trial, and thereafter makes two additional catches each trial. What is the total number of catches he will make in seven trials?" If, in addition to such assigned examples, the students had also been encouraged to think of further applications of the principle, it is very likely that more students would have applied it to the pyramid problem.

Our review and theoretical explanation of some transfer experiments indicate that, although transfer in some learning sequences is potentially very significant, whether or not it actually occurs depends on certain conditions. We now turn to a more intensive study of these determinants of transfer.

ESSENTIAL CONDITIONS OF TRANSFER

In order to transfer the elements learned in activity A to the learning of activity B, the two activities must be alike in some ways. But identity of elements alone is insufficient. As the generalization theory implies, transfer in learning and teaching depends upon (1) developing generalizations which extend to other situations, (2) providing for varied application of them, and (3) building up mental sets and alertness for continually making new applications of the principles learned.

1. *Generalizing.* Generalizing is the heart of transfer; it enables us to apply general concepts or principles to innumerable situations without having to learn a new response to each specific situation. Let us see therefore how it multiplies learning power in specific examples, in especially designed experiments, and in the practical tasks of the curriculum.

We shall observe first a resourceful child's discovery of the importance of generalizing in learning to spell. Whenever the children in a first grade classroom needed to spell a new word they asked their teacher how to write it. In this way they accumulated a small vocabulary of words which they could remember and use in writing about some event which interested them. But this did not save them the separate task of learning to spell each new word as they needed it. Such learning did not generate the spelling of new words. But one day Billy made a discovery. When his teacher wrote "think"—a word he had asked his teacher to spell—he at first thought she had made a mistake. He said: "I said 'think' not 'thank.' I already know how to write 'thank.'" She assured him that the word she had written for him *was* "think." He examined it more closely and then announced an important discovery—a generalization which could be used to facilitate the spelling of new words. He remarked: "'Thank' and 'think' are alike, except for one letter— one has an 'a' and the other has an 'i.'"

Billy had discovered the vowels and with his teacher's help he found other words which differed only by a vowel—such as *bag, beg, big*, *bog*, and *bug*. He went on—with teacher guidance—to discover the role of the initial consonant in such words as *big*, *dig*, and *pig*. Since he already knew how to spell these particular words and now knew the vowels and the initial consonants, he could transfer these generalizations to the spelling of such words as *drink*, *drank*, and *drunk* or *rig*. The generalizations saved him many subsequent specific learnings.

Forgus and Schwartz have demonstrated experimentally that generalized organizational principles facilitate original learning, retention, and transfer to related tasks. They taught one group of college women to memorize by rote new symbols for the alphabet, presented in irregular order, such as: $F = \square$, $C = \triangle$, $K = \int$, $R = \theta$, and so on, for the 26 letters of the alphabet. A comparable group of 13 women was directed to discover from studying the following organized presentation of the two alphabets the general principle of construction, and to use it as an aid in memorizing the new symbols:

A B C D E F G H I J K L M N O P Q R S T U V W X Y Z

ΛΔᐃᗡⵎ◨ᗺᗷΙΓ∫ᒧᐯᐯᐯᐯ∨Oθθθϙϙϙϙⵘ⟨⟨

For original learning, the rote memorization group took twice as long as the group guided by the organizational principle. One week after the original learning, a retention test was given which required translating a passage in symbols into English. On this test, the rote memorization group scored 37 and the generalization group scored 52. And on a different transfer test requiring translation of letters into digits (each letter being represented by a pair of digits: A, B, C, D = 11, 12, 13, 14 and E, F, G, H = 21, 22, 23, 24), the rote memorization group scored only 10 while the generalization group scored 37 [13].

Both school experience and experiments confirm the advantage of generalizing. In the primary grades it simplifies mastery of the following simple letter formations in manuscript writing: a b c d e f g h i j k l m n o p q r s t u v w x y z. From examination of these letters, it is apparent that they are *all* formed by simple circles and straight or curved lines. This generalization greatly facilitates mastery of them. Instead of learning specifically how to write 26 different letters, the child learns 26 applications of only three simple forms. Moreover, he recognizes these forms as some he has already learned to make in pre-writing drawing activities [33].

In experimental confirmation of the advantage of generalizing, Overman found that the derived rule of "adding ones to ones and tens to tens" transferred substantially from taught to untaught column additions [39]. Olander showed that the generalizations developed in mastering half of the hundred addition and hundred subtraction combinations in his experiment were transferred almost completely to the untaught combinations [35]. Archer found that fifth and seventh grade children effectively transferred concepts acquired in learning to spell certain verb forms to the correct spelling of untaught derived forms of these verbs. For example, children who learned to spell *reflect* or *assign* were also able to spell *reflects*, *reflected* and *reflecting* or *consigned* with-

out specific study of these related words [1]. In these experiments, the content studied was presented not as isolated facts, but as interrelated concepts—from which it was possible to derive useful generalizations.

2. Varied applications. Billy did not achieve an understanding of the principle of consonant substitution or of the role of the vowels in word structure from merely seeing their application in single words. In order to generalize the principles, he needed to see them applied in several different words. From varied pertinent experiences, generalizations are inductively derived and extended to further applications. As a demonstration of the role of varied applications of a principle in determining transfer, Roberts's experiment is worthy of study in some detail. Using as subjects 21 preschool and 19 orphanage children, aged three to seven and varying in IQ from 80 to 150, she presented to them, individually and in succession, nine varied learning problems. Although the problems were all different each could be solved by the application of the same principle [44].

Through a glass window in each upper compartment of the six-unit problem box shown in Figure 10.1, a toy airplane or a box of toys could be seen. The directions were: "See all these airplanes [pointing to each one] and see all those doors [pointing to the lower tier of

For effective and creative applications in new situations, children need to generalize and see varied applications of the concepts they learn. (Adams School, Logan, Utah.)

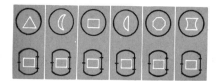

Fig. 10.1. *Diagrammatic front view of six 2-story boxes arranged for multiple-choice problem solving (Situation IIB, Trial 1).* (From K. E. Roberts, Univ. Iowa Stud. Child Welf., 1933, vol. 7, no. 3, p. 31.)

compartments]. All these doors open, but just one door will make an airplane fall so you can get at it to play with. You look at all of the airplanes and all of the doors, and then you open one door and see if you can make an airplane fall." The guiding principle to be discovered was that, although the correct door was different for each trial, it always matched in some identifiable way a clue in the windows above.

The nine different situations included three major variations: I (color), II (form), and III (size). Within each of these major variations there were three minor variations: A, B, and C. In IA, the upper compartments contained six airplanes, all of the same color for any one trial; and each of the doors below was marked with a different color, only one of which matched the color of the airplanes. In IB, each of the six airplanes was a different color; only one matched the doors, which in this trial were all of the same color. In IC, both airplanes and doors varied through six colors, only one pair being matched for color. These three subvariations were similarly applied for the form (II) and size (III) series.

Figure 10.1, of course, illustrates one trial in the IIB series in which the six geometrical patterns on the boxes above vary and the patterns on the doors below are all the same, with only the third pair matching. Each successive trial required a response to a different stimulus cue in a random order which was kept constant for each child. For each of the nine situations (IA, IB, IC, IIA, IIB, IIC, IIIA, IIIB, and IIIC), twelve trials were given per day and continued until mastery, which was defined as four correct choices in succession.

Because the situations are of approximately equal difficulty as initial problems and because of the counter-balanced order of presentation for the three subgroups, a tendency toward a decrease in the mean number of trials required for each succeeding problem is evidence of transfer from earlier to later problems. In situations (1), (4), and (7), which are the initial problems starting each major variation, the successive means of 36.78, 9.03, and 1.23 indicate transfer through application of the principle to quite radical variations.

The most striking indication of transfer—in the form of learning how to learn—is revealed in Figure 10.2. The figure shows the percentage of children in the two groups who demonstrated immediate mastery of the principle and therefore reached the criterion on the first trial in each of the nine situations. The curves in the figure show that within each major variation, after success on an initial problem, increasing percentages of children—with minor fluctuations from situation (4) to (6) for the orphanage children—applied the principle immediately to a related problem. And the increasing percentage of children applying the principle by transfer to the initial problem in each major variation—from color to form to size (or in reversed order) in situations (1), (4), and (7)—shows marked cumulative transfer. This transfer appears to have resulted from *varied applications* of the principle. Only because the children had experienced application of the principle, not only to the first series—situations (1), (2), and (3) —but also to a second, quite different series—situations (4), (5), and (6)—could so many of them (about 70 per cent) apply the principle to the new condition met in situation (7). We see, then, from this experiment that transfer not only of knowledge, but also of modes of attack, is facilitated by experience with varied applications of principles learned.

Such opportunities for varied applications of initially and only partially mastered concepts and skills are provided in the developmental sequences of many curricula. For example, we have seen that during her year in the sixth grade a child wrote 14 independent reports on such different topics as "Strange Animals," "Babylonia," "Norse Myths," "Japanese Architecture," and finally "Denmark"—the land of her great-grandparents. In these varied applications of report writing, she learned to do each job more effectively. For each succeeding report, more and better references were sought. Organization was improved. Reports became longer and more elaborate. Artistic illustrations were included, and increasingly more attention was given to spelling, punctuation, and sentence and paragraph structure. She developed a generally effective procedure for learning about any topic in which she might become interested. When, during the summer

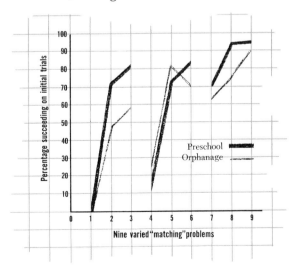

Fig. 10.2. *Transfer from varied applications of a principle is indicated by percentages of children successful on first trials in each of nine different situations (for 21 preschool and 19 orphanage children).* (From K. E. Roberts, *Univ. Iowa Stud. Child Welf.*, 1933, vol. 7, no. 3, p. 50.)

vacation, her family planned an automobile trip to Canada, she immediately initiated a report on the country and independently employed the same systematic techniques she had learned to use so skillfully and confidently in school.

3. *A mental set for transfer.* Out of such sequences of learning activities in which general principles are applied in varied situations, a mental set of readiness for further applications should emerge. Some resourceful children *are* sensitive to further opportunities for application of newly mastered concepts and skills and may even seek them out. Many other children fail to make appropriate application of learned principles in situations that confront them. Both such observations and experiments indicate the need for specific teacher guidance in helping children become alert to opportunities for using the knowledge, skills, and ideals that they have [3, 46]. For example, the results in the previously reported experiments of both Hendrickson and Schroeder and Buswell and Kersh remind us that transfer is not automatic. In the former experiment, the principle of light refraction was helpful in aiming at the submerged targets only when the subjects were told how to apply it. And in the latter experiment, many of the subjects failed to apply in counting the x's in the pyramid the mathematical principle they had previously mastered.

Dorsey and Hopkins demonstrated that transfer is more likely to occur if students are given explicit directions to apply their knowledge. First, they taught two equated groups of college students more efficient reading techniques, college Latin, and descriptive geometry. Then they tested both groups on (1) reading comprehension, (2) a vocabulary list comprised of Latin derivatives, and (3) miscellaneous items related to geometry. The only difference in preparation for the tests of the two groups was that the experimental group was warned before each test to use the appropriate previously learned concepts and skills. The control group, although they had acquired the same knowledge, did not receive explicit direction to apply it in the tests and failed to do so as effectively as the warned group [11].

These experiments indicate that building mental sets for transfer—encouraging children to be alert, to expect to find occasions for using concepts, to seek continually for application of principles, and to develop expanding, functional organizations of the concepts learned—needs to be a definite teaching objective. For example, one way of increasing the scope of application and likelihood of transfer of mathematical concepts and skills is to correlate high school mathematics and science classes. Mathematical concepts can be illustrated by applying them to concurrently studied science problems. And the science teacher can motivate and reinforce mastery of mathematical concepts as they are being learned by providing functional applications in the science course [9].

From satisfying teacher-guided self-discovery applications and extensions of generalizations, the general habit of looking for further applications should be developed. Then the explicitness about specific applications which was employed in Dorsey and Hopkins's experiment above should not be necessary. Such a habit will be developed best in interrelated curricula arranged in sequences so that applications for both old and newly acquired principles occur continually.

COMPLEMENTARY CONDITIONS OF TRANSFER

In addition to the essential dynamic conditions of transfer, there are several complementary conditions which determine its effectiveness. These include the degree of relationship between transfer principles and the areas of application, the improvement of learning methods, the extent of mastery of the concepts, skills, or principles to be transferred, and the ability of the learner to generalize.

1. *Applicabilities.* Although a degree of relevancy between transfer content and areas of application is not alone sufficient to ensure transfer, it *is* necessary. For generalizations learned in activity A to transfer to activity B, they must be applicable to both A and B. Sometimes, however, we assume that transfer will occur when, in reality, the relevancy of the generalization to the new activity or area is too superficial for it to occur.

Gates and Taylor demonstrated this principle in an experiment to determine the transfer effect of mechanically guided tracing of letters over transparent paper on learning to write (copy letters). Two equated groups of kindergarten children without prior experience in writing were trained to write letters—one group by actually writing letters, the other by tracing them. Fourteen children in the writing group were given 14 daily five-minute guided-practice periods in copying letters from models. For the first seven days, they practiced the letters *a, b, c, d, e* and for the second seven days the letters *f, g, h, i, j*. Twenty-one children in the tracing group practiced for 19 days, including, in sequence (1) five days of tracing the letters *a, b, c, d, e* over transparent paper; (2) a copying test on these letters; (3) five

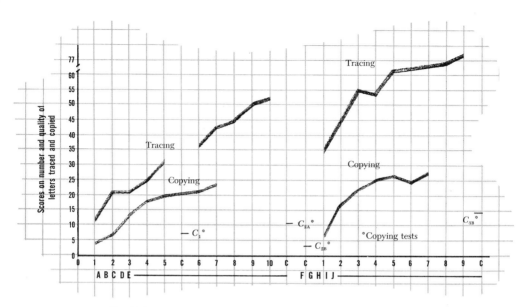

Fig. 10.3. *Transfer from tracing letters to copying letters is shown to be very slight for kindergarten children.* (Adapted from A. I. Gates and G. Taylor, *Teachers Coll. Rec.*, 1923, vol. 24, pp. 459–469.)

days more of tracing them; (4) two tests on copying—one on *a, b, c, d, e* and one on *f, g, h, i, j*; and (6) a final copying test on *f, g, h, i, j*.

The progress curves of both the copying and the tracing groups, as well as the copying-test scores for the latter group, are graphed in Figure 10.3. Scoring for both the copying and the tracing groups was based on the quantity and quality of letters written or traced.

As Figure 10.3 shows, the progress from practice in tracing letters —which, of course, is a much easier skill than writing—is much more rapid than the progress made in independent writing (copying). But the transfer from practice in tracing to writing is extremely meager. After five practice periods on tracing *a, b, c, d, e* the copying transfer score is only 8, which score is almost achieved with only two practice periods on actual copying. Five days of direct practice in copying yields a score of 20, which is more than twice as high as that transferred from tracing. Similarly, after nine practice periods on tracing *f, g, h, i, j*, the copying-test score from transfer is only 15, which score is achieved by only two practice periods in copying these letters.

Another aspect of these results brings out sharply the role of identical elements. Transfer from tracing *a, b, c, d, e* to tracing *f, g, h, i, j* is considerable. This results from the close identity of the two tasks. Mechanically guided tracing does not require conceiving the unique features of each letter, as is required in writing them. Therefore, there is little difference between tracing *a, b, c, d, e* and tracing *f, g, h, i, j*; both involve only following lines. The transfer from independently writing *a, b, c, d, e* to writing *f, g, h, i, j*, however, is less. Here the dissimilarity is greater, because writing *does* require conceiving the unique characteristics of five different letters. There is appreciable transfer, however, from copying *a, b, c, d, e* to copying *f, g, h, i, j*, as is indicated by the fact that it took only three practice periods on the latter to attain the same degree of skill attained after six days' practice on the former letters.

On the whole, of course, the experiment demonstrates that practice in tracing letters is a very poor way of learning to write. Three periods in actual copying practice results in as much improvement in writing as is achieved by 19 days of tracing! But why does not tracing transfer to writing? Our answer is simply that these processes have very little in common. Writing is largely a conceptual-perceptual-motor process, and tracing is largely a motor process. There seem to be few, if any, pertinent applications to be made from tracing to writing.

There are other areas where, because of insufficient identity between processes, expected yields from transfer have been disappointing. Gates has found that flash-card exercises as an ancillary approach to improving comprehension and speed of reading is less effective than practice on regular reading material [15]. Reading passages for comprehension of ideas, of course, is a complex reasoning process in which the context contributes significantly to the comprehension of each word or phrase. Recognizing a word or a phrase in a flash out of its context is a quite different process.

Some teachers have also been surprised to discover that such subjects as Latin, geometry, or physics contribute no more (or less) to improved general reasoning with verbal, numerical, and spatial symbols than do courses in English, sociology, bookkeeping, or almost any other high school subject. For 8,564 high school students, Thorndike compared the gains made during a year on a *Test of Selective and Relational Thinking* for students taking different patterns of subjects. For example, to determine the differential effect of Latin and shopwork on growth in reasoning ability, he compared the gains made by students taking English, history, geometry, and Latin with those taking English, history, geometry, and shopwork [52]. Later studies have confirmed Thorndike's original finding that the small test-retest gains achieved on tests of general reasoning ability are unrelated to differences in patterns of high school students' courses [7, 57].

Such illustrations as these should alert teachers to the desirability of critically examining ancillary approaches to learning in order to determine whether the components really are applicable to the goals sought. Many concepts and skills, however, have widespread transfer possibilities. Earlier-acquired mathematical concepts and skills have continuing applications in learning the physical and social sciences.

Effective methods of vocabulary building, reading, and writing are intrinsically applicable in nearly every area of the school curriculum. There are probably certain components of industrial and recreational motor skills which, if introduced in certain early-learned motor activities, would have widespread application in many other specific activities [61].

Some specific concepts or skills recur frequently as identical elements in many different situations. If teachers give early and special emphasis to mastery of these common facts or skills, they facilitate their transfer to sequences of learning activities. For example, Kyte and Neel have pointed out the high frequency of certain words that children write. They note that the 500 most frequent words in Rinsland's list account for 82 per cent of the total words that elementary school children write. Using both Rinsland's *A Basic Vocabulary of Elementary School Children* and Horn's "A Basic Writing Vocabulary" for adults, they have derived a core vocabulary of 501 spelling words which both children and adults are most likely to need [32].

Teaching this list early to all children should prepare them for many of their writing needs. For mentally retarded children or for other children and youth who have difficulty in learning to spell, the list is a manageable and useful list of minimum essentials. But mastery of the list, besides having transfer value in many applications, also should produce transfer through generalizing. If spelling is taught according to transfer principles, generalizations learned in studying these 501 words should lead to ready mastery of additional words. For example, learning *men* and *send* from the list should produce, as generalized by-products, the ability to spell such other words as *mend, lend,* and *tend.*

Analysis of words according to roots, prefixes, and suffixes and other visual and phonetic components yields a few common elements applicable to reading and spelling thousands of words. For example, only 45 different key syllables are employed in spelling nearly all of

veni, vidi, vici?

9,000 polysyllabic words in the Rinsland list [38]. A child who learns to spell such words as *going, morning, playing,* and *counting* and generalizes that the final syllable is always spelled *ing* will be able to spell this part of 877 words in the Rinsland list which end in *ing.*

Despite the many exceptions and variations [23, 24] in phonetic spelling of English words, there is sufficient consistency in the spelling vocabulary of school children for the effective transfer of phonetic generalizations. According to Hanna and Moore, approximately four-fifths of the sound elements of these words are represented by regular spelling. Three-fourths of the vowel sounds in the great majority of these words are spelled consistently. And even more of the consonant sounds are spelled consistently [19, pp. 333–334].

2. *Learning how to learn.* Varied applications of a principle, skill, or concept make it possible for a learner to grasp the possibility of other applications and to discover more effective work methods. Both of these aspects of practice facilitate transfer. However, practice without guidance or scope and incentive for self-improvement often fails to yield transfer gains.

In the interim between a variety of "before" and "after" memory tests, Sleight had three subgroups of 21 sixth-standard pupils each practice memorizing. Group 1 listened as the experimenter read poetry, and repeated it after him line by line. Group 2 listened as the experimenter read tables of number combinations, and repeated them after him part by part. For Group 3, prose selections were read twice, and the children wrote what they could remember of them. Another 21 children serving as a control group only took the pre- and end-tests. There was no teacher guidance on ways of memorizing, and the stereotyped method of practice permitted the children little scope for self-discovery of more effective procedures. It is not surprising, therefore, that on the various postpractice memory tests, gains beyond those made by the no-practice control group were neither consistent nor significant [49].

William James, acting as his own subject, found that extensive practice in memorizing one kind of poetry did not improve his ability to memorize another kind. As his pre- and post-tests, he used comparable 158-line parts of Victor Hugo's "Satyr." In a 138-day interval between the tests, he memorized, working about 20 minutes daily, the entire first book of Milton's "Paradise Lost." Memorization of the pretest material required 132 minutes; memorization of the second part of Hugo—the post-test material—required 151 minutes. He was astonished to find that after the 38 days of practice, the time required to memorize the 158-line passage increased, rather than decreased [26, pp. 666–688]. As an explanation of James's failure to improve his memorizing efficiency, we suggest that as a mature adult he simply *used* already-developed memorizing procedures—without attempting to improve them. As we have learned, repetition alone produces neither improvement nor transfer. Teacher guidance or self-improvement efforts, however, *can* enhance proficiency in memorizing.

Woodrow tested and retested three comparable groups of college students on a variety of memorizing tasks—poetry, prose, facts, dates, vocabulary, and digits. Between the tests, one group did no memorizing. A second group simply practiced memorizing poetry and nonsense syllables without guidance, as William James did. A third group, on the same materials, was given practice plus teacher guidance in effective memorizing techniques, such as learning by wholes, making a meaningful approach, employing active self-recitation, using rhythm, and grouping facts and ideas. When Woodrow compared the scores from pretests with those from end-tests, he found small and insignificantly different gains for both the control and practice-only groups. But on all six memory tests, the group given practice plus guidance in effective memorizing techniques made substantially greater gains than either of the other groups [60].

Winch's experiment suggests that, given scope for development of new methods, some children can improve their own memorizing techniques and transfer the new techniques to other memory tasks [59]. With freedom to try out varied ways of memorizing poetry, the children discovered effective procedures which they could also apply in memorizing passages of history and geography. Haslerud and Meyers have suggested that self-discovery learning is especially effective in facilitating transfer. They found, for college students, that teacher-guided learning is better than self-discovery learning in the original mastery of concepts. But in the transfer of the concepts to the solution of different problems, they found that self-discovered concepts are more transferable than teacher-given concepts [20].

Some experiments suggest that the contributions of high school chemistry, physics, biology, and other science courses to development of understanding, appreciation, and generalized skill in scientific problem solving also depends on the methods of learning in these courses.

A group of 21 high school students followed an inductive-deductive procedure in studying chemistry. They used the laboratory to solve "real" problems in which they were genuinely interested. Working with the teacher, the students experimented, generalized, and drew conclusions from their own data and applied their generalizations to other related problems. A comparable group of 20 students, following a deductive-descriptive method, carried out laboratory experiments illustrating general principles according to directions given in a manual. With this method, there "was little call upon the student to develop and use generalizing ability." Transfer tests on attitudes and on knowledge of scientific methods and of applications of principles in new situations favored the inductive approach [6, pp. 248–249].

3. *Degree of mastery of general principles and techniques.* Generalized responses learned initially in one activity facilitate learning subsequent activities in which they are applicable. Being already available, these responses are more easily elicited in the new situations. If one has already learned to operate an automobile or typewriter, for example, it is easier to learn to use another vehicle or office machine, the operation of which requires the same skills.

Janet interrupted her violin lessons over a summer during which she studied the cello. In the fall, her violin teacher observed that she had improved her skill in playing the violin. Certain skills applicable to both instruments were transferred from cello playing to violin playing.

Experiments indicate—for both verbal and perceptual-motor learning—that the extent of such transfer is related to the original degree of mastery of such transferable concepts and skills. In one of these experiments, Duncan taught 300 college students a complex percep-

Transfer: generalizing in learning

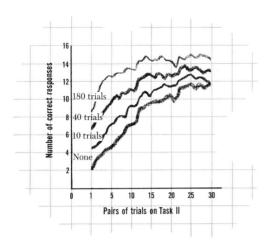

Fig. 10.4. *Transfer to mastery of Task II varies with the extent of practice (0, 10, 40, or 180 trials) on similar Task I.* (After C. P. Duncan, *J. Exp. Psychol.*, 1953, vol. 45, p. 5.)

tual-motor task which required them to make a pattern of bimanual responses to a sequence of light signals. By giving different groups 10, 40, 80, and 180 trials on this original task, he produced varying degrees of mastery, as is indicated by their mean scores on the 16-signal task of 4.63, 10.54, 13.20, and 15.63, respectively. Then he presented to these four groups plus a control group (who had had no practice on the original task) a second task requiring the same responses, but to a changed sequence of light signals.

In Figure 10.4, the graphed performance on the second task clearly shows that the degree of mastery of transferred skills affects their usefulness in subsequent similar tasks. Ten trials on the first task aids somewhat in learning a second similar task. But the increased mastery from 40 and especially from 180 trials greatly facilitates transfer of skills from Task I to Task II.

4. *Intelligence as a factor affecting ease, level, and extent of transfer.* Since performance on intelligence tests and ability to generalize concepts and skills depend on reasoning and symbolic representation of ideas and relationships, it is not surprising to discover that bright children tend to transfer their learning more effectively than do dull or even average children. Both the level of abstract conceptualizing which children can attain and their ability to apply and to extend generalizations are related to differences in intelligence.

Using as subjects both bright (IQs of 117 to 137) and dull (IQs of 66 to 81) 12-year-old children, Ray has demonstrated that bright children are more efficient in generalizing. To each child (six in each group), he presented repeatedly until mastered several 20-item problems requiring a succession of choices of the "correct" one between pictures of pairs of objects. Which of each pair was correct could be determined by the trial-and-check process and remembered as a specific fact. But for each problem a general abstract characteristic differentiated the pairs of objects. When this concept was discovered with a few items, it would—by transfer—predict the correct choice in new items. For example, once a child noticed that the correct choices between cat or hawk, alligator or fish, man or horse, and deer or sea horse were all four-legged animals, he could predict (and confirm in a provisional trial) that goat would be correct for the rooster or goat pair; and in the remaining pairs of the 20-item set he would, of course, choose the quadruped. Such efficient learning depends on transfer of already-mastered concepts. The trial-and-check process by which both bright and dull children achieve generalizations and the difference in the quality of their solutions to problems are suggested by the recorded verbalizations which accompanied the problem solving of specific children.

Among other comments made at different stages of solution, a bright child, with an IQ of 127, said: "If it's an animal it's right, but I think something is wrong." Obviously, he had made a restricted interpretation of the word "animal." Later, "If I'm not mistaken, it's an animal that has legs." Next pair, "It's either the largest or a mammal." Then, with clear awareness of the trial-and-check process, "Wait a minute, let me go through once more." After another checked provisional choice, "I think it's an animal with four legs. The thing that got me puzzled was the snake and the turtle. Couldn't see any difference hardly [41, pp. 93–94]."

On the same problem another 12-year-old child, with an IQ of 81, also verbalized certain aspects of his problem solving: "Ain't no animal [the alligator], but I'll try it." On another choice, "Fish ain't right is it? Fish and snake ain't lucky. I won't try them." Finally, "It's animals. Course there's some snakes and frogs in there, but they ain't no good [41, p. 91]."

Ray's quantitative data and illustrations show that bright children achieve generalizations in fewer trials, apply them more effectively, and formulate them more precisely.

Carroll has shown that both "bright" (mean IQ: 125) and "dull" (mean IQ: 92) fourth and fifth grade children tend to generalize from already-achieved spelling concepts when asked to spell unfamiliar words. Both the bright and dull children made "reasonable" (negative transfer) errors on words dictated from spelling lists a year in advance of their grade placement. However, the bright children, besides missing fewer words, misspelled relatively more words according to transfer principles. Relatively more often than the dull children, they doubled single letters (as *advise* spelled *addvise*), omitted a double letter (as *rabbit* spelled *rabit*), or transposed or substituted single letters (as *fairly* spelled *farily*). Dull children exceeded the bright children in frequency of erratic errors, such as writing *boat* for *picture* and in such sheer guessing as writing *rszilon* for *defeated*. As Carroll concludes: "It appears that phonetic generalization is the dominating factor in the [different] kinds of spelling errors made by bright and dull children." The bright child possesses in greater degree an ability to translate sounds into letters [10, p. 499].

The level of abstractness of the concepts that individuals achieve and apply is also related to intelligence. For example, Pratt noted that in solving the numerical problems of the *American Council on Education Psychological Examination*, approximately 55 per cent of 1,229 college freshmen employed arithmetic processes and 45 per cent used algebraic processes. The students using the more abstract algebraic approach were superior in intelligence to those using the arithmetic procedures, and they achieved more correct solutions [40].

On first thought, we might conclude from some of these studies that generalizing is the best way for the bright child to learn and that rote memorization is most suited to the dull child. But this would be an unfortunate mistake. Although the dull child achieves generalizations more slowly and with greater difficulty, and although some abstract principles are beyond his comprehension, even mentally retarded individuals discover generalizations and use them to advantage in learning [5]. Transfer principles enhance the effectiveness of learning for individuals at *all* levels of intelligence. Since dull children achieve generalizations less easily than brighter children, however, they need more and simpler concrete inductive experiences as a basis for their generalizing. Abstract levels of reasoning must be approached more gradually. Average and below average children need more varied applications of principles and more explicit guidance as to when and how to adapt them for new applications.

HOW TO TEACH FOR TRANSFER

The tremendous advantages of transfer principles in learning are not automatic by-products of all learning effort. They are achieved only by appropriate learning and teaching procedures.

1. Transfer depends mainly upon the inductive derivation of general principles. Principles are developed by emphasizing meaning, by studying organized experiences inductively for the purpose of arriving at significant generalizations, and by looking for interrelationships among ideas and techniques.

2. General principles are both discovered and extended in application by varied applications in the initial mastery of them. Only by applying a principle to different kinds of situations will children come to understand its generalized nature—that it is a concept or skill which is not limited to a specific situation. From a sufficient number of varied

applications of a principle there should emerge the mental set to expect further applications.

3. Experience and experiments indicate, however, that the emergence of the set to make new applications of one's background of general concepts and skills cannot safely be left to chance. To develop in children and youth the habit of seeking new applications and extensions or adaptations of previously learned principles, specific procedures are required. Alertness to opportunities for appropriate applications of already-mastered principles is facilitated by learning sequences which provide expanding uses of them, by the learner's functional organization of his accumulating concepts and skills, and by methods of teaching which encourage initiative and which reward his efforts to discover new applications of his growing resources for problem solving.

4. Although generalized experience is the dynamic factor which determines transfer of learning, transfer is also dependent upon the actual presence of "identical" elements between the transfer content and the areas of application. The principles transferred must be related to the areas of application. Superficial similarities, such as between tracing and writing letters, do not permit transfer. There are, however, many general concepts and skills which recur frequently as components in long sequences and in a wide area of school curricula, such as scientific problem solving, phonetic and structural analysis of words, and fundamental mathematical procedures. Early learning of these frequently used concepts and skills yields high returns in wide-scope application.

5. As Judd observed, whether transfer is significant or inappreciable depends upon the method of learning. Static repetition of already-mastered techniques does not yield transfer gains. Attention to *how* to learn, to better ways of solving problems, and to acquiring more efficient work methods do produce both more effective original learning and significant transfer gains in related learning activities.

6. Mastery facilitates transfer. If earlier-learned concepts and skills are incompletely learned, they are not readily available for transfer in new situations. Well-mastered principles are more easily elicited, and thus the probability of their application in appropriate situations is enhanced.

7. Besides being affected by content and methods of learning, transfer is also related to individual differences among learners. Bright children learn generalizations more easily and with fewer varied applications, attain higher levels of abstraction, and apply or extend principles more readily than average or below-average children. Dull children fail to reach the higher levels of abstraction and some generalizations are, of course, beyond them. They often need more guidance, greater variety of simpler, concrete, inductive experience, and

reminders of opportunities for application of the general concepts and skills they learn. Their curriculum in the basic skills should be reduced to the most frequently used elements, such as a spelling curriculum comprised of the 500 words children and adults write most frequently. But generalizing enhances the efficiency of learning for *all* children. Therefore, with appropriate modifications, transfer principles should be employed in teaching children at every level of intelligence.

SUMMARY

Transfer is a pervasive factor which significantly influences the efficiency of learning. The new learning tasks which students meet continually in their progress through school are accomplished more easily by applications of earlier-achieved generalizations and by improved methods of learning. Multiple-element tasks that would otherwise be difficult or impossible are reduced in complexity, by inductive generalizing, to the need for mastering only a few unifying principles. And by transfer principles, learners continually interrelate and creatively extend their accumulating concepts and skills for more effective application to the problems they find or create in and out of school.

Mastery of the skills and concepts involved in learning activity A often facilitates the subsequent learning of activity B. But sometimes transfer from A to B is negative or inappreciable. To explain these transfer phenomena, two general theories have been proposed. The theory of identical elements assumes that transfer from A to B depends upon the extent of similarity of the elements (facts, methods, principles, or attitudes) involved in the two activities. In the absence of common elements, no transfer is expected. The existence of many common elements allows for considerable transfer.

The generalization theory assumes that transfer occurs from A to B when the generalizations learned in activity A are applicable to *both* A and B. However transfer is explained, both experience and experiments indicate that it is not an automatic by-product of *all* learning. It depends upon three essential and four complementary conditions.

Effective transfer is a product of (1) generalizing concepts and skills, (2) practicing them in varied applications, (3) developing a mental set for further applications and extensions of learned concepts and skills in new problem situations, (4) sufficient relationship between principles to be transferred and intended areas where they may be applied, (5) learning how to learn—that is, discovering continually more effective work methods, (6) thorough mastery of concepts and skills to be applied, and (7) adapting curricula and methods of teaching for transfer to individual differences in abilities of the learners.

GUIDES FOR STUDY, REVIEW, AND APPLICATION

1. Each of us needs hundreds of thousands of specific concepts and skills. Is there a short cut to mastery of them? How does effective application of transfer principles in present learning multiply our efficiency and save us subsequent learning?
2. How frequently and extensively does transfer occur in school learning?
3. Describe instances of positive, negative, and unexpected failure of transfer.
4. Explain the two major theories of transfer, cite the data they were constructed to explain, and apply them in explaining examples of positive or negative transfer.
5. Cite experiments and observations which evaluate and illustrate the three dynamic and four complementary principles of transfer. How does the teacher facilitate positive transfer?
6. Describe an interesting example of learning or teaching and point out as many applications of transfer principles as you can find. Many of them are illustrated in *Making Learning More Meaningful,* McGraw-Hill Text-Film Department.

Chapter 11

REMEMBERING AND FORGETTING

It has been said that "knowledge keeps like fish." Actually, we are continually learning, remembering, and forgetting, and sometimes it seems that the accumulation of knowledge is a process of taking two or three steps forward and one step backward. As students and as prospective teachers, we are concerned both with how efficiently we can learn and how well we can remember what we learn. It has perhaps occurred to each of us that the tasks of educating ourselves and of teaching children and youth would be very much easier if we remembered everything that we learn. If retention of learned facts, concepts, and skills were perfect, consider how easy the examination in this course would be and how many things we should now know. Sometimes the net gain from a year's study of a subject is indeed small. Observe, for example, how much (or little) you presently remember of the foreign language you studied in high school but have not spoken or read since. Or try to recall from your biology course the phyla of the animal kingdom. When retention tests of specific facts—

relatively isolated items of knowledge—are administered to elementary, high school, and college students a year or two after they completed courses in such subjects as history, Latin, chemistry, or botany, marked forgetting is often revealed. Average retention scores are sometimes as little as one-third of the end-of-course score [46, p. 262].

Fortunately, not all the concepts and skills we learn are so quickly forgotten. Moreover, there are things we can do—as we shall discover in this chapter—to prevent forgetting and to enhance our effectiveness in the application of previously learned concepts and skills. Such principles, for example, as learning how to learn and transfer of training are just as effective in sustaining as they are in facilitating original learning. But before we begin a systematic study of the causes of forgetting and of ways to improve remembering, let us explore some informal illustrations of the factors involved.

EXAMPLES OF REMEMBERING AND FORGETTING

In her fifth grade geography class, a bright 10-year-old child barely succeeded in learning to associate the states of the United States with the names of their capital cities. When she was asked two years later to recite them, she recalled correctly only Salt Lake City (in her home state), Indianapolis (in the other state in which she had lived), Sacramento, Boise, Cheyenne, Phoenix, Santa Fe, Oklahoma City, and Austin. Since in her home state and in the state in which she lived temporarily the capitals are the largest cities, it probably seemed logical to reconstruct in her recall the capital of Nevada as Reno and of New York as New York City. Butte, Kansas City, and Miami intruded as capitals, possibly because they are frequently associated with their respective states. Mobile, Alabama, was perhaps incorrectly recalled for a similar reason. But for the remaining 32 states she could not make even a plausible guess.

Apparently, for such extrinsic associations, poorly mastered and rarely reviewed, retention is very limited and inaccurate. We note also in this illustration the operation of transfer (both positive and negative) in the child's assumption that the capitals are big cities. The following illustration contains evidence of having learned how to learn and of effective transfer.

In an eleventh grade physics class, the same child was given a quiz on work and machines which called for the names of the six simple machines. The child remembered that she had learned the names of the machines in the eighth grade. Now she needed to recall them. Thinking of the ways in which simple machines give the worker a mechanical advantage (their *general* function), she recalled first the *lever*. Then she recalled the *pulley* which provides a similar advantage, since both the lever and the pulley lift. The idea of the pulley then suggested the *wheel* and *axle*. In another group, the *inclined plane* was remembered. The *wedge* was then recalled as a variation of the inclined plane. Finally, the *screw* was recalled as a combination of a wedge and an inclined plane wrapped around an axis. The better retention of the simple machines than of the state capitals suggests that meaningful, integrated concepts are easier to remember and to recall than detached details.

The factors of mental set, interference, transfer, and saving in relearning are all illustrated in Janet's recall of some piano pieces she had memorized for recitals two or three years earlier but had not reviewed since. Asked to play "Soldier's Chorus," she at first thought she could not recall it. Then, as she reestablished an appropriate mental set in thinking about it, the general nature of the melody came to her. In a few trial-and-error attempts, she reconstructed it. She recalled the gay mood of "Playful Rondo"; but she could recall only bits of the melody. As she worked at its reconstruction, she observed: "I don't know whether all these parts are from 'Playful Rondo' or from the 'The Doll's Dream.'" Actually, when the music was checked, she discovered that she had been confusing bits of "Playful Rondo" with parts from "The Music Box" rather than from "The Doll's Dream." Both of them, she said, "have gay things in them." Since these two pieces are alike in mood and in pattern, and had been learned in close succession, bits from "The Music Box" intruded to interfere with accurate recall of "Playful Rondo."

But the relearning of these pieces now revealed that more was retained than seemed apparent from the recall efforts alone. Originally, it had required approximately 50 trials to memorize "Playful Rondo" for the recital. Now, when Janet practiced to relearn "Playful Rondo," it required only 11 trials, or 39 fewer than were originally needed. In other words, because of the original learning three years earlier, she was now saved 78 per cent of the trials which would otherwise have been required. This may be an overestimate, however, of the degree of her retention. In her continued study of other pieces following original mastery of the recital pieces, she probably had learned something about how to learn music which she was able to transfer in relearning "Playful Rondo." Such a transfer effect plus the warm-up effect were clearly demonstrated in the relearning of "The Music Box," which she undertook immediately after relearning "Playful Rondo." Relearning "The Music Box"—similar to "Playful Rondo" in key, mood, and pattern—required only six trials.

The role of active reconstruction in memory is suggested in all these illustrations. It is more explicitly revealed, however, in testing seven-year-old Brant's immediate recall of the items of the following story which was read to him:

"THE WET FALL"

Once there was a little girl named Betty. She lived on a farm with her brother Dick. One day their father gave them a Shetland pony. They had lots of fun with it. One day, when Dick was riding on it, the pony became frightened and ran away. Poor Dick fell into a ditch. How Betty laughed when she saw him! He was covered with mud from head to foot [55, p. 89].

Anxious and easily distracted by his worries, Brant had unusual difficulty in answering questions about the story. Asked, "What is the name of the story?" he constructed the plausible title "Rain, or something." Asked, "What was Betty's brother's name?" he reasoned: "Could be Tom." For, "Who gave the pony to them?" he also imagined a credible response: "A man—should be, or one of their friends . . . or their father." On the most dramatic parts of the story, however, he reproduced the items correctly with only slight elaboration. For "What did the pony do?" and "What happened?" he said: "It ran away," and "The boy fell into a puddle of water—a big puddle."

These informal observations reveal that learning, forgetting, remembering, and transfer are interrelated processes. They also indicate that remembering is not a passive process of reproduction, but an active process of reconstruction. Some of the factors affecting both forgetting and remembering have been suggested. We now turn to some of the experiments which psychologists have conducted and the theories they have proposed with respect to these processes.

Bull's eye?
Remember how you did it!

A mental set
to remember

Remembering
is a
creative
process

Meaningful material related to interests

The things we learn are not equally well remembered: studies show that what has been learned may be forgotten rapidly and almost completely; it may be retained without appreciable loss; or it may be recalled more efficiently after an interval of time has lapsed than it was immediately after learning. For example, Elder found that, over the summer vacation, 27 per cent of 203 pupils in grades 3 to 6 sustained losses of knowledge, 15 per cent of them had neither gains nor losses, and 59 per cent showed gains [20]. For primary grade pupils, whose skill in reading is less mature, slight losses often occur over the summer [52]. Largest losses are usually reported in arithmetic—varying, however, from inappreciable [44] to considerable [10, 32]. At the intermediate grade levels, where the majority of pupils have developed greater mastery and interest in reading, average gains in reading skills over the summer are quite uniformly reported. In these simply designed experiments, the specific factors causing losses, sustained retention, or gains are not clearly indicated. Other experiments, however, reveal the factors more clearly.

Rapid forgetting. In his historically important study of the retention of nonsense syllables, Ebbinghaus found that forgetting of such meaningless material is extensive and rapid, especially immediately after learning [23]. A schematic representation of his results is shown in the bottom curve of Figure 11.1. Relatively meaningless lists of associations, such as the states and their capitals, and the detached facts of many school subjects are forgotten almost as quickly and completely as are nonsense syllables [46, p. 262]. As the middle curve of Figure 11.1 shows, 3 months after completing a course in botany,

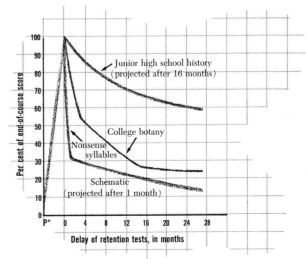

Fig. 11.1. *Retention varies for different materials: understanding of junior high school history (7), top curve; specific facts in college botany (30), middle curve; and nonsense syllables (23), bottom curve. P* designates the pretest, for botany only, prior to the learning experience.*

college students had forgotten almost half of the numerous facts they had learned. After 27 months, they remembered only 24 per cent of these facts [30].

Sustained retention. The retention of interesting and meaningful concepts, such as the six simple machines which give man a mechanical advantage, is often much better. As the top curve of Figure 11.1 shows, under conditions favorable to retention, certain kinds of school content are retained very well over long intervals of time. This curve represents junior high school students' retention of material learned in a world history course, as reflected in their answers to such questions as the following: "Alfred improved his kingdom by (a) gathering all the best laws into one book, (b) fighting the Huns, (c) going on a crusade, (d) teaching the French language [7, p. 683]." Continued study, after the world history course, of the social studies in the seventh and eighth grades and the added practice afforded in retaking the test in a sequence of four 4-month intervals also probably facilitated retention of these facts.

Augmented retention. Under certain especially favorable conditions the performance on delayed-retention tests may exceed that on tests taken immediately after the original learning. Two different kinds of experiments suggest that if, after original learning, the individual achieves an attitude more favorable to effective recall or enhances his understanding of pertinent general principles, his recall of the related specific content may be augmented.

For school children who memorized long selections of poetry under time limits *insufficient for mastery,* Ballard discovered that the score on retention tests taken two or three days later often exceeded the immediate-recall score [5]. To different subgroups of his 5,192 subjects, he gave recall tests immediately and again, without prior notice, one, two, three, four, five, six, or seven days later. The immediate and delayed average recall scores on "The Ancient Mariner," expressed as percentages of the mean immediate-recall score, are presented in Figure 11.2. As the figure shows, the recalls delayed two and three days are 6 to 9 per cent better than the recall immediately after learning.

Several hypotheses have been proposed to explain this phenomenon, which has been named "reminiscence [27]." The effect of practice from the initial test, although a likely factor, is probably not the full explanation. The most acceptable hypothesis seems to be that between immediate and later recalls the individual adopts a more effective approach to the task. For example, in the immediate attempt to recall the incompletely memorized selection, the individual may strive to recall it as a maze of details—a situation in which "the trees obscure the forest." Later, when his attention is returned to the recall task, the learner may consider the selection as a more integrated whole.

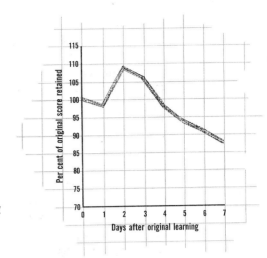

Fig. 11.2. *Reminiscence curve of 12-year-old children's recall of "The Ancient Mariner," tested immediately or after varying delay intervals.* (From P. B. Ballard, *Br. J. Psychol., Monogr. Suppl.,* 1911, vols. 1–4, no. 2, p. 5.)

Having first recalled it as a whole, he may then in the reconstruction process, which we observed in our introductory examples, fit in the specific details more efficiently than he could have done initially.

In another kind of study of longer-delayed retention, Tyler discovered that college students applied certain of the concepts they had learned more effectively 15 months after completing a course in zoology, than they had in the end-of-course test. In the part of the test concerned with interpretations of new experiments in zoology, the delayed-retention score was 25 per cent higher than the end-of-course score. Although in the meantime these students had not taken additional courses in zoology, they had—through the study of other science courses—enhanced their understanding of the scientific principles of experimentation. In the delayed-retention test, they transferred this enhanced understanding to zoology, with improved interpretation of the experiments [59].

THE CAUSES OF FORGETTING

Our illustration of the child's recall of the several piano recital pieces suggests that forgetting is not merely the fading away in time of memory traces (hypothetical residues of experience) in the nervous system. In trying to recall a specific piece, she found that bits of other later- or earlier-learned pieces intruded and interfered with accurate recall. As the individual remembers and learns, there is continuous interaction between memory traces (the retained effects in the nervous system of prior learning) and new learning. This "interaction works both ways, modifying both" the organization of the traces and the new learning [62].

Our illustrations have suggested that forgetting, like learning, is an active process. Experiments showing that forgetting is more rapid during the activities of wakefulness than during the relative inactivity of sleep also indicate that forgetting is an active process. It is a process in which new experiences interact with the trace systems from prior learning to interfere with accurate recall of them. As is shown in Figure 11.3, Jenkins and Dallenbach's subjects forgot the nonsense syllables they had just learned more rapidly while they were awake than when they were asleep. But let us explore the problem further. What are the kinds of activities and situations which cause forgetting? In answering this question, Deese lists six causes [19].

1. *Interactive inhibition.* At the recall of either of two sets of facts or concepts which have been learned in succession, there is the likelihood of competition between them. At the recall of the first set, intrusions from the second set may occur (retroactive inhibition). And when the second set is recalled, elements from the first set may interfere (proactive inhibition). Such interactive inhibition is probably the single most important cause of forgetting. In the child's recall of the state-capital associations, later-learned pairs inhibited accurate recall of earlier-learned pairs. And the accumulating earlier-learned associations interfered with memorization and recall of the later-learned associations. On experiencing such interference, a student in a college course, Theories of Personality, recently remarked: "The more different theories we study, the more difficult it is to remember and to distinguish between them. I grasped and differentiated the theories of Freud, Jung, and Adler. But now as we take up the theories of Fromm, Horney, and Sullivan, I am becoming confused. For example, I believe it was Adler who proposed the concept of 'inborn social interest,' but I am not sure; it might have been Jung."

These observations of the effects of retroactive and proactive

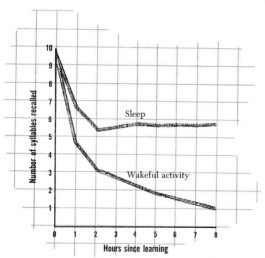

Fig. 11.3. *The comparison of retention of nonsense syllables after sleep with that after equal periods of wakeful activity suggests that forgetting is an active process.* (From J. G. Jenkins and K. M. Dallenbach, *Amer. J. Psychol.*, 1924, vol. 35, p. 610.)

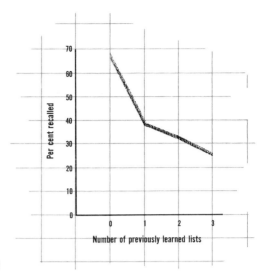

Fig. 11.4. *Because of proactive inhibition, the recall of subsequently learned lists of paired adjectives becomes less efficient as the number of previously learned lists is increased.* (From B. J. Underwood [cited from B. J. Underwood and R. Greenberg], *Psychol. Rev.*, 1957, vol. 64, p. 51.)

inhibition have been confirmed by several experiments. Following their study of the meanings of 25 French words, 94 high school students were divided into two equal groups. One group was directed to study a second list of French words, while the other group rested. Jenkins and Sparks report that retention of the initial list was significantly better among the students not subjected to the retroactive effect of learning a second list [29]. Another study shows that the exent of loss in retention of unmeaningful content varies with the amount of similar learning interpolated between initial learning and delayed recall [58, p. 498].

Underwood believes that proactive inhibition from previously learned content is even more important as a cause of forgetting than retroactive inhibition. His review of several studies indicates that "the greater the number of previous lists [learned], the greater the proactive interference" [60, p. 53]. As is indicated in Figure 11.4, retention-test scores, after 48 hours, on lists of pairs of associated adjectives become increasingly poorer as the number of previously learned lists is increased from none to three. Both the drop in mean score—from 69 per cent on the first list to 25 per cent on the fourth list—and the intrusions of adjectives from the previously learned lists demonstrate that proactive inhibition is a major cause of forgetting.

2. Changes in cognitive structure, attitudes, and interests. The delayed recall of learned concepts or of observed events depends both upon the original experience and upon the cognitive structure, attitudes, and interests of the person at the time of recall. If, between initial learning and delayed recall, children acquire different ways of thinking and reasoning, different beliefs, attitudes, or interests,

the traces from these intervening learnings can be expected to modify their recall of the originally learned concepts or observed events.

Such forgetting, or distortion of memory, is illustrated in Bartlett's report on his subjects' long-delayed recall of stories read to them [6]. In one of the stories which Bartlett read to his subjects there were references to a young man who joined some ghosts in a war party. The structure of the story as a whole was not very logical or coherent. In succeeding recalls of this story, Bartlett's subjects —in order to make it conform to their naturalistic beliefs and logic—often deleted the ghosts and constructed the story more logically. Another study shows that if we feel competent, successful, and satisfied with ourselves as adults, we tend to recall our high school experiences as constructive and as contributing to our needs. On the other hand, if we presently feel unsuccessful and inadequate, we tend to look back critically on our high school experiences and to recall them as unsatisfactory and unsuited to our needs [1].

3. *Changes in the recall situation.* Concepts and skills learned in a particular setting are sometimes unrecallable in a different situation. When some of the cues guiding the original learning are absent, or when distracting cues are introduced, the once-remembered concepts or skills seem to be forgotten. A variety of illustrations of this cause of forgetting are at hand.

At home, a six-year-old had successfully rehearsed a song to sing at a PTA meeting. When the child suddenly found himself perched on a high stool facing his audience, however, he could no longer remember the beginning line. The radically changed situation presented too many distracting cues. Another child sometimes, although not always, confused the reading of *then* and *there, boy* and *dog,* and *pig* and *big.* In the original piece in which he had learned to recognize *then, boy,* and *pig,* the accompanying pictures and other cues supported perfect recognition of these words. His recall of them was faulty only in different situations in which some of the original cues for recall were absent and in which new and distracting cues were present. A high school orchestra demonstrated the same phenomenon. After coming to rely on the cues of the regular orchestra conductor during rehearsals for the school operetta, the orchestra was unable to perform at its best when the choral conductor (who was more concerned with signaling the chorus than the orchestra) took over the conducting role at the presentation of the operetta. Grossnickle's experiment, which we discussed earlier, also illustrates this point. In division problems, his pupils were unable to use the multiplication facts which they had previously used only in the multiplication situation.

4. Incompatible mental set. As an individual learns concepts or skills, he develops a functionally effective mental set for the activity, including the needed confidence and ready availability of appropriate responses. If intervening activities cause the mental set to change during the time between original learning and the retention test, recall will be more difficult. Bartlett's subjects failed to recall the role of the ghosts in the story he read to them because belief in the existence of ghosts was incompatible with their naturalistic training. We have all experienced such examples of forgetting as that of a student who intended to ask her English teacher whether to hyphenate "blue" and "green" in the phrase "blue-green lake." Once in the classroom, she forgot to ask the question because ongoing activities distracted her from her original set. She remembered the question again only when she returned to her incomplete composition and needed the answer.

An experiment by Carmichael, Hogan, and Walter demonstrates how different mental sets can alter remembered reproductions of the same perceived objects. As three groups of subjects viewed a list of 12 drawn figures, such as those in the middle column of Figure 11.5, Group I heard them named with the words in the left-hand column and Group II heard them named with the words in the right-hand column. For the third group, the objects were unnamed. Directed to reproduce all 12 patterns, the subjects in all three groups reproduced many of them correctly. However, of the poorest drawings of Groups I and II, about three-fourths of the distorted reproductions tended to resemble the forms each group had heard named, in the ways indicated in the left- and right-hand drawings of Figure 11.5.

Remembering and forgetting

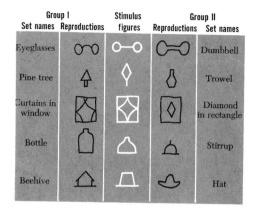

| Group I | | Stimulus | Group II | |
Set names	Reproductions	figures	Reproductions	Set names
Eyeglasses				Dumbbell
Pine tree				Trowel
Curtains in window				Diamond in rectangle
Bottle				Stirrup
Beehive				Hat

Fig. 11.5. *The reproductions of the stimulus figures in the middle column are affected by the mental-set words in the left- and right-hand columns.* (After L. Carmichael, H. P. Hogan, and A. A. Walter, *J. Exp. Psychol.,* 1932, vol. 15, p. 75.)

The different names heard by Groups I and II had created mental sets, and many of the reproductions conformed to those sets rather than to the original drawings. For the third group, distorted reproductions did not take either of these particular directions.

5. Repression. As a protective device for avoiding anxiety, an individual may fail to recall certain emotionally disturbing ideas. Because they are repressed, embarrassing or threatening concepts are forgotten more readily than satisfying concepts. For example, Levine and Murphy discovered that students forget more rapidly propaganda which is contrary to their biases than that which is in agreement with them [37]. There is also the example of Helen, who could not remember the content of a unit on health in her science course because to do so would re-arouse earlier-established anxiety. As a child she had responded to hospitalization with anxiety. In adolescence, when the health unit content reminded her of the painful, anxiety-provoking treatments and of what she had interpreted as abandonment by her parents, she avoided the full recurrence of the anxiety by repressing or forgetting ideas which would remind her of the earlier conditioning experience [47].

6. Disuse and metabolic changes in the nervous system. It seems plausible to assume that the residual traces imprinted in the nervous system by experience should fade with time. Indeed, this factor was at one time believed to be the primary cause of forgetting. In the face of the accumulating evidence of other active interferences with retention, it has come to be considered less and less important. But since the five psychological factors named above do not appear to account completely for the observed decrements in retention, the physiological factor is also assumed to be a possibility. Woodworth and Schlossberg have said that, although they consider interactive factors primarily responsible for forgetting, they also believe that "there is evidence that metabolic activities play some part" in erasing memory traces from the nervous system [62].

How well children and youth remember what they learn depends upon their curricula, the nature and effectiveness of the conditions of learning, the degree of mastery attained, and individual differences in their interests, other motives, and talents.

1. *Meaningfulness of content and approach.* Meaningful content and a meaningful rather than a rote approach to learning facilitate both original learning and retention. As our introductory examples illustrate, meaningful concepts—especially those related to general principles—are retained much better than rote-learned detached details or nonsense syllables. This difference was clearly indicated in the child's perfect retention of the functionally interrelated six simple machines and her marked forgetting of the detached state-capital associations.

The better retention of meaningful content than of meaningless content is demonstrated in the composite of experimental findings collected by Davis and Moore, presented in Figure 11.6 [16, p. 211]. In their review of these studies, Davis and Moore point out that the retention curves for both kinds of material are similar—they show rapid early loss and then a leveling off; but, as the curves also show, the retention of meaningful prose and poetry is maintained at a much higher level than the retention of nonsense syllables [17].

Several studies of school learning show that meaningful, organized content is better remembered than are isolated details. Pressey, Robinson, and Horrocks have summarized studies indicating that as much as two-thirds of the detailed facts students acquire in high school and college courses is forgotten within two years [46, p. 262]. In contrast

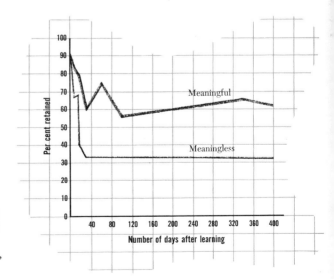

Fig. 11.6. *Composite retention curves for 18 studies of meaningless material and 24 studies of meaningful material* [17]. (From R. A. Davis, *Psychology of Learning*, McGraw-Hill, New York, 1935, p. 211.)

with these reports of extensive forgetting of unrelated facts, there are also several reports of generalizations and meaningful principles which have been retained over long periods of time. Schrepel and Laslett have reported that, although junior high school pupils lose some computational skill over the summer vacation, their ability to apply general principles of arithmetic is retained [49]. Frutchey [21] with high school students and Tyler [59] with college students, confirm the findings on rapid and extensive forgetting of isolated details, but show that general principles and the ability to apply them are well retained a year or more later.

As a consequence of our discoveries of the kinds of content students retain, we are learning how to make better achievement tests. For example, recent studies show good delayed retention of the general concepts students learn both in general [39] and in educational psychology [38]. Delayed-retention scores on tests given four to eight months after completion of the courses ranged from 71 to 79 per cent on such items as "Accepting pupil diagnosis as a major function of testing, which of the following is the best test: (a) a comprehensive achievement battery at the end of high school, (b) an achievement battery given early in the year, (c) an intelligence test, (d) a series of tests used to determine a student's grade [38]."

In order to enhance the retention of meaningful content, teachers should also see that the *learning approach is meaningful.* Many children do not approach a retention task so meaningfully as did the child who based her recall of the six simple machines on the observed functional interrelations between them. Some students try to recall such concepts as separate, unrelated facts. In rote fashion, they memorize numerous geometry theorems or chemical formulas as relatively meaningless facts rather than as differentiated elaborations of a few meaningful principles. Both our experience and experiments, however, demonstrate the advantage of the meaningful approach.

Steele found, with equated groups of fifth and sixth grade pupils, that the group which was taught fractions with emphasis upon understanding and the inductive discovery of principles did better both on end-of-course tests and on retention tests seven months later than did the group whose emphasis was on verbatim mastery by repetitive drill [51]. Using two groups of 35 college students as his subjects, Carpenter [12] directed them in learning to classify blocks—differing in color, size, and shape—into four categories: *cevs, biks, lags,* and *murs.* For example, in successive teacher demonstrations, the group taught by rote memorization, observed that the *mur* class included a white hexagon, a white circle, a blue circle, a yellow square, and a yellow triangle. The group instructed in a meaningful approach observed that *murs* were "tall and small," that *cevs* were "short and small," and so on. On a retention test one week later, in which the subjects were given a block of each class and required to pick out the remaining members, the rote-memorization group correctly identified only 29 per cent of the blocks while the meaningful-approach group correctly identified 77 per cent of them.

One of the important aspects of meaningfulness, as a factor favoring learning and retention, is organization of the material to be learned.

2. *Organization.* Retention of the thousands of facts, concepts, and skills—in language, science, mathematics, social studies, and other subjects—which elementary and secondary school children learn is greatly facilitated by effective, functional organization. Especially over long intervals, organizational categories for classifying or interpreting separate details determine the number and quality of ideas students retain. Postman has experimentally demonstrated that "learned rules of organization can systematically influence both the amount and quality of retention." When his subjects were given explicit verbal formulations of principles governing the content to be remembered, they improved their retention [45].

Let us illustrate the role of organization on recall in some recent experiments. In recalling a randomly arranged list of 40 words—such as *collie, lance, Belgium, Wallace, panther, Brazil, husky, Susan, revolver, bayonet, Homer, musket, Rumania, leopard, Chile, Elaine*—college students tended to group them into classes and subclasses. For example, there were ten animals divided into two classes: canine—collie, husky, etc., and feline—leopard, panther, etc. According to Cohen and Bousfield, the greater use students make of organizational concepts, the more effectively they recall words read to them [15]. In explaining the process of clustering items in recall, and its facilitating effect upon recall, Sakoda says that the individual "naturally" tends to organize the miscellaneous ideas he has learned into meaningful categories or under general concepts. In such an approach, an item suggests its class; the class concept then generates its members. Retention is thus facilitated by transfer of previously achieved generalizations [48].

In another recent study, Hall has shown that meaningful, well-organized verbal content is quite resistant to retroactive inhibition. Forty-five college students, subdivided into three groups, studied for three minutes a story about the customs and characteristics of a hypothetical primitive tribe. The story consisted of an introductory statement and 30 sentences, such as: "Women perform most of the *domestic* tasks." Immediately following the study, all three groups were given recall tests. Before a delayed-retention test, given 45 minutes later, Group I, the control group, took mechanical aptitude tests whose content had no relation to the original content but prevented them from rehearsing the story. Group II studied a quite different story

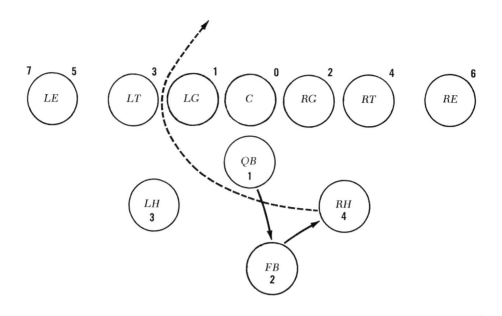

about another hypothetical tribe. And Group III studied a story similar to the original story. It was anticipated, of course, that in the process of trying to recall the original story, items, especially from similar sentences in the interpolated stories studied by Groups II and III might intrude. Despite the possibilities of retroactive effects, however, the percentages of items recalled by all three groups ranged from 91 to 101 per cent of the immediate-recall score. Even after 21 days, these retention scores ranged from 81 to 83 per cent. These short, fairly well-learned, coherent paragraphs probably left as a trace a unitary impression from which the details could be logically reconstructed. Because of their mental set to recall customs about a primitive tribe, and because of their ability to transfer generalizations about their own culture to the test situation, the students might very logically have inferred the missing word in such a sentence as: "Women perform most of the .... tasks." To assume that women perform domestic tasks is in harmony with well-learned cultural concepts [25].

These experiments suggest that one way to facilitate retention and effective recall of many concepts of the school curriculum is to develop interrelated functional classifications of them. The adolescent could recall the six simple machines because she had learned them as interrelated ways of giving a worker a mechanical advantage. Similarly, a child will effectively remember numerous concepts of physiology if he learns them in connection with understanding the *systems* of circulation, digestion, respiration, reproduction, etc. Similar functional integrations of the numerous concepts of English usage, of mathematics, and of every other phase of the school curriculum should lead to better retention and appropriate recall of them.

As a specific illustration of the advantage of good organization, consider how it enables high school football players to remember the 100 to 200 differently signaled plays they learn in a single short season. How do they remember for example, the particular one signaled by the call "four-three—on two," which is diagramed on page 380?

The players instantly recognize the play because the *system* they have learned gives the call meaning. For example, one system is organized in the following way: (1) All even-numbered plays go to the right and odd-numbered plays go to left; (2) signals beginning with 1 are quarterback plays, those beginning with 2 are right halfback plays; (3) a running play begins with a number; a passing play begins with the word "green"; (4) the first number called indicates the player to carry the ball, the second number is the hole number (over the right hip of the offensive players), the third number is the flanker, and a fourth number is the charging signal. If it were not for such organizational patterns, the signals would be a confusing jumble for both the quarterback and his teammates.

3. Thorough mastery. Poorly or barely mastered concepts and skills are soon forgotten. "Material that one wishes to retain for long periods needs to be studied and restudied [62, p. 730]." As Krueger has demonstrated, the additional practice beyond that required for minimal or uncertain performance of a skill pays dividends in sustained retention. After his three groups of subjects had taken the minimum number of trials needed to be able to trace a finger maze correctly, he gave one group 50 per cent more practice and a second group 100 per cent more. The added overlearning trials were not merely perfunctory repetitions, but were active efforts to improve proficiency and confidence on the maze. As the curves of Figure 11.7 show, the more thoroughly the material is mastered, the better it is retained. Other experimental studies indicate that on recall there is less interference of retroactive inhibition if there has been thorough

mastery, both of the material originally learned [29] and of the material interpolated [40] before the retention tests.

The role of original mastery in sustaining retention is also indicated in delayed retention studies of school subjects. For primary grade pupils, whose skills in reading, spelling, and arithmetic are developed to only minimal levels of proficiency, slight losses often occur over the summer vacation. For the intermediate grade levels, however, where the majority of pupils have developed higher degrees of mastery and interest in reading, average gains over the summer are quite uniformly reported [52]. Ashbaugh found that third grade children sustained net losses in spelling over the summer, but that fifth and sixth grade children, who had accumulated a greater background of spelling generalizations and skill in learning how to spell, experienced gains [2]. Brueckner found that second grade children retain, over the summer, the relatively well-learned easy addition and subtraction facts, whereas they tend to forget the harder, less well-learned subtraction facts [8]. On retention of American history, Kolberg reports that seventh grade pupils retain familiar, well-learned information items better than they do new, less well-learned facts [33].

Two studies, similar in design to Krueger's, show the effects of added amounts of practice on sustained retention. During the spring semester, Morgan gave his experimental group of sixth grade pupils two weeks of intensive remedial teaching in reading and arithmetic based on the diagnostic-test-discovered needs of individual children. An equated control group was given no special attention. It was found that the pupils whose spring achievement levels were raised by the remedial teaching maintained the higher levels without loss over the

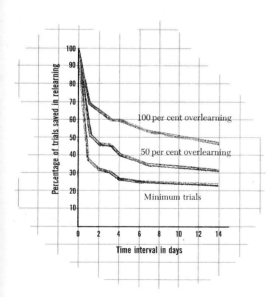

Fig. 11.7. *Comparison of the retention curves on finger-maze performance of groups given* (a) *the minimum trials for mastery;* (b) *50 per cent added trials;* (c) *100 per cent added trials shows that overlearning sustains retention.* (Data from W. C. F. Krueger, *J. Exp. Psychol.*, 1930, vol. 13, p. 155.)

summer vacation. The control group, who ended the spring term at lower achievement levels, sustained a loss in computation skill and maintained only their lower levels in arithmetic reasoning and in reading [41]. Brueckner and Distad compared the summer-retention of first grade children who had had 12, 24, and 36 weeks of reading instruction, and who attained corresponding levels of proficiency. For the children given only 12 weeks of instruction in reading, a significant loss occurred. For the children given 24 or 36 weeks of instruction, there were no appreciable losses [9].

Added practice is not, of course, the only way to facilitate mastery or retention of concepts and skills. Giving proper attention to *all* the conditions of effective learning—readiness, motivation, appropriate guidance of the trial-and-check process, emphasis on transfer principles, and the cultivation of mental health—will enhance both original learning and retention.

4. *Reviewing.* Interactive inhibition and other causes of forgetting take their toll of even well-mastered, meaningful concepts and skills unless they are reviewed. For example, without further instruction or review, ninth grade students in one year forgot two-thirds of the knowledge they had mastered in elementary algebra [36]. However, effective review, systematically scheduled review sessions, periodic retests, continued use of concepts, or expansion of previously accumulated concepts and their integration with new concepts can prevent such forgetting.

By means of relearning reviews in the fall, school children soon recover the losses sustained in some subjects over the summer vacation. In an experimental demonstration of the role of review in recovering losses from forgetting, Stroud and Johnson had about six hundred pupils in grades 7 to 9 read a 1,750-word article on paper making. Preceding the retention tests taken by different experimental and control groups after 1, 15, and 29 days, the experimental groups were permitted a 12-minute rereading review of the material. Control groups were denied this opportunity. Groups permitted the review earned retention scores 15 to 60 per cent higher than the control groups. As these data show, the need for review increases as the retention interval is lengthened. After only 1 day, the review produces an advantage of 15 per cent; after 29 days, the advantage is 60 per cent [53].

In order to prevent the losses which would otherwise occur from forgetting, the reviews need to be systematically spaced in a way to take into account the findings from curves of forgetting. To prevent the typical rapid forgetting which follows shortly after initial learning, a thorough review should be given early. Then comprehensive reviews, but with smaller samplings, can be spaced at longer and longer intervals. In spelling, for example, the words learned during the week are reviewed on Friday. Those missed on Friday are included in the next week's lesson. Other comprehensive reviews may be spaced at the end of the month, at the end of the term, and at the beginning of the following school year.

Periodic retesting of earlier-learned concepts and skills is an effective reviewing device. When children have opportunities to confirm or to revise concepts by study of their corrected test papers, they not only sustain retention but often achieve improvement. For example, of the addition problems which children missed on the second test—after having correctly solved them on the first—Davis and Rood found that 82.5 per cent were corrected on the third test, 8.8. per cent more were corrected on the fourth test, and an additional 2.9 per cent were finally corrected on the fifth test. The five successive tests, given at intervals of four to seven months, resulted in the eventual recovery of 94.2 per cent of concepts initially forgotten [18]. Studies by Tiedeman [56], with fifth grade pupils, and by Spitzer [50], with sixth grade pupils, show that multiple-choice review tests, given immediately after learning and spaced appropriately over the retention interval, aid in sustaining retention. As a comparison of the curves in Figure 11.8

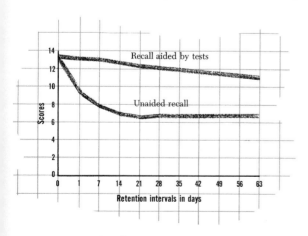

Fig. 11.8. *Test-aided retention of geography facts is superior to unaided recall of such content.* (From H. F. Spitzer, *J. Educ. Psychol.,* 1939, vol. 30, p. 647.)

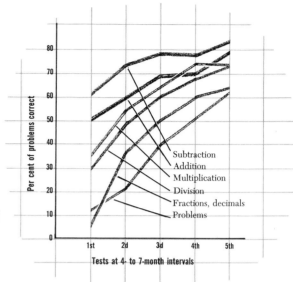

Fig. 11.9. *Retention and improvement of concepts and skills occur when review, need, and use of them are provided.* (From data by R. A. Davis and E. J. Rood, *J. Educ. Psychol.*, 1947, vol. 38, pp. 216–222.)

shows, retention aided by intervening tests is superior to unaided retention. The advantage of the test-aided recall could have been greater, however, if the corrected tests had been utilized more effectively in confirming correct test responses and in revising incorrect ones. Unless wrong answers are corrected, they tend to be repeated.

Although systematic reviews and appropriately spaced retention tests help children to remember school content, perhaps the best way to promote retention and to improve understanding of earlier-learned concepts and skills is to provide opportunities for their continuing use. Davis and Rood demonstrated that junior high school pupils who were given such opportunities improve in rather than forget the computation and problem-solving skills they learn in the elementary grades. During the four- to seven-month intervals between retention tests, their continued study of arithmetic required them to use the previously learned concepts and skills. For example, during the first semester of the seventh grade, they reviewed the four fundamental processes in studying decimals and fractions. In the eighth grade, they reviewed percentages by applying the concepts to interest, insurance, and other problems. In the succession of retention tests given over a two-year period, each child was encouraged to try to better his previous record. As is revealed in Figure 11.9, such continued and extended application of concepts not only prevents their loss but increases understanding of them. The orderly arrangement of sequences of topics so that new problems provide for functional applications of significant facts and principles will ensure both their retention and expanded development.

5. *Integration.* Two studies point out especially clearly how re-

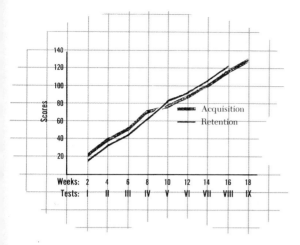

Fig. 11.10. *Reviewing sustains retention and facilitates new learning, as is shown by acquisition and retention scores plotted cumulatively.* (From A. H. Word and R. A. Davis, *J. Educ. Psychol.*, 1939, vol. 30, p. 121.)

tention can be improved by the *integration* of topics in a sequence. When pupils study a sequence of topics—as in science, social studies, or literature—each new topic should be related to or developed as an extension of the organized accumulation of preceding topics. With such integration of topics in a sequence, studies show that the kind of interactive inhibition complained of by the student in the previously mentioned course in theories of personality does not occur.

In a study of seventh grade science pupils, Word and Davis demonstrated the role of integration in retention of general science concepts. As review devices, they employed repeated testing, continued use of previously learned facts, and attempts to interrelate or integrate new concepts with previously accumulated and organized concepts. At the conclusion of each two-week assignment, the pupils were tested both on the newly acquired content and on retention of content from the preceding two-week assignment. Their accumulated scores on both the old and the newly acquired concepts, recorded biweekly over a period of 18 weeks, are presented in Figure 11.10. The figure shows that the integration of new concepts into the student's functionally organized background of concepts not only keeps the background facts alive but probably gives them broader and enriched meaning. As a consequence, the possibilities of both retention and transfer are enhanced.

In another study of the effect of integration on the retention of social studies content, Ausubel, Robbins, and Blake [3] had 188 college students first study for 25 minutes a 1,700-word passage on Buddhism (its history, sacred literature, doctrine, and ethical teachings). Immediately after this initial study, the students took a multiple-choice test on the content of the passage. Twenty-four hours later, different subgroups of the 188 students studied different interpolated materials.

A nonintegrative group read a new 1,700-word passage on Christianity (its history, sacred literature, doctrine, and ethical teachings). An integrative group read a comparative 2,100-word essay on Buddhism *and* Christianity, recapitulating the content on Buddhism and pointing out the similarities and differences between it and Christianity. Eight days later both groups took a delayed-retention test on the content of the original passage on Buddhism. For the nonintegrative group who studied the passage on Christianity without relating it to Buddhism, retroactive effects reduced the mean score on Buddhism to 82.3 per cent of the original score. However, for the integrative group who compared Buddhism and Christianity, the delayed-retention score on Buddhism was 107.7 per cent of the original score. Instead of experiencing interference from study of the second topic, the students who integrated their study of the two religions enhanced their understanding of Buddhism.

6. *Dynamic factors in retention.* Such dynamic factors as interests, intention to remember, mental set, and attitudes affect both the learning and retention of concepts and skills.

Interests. As children and youth develop specialized interests—in science, art, literature, or other curriculum activities—these interests become dynamic cores for the organization, extension, and search for new related knowledge or skill. For example, the child who enjoys constructing crystal, tube, and transistor radio sets becomes preoccupied with his creative interest. In extending his insights into the principles of radio and the general field of electronics, he is continuously reorganizing his accumulating background of concepts for more effective use. Such highly motivated learning and *use* of concepts reinforce them for permanent retention.

Intention to remember. The interest-motivated child learns concepts with intention to remember them, and, as experiments show, intention to remember facilitates retention. Karen [31] directed two groups of students to look over long lists of words and nonsense syllables; one group was told to draw a line through 30 of them, and the other group was told to "study and remember" these 30 words and syllables. In a retention test requiring the subjects to recognize the 30 items when mixed with 30 other words and syllables, the group which had *intended* to remember them recognized 9.47 of the items while the *incidental-learning* group recognized only 5.70. Another experiment indicates that for "intention to remember" to be effective, it must operate during, not after, learning [4]. These experiments remind us that effective learning is goal-directed; and that anticipation of using the concepts and skills we learn enhances our retention of them.

Set to recall. Retention depends upon intention to remember

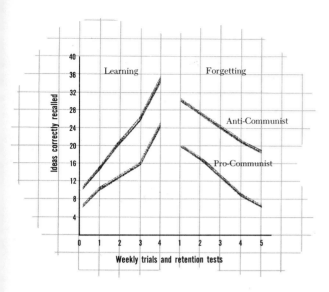

Fig. 11.11. *Students with anti-Communist attitudes surpass those with pro-Communist attitudes in the learning and retention of anti-Soviet material.* (From J. M. Levine and G. Murphy, *J. Abnorm. and Soc. Psychol.*, 1943, vol. 38, p. 513.)

during learning and upon an appropriate mental set at the time of recall. Often before earlier-learned concepts and skills can be recalled, the individual must "warm up" to the specific task. Suddenly confronted with a request to play the piano-recital pieces she had not practiced for two or three years, the child of our earlier example was at first baffled. She seemed completely unable to remember "Soldiers' Chorus," but as she persisted in her efforts to recall it, an idea of the melody occurred. Then, in a goal-directed trial-and-check process, she reconstructed the piece—first the melody and then even the accompaniment. As the warm-up proceeded, she became able to recall pieces which had seemed completely forgotten. In reestablishing an appropriate mental set for playing these pieces, traces from general musical concepts and related clue traces were reactivated and attention was diverted from distracting traces and cues.

Unless children come to understand the role of mental set in recall, they may assume that it is useless to try to recall partially forgotten concepts or skills. It often seems futile to attempt some recall tasks because they seem too difficult, and they *are* difficult until one gets into them. Children need, therefore, to learn to make trial efforts. By encouraging resourcefulness generally, we may aid children in getting through the warm-up period. If we can develop in our pupils a mental set to remember and to apply, to transfer general concepts and skills, we shall also aid the development of their retentive power.

Beliefs, attitudes, and self-concept. A motivational bias in harmony with the concepts being learned tends to facilitate both the learning and retention of such material. In testing this hypothesis, Garber found that students who believed and approved the concepts in a passage they read twice in *Russia Today* retained more of the essential ideas than a group who disbelieved and disapproved them [22]. In another study, Levine and Murphy had pro-Communist and anti-Communist college students read and recall, in five weekly practice periods, both pro-Soviet and anti-Soviet prose selections. Then, in five weekly delayed-retention tests, they measured the number of ideas which the students could correctly reproduce from the earlier-read selections. As Figure 11.11 shows, each group learned more and forgot fewer of the concepts with which they could agree. The anti-Communist students retained more of the anti-Soviet ideas; and, as a similar graph in Levine and Murphy's article shows, the pro-Communist students retained more of the pro-Soviet ideas [37, p. 512].

One's self-concept is another dynamic factor which affects retention. In demonstrating the role of this factor, Cartwright read to 80 adults lists of adjectives and names of objects, both consistent and inconsistent with their self-concepts. Self-consistent or self-inconsistent adjectives and names had previously been sorted by the subjects as "most like [or least like] me" and as "most like [or most unlike] me to own," respectively. On immediate-retention tests, the subjects recalled significantly more of the self-consistent items [14, p. 214]. Adjectives inconsistent with the self-concept were sometimes distorted in the direction of greater self-consistency. For example, *satisfied* was misrecalled as *dissatisfied*, *hopeless* as *hopeful*, and *hostile* as *hospitable*.

A GENERAL THEORY OF REMEMBERING

The introductory examples of remembering and the experiments both on the causes of forgetting and on the factors which facilitate retention all indicate that remembering is not a passive reproduction of previous experience. On the contrary, they indicate that remembering is a complex creative process. In the specific acts of remembering described—

recalling the capitals of the states, the six simple machines, the events in "The Wet Fall," and the piano pieces—the roles of both past experience and current problem solving are evident. From past experience, there are the residue of the events to be recalled, transferable beliefs and generalizations, and conditioned attitudes and interests. Operating at the moment of recall are the

present mental set and the goal-directed trial-and-check process of problem solving. For example, in remembering a story children often recall the story's general outline and some especially significant details from the original learning experience. But in the process of recalling it—by additions, deletions, substitutions, and distortions—they tend to mold the original story into a form in harmony with their present concepts, beliefs, and attitudes [13, 43].

We have learned in this chapter that the delayed recall of concepts or skills is affected by interactive inhibition and by changes in both the situation and in the cognitive structure, attitudes, emotions, interests, and mental set of the learner. How well we recall them depends upon their meaningfulness, our mastery of them, and on how thoroughly we have reviewed them in the meantime. In recalling miscellaneous facts or events, we give them more economical and satisfying organization. Such dynamic factors as individual difference in interests, beliefs, attitudes, self-concepts, and mental set tend to shape each individual's recall to suit his needs.

Other data are in agreement with these findings. Morris reports that as each of six children reproduced in a succession of retellings a story read to the first child, the story became shortened. Details were deleted. The titles and names of persons and places were either changed or omitted. Events were transposed. And complex sentences were simplified and put into more childlike language [42]. Talland found that when college students from different nations, working in teams of four, retold in serial reproduction essays from various areas of interest, there was some tendency to restructure the concepts in terms of the students' different cultural attitudes. For example, Americans misinterpreted cricket scores as baseball scores, and then marveled at a player's 95 consecutive runs. British students reproduced "the difference goes deep" with "the cleavage goes deep [54, p. 80]." Tiernan found that in delayed reproductions—at intervals of 11, 46, and 120 days—children aged 7 to 14 tended to complete such uncompleted figures as hearts, circles, or diamonds [57]. Their reproductions tended to conform more nearly than the uncompleted drawings to their concepts of these figures. Williams and Knox, in summarizing some of the dynamic factors affecting memory, note that (1) reproductions are affected by naming objects; (2) they tend toward symmetry, simplicity, and completeness; and (3) their traces are affected by organizational processes, by interaction with other traces, and by attitudes [61].

As a concrete illustration of these tendencies, let us examine a nine-year-old child's reproduction of the left-hand pattern in Figure 11.12. After observing the stimulus figure for 10 seconds, with intent to remember it, he was asked to reproduce it from memory. His drawing, on the right-hand side of Figure 11.12, shows that it is partly a reproduction and partly a logical reconstruction. He first reproduced the larger rectangular pattern and, with some variation, included a smaller enclosed rectangle. Next, he drew the enclosed triangle on the left side. Instead of the right-hand enclosed triangle, however, he first drew the dotted line, which he immediately erased. Then, apparently to make the whole more symmetrical, he completed the drawing with the other self-contributed triangle.

Our review of the experiments on remembering and our observations of particular examples, such as those above, indicate that remembering is more a process of construction than of reproduction. According to Bartlett, whose theory has guided us in this discussion, "Remembering is an imaginative reconstruction, or construction, built out of the relation of our attitude towards a whole active mass of organized past reactions [traces], and to a little outstanding detail which commonly appears in image or in language form [6, p. 213]."

An act of remembering involves the trace left by the experience to be remembered, interaction of this trace with the integrated organization of traces from the individual's entire background of experience, and the creative process of reconstruction. As Bartlett says, "Remembering obviously involves determination by the past." From past experience the individual develops an active organization of traces, which Bartlett calls "schemata." In remembering, however, the individual, at least in part, *infers* the past from his present cognitive structure—of hypotheses, assumptions, interests, and attitudes. It is as though the individual said to himself: "This and this and this must have occurred in order that my present state should be what it is." In remembering something, often the first thing to emerge is an attitude. The constructed recall justifies the attitude. The original trace

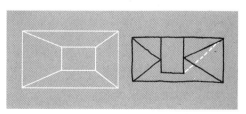

Fig. 11.12. *In reconstructing from memory the stimulus figure on the left-hand side, a nine-year-old child "corrects" his drawing (the dash line) to make the whole more symmetrical.*

probably determines the attitude, the general form of the event, and some vivid detail. From these the individual "constructs the probable detail."

SUMMARY

Accumulating knowledge for both present and lifetime goals is a complex function involving the interrelated processes of learning, remembering, and forgetting. In the elementary and secondary school, children do not simply march forward, mastering the sequences of concepts and skills as they are presented. Earlier-learned concepts and skills can either interfere with or facilitate their mastery. And later-learned concepts and skills can either impair or facilitate their retention and application. As teachers, we are concerned with efficient learning, sustained retention, and effective application of the concepts and skills children learn. Hence we need to understand and to control the complex of factors involved.

Delayed tests have revealed that retention depends upon the nature of what is learned and upon the opportunities for review and applications. There is often rapid and extensive forgetting of unrelated details. But meaningful, well-mastered, and frequently reviewed or applied concepts are retained for long periods of time. And when conditions are such that transfer can operate, delayed retention and application of concepts and skills may be better than immediate recall.

Forgetting, like learning, is an active process. It does not consist merely of the fading of memory traces in the nervous system. On the contrary, several factors cause us to forget the concepts and skills we learn. Because of proactive inhibition, our accumulating stores of knowledge sometimes make it more difficult to memorize and to recall subsequently placed material. And later-learned concepts sometimes retroact to inhibit accurate recall of earlier-learned content. The changes an individual undergoes—changes in his way of thinking and reasoning, and in his beliefs, attitudes, and interests—are likely to modify his recall of earlier-learned concepts. Changes in the original learning and the recall situations, such as the elimination of certain relevant cues and the addition of distracting ones, can also prevent accurate recall of once-remembered concepts or skills. Moreover, an incompatible mental set at the moment of recall can divert an individual from accurate recall of an earlier-learned behavior pattern. And sometimes our need to avoid anxiety can cause us to repress recall of a painful experience. In addition to these active causes of forgetting, ongoing metabolic activities play some part in erasing memory traces from the nervous system.

In the light of our understanding of the causes of forgetting and of other conditions which favor retention, we can suggest several ways of facilitating retention of the concepts and skills children and youth need to remember. The curriculum should be comprised of meaningful material organized for the discovery, developmental expansion, and continuous application of significant principles. The approach to learning should emphasize understanding and the inductive discovery of principles rather than rote memorization. By conscientiously providing for the conditions of effective learning, teachers can guide children to the attainment of high levels of mastery and effective functional organizations of the concepts they learn. Even meaningful, organized, and well-mastered concepts and skills are forgotten, however, unless they are reviewed. Review is essential for sustained retention. It should consist of systematically scheduled periods for the relearning of test-discovered forgotten concepts, of the integration of new concepts into functional organizations of accumulating knowledge, and of provisions for continuous and extended applications of the expanding systems of principles being learned. Retention is also facilitated by relating the curriculum to children's interests; by appropriate consideration of and guidance in the development of their beliefs, attitudes, and self-concepts; by establishing intentions to remember useful concepts; and by developing mental sets for the recall and application of them in an ever-increasing variety of problem situations.

An integration of all the facts we have reviewed, both on the causes of forgetting and on the ways of facilitating retention, suggests that remembering is not a passive reproduction of previous experience. Our review supports Bartlett's theory that remembering involves both reproduction and creative reconstruction. In remembering an experience, the individual often reproduces only its general form and some of the vivid details and then constructs the probable details in harmony with his present cognitive structure. The condensations, elaborations, substitutions, and inventions characteristic of memory are contributed from the individual's general system of traces—to suit his present logical assumptions, beliefs, interests, and attitudes.

At any particular moment in the individual's sequence of learnings, his present cognitive structure provides a probable solution in both the learning and memory problems he meets. Each new learning experience, however, leaves a residual trace in the nervous system which interacts with the organization of trace systems previously established from his entire background of prior experiences. Thus new experiences are constantly changing the organization of trace systems. When a learned behavior pattern is recalled, the reproduction is affected both by the residual trace from the specific experience to be recalled and by the individual's total organization of trace systems, with which the original trace and traces from all intervening experiences have interacted. It is more correct, therefore, to think of learning as a *reorganization* than an addition to the individual's cognitive structure. And in this manner of thinking, it is more accurate to think of memory as a process of reconstruction than of reproduction.

In Chapters 3 through 10 we have presented the functions, supporting experiments, and varied applications of six essential conditions of effective learning: readiness, motivation, guidance in structuring approaches to learning tasks, repeated trials and perception of the effects in the trial-and-check process, and transfer. In the present chapter we have discovered that these same conditions facilitate sustained retention. They are pervasive factors in the acquisition, retention, and application of the concepts and skills we learn. Transfer, for example, is both an essential condition of effective learning and retention and an effective test of retention. But as we learned in Chapter 2, there is a seventh condition of effective learning. Like readiness, it is a supplementary, although nonetheless essential, condition.

For effective operation of the first six conditions of learning, the learner also needs confidence, a self-concept of competency, and healthy relations with his classmates—with whom he achieves both academic and personal-social-development objectives. Otherwise, anxiety, feelings of inferiority, and social maladjustment may produce self-protective defenses which impair his intellectual efficiency. In the next three chapters we shall consider this condition of effective learning—mental health and social adjustment.

GUIDES FOR STUDY, REVIEW, AND APPLICATION

1. Explain the following quotation: "Good teaching involves not only efficient guidance of initial learning, but the fostering of sustained retention and extended applications of the concepts and skills learned."

2. Using a child or yourself as the subject for your experimenting, collect some examples of remembering and forgetting. What *general factors* affecting remembering and forgetting can you identify in these examples?

3. What kinds of learning material and methods of learning seem to produce retention curves showing (*a*) rapid forgetting, (*b*) sustained retention, (*c*) augmented retention?

4. List a variety of things once learned which are now partially or almost completely forgotten. Can you explain the forgetting as caused by (*a*) interactive inhibition, (*b*) changes in cognitive structure, (*c*) changes in the recall situation, (*d*) incompatible mental set, or (*e*) repression?

5. In a plan for teaching the subject of your major interest to elementary or secondary students, incorporate provisions for sustained retention of the concepts or skills to be learned. Try to apply as many as you can of the six factors which facilitate sustained retention.

6. Summarize all the facts you have learned about remembering and forgetting. Is Bartlett's creative "reconstruction" theory an adequate explanation of these facts? Can you construct a better theory?

7. Can you extend our general cognitive theory of learning, outlined in Chapter 2 and elaborated in the intervening chapters, to incorporate the "reconstruction" theory of remembering? Are the "seven conditions of learning" essential for both effective learning and sustained retention?

Part 4

MENTAL HEALTH AND SOCIAL LEARNING

Chapter 12

MENTAL HEALTH: ITS ROLE IN LEARNING

Mental health and success in learning are very closely related. There is a complex cause-and-effect relationship between them, and between their opposites, emotional maladjustment and intellectual inefficiency. Mental health is essential for effective learning; and zest for the discoveries and self-enhancements of learning is a sign of mental health. In activities which appeal to their interests, curiosities, and problem-solving propensities—in the classroom, peer group, family, and community—children and youth find great joy in the full use of their intellectual talents. Therefore, the individual with a healthy, well-integrated personality—in cooperative and complementary relations with other individuals—develops and utilizes his potentialities for constructive, creative productivity. With his distinctive intellectual capacities—for learning, remembering, projecting generalizations into the future, forecasting the consequences of his behavior, creating new tools and products, and formulating self-guiding ideals—his normal course of growth is toward "a more productive, contributory, and satisfying way of life [65, p. 183]."

A pupil who normally engages in creative and productive activities and who approaches learning and problem-solving tasks constructively has, we say, a healthy personality. There are, of course, other complementary characteristics which underlie this child's healthy behavior. For creative productivity, he needs to feel socially secure, personally worthy, and confident of his talents. He needs to have self-respect and a comfortable feeling of self-acceptance. Healthy individuals appraise themselves realistically; they accept their shortcomings and respect their talents and virtues. On the basis of realistic self-appraisals, they set for themselves attainable goals. Mental health also implies a feeling of being wanted and of belonging to groups, of trusting and being trusted, of loving and being loved in family, peer, and teacher-pupil relationships. Because of the deep joy individuals find in fellowship, they "can achieve fulfillment only through full participation in activity which leads to fulfillment of group goals [46, p. 7]." Mentally healthy children and youth learn, as they mature, a problem-solving approach to life's problems. They accept their responsibilities, make their own decisions, plan ahead, set realistic goals for themselves, and, in problem-solving fashion, do the best they can in the problem situations they encounter or create. They learn how to learn and to solve problems, and they take pride in enhanced intellectual efficiency. They commit themselves wholeheartedly to significant personal-social ideals. Although they often conform comfortably to interdependent group patterns of behavior, they also feel free to be original when it seems desirable, and they take spontaneous, uninhibited pleasure in the full development and expression of their personal resources.

School accomplishment and mental health. In our study of the essential conditions for effective learning, we have found many reasons why the school achievement of some children and youth exceeds or falls below what we might ordinarily expect of individuals of similar intellectual capacities. An important factor is mental health. Compared with underachievers, overachievers enjoy greater self-esteem and a more satisfying sense of personal worth. They are happier about their aspirations, intellectual efficiency, and scholastic programs, and they are more content in their social relations [13]. Among intellectually superior students, the high achievers tend to be mentally healthy and well adjusted to their social environments. The underachievers, on the other hand, often exhibit symptoms of self- and interpersonal conflict [30]. In contrast to the underachievers, the overachievers appraise themselves as more intellectually efficient, confident, ready to accept social responsibilities, mature in interest development, and as enjoying intellectual pursuits [45]. Adolescent underachievers tend to have more aggressive feelings and other negative attitudes about their relationships with their parents; consequently, they sometimes tend to feel anxious and guilty [35]. Such obstacles to mental health as inappropriate educational and vocational goals, lack of confidence, fear of criticism, unhealthy parent-child relations, poor adjustments with peers, and other unresolved problems too often divert intellectually gifted children from the full development of their superior talents. Indeed, scientific studies indicate that because of such handicaps, 10 to 40 per cent of these children are underachievers [22]. Frustrated as they are, their natural eagerness to learn is dulled. Such children and youth resign themselves to boring, uninteresting routines and come to think of themselves as incapable of creative and productive work [46].

WHY EMOTIONAL HEALTH IS ESSENTIAL TO LEARNING EFFICIENCY

Efficient learning requires an integrated, systematic attack upon problems. It involves anticipation, planning ahead, persistence balanced with variability of approach, the application of a functionally organized background of experience, and a set to learn—to be guided by prior experience in a new problem situation. It is a goal-directed trial-and-check process requiring concentrated attention and sustained effort, despite delays and feelings of uncertainty about the outcome. Efficient problem solving requires self-confidence, self-reliance in the face of difficulties, and a willingness to follow up promising leads even while experiencing some frustration. Emotionally healthy children often demonstrate this pattern of problem solving both in classroom activities and in their approach to problems in psychological tests. In contrast, emotionally maladjusted children often exhibit symptoms of impaired efficiency in learning and problem-solving situations.

*Good mental health
is an essential condition
of effective learning*

*Opportunities
for creative expression . . .*

*provide constructive outlets
for tensions*

A zest for discovery

Well-adjusted children are curious

Confident youngsters try difficult tasks

Let us try to pinpoint some of these symptoms in the case of a ten-year-old fourth grade girl who has not yet learned to read. Mary has an S-B IQ of 107, but, at best, she reads only a relatively few words which she remembers as sight words. Lacking the confidence to try to remember words which are pointed out to her and lacking any skill in the independent identification of unfamiliar words, she waits dependently for her mother or teacher to prompt her when she comes to a word she does not know. Failing to meet the standards of accomplishment expected by her parents, teacher, or classmates, she feels anxious, inferior, and guilty. Her mother alternates between exasperation—because she sometimes feels that Mary could learn if she would only try harder—and discouragement about the futility of her efforts to help her. Nightly practice sessions have been tense experiences for both of them. Mary always feared that she would guess a word wrongly and that she would immediately hear her mother's reproof or sense disapproval in her mother's facial expression. Finally, she has become so fearful of risking a provisional trial—even on a word which she should easily infer from the context—that she inhibits the trial-and-check process, and thus severely impairs her learning efficiency.

Such emotional disturbances develop from frustration and conflict experienced in school, from unhealthy parent-child relationships, or from other unfortunate personal or social experiences. Sibling jealousy, parental overprotection, parental rejection, social-class differences, general home insecurity, personal handicaps, and other conditions producing feelings of anxiety, aggression, inferiority, and guilt have all been associated with learning difficulties [76]. Children differ, however, in their reactions to such frustrations.

Aggressive reactions can impair intellectual efficiency in a variety of ways. An eight-year-old boy of average intelligence resisted learning to read as an unconscious counteraggressive reaction to his mother. When he was six, he developed the feeling that his mother had rejected and abandoned him in favor of a new baby sister. But being afraid to express his aggressive impulses openly, he symbolized them in reversed writing of words and letters and in a resistance to reading [9]. An intellectually superior 12-year-old developed a hostile attitude toward her parents. Although this attitude did not prevent her mastery of skills, it distorted her interpretation of certain concepts. In reading a passage on parent-child relationships, she overemphasized the superficial details and slighted the deeper broad meanings. She mistakenly described the authors as "preaching," as biased toward parents, and as believing that "you ought to resign yourself to staying at home with your parents [51]." Another intellectually superior 18-year-old girl who felt anxious and unworthy readily abandoned

systematic problem solving when she could not achieve immediate solutions to problems. She was presented with the problem: "If a man buys eight cents' worth of stamps and gives the clerk twenty-five cents, how much change should he get back?" She tried for only a few seconds to solve it, then she remarked angrily: "Might as well forget it, I'm no good at that." But she continued: "Eight?" Resuming her self-attack, however, she added: "Oh how dumb can you get—that's wrong, it's thirteen." The distracting self-aggressive attitude which she assumed seriously interfered with her efficiency.

Overconformity as a reaction to aggressive impulses can also impair learning efficiency. Johnny, age seven, had until recently been quite successful in school, but now he began to fall behind. He tried to please his teacher and his parents; but in order to please his dominating mother, he felt a compulsion to do everything perfectly. Because of his overcautious and excessively slow approach to learning projects—rechecking them, erasing, and doing things over—he could rarely complete tasks. He would have preferred being more like his easy-going and somewhat careless father, but his anxiety compelled him to try to live up to his mother's demands. This anxiety resulted in part from fear of his own irrepressible aggressive impulses toward his mother—both for her strict discipline and for imposing on him so many irksome home chores. Fearful of the consequences, should these impulses be expressed, Johnny overcompensated by being "as good as gold," and, as is usual in anxiety-motivated behavior, his efforts proved self-defeating [32].

Lack of confidence impairs the efficiency of many children. Feeling inadequate and distrusting their own problem-solving efforts, unconfident children hesitate to undertake tasks, make excuses, behave overdependently, or, in great stress, give way to panic. Of Bruce, who has an S-B IQ of 122 and is in the third grade, his teacher says: "He is capable of doing many things, but he sits at his desk chewing a pencil or his shirt sleeve and never does any work except when I sit with him." Glen, who often responds to tasks with "I can't get that," was asked to draw a man. Rather than risk the possibility of failure in an attempt to draw it, he preferred to show how he would go about doing it. Intellectually superior Rolf, at age five, revealed his insecurity and self-distrust by drawing very tiny circles, squares, and diamonds when asked to copy models of these figures. His low self-concept was suggested by his self-depreciatory comments. About paper folding he remarked: "Mine isn't as good as yours." While watching the examiner demonstrate how to make a bead chain, he said: "Maybe I'll forget to make mine like yours." Although Rolf succeeded on these items, his insecurity and self-distrust led to error in the block-counting test. When asked for three blocks, he first correctly placed three blocks on the paper before the examiner. Then, prompted by anxiety over the possibility of being wrong, he added two more, remarking: "That's not enough, is it?" When asked for seven blocks, he placed the correct number on the paper. Then, again distrusting himself, he removed some, commenting: "No, that's too many." The comments of a 14-year-old who feared a geometry examination illustrate how panic can disorganize our thinking: ". . . suddenly, I couldn't for the 'life of me' remember a single axiom or postulate; I didn't know why and when angles or sides are equal; my mind seemed a total blank! [69, p. 100]"

Other individuals, embarrassed by their limitations, seek persistently to hide them instead of working to overcome them. Ann—in the fifth grade and unable to read at all, except for the recognition of a few sight words—sought to protect herself from more painful feelings of inadequacy by being very nice to people and by trying to avoid situations in which her deficiency would be detected. When her intraclass group joined the teacher at the reading table for oral reading, she sat quietly, watching for a clue to turn the page in her book at the right time. When her group returned to their individual seats for silent reading, the school psychologist, interested in determining the level at which she could read, joined her at her desk and suggested that she read something to him. She looked startled for a few seconds. Then smiling up at him, she said, "Let's read silent." Next day, however, fearful that her deficiency had been revealed, she brought a book to show him that she could read. That she had tried to memorize the selection was shown, however, by the frequent mismatching of the words she "read" with those printed.

A tentative explanation of emotional disturbances of learning. Although these cases suggest that emotional disturbance can impair learning efficiency in a variety of ways, they also reveal some common features. These children, like every child in our culture, seem to have learned that school achievements and other accomplishments win rewarding approval from teachers, parents, and peers. Thus successful children come to feel worthy, esteemed, and confident. However, when they fail persistently to meet the accomplishment, social, and moral standards of their parents, teacher, or peers, they are often disapproved. Threatened with loss of esteem and love, they come to feel inferior, guilty, and anxious. In panic about preventing or retrieving their loss, but impaired in intellectual efficiency by these handicapping self-attitudes, they often develop such self-defeating modes of adjustment as inhibition of problem solving, misdirected interpersonal- or self-aggression, compulsive overconformity, overdependency, or unwillingness and inability to face or correct any limitations. These shortsighted, although natural, modes of adjustment impair learning efficiency rather than facilitate the accomplishments needed for feelings of security, personal worth, esteem, and confidence.

The cause-effect relationship between emotional disturbances and learning difficulties is complex. Emotional disturbances growing out of unfortunate parent-child or peer relations may impair learning efficiency, or, if they are severe, even preclude school learning [66]. From a history of harsh treatment and parental rejection, some children become so counteraggressive toward adults that they use their intelligence only in pursuing and in defending the delinquent roles with which they have identified. After having studied the behavior of a group of aggressive, preadolescent delinquents, Redl and Wineman said that "for a good educational diet to take hold of these children at all, their basic ego disturbances must be repaired first [53, p. 242]." But learning difficulties themselves can cause anxiety and guilt which, in turn, can intensify the learning difficulties. On the other hand, successful learning experiences can lead to restored confidence and improved mental health. Some resourceful children learn to manage emotional disturbances without any obvious impairment of their learning efficiency. Because of these complications, it seems desirable to explore more systematically the experimental studies of the problem.

REACTIONS TO FRUSTRATION, CONFLICT, AND THREATS

The reactions of children and youth to frustration of their needs and strong desires vary and include a wide range of behavior patterns. Frustrating situations frequently provoke aggressive behavior. They often produce a loss in constructiveness of behavior. Some individuals, however, increase their constructiveness when challenged by difficulties. In other children, levels of aspiration may be disturbed. As we have already seen, intellectual efficiency may be impaired in a number of ways. And when a self-concept of adequacy is threatened, individuals may develop a variety of defensive modes of adjustment.

Aggression and frustration. Barker, Dembo, and Levin observed the behavior of 30 bright four-year-old children both before and during frustration, as they played in a standardized playroom equipped with doll and housekeeping toys, a truck and trailer, boats and water toys, and crayons and paper—all arranged in three squares on the floor. In the prefrustration period, each child played in a part of the room where only the toys mentioned were visible. Frustration was introduced during a second play period by removing the partition which had divided the room and exposing a larger assortment of much more interesting and attractive toys. After a child had become interested in the more attractive toys, the experimenter suddenly led him to the "old" part of the room and directed: "Now let's play at the other end." A wire screen was then drawn across the room, preventing the child further access to the more attractive toys but leaving them visible to him. Thus frustrated, many of the children reacted aggressively—by hitting, kicking, breaking, and destroying [3, p. 456]. Besides observing these aggressive acts, the examiners noted an increase in unhappy verbal expressions, motor restlessness, and loud singing and talking. Friendly conversation and happy expressions decreased. A few of the more resourceful of these children, however, made the best of the situation. Deprived of the more attractive toys, they utilized those left to them more constructively.

In an exploration of the factors determining reactions to frustration, Davitz studied the influence of specific training [15]. Using as subjects 40 seven- to nine-year-old children, he subjected them to the following sequence of ratings and experiences: (1) ratings on aggressiveness and constructiveness during free play with toys permitting either aggressive or constructive activities; (2) training of 20 children in aggression and of an equated group of 20 in constructive behavior; (3) frustration of both groups; and (4) reratings of both groups for aggressiveness and constructiveness.

The aggressive training consisted of seven 30-minute sessions of aggressive play, such as competing in tearing the "scalp" (a piece of cloth attached to each child's arm) from other children while protecting one's own "scalp." The constructive training consisted of an equal · number of sessions in which the subjects were rewarded for constructive work in making murals and assembling jigsaw puzzles. The frustrating experience for both groups consisted of taking away some candy they had just been given and of abruptly interrupting films they had just begun to watch.

In response to the two different types of training, the majority of the children in each group changed in the expected directions. Aggressive training tended to make the children more aggressive, and constructive training tended to make them more constructive. But neither kind of training was universally effective in these ways. Moreover, there were inconsistencies within the two groups. A few constructively trained children became more aggressive; and a few children trained in aggression became more constructive. Specific training is apparently only one factor affecting children's reactions to frustration. Whether or not a given child reacts aggressively in a frustrating situation depends upon such other factors as the strength of the frustrated motive, the extent of accumulated past frustrations, the availability of alternative modes of adjustment, and the likelihood of punishment. How an individual reacts in particular situations depends upon his personality and total life history [6, 15].

Loss in constructiveness and frustration. The experiment by Barker, Dembo, and Levin described above, in which familiar toys were abruptly substituted for more-preferred new toys, showed that frustration can cause a loss in constructiveness. In this experiment, play constructiveness was measured on a 7-point scale ranging from "rather primitive, simple, little-structured activities to elaborate highly developed play." For example, the child who merely sits on the floor and picks up a truck and trailer is rated 2 on the scale. For such imaginative play as equipping a truck and going fishing (which involves taking off the trailer, attaching a motorboat, getting gasoline, and an integrated verbalization of the sequence of activities), the rating is 7.

In the prefrustration free-play situation, the mean constructiveness rating was 4.99. During frustration, it dropped to 3.94. This decrease in play constructiveness is equivalent to a loss of 17.3 months in mental age. In other words, after frustration, the play of these children corresponded—on the average—to that of children about 17 months less mature than their normal, or before-frustration, standard. Of the 30 children, however, only 22 of them regressed to a lower level of constructiveness, despite the frustration. And 5 children met the challenge of restricted play resources by improved constructive effort. One child raised his constructiveness rating from under 3 to approximately 5 [3].

Level of aspiration and frustration. Frustration of success in learning often upsets the aspiration levels of children. Lantz found nine-year-olds reluctant to begin a second test following a significant failure in a prior test [38]. Sears discovered that, in a succession of arithmetic and reading learning tasks on which small increments of gain in score could be expected, nine- to twelve-year-old children who had experienced repeated failure on tests and who had earned consistently low marks estimated "next scores" unrealistically—either much too low or much too high [61]. And in a series of trials on a motor-skills task, Wenar found that motor-handicapped children persistently overestimated their "next trial" scores. Frustrated both by initial low scores and failure to improve during five successive trials, many handicapped children continually said that they expected to do better next time. What they would have liked to accomplish interfered with realistic self-appraisals [74].

Impairment of intellectual efficiency and frustration. It is claimed that frustration or stress (from failure, threat, pressure, excessive demands, or distraction) prior to or during problem solving is likely to impair intellectual efficiency in a variety of ways. Under stress, many individuals are prone to adhere to the familiar and to become mechanical and rigid in their thinking. They often have difficulty in shifting to alternative approaches in the trial-and-check process of problem solving. Their perception of a problem situation is often restricted, distorted, or confused. They sometimes have difficulty in grasping the essence of a problem. Instead of generalizing from the facts they observe, or organizing or classifying them in some useful way, they become disorganized in their thinking. Stress is also likely to disturb the processes of attention, memory, and symbolic representation. Thus handicapped, individuals are often unable to hold in mind simultaneously the several aspects of a complicated problem. Because of these difficulties, they readily abandon systematic problem solving and begin to guess and make free associations—or they develop counteraggressive resistance to learning or become overdependent. Such disturbances of intellectual efficiency are most likely to impair learning and problem solving in situations calling for complex, novel, and creative thinking [54]. Let us review some of the experimental support for these claims.

Experiments on the effect of stress on intellectual efficiency. Beier tested two groups of college students on complex problems which required the discovery and application of abstract principles, the shifting of mental set, and the reorientation of their normal work habits. One group was threatened by the negative implications of a personality-test interpretation which cast some doubt on their intelligence, productivity, and social adjustment. It was found that the threatened group performed less effectively on the problem-solving tasks than did the nonthreatened group [4].

In an experiment in which college students were asked to respond to "ambiguous, hard-to-answer" interview questions, Gynther found that the communicative efficiency of the students was poorer when they thought they were submitting to a personality test than when they assumed they were merely producing a sample of anonymous talk [25].

Efficient problem solving requires free consideration of alternative approaches on each new problem. Some individuals, however, are prone to perseverate, that is, to naïvely employ on some new problem a solution recently found workable in solving earlier-met problems. They tend to perseverate on the new problem, even though —with a little flexibility—a much more efficient mode of attack might easily be discovered. Assuming that rigid persistence with familiar, although inefficient, approaches is more likely when individuals are under greater stress, Cowen compared the rigidity in problem solving of three groups of 25 college students who had been previously subjected to three different degrees of psychological stress—none, mild, and strong. Mild stress was produced by subjecting the students to failure on an unsolvable puzzle which appeared to be soluble. The group subjected to strong stress were told that a personality test they had taken a week earlier had yielded some ambiguous evidences of maladjustive personality features, which the additional testing would check.

Rigidity in problem solving was measured by a series of 11 water-jar problems, 7 of which could be solved by alternative approaches. A set for a roundabout, indirect approach, however, was first established by guided practice on three such problems as the following: Given three jars of different capacities—A, 42; B, 71; and C, 5 pints—measure out exactly 19 pints of water. In establishing the set for an indirect approach, the students learned to solve this first problem according to the formula, $B - A - C - C$, filling the 71-pint jar and subtracting from it 42 pints once and 5 pints twice. Then to test for rigidity of the previously established approach, the experimenter gave the subjects problems permitting either the roundabout or a more direct and efficient approach. For example, to obtain 12 pints—using jar A, 21 pints; B, 51 pints; and C, 9 pints—the student could either continue with the indirect formula, $B - A - C - C$, or he could invent the direct, easier formula, $A - C$.

The average number of roundabout solutions on the 7 alternative-approach problems—which is assumed to be indicative of rigidity— was, for the nonstress group, 1.20; for the mild-stress group, 2.48; and for the strong-stress group, 5.12. From these results, Cowen concludes that problem-solving rigidity "increases under increasing degrees of psychological stress [14, p. 518]."

After observing the influence of stress on intellectual efficiency, we are not surprised to discover that students learn biology, chemistry, physics, history, and psychology content more effectively under nonstress than under stress conditions. Gochman found that the student tends "to stick to 'what he knows best'" when studying under stress conditions [21]. Since he tends to rely on or regress to familiar modes of attack, his efficiency on problems requiring the invention of new strategies—learning how to learn—is impaired.

In none of the experimental tests of reactions to frustration—revealing aggression, loss in constructiveness, disturbances of aspiration, and impairment of intellectual efficiency—were the negative reactions universal. Apparently some individuals learn to tolerate frustration and even to enhance their efficiency in difficult situations. Let us explore further the role of differences in mental health which are associated with the negative and positive reactions to frustrations.

FRUSTRATION TOLERANCE OF WELL-ADJUSTED AND MALADJUSTED INDIVIDUALS

The intellectually inefficient children presented as introductory case studies were all emotionally maladjusted. Mary, fearful of failure, inhibited problem solving. Three children distracted themselves from problem solving by aggressive reactions—toward parents, teachers, or themselves. Johnny, afraid to express aggressive impulses toward his mother, became so perfectionistic that he failed to complete tasks. Bruce, Glen, and Rolf, feeling inadequate, either refused to try tasks or distrusted their solutions of problems. Ann became preoccupied with hiding her deficiency in reading rather than correcting it. All of them were worried and anxious about themselves.

Anxiety is a characteristic of all maladjusted persons [63]. It is a vaguely defined feeling of impending disaster and of apprehension about being inadequate to meet the inevitable problems of life. Having failed in important life activities, maladjusted children develop pervasive feelings of inferiority, unworthiness, and guilt. They come to anticipate failure in any challenging task; and as consequences of failure, they fear loss of acceptance, esteem, and love. As a defense against the painful anxiety thus frequently aroused, they are constantly ready for a variety of self-defensive reactions. As the experiments we shall now review indicate, it is these competing reactions which often interfere with the anxious person's efficiency in complex problem-solving tasks.

Anxiety and learning. In determining the effects of anxiety on learning, psychologists have compared the efficiency of anxious and nonanxious individuals. Differences in degree of anxiety are often appraised by an inventory of "worries." For example, a certain children's anxiety scale [11] includes items such as the following: "It is hard for me to keep my mind on anything." "I get nervous when someone watches me work." "Others seem to do things easier than I can." "I worry about what my parents will say to me." "I get angry easily." "I often do things I wish I had never done." An individual's anxiety score is the total number of such complaints which he indicates are characteristic of him. High scoring (anxious) and low scoring (nonanxious) individuals have been compared on a variety of learning tasks.

On familiar, simple, or easy learning tasks, anxious individuals often equal or surpass nonanxious subjects [19]. However, on novel and complex learning tasks, the efficiency of anxious subjects seems to be impaired by self-defensive distracting or competing impulses.

In a complex learning problem—which required discovering and remembering which of two buttons turned out which of a randomly presented series of red, blue, amber, and white lights—the most anxious 20 per cent of the 36 fourth grade children made more errors in each of 20 trials than did the least anxious 20 per cent [49]. On the most difficult of five levels of complex multiple-choice learning tasks, fifth grade children scoring below the median on an anxiety scale surpassed those scoring above the median [12]. On the easier levels, however, the anxious and nonanxious children did not differ in learning efficiency.

The efficiency ratings of anxious and nonanxious college students (very high and very low scorers, respectively, on anxiety scales) have been compared on such complex tasks as discovery and mastery of concepts [68]; learning of novel, false multiplication tables, like $3 \times 5 = 6$ [36]; verbal proficiency in answering difficult, ambiguous questions [25]; and memorization both of nonsense syllables [48, 57] and of relatively meaningless words [58]. These learning tasks were usually associated with some stress, such as having just failed a prior task [57] or working under the assumption that performance on the task was indicative of intelligence [48]. In all these experiments, the learning of the most anxious students was less efficient than that of the least anxious students.

As typical of the greater learning efficiency of nonanxious students, the results from Nicholson's experiment are presented in Figure 12.1. During 45 trials in learning to anticipate 12 difficult-to-learn nonsense syllables, 31 anxious students (from the upper 8 per cent on the *Taylor Anxiety Scale*) progressed more slowly and attained a lower level of mastery than 32 nonanxious students (from the lower 10 per cent on the anxiety scale). Working under the stress of the need to demonstrate intelligence, the anxious subjects sometimes hesitated to respond (for fear of being wrong) or distrusting memory, substituted invented syllables.

McCandless and Castaneda have demonstrated such anxiety-impaired learning in the classroom. They found that the negative correlations between anxiety-scale scores and academic achievement

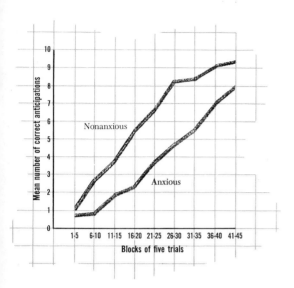

Fig. 12.1. *Anxious students are less efficient than nonanxious students in learning to anticipate a list of 12 difficult-to-learn nonsense syllables.* (From W. M. Nicholson, *J. Personality*, 1958, vol. 26, p. 310.)

were —.32 for 55 sixth grade boys and —.59 for 45 sixth grade girls [42].

Personal-social adjustment and learning. That anxiety is a handicap has been indirectly indicated in comparisons of the learning efficiency of teacher- or counselor-selected well-adjusted and maladjusted children. For example, of 100 four- to six-year-old children of "normal intelligence," 30 who exhibited such maladjustments as withdrawal, lack of interest, lack of self-confidence, overdependency, negativism, bullying, and showing off required "twice" as much practice in learning to read as did the 33 best-adjusted children [8]. Edelston has reported that 17 in a group of 18 emotionally maladjusted children, despite "average" to "superior" intelligence, failed to make satisfactory progress in school [17].

The weak frustration tolerance of maladjusted children is revealed in their reduced intellectual efficiency in taking the S-B test according to standard directions, which involve proceeding from the lower to the higher levels of the test. In completing the scale, a child sometimes meets failure in the last 6 to 11 items. It is possible to minimize this failure frustration, however, by presenting easy and difficult items alternately. Well-adjusted children—able to tolerate the frustration of several successive failures—do equally well whether the test is given according to standard or adapted (minimal-frustration) directions. Of 24 matched pairs of maladjusted children, however, those taking the test according to reduced-frustration directions earned a mean IQ of 102.7—11 points higher than the mean of 91.7 earned by those who took the test according to standard directions [31].

As we have already observed, achievement frustration disturbs the aspirations of children. Gruen found that the aspiration levels of maladjusted adolescents were more sensitive to failure, less stable, and more unrealistic than for well-adjusted adolescents [23].

Severely disturbed children have very little frustration tolerance. Sherman has observed that when neurotic children are frustrated in a learning task, they exhibit both physiological and psychological symptoms of disintegration of behavior. "Not only did the neurotic children react [emotionally] more quickly to frustration, but they also returned more slowly to the normal level [63, p. 98]." Redl and Wineman have found that seriously disturbed delinquent children are extremely susceptible to frustration. "Even in the midst of a happily enjoyed game the slightest additional hurdle to be met or mild frustration to be added would throw the whole group into wild outbursts of unstructured bickering, fighting, disorganization, and griping [53, p. 77]."

Attitudes of well- and poorly-adjusted children. As Anderson and associates have shown, the tendencies toward efficient or inefficient approaches to problems are rooted in deep-seated attitudes. In a study of 3,200 children ages 9 to 18, they discovered a relationship at all ages between the affective attitudes of these children and their classification on adjustment inventories and on teachers' ratings which judged them well adjusted, fairly well adjusted, or poorly adjusted.

The affective attitudes (pleasant, neutral, or unpleasant) were appraised by classifying the children's responses to a 30-item sentence-completion test, including such items as: "When I go home from school, _____." The child who filled the blank with: "I have a good time," would be credited with a pleasant attitude on this item. "I go by the stores" would be classified as neutral. And "The boys tease me" would be rated unpleasant. The mean ratios of the number

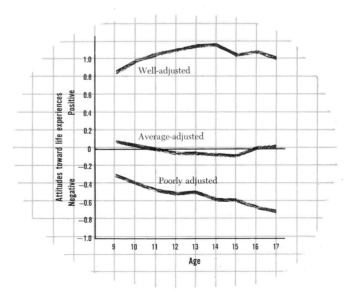

Fig. 12.2. *The projectively measured attitudes of children and youth toward life experiences indicate that the well-adjusted expect them to be pleasant and the maladjusted expect them to be unpleasant.* (From J. E. Anderson and others, A Survey of Children's Adjustment over Time, Inst. Child Developm. and Welf., Univ. of Minn., Minneapolis, Minn., 1959, p. 14.)

of pleasant responses to the number of unpleasant responses, converted to standard scores for the three adjustment groups at each age, are graphed in Figure 12.2.

How can we explain the relationship between maladjustment and unpleasant attitudes? It seems plausible to assume that the maladjusted child, because of frustration at school, unhappy peer relationships, unmet needs in parent-child relationships, and frequent ineffective and unrewarding behavior in many situations, becomes conditioned to expect life generally to be unpleasant. As is suggested by the gradual separation of the curves, the frequently confirmed negative consequences of such attitudes and behavior tend to intensify this pattern of expectations, and as the child grows older the pattern becomes more generalized.

Impaired in intellectual efficiency, inferior in school accomplishment, personally and socially ineffective, and with persistent pessimistic attitudes toward life, maladjusted children and youth are painfully anxious. In self-protection from constant threat of worse failure and consequent intensified anxiety, they develop and over-employ various defense mechanisms. In order to get a better understanding of these defenses, let us see how psychologists have classified them.

GENERALIZED MODES OF SELF-DEFENSE

Every individual, as we have already observed, needs to feel socially secure, personally worthy, esteemed, and self-respecting. He achieves these needs by becoming personally and socially effective, competent, and productive. If he fails in these personal achievements, he is likely to feel inferior, guilty, anxious, and threatened with loss of acceptance, esteem, and love. Psychologists and psychiatrists have observed that individuals learn a variety of self-deceptive adjustment mechanisms in order to maintain, enhance, or protect their self-concepts of adequacy and to allay threat-induced anxiety. In a moment we shall describe some of these defense mechanisms, but first, let us observe a typical instance of how they are learned and how they are used in coping with life's problems and frustrations.

Learning mechanisms of defense. In learning to cope with her fear of thunder and the noise of jet planes, Molly exhibited a developmental sequence of adjustments [47]. At 2 years of age, when terrified during thunderstorms or at the passing of a jet plane, Molly discovered that her helpless crying would bring her mother's comforting attention. At age 3–3, she learned to seek comfort and also to comfort herself. She discovered the comfort of getting into bed with an older sister during a thunderstorm. And she also learned to reassure herself with such verbalizations as "It's just noise and it really won't hurt you a bit." By age 3–5, she had learned to protect her developing self-concept—of not being afraid of things—by projecting her fear onto others, and to seek comfort in a symbol (an open door). Opening the door to her parents' room during a thunderstorm, she said that her younger brother (who was fast asleep) was afraid. At age 4–2, she had learned both to comfort herself with a developing self-image of pride and mastery and to deny her fear. Awakened from a nap by a thunderstorm, she remained quietly in bed; later she said: "There was lots of thunder, but I just snuggled in my bed and didn't cry a bit." At age 4–6, she had learned the self-defense mechanism of "reaction formation," the replacement of shameful fear with its opposite, self-enhancing bravery. Showing no fear herself as she comforted her little brother during a thunderstorm, she said: "I remember when I was little baby and I was scared of thunder and I used to cry every time it thundered."

Comfort seeking, self-assurance, denial, projection, and reaction formation are only a few of the defense mechanisms we develop to allay anxiety. Let us extend our outline of them.

Substitute self-gratifications. Individuals who are frustrated in their attainment of the goals in our culture which usually bring safety, esteem, and love sometimes assuage their anxiety by such substitute satisfactions as self-reassurance, physiological comforts, or daydreaming. Nan, like Molly, reassured herself about her failure to learn to read in the first grade: "When I grow bigger, I'll know everything. I'll catch up with my work and do everything." Eight-year-old Isabel found comfort in food.[1] Feeling rejected by her peers, who called her "Fatso" and "Baby Tank," and by her mother who was too busy to spend any time with her, she comforted herself by overeating. After a lonely day at school, in which she felt that no one liked her, she could find solitary comfort in a double chocolate sundae [32, p. 161].

Paul found daydreaming a pleasant substitute for the harsh realities of his life.[1] Despite "adequate ability to do schoolwork," he was repeating the fourth grade at 12 years of age. Lost in daydreams—of being big and strong, of living in a world in which everyone was cheery and easygoing, and of being free from unfavorable comparisons with his superior brother and from the harsh tirades of his father—Paul no longer heard his teacher's demonstrations and explanations of tasks which he felt were beyond his ability. He had learned to let his thoughts wander away from unpleasant experiences, such as the time when his father criticized his poor reading or when he roared in anger when Paul complained about the many chores imposed on him and the few required of his brother. Now he substituted

[1] From *These Are Your Children*, Expanded Ed., by Gladys Jenkins, Helen Shacter, and W. W. Bauer. Copyright 1953 by Scott, Foresman and Company, Chicago.

the delights of daydreams for all sorts of unpleasant experiences—in the classroom, with his peers, or at home [32].

Denial. Some children alleviate anxiety by denying either self-inadequacy or the threats in their environment. Jerald, in the seventh grade, completely lacked word-identification skills. He said, "I took remedial reading [six weeks] and got 'A's' in it, so I guess I'm all right." Another child, who feared the loss of love and whose teacher had slapped him, denied any counteraggressive impulse. On the contrary, he said that the teacher was right to have slapped him because it made him remember the date he was trying to recall. He thought she was a "nice person" and wanted to remain in her class [67].

Repression. Some dangerous impulses and past experiences are so threatening or painful that the individual is unable to tolerate thinking of them. As a result of associating actions, words, or ideas with guilt- and anxiety-producing experiences, the actions, words, or ideas become, through conditioning, effective conditioned stimuli in eliciting anxiety. In using repression to protect himself from anxiety, however, the individual impairs his effectiveness in learning, remembering, and perceiving. As a defense against such anxiety, the individual unconsciously learns (problem-solving fashion) to divert his attention from the incipient anxiety-producing symbols.

For example, the five-year-old child, who learned to recognize the word "school" after 18 exposures of the word, could not recognize "street" after 98 exposures. He could not learn to read "street" because it had previously become a conditioned anxiety-arousing stimulus. "Instead of looking at the word fixedly as was his custom with other words, he turned away from it." His anxiety and negative reaction to the word "street" had been previously produced by the command that he "must never cross or go near the street," which was separated from the family home by a fence [27].

Repression also disturbs memory. As we observed in the preceding chapter, Helen, as a small child, became anxious when she was hospitalized and, as she thought, abandoned by her parents. Later when the health-science content she studied threatened to rearouse the earlier-established anxiety, she repressed ideas associated with it. In self-defense, she forgot the class meetings, lost her textbook, and could not recall a single fact of a film on immunization [52, pp. 195–196].

Perception of the environment is also affected by repression. Eleven-year-old Alexander, who felt frustrated and aggressive but was fearful of expressing his impulses, misinterpreted a picture showing a pioneer foolishly aiming his rifle at a distant Indian, while two nearby Indians are about to attack him with tomahawks. Asked what was *foolish* about the picture, he said: "They should be friends instead of fighting each other."

Rationalization. Individuals who feel guilty but need esteem often give false, socially acceptable rather than true reasons for behavior which they expect would otherwise be disapproved. When he was asked what was foolish about a picture of a couple sitting outside their house while it was raining, Harold, fearing failure on this S-B item, invented an excuse for not risking a trial: "I can't tell a story about that picture because it's too dim." (The crosshatching to indicate rain gave him his flimsy rationalization.) Lyman was disturbed by guilt over his resistance to his parents' coercive discipline; he rationalized: "Sometimes I can't hear my mother and father because of something in my ears or something." Pete, who is awkward and uncomfortable with his adolescent peers, rationalized his absence from school dances: "I don't have time for such kid stuff [70, p. 24]."

Projection. The individual sometimes disowns his socially disapproved characteristics, and projects them onto other people, because he feels inadequate or guilty. Sears found that college students who were rated as most "stingy" or "obstinate" by their classmates, but who rated themselves favorably, tended to rate their classmates unfavorably on such reprehensible traits [62].

Eleven-year-old Ronald, feeling embarrassed about his inadequacy in reading, eases his anxiety about it by projecting the blame onto his first grade teacher, saying: "She didn't teach me how to read the little words." Sometimes self-criticism is projected. Philip *himself* feeling inadequate in baseball projected his own self-appraisal to his classmates: "*They* don't think I'm any good [24]."

Identification. Fearful that his own personal resources are inadequate to attain his ideal self-image, the individual identifies with—perceives himself as like—an admired model, as a means of providing enhanced satisfaction of his needs for mastery, esteem, and love. He perceives the model (a parent, teacher, peer, hero, or fictional character) as better able to satisfy these needs. By perceiving similarities between himself and the model, or by actually becoming more like the model, he takes symbolic (imagined) satisfaction of these needs [34].

Realistic, appropriate sex identifications of children and youth are important in the development of healthy personality. Lacking rewarding relationships with appropriate models, however, individuals sometimes make inappropriate identifications. Because of a guilt-producing sex experience in preadolescence and a long-continued annoyance with and lack of respect for her mother, a seventeen-year-old rejected a feminine role. She refused dates. Her resistance to a feminine role also affected her choice of an occupation. She said: "I thought and thought and thought—nursing, medicine, law, farming, teaching, music." Then, one day a decision came to her: "Try the foreign service; see the world and what makes it turn. Improve yourself by associating with the people who are doing things—the *men*

who have gone somewhere and are guiding the world. . . . That's my goal, and all the talent, ability, and ambition I can gather won't be one whit too much to take me on from here [37]."

Reaction formation. Severely threatened by the hazards and unacceptability of their spontaneous impulses, some individuals allay their anxiety by compulsively directing their behavior in the "opposite direction from its normal expression [71]." James, naturally suited to the role of the scholar but insecure in his new peer relationships, became the tough anti-intellectual. Individuals whose aggressive impulses have proved dangerous (have been severely punished or disapproved) may learn conformity as a reaction-formation defense to keep hostile impulses repressed [29].

Inappropriate identifications are often reaction formations. Felix, for example, was fearful that becoming a scholar like his lawyer stepfather would mean being disloyal to his daredevil father, who had been killed in an automobile speed test. Therefore, he compulsively overemphasized his identification with his own father. "By not studying, he flaunted his disapproval of knowledge." He "climbed over high fences, performed numerous stunts, and wound up as the leader of a gang, thus defying the values of his stepfather-as-lawyer. In this way he tried to show that it is not those who study and live carefully [like his stepfather] but those who dare [like his father and himself] who are the leaders of men [7, p. 138]."

Displaced hostility. As we have already observed, aggression is a frequent reaction to frustration. Children conform to the guidance of people they love and admire. Rejected or otherwise frustrated by parents or teachers, they often react counteraggressively. They may resist teacher guidance, disrupt class activities, or attack "model" pupils. One boy, who said his teacher "scolded, yelled, and pinched," exclaimed: "I wouldn't learn nothin' for that old battle-axe [41, p.

783]." When a direct attack on the frustrating agent is dangerous or impossible, however, it may be suppressed. Frustrated and anxious, such individuals harbor an idling hostility which is often impulsively displaced toward all sorts of innocent victims.

Elaine, for example, abandoned by her own parents, overstrictly disciplined by the aunt with whom she lived, and feeling inferior because of her color in a class of white children, is constantly engaged in unprovoked attacks upon someone. According to her teacher's report, "She takes great pleasure injuring or tormenting other children, and never passes up an opportunity to trip, poke, pinch, slap, or throw ink on them. . . . She is defiant and sullen with her teacher, and talks and mutters to herself a great deal." Some self-insight into the displaced nature of her aggression, however, is suggested in a story she told about a picture: ". . . she [the heroine of her story] started calling other kids names that never bothered her and that's how she got into so much trouble."

Self-punishment. Some individuals, feeling inferior and guilty and finding in punishment some reduction of anxiety (as in expiation for sin), continually seek punishment. Nine-year-old Johnny, for example, despite repeated warnings and reprimands, persisted in jeopardizing the safety of himself and his classmates by recklessly riding his bicycle through the school playground and even by darting toward the bus. In telling his mother about such incidents, Johnny would announce: "Mother, I did a bad thing today." His punishment-seeking behavior was the consequence of guilt feelings he had about wishing to get rid of his baby brother (who had died six months after displacing Johnny as his mother's major interest) and about being a rival of his father for his mother's affection [10].

Regression and overdependency. Although functioning at his highest level of proficiency on challenging tasks brings the healthy individual his highest satisfactions, it also involves the hazard of failure. Since the insecure, inadequate, and unconfident individual feels threatened by the possibility of failure, he is prone—when challenged or frustrated—to regress to a lower level of maturity of behavior. As an experimental demonstration of regression, we have already observed the general loss in play constructiveness of frustrated preschool children. The sudden change in the maturity of Carla's behavior provides a specific illustration.[1] Carla had been an unusually independent, competent five-year-old. At home she had learned to dress and wash herself, keep her belongings neat and tidy, and to help her mother with such chores as drying the spoons and emptying the wastebaskets. In kindergarten she managed independ-

[1] From *These Are Your Children,* Expanded Ed., by Gladys Jenkins, Helen Shacter, and W. W. Bauer. Copyright 1953 by Scott, Foresman and Company, Chicago.

ently to take off and put on her own wraps and boots; she took falls without crying, and "took upon herself" the task of setting and clearing the table "for the mid-morning orange juice and graham cracker period [32, p. 104]." But all this was changed when Carla suddenly felt supplanted in the family's affection by new twin sisters. She no longer dressed herself either at home or in school. She insisted on having her milk in a bottle. She wet the bed at night and whimpered when she was bumped. She wearied of the juice and cracker serving and spilled the juice when she tried to fill the cups. Carla, it seems, as a way of regaining the love she feared she had lost, regressed to an earlier-enjoyed dependency relationship with her mother and other adults.

Avoidance of learning. Fearful of failure and the consequent loss of esteem, of the developmental responsibilities of maturing, or of facing certain embarrassing facts of life, some insecure and anxious individuals avoid trying to learn new concepts and skills. As an illustration of this defense mechanism, we have already mentioned Mary's inhibition of the trial-and-check process in learning to read and Ann's zealous efforts to hide the fact that she could not read. Liss has suggested that because of the anxiety-arousing implications (sexual, aggressive, competitive) of certain knowledge for some individuals, they try to allay anxiety by avoiding all knowledge [40].

Some individuals avoid learning effort in some areas where they feel threatened with potential failure and overemphasize accomplishment in other areas in which they feel more confident. Jackie, despite being a little above average in intelligence, vocabulary, and maturity of oral language, is helpless in reading and avoids it. He is absorbed in art, however, and produces a daily stream of pictures which his teacher and classmates enthusiastically admire.

A problem-solving approach to frustration. As modes of defense and self-enhancement, both well-adjusted and maladjusted individuals sometimes employ defense mechanisms. The mentally healthy individual, however, is also ready to meet frustration with a problem-solving approach. He corrects limitations and enhances his problem solving by mastering appropriate concepts and skills and by learning how to learn efficiently. Achieving self-understanding and self-acceptance, he substitutes attainable goals for unobtainable ones. The unhealthy individual, driven by anxiety and impaired in intellectual efficiency, too often completely substitutes defense mechanisms for more effective problem solving.

A DYNAMIC THEORY OF MALADJUSTMENT AND IMPAIRED LEARNING

A healthy personality is a developmental achievement. The healthy individual is confident and efficient in learning and problem solving, constructively productive, realistic in self-appraisal and in goal setting, able to accept and to give esteem and love in interpersonal relations, and happily committed to significant personal and social goals. The infant is born relatively helpless; but if, as he matures, he manages his developmental tasks successfully, then he will develop a concept of himself in dealing with tasks and with interpersonal relations as adequate, worthy, esteemed, and loved. Such a developing child is free for constructive and creative expression of his talents in various fields of interest.

Development of mental health. In an adaptation of Erickson's concept of the "eight stages of man," Heffernan has presented a concise overview, which we shall paraphrase, of the development of a healthy personality [26].

In attaining a healthy personality, the individual needs to achieve, as he develops—

1. *A sense of trust*—from the care and love of adults during his first year of relatively greatest dependency.

2. *A sense of autonomy*—from being permitted choices, independent action, and individuality in a safe environment during the second and third years when he is making great strides in basic motor abilities, in language, and in exploration of himself and his environment.

3. *A sense of initiative or confidence*—from trying himself out in a variety of constructive and tentative role-playing experiences during the fourth and fifth years when he is growing very rapidly in knowledge and skills, in independence, in effective social participation, and in ability to do things for himself.

4. *A sense of worthwhile accomplishment*—from successful achievement in school, at home, and in play, during the period from six to twelve years.

5. *A sense of identity*—from discovering, clarifying, and accepting himself more thoroughly and from becoming more effective in his major life roles as he works through the "developmental task of adolescence."

6. *A sense of intimacy* in the relations of friendship and love, and a sense of inspiration as he accomplishes the social adjustments of courtship and marriage.

7. *A parental sense*—from productivity and creativity in work, family, and community roles during the occupational, family-rearing, productive years of life.

8. *A sense of integrity*—from satisfaction and self-respect with his long-range roles in life.

These eight major attainments are not, of course, confined to the age periods mentioned. Once achieved, each attainment continues to function and to develop throughout the person's life. But cumulatively, accomplishment of the preceding attainments constitutes preparation for the next developmental stage, and they all culminate in the sense of integrity mentioned last.

As a product of these socializing experiences, the growing individual develops a concept of himself or a self-image. Modeling his behavior in a variety of situations after persons he has come to love and admire, he incorporates into his personality and self-concept those patterns of behavior and ideals which significant adults in his environment reward. For full acceptance and approval in the culture of Western civilization, he discovers that he must achieve "personal competence [5]." Trying out various modes of adjustment, he finds that success in school, persistent effort in acquiring skills, an effective problem-solving approach to tasks, sharing, fair play, and a respect for teachers usually win him rewards and approval. Thus, because they are so universally rewarded in our culture, such goals as self-adequacy, competency, and constructive productivity become incorporated into the ideal self-image. Every individual in our culture—in ways suited to his own particular talents, interests, and personality—strives to attain, to protect, and to enhance such an ideal self-image. But, as we have discovered in this chapter, many individuals are frustrated in these efforts and often find their ideal self-concepts threatened.

Development of maladjustive behavior. When a child's life at home, in school, and with his peers fails to provide opportunities for developing a sense of trust, autonomy, confidence, accomplishment, and comfortable identity with worthy life roles, and when fulfillment of his ideal self-image of adequacy is threatened, he is vulnerable to the development of maladjustive modes of behavior. Children who are neglected, harshly punished, or rejected by one or both parents tend to react with fear and withdrawal, overaggressiveness, self-distrust, irresponsibility, and with generally destructive rather than constructive patterns of behavior. Constantly experienced failure at school or persistent rejection in the peer culture also contribute to the development of destructive and nonconstructive modes of adjustment. These maladjustive behavior patterns, whatever their origin, are generalized to a wide range of interpersonal situations—to parents, teachers, peers, to people generally [43]. Such nonconstructive or destructive behavior often elicits counterpunishment and continued rejection, which in turn reinforce the maladjustive behavior. As a consequence, the child's fear of punishment and rejection in all his interpersonal relations is confirmed. Frustrated in his needs for safety, love, and esteem at home, in school, and among his peers, the child comes to feel inferior, guilty, and anxious [16, 64].

In striving to allay his anxiety and to protect his self-concept, the maladjusted individual often suffers a loss in constructiveness of behavior, a distortion of aspirations, and impairment of intellectual efficiency. Mary's inhibition of the trial-and-check process in learning, James's abandonment of his scholarly interests for the false role of the anti-intellectual tough, Ann's hiding of her deficiency in reading, Johnny's overperfectionistic standards, and the self-defeating behavior patterns of many of the other cases presented in this chapter reveal a great variety of ways in which aspirations, constructiveness, and intellectual efficiency are impaired.

Despite the self-defeating consequences of such maladjustive patterns, they are persistent and pervasive [64]. Maladjusted individuals cling tenaciously to them for a number of reasons. Anxiety is painful, and by them a measure of anxiety-reduction is achieved. Rigidity and other intellectual impairments handicap the individual in discovering alternative approaches. And by employing such mechanisms as denial, repression, rationalization, projection, and reaction formation in defense of his self-image, the individual distorts his perception of himself and the consequences of his maladjustive behavior. The maladjusted individual's capacity for self-improvement is then severely impaired.

The vicious cycle of the maladjusted. In maladjusted children a vicious cycle becomes firmly established. Punishment and rejection of children elicit fear and obnoxious behavior. The obnoxious behavior provokes parents, teachers, and peers to further disapproval and rejection, which reinforce the anxiety and consequent self-defeating behavior. The anxiety is anticipatory and it is attached primarily to impulses which have been forbidden—including sexual impulses, unjustified aggression, overdependency, unfair competitive attacks, and culturally disapproved identifications. By generalizing, *all* such impulses become conditioned cues for anxiety which "may be conceived as fear of one's self [64, p. 132]."

Driven "by anxiety and unable to symbolize the sources of the stress in his impulses," the maladjusted individual "desperately pursues first one set of goals and then another, giving up each as his strivings fail to bring him satisfaction. Forever dissatisfied, he develops an image of himself contrary to his self-ideal." Instead of feeling successful and competent, he perceives himself as inadequate —as unable to cope with the demands of his own existence. "And these self-concepts lead to even more intolerable anxiety, under motivation of which he develops various strategies [being perfect, being anti-intellectual, inhibiting the trial-and-check process, hiding deficiencies, etc.] for rationalizing or denying his experiences to himself and to others." But these adjustments, although they partially allay anxiety, lead to failure in important life activities and therefore to social disapproval and self-blame—"thus producing an ever-increasing spiral of neurotic involvement [64]."

Because of their ineffective efforts and consequent self-recrimination and social disapproval, maladjusted individuals are eventually forced "to the painful realization that they have fallen short"—that they are failures. Since feeling inadequate, inferior, and guilty is incompatible with their incorporated cultural ideals, they have a powerful tendency to deny this embarrassing self-image, to attribute it to others, to seek protection in withdrawal and avoidance of challenges, to rebel, to be counteraggressive, to be compulsively perfectionistic, or to demonstrate in some other way the untruth of the painfully felt inadequacy. But this irresponsibility and these false pretensions lead to further disapproval and guilt. The whole trend becomes a vicious cycle: sexual, aggressive, nonconstructive, and other culturally disapproved impulses→(lead to) punishment→anxiety and general fear of self→repression and perceptual distortion→"neurotic stupidity"→ increased social- and self-disapproval→intensified anxiety and guilt→ more perceptual distortion and neurotic stupidity—all become a self-sustained cycle.

This theory of how emotional maladjustment may impair learning efficiency can be summarized in the light of the two-factor theory of learning. As a result of an unfortunate psychological history, the individual becomes conditioned to respond with anxiety to a wide variety of tasks and interpersonal situations. As defenses against anxiety, he learns by trial-and-error problem solving a variety of self-attitudes and techniques which, except for partially and temporarily reducing anxiety, are ineffective and self-defeating. But despite their ineffectiveness—and since they do reduce anxiety and are not perceived as contributing to the individual's maladjustment—they are maintained and applied generally in school, at home, and in other social and personal situations.

SUMMARY

Mental health and effective learning are reciprocally related; each is a condition or symptom of the other. Efficient learning requires a confidence-inspired integrated and systematic attack upon problems. Anxiety, feelings of inferiority, and social maladjustment produce self-defensive reactions which impair intellectual efficiency. Thus mental health is an essential condition of effective learning.

Although psychological stress or frustration can sometimes disturb the efficiency of learning and thinking of anyone, the anxious, maladjusted person is especially prone to such disturbances. In maladjusted children and youth, varying in personality and psychological history, mental health disturbances impair learning in a variety of ways. Poor mental health can inhibit the basic trial-and-check process of learning, produce diverting aggressive reactions, reduce the level of constructiveness, disturb levels of aspiration, undermine the confidence and initiative required for problem solving, and in other ways impair intellectual efficiency.

An explanation of emotional disturbances of learning incorporates the following aspects of development: Children observe that *accomplishments* win them rewarding approval from their parents, teachers, and peers. Thus the achievement of competency becomes a cultural ideal and the basis for feelings of personal worth, esteem, and confidence. Failure to meet the standards of parents, teachers, and peers threatens the child with loss of esteem and love and leads to feelings of inferiority, guilt, and anxiety. As generalized modes of adjustment to threats (to the self) and to the accompanying anxiety, individuals learn such defenses as substitute gratifications, denial, repression, rationalization, projection, identification, reaction formation, displaced hostility, self-punishment, regression, and avoidance of learning. Excessive dependence on these defensive modes of adjustment account for the ineffective learning and problem solving of the maladjusted individual.

Both healthy and maladjusted modes of adjustment are products of the individual's psychological history. According to the two-factor theory of learning, the maladjusted individual, because of an unfortunate psychological history, becomes conditioned to respond with anxiety to impulses associated with behavior for which he has been punished and to a wide variety of challenging or threatening situations. As defenses against anxiety, he learns by trial-and-error problem solving a variety of self-attitudes and techniques which, except for partially and temporarily reducing anxiety, are self-defeating. But despite their ineffectiveness, these attitudes and defensive techniques reduce anxiety and divert the individual from perceiving the causes of his maladjustment; thus they are maintained and applied generally —in school, at home, and in other social and personal situations.

In this chapter, we have demonstrated the role of mental health in effective learning. In the next chapter, we shall study the factors which affect mental health, how to appraise it, how to correct maladjustments, and how to foster its development.

GUIDES FOR STUDY, REVIEW, AND APPLICATION

1. Define mental health, and indicate how it is related to school accomplishment and creative productivity. As possible illustrations of your definition and the mental health–accomplishment relationship, study the cases of Larry, Jimmy, Johnny, Isabel, Marlene, Paul, Alec, and Agnes in *These Are Your Children*, by Gladys O. Jenkins, Helen Shacter, and W. W. Bauer, Scott, Foresman and Company, 1953.
2. Outline the significant features of problem solving and describe a va-

riety of ways in which emotional disturbances can impair the efficiency of the process.

3. List all you can find and then classify the informally observed and experimentally demonstrated reactions of individuals to frustration, conflict, and threat.

4. How do well-adjusted and maladjusted individuals differ in their reactions to frustration? How can we explain this general difference?

5. How do we acquire defenses from the anxiety which feelings of inferiority, unworthiness, and guilt provoke? Cite examples of self-defense by (a) substitute self-gratifications, (b) denial, (c) repression, (d) rationalization, (e) projection, (f) identification, (g) reaction formation, (h) displaced hostility, (i) self-punishment, (j) regression and overdependency, and (k) avoidance of learning. As an example see the film *Angry Boy* (35 minutes), Mental Health Film Board.

6. How can we explain the development of maladjustive behavior?

Chapter 13

FOSTERING MENTAL HEALTH

Mental health, as we discovered in Chapter 12, is essential both for efficient learning and for achievement of self-realization and social effectiveness. It is, therefore, an important educational objective. In this chapter we shall see how the teacher, working cooperatively with parents and mental health specialists, can contribute to the attainment of this objective. We shall study the incidence of mental health handicaps in school children, procedures for appraising the quality of children's mental health, the home and the school as important determinants of mental health or maladjustment, and the specific ways in which teachers can aid in correcting maladjustment and in fostering the development of mental health. Let us begin with a case study which illustrates all of these problems.

AN EXAMPLE OF MENTAL HEALTH GUIDANCE

The identification, diagnosis, and corrective treatment of Elaine's problem illustrate the cooperative efforts of the classroom teacher and the school psychologist to foster the mental health of maladjusted school

At school: guidance in constructive play . . .

and in group activities

Mental health is essential
for self-realization and social effectiveness

At home: adequate provision for physical needs . . .

a sense of belonging . . .

joy in being together

children. This 11-year-old child was described in the preceding chapter as an example of "displaced hostility." She was "constantly involved in quarrels," seemed to take pleasure in "hurting or tormenting other children" and was "defiant and sullen with her teacher [20]." The discrepancy between her low achievement and above-average intelligence is another symptom of her maladjustment.

In her exploration of the possible causes of such behavior, the teacher observed that Elaine often initiates quarrels, but that the other children do not "pick on her," as Elaine says they do. On the contrary, they invite her to join their games. Elaine, however, "makes no effort to win friends on her own account." When she visited Elaine's home, the teacher found that she lives with her aunt and uncle, "who seem genuinely interested in her, keep her clean and nicely dressed," and are "trying to teach Elaine to be a lady." Shocked by the report of Elaine's misbehavior at school and annoyed by her frequent out-of-school fights, the aunt decided that Elaine should not be permitted time for loitering on her way to and from school. The teacher also learned that Elaine's parents are separated, and that she is not sure where they and her two brothers and two sisters live. Elaine hopes, however, that she will someday have the opportunity to live with her mother again.

Abandonment by her parents, placement with kind but strict and strange relatives, and the problem of adjusting to new classmates could understandably frustrate Elaine's needs for security, love, and esteem. Thus frustrated, she exhibited a displaced aggression which was not surprising to her teacher, once she understood her background. Wishing to understand the problem more fully, however, she sought to learn something about Elaine's specific attitudes and feelings. In a pupil-teacher interview, Elaine admitted all her misbehavior but she could not explain it, except to say: "The kids are mean to me." The teacher therefore decided, in consultation with the school psychologist, to give Elaine another medium for revealing her motives, her attitudes

toward herself and her environment, and her potential modes of adjustment.

In a session with the school psychologist, Elaine was asked to make up stories about pictures selected from the *Thematic Appercep- tion Test*. For each picture, she was directed to "tell what has hap- pened before and what is happening now," to "say what the people in the story are feeling and thinking, and how it will come out [51]."

According to Tomkins, the "fabric" of such stories "is woven of many and diverse strands. The deepest unconscious recesses, the pri- vate solipsistic world, the shared intimacies, the publicly avowed behavior and sentiments, fragments of the past, cross-sections of the present and anticipations of the future, the person at work and at play, in the family setting, among friends, and in love, the person reacting to older and younger people and to those of his own age—these are a sample of what finds representation in the individual's stories [67, p. 358]."

From this potentially rich source of personality data, the psy- chologist abstracts content classifiable under five headings:

1. *Personal identifications and interpersonal relations*. It is as- sumed that the storyteller projects onto the "hero" and onto other significant characters in the stories what he is, wishes he were, or fears he may become.

2. *Motives and goals of the hero and of other characters*. The storyteller's own motives, goals, and conflicts may be represented directly or symbolically in the behavior of the hero and sometimes the other characters.

3. *Problems and environmental barriers or supports*. Here the storyteller's "view of the world" is noted. For example, are parents, teachers, doctors, and other persons trusted, loving, kind, helpful, and protective, or are they rejecting, coercive, critical, punitive, and threatening?

4. *Modes of adjustment*. Does the hero attack his problems *directly*—by learning, working, problem-solving effort and by setting attainable goals—or does he, because of excessive anxiety, shame, or loss of esteem, adjust defensively by rationalizing, reaction formation, repression, displaced aggression, and other such mechanisms?

5. *Outcomes*. Is the hero realistic or fanciful, optimistic or pessi- mistic, happy or depressed about the past, present, or future?

From this orientation, let us interpret excerpts from some of Elaine's stories.

In her story about a picture of an outdoor scene—showing a man plowing a field, a woman leaning against a tree, and a girl holding some books—she said: "The girl is going to school. . . . She is sad. . . . The man is glad to plow his garden because he wants to have something to eat. . . . They are there because the Indians ran them away; and the girl likes to go to school because when she grows up she'll get an education and be a school teacher."

Possibly threatened by a hostile "other race" and feeling sad, the schoolgirl with whom Elaine identifies finds security both in a protecting father figure (the man producing food) and in her own self-development. In imagining herself as growing up, getting an education, and becoming a teacher, she satisfies her needs both for security and self-enhancement.

But Elaine's projected heroes alternate between optimism and despair. In a story about a girl running along a beach and being watched by another girl hidden behind a tree, she said: "This girl is running away because she stole something—maybe she did something she shouldn't have done and the police are after her. . . . She stole because she wanted something real bad. . . . The other girl is going to call the police and show them where she has gone. . . . She is happy now, but when they take her to jail she'll wish she hadn't done it."

Frustrated by demanding, unsatisfied needs, Elaine's hero commits aggressions. Feeling guilty, she sees herself spied upon, caught and punished by hostile people. The acceptance of punishment and wish for self-reform are her ways of allaying the guilt-produced anxiety.

In another story about a woman reading to a girl, Elaine projects her anxiety over the loss of her parents and her needs for comforting (as a temporary relief from anxiety) and love: "This lady is reading to her little girl. Maybe the girl's daddy died in the war and she is thinking about her daddy. The mother is reading to her to make her not think about her daddy, so she will probably forget it for that day. They are going to be happy because she is going to get some presents and the little girl already has some new shoes." (Elaine's symbolized wish for love?)

In another story about a picture of a solitary girl standing with her forearm over her head, Elaine is almost autobiographical: "Once there was a girl and her mother died. Then the girl went away to her aunt's house. She kept going to school and she liked it at school. But someone beat her up because she called them a name they didn't like and now the girl is crying. The girl started it so her aunt isn't going to do nothing. They will send her to the juvenile school and she will have to work. The kids talked about her and then she started calling other kids names that never bothered her and that's how she got into so much trouble. When she comes out of the reform school, then she'll work and be a secretary and get married."

Here Elaine again symbolizes the loss of her parents, her guilt in wrongdoing, her acceptance of punishment and desire for reform, her ambivalence about school, and her need for self-enhancement, status, and love. By her fantasies of continuing in school, working, and becoming a secretary, she suggests her own potential resources.

Elaine's need to escape her unhappy predicament, her anxiety, and her feelings of inferiority are suggested in a story about a girl leaning on the railing of a high bridge from which position she looks down at the boats in the river: "The girl is looking into the sea. She is watching them loading and taking boxes off the boats. It is going to rain and she feels *cold and scared* [anxiety symbols]. She is thinking [daydreaming] she'd like to go to the place where those people came from. She's thinking 'how could she get on the boat?' She is going to run away [escape from her unhappiness] and see that land, and next time when the ship comes back she will come back home. [The anxiety associated with venturing brings her back.] But she falls in the water and drowns because she couldn't swim. [She feels too inferior to solve her problems.]"

Summarizing our interpretation of Elaine's stories, we note that she identifies with an unhappy, anxious, aggressive, guilty, and unconfident "little girl," who feels rejected by both parents and peers and who expects or seeks vague punishments. The dominant motives in her life are for acceptance, love, security, status, and achievement. But since these needs are severely frustrated, she is pained with anxiety, guilt, and feelings of inferiority. The barriers to satisfaction of her desires are perceived as peers who "don't like her," other hostile people, the loss of the loving care and protection of her parents, her own inferiority, and a somewhat unsympathetic, coercive mother-aunt. But her environment is also supportive. Sometimes her aunt comforts her; and the school, despite the conflicts with her peers and her lack of confidence, provides a means to achievement and status. Thus, although she is in the main thwarted, what are Elaine's fantasied modes of adjustment?

She considers a variety of possibilities—half-hearted attempts to escape, self-abasement, repression, fantasy, aggression, and appeals for comforting and sympathy. But she also recognizes her own resources and potentialities for reform and self-improvement. She will study, work, and win an esteemed position in life. Although Elaine feels guilty, lacks confidence, and is resigned to or unconsciously seeks punishment, she is not completely unoptimistic about her life. Given fair opportunities—in her home, school, and out-of-school peer relationships—for satisfaction of her needs for acceptance, security, love, esteem, and achievement, she will likely employ her learning and problem-solving abilities in constructive efforts to attain praiseworthy goals.

In guiding Elaine toward better mental health, her teacher and the school psychologist decided to try a combination of four procedures: (1) counseling, (2) promoting better relations between

Elaine and her classmates, (3) helping her to achieve greater efficiency and satisfaction in schoolwork, and (4) motivating Elaine's aunt to give her more acceptance and love.

To contrive occasions for informal counseling, the teacher invited Elaine to assist after school with such chores as decorating a corner of the room or preparing materials for the next day's activities. As they worked together in an accepting and friendly relationship, the teacher helped Elaine to reinterpret some of the feelings and attitudes she expressed. For example, to Elaine's complaint that "the kids pick on me," the teacher responded with the comment that while that often seems true, sometimes children's teasing is their peculiar way of getting acquainted. She said that when she herself corrected Elaine, it didn't mean that she had ceased to love her. And she explained that another child or the teacher might—because of their own frustrations —be cross some days, but that friends learn to tolerate such things in each other. In these talks and from the simultaneous results of other procedures, Elaine achieved greater self-understanding and more satisfying interpersonal relations. In one of the after-school talks, as she related the fun she had had at recess, Elaine said: "You know, I used to shove the kids 'cause I was mad, but now when I do it, it's just for fun." On another occasion, when the teacher had reprimanded a boy for playing too roughly, Elaine said: "Oh, it's all right. He didn't hurt me. We were only playing." As her teacher remarked, "This was quite a change in a girl who would turn fiercely and fight if anyone accidentally brushed against her."

In order to initiate better relations between Elaine and her classmates, the teacher suggested to them—during Elaine's temporary absence from the classroom—that Elaine's fighting probably resulted from her unhappiness and that she really wanted friends. She encouraged them to think of ways to enhance Elaine's happiness and to win her friendship. Not being antagonistic toward her, the other children had simply avoided her lest they be involved in a fight. They now began to make friendly overtures. Formerly, Elaine had walked to and from school alone. Now another child joined her on these walks. Still another child, as they came in from recess, proudly announced that "Elaine can jump pepper."

By diagnostic and remedial teaching, the teacher also aided Elaine in becoming more effective in schoolwork. For example, with guidance in correcting her slow, cramped handwriting, Elaine overcame her difficulty with written assignments. And more frequent checking and guidance at just the right time gave her the satisfaction of completing more projects.

Finally, the teacher helped Elaine through her aunt. Earlier, when the aunt was informed of Elaine's misbehavior, she became more strict, coercive, and punitive. She refused Elaine the sewing materials

she had requested until she improved her behavior. The teacher now discovered that reward motivation is effective with both children and parents. When she reported to the aunt some specific improvements in Elaine's schoolwork and conduct, the aunt's attitude changed from embarrassment to pride, and her treatment of Elaine became consistent with this new attitude. Sewing materials and other gestures of love were immediately forthcoming. Obviously pleased, Elaine announced to her teacher: "My aunt says that pretty soon she is going to buy me some of that stuff you make pretty towels out of and show me how to make them."

Elaine's own constructive efforts were also an important factor in her improvement. As we learned in the picture-stimulated stories, her self-improvement efforts were well-motivated. That they were also goal-directed is suggested by her occasional question, "Am I doing better?"

Elaine's progress toward better mental health also pleased her teacher. Furthermore, as the teacher observes, "The entire class is happier." As one concrete indication of the class's genuine liking for Elaine, her teacher says that she was nominated for a class office. In summarizing the progress, the teacher said: "The change has not come overnight and there are still occasional bad days, but they are getting farther and farther apart. She still needs guidance and reassurance; but she has practically no conflicts with her classmates any more. In fact, one of her best friends is a girl with whom she quarreled violently in the fall."

Elaine's maladjustment interfered with her academic accomplishments, and therefore her teacher was indirectly concerned with correcting her problem. She was also directly interested in the positive enhancement of Elaine's mental health. In order to appreciate the teacher's task in fostering mental health, let us consider the frequency with which teachers meet mental health problems.

The proportions of children identified as maladjusted have varied in different surveys. In one populous county, teachers trained to identify children with problems discovered that 11 per cent of the elementary and junior high school pupils were "seriously emotionally disturbed." In different school districts within the county, however, the proportion ranged from 5 to 35 per cent. Included among the seriously emotionally disturbed children were 30 per cent who were classified as unable to get along with their peers; 25 per cent who were quarrelsome and refused to do schoolwork; 24 per cent who adjusted by withdrawal; 16 per cent who were excessively nervous; 15 per cent who were too easily distracted; 12 per cent who were characterized as immature; and smaller percentages who were characterized as overly conscientious, moody, or lacking interest in school [13]. In another similar survey of emotional disturbances in elementary school children, 12 per cent were classified as seriously maladjusted and 30 per cent as poorly adjusted [35].

When the criterion of mental health handicaps is extended to include children with *any* deficiency in positive mental health, the proportion found handicapped is, of course, greatly increased. In one fourth grade class in which frustration of such needs as belonging, love, achievement, security, understanding, and self-esteem was used as the criterion of emotional handicap, 55 per cent of the children were classified as handicapped [8]. And when *all* the emotional disturbances sufficiently severe to disrupt an individual's efficiency and happiness are considered, Dr. William C. Menninger believes that the proportion in our population for whom mental ill-health is a hazard is "one in one [18]." Everyone, he says, suffers sometimes from mental ill-health. And better mental health would improve the efficiency and happiness of everyone.

APPRAISING THE QUALITY OF MENTAL HEALTH

Since mental health is an essential condition of effective learning and its cultivation is an important educational objective, we need to become sensitive to the signs of positive mental health and to the symptoms of emotional disturbance. As we described it in the preceding chapter, positive mental health is more than the absence of ill-health. It has its own characteristics, such as intellectual efficiency, creative productivity, effective and satisfying interpersonal relations, frustration tolerance, and buoyant joy in life. The absence of these characteristics and the presence of other personally and socially handicapping patterns of behavior are indicative of emotional maladjustment. In the development of several procedures for appraising the quality of mental health, the negative symptoms have been emphasized.

Observation. As the personality sketches in the preceding chapter suggest, children exhibit a wide variety of signs of mental health or of maladjustment in many individual and social activities. Underachievement, frequent displaced aggression, loss in constructiveness of behavior, unrealistic aspirations, withdrawal from schoolwork and social activities, depressed and pessimistic attitudes, symptoms of insecurity and anxiety, excessive and inappropriate use of defense mechanisms, and various impairments of intellectual efficiency are all indicative of serious emotional disturbance. As a guide to teachers in identifying emotionally maladjusted school children, Topp has collected a list of 40 signs which 25 experienced child psychologists and psychiatrists agree are indicative of emotional malfunctioning. In addition to several of the above-mentioned indexes, his list includes such symptoms as "excessive worriedness," repeated thefts despite punishment, being lost in daydreams, habitual facial grimacing, being constantly active and restless, oversensitivity to real or imagined slights, cruelty to younger children or animals, being perfectionistic about schoolwork, hating many people, lacking in affection for anybody, "just sitting" for long periods of time, indecisiveness, "restricted emotional expression," always being tired, often perplexed and confused, self-punitive, continually in accidents, destructive of things, and complaining of medically unconfirmed ailments [68].

Anecdotal records. For a more reliable and comprehensive picture of a child's developmental trend toward maladjustment or toward mental health, it is often desirable for the teacher to record a sequence of observations of significant behavior episodes. Such anecdotal records, as they are called, should sample the child's actual behavior and the reactions of other individuals to him in a variety of situations. Two such recorded observations of John Sanders illustrate the method. At about age 14½—because of his delayed preadolescent growth spurt and a combination of other unfortunate personality traits and circumstances in his life—John was at the depth of his unpopularity. The frustrations of his desires for acceptance, affection, and esteem from his peers are dramatically indicated in the following anecdotes:

> (Clubhouse porch. John came in with his lunch. Asked if someone would play backgammon with him.)
> DOUGLAS: I can play but I wouldn't play with you.
> MARILYN (to John): He's beat better people than you.

(John dropped the backgammon board, and Douglas and Marilyn laughed at him. He was disconcerted, but still remained on the porch and later played a game with Bill. Bill trotted away abruptly as soon as the school bell rang.)

JOHN: I'm always the one that's left to pick things up [37, p. 54].

(Evening party at the clubhouse. Most of those present are playing a game which involves penalties. John is reading magazines in a corner. Louise is given the penalty: "Go up to the best looking boy in the room and vamp him." When she balked, one girl said, "Oh, you just go up and say 'I love you,' and then give him a kick." Louise looked relieved at the apparent simplicity of this assignment, but still hesitated.)

DOROTHY: Say it to sissy-babe John. He doesn't know the difference anyway.

(John responded with a sarcastic "Thank you," without looking up from his reading) [37, pp. 54–55].

Rating scales and check lists. For economically summarizing, organizing, and quantifying the teacher's accumulated prior observations of children's behavior, rating scales and check lists are useful. The *Haggerty-Olson-Wickman Behavior Rating Schedule* [25], for example, includes 11 items indicative of emotional adjustment. One item reads: "How does he react to frustration or to unpleasant situations?" It is answered by checking the appropriate position on the graphic scale describing his typical behavior, as the teacher judges it from recollected observations.

Very submis-sive, long suffering	Tolerant, rare-ly blows up	Generally self-controlled	Impatient	Easily irri-tated, hot-headed explosive
(3)	(2)	(1)	(4)	(5)

As the numerical values beneath the described degrees of emotional control indicate, the scores on each item range from 1 (favorable) to 5 (unfavorable); and on the 11 items, the totals, of course, range from 11 to 55.

The check list is illustrated in Table 13.1, where the first 10 of Topp's behavior patterns indicative of emotional maladjustment are listed. It is assumed that the more items a teacher checks as applicable, the more severely maladjusted the child is.

Classmates' opinions. In the identification of maladjusted or of mentally healthy children, devices involving quantification of peer observations are sometimes utilized. For example, opposite such questions as "Who flies into fits of anger on the slightest provocation?" or "When things go wrong, who is most likely to work out a good solution?" children are directed to write the names of their classmates whom the descriptions fit best. Scores on such traits are determined by computing the percentage of times each individual is mentioned as

Table 13.1. *Check list of behavior patterns indicative of emotional maladjustment (first 10 items from a list of 40)*

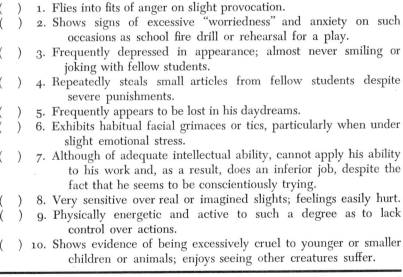

( ) 1. Flies into fits of anger on slight provocation.

( ) 2. Shows signs of excessive "worriedness" and anxiety on such occasions as school fire drill or rehearsal for a play.

( ) 3. Frequently depressed in appearance; almost never smiling or joking with fellow students.

( ) 4. Repeatedly steals small articles from fellow students despite severe punishments.

( ) 5. Frequently appears to be lost in his daydreams.

( ) 6. Exhibits habitual facial grimaces or tics, particularly when under slight emotional stress.

( ) 7. Although of adequate intellectual ability, cannot apply his ability to his work and, as a result, does an inferior job, despite the fact that he seems to be conscientiously trying.

( ) 8. Very sensitive over real or imagined slights; feelings easily hurt.

( ) 9. Physically energetic and active to such a degree as to lack control over actions.

( ) 10. Shows evidence of being excessively cruel to younger or smaller children or animals; enjoys seeing other creatures suffer.

SOURCE: Topp, R. F. *Elem. Sch. J.*, 1952, 52, 340–343. Reprinted by permission of the University of Chicago Press. Copyright by the University of Chicago.

fitting a particular description. John Sanders, for example, whose unpopularity was indicated in the anecdotal records, was mentioned most frequently by his peers as "someone nobody seems to care much about [37, p. 36]."

Self-inventories of emotional adjustment. To complement teacher, counselor, and peer observations, children and adolescents are often invited to appraise the quality of their own mental health. Their approach is likely to be different from that of an outside observer. Rather than rely on manifest behavior, the individual, in appraising himself, is likely to consider his inner thoughts, feelings, and attitudes. However, in order to protect himself from the anxiety of facing an unacceptable or guilt-producing self-image, he is prone to distort his appraisal because of repression and other self-defensive mechanisms. Despite the difficulties in self-appraisal of emotional adjustment, psychologists have developed a large variety of adjustment inventories.

Inventories of anxiety and insecurity. An adaptation for children of the *Taylor Manifest Anxiety Scale* [1, pp. 49–51] was mentioned in the preceding chapter as an inventory of anxiety symptoms. It includes 52 such items as "I get nervous when someone watches me work [11, p. 318]." Maslow's *Security-insecurity Inventory,* intended for adults, is also a measure of anxiety. Maslow believes that freedom from anxiety is an important factor in mental health. He says that this inventory will reveal the individual's "inner conscious feelings" of being unloved and rejected, of isolation, of being threatened in a dangerous world of hostile people, of pessimism, discontent, and tension— or of being loved, of belonging, and of being safe, content, and happy in a pleasant world of benevolent, friendly people. Answers of "Yes," "No," or "Undecided" to 75 questions such as "Do you have a vague fear of the future?" and "Do you ordinarily feel contented?" yield scores which have ranged from 0 to 69 for college students. The mean score of 19.5 on the inventory, for "normal" college students, indicates that everyone is likely to confess some mental health handicaps. For maladjusted groups, it is assumed that mean scores are higher. For 51 women in a city jail, for example, the mean score was 29.2 [45].

Life-situation adjustment inventories. Several adjustment inventories yield profiles of scores indicative of adjustment in different life activities [1]. For example, the *Bell Adjustment Inventory* for high school and college students inventories the individual's feelings of satisfaction or discontent about his home and his health, whether he feels confident or retiring in social contacts, and his feelings of emotional control in general. An item from each category suggests its content. *Home:* "Did you ever have a strong desire to run away from home?" *Health:* "Do you have many headaches?" *Social:* "Are you troubled by shyness?" *Emotional:* "Do you get discouraged easily?" Answers of "Yes," "No," or "Undecided" yield, in each category, a range of scores which is interpreted according to norms, from "Excellent," "Good," "Average," "Unsatisfactory," to "Very unsatisfactory." Bell reports that students judged by school counselors as "poorly adjusted" tend to give more maladjustive answers to these questions than students considered "well-adjusted [6]." It is noted, however, that self-inventoried appraisals of mental health and teacher estimates based on observation are usually not closely related. We shall discuss this topic more fully further on in this chapter.

Multiple-aspect personality inventories. Other adjustment inventories evaluate the quality of an individual's mental health in terms of differentiated strengths and weaknesses of personality. The *Minnesota Multiphasic Personality Inventory,* the interpretation of which requires training in clinical psychology, was empirically constructed to differentiate between "normal" and maladjusted individuals and, to some extent, between individuals with different kinds of mental illnesses [29]. The test includes over 550 items such as the following: "I cannot keep my mind on one thing." "I am worried about sex matters." "The future seems hopeless to me." In addition, there are such apparently normal items as "I like to read about science." The individual taking the test indicates whether they are true, false, or impossible to decide, as applied to himself. The items cover a wide range of content in such areas as health and psychosomatic symptoms; personal and social attitudes; educational, occupational, and family adjustment; and neurotic and psychotic symptoms. From this pool of diverse items, nine originally standardized and several added scales have been developed. As an illustration of the added scales, *Wa* (work attitudes) differentiates between over- and underachieving college students [64].

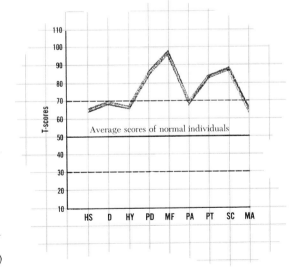

Fig. 13.1. *The* MMPI *profile of a 22-year-old high school graduate, whose symptoms of mental illness had earlier included delusions, depression, and anxiety.* (From L. R. Harmon and D. N. Wiener, *J. Appl. Psychol.,* 1945, vol. 29, pp. 132–141.)

For the construction of interpretive profiles, such as that illustrated in Figure 13.1, the raw scores on the nine original scales [29] and also on the added scales [28] are converted into standard T-scores for which the mean is 50 and the standard deviation is 10. This device makes it possible to compare any individual's scores with those of the normal standardization group [1, p. 120], and it also renders the several scores comparable. T-scores above 70 (the upper 2½ per cent) are considered indicative of maladjustment and sometimes of serious mental illness.

The high school graduate whose *MMPI* profile is presented in Figure 13.1 requested vocational guidance because he was dissatisfied with his job as a shipping clerk. He said that he lacked confidence and was unable to perform effectively in situations requiring quick thinking. Although he tested above average in academic ability, his ineffectual behavior in the interview (lack of initiative, whispering, and confusion), together with the extremely high scores on several of the *MMPI* scales, indicated to the counselor that the young man needed psychiatric help.

Although the *MMPI* has not proved especially effective in differentiating between different kinds of mental illness [2], differences between normal and maladjusted groups have often been demonstrated. As is indicated in Figure 13.2, the mean *MMPI* profile of delinquent girls is elevated, especially on the scale indicative of social irresponsibility, while the mean scores for a comparable group of normal adolescent girls is near 50 [10].

Inventories of both personality and life-situation adjustment. Intended for self-appraisals of both self and social adjustment, the *California Test of Personality* [66] yields a profile of scores on several personality traits, plus scores on adjustment in family, school, and

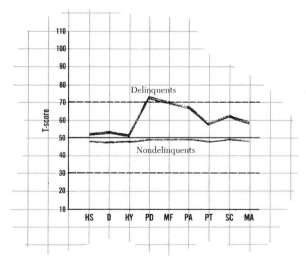

Fig. 13.2. *Mean* MMPI *profiles for 99 delinquent and for 85 nondelinquent adolescent girls.* (From Dora F. Capwell, *J. Appl. Psychol.*, 1945, vol. 29, p. 291.)

community relations. A sample question and its favorable answer, from each of the 12 subdivisions, will suggest the test's content:

[*Self-reliance*] Do you usually keep at your work until it is done? (Yes)

[*Sense of Personal Worth*] Can you do most of the things you try? (Yes)

[*Sense of Personal Freedom*] Are you allowed enough time for play? (Yes)

[*Feeling of Belonging*] Do you think that nobody likes you? (No)

[*Freedom from Withdrawing Tendencies*] Are people often mean or unfair to you? (No)

[*Freedom from Nervous Symptoms*] Do you bite your fingernails often? (No)

[*Social Standards*] Is it necessary to thank those who have helped you? (Yes)

[*Social Skills*] Do you help new pupils talk to other children? (Yes)

[*Freedom from Antisocial Tendencies*] Do you often have to make a "fuss" or "act up" to get your rights? (No)

[*Family Relations*] Do your folks seem to think that you are just as good as they are? (Yes)

[*School Relations*] Does it seem to you that some teachers have it in for pupils? (No)

[*Community Relations*] Do you sometimes help other people? (Yes)

For interpretation, the sums of favorable answers, ranging from zero to 12 in each subdivision, are converted into percentile scores. The higher the percentile, the better the adjustment is presumed to be. In phrasing the questions, the authors of the test attempted to minimize the unacceptability of "unfavorable" answers. For example, rather than ask a child whether or not he has temper tantrums, the test item asks: "Do you often have to make a 'fuss' or 'act up' to get your rights?"

Despite the effort to avoid asking questions which arouse self-defensiveness, it has been found that children tend to answer most of the questions in the direction of social acceptability. For example, a fourth grade girl earned the unfavorable 25th percentile score—indicative of restricted "personal freedom"—by only three unfavorable answers. She answered "No" to the items: "May you usually choose your own friends?" "Are you allowed to do most of the things you want to?" "Are you given some spending money?" Since she gave favorable answers to nine such questions as "May you usually bring your friends home when you want to?" we should, of course, be cautious in assuming that such a profile is really indicative of a restricted sense of personal freedom.

Inventories of self-conflict. Because the understanding of self-conflict is significant in the diagnosis of maladjustment, the inclusion of 16 items on which a child compares his actual self-image with his ideal self-image is an important feature of the *Roger's Test of Personality Adjustment* [56]. In answering such questions in the test as the one below, the child is directed to check "Yes," "No," or an appropriate cell between them, to express both his own self-estimate and a wish.

John is the most popular boy in school. Everybody likes him.

	1	2	3	4	5	6	7	8	9	10	
Am I just like him?	Yes										No
Do I wish to be just like him?	Yes										No

The conflicts which the device sometimes reveals is illustrated in the case of John Sanders, who was mentioned earlier in illustrating anecdotal records. At 14½ years of age, it will be remembered, he was exceedingly unpopular with his peers. Being both aware of and able to accept this fact, he rated himself 8, that is, as quite unlike the most popular boy in his class. In contrast with his actual self-image, John checked 1 for his wish, thus expressing his desire to be just like the most popular boy [37, pp. 132–135].

Self-inventories and observational appraisals of adjustment. Since the inner feelings of which only the individual himself is aware are not always expressed in observable behavior, we should not expect high correlations between self-inventory scores and observational appraisals of mental health. Several studies have revealed only slight relationships. For example, among 66 boys, self-inventoried adjustment on the *California Test of Personality* was found to correlate .26 with counselor's ratings, .28 with peer opinions [65], and, in another study of 120 ninth grade students, .32 with teachers' ratings of adjustment [12]. The correlations between high school students' self-inventories of home, health, social, and emotional adjustment on the *Bell Adjustment Inventory* and teachers' or counselors' observational ratings on these same traits have ranged from zero to .30 [14, 40, 69]. Some studies, however, have revealed higher correlations between self-inventory appraisals and overt behavior. For example, certain elevated scales on the empirically constructed *MMPI* for ninth grade boys and girls have proved significant in predicting their subsequent delinquency [30].

The typically low relationships between self-inventories and observationally appraised adjustment indicate that many discrepancies between these ways of identifying maladjusted students should be expected. Regardless of the actual quality of their personal and social adjustment, many individuals tend to perceive themselves as socially acceptable—as approximating the ideal self-image. For example, among 277 college students, the correlation between the total self-inventory score on the *California Test of Personality* and a derived score of idealized social acceptability—based on items such as "Do you try to get better acquainted with the people you don't like?"—is .85 [42].

Because of our almost universal need for social acceptance, favorable self-inventory profiles are often ambiguous. Instead of being an objective appraisal of mental health, they are sometimes indicative of "culturally acceptable defensiveness," of a tendency to "see oneself in the best possible light [42, p. 90]." As an illustration of this tendency, it was discovered that a third of the college students judged "seriously" or "critically" maladjusted by a faculty committee (including two psychologists) appraised their own adjustment on the *Bell Adjustment Inventory* as either "good" or "excellent [44]." In another study, a student who later developed delusions of persecution which required psychiatric treatment checked as "moderately disturbing" only two items on the *Thurstone Neurotic Inventory* [50].

Interviewing to check self-inventories. Because of such inconsistencies between procedures for appraising mental health, it seems desirable to check the inventory results by a multiple approach. One such check is to inquire in an interview about the meaning of an individual's answers to significant inventory items. This procedure also facilitates freedom of expression and self-analysis in the interview. Having described himself in a self-inventory (without the presence of another person), an individual is often readier to observe and evaluate himself in the face-to-face situation. Thus the inventory and the interview become complementary devices.

To illustrate the use of the interview as a check upon the self-inventory, we quote below some excerpts from Channell's interview with Kathy, whose *California Test of Personality* profile appears in Figure 13.3. The unfavorable scores in the areas of *Personal Freedom, Withdrawing Tendencies, Nervous Symptoms,* and in *Family* and *School Relations* suggest that Kathy feels frustrated and anxious about her family and school interpersonal relations. Despite feelings of adequate self-reliance, personal worth, and of social competency, she indicates that she tends to withdraw. Guided by the specific items which led to Kathy's unfavorable scores, the interviewer directed her to elaborate on her original answers to them. Referring to the inventory, he said: "You checked 'No' as your answer to the question 'Do your folks give you a reasonable amount of spending money?' Why?" Kathy, with some expression of bitterness, replied: "My folks give me *no* allowance. I do baby sitting for what money I get." In this way several items were reconsidered. To the question "Are you scolded for little things that do not amount to much?" Kathy answered: "Yes, my parents scold me for things, little things. My brother gets scolded too, but not as much as me." And in answer to "Are people frequently so unfair to you that you feel like crying?" she said:

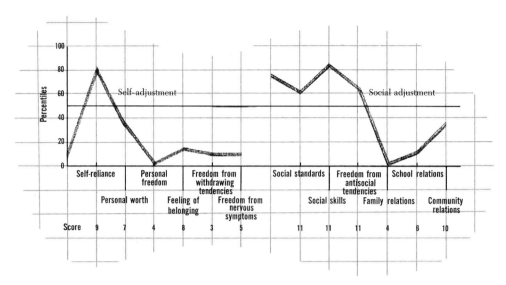

Fig. 13.3. *The* California Test of Personality *profile for Kathy, a ninth grade girl, indicates that she feels anxious, restricted in personal freedom, poorly adjusted to family and peers, and socially isolated; but that she has adequate feelings of self-reliance and of social competency.*

"Yes, sometimes people make me so mad I could bawl. . . . Once last year I had a teacher who made me so mad. She didn't like my mother so she gave me a D [12, pp. 23–24]."

These and other similar answers to the interview questions confirm the interpretation given of Kathy's profile. She apparently does feel restricted in personal freedom, unfairly treated by people, and, with some anxiety, withdraws from them. Her responses on the inventory and in the interview agree.

In contrast to Kathy, Cyril, who made a favorable self-appraisal on the inventory, mentioned many complaints in the interview. When he was asked about missing classes, he said: "It doesn't seem like I can get out of trouble when I get into it. I don't like school. I know that. I just can't make myself get up in the morning and come."

The interview appraisal confirmed the inventory for only about one-half of the 23 pupils whom Channell interviewed. Nearly 50 per cent of these children, the interviewer felt, gave defensive pictures of themselves—most frequently in the inventory but sometimes in the interview.

Projective methods. Projective tests are attempts to overcome the inhibitions and self-deceptions which often distort conscious self-appraisals of personality or adjustment. It will be remembered from the introductory case study that when Elaine was asked why she often attacked other children, all she could say was "I don't know, except that the kids are mean to me." However, in the picture-stimulated stories—in which she seemed unaware of her self-revelations—her inhibitions were relaxed and in place of overtly expressed hostility, she revealed herself as wanting acceptance, security, love, and esteem, and as willing to work constructively for these satisfactions.

Such disparities between the personality projected into *TAT* stories and that revealed in overt behavior are especially characteristic of maladjusted individuals. For example, Laura revealed hostility toward her mother both in *TAT* stories and in marrying a man of whom her mother disapproved. She allayed the guilt from her hostile impulses, however, by a reaction-formation pattern of overly polite, prim, sweet, and submissive conduct [63, p. 91]. Catherine revealed hostility to her mother in *TAT* stories by referring to mother figures as bad and punitive. But, employing denial as a defense from the anxiety these feelings aroused, she said about her parents: "They are the best parents in the world [63, p. 82]." After therapy, however, she confirmed the validity of the *TAT* interpretation by freely admitting her dislike of her mother.

By freeing the individual from self-conscious restraints, the *TAT* and other projective devices provide him a medium for symbolizing his self-concept, basic motives, attitudes toward his environment, and latent modes of approach to frustrations and problems. Expertly interpreted, such fantasied projective content yields significant clues indicative of individual trends in the development of mental health or of maladjustment. The interpretation of such projective symbols, however, requires extensive psychological training, and, like the other devices described here, the *TAT* is far from infallible. It is one tool in a combination of procedures by which the psychologist enhances his effectiveness in working jointly with teachers in the identification, diagnosis, and treatment of maladjusted school children.

The stimuli and media for eliciting and expressing projective content are not limited to picture-stimulated stories. There are many other devices, including projective interpretations of drawings, cartoons, dramatic sets, and ink blots; completions of sentences and stories; and autobiographical sketches [3]. There are also such informal media for revealing underlying motives and attitudes as a child's reaction to the things he reads.

For example, even after she had finally begun to read, Mary—who in fear of her mother's criticism for mistakes had inhibited the trial-and-check process in word identification—revealed a general, pervading fear of parental disapproval in her reaction to a story. When she read that "Some boys tried to climb the pole [at the Fair] to get a five-dollar bill fixed at the top, but could not get even a handhold [because of grease on the pole]," she remarked with evident consternation: "Joe [the story's hero] isn't going to do that, is he?" When her teacher asked her why she thought he should not do it, Mary replied: "His mother would spank him for that!"

As our review has shown, the teacher and school psychologist, working together, have available a variety of procedures for the identification and diagnosis of mental health problems. The devices include observation, anecdotal records, rating scales and check lists, classmates' opinions, self-inventories, the interview, and projective methods. But in order to foster the development of mental health effectively, teachers also need to understand both the causal factors in its development and ways of improving its quality.

THE HOME AS A FACTOR IN THE DEVELOPMENT OF MENTAL HEALTH

Our discussion of Molly in Chapter 12 illustrates the early acquisition of basic modes of adjustment. Before she was five years of age Molly had learned to cope with her fear of thunder and the noise of a jet plane. She had learned comfort seeking, self-assurance, denial, projection, and reaction formation as defense mechanisms for dealing with anxiety. Since the basic approaches to life's problems develop early in childhood, the home is an especially significant factor in fostering or in hindering the development of mental health. Later, the school, the peer culture of childhood and adolescence, and the adult's occupational and other social relationships become important. But the home starts the child along the way to mental health or maladjustment.

Mental health–fostering parent-child relations. A confident, constructive, and happy approach to school learning is largely a product of good parent-child relationships before the age for beginning school. As Heffernan has pointed out, and as we learned in Chapter 12, appropriate parent-child experiences are most influential in the early years; the emotionally healthy child develops by six years of age a sense of trust, a sense of autonomy, and a sense of self-confidence and constructive initiative. Moreover, according to Maslow's hierarchical concept of motives, which we presented in Chapter 6, the child who is accustomed to adequate provision for his physiological needs and who feels safe, loved, and esteemed is free for constructive and creative use of his talents. These basic conditions for the development of mental health and its expression in constructive achievement are effectively elaborated elsewhere [34, 55]. Here, guided by the ideas of Nimkoff [52] and Katz and Lehner [39], we shall merely list some of the parent-child relationships needed for the development of optimum mental health in children.

1. Every child needs two mentally healthy parents who love each other, who themselves have developed a sense of integrity in their

life roles, and who strive to meet life's problems with a confident, constructive, problem-solving approach. This, of course, is an ideal. While moving toward it, without, perhaps, fully attaining it, parents can also provide the conditions of mental health for their children. Moreover, when a child loses one parent, the resourceful parent left alone to raise his child often can make adequate compensation for the lack of the other parent. We are reminded here that mental health is not the automatic product of ideal conditions. It involves learning to deal with both frustrating and satisfying conditions.

2. In helping the child to achieve feelings of security, trust of people, personal worth, and confidence, parents need to demonstrate amply their love for him.

3. As he matures, the child needs his parents' recognition and their understanding of his developing talents, interests, and aspirations.

4. He also needs parents who take an active interest in providing adequate and self-realizing opportunities for his physical, intellectual, social, and moral development; who provide appropriate guidance in structuring approaches to developmental tasks; who approve his achievements but also encourage him in his failures and reward his constructive efforts; and who employ democratic principles of discipline.

5. Each child needs parents who show respect for his continual growth toward maturity and for his unique individuality, who, at every emerging stage of development, give judicious amounts of help and guidance, ample opportunities for independence, sincere respect and appreciation for his developmental achievements, and freedom for development—at his own rate, following his own interests, and in harmony with his own talents.

6. Since children have limitations and meet frustrations, every child needs parents who accept him as he is—without competitive standards of value—and who are permissive with respect to his needs for emotional expression, even of fears, angers, and jealousies.

7. Every child also needs within the family a sense of belonging, occasions for democratic planning and social action, and opportunities to participate as a family member in the group approach to both individual-member and entire-family problems.

Maladjustment-producing parent-child relations. When children experience rejection, are restricted in opportunities for self-realization, have inadequate guidance, and suffer harsh treatment, they are vulnerable to emotional maladjustment and sometimes to consequent impairment of intellectual efficiency. As examples of such development, we are reminded of the maladjustments of the children mentioned earlier: Mary's inhibition of the trial-and-check process in learning to read—because of fear of her mother's inevitable criticism of a mistake;

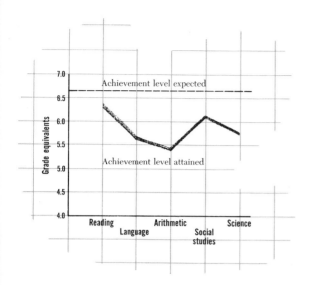

Fig. 13.4. *Because of impaired mental health and intellectual efficiency, 138 orphanage-reared children fail to attain the achievement level expected for their chronological and mental maturity levels.* (Adapted from H. Feinberg, *J. Genet. Psychol.*, 1954, vol. 85, pp. 217–229.)

Johnny's self-defeating, perfectionistic approach in school, which he adopted to allay the anxiety aroused by periodic impulses of resentment toward his dominating mother; and Elaine's self-ostracizing displaced aggression toward her classmates, because of abandonment by her parents and the insufficiently demonstrated love of her foster parents.

Both the accumulating experience in working with maladjusted children and youth and the findings of several studies indicate that the development of mental health or of maladjustment depends significantly upon the quality of early home experiences. Bender, for example, as a result of her study of "more than six thousand maladjusted youngsters, feels that almost all of these children have suffered from lack of adequate parent-child relationships in infancy and early childhood [34, p. 222]."

Orphanage-reared children—handicapped by frustration of their needs for security, love, and esteem; by developed attitudes of hopelessness, unworthiness, and guilt; and by naïveté about their environment—often fail to achieve our first criterion of mental health, the full and constructive use of their talents. As is shown in Figure 13.4, the average achievement level attained by 138 orphanage children is approximately one year below that expected of children of their chronological and mental maturity [19]. One study compared the intellectual efficiency of 15 normally reared adolescents with that of 15 adolescents who had spent a part of their early childhood in an orphanage. This study suggests that deprivation of the guidance and love given in intimate parent-child relationships can disturb our patterns of thinking [21]. The previously institutionalized adolescents, when directed to sort a variety of figures of different color and shape, failed to conceptualize their abstract features. Neglecting the features of color and shape—on the basis of which the various objects could be efficiently classified into groups of green, yellow, triangular, and square figures—they arranged them into unplanned designs and patterns of concrete things.

Not only deprivation of intimate parent-child relationships, but also inadequate parent-child relationships can produce maladjustment and consequent impairment of intellectual efficiency. Hattwick and Stowell found that children whose parents either push or baby them are inferior—both in social adjustment and in the efficiency of their schoolwork habits—to children who enjoy more self-reliance and maturity in relations with their parents [31]. McCarthy believes that the emotional insecurity produced in children by such unwholesome parental attitudes as rejection or overprotection often leads to maladjustment and learning disabilities. She reports that three-fourths of the intellectually normal nonreaders referred to her clinic "show clear evidence of parental rejection, or over-protection, or both [43, p. 95]." In reaction to the frustration of parental rejection or overprotection, these nonreaders developed one or the other of two maladjustive patterns of behavior. An aggressive group was comprised of children who, like Elaine, were characterized by quarrelsomeness, defiance, jealousy, bad temper, stubborn and demanding attitudes, fears, and lack of friends, but who were of normal ability and had a normal interest in athletics. The submissive group exhibited jealousy, lack of skill in sports, immature helplessness, anxiety, fear of showing antisocial behavior, and, like good-as-gold Johnny, they were quiet and docile.

In another study of poor readers who ranged in age from seven to thirteen and in IQ from 91 to 140, Missildine reports a variety of poor parent-child relationships. Of these 30 underachieving school children, the mothers of 10 were characterized as "critical, hostile, and rejecting." Ten other mothers, like Johnny's mother, were described as "tense, coercive, and perfectionistic" and as demanding strict obedience. The fathers of these 20 children also were in various ways lacking—in their support, guidance, or love. Among the remaining 10 children, 4 had problems of sibling rivalry over a new baby; 2 were overindulged until they entered school and then were neglected; 2 were considered overprotected, and 1 child was disturbed over adjusting to a new school. Although all of these maladjusted children were intellectually inefficient, they reacted differently to their unhappy family relationships. "Some assumed a restless, indifferent, happy-go-lucky pose. . . . Others felt crushed, unhappy, inadequate [49, p. 271]."

The attitudes and modes of adjustment which children learn in their relations with their parents are often generalized and extended to pupil-teacher relationships and to other interpersonal relationships. Children enjoy pleasing and imitating their loved and admired parents. When they feel rejected, unfairly or harshly treated, they may become counter-aggressive and consciously or unconsciously resistant to parental guidance. Children often transfer these home-established positive or negative attitudes to their teachers, with consequent enhancement or impairment of school achievements [7].

Because anxious children tend to imitate the modes of adjustment of their parents, overdependence as well as resistance may be transferred from parent-child to teacher-pupil relations. For example, the parents of children who avoid or inhibit learning—like Mary, who didn't dare to risk an uncertain provisional trial in learning to read—also adjust to challenging tasks by intellectual inhibitions and dependency.

Children adopt these modes of adjustment both because they are guided by their parents as models and because their parents tend to reward such behavior. As Staver has shown, some mothers, dreading separation from their children, take vicarious satisfaction in and subtly reward their children's helplessness, and thus bind their children to them [62].

Several other direct or indirect relationships between parent and child behavior patterns have been suggested. Children of rejecting mothers tend to be overaggressive. Children of dominating mothers are prone to submissiveness [59]. Children who aggressively dominate their peer groups have often experienced coercive, restrictive, and discordant parental discipline [48]. On the other hand, a child's cooperative behavior is developed by parental acceptance, understanding, sympathy, shared formulation of standards, and readiness to give help when it is needed [48]. The development of initiative and leadership in adolescents seems to be related to parental provision of appropriate responsibilities, adequate independence, opportunities to make decisions and to experiment with new situations, and respect for their opinions in family discussions [4].

THE ROLE OF THE SCHOOL IN MENTAL HEALTH

Since the development of mental health is both an important educational objective and an essential condition of effective learning, good teachers utilize every resource available to them to cultivate it in children and youth. They find in the school itself several important mental health resources.

Having developed feelings of trust, of autonomy, of self-confidence, and of initiative before coming to school, healthy children extend their development of mental health by successful school learning and exploratory experiences which produce a sense of accomplishment and a more differentiated sense of self-identity. For children and youth who feel safe, loved, and esteemed, the school can both reinforce these satisfactions and provide for self-actualization—in opportunities for constructive and creative expression. These satisfactions further enhance the individual's feelings of personal worth and confidence and his interest and efficiency in learning and problem-solving activities. Furthermore, the opportunity for identification and constructive participation in orderly group life contributes to each individual's feelings of security and belonging.

Unfortunately, the school, like the home, often fails to provide these mental health–building resources for *all* children. Because of frustrating school experiences, some children develop a sense of inferiority rather than a sense of accomplishment. Instead of discovering satisfying roles for expression of their unique talents and interests, they become bored with unsuitable tasks. Instead of feeling safe, loved, and esteemed, they come to feel threatened, unlovable, and guilty.

There are six provisions in the areas of school experience or service by which we can facilitate the child's development of mental health and concomitant efficiency of learning: (1) a suitable curriculum, (2) effective and appropriate instruction, (3) guidance of the child's in-school social experiences, (4) help with his personal problems, (5) indirect aid through cooperation with his parents, and (6) the utilization of professional mental health services.

Suitable curriculum. Being able to do something well enhances a child's healthy self-acceptance, feelings of worth, and self-confidence. Since children typically exhibit wide intraindividual trait variations— differential motor, intellectual, artistic, and social abilities—each child is most likely to find something he can do well if his school provides a great diversity of curricular opportunities and guidance in discovering and in relating his talents to them. A curriculum of learning activities for a child—suited to his maturity, interests, patterns of abilities, and needs—should lead in the main to experiences which produce in the child a satisfying sense of accomplishment. Progress in such a curriculum should give the child a feeling of enhanced worth as a person. Furthermore, from success in varied learning and problem-solving tasks, the child learns how to learn more effectively and develops increasing confidence in learning and problem solving as general modes of adjustment. As Buswell has shown, a child's success in schoolwork enhances his acceptance by his peers [9]. With these mental health assets, the child does not need to develop self-defeating, defensive modes of adjustment. Thus free of anxiety, and with increasing skill and confidence as a learner and problem solver, he should make better adjustments in all his life activities—with his peers, siblings, parents, teachers, and in other interpersonal relations.

Such a curriculum and appropriate guidance may not only further the development of good mental health begun in the home—it may sometimes compensate for inadequacies in the home. Mike's story illustrates this point. With his home-based security threatened, Mike developed a fiercely aggressive pattern of reaction. But with patient, constructive guidance and a curriculum in which he could adequately express his talents and interests, he finally began to feel security, confidence, and self-respect in his own potentialities.

Mike began school as a normal, happy, first grade boy. But when his mother was permanently hospitalized and he was left alone with his overindulgent and otherwise indifferent father, his life was disrupted. In the second grade he lost interest in schoolwork. He became noncooperative, sullen, and often had fights or temper tantrums. His third grade teacher frequently isolated him because of his temper tantrums and his destructive behavior on the playground and in the classroom. During his fourth year in school, he alternated between exhibiting sparks of interest and relapses into aggression. For a unit on birds, Mike brought a robin's nest to school, made a birdhouse, and found a sparrow with a broken wing. During this time he had only two fights. He lost interest, however, during the unit on plants, and resumed his aggressions, even to the extent of threatening a boy on the playground with his knife. He concluded the year, however, by contributing a nicely constructed birdhouse to the May Day parade.

In grades 5 and 6, his interest in science—insects, birds, and snakes—deepened, and he became more emotionally stable. Now, in junior high school he has developed a serious interest in natural science—in excursions, projects, reading, and in writing reports. Experiencing the joy of constructive achievement and enjoying the gratifying esteem of his classmates, he has developed a healthier self-concept. According to his teacher, "Mike's attitude is now one of pride in his ability to do the things in science that he likes to do. He can still swear like a trooper when he is crossed. But temper tantrums are infrequent. And he no longer feels threatened by everyone."

In order to provide ample opportunities for discovery and expression of individual talents during the elementary school years, children should be exposed to many media for creative expression and should be encouraged to try their hand at using them. Art activities, crafts, puppets, dramatic play, rhythms and dancing, music, creative writing, construction, and science and social studies projects are all rich in opportunities for creative expression. Among these varied experiences each child should find something he enjoys and feels he can do well.

At the junior and senior high school levels, curricula are more differentiated. The child's self-discovery experiences in diverse curricular activities can be supplemented by the procedures for appraising abilities described in Chapter 4. Thus the school can help adolescents define their talents more clearly. Guided by such appraisals, and by self-exploratory experiences in various learning activities, each child should, with teacher guidance, plan a curriculum suited to his talents and interests. Every worthwhile area of the curriculum deserves consideration and respect. As Rotter has suggested, bricklayers, plumbers, baseball players, musicians, sign painters, dancers, and many kinds of businessmen enjoy their work and achieve satisfying personal and social lives without superior abstract-verbal ability (although they may have it) [58, p. 420].

A uniform, undifferentiated curriculum ignores the extensive intra- and interindividual differences we have discovered in and between children. For the many children who are denied success in such a curriculum, it produces only boredom, frustration, and failure. From such experiences, children are likely to develop self-attitudes of inferiority, counteraggressive rebelliousness, and guilt. As Layton has shown, the frustration caused by school failure produces dislike of school, hostility toward teachers, feelings of inferiority, and the desire to escape school situations. Since these attitudes become generalized, school-frustrated children do not develop skill and confidence in learning and problem solving. Instead, they reject learning and problem solving as general modes of adjustment and thus are handicapped in many life activities [41].

Teaching procedures. Satisfying school accomplishments contribute to mental health, and improved mental health enhances the efficiency of learning. Thus, mental health–oriented teacher guidance

Ample, diverse opportunities for discovery, development, and expression of individual talents contribute to mental health. (Adams School, Logan, Utah.)

facilitates growth in both of these reciprocally related aspects of development. Such guidance integrates the principles of mental health with the other conditions of effective learning. Emphasizing our seventh condition of effective learning, such teaching aims to establish and maintain the learner's self-confidence and to avoid the efficiency-impairing anxiety to which maladjusted children are prone.

Although the application of mental health principles in teaching is important for every child, it is especially necessary in teaching maladjusted children. Such children need abundant and patient demonstrations of the acceptance, love, and esteem of their teacher and classmates. They need to participate constructively in group activities in which they feel that they belong and are valued [38]. To overcome their feelings of inadequacy, maladjusted children need to cultivate resourcefulness in problem solving—both in school tasks and in dealing with the frustrations of their lives. They need the self-confidence which comes from mastery of useful academic, social, and play skills. These achievements take time. In the meantime, maladjusted children need tolerance and understanding of their anxiety-motivated, self-defeating, and often class-disturbing behavior. The child's impulses to constructive achievement and his sporadic manifestations of self-confidence must be nurtured.

In the case of the maladjusted child, the other six conditions of effective learning take on even greater significance. While the teacher seeks to improve the child's mental health, she gives extra attention to factors which will increase his learning efficiency. In order to ensure the confidence-building success the child needs, the teacher adjusts his curriculum to his level of *readiness* and pattern of abilities. Besides ensuring successful completion of worthwhile tasks, the teacher supplements such *motivation* with encouragement and manifestations of confidence in the child's potentialities. In periods of problem-solving difficulties and uncertainty of outcome, the teacher rewards the child's willingness to try, his initiative, and his participation. The teacher avoids such anxiety-provoking motivation as threats, competition, and excessive concern for success and avoidance of failure. Since the maladjusted child is often especially anxious and unconfident in approaching new problems, his teacher clearly *structures* new tasks for him. At each level of progress, he is given sufficient and varied *trials* of a concept or skill so that he will establish confidence before proceeding to the next level. The *checking* of provisional trials is managed in self-enhancing ways which avoid arousing anxiety or inhibiting the trial-and-check process.

For example, when a retarded reader read "seventeen" as "silver," the mental health–oriented teacher still found occasion for encouragement. He said: "That was a good trial on 'seventeen'; you got both the 's' and 'v' sounds, and we have discovered that we need to examine such words more completely." In proceeding, however, the child needs more than correction of the specific error. By learning to apply *transfer* principles, he increases his learning power. The maladjusted child needs to feel the self-enhancement that comes from seeing that he is becoming more effective as a learner and problem solver. Therefore, in this instance of learning to read "seventeen," the child is taught *generalized* word-identification procedures.

Since each maladjusted child is a unique personality, we need to individualize mental health guidance. Seeing the child and his situation from the point of view of his particular needs—as we succeeded in doing in the case of Elaine—the teacher is able to give appropriate help at the right time. The general principles developed here and in Chapter 12 suggest tentative hypotheses for meeting the needs of individuals.

For overaggressive children, we try to reduce the frustrations in their lives—at home, in school, or in their peer relations. When the frustrations arise from unfortunate parent-child relations, as they did for Elaine and Mike, the school can often provide security-giving and confidence-building compensations. When the anger-provoking frustration occurs in the classroom, teacher guidance of the right kind and at the right time can prevent its disruption of learning and at the same time instill in the child feelings of trust, worth, and self-confidence. For example, "Ned was having trouble with decimal points in a multiplication problem." Noticing the frown on his face, his teacher "walked to his seat and asked him what was wrong. He said he couldn't do the problem. With patient questions she helped him figure out the answer and, in doing so, helped him to understand the rule and the reason for it. Then she gave him another problem. Later, when he had solved it, he brought the paper to her desk. All she said was, 'That's right [55, p. 191].'" But in this strategic incident, she helped Ned over a specific frustration, guided him in generalizing an effective and more confident approach to such problems, and enhanced his self-respect.

Helpless and overdependent children like Mary—who inhibited the trial-and-check process because she could not risk making a mistake—also need appropriate help at the right time. The following case illustrates what is needed. Jack was in the habit of leaving his work unfinished for fear of failure and criticism; now he merely stared at his just-begun arithmetic problem. His alert teacher, sensitive to Jack's need on such occasions, relieved his fear by her manifestation of interest and encouragement: "It's right as far as you have gone [70, p. 134]."[1] By appropriate guidance in getting started, by encouragement for a beginning, and by occasional checks on the child's

[1] Reprinted from Vol. 74, 1953, of *Education*, used by special permission of The Bobbs-Merrill Company, Inc., Indianapolis, Indiana.

*Encouragement and teacher guidance at the right time ensure a completed assign-
ment, plus increased confidence and worth instead of inferiority and guilt.* (Edith
Bowen Laboratory School, Utah State University, Logan, Utah.)

progress through a problem, helpless and overdependent children can
be guided to the completion of school tasks. Because of such help
they leave school not with the guilt of unfinished assignments on their
minds, but with confidence and esteem-building satisfaction of constructive achievement.

Children like Ann, who withdraw from school learning activities
to self-isolation, artificial roles, or daydreaming, need gradual reintro-
duction to the greater satisfaction of constructive participation. Otherwise, they continually reinforce their self-defeating escapes—as Ann
did in merely acting as though she could read. Johnson suggests that
mental health guidance for such children involves enhancing the
child's self-concept and confidence—by legitimate praise for any constructive effort, by giving the child responsibilities within the areas
of his competency, and by inviting his active participation in classroom activities where his success is assured. All these activities, he

further suggests, should be conducted without pressure—in an atmosphere conducive to feelings of security and relaxed calmness [36].

Supervision of peer relations. Academic achievement and good social adjustment are to some extent reciprocally related. Each favorably affects the other and both are conditions of mental health. Every child needs the acceptance, love, and esteem of his peers. If he feels rejected and disapproved by them, he may react counteraggressively, as Mike and Elaine did. With differences in personality and circumstance, other maladjusted children try to adjust in other ways. In most such instances, however, the child's anxiety-motivated behavior proves ineffective in winning friends, and his self-defeating efforts often interfere with his constructive and creative efforts in the classroom.

For such children, teacher guidance in social activities and the enlistment of aid from the child's peers are helpful. We have already observed the sympathetic response of Elaine's classmates to the teacher's invitation: "Are there things we can do to make Elaine feel happier with us?" In a similar teacher-led discussion, it was decided that Ray's belligerent behavior on the playground resulted from his feeling that the other boys didn't like him, since they never chose him as a leader in their games. When his classmates began to give him such recognition and encouragement as election to the position of class treasurer, his behavior became more constructive. For several weeks he was not involved in a fight. He made praiseworthy contributions to class discussions which won the respect of his classmates. And his general interest in schoolwork improved [15, pp. 68–69]. Cathy, who was new in the school, was helped to overcome her shyness by teacher guidance which enhanced her relations with her peers and gained their acceptance of her [23].

The sensitive teacher understands the social needs of children and is resourceful in suggesting and arranging satisfying and confidence-building social activities for them. She finds many opportunities to help maladjusted children—in the classroom, lunchroom, at school parties and in other student gatherings, and on the playground. The teacher can find opportunities for children to use their special talents in these situations and thus enhance their confidence. Children who have difficulties in establishing friendly relations can be given opportunities to come into contact with potential friends—through seating arrangements, appointments to committees and special work groups. Children whose social skills and standards are unacceptable to their group can be given special coaching to make them both more socially acceptable and self-confident. Children who need confidence-inspiring experiences and aid in making social contacts can be selected to help with school routines, such as distributing materials, arranging materials on the bulletin board, or aiding in conducting a science demonstration [17].

It is sometimes suggested, however, that special social treatment of the maladjusted child is undemocratic and, furthermore, that his presence in the classroom is an unjustifiable disturbance to other children. But there are good reasons why he should be accepted in the regular classroom whenever it is at all possible. For his recovery, the disturbed child needs to participate as much as he can in the normal academic and social activities of the school [24]. Moreover, normal children can learn to understand the unusual behavior and special needs of maladjusted children. With developed confidence in their teacher, they can appreciate his acceptance of the disturbed child, despite the child's annoying behavior. Since healthy children are free of the anxiety which motivates the maladjusted child, there is no danger that they will automatically imitate his behavior. On the contrary, with their sympathetic helpfulness—which appropriate interpretation of the maladjusted child's behavior can elicit—he is likely to begin emulating the healthy children [32]. Understanding why the maladjusted child needs (because of anxiety) to express his unusual symptoms helps other children both to accept the special arrangements and things done for him and to realize (with greater security) that, should they meet similar problems, they also would be treated tolerantly and helpfully [24].

Teacher counseling of children. Although the classroom teacher is usually unqualified to function as a psychotherapist or as a professional school counselor, there are many informal counseling situations in which he can serve effectively [22]. In occasional individual pupil-teacher conferences in the classroom and in short counseling sessions during the teacher's free periods, he can provide a warm, friendly atmosphere in which the maladjusted child feels accepted and free to express his fear, anger, and other disturbing feelings, as well as his aspirations and hopes. By openly recognizing the child's view of himself and his problem situation and by giving his problems a simple interpretation which he can understand, the teacher-counselor can often help a child achieve both self-understanding and a more healthy concept of himself and his world. Such reorientations of self-concepts and of interpersonal attitudes came out in the teacher's afterschool interviews with Elaine. At first, Elaine complained of her supposed maltreatment by her classmates. But in later interviews she could evaluate the situation more objectively.

As the child works through his adjustment problems, the teacher-counselor can play several different roles, depending on the child's needs. Sometimes he supplies information which helps the child understand and solve a problem. At other times he becomes the security-giving, reassuring substitute parent. At still other times, he plays the role of a peer with whom the child has troubled relations—permitting the child vicarious trial and checks of alternate modes of approach to a better relationship. Often he is the confidant who listens sympathetically and, by his reactions, helps the child to achieve a greater understanding and acceptance of his feelings and to gain increased confidence in his decisions [57].

The last-named of these teacher-counselor roles is illustrated in some excerpts from Arbuckle's report of the latter half of a free-period interview between Peter and his teacher [5, p. 135]. Peter's unhappiness over his mother's objection to the girl he had chosen to take to the senior prom had precipitated a critical decision he had been considering.

S: Miss Foster, I've been wanting to tell you about my mother and father. Did you know they just got a divorce?

C: No, I didn't, Peter. (By this simple response, Peter is sympathetically invited to continue.)

S: Well, it was in the paper. I thought you might have seen it. I felt pretty bad about it.

C: You felt pretty bad about . . . (Reflecting his expression, the teacher indicates that she understands how Peter feels.)

S: Yes, you see my sisters and I are with my mother now. My sisters are in the fourth and sixth grades, and I think it would be nice if the family were all together for their sake, but I realize it wouldn't be pleasant hearing my mother and father quarrel all the time. My father was pretty unreasonable and I guess my mother will be better off without him, and so will my sisters. They were afraid of him. As for me, I could always get along with him. It doesn't matter too much to me, though, because I've just about made up my mind to go to Florida to work with relatives who own some orange groves. Don't you think it would be O.K. for me to go?

C: Well, there are many things to consider, Peter. (Peter's request for support for his decision is met with a suggestion for an approach rather than with an evaluation of his decision.)

S: I have thought it all over. My father sends my mother money and she is going to work, so I won't have to worry about helping to support them. Besides, my ideas and my mother's are entirely different on so many things. You know that, Miss Foster, as I've talked with you a lot about them. And when I'm on my own, making my own living, I can do what I think right without hurting her. I know my ideas are just as right as hers, only my ideas are American. Hers are Old World and she won't change. Yes, I'm going to go to Florida. After all, I'll be 19 before I graduate next month, and I think I'm old enough to make up my own mind. Aren't you going to wish me luck, Miss Foster?

C: Of course, Peter. I hope you get the job you want out in Florida, and that you are successful. Good luck to you! (Leaving the

decision entirely to Peter, he is still reassured by his teacher's acceptance of his thoughtful, problem-solving procedure.)

Feeling that he is understood and accepted by an interested and sympathetic person whom he trusts, Peter is now able to act more confidently on his decision.

As in the case of Elaine, sharing some work with his teacher—such as getting the art materials ready for the next day's project—can provide a therapeutic relationship for the maladjusted child. Jersild says [35, pp. 282–283]:

> The common task makes it possible for the child to be silent when he chooses, yet his nearness to the adult makes it possible for him to talk about the work or about himself if he so desires. The work makes it possible for him to make mistakes and to observe that he will not be condemned, to proceed slowly and observe that this adult is not going to hurry him, to venture a little criticism while observing that it brings no retaliation, to express self-reproach about his own lack of skills while observing that he is not therefore abandoned as a failure, and so on. The child, without having to ask for help, or seeming like a weakling or a beggar, can explore this relationship, exploit it, and venture into an expression of his feelings and grow in his understanding of what might be expected of others as well as in awareness of his own wishes and his own rights.

Parent-teacher cooperation. Since parent-child relationships are usually significant in causing and in correcting a child's maladjustment, ways of helping him are often suggested in parent-teacher conferences. Such conferences enrich both the teacher's and the parent's understanding of the child, and together they can plan the home and school experiences a child needs for better mental health. For example, when Randy's teacher learned about his talent and interest in model-plane and boat building, she found an effective lead for motivating his remedial reading efforts [23]. The discovery in a conference with Cathy's mother that Cathy was confident and full of fun at home indicated to the teacher that Cathy had the personal resources for overcoming her shyness at school [23]. She seemed to need, not psychotherapy, but only guided social opportunities. And by arranging more rewarding experiences for Elaine both in her home and at school, the teacher helped her to improve her social adjustment and mental health.

For effective, cooperative parent-teacher efforts in the child's behalf, the teacher should take the initiative in establishing a friendly, nonthreatening, working-together relationship with the child's parents. Meeting the parents at school or at their home, the teacher might suggest that by learning something of the child's behavior at home and by working cooperatively with his parents, he will be able to help the child more effectively at school. By listening with sincere interest and by being accepting and noncritical of parents as they talk with him, a friendly teacher can help them to allay some of their probable anxiety, guilt, and defensiveness with respect to the child's maladjustment. As the teacher discovered in working with Elaine's foster mother, it is often better to focus on the child's potentialities or on some minor steps already taken toward better mental health than to complain of his deficiencies. If a calm, objective, and interested attitude toward the child's problem can be achieved, the teacher and parent can proceed in problem-solving fashion to consider the child's needs and potential resources, and to work out specific ways of helping him grow toward more healthy development. If, however, the parents remain anxious and defensive, or if the child's problem seems to require it, more expert professional help should be sought [54].

Professional mental health consultants. Schools and school districts are increasingly providing such mental health consultants as school counselors, school psychologists, social workers, specialists in remedial teaching, and psychiatrists. When they work as a team, the specialists and the teacher can contribute substantially to the mental health development of school children. The joint efforts of the teacher and the school psychologist in identifying, diagnosing, and treating Elaine's mental health problem illustrate the effectiveness of the team approach. When children with severe emotional or social problems are identified, the teacher's professional responsibility is to refer the child to such mental health specialists. He should not, of course, assume diagnostic or treatment responsibilities beyond the limits of his training.

Although we have included in this discussion several criteria of mental health and maladjustment, it is not easy to apply them in judging the severity of mental health problems. It is always safer to err on the side of seeking the help of specialists than to assume that the teacher alone can manage a borderline problem of maladjustment. Although the teacher was probably right in helping Cathy to overcome her shyness, in the case of Evelyn, who was deeply withdrawn both at home and in school, the teacher was wise in referring her for psychiatric help [23]. And in the case of Peter, Miss Foster (who had some training in counseling) probably did not exceed her responsibility in reflecting Peter's feelings as he reconsidered in the interview his decision to leave home for work elsewhere.

Working cooperatively with teachers, the mental health specialists help identify children who need mental health guidance. By an integrated consideration of all the behavior- and test-determined symptoms, they contribute to a diagnosis. They participate in a comprehensive search for the causes of maladjustment—in the child's school activities, family relationships, peer relationships, and in the personality study of the child. And on the basis of a better understanding of the child and of the factors affecting his behavior, the teacher-specialist team plans and arranges for the experiences which will satisfy his basic needs for security, love, mastery, and esteem; for expression of his talents and interests; and for developing healthier, more effective modes of adjustment.

The specialist's job is to supplement the teacher's guidance; the joint efforts of the specialist and the teacher help the child to improve in both mental health and academic achievements. There are several reports, such as the one we have on Elaine, which deal with the response of individual children to multiple mental health efforts. For example, 10-year-old David, in the fifth grade and with an IQ of 115, earned grade equivalents of 3.2 in reading, of 3.4 in spelling, and of 5.4 in arithmetic. Probably as a consequence of poor parent-child relationships (related to the divorce and subsequent remarriage of his mother), he had become both emotionally maladjusted and educationally retarded. He felt inadequate, cried easily, was restless, anxious, and unhappy. During four months of both remedial teaching and psychotherapy, however, this bright boy gained one year in spelling and two years in reading; he grew more confident in his relations with his peers and became better adjusted to them [47].

An evaluation of group counseling—in which underachieving junior high school students discussed school frustrations, parent-adolescent conflicts, unhappy peer relations, and personality problems —revealed that the counseled group made slightly greater gains in achievement, social acceptance, and in self-inventoried personal and social adjustment than did a comparable noncounseled group [16].

SUMMARY

The case study of Elaine illustrates the cooperative roles of the classroom teacher and the school psychologist in the identification, diagnosis, and mental health guidance of a maladjusted school child. Such children are not rare in our schools. Estimates of their frequency range from about 10 per cent seriously maladjusted children to about 30 per cent poorly adjusted. And it is possible that better mental health would improve the efficiency and happiness of every school child.

Since mental health is both an essential condition of effective learning and an important educational objective, teachers need to understand procedures for appraising its quality. They also need to be aware of the factors in its development, and they need to learn ways of improving it. Observation, anecdotal records, rating scales and check lists, classmates' opinions, self-inventories, interviews, and projective methods are all ways of identifying maladjusted individuals or of appraising the quality of an individual's mental health. In early childhood, parent-child relationships are especially significant in fostering or in hindering the development of mental health. Later, the school, the peer culture, and various social relationships become important. Like the home, the school can contribute to either the mental health or the maladjustment of children. Mental health is fostered and maladjustment prevented or corrected by appropriate procedures in six areas of school experience or service: a suitable curriculum for every child, the application of mental health principles in teaching procedures, supervision of peer relations, teacher counseling, parent-teacher conferences, and the joint efforts of teachers and professional mental health consultants.

GUIDES FOR STUDY, REVIEW, AND APPLICATION

1. Dr. William C. Menninger estimates that the proportion in our population for whom mental illness is a hazard is 1 in 1. Is this true for school children? What proportion of them would probably fail to attain both the academic and mental health objectives of the school without special mental health guidance?
2. What resources for correcting maladjustment and for fostering mental health are brought out in the case study of Elaine? Can you find illustrations of other resources for mental health guidance?
3. For appraising the quality of children's mental health, what procedures are available to the teacher—for his own or an assisting specialist's use? What are the distinctive features, uses, and limitations of each procedure?
4. What kinds of parent-child relationships foster (or hinder) the development of mental health?
5. Teachers foster the development of mental health in children by providing (a) a suitable curriculum, (b) effective and appropriately modified instruction, (c) guidance of the child's in-school social experiences, (d) direct help with his personal problems, (e) indirect help through cooperation with his parents, and (f) for utilization of professional mental services. Explain and cite examples of these procedures. They are well illustrated in the film *Meeting Emotional Needs in Childhood: The Groundwork of Democracy* (32 minutes), New York University.

Chapter 14

SOCIAL LEARNING IN THE CLASSROOM

Social interaction is an important feature of the typical classroom. For example, out of 166 classroom behavior episodes recorded for Raymond in a single day, 70 per cent of them involved interaction with one or more other persons [82]. Such social interaction provides significant opportunities for both self-discovery and teacher-guided social learning. And since the development of effective social interaction is both an important educational objective and a condition of effective group learning, we are interested in taking full advantage of the opportunities which these contacts present. As an illustration of teacher-guided social learning, let us observe how an alert teacher utilized an especially significant social-interaction episode in the attainment of both social and academic objectives.

The fourth grade boys were playing chase on the school playground. As Billy dashed around the corner, he ran smack into Johnny's brand-new bike. There was a loud report, and everyone saw that the back tire of Johnny's bike was flat. Billy, who had never been well accepted by the group, stood facing the anguished Johnny. The teacher approached the group just in time to hear Johnny's accusation: "You'll have to pay for this. My dad will be so angry!"

As he listened to the clamoring reports, the teacher discovered that the front tire of the bicycle was highly inflated. He questioned Johnny and learned that he had added air to his tires in the morning—without the help of the garage attendant. He directed Johnny to feel the front tire and advised him to let out some of the air. Then, postponing the problems of Johnny, his bike, his father, and unpopular Billy's part in it, the teacher sent Johnny to a nearby store to purchase some penny balloons.

When Johnny returned with the balloons, the teacher blew one of them up to average size, tied it securely, and had one of the children get permission to put it in the lunchroom refrigerator. Then, blowing up another balloon, the teacher explained that air takes up space. The children contributed to the discussion: "The more air you blow into the balloon, the bigger it gets." "If you put in too much, it will break the balloon." Later, when the refrigerated balloon was examined, the children noted that it had become smaller. They speculated that perhaps some air had escaped because the tie was not secure. Then the teacher placed the balloon over a lighted candle, being careful not to get it too near the flame, and the children saw the balloon slowly inflate. The teacher explained that warm air takes up more space than cold air and that was why the balloon had seemed to lose air when put into the refrigerator. As the children watched, the heated balloon continued to enlarge and finally—since the air could not escape in any other way—the balloon burst. Immediately the children applied their newly discovered principle to the problem of Johnny's ruptured tire. "Then Johnny's tire was something like that. The sun made the air expand." "Then Billy isn't really to blame." "This is something like Badge 714. You think someone did something, and they prove by science that he didn't."

Now that he could not blame "bad boy" Billy, Johnny had a new worry. "What will I tell Dad? He is going to scold me—he'll be so angry." One of the children suggested that Johnny show his father with the remaining balloons what had happened. Since Johnny had really been trying to take good care of the new bike, but had not known the principle he had just learned, his classmates believed that his father would understand and not blame Johnny.

Such social-behavior episodes make the classroom a unique laboratory for multiple learnings. The social situation often gives both significant meaning and high motivation to academic lessons. As a laboratory for lessons in human relations, the classroom facilitates self-

*Sensitive teachers
help children
understand themselves*

Sympathetic classmates help, too

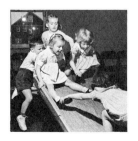

*In group activities,
youngsters take turns ...*

play various roles ...

Or are you
the do-it-yourself type?

The school is a miniature society:
children learn to work and play together

and learn to cooperate

and social development, understanding and tolerance of other individuals, and mastery of the concepts and skills needed for effective participation in many group activities.

Full utilization of such episodes and also the less dramatic social behavior which goes on every day in our classrooms and on our playgrounds requires that we understand personal-social development. We shall therefore study in this chapter the opportunities in the classroom for social satisfactions and for learning appropriate social behavior; the "self" and the factors affecting its development; the relationship of an individual's self-concept to his social behavior; teacher guidance of self- and social development; the problem of classroom discipline; and how to appraise progress in social learning.

SOCIAL DEVELOPMENT AND SATISFACTIONS IN THE CLASSROOM

As a laboratory for social learning, the classroom provides opportunities for (1) satisfaction of social needs, (2) self-discovery social learning and development, (3) guidance in learning the techniques of effective group action and problem solving, (4) learning differentiated social roles, (5) development of responsiveness to social motives, and (6) development of healthy self-concepts and self-acceptance.

Satisfaction of social needs. The school, as a miniature society, provides for many of the social needs of children and youth. These needs, according to Fromm, include a uniting of independent personalities in a loving relationship with others, social opportunities for creative contributions, freedom for the individual to be original within the security of his group, feelings of confidence and worth in his concept of self-identity, and the satisfaction of wholehearted devotion to group goals [24]. Because of the deep joy individuals experience in being united in satisfying relationships with others, each child should find and develop in school a number of complementary, cooperative, group-serving roles suited to his unique talents and personality [56].

Social learning in the classroom. The many school projects on which children and youth work together provide functional opportunities for effective guidance of social learning. They provide opportunities in which pupils come to understand their social world, experience the joy of being contributing participants in it, and acquire the skills and appreciations of democratic living. In real-life school projects they discover or confirm the merits of cooperative planning and work. For example, although Stephen could make a small map by himself, the class working together could produce a better one—one on which the children could walk down streets, stop at crossings, and work the stop lights [40].

Children learn, however, that group achievement is dependent upon the individual participants, who can either aid or hinder the attainment of group goals. In experiencing group appreciation for their contributions, children learn both self-respect and respect for others. They learn that group morale—friendly, mutually helpful, coordinated effort—enhances both the efficiency and enjoyment of group work. In varied group projects, children find opportunities both for leadership and varied participant roles. Despite differences in original opinions, they learn that, by democratic processes, workable plans and actions can be achieved. And they learn both to enjoy and to share with others the satisfaction of constructive participation in class projects, such as the contribution of murals by the art class to the cafeteria.

Social learning is a concomitant of many academic activities, at both the elementary and secondary levels. Social interactions in secondary school social studies, language arts, home economics, physical education, science, mathematics, art, music, crafts, shop, and other subjects all provide rich opportunities for social learning. A high school debating coach, for example, says that "each member of the team must learn to work smoothly and efficiently with other members of the squad, the coach, and the critics. He learns to profit and to contribute in discussion with many other people."

Because their pressing personal needs are involved in academic-social learning, children are ready to do everything possible in such projects to accomplish their purposes. The demand for the success of their efforts often ensures provision of the conditions of effective learning in such functional learning activities. Academic-social learning should, therefore, be especially efficient. As the introductory illustration indicates, both the academic and social learning in such projects can be *well motivated*. The high motivation of such learning is exhibited in a child's comment as she worked on a stained-glass window as part of the preparation for a school Christmas play: "You don't need to worry—as soon as I see I'm not doing a good job, I'll put this brush down as quick as a wink [62, p. 139]." As the introductory illustration also suggests, the social-interaction problems which occur in the classroom invite *teacher guidance in structuring effective approaches*. The many projects of the classroom involving children working together provide the ample and varied *repeated opportunities* needed for improvement of social skills. Children also find occasions in the classroom to *evaluate the results* of their goal-directed social efforts. For example, one child observed: "Do you remember last year we never got much done because we never got started? Everybody wanted his way. Nobody is trying to push anybody around [now]. It's much nicer and I expect it will be nicer every year [40]."

Because applications of such social-behavior patterns as cooperation, self-controlled discipline in coordinated efforts, respect for the unique talents of individuals, group morale, democratic procedures, and the joy of sharing recur in many varied situations, they are generalized as principles, and thus children *transfer* them effectively to other situations.

Group problem solving. In our complex civilization, many problems—such as the development and use of atomic energy, the conquest of disease, the economical production and distribution of food, the improvement of education, and complex problems in many other areas —must be solved, not by individual workers, but by teams of several differently trained specialists. Besides these problems which *demand* a team approach, there are probably many other problems, ordinarily attacked by individuals, which might be more efficiently solved by groups. Recognizing the growing need for cooperative problem solving, teachers and psychologists are interested in exploring its possibilities and in improving its effectiveness. The production of a school operetta, the discovery of the several ways of solving quadratic equations, or the study of the unit "The Water Supply in Our Community" are typical of the problems which provide practice in group problem solving.

Like the individual problem solving we studied in Chapter 7, effective group thinking involves developing sensitivity to problems, the structuring and restructuring of approaches, the production of provisional solutions, tentative evaluation of the implications of suggested solutions, the testing of plausible solutions, generalizing, and extending the implications of generalized principles. It is quite possible that a trained group approach is more effective than a single person attack in all these aspects of problem solving. It seems probable that it is more effective especially in the flexible restructuring of approaches, in the production of varied provisional solutions, in the critical evaluation of tentative solutions, and in extending the implications of generalizations. Although these specific aspects of problem solving have not.been studied from this point of view, a few experiments indicate that for some kinds of problems, the group approach is more effective in general than is individual problem solving [48].

In preparation of school assignments and in complex problem solving, a group attack has proved advantageous. Klugman found that fourth to sixth grade children working in pairs solved more arithmetic problems, although at a slower rate, than children working separately [43]. Blue found that college psychology students who studied together in preparing complex assignments and in preparing for examinations earned higher grades than students who worked alone [6]. Although Marquart [51] found individual and group problem solving equally effective on mathematical problems, Taylor and Faust found the group approach more effective on complex Twenty Questions problems [74].

Told only whether the object they are to identify is animal, vegetable, or mineral, the participants in Twenty Questions ask a sequence of goal-directed, provisional questions by which they narrow the range

In solving problems, groups are sometimes more effective than individuals in using flexible approaches, producing varied provisional solutions, and critically evaluating such solutions. (Logan High School, Logan, Utah; photograph by Arlen Hansen.)

of possible solutions and finally identify the particular object. It is a trial-and-check process in which the checked information from each answered question leads progressively to the formulation of more revealing questions. Productivity of hypotheses, functional organization of accumulating information, and critical evaluation of tentative provisional trials are all needed. As Figure 14.1 shows, the average performance of 60 college students assigned to work in groups of 4 surpassed the average performance of 15 students who worked individually. The groups asked fewer questions, needed less time, and reached more solutions. It is suggested that the superiority of the

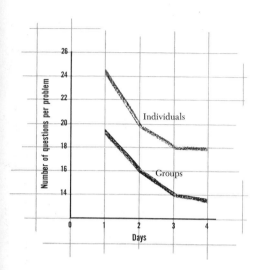

Fig. 14.1. *In complex, inductive problem solving, such as in Twenty Questions, teams of four college students are more efficient than single individuals in terms of the number of questions asked in reaching a solution.* (From D. W. Taylor and W. L. Faust, *J. Exp. Psychol.,* 1952, vol. 44, p. 362.)

students working in groups—in which they were allowed to talk freely —resulted from their possession of complementary stores of information, greater flexibility of approach, and more thorough checking of proposed hypotheses.

The effectiveness of group problem solving depends both on the nature of the task and upon the training and experience of the participants. When productivity per man is the criterion of achievement, individual work is usually better [48]. On some problems, however, where the attainment of a good solution is more important than the number of solutions reached per person, group problem solving is, as we have discovered, very effective. By learning how to work in groups, the efficiency of group problem solving can be improved. Yuker, for example, discovered that groups of students instructed to work co-operatively to produce a group product surpassed groups in which each individual was directed to see how much he himself could contribute [85]. And Perlmutter and De Montmollin found that experience in group problem solving improves the efficiency of subsequent individual work [59].

Two investigators report having improved children's effectiveness in group work. Chittenden, by training preschool children in better understanding of social situations, decreased their dominative and increased their cooperative behavior [12]. Rehage compared two groups of eighth grade social studies classes for both the mastery of social studies concepts and social learning. One of the groups participated in planning the aims and activities of the course. Without any loss in mastery of academic concepts, the planning participants surpassed the teacher-directed group in understanding group work and in the number of home-room projects initiated and carried out [63].

Productive group work depends upon the learning of effective cooperative and leadership roles. For successful participation in problem-solving discussion, for example, children and youth need to learn such leadership techniques as (1) formulating a clearly stated goal to guide participants; (2) taking initiative in making and evaluating problem-solving suggestions; (3) listening to others' suggestions, being sensitive to them, and integrating them into one's own thinking; (4) building on what others have said so that group problem solving is carried forward toward the ultimate goal, rather than being diverted or sidetracked along the way; and (5) making constructive rather than destructive criticisms. The classroom can make significant contributions to the mastery of such techniques and other aspects of group problem solving [64].

Differentiation of social roles. From discriminating observation of themselves and other participants in group problem solving and in other social activities, children discover that they play different social roles. Some children, like unpopular Billy, tend to play the same role in different activities. Most children, however, play a succession of roles at different times or in different situations.

The social and group problem-solving roles they play include (1) the initiator, who suggests new ideas, provisional solutions to problems, and alternative modes of action; (2) the information seeker, or information giver, who asks for or gives facts, clarifications, pertinent experiences, or generalizations related to group problems; (3) the elaborator, who develops the initiator's suggestions, works out the implications, and figures out how ideas would work in practice; (4) the coordinator, who pulls ideas together, integrates subfunctions, and coordinates the efforts of the participants; (5) the evaluator, who evaluates group accomplishments in terms of progress achieved, practicality, and goals attained; and (6) the follower, who goes along with the group. There are also, of course, such nonconstructive roles as the blocker, recognition seeker, dominator, help seeker, and special-interest pleader. Group accomplishments are achieved by the combined constructive and obstructive role-playing of individuals [4].

Responsiveness to social motives. Effective self- or teacher-guided participation in group activities provides many satisfactions. These satisfactions increase the attractiveness of group membership and cause individuals to strive for group esteem. The development of social responsiveness is expressed in several ways.

As children mature—from early childhood to adolescence—their identification with admired and loved persons in varied social roles becomes increasingly important, more important than the possession of material things. Preschool and kindergarten children learn to adopt the behavior patterns of the peer leaders with whom they establish agreeable and satisfying relationships. As children and adolescents become aware of group norms of performance, they tend to conform to them. For example, in setting aspiration levels on a series of tasks, both elementary school children and college students tend to regress toward the *average* of the announced performance of the group. Low scorers tend to aspire to relatively higher future performances and high scorers are satisfied with relatively lower performances [2, 35]. Depending on the goals and the guidance of groups, the pervading style of group life can make its members constructive, competitive, or hostile. However, by appropriate teacher guidance of the trial-and-check process through which individuals learn group techniques and loyalties, constructive group cohesiveness can be strengthened and the disruption of coordinated group efforts can be avoided [77].

In addition to affording opportunities for the satisfaction of social needs, for learning how to participate constructively in democratic group life, for becoming effective in group problem solving, for acquiring understanding of the differentiated roles individuals can play in group projects, and for becoming sensitive to social motives, the classroom is also one of several factors which contributes to the development of the self.

THE SELF AND ITS DEVELOPMENT

The self—organized in terms of the individual's unique talents and temperament and molded by society's conventions—emerges out of social experience.

The self-concept defined. According to Jersild, the self is "a composite of thoughts and feelings which constitute a person's awareness of his individual existence, his perception of what he has, his conception of who he is, and his feelings about his characteristics, qualities, and properties [39, p. 179]." As Mead has explained, it is comprised of the "me" (the observed and conceptualized self) and the "I" (the striver, the self-creator). By taking the attitude of others toward himself, the child becomes aware of himself as an object—as a "me [52, p. 226]." Thus, the "me" is the assumed, organized attitudes of others toward the individual. The "I" is the unique, self-assertive, impulsive doer. It is in the "I" that "our most important values are located [52, p. 204]." The "I," in striving for self-realization, seeks personal worth and esteem by worthwhile accomplishments, by acceptance of the moral responsibilities of his society, and by identification with admired people [52, p. 205].

The social origins of the self-concept. In his development of a self-concept, the individual introjects into himself the roles and attitudes of the community. He comes to view himself (as a "me") from the point of view of the generalized concepts he thinks others have of him.

The responses of other people to us are mirrors in which we see ourselves reflected, and from which we develop our conceptions of ourselves. From evaluative relationships with parents, siblings, teachers, and peers, the child builds a dynamic and expanding concept of himself—of his appearance, talents, habits, worth, and the ideal self he strives to become. Accepting the appraisals which the significant people in his life make of his characteristics and accomplishments, he incorporates these evaluations into his own self-concept as the "me" component of the self. The "I" is the knower and evaluator of the self as a "me." As an "I," the individual reacts to the introjected attitudes of others. In the harmonious self, the "I" accepts the "me" as it is reflected in the appraisals of others. In instances of self-conflict, however, the "I" rejects the "me." In either event, the child's developing self-concept—of competence and worth or of inferiority and badness—is an important determinant of his social behavior. For example, when a child feels accepted as a competent first grader or a worthy Boy Scout, he tends to shape his behavior to meet the social expectations of these roles [42].

Since language stimulates at the same time both the individual himself and others, it is the major medium through which the child takes the role of the other. As an example of a child taking the role of the other (in this case, the "me"), listen to this six-year-old in the role of mother, admonishing her doll: "Now you drink your milk. Drink it all down." In a more complex example both the "I" and the "me" are illustrated. On observing her picture in the local newspaper, a thirteen-year-old said: "I feel sort of guilty having the picture of *me* and my one-tube radio set in the paper when Ronald has a much more advanced set." Here the child is applying to herself the introjected community attitude that only distinctive merit (the best) should be awarded social recognition. As an "I" she responds to the "me" from the point of view of the introjected community attitude.

For effective, organized, cooperative action, the individual learns to take the attitudes of everyone else in the activity. The complementary, cooperative roles of individuals in a game or problem-solving group, for example, require that each individual be controlled by the expectations of everyone else on the team. From such social experiences, the individual introjects into his "self" an "other" which "is an organization of the attitudes" of the other individuals "involved in the same process [52, p. 154]."

DETERMINANTS OF THE SELF-CONCEPT

Coming to know oneself—as a doer and as a differentiated personality of unique characteristics—is a developmental, lifetime achievement in self-exploration. Early experiences begin to supply answers to one's questions: "Who?" "What am I?" And the answers are forthcoming throughout an individual's life. But, because the human personality is so complex and is continually changing, the answers are never complete or final.

During the first six months of life, the individual probably becomes aware only of comfortable and painful body states—of tension and quiescence. By the end of the first year, from varied social-interaction experiences, he begins to differentiate between approval and disapproval. He also differentiates agents, objects, persons, and acts of persons [66]. In the second year, he succeeds in mastering locomotion, manipulation of things, speech, and some eating and toilet functions —both with the support of and sometimes against the opposition of parents, siblings, and others—and the concept of "I" as a doer emerges. During the third and fourth years—from exercise of growing skills and initiative in many self-assertive situations—children begin to differentiate themselves from others as unique personalities. Three-year-old Alice, for example, announced, as she asked her father to retrieve her lost ball from under the couch: "I can't do it 'cause I'm too little." By five or six years of age, children develop both somewhat differentiated and evaluated self-concepts. They choose differentiated sex roles. They recognize what makes them secure and happy or frightened and angry. They interpret and are sensitive to the attitudes of others toward them. And they begin to feel competent ("I'm doing pretty good," says the proud five-year-old), worthy, and loved or inadequate and rejected [55].

With more maturity and experience, the child comes to understand the complexities of self and the differential and multiple roles an individual plays. Six-year-old Dave, for example, when asked, "Can you be American and Jewish at the same time?" says, "No." Nine-year-old Eddie, however, perceives himself as consisting of all the roles he occupies, and can say that he is both American and Jewish, all at the same time [29].

Let us now study some of the factors which affect the development of the self-concept. As we shall see, each child's developing concept of self is a product of parent-child relations, of teacher-pupil relations, of peer relations, of the inherent aspects of personality, and of the creative self.

Parent-child relationships. The child whose parents see him as a contributing, worthy, lovable family member comes to view himself in the same way. The child whose parents subtly convey to him that they consider him unworthy, a burden, and an unpleasant responsibility with nothing to contribute often appraises himself as reprehensible. Instead of recognizing the specific sources of his frustrations, however, he is prone to develop generalized attitudes of aggression— toward everything and everyone. Because of the guilt and anxiety which such attitudes engender, he comes to "operate as a superficial self in order to protect the real self within him [55]."

Nance has observed some concrete ways in which children's self-concepts come to mirror parent appraisals of them [57, p. 15]. When Bill's mother says: "Yes, at home we call Bill our artist. He made our Christmas cards last year," Bill is likely to incorporate this evaluation of his competency into his developing self-concept. Such a reflection of a parental attitude is explicit in Johnny's self-appraisal: "I'm the one . . . to see if doors are closed and lights are out when we go away. Dad says I never miss a thing." Unfortunately, some parents also express such negative appraisals as "I can't do a thing with him; he's stubborn just like his grandfather." Such appraisals often lead either to the development of a self-concept of unworthiness or to a counter-aggressive attack against the parents.

Despite the tendency of the child to accept certain parental attitudes, studies reveal only low correlations between parents' and children's attitudes, and indicate that parents are only one of several factors which shape children's self-concepts [33].

Teacher-pupil relationships. Successful experience in school and teacher approval contribute significantly to children's self-concepts of competency and personal worth. "Doing well in school subjects," "playing games skillfully," and "helping teacher" are the things which nine- to twelve-year-old children mention most frequently as making them "feel important." Being able to achieve satisfying goals, to help his classmates or teacher, to lead in some class activity, and to enjoy expressions of appreciation for his contributions—all of these enhance a child's sense of personal worth [22]. In the contrasting situation—of "constantly [seeing] himself with half-finished problems, incorrect answers, partially completed papers, with pottery which falls to pieces, or a picture he does not like," a child is likely to develop a self-concept of inferiority and unworthiness [44, p. 175]. As the following case study illustrates, however, teachers can help such children to change their self-concepts.

Charles, a 15-year-old high school boy with an IQ of 128 was receiving below-average marks in all his subjects. Furthermore, he was shy and retiring about participating in the classroom and in other peer groups. His small stature, low family economic status, the fact that his brother and sister were victims of cerebral palsy, and a humiliating experience when he was younger—all probably contributed to his feelings of inferiority, social timidity, and unproductivity. The humiliating experience occurred in oral reading when he mispronounced the word "washer" as "was-her." The reaction of his sternly critical teacher and jeering classmates made him feel that they thought he was "dumb." Apparently Charles accepted this evaluation, but he defensively tried to hide it from others. Because of his background of insecurity and

because of this precipitating incident, Charles learned to avoid further humiliation by not participating. He rationalized his underproductive behavior: "Why try—I couldn't do it, anyway."

Charles's selection of art as an elective course in the tenth grade provided the opportunity he needed to change his self-concept. His design for a linoleum block–printed Christmas card won from his teacher the comment: "Unusual and very artistic." The increased confidence this approval gave him and his teacher's guiding questions led Charles to think of ways to improve the design. Following his teacher's leads and other original ideas of his own, he produced a greatly improved design. It won the immediate approval of his teacher and the request that he exhibit and explain it, not only to his own classmates, but to another art class as well. He continued to excel in the art class. He was undaunted by any project, however challenging, and he was satisfied only with his maximum effort. This opportunity for constructive expression of his talent, his teacher's understanding, and the admiration of his peers helped Charles to achieve a generally enhanced self-concept and behavior consistent with it. As a consequence, his schoolwork improved; by the end of the second semester, he had raised his average mark from C to B.

Peer relationships. Children's self-estimates tend to agree with the appraisals of their peers. The self-ratings of fourth to eighth grade pupils on such desirable social traits as courtesy, popularity, generosity, dependability, honesty, sociability, and cooperativeness tend to correlate with ratings of them by their peers [1]. For adolescents, the correlation is approximately .40 between self-appraisals of competency and satisfaction in leadership roles and social activities and the reputations they establish with their peers in these activities [41]. The cause-effect direction of these relationships are, of course, ambiguous. In the light of our theory of the social origins of the self-concept, however, the correlations suggest that children and adolescents tend to incorporate into their self-concepts the appraisals of their peers. According to this theory, we can see that all children and adolescents need opportunities to gain the respect and approval of their peers. The following cases indicate that teachers can help in arranging such opportunities [44].

Matthew, an intellectually gifted twelfth grade student, isolated himself from his classmates because he did not share their interests in sports and was self-conscious with girls. Believing that Matthew needed social participation with his peers, his science teacher guided him in a project which not only permitted him to use his talent but gave him an opportunity to make a social contribution. Matthew extended his work in physics and installed a broadcasting system in the school. This successful experience enhanced his self-concept and won him more social recognition and peer acceptance.

Martha, a shy but intellectually superior eighth grade girl, revised and unified a group-prepared script for a class play and thereby increased the satisfaction of every participant. This role of inconspicuous leadership provided scope for her special talent and opportunity for making a social contribution, as well as enhancing social recognition and esteem.

Bert was handicapped in achieving social esteem by his small stature and low academic ability. By virtue of his craftsmanship, talent, and two weeks' zealous work in the shop, however, he made a satisfying contribution to the annual high school Christmas program. When his lighted decoration was placed on the front of the high school building, his needs for self-pride and social esteem were fulfilled.

The socioeconomic status of children affects peer appraisals of them. For example, of tenth grade students—from upper, middle, and lower classes—those in the upper class were judged more frequently as "best liked, most fun, and real leaders." Children from the lower class were checked more often as "not liked," "fights a lot," and "dumb" and they were chosen less frequently as best friends [13, p. 253]. Through individual guidance and structured participation in group projects, however, the social acceptance of the lower-class children was improved.

Physique, aptitudes, and temperament. Since favorable social and self-appraisal depend, at least in part, upon distinctive accomplishment in some activity, the individual's self-concept is affected by his basic capacities. Best-liked elementary school children, for example, tend to be high in athletic ability [49]. Because of Philip's ineptitude in baseball, his classmates avoided choosing him for their teams and he came to feel inferior and unwanted. Especially during the crucial years of rapid growth from preadolescence into adolescence, the child's degree of physical maturity is important in determining his self-concept of adequacy and confidence in such sports as football, basketball, or tennis [70]. Social acclaim and enhancement of the self-concept, however, may be based on any worthwhile talent—intellectual, artistic, musical, or mechanical. Different children achieve social and self-esteem by whatever discovered and developed talents they have—Matthew, for example, by his talent in physics, Martha by her talent for writing, and Bert by his talent in crafts. One experimental support of this generalization is Froelich's finding that individuals' self-ratings of different abilities tend to match their scores on tests of these same abilities [23].

The creative self. The self is not the passive product of biological endowment and of parent, teacher, and peer approval or disapproval. The "I" component of the self is a striver, a self-creator. Symbolizing the self and its development in time—including both remembered past experiences and imagined future attainments—the individual tries to shape his own life. Through his self-selected experiences and learning efforts, he creates his self—in so far as his talents and opportunities permit—in harmony with his symbolized aspirations. Each individual tends to become the self-actualization of his potentialities. According to Adler, the self searches for or creates experiences for development of the individual's unique talents for self-satisfying and socially constructive accomplishment. Motivated by his symbolized expectations of enhanced self-actualization in the future, the individual constantly strives for self-improvement. Being socially oriented and enmeshed in social interactions throughout his life, however, the individual strives for self-actualization in socially constructive achievement [28, pp. 96, 109, 117, 120, 122].

In such experiences, the individual supplements social appraisal with self-appraisal of the "me." We get a glimpse of this as we observe five-year-old Johnny's delight with the results of his self-improvement effort in pitching a basketball into a low-hung hoop on the family garage. After three or four attempts, he exclaimed to his mother, who stood by watching: "I got one in!" Then, rewarded with success once in every three or four trials, he continued: "I got another one—again—again—another one." Summing up both his satisfaction and self-appraisal, he observed: "I'm getting pretty good." In our society, such self-striving often goes beyond social-class expectations. For example, Bart, despite parental opposition to his educational aspirations, says: "I'll take 50 tests if it will help me get a scholarship . . . to go to college [32, p. 128]."

Identification with self models. As an aspect of self-actualization, the individual selects admired and loved persons as models to emulate. By incorporating the admired characteristics into his own personality —in a process which we learned in Chapter 12 to call identification—

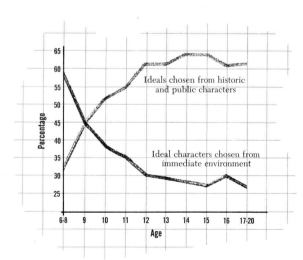

Fig. 14.2. *As children mature, their models for self-ideals shift from the immediate to the more remote environment.* (Adapted from D. S. Hill, *J. Soc. Psychol.*, 1930, vol. 1, pp. 379–392.)

the individual experiences satisfying enhancement of his self-concept. Self-models may be admired parents, siblings, teachers, classmates, relatives, or acquaintances, public figures, historical persons, fictional characters, or a composite of such figures.

Figure 14.2 shows us that younger children tend to choose the person they "most wish to be like" from their immediate environment —from among parents, relatives, friends, and teachers [36]. As they mature and extend the range of their experiences, children may broaden or extend the sources of their self-ideals. After ages nine to ten, children and adolescents select their self-models more frequently from the remote environment—from public heroes, historical and fictional characters, and from composites of ideal traits.

SELF-CONCEPT AND BEHAVIOR CONSISTENCIES

As the self-concept emerges and develops—a product of social experience, innate characteristics, and self-striving—it becomes generalized, stable, and an important determinant of social behavior.

Assured of being wanted and of being adequate in the groups to which he belongs, the child develops a generalized self-image—of being adequate, worthwhile, and esteemed. Feeling unwanted and rejected by his parents, teachers, or classmates, he may develop a generalized self-image of inferiority. But since such a self-image provokes painful anxiety, the child may defensively reject it, create an artificial self-image, or remain deficient in self-definition. As we saw in the preceding chapter, however, the child, in appraising himself on different personality inventories, tends to achieve a profile consistent with the needs of his self. Moreover, he tends to present himself to others in the same way in different situations. For example, Gronlund and Whitney found that for junior high school students correlations ranged from .67 to .78 between social-acceptability scores in three different situations—the classroom, the school, the neighborhood [27]. Gronlund also reports that when pupils are asked to choose the work and play companions they most prefer and when teachers are asked to select the children they most prefer in their classes, the same children tend to be chosen [25].

Because healthy self-concepts are continually rewarded and unhealthy self-concepts are defensively protected, the self-concepts of individuals tend to remain stable in time. Cantoni, for example, has shown that adolescents' and young adults' self-appraisals of the quality of their family, health, social, and emotional adjustments tend to remain stable, although they fluctuate in some ways [10]. He found correlations between test-retest *Bell Adjustment Inventory* scores on 211 subjects of .51 between ninth and twelfth grades, and of .35 between ninth grade scores and scores obtained nine years later.

The individual's generalized and stable self-concept becomes an important determinant of his behavior. By motivational control of his behavior, the individual strives to achieve performance levels—in schoolwork, on tests of proficiency, and in social activities—consistent with his self-concept [3]. The child who thinks of himself as apt in art, baseball, science, or social leadership strives especially for proficiency in these activities. Socially esteemed (and thus likely self-esteemed) individuals tend to participate effectively in group projects. For example, when individuals who are rated high on such traits as morale, productivity, interest in job completion, leadership, and friendliness work together in small groups, the quality of their group functioning also tends to be high [31]. As we have already seen, there is a significant correlation between adolescents' self-appraisals of their capacities for leadership and friendliness and the reputations they establish for themselves with their peers in these areas [41].

Self-concepts affect not only our behavior but our attitudes toward other people. The general attitudes one takes toward himself are often extended to other people. Among groups of adolescents and young adults, Phillips discovered substantial correlations between their self-attitudes of acceptance and respect and their appreciation of other people [60]. The self-attitudes were appraised by summing appropriate "True" or "False" answers to such self-inventory items as this: "I feel that I have very little to contribute to the welfare of others." The attitudes of these same individuals toward other people were appraised by summing appropriate "True" or "False" answers to such items as the following: "One soon learns to expect very little of other people." Among different groups of both high school and college students, the correlations between attitudes toward self and toward others ranged from .51 to .74.

Self-consistencies—within the self, between the individual's own and other people's appraisals of him, and between the self-concept and behavior—are not perfect. There are discrepancies. Because we strive for self-consistency, however, the discrepancies between different views of the self are frustrating. For maladjusted individuals, discrepancies are both more frequent and more disturbing. As Brownfain's research suggests, individuals whose "true," "hoped for," and "feared" self-ratings are consistent tend to feel self-esteemed and confident and to be judged as popular and well liked [8]. On the other hand, individuals with discrepancies between these different self-ratings tend to feel more inferior and anxious and to be judged as less popular and well liked.

Although self-concepts tend to be stable, they can be changed, as the earlier-mentioned case study of Charles suggests. And when self-concepts shift, behavior changes in corresponding ways. When Charles's self-concept was changed from one of inferiority to confi-

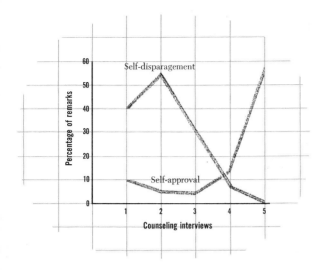

Fig. 14.3. *Individuals change from self-disparagement to self-approval in mental health–fostering experiences.* (From V. C. Raimy, *J. Consult. Psychol.*, 1948, vol. 12, p. 159.)

dence, his behavior changed from timidity and underproductivity to constructive social participation and productive scholarship. The relationship between the self-concept and effectiveness of behavior, however, is reciprocal. As is indicated in Figure 14.3, when maladjusted individuals achieve more healthy adjustments in their life activities—through counseling or mental health–fostering classroom experiences—they tend to "shift in self-evaluation from an original preponderance of disapproval to a preponderance of self-approval [61, p. 159]." This shift suggests that an important concomitant of mental health is a comfortable, satisfying self-acceptance. Such changes also suggest that the development of healthy self-concepts in children and youth enhances their personal and social effectiveness. Let us therefore inquire how the teacher can foster such development in the classroom.

TEACHER GUIDANCE OF SELF- AND SOCIAL DEVELOPMENT

The concepts, skills, and attitudes of congenial and productive human relations in the classroom are learned in the day-to-day interactions of the teacher and pupils. To foster such self- and social development is not inconsistent with efficient mastery of academic concepts and skills. In fact, the fostering of happy and effective social relations facilitates academic achievement. Classroom management—for both efficient academic learning and healthy self- and social development—is based on the application of the following principles.

Full use of resources. All the modern classroom's resources for developing effective social participation and leadership should be utilized. The classroom should provide children opportunities for success in worthwhile group projects, self- and social esteem in appropriate leadership roles, and exhilarating creative experiences in a social setting of secure, sympathetic, and loving teacher-pupil and peer relationships. All children should find suitable complementary and cooperative roles in which they work toward personal and group goals. In projects involving the complementary, cooperative efforts of several people, individual differences should be sources of group enrichment rather than causes of rejection.

The subject-child-society-centered curriculum of the modern school increases such opportunities. As we saw in Chapter 1, the group problem-solving approach illustrated in the project "The Water Supply in Our Community" provides rich opportunities for leadership and constructive social interaction. The high school core curriculum (which focuses on such otherwise separate subjects as English and social studies on community problems) and the often more comprehensively integrated elementary school curriculum produce both effective mastery of academic concepts and skills and superior social development. But when emphasis is directed to social objectives, the separate subjects, such as literature also contribute importantly to self- and social understanding [11, 14, 21].

Because democratic leadership is flexible and adaptable to the needs of varying situations, nearly every child in a socially oriented classroom is a potential leader. In the construction and management of a classroom store, for example, several different children emerged temporarily as leaders—as competent for a worthwhile job whose accomplishment was valued by the group. Because of his mechanical skill and experience, Chris took the initiative in building the store. Because of Jerry's talent in art, everyone recognized that he should create and paint the front sign. Laura served the group effectively by organizing relays of children to serve as clerks. Harry, because of his competency in arithmetic, was chosen first to keep the records. Other children labeled the merchandise. Since different talents, skills, and resources are needed in each new situation, leadership opportunities change. Thus, in this and in other projects, the leadership talents of

nearly every child are recognized. Teacher guidance of such student leadership should foster both constructive initiative and teamwork.

Teacher direction and pupil initiative. For effective academic and social learning in the classroom, we need to provide scope for both pupil initiative and expert leadership. Because of his maturity, professional training, greater experience, and the responsibility of his position, the teacher is responsible for the leadership functions of the classroom. By socially integrative leadership, he can provide pupils the opportunities for participation and initiative which they need for their social development.

Socially integrative leadership of group problem-solving projects is an experimental, trial-and-check process. On the basis of an appraisal of the goals, needs, and problems of the group, the leader guides the participants in the formulation of a plan of action, in trial courses of action, in the evaluation of observed consequences, and, if necessary, in reinterpretations and formulations of different plans and courses of action. Structuring and restructuring the situation to utilize the contributions of every member of the group, he guides the participants in defining goals, in exploring roles, in producing solutions, and in setting up criteria of progress toward their goal. The socially integrative leader aids the group in deciding courses of action by helping the participants to consider action in relation to goals, to anticipate possible consequences, and to see how action will, when evaluated, test the correctness of their approach. By getting volunteers, by integrating the efforts of participants in carrying through the project, and by continuous self-corrective evaluation, he steers the group toward their goal [75].

To facilitate group productivity and the satisfactions of the participants, the leader needs to establish cohesive, harmonious, and nondistracting interpersonal relations and to coordinate problem-solving efforts toward the accomplishment of curricular goals. In organizing individuals for effective group work, both the leader and the participants need to recognize, respect, and reward the talents, resources, designated responsibilities, and assigned or elected leadership positions of individual members. And each individual needs to feel free to make original contributions and to express criticism without fear of disapproval in secure, supportive, friendly relations within the group [38].

Although the teacher often assumes the major role of leadership, the democratic teacher also provides ample opportunities for student leadership to emerge and develop. In one such group, a child said of his teacher: "She works right along with you, but she knows more than you do so she can help you when you get stuck [17, p. 147]." To win socially approved leadership roles, students must develop leadership competency and skills. In assessing pupil leadership, children say they value the leader who (1) "sees that everyone gets to give ideas," (2) plans "things like we wanted him to," (3) knows "how to get started," (4) doesn't "act silly," (5) learns and improves his leadership skills as he leads, (6) creates a friendly atmosphere such as is implied in the comment "Mabel was nice to us so we had to be nice to her," (7) "gets things done," and (8) meets group standards as did Norma, who handled planning as well as any child could [17, p. 127].

As we explained in Chapter 7, teacher guidance varies in directiveness. For both effective academic learning and healthy social development, teacher guidance should not be autocratic and dominative. Imposing goals, giving arbitrary orders, demanding conformity, threatening penalties for deviations, and refusing pupils opportunities for initiative—all produce in children either submissive conformity or aggressive resistance to leadership. Such autocratic leadership also stifles creative productivity and arouses interpupil hostility, discontent, and anxiety. Moreover, when such leadership is relaxed, children are left without developed self-control, and they are then prone to become aggressive, unproductive, and destructive. At the opposite extreme of teacher directiveness, laissez-faire abandonment of the roles of leadership and authority also result in underproductivity, discontent, and anxiety [20, 46, 65].

Democratic, socially integrative teacher guidance—under which pupils share, as respected participants, in goal setting, in planning, in responsible problem-solving roles, and in evaluation of attainments—produces in pupils an enhancement of the self-concept, confidence, spontaneity, and resourcefulness. Under such guidance, children learn self-reliance; and in the absence of the teacher, pupil productivity and control are sustained [46]. As we have already implied, however, democratic teacher guidance does not mean laissez-faire abandonment of the role of authority. For his security and for constructive social development, the maturing child needs guidance, he needs to know what the limits to his freedom of action are, and he needs discipline. As Sanford has said, however, the authority should be of a kind the child can understand as desirable and can come to accept as his own. It should be imposed in the interest of group-accepted goals and in "a context of love and respect for the child." As the child gradually develops genuine social interest and self-control, teacher authority can be relaxed, and the child can be trusted as his own authority [65, p. 114].

On the question of the optimum proportion between teacher direction and pupil initiative, we have no precise answer. Some comparisons of teacher-dominated classrooms with those in which leadership is democratic and socially integrated, however, indicate that, while academic achievement remains about the same in both situations, healthy development of the self and social learning are favored in the democratically guided classrooms. Bills compared a control group of teacher-directed college students with a comparable group (in a course in mental health) which was taught according to democratic, student-centered principles. He found that the latter achieved more realistic concepts of themselves, became more self-accepting, and reduced the discrepancies between their real and ideal self-concepts [5]. In an elementary school classroom where pupils felt free to express themselves, participate in planning, criticize, discuss, create, and move about, Spector reports marked gains in social acceptance, as measured by test-retest scores on the *Ohio Social Acceptance Scale* [71].

Students vary, however, in their reactions to directive versus nondirective teacher guidance. According to Wispe's findings, preferences for teacher direction or pupil initiative are related to personality patterns [80]. Students who prefer directive teacher guidance tend to feel insecure, dependent, intropunitive, and critical of their teachers and classmates. Students who desire more freedom tend to be more independent, more extrapunitive, more favorable toward the course, and less tense.

The implications of such studies are that students need both teacher direction and opportunities for initiative in active participation in socially integrative projects, and that they vary in the relative degree of these needs. As children grow in self-reliance, in leadership qualities, and in group-participant skills, teacher guidance should provide for more independence, initiative, and creativeness—in terms of each student's particular pattern of interests, talents, and personality.

Self-enhancing teacher-pupil relations. By being sensitive, democratic, outgoing, warm, and loving; by giving sympathy and help when they are needed; and by sincere, respectful, and constructive guidance of children in problem solving, the teacher gives children the acceptance and appreciation they need for the development of these attitudes in themselves. By emphasizing children's positive characteristics, by avoiding calling embarrassing attention to weaknesses, and by self-respect-preserving discipline, teachers help children to feel accepted and worthy. By recognizing each child's unique contributions, by providing opportunities for the sharing of experiences, by cultivating group-work skills, and by developing understanding and appreciation of the different people of the world, teachers help children to value each other [78]. These are also the teacher characteristics which 14,000 children in second to twelfth grades mentioned most frequently in describing "the teacher who has helped me most." Such a teacher is "cooperative," "democratic," "kind," "patient," "fair," "consistently good dispositioned," "interested in pupils' problems," "flexible," "approving of pupils," and "proficient in teaching [81, p. 345]."

Sensitivity to social learning opportunities. Early in this chapter, we described an instance of a teacher's sensitivity to a significant social learning opportunity—an incident for learning a practical science concept and for learning how to be fair to an unpopular child. The more commonplace and less exciting classroom activities also present important social learning experiences. As Henry has suggested, the structuring of social relations in the classroom and the reinforcement of certain patterns of behavior affect the development of both children's self-concepts and their social behavior. Teachers who are sensitive to the social implications of classroom situations can facilitate the development of confident, creative, and democratic group participation. Other teachers unintentionally guide children to satisfy their needs for acceptance, security, and alleviation of anxiety by developing tendencies to docility, competitiveness, or intragroup aggression.

For example, when Charlie finished reading his self-created story of an exciting experience, his teacher invited criticisms. Lucy said Charlie should have written better sentences. Gert said they were too short. Jeanne criticized the position of a word in a sentence. Because Charlie had read "cracked" where he meant "creaked," Jeff sarcastically asked: "Did they [Charlie and his friend] fall through the stairs or what?" Gwynne and Rachel both said he should have read with more expression. No one mentioned any of the obvious merits of the composition. Charlie meekly accepted the avalanche of negative criticism. And his teacher—reinforcing the attack—finally added: "I guess we've given you enough suggestions for one time, Charlie, haven't we? [34]"

In another classroom interaction episode, a more sensitive teacher —by a few appropriate structuring and rewarding comments while acting as a democratic guide of self-discovery learning—led children to more constructive criticism [54].

HENRY: The other day I was painting at the easel. I left the easel to throw my paper in the basket and when I came back Leland had my place. I tried to tell him that I just went to put my paper in the basket but he wouldn't listen to me. So today when I went up to the easel Leland came and wouldn't let me paint again. He said he just threw a paper in the basket. He made me let him have the easel the other day, but when I did the same thing today he still wouldn't let me paint. I don't think he's being fair about it.

SANDY: Leland, if you made Henry give it to you, you should have done the same thing when Henry wanted it.

LELAND: Yes, but I had started to paint and I wanted to finish.

TEACHER: Henry wanted to paint too.

HENRY: Leland, you could take your picture off and finish later.

CYNTHIA: Henry, why didn't you put your name on the paper? Then no one could paint on it.

TEACHER: A very good suggestion, Cynthia.

PAMELA: Could we move the waste basket over near the easel? Then you wouldn't have to leave your place. I think it would be better anyway 'cause you wouldn't have to walk so far in quiet time.

TEACHER: We could try that. Leland, what do you think about this problem?

LELAND: I think, maybe, I should have let Henry paint.

TEACHER: But you are not quite sure?

LELAND: Yes, I am. If I did it to him I should let him have it. I'll take my paper off, Henry, and finish later.

Individually arranged social experiences. We have suggested how individuals—because of differences in their talents—can make unique and complementary contributions to their groups. Children also have *needs* for unique kinds of social experiences. For example, to enhance his feelings of competency and social acceptance, Philip especially needed esteem in a leadership role. Shy Cathy needed welcoming into her new classroom and social experiences in which she could feel wanted and able to contribute to the group. Elaine, in order to control her self-defeating displaced aggressions, needed warm acceptance, love, and indications of being valued by her group. In fostering healthy self- and social development, teachers need to diagnose such needs and then—guided by understanding of the principles of mental health and social relations in the classroom—to arrange the appropriate social experiences for each child. This principle is especially important in managing problems of pupil discipline.

Classroom discipline is a byproduct of effective guidance of academic and social learning. Thus, what we have already said about guidance of constructive social learning is applicable to the maintenance of classroom discipline. Let us, however, apply the principles more specifically to this problem.

DISCIPLINE

As we learned in the two preceding chapters on mental health, a child's neglect of schoolwork, resistance to compliance with school regulations, aggression toward classmates and teacher, or disruption of group activities are usually his reactions to frustration. He is sometimes striking back against his peers and teacher, who he feels have rejected him. But, as Elaine's classroom aggressions illustrated, a child's misbehavior in the classroom is often displaced aggression, the cause of which is frustration in out-of-school situations—in the family, peer relationships, or in self-development. Feeling rejected, inferior, unworthy, and guilty, and deprived of opportunities for satisfying development, some children behave uncooperatively or destructively in school activities.

Such children need constructive help. In Chapter 13, on fostering mental health, and in the present chapter, we have considered many of the opportunities which teachers have for helping children whose maladjustment is expressed in disruptive classroom behavior. As was illustrated in the study of Elaine, the general approach to discipline problems involves (1) a diagnostic study of the possible frustrations in a child's life and of his characteristics, resources, and needs; (2) help in providing opportunities for achieving security, self-confidence, and a self-concept of personal worth, social acceptance, and esteem; (3) guidance in more constructive social behavior; and (4) provision of other intrinsic and social rewards for better behavior.

Both mental health experts and children themselves agree that this plan of treatment is effective. In order to prevent or correct classroom misbehavior, 92 eighth grade children say that they want guidance rather than punishment or permissiveness. They say that interesting lessons, guidance, and encouragement would prevent their neglect of homework. To eliminate cheating on tests, they want help in succeeding and a chance to take the test over. And as encouragement in self-discipline when the teacher leaves the room, they want interesting work, trust and reward for self-discipline [68].

Self-discipline. The teacher's ultimate aim in guiding her pupils toward social development is to help them achieve rational self-discipline. Ordinarily, self-discipline involves some curbing of selfish desires both for the greater satisfaction of long-range self-interests and for the attainment of group goals. This means that children and youth come to be guided by developed ideals and goals toward which they strive—such as the mutual sharing of responsibilities, conforming to group standards (or deviating from conformity) in the light of long-range consequences, being dependable in relations with others, and being constructive, contributing participants in society [67].

As children and youth gradually achieve rational self-discipline, they are likely to pass through the following developmental levels which Cronbach has defined [16]. In infancy and early childhood, the child's social behavior is *amoral.* He makes choices without realization of the consequences of his behavior for other people. At the self-centered level, the child acts selfishly—impulsively, thoughtlessly, or sometimes with full awareness of the unfavorable consequences of his acts on the welfare of other individuals.

At the level of *conventional conformity,* the child chooses and acts according to his group's standards simply because he finds such behavior expedient and approved. He is not, however, guided by his ideals; he acts without thinking whether his behavior is right or wrong.

At the *irrational-conscientious level,* the child conforms to expected social standards, not from reasoned consideration of the welfare of others, but because of anxiety over the consequences of misbehavior. Johnny, for example, adopted the perfectionistic standards of his mother, not because of love and admiration for her, but because he feared harsh punishment if he should fail to conform.

At the highest level of self-discipline—the *rational-conscientious level*—the individual, guided by thoughtful foresight of the consequences of his behavior, acts to achieve his social ideals. Motivated by his love for other people and strongly committed to social ideals, he finds joy and self-enhancement in constructive contributions to his group and to society in general.

Rational self-discipline is the educational goal for every child, and mentally and socially healthy children attain this level, although not always at the same age. Many individuals, however, are arrested in their social development at the irrational-conscientious level, and some socially immature adults do not develop beyond the levels of conventional conformity or even of self-centeredness. By appropriate mental health therapy and social guidance, however, some children who are arrested in social development can be helped to attain higher levels. For example, when seriously hostile and delinquent adolescents were given acceptance, understanding, love, and constructive guidance in meeting the real problems which worried them, their interpersonal relations became more democratic, harmonious, cooperative, and friendly [15].

As an illustration of these principles and of the conditions of effective learning, let us observe a classroom example in learning self-discipline.

A lesson in self-discipline. A student teacher's report and analysis of an incident in which sixth grade pupils achieved greater self-discipline provides us a typical example of what any of us might find in a nearby school.

I had never realized before that teaching children to be respectful and courteous to other people requires the same conditions for effective learning as learning to read or to write. My observations of an effective lesson in courtesy, however, have taught me that these conditions of learning are general.

All over the nation, people were observing *United Nations Week*. The sixth grade I visited was planning and preparing a play about the *U.N.* for presentation to the children of the entire school. While their regular teacher, Miss M, was rehearsing a few members of the class in the auditorium, the remainder of the pupils in the classroom were taught by Miss H, a student teacher.

As soon as Miss M had left the room, the children began to see just how far they could go with Miss H. There was much whispering and giggling and throwing of paper. Miss H, being unprepared for such behavior, became nervous and upset. Fortunately, it was soon time for the recess and the children went out to play.

When the children returned to their classroom, they found Miss M again in charge of the class. And having had a report about their misbehavior while Miss H had been in charge, she was displeased.

Miss M explained to the class that she was not angry, but was very disappointed to learn that her class would act so disrespectfully to

anyone. Then she asked if anyone could explain the meaning of respect. Several children volunteered definitions. She then asked if they were reminded of any recent discussion of respect. Several immediately recalled the discussion of respect in connection with their study of the *United Nations*. They had learned that one of the purposes of that organization was to create respect for all people.

The children were then asked if anyone would like to express his feelings about his recent behavior in the classroom. No one was forced to say anything. No one was called upon. But several children said that they had participated in the mischief making, and they were now sorry and ashamed of their actions. Miss M then asked the children for suggestions about better behavior in such situations. One boy suggested that he should apologize to Miss H for his disturbing conduct in the class. Several believed that they had behaved much too childishly for sixth graders. The class also concluded that if they could make the practice teacher feel more comfortable with them, she would probably be a better teacher, which would result in a happier and more interesting class for all.

The student teacher goes on to report that—

. . . the children soon had an occasion to put into practice their new plans for being respectful to their practice teacher, and they experienced the improvement they had predicted.

Social learning in the classroom 491

Moreover, the student teacher also learned—

> . . . that the children became increasingly respectful to other people, not only to other student teachers and to classroom visitors, but also to each other. They didn't abandon all mischief. That couldn't be expected of active eleven- and twelve-year-olds, but the social relations in their classroom became much more courteous.

In her analysis of this social-learning episode, the student teacher points out applications of the seven conditions of learning:

1. *Readiness.* The children showed their readiness and maturity for this lesson by their immediate recognition that their conduct had been inappropriate and disrespectful and by their suggestions for improving their classroom behavior.

2. *Motivation.* Probably the main motive for their changed attitude and behavior was the "enhanced value" these children experienced in their more mature self-concepts. They enjoyed identifying with the "respectful" leaders of the *United Nations.* Acting like "second graders" was perceived as inconsistent with this self-concept; and they experienced greater satisfaction in playing more mature sixth grade roles.

3. *Structuring.* By her leading, thought-provoking questions, the teacher guided their thinking toward the self-discovery of more appropriate social behavior and attitudes.

4. *Trials.* The initial class discussion, the opportunity for trying out their new plans for more respectful behavior with the student teacher, and subsequent opportunities with other student teachers and visitors provided practice in self-discipline in the classroom.

5. *Perception of effects.* Because pupils perceived that the improved and happier classroom situation resulted from their more respectful behavior, and because they experienced greater satisfaction in it, the new patterns of behavior were reinforced.

6. *Transfer.* Understanding of respectful behavior was generalized from the *United Nations* discussions to their own social behavior. Transfer was illustrated in the spread of courteous behavior to everyone in the classroom and possibly elsewhere.

7. *Confidence.* The teacher, by "criticizing" the mischief of these children without anger or threat, provoked no fear or anxiety. They

did not need to become defensive about their behavior. And she gave them an opportunity to solve the social problem themselves; thus they felt more mature and confident.

APPRAISALS OF SOCIAL LEARNING

Like other kinds of learning, social learning is a goal-directed, trial-and-check process. Therefore, in order to give more effective guidance in this kind of learning, we need devices for measuring status and checking progress.

The teacher's observation of student behavior in interaction episodes will give some evidence of progress or change. Teachers can observe the quality of children's acceptance and participation in group activities, self-initiated activities, participation in complementary group roles, leadership in suggesting ideas or in directing and organizing work, group morale and efficiency, and group problem solving and accomplishments. By observing and interpreting children's behavior in the classroom, on the playground, and in other social situations, the teacher becomes aware of the unique social needs of individual children and of their progress in social development [84].

For appraising the different facets of social development and adjustment of children, the teacher supplements observation with the procedures described in the preceding chapter for appraising mental health: interviews, anecdotal records, check lists, rating scales, social-adjustment inventories, and the projective testing of the school psy-

Table 14.1. *Sociometric chart of responses of pupils requested to list their very best friends*

	A	B	C	D	E	F	G	H	I	J	K	L	M
A		X		X									
B			X		X								
C		X				X		X					
D		X			X						X		
E			X				X		X				
F		X	X									X	
G			X					X					
H						X							
I		X											
J				X			X						
K			X										
L					X								X
M												X	
Total	0	5	0	6	1	4	1	2	2	1	1	2	1

chologist. In addition to these procedures for measuring the quality of social acceptance and social interaction, teachers use such devices as sociometry and social-participation charts.

Sociometrics. Sociometry provides a means of summarizing, organizing, and quantifying children's opinions on the social acceptability of their peers and of their interpersonal relationships with them. It is especially useful in appraising status and changes in the friendship patterns and other interpersonal relations among pupils. A sociometric appraisal of a group produces a graphic picture of the verbally expressed interpersonal relations among the members. The technique usually involves four steps. First, the social factors on which the children's preferences are to be elicited are decided upon. Typical directions are: "List your best friends." "With whom in the class would you like to sit?" "Whom do you prefer as a companion in a work project?" First, second, and third choices or the naming of one to three or five individuals is sometimes requested. Second, sincere answers to such questions are obtained from all the members of a class or other group. Third, these answers are charted in a form such as Table 14.1, which shows the very-best-friend choices of the girls in a fifth grade classroom. Finally, the choices are graphically represented on a sociogram, such as Figure 14.4 [26].

In Figure 14.4, each girl is represented by a circle. Lines with arrows indicate the direction of choice of the friendship relations. Children D, B, and F—the "stars"—are the most popular children. Arrows pointing both to and from each of them indicate also that they are reciprocal friends. The single arrows from E, G, K, and A to D indicate that these children aspire to friendship relations with D, but that their preferences are not reciprocated. Both A and C aspire to friendship relations with other children; but since no other children choose them as best friends, they are regarded as isolates in friendship patterns.

The validity and significance of such friendship classifications need to be checked and interpreted in the light of information obtained

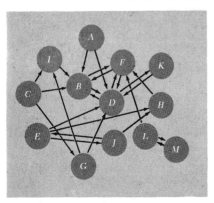

Fig. 14.4. *The sociogram shows the relative acceptability as a very best friend of each of the 13 girls in a fifth grade class.*

from teacher observation, anecdotal records, interviewing, and other procedures. If such further study confirms the sociogram in indicating that pupils A and C have no friends among their classmates, the teacher is alerted to try to provide for them the specific kinds of social experiences which further diagnostic study indicates they need. Remedial social guidance should be planned in the light of understanding each child's characteristics, resources, and needs. A knowledge of the general factors affecting social acceptance, however, is a helpful source of hypotheses.

In general, children who succeed in their schoolwork also establish good social relationships with their peers [9, 47]. Sociometrically popular children tend to be characterized by their teachers as well adjusted, dependable, and friendly. The social isolate is more often maladjusted, dominating, uncooperative, shy, or new to the class [25]. Olsen has found that a child's friendship status (star to isolate) on the sociogram is related to (1) his opportunities for home and other out-of-school association with his classmates, (2) the socioeconomic status and education of his parents, (3) his general maturity of development, (4) his mental health and social adjustment, and (5) teacher-provided opportunities for classroom responsibilities [58]. When any factors seem unfavorable for a child who needs better friendship relations, some of them can be improved for him. As general procedures for improving a child's friendship relations in the classroom, Elliot has suggested the provision of ample interaction opportunities for developing friendly peer relations, enhancing children's social attractiveness by improving their skills and social standards, and building appropriate social attitudes and confidence in friendship roles [18].

Participation charts. Leadership and other participant roles in class recitations, panel discussions, committee work, and other group activities provide opportunities for improving important social concepts and skills. In the goal-directed practice of social skills, periodic evaluation of the behavior patterns employed should facilitate improvement. Participation charts, like sociograms, give organization and some quantification to evaluative observations of behavior in such social situations. As a standard for evaluating social behavior, Thomas has defined effective group participation as including willing acceptance by a child of his share, contributing to discussion, keeping to the topic or problem, abiding by majority decisions, and permitting others to express their views. By observation of the discussions of such groups, a teacher can make general appraisals of the present effectiveness and development of the participants. By systematically charting their participation, the teacher can sharpen the accuracy and meaning of his observations.

The chart below shows a teacher's charted observation and evaluation of children's participation in a committee appointed to plan a phase of a social studies project. By drawing a line of appropriate length and in the appropriate cell as each child contributed to the discussion, the teacher produced a graphic record of the frequency, length, and value of each child's contributions. Excerpts from the discussion on which the chart was recorded follow [76, pp. 230–232].

Evaluation of Contributions	Participants					
	Chuck	Lyle	Doris	Gerry	Margaret	Kent
Major	/''''/	/' '	//'//	/		
Minor	'/'/' '/	'/	//'/	///		
Passive or doubtful	/	/// ''		/	'/	'/
Distracting		///	'			

CHUCK (the chairman): Well, now here's what we're supposed to be doing . . . Make a plan for showing how our town depends a lot on modern transportation for the way we live.

LYLE: You mean some way to show the rest of the class? A report or something?

DORIS: Of course, that's why we're doing it.

CHUCK: Kent, you have any ideas?

KENT: No.

GERALDINE: Well, some way we ought to show all the different kinds of modern transportation . . . like trains and the airfield and cars and trucks.

LYLE: Oh, sure, and bikes and scooters and kiddy-cars. Ha!

CHUCK: Well, Gerry's idea is a start. Margaret, any other ideas?

MARGARET: Gerry's suggestion is all right. The different kinds of modern transportation. But then that really doesn't show how important transportation is.

DORIS: That's right. Just think what it'd be like if all the cars and trains and trucks and airplanes stopped. What would it be like then?

LYLE: Maybe there's an idea. Maybe we could figure out what would happen if all kinds of transportation stopped. Like she says.

CHUCK: Then put on some kind of thing so the class would understand it?

LYLE: Sure.

GERRY: Thing? You mean a program, like a talk or a committee report?

CHUCK: Look. We have to give a report, but we don't want it dull. So why don't we make it like a radio program? You know, like trucks and trains all stopped and this is a news broadcast?

LYLE: You mean, a war or death rays stop everything. And then we see what our town would be like?

GERRY: That might be all right.

DORIS: Say, I know. You know that microphone and that . . . that big thing they use for the square dances in the gym.

CHUCK: You mean the loudspeaker?

GERRY: How would they hear us if we're in the other room?

DORIS: You just put the microphone in the other room and then run the cord out and put the loudspeaker in this room.

LYLE: Yeah, those P-A systems have a long cord. That'd work.

CHUCK: All right, now let's see what we've decided so far. We'll have a radio program and broadcast like news flashes. Have maybe some kind of rays shot down from Mars that stop all transportation. And the news broadcast will tell what it would be like if all modern transportation stopped. Agreed? (All nod and say yes.)

The chart indicates that Chuck and Doris participated frequently and most constructively. Lyle participated as frequently as they did, but his contributions were as often passive or doubtful and distracting as they were constructive. Gerry's participation was moderate but tended to be constructive. Margaret and Kent participated only rarely, and then only passively.

When such charts are examined and discussed freely by the participants, they become useful in facilitating social learning. During the group discussion, the participants are often distracted from self-observation of their own roles. The chart permits them to perceive clearly the extent and nature of their participation. It thus becomes a basis either for confirming the adequacy of their social efforts or for improving them. And subsequently made charts of other group discussions may reveal progress and thus motivate further effort.

SUMMARY

The numerous and varied social interactions which occur among elementary and secondary pupils make the modern classroom a laboratory for significant lessons in human relations, in which both academic and social learning are facilitated. For full utilization of the social interactions in the classroom, we need to understand (1) how they contribute to social satisfactions and how they facilitate mastery of social concepts and skills, (2) the "self" and the factors affecting its development, (3) the relationship of an individual's self-concept to this social behavior, (4) the principles of effective teacher guidance of self- and social development, (5) how these principles can be applied to classroom discipline, and (6) how to appraise progress in social learning.

The social relations in the classroom provide opportunities for the growth of love, group security, and feelings of confidence and worth in constructive group achievements; for mastery of group problem-solving techniques and other social concepts and skills; for differentiation and understanding of different social roles; for becoming responsive to social motives; and for development of self-understanding and acceptance.

The child's self-concept—of his appearance, talents, personal-social characteristics, and worth—emerges and develops as a product of his inherent potentialities and social experiences. The specific determinants of the individual's expanding and differentiating self-concept are his parent-child, teacher-pupil, and peer relationships; the quality of his physique, aptitudes, and temperament; and his own self-creative striving, for which loved and admired real or idealized persons often serve as models.

Although there are sometimes discrepancies within the self—between the individual's own and other people's appraisals of him, and between the self-concept and behavior, especially in maladjusted individuals—the developing self-concept tends to become generalized, stable, and a determinant of the individual's behavior. Whether a child behaves constructively or maladaptively depends importantly on his self-concept. And just as the child's self-concept is shaped by the attitudes of other people toward him, so his self-concept affects his own attitudes and behavior toward other people.

Effective teacher guidance of healthy self- and social development is democratic, integrative, teamwork-oriented, constructive, and loving. It utilizes the full resources of the modern subject-child-society-centered curriculum. It gives teacher direction as needed and also fosters pupil resourcefulness and leadership. It creates self-enhancing teacher-pupil and pupil-pupil relations. And it arranges the unique social experiences which personal-social diagnosis indicates each pupil needs.

Classroom discipline is a product of healthy self- and social development in constructive and rewarding socially integrated learning projects. In fostering self-discipline, the teacher applies the principles of mental health presented in the two preceding chapters, the principles of social learning developed in this chapter, and, in fact, all the seven conditions of effective learning which we have found applicable to both academic and personal-social learning.

In a goal-directed trial-and-check process, effective guidance of social learning requires periodic appraisals of status and progress. For appraising the multiple facets of self- and social development, the teacher uses observations of behavior, interviews, anecdotal records, check lists, rating scales, social-adjustment inventories, sociometry, participation charts, and psychologist-conducted projective tests.

In the next and final chapter, we shall study in greater detail both the general principles of appraisals of learning and the tests specifically appropriate for appraising academic achievement.

GUIDES FOR STUDY, REVIEW, AND APPLICATION

1. Despite the needs we have found for some individualized instruction of school children, why would a *completely* individualized program be unwise? Why is group instruction also desirable?
2. From observation and study of classroom group activities, point out both the valued products and the problems they produce. As examples of social learning in the classroom, see the films *Learning through Co-operative Planning* (20 minutes), Teachers College Bureau of Publications, and *Near-Home* (25 minutes), International Film Bureau.
3. For what kinds of problems does a group approach seem more effective than an individual attack? How can the effectiveness of group problem solving be improved?
4. Define the self-concept and show how it develops as a product of inherent potentialities and social learning. For a particular person whose self-concept you think you know, point out the roles of the major determinants of it.
5. How does the individual's generalized and somewhat stable self-concept affect his social attitudes and behavior?
6. In fostering healthy self- and social development in the classroom, illustrate the following principles of teacher guidance: full use of resources, balance between teacher direction and pupil initiative, self-enhancing teacher-pupil relations, sensitivity to social learning opportunities, individually arranged social experiences. For illustrations, see the films *First Lessons* (22 minutes), International Film Bureau, and *Elementary School Children*, Part I: *Each Child Is Different* (17 minutes), McGraw-Hill Text-Film Department.
7. Illustrate applications of the principles of mental health, social learning, and the conditions of effective learning to the problem of managing classroom discipline.
8. Describe the appraisal procedures and show how appraisals of status and progress in self- and social development can facilitate social learning.

Part 5

THE EVALUATION OF LEARNING

Chapter 15

APPRAISING LEARNING

Throughout this study of the contributions of educational psychology to teaching, we have cited many illustrations of how we appraise learning. Appraisals of achievement status and progress in learning are directly or indirectly related to all the major functions of teaching —to the formulation of attainable objectives; to the selection and organization of appropriate curriculum content; to the adjustment of curricular experiences to the levels of readiness and patterns of abilities of pupils; to teacher guidance of the trial-and-check process of learning; to determination of the needs for and effects of developmental social experiences; and, in general, to the periodic evaluation of the outcomes of instruction.

HOW EVALUATION FACILITATES LEARNING

We have seen that appraisals of pupil accomplishment facilitate learning because they guide teachers in providing more adequately for all the conditions of effective learning.

We saw in Chapter 3 that as children grow and learn they continually reach higher levels of readiness for learning. And we learned in Chapter 4 that, among the indexes of capacity for subsequent achievement, the best single index is a measure of earlier achievement. Therefore, periodic assessment of progress—in reading, language, mathematics, and other subjects—effectively guides both teachers and pupils in adjusting the curriculum to each child's emerging stages of readiness. Moreover, appraisals of differentiated talents guide us in providing curricula and teaching procedures adapted to each child's unique pattern of abilities.

In our study of the problem of teaching unique individuals in groups, we learned in Chapter 5 that measures of achievement can aid us in several ways. Since they are indicative of both present status and potential learning, our interpretations of achievement-test scores guide us in adjusting school progress to individual rates of maturation, classifying children into appropriate homogeneous groups, and arranging intraclass groupings of heterogeneous classes of children. The profiles of differentiated achievement of secondary school students guide them and their counselors in choosing appropriate elective courses. And diagnostic achievement tests contribute to the efficiency of individualized and remedial teaching.

We saw in the chapters on the conditions of learning that when pupil growth is broadly conceived, testing facilitates several facets of the actual process of learning. Test-revealed evidences of progress intensify and sustain the pupil's motivation. Interest inventories, as we learned in Chapter 6, can guide students and teachers in relating learning to pupils' individual interests—in science, social studies, biography, or fiction. The diagnostic evaluations of modes of attack in learning and the inventories of study skills described in Chapter 8 give students effective guidance in improving the efficiency of their learning procedures. We discovered in Chapter 8 that effective learning requires informative, precise, and prompt checking of provisional goal-directed trials. In a continual schedule of testing, teaching, retesting, and reteaching, tests facilitate the trial-and-check process of learning. Furthermore, as we learned in Chapter 11, review tests—requiring the integration and functional organization of accumulating concepts—facilitate the retention and application of the concepts and skills children learn.

Appraisal of learning is also important in fostering mental health and social development. As aids both in identifying children who need mental health guidance and in appraising their progress toward better mental health, we described in Chapter 13 the usefulness of teacher observations, anecdotal records, check lists, rating scales, self-inventories, and projective devices. These same procedures, plus the sociogram and participation chart described in Chapter 14, also guide us in arranging the social experiences children need for appropriate social development.

The foregoing illustrations suggest several different purposes of appraisals of learning, but in concluding this section, let us define the functions more precisely. In achieving the general goal of appraisals of achievement—the facilitation of learning—tests and other evaluation procedures are used specifically for (1) placement of pupils, (2) diagnosis of learning difficulties, (3) guidance of learning, (4) assessment of progress, (5) prediction of subsequent learning, and (6) evaluation of curricula and methods [34].

Placement. Appraisals which reveal individual differences in level of achievement guide us in the appropriate school placement of children. Knowledge of where a pupil is—his position in a curriculum sequence—indicates the next step for which he is ready. Such information, as we have already suggested, guides us in intraclass and homogeneous grouping, in assignments for remedial instruction, and in the placement of exceptional children in special classes.

Diagnosis. Analytical tests which make possible intraindividual comparisons of achievement in different subjects, or in the different aspects of a single subject, guide us in individualized instruction. Knowledge of a pupil's proficiencies, of gaps in his understandings and skills, and of his learning difficulties enable us to "pinpoint individual remedial work" and to adapt curricula and methods to his needs [33, p. 16].

Guidance. In addition to yielding specific diagnostic clues for the alleviation of learning difficulties, intraindividual comparisons of achievement provide general guidance of learning. For example, an inventory of study habits, like that described in Chapter 9, can indicate the specific goals—such as the improvement of reading, note taking, or reviewing—toward which a student should strive. In addition to directing the student toward desirable educational objectives, tests which yield knowledge of progress motivate sustained learning effort. As the student moves through each unit of instruction, comparable test scores in differentiated areas indicate the concepts he has mastered, the areas in which he needs further study or those in which he needs to revise his concepts [8].

Assessment. Comparisons of a succession of scores on tests with equal units of measurement yield indexes of pupil change or growth. Such measures of development—obtained by comparing status before and after instruction—are useful in assessing pupil progress and in appraising the effectiveness of instructional programs.

Prediction. The correlations mentioned in Chapter 4 between the earlier- and later-administered achievement tests show that present status on achievement tests is indicative of future achievement. Because of these established relationships, our confidence in estimating a student's probability of success in a given course is enhanced by knowledge of his prior achievement in the same or similar subjects. For example, as we learned in Chapter 4, a student's junior high school general science achievement is a good forecast of his probable achievement in high school physics or biology. Achievement-test scores earned in the first weeks of a course are indicative of final achievement. And, as we saw in Chapter 5, very high scores on an English usage test predict that college freshmen may safely bypass English 1 and succeed immediately with English 2.

Evaluation. In addition to the foregoing instructional and guidance functions of achievement tests, we also use them to answer the question "How well have we done?" We make evaluative uses of tests when we compare achievement under different curricula or methods, when we compare the achievement of a given school against national norms, or when we compare achievement "then" and "now," as we did in evaluating the modern school in Chapter 1.

EFFECTIVENESS OF TESTING IN FACILITATING LEARNING

By enhancing in several ways the conditions of effective learning, measurement improves school achievement—especially in the areas tested. Henmon, for example, has demonstrated that monthly testing of fourth grade pupils in reading, writing, spelling, and arithmetic produces gains beyond those otherwise expected [24]. Keys has shown that more frequent testing is even better. He found that 143 students given weekly tests in educational psychology exceeded by 12 per cent the final achievement of a comparable group tested monthly [29].

Tests facilitate learning in still another way. They tend to define for the student the particular objectives which are most important and which he must strive most intensely to attain. This effect of testing was demonstrated by the growth in mean score of a succession of tested shop classes. When a test of the specific shop skills needed for performance on the job was administered to the first of a series of classes, the students earned from 20 to 25 points out of a possible 100. As each successive class passed through the in-structural unit covered by the test, the scores increased. The sixth class attained a mean score of approximately 85, which is 300 per cent higher than that of the first class [13, p. 80]. In this instance, both the teacher and the students learned to work more economically for attainment of the test-defined objectives.

THE SCOPE OF ACHIEVEMENT TO BE APPRAISED

Since testing tends to set learning objectives for pupils and teachers, it is important to encompass in our evaluation of school accomplishment *all* the important educational objectives. Otherwise children would be effectively directed and motivated to attain only certain objectives and diverted from the pursuit of other equally important but untested objectives [8].

The wide scope and varied characteristics of educational objectives make their appraisal a complicated task. In addition to being concerned with the academic achievement of children and youth, we also want to develop constructive interests, aesthetic appreciations, mental health, worthy self-concepts, social effectiveness, and ethical character. Moreover—as we learned in Chapter 1—the elementary and secondary school objectives of self-realization and social effectiveness include the acquisition of different kinds of behavior: knowledge and understandings, skills and competencies, attitudes and interests, and

Table 15.1. *Procedures for appraising attainment of elementary and secondary school objectives*

Procedures	Knowledge and understandings	Skills and competencies	Attitudes and interests	Action patterns
1. Academic achievement survey tests	√	√		
2. Diagnostic tests of achievement	√	√		
3. Teacher-made achievement tests	√	√		
4. Observation of performance and products	√	√	√	√
5. Interviews with pupils and parents	√	√	√	√
6. Anecdotal records of behavior		√	√	√
7. Rating scales and check lists			√	√
8. Sociometrics			√	√
9. Participation charts			√	√
10. Self-inventories			√	√
11. Projective methods			√	

action patterns—in both the academic and the personal-social areas of the curriculum. Appraising attainment of this broad range of objectives requires multiple, diverse procedures. Fortunately, educational psychologists and teachers have developed several different types of evaluation and measurement procedures. In Table 15.1, we have listed the major types and suggested the kinds of objectives for which they are applicable [23].

Standardized or teacher-made tests of academic achievement, teacher observation, and interviews are appropriate for appraising the understandings and skills in Kearney's [27] areas of the social world, the natural environment, communication, and quantitative thinking, or in French's [15] areas of intellectual growth, cultural orientation, health, and economic competence. Such action patterns as "habits of eating wholesome food" or "living up to safety precautions in driving the family car" can be evaluated by observation or in a parent-teacher interview. Such attitudes as "interest and pride in his physical growth and development" or "not worrying continuously about physical or mental health" can be evaluated by a parent-teacher or teacher-pupil interview, or by a self-inventory. Such social and emotional development objectives as "volunteering to assume responsibilities and to carry them out" can be evaluated by pupil sociograms, teacher observation, anecdotal records, or a rating scale. These same devices are appropriate for evaluating such ethical-behavior objectives as "cooperating, sharing, taking responsibility, and subordinating self-interest in working with others." Such social-skills objectives as "leadership and cooperative membership in peer groups" or "being a courteous speaker or listener" can be evaluated by observation, sociograms, or a participation chart. Such intellectual skills as "observing accurately and describing carefully the results of individual investigations" or "practicing good study and other work habits" can be evaluated by observation of performance or by examination of student notes, reports, creative constructions, and the like. Quantitative skills such as "measuring, weighing, constructing, and reading graphs" can be evaluated by observation or by tests of actual performance.

These few illustrations suggest that effective appraisal of each objective outlined in Kearney's and French's long lists depends upon the appropriate use of one or more of a variety of evaluative procedures. In both elementary and secondary classrooms, teachers need to understand and become skillful in the use of all these devices.

At appropriate places in preceding chapters, we have described and explained the procedures in evaluating nonacademic achievement —procedures such as interviewing, anecdotal records, rating scales, check lists, sociometry, participation charts, self-inventories, and projective methods. Therefore, in this chapter we shall consider in detail only the procedures for appraising academic achievement.

Survey, multiple-subject tests appraise the achievement of pupils in the basic academic areas of the elementary and secondary school curriculum. The comparable scores and national norms of these standardized tests yield interpretations which indicate relatively how much a pupil has learned—both in the different areas of the curriculum and in comparison with representative pupils in the country. Since the tests cover broad areas of the curriculum, the sampling of concepts and skills is extensive rather than intensive. Although the several survey tests available are similar, they differ in the scope of objectives measured, in the span of grades covered, and in the specific content of the test items.

Such tests as the *Stanford Achievement Test* [28] and the *Metropolitan Achievement Test* [3], for grades 1 to 9, the *Essential High School Content Battery* [22] and the *Iowa Tests of Educational Development* [25], for grades 9 through 13, and the *Sequential Tests of Educational Progress* [9], for grades 4 through 14, are comprehensive in scope. They cover both the basic skills of language, reading, and computation, and also such subjects as social studies, natural science, and mathematics. These five tests differ, however, in specific content. The first three are intended to measure mastery of curriculum content. Consequently the items reflect the content of commonly used textbooks and courses of study. The last two, however, focus on more ultimate objectives and claim to measure children's abilities to use what they have learned. And instead of measuring the concepts derived from specific school courses, they are designed to measure general concepts which can be acquired either in the classroom or in out-of-school reading, work, travel, or other educational experiences.

Other tests are more restricted in scope. Such tests as the *Iowa Tests of Basic Skills* [31] and the *SRA Achievement Series* [36], for grades 2 to 9, and the *California Achievement Tests* [39], for grades 1 to 14, are designed to measure the "generalized intellectual skills" children *use* in academic activities. They include only language, reading, arithmetic, and work-study skills. Confining the content of the tests to that "most universally taught," these tests exclude subject concepts, such as those in science and social studies, which different school systems handle differently.

Since a single test which spanned several grades would contain many items too difficult for the younger children and other items too easy for the more mature children, each of these tests is arranged for several levels. For example, the *California Achievement Test* is arranged in five levels which span the grades from 1 to 14. The *Iowa Tests of Basic Skills* has a different set of overlapping items for each of the grades, 3 through 9.

Each of these briefly mentioned tests, and several others [7], has its distinctive features. We hope that interested students will find the opportunity to examine specimen sets of some of them. Here we shall take a closer look at only two of them—one which reflects curriculum content and one which is constructed to appraise ultimate objectives.

The Stanford Achievement Test. This is a comprehensive battery designed to measure the important understandings, knowledge, and skills "commonly accepted as desirable outcomes" of the elementary and junior high school curriculum [28]. Arranged in four developmental levels, the primary level covers grades 1 to 3; the elementary level, grades 3 and 4; the intermediate level, grades 5 and 6; and the advanced level, grades 7, 8, and 9.

The scope covered expands through the successive levels. At the primary level, there are tests of reading, spelling, and arithmetic. Language is added at the elementary level. And at the intermediate and advanced levels, tests of study skills and of concepts in social studies and science are added. The authors of the test claim that "the content is closely attuned to what is actually taught in the school" and that the norms "reflect accurately the current accomplishments of pupils of varying grades and ages [28, p. 1]." For a firsthand glimpse of the content of these tests, let us examine some representative items from the *Intermediate Battery, Form J.*

Reading proficiency is measured by tests of paragraph meaning and of word meaning.

Paragraph meaning. "Reading as reasoning" is measured by 20 very short paragraphs which require the student to select among sets of four alternatives two to four words which appropriately complete the thought of each paragraph. Example [28, p. 3]:

> A long time ago the people of Peru did not know how to write. In order to count, they tied knots in threads of different colors. Each color meant a different kind of thing. The_____a_____in a thread stood for the things being_____b_____. a: (1) knots, (2) colors, (3) loops, (4) twists. b: (5) counted, (6) named, (7) written, (8) used.

Word meaning. To sample his understanding of the words which children frequently read, the student is directed to complete 48 sentences by selecting among four alternatives the appropriate synonym, definition, or association. Example [28, p. 5]:

> A thing is gigantic if it is_____ (1) very important, (2) huge, (3) exploded, (4) far away.

Spelling. Guided by the curriculum criterion of social utility, the authors chose half of the 72 words by which pupils' proficiency in spelling is sampled from the 2,000 different words children write most frequently. The other half of the words in the test include less frequently written words. The particular aspect of spelling tested is identification of the correctly spelled word among four alternatives. Example [28, p. 8]:

> The guards moved (1) quitly, (2) quietly, (3) quitely, (4) not given.

Language. In 70 items (27 of which are organized into paragraphs) sampling capitalization, punctuation, sentence sense, usage, and grammar, students are directed to choose between pairs the correct or acceptable possibility. Example [28, p. 10]:

> Don't you want (no more, any more) ice cream?

Arithmetic reasoning. Since arithmetic problem solving involves a combination of factors—information, reading ability, reasoning, and computational skill—the reasoning test (in two parts—problem solving and concepts) samples, in 45 items, this complex of factors. Example [28, p. 12]:

> A lock for the clubhouse will cost $1.35. What will be each boy's share if 9 boys share equally? (a) 9¢, (b) 14¢, (c) 37¢, (d) $12.15, (e) not given.

Arithmetic computation. With "generous" time limits, 45 items—involving the four fundamental operations with integers, decimals, fractions, and denominate numbers—sample the student's computational skills. Example [28, p. 16]:

> $\frac{3}{4} \div \frac{1}{2} =$ (a) ⅜, (b) ⅔, (c) ¾, (d) 1½, (e) not given.

Study skills. Supplementing other appraisals of reading skills, the study skills test measures proficiency in reading maps, charts, graphs, and tables, and the use of references, indexes, and the dictionary. These skills are measured by 49 multiple-choice questions which require the actual interpretation of these media. For example [28, p. 22], from reading a bar graph, the student answers such questions as—

> How many of the states listed on the graph have average elevations of 2,000 feet or more?   (a) 1, (b) 2, (c) 3, (d) 4.

Social studies. In 70 items from history, geography, and civics, the test samples the student's mastery of the concepts and facts commonly included in textbooks and courses of study in the social studies subjects. Example [28, p. 18]:

> An important occupation in colonial days was that of (1) locomotive engineer, (2) plumber, (3) blacksmith, (4) telegraph operator.

Science. The student's range of general science information and understanding is sampled by 49 items from the physical, life, and earth sciences, and from conservation, health, and safety concepts. Example [28, p. 21]:

> For his bones to harden well, a child needs plenty of (1) sugar, (2) starch, (3) fat, (4) calcium.

Interpretation of scores. Since this is a standardized test, a child's raw scores on the eight subtests are interpreted by comparing them with the distributions of scores of the 13,000 to 55,000 representative children in each grade (1 through 9), drawn as a norm group from 363 school systems in 38 states. A pupil's scores can be compared with *all* the norm pupils of a grade or with those in the modal-age group (those at the typical age for grade, that is, those pupils who enter at the typical age and advance one grade per year).

In order to interpret a given child's raw scores, such scores are converted to age equivalents and grade equivalents, according to *modal* and/or *total* group norms, and within-grade percentiles, according to modal-age grade norms—for the beginning, middle, or end of each grade. The age- or grade-equivalent score indicates the age or grade *level* at which the typical pupil earns the converted raw score. They are approximate indexes of educational progress. A grade equivalent of 5.5, for example, indicates that the raw score from which it was converted is earned by the typical norm pupil in the fifth month of the fifth grade. The within-grade percentile indicates the percentage of the appropriate norm grade pupils who fall below the given score. The percentile scores thus indicate more precisely than the grade equivalents a child's position *within* his grade group. Although the

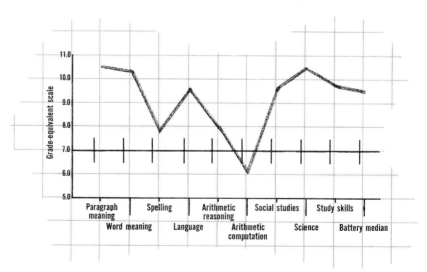

Fig. 15.1. A Stanford Achievement Test *profile for a child about to enter the seventh grade at age 11–8.*

yearly advances in grade equivalents are rough indexes of growth, development throughout the entire range of the test can be assessed more accurately in the approximately equal standard deviation units of the K-scales into which raw scores can be converted [28, p. 21].

As an illustration of the uses and interpretations of the scores of this test, let us examine in Figure 15.1 the profile of comparable scores it yielded for a child at age 11–8. The midline opposite grade equivalent 7.0 indicates that this child is just beginning the seventh grade. Compared with the total-grade national norms, the over-all profile of grade-equivalent scores and the battery median indicate that her general achievement is very superior. In reading and science, she reaches the projected tenth grade norms. In language, social studies, and study skills, she has attained average ninth grade levels. And in spelling and arithmetic reasoning, she approximates the average eighth grade level. Only in arithmetic computation is her achievement below the average of her grade level.

Looking at the relatively advanced grade equivalents from the point of view of *placement*, we can see that some acceleration in grade progress is suggested. The child's status among her seventh grade classmates can be indicated more precisely, however, by reading from a table in the manual the within-grade percentile equivalents of her scores [28, p. 15]. They range from 30 in arithmetic computation to 93 in reading comprehension or 95 in understanding of science. The relatively high percentiles in all the areas except arithmetic computation suggest the desirability of *placement* in the most advanced homogeneous or intraclass group. From the point of view of *guidance of learning*, enrichment in science, social studies, and language is suggested. The relatively low score in arithmetic computation suggests that, despite her generally superior achievement, she may profit from specific remedial instruction in arithmetic. A *diagnostic* examination of the arithmetic computation items reveals that all the items she completed are correct and that the relatively low score resulted from proceeding too slowly. She needs, therefore, to cultivate greater speed and confidence in this skill.

Should the teacher wish to *assess* the gains made in each of these areas during the year in the seventh grade, the K-scale scores earned in the fall could be compared with the K-scale scores earned on another form of the test given in the spring.

A profile of comparable achievement scores such as that illustrated in Figure 15.1 is an index of general academic proficiency and—to some extent—of differentiated educational development. This interpretation is justified by the moderately high but not perfect correlations between the several subtests comprising such a profile. For example, on the *Iowa Tests of Basic Skills* the correlations between pairs of the five subtests range from approximately .60 to .80 [31, p. 77]. And on

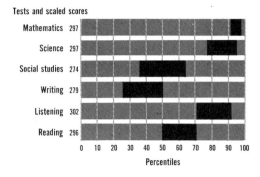

Tests and scaled scores

		Percentiles
Mathematics	297	
Science	297	
Social studies	274	
Writing	279	
Listening	302	
Reading	296	

0 10 20 30 40 50 60 70 80 90 100

Percentiles

Fig. 15.2. *The profile of percentile bands of scores on the* Sequential Tests of Educational Progress *earned by 16-year-old Lawrence in the eleventh grade.* (From *Manual for Interpreting Scores, Social Studies,* Educ. Testing Serv., Princeton, N.J., 1957, p. 12.)

the *Iowa Tests of Educational Development* the median correlation between pairs of the nine subtests is .65 and the range is from .40 to .78 [25, p. 32]. These less-than-perfect correlations between highly reliable tests indicate that, although the battery median is indicative of general achievement, the separate tests discriminate to some extent the differences in a pupil's pattern of achievement. Thus the profile is also useful in differential guidance.

Sequential tests of educational progress. This comprehensive battery of tests—the cooperative product of test experts, of teachers, and of research—"measures critical skills in the *application* of learning in seven major fields": reading comprehension, listening comprehension, quality of essay writing, knowledge of how to write, mathematics, science, and social studies [9]. Embodied in realistic problem situations, the test items sample the students' abilities to use in real-life activities "what they have learned in the classroom." Developmentally oriented, the tests appraise the continuous growth in these skills from the fourth grade of the elementary school through the sophomore year of college. To span this range, the tests are arranged in four levels: grades 4 through 6, grades 7 through 9, grades 10 through 12, and grades 13 and 14. In long, 70-minute tests in each field (except for the 35-minute essay test), "the depth and power" of skills are reliably appraised.

Within-grade percentile scores, as illustrated in Figure 15.2, implement the placement and guidance functions of the test. For assessment of growth, the raw scores are converted to standard scores, which are approximately comparable from age to age, and, between the seven different tests, for the full range from grade 4 through grade 14.

In their attempt to construct valid items for the test, the authors have tried to appraise attainment of *significant educational objectives* rather than memorization of specific curriculum content. Since it appears that the authors have been unusually creative in constructing the items for this purpose, we shall quote one from each part of the test:

Reading comprehension. On passages of ample length and representative of the major types of reading material, students are tested
for "ability to understand direct statements, to interpret and summarize
passages, to see the motives of authors, to observe organization of
ideas, and to criticize passages with respect to ideas and purposes of
presentation [9, Manual, p. 7]." This atypically short passage and one
of five different kinds of multiple-choice questions on it illustrate an
item for grades 10 to 12 on observation of organization of ideas
[9, Brief, p. 11].

> In turn-of-century vaudeville, folding beds were favorite comedy
> props, but many descendants of those early folding beds are no laugh-
> ing matter. Today's smaller homes call for furniture that conserves
> space by serving more than one purpose, and the modern "convertibles"
> are going far toward satisfying that need. They can turn the most
> proper living room into a dormitory that will sleep nine people. Con-
> vertible furniture is giving American homemakers the imaginative
> engineering, improved design, and remarkable mass-production prices
> associated with home appliances. This development has provided the
> biggest home-furnishing news in recent years. In 1940, United States
> families spent about 22 million dollars for convertible sleep furniture;
> now, they are spending six times that amount for beds that hide in
> the living room during the day.
>
> Which of the following techniques does the author use to make
> his presentation of ideas effective? (a) supporting a statement with
> specific proof, (b) giving figures, (c) listing advantages, (d) all of
> these.

Listening comprehension. On material read to them—typical of
that spoken to students, such as directions, expositions, narrations,
arguments, and aesthetic pieces—students answer 72 to 80 multiple-
choice questions which measure their ability to comprehend, interpret,
evaluate, and apply the concepts they *hear.* From a test for grades
7 to 9 comprised of 12 selections, the first paragraph of a student's
speech and one of five questions on it illustrate the items [9, Brief,
p. 9].

> A students, B students, C students and my friends. As you know,
> I am running for the office of President of the Student Council. I'd
> like to tell you what I'll do if I'm elected. In the first place, I think
> several students ought to sit in on teachers' meetings. They settle too
> many things for us. I don't think that the teachers always know what is
> best for us.
>
> It is likely that in the past the speaker has (a) disagreed with
> the teachers' decisions, (b) disagreed with the opinions he has stated,
> (c) agreed with the doctor about the candy machine, (d) agreed with
> his other opponents about decisions of teachers.

Quality of essay writing. Using as a guide a scale of student essays
representative of different levels of writing quality, the teacher evalu-

ates his students' essays written on the same topics [9, Brief, p. 7].
An essay topic for grades 13 and 14, for example, is—

> Looking back over the critical decisions of your life, "where you took one path rather than another," describe "a decision and indicate the influences—person, book, experience, event—which prompted you to make the choice you did."

Knowledge of how to write. On various student-written materials, the examinee identifies errors or weaknesses. Then, in multiple-choice items, he selects the most appropriate revisions to achieve the purposes of the original authors. The 60 items at each level are constructed to measure critical thinking in writing; organization of ideas; and correctness, effectiveness, and appropriateness of expression. The first two lines of an eight-sentence selection, "My Favorite Magazine," and one of seven questions on it, for grades 10 to 12, illustrate the items [9, Brief, p. 13].

> 1. Many young people of today are taking a great interest in the magazine *Suburbia*. 2. It is of fairly large size with a considerable number of pages . . . Etc.
> In Sentence 2, how could the size of the magazine be indicated most effectively? (*a*) By comparing it with one or two well-known magazines, (*b*) By giving length, width, thickness, weight, and number of pages, (*c*) By drawing a scale model, (*d*) By telling how many articles each issue contained.

Mathematics. On everyday-problem situations, students at each level answer multiple-choice items covering the development of concepts and skills in number and operations, symbolism, measurement and geometry, function and relation, deduction and inference, and probability and statistics [9, Manual, p. 7]. Item 21 is typical of 50 items for grades 10 to 12 [9, Form 2A, p. 4].

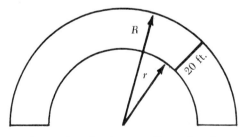

Mr. Smith wanted to reduce the area of the driveway without changing its 20-foot width or its semicircular shape. He could do this by (*a*) reducing only the outer radius *R*, (*b*) increasing only the inner radius *r*, (*c*) reducing the outer radius *R* and increasing the inner radius *r* by the same amount, (*d*) reducing both radii by the same amount.

Science. Sampling scientific concepts from biology, chemistry, physics, astronomy, geology, and meteorology, this test appraises the student's scientific problem-solving ability by means of 60 multiple-choice problems which emphasize science applications in home, economic, cultural, and social situations. An example, for grades 10 to 12 is given here [9, Brief, p. 17].

> You and your family are visiting the Grand Canyon National Park in Arizona. . . . Upon reaching the bottom of the canyon, you find the Colorado River extremely turbulent and muddy. To determine how much mud and other eroded material is in the water, it would be best to take measured samples of the river water and (*a*) determine the average molecular weight of the samples, (*b*) evaporate the water and weigh the residue, (*c*) add reagents to precipitate dissolved minerals, filter, and weigh the residue, (*d*) filter, evaporate the water, and weigh the residue from the filtrate.

Social studies. On varied materials from history, geography, economics, government, and sociology, the student answers sets of multiple-choice questions (totaling 70 at each level) which measure (*a*) his understanding of such concepts as social change, effects on man of the geographic environment, democratic society, the interdependence of individuals and of communities, man's economic wants and his increasing control over the forces of nature; and (*b*) his skill in reading and interpreting maps, charts, graphs, cartoons, and diagrams.

To illustrate the concepts tested, we quote only the second and fourth of four paragraphs of an item on the different periods of American history and one of seven questions on it for grades 10 to 12 [9, Form 2A, p. 3].

> II. The right to enjoy liberty is inalienable. According to Scripture man cannot hold property in man. In view of the religious and civil privileges of this nation, the guilt of its oppression is unequalled by another on the face of this earth; and, therefore, it is bound to repent instantly and to let the oppressed go free.
>
> IV. The main threat to liberty and the Republic is the money question. If protection has enslaved its thousands, the gold standard has enslaved its tens of thousands. What if the great cities are in favor of the gold standard? The cities depend upon these broad prairies. Destroy the farms and grass will grow in the streets of every city.
>
> Which statement was made by an abolitionist? (*a*) I, (*b*) II, (*c*) III, (*d*) IV.

An item illustrating the skills test presents a graph showing increases in average weekly earnings and in consumer prices from 1900 to 1955, and asks four questions testing reading and interpretations of it. Example [9, Form 2A, p. 5]:

> Which of the following is the best title for this graph? (*a*) Wages and Prices, (*b*) Earnings of Workers and Consumers, (*c*) The Cost of Living, (*d*) Changes in Income.

SEPARATE-SUBJECT TESTS OF ACHIEVEMENT

Elementary teachers, interested in every aspect of the child's educational development, and school counselors and administrators, concerned with problems of differential placement and guidance, prefer the multisubject tests. Junior and senior high school teachers of single subjects, however, often need a unisubject test of achievement. For this reason, the different parts of the survey batteries are usually available as separate-subject tests. In addition to the tests already described, the test publishers referred to in this chapter and others have constructed tests for appraising achievement in many separate subjects—English, foreign languages, mathematics, general science, biology, chemistry, physics, government, history, home economics, industrial arts, music, art, and several other subjects. For example, a *Cooperative Physics Test* is described by the publisher as suitable for measurement of end-of-course achievement in standard high school courses. With appropriate emphasis on each part, it samples knowledge of mechanics, heat, light, sound, and electricity [10, p. 19]. For both a comprehensive list of guidance and achievement tests and critical evaluations of them Buros's *Fifth Mental Measurements Yearbook* is an excellent reference [7].

DIAGNOSTIC TESTS OF ACHIEVEMENT

Primarily, survey tests measure how much a student has learned. Diagnostic tests reveal his learning difficulties and sometimes suggest the causes of them. Since these functions are so important in individual guidance of learning and in remedial teaching, constructors of survey batteries and of separate-subject tests have exploited their diagnostic possibilities by comprehensive coverage of objectives and by classifying the items into diagnostic categories. For example, in subdivisions of the language subtest of the *Iowa Tests of Basic Skills,* the subsidiary category on punctuation includes items on the period, question mark, comma (13 uses), apostrophe, double quotation mark, colon, semicolon, and exclamation mark [31]. But as samplings of comprehensive areas of achievement, survey tests often have too few items in each diagnostic category for reliable measurement. Diagnostic tests attempt to sample each category more thoroughly, so as to yield reliable measures of the pupil's strengths and weaknesses. And they sometimes point up the probable causes of failure to make normal progress in learning. Although there are diagnostic tests in several subjects, we can suggest their general characteristics by describing a diagnostic study of reading.

The Gates reading tests. In a comprehensive system of tests for appraising several facets of reading, these tests combine both survey and diagnostic features. They assess the development of reading skills from the primary level through tenth grade, and they yield comparable measures on several aspects and types of reading.

The *Gates Primary* and *Advanced Primary Reading Tests,* for grades 1 through 3, are designed to measure the initial development of proficiency in (1) recognition of *words,* (2) understanding of *sentences,* and (3) comprehension of the thought in *paragraphs* [17, 18]. There are 26 to 48 items in each of the three word-picture tests. As an illustration of them, the *Paragraph Reading* test—consisting of 26 paragraphs of increasing complexity, difficulty, and length—requires the child to grasp the meaning and to execute a direction such as in item (13), *Form 3.*

13. The postman comes to the gate. He stops when he has mail to deliver. To signal him to stop, we put up the little red tin flag. Put an X on the thing that is used as a signal.

Beyond the primary level, from grade 3 through grade 10, the *Gates Reading Survey* tests [19] measure development of four aspects of reading effectiveness: (1) the range and level of complexity of the child's proficiency in *identification and understanding of words;* (2) the level of his reading *comprehension*—in 21 passages arranged in order of increasing difficulty; (3) his *speed* of reading—in 21 paragraphs of uniform difficulty; and (4) his percentage of *accuracy*—the ratio of the number of items read correctly to the number attempted of the 21 paragraphs read for speed. Since the word-identification items are in the by-now familiar multiple-choice form and the reading comprehension items are like the very short passages in the *Stanford Achievement Test,* we shall illustrate only the easily comprehended paragraphs of uniform difficulty, scored for both speed and accuracy. As the item [19, No. 28, *Form 3*] shows, only a minimum of reasoning or discrimination between meanings is required in answering it.

> Read the paragraph and draw a line under the word which completes it.
> Owls can fly without making any noise. Their wing feathers are

formed in such a way that they move through the air silently. The owl flies—(1) quickly, (2) noisily, (3) winglessly, (4) quietly.

The *Gates Basic Reading Tests*, for grades 3 through 8, overlap the preceding tests by including measures of development in (1) reading vocabulary and (2) level of comprehension. Three other different subtests in the series, each comprised of 18 to 24 paragraphs of uniform difficulty, measure speed and accuracy of reading for (3) appreciating the general significance of passages, (4) understanding precise directions, and (5) noting details [20]. Let us illustrate this test by quoting an item which is read for an appreciation of its general significance only, and one which is read for understanding and executing precisely a set of directions [20, No. 13, *Form 3*].

[GS] Man has long wanted to take a trip to the moon. It is not yet time for us to start packing our suitcases, but our visit to the moon is closer today than ever before. Early stories told of man being carried to the moon by winds or birds. Today we know it will not be that easy, and scientists are working hard to make the trip possible.

Draw a line under the word that tells what kind of travel is becoming more possible: bird, wind, undersea, scientific, space.

[UD] "To make an aquarium, you need a large glass tank. Green plants and 'garbageman' snails will help keep the water clean. A hose and net are needed, too. And don't forget the fish—and their food. Draw a line around the thing not needed in an aquarium.

From the distribution of scores of representative children at appropriate grade levels, scores on all of the Gates reading tests are convertible to age and/or grade equivalents and to within-grade percentile scores. By a quintile classification of ratings (very high, high, medium, low, very low), the percentage of accuracy scores are related to the pupil's grade equivalent (GE) in speed of reading. For example, a percentage of accuracy of 80 with a GE of 3.0 to 3.4 for speed is rated "high"; with a GE for speed of 5.5 to 5.9, the same percentage of accuracy is rated "low [19, Manual, p. 6]." These comparable scores make it possible to compare a child's relative proficiency in the several aspects of effective reading measured—reading vocabulary, identification of words, speed, accuracy, level of reading comprehension, appreciation of general significance, understanding of precise directions, and the noting of details. The comparisons show significant strengths and weaknesses.

These several aspects of reading are not, however, highly differentiated. The correlations between pairs of the *Basic Reading Tests* range, like those typically found between pairs of different academic subjects, from .60 to .80 [20]. Correlation of these magnitudes indicate that 36 to 64 per cent of what the five tests measure is common to all of them. On the other hand, and indicative of their use in differential diagnosis, 36 to 64 per cent of what any one of the tests measures is independent of what the others measure.

For the school psychologist and for teachers who achieve the expert's understanding of how children learn to read, the *Gates Reading Diagnostic Tests* [16, pp. 577–652] supplement the diagnostic clues obtainable from the survey-diagnostic tests. These more intensive diagnostic tests are given individually and include—

1. Observation and analysis of the child's oral reading, from which the examiner appraises expression, versatility and effectiveness of word-identification techniques, other modes of attack, maturity and correctness of articulation, nature of errors, and signs of confidence or anxiety.

2. Oral vocabulary.

3. Tests for tendency to reverse words.

4. Ability to perceive phrases such as "the big ship" in ½-second flashes.

5. Perception of single words both in flash exposures and with ample time and encouragement to try to identify them by phonetic- and visual-analysis techniques.

6. Specific tests of visual-perception techniques, such as combining syllables into words, recognition of syllables and phonograms, blending letter sounds (such as *f-o in fo*), and giving the sounds of letters.

7. Tests of auditory perception and techniques, such as giving letters for sounds, supplying other words that begin with the same initial sound, and giving words that end in the same sound.

Used as a flexible system of diagnostic tools, the *Gates Reading Tests* are designed to provide a comprehensive analysis of the component abilities and skills required for an effective mode of approach in reading. Guided by the results of the survey-diagnostic testing and by hearing the child read, the examiner employs whichever of the individual tests he thinks may aid in revealing the child's strengths and weaknesses and the specific causes of his reading difficulties. In a thorough diagnostic study of reading or of other learning difficulties, the findings from the proficiency tests are supplemented by nonverbal tests of intelligence or differential abilities, of interest, and of mental health. Remedial instruction is then adapted to the child's learning needs and to the pattern of reading and other abilities revealed. How to correct the specific causes of ineffective reading revealed in the

Gates tests is suggested in Gates's book *The Improvement of Reading* and in Chapter 5 of this volume.

TEACHER-MADE ACHIEVEMENT TESTS

For pupil placement, assessment of long-range growth, differential guidance, and formal diagnosis of learning difficulties, teachers and counselors will probably administer standardized achievement tests at least once a year. But in connection with the day-to-day guidance of learning, the assessment of growth from unit to unit, and the continuous, informal diagnosis of learning difficulties, teachers use teacher-constructed tests much more frequently. Supplementing their informal observations of pupil performance and products, they construct and apply a variety of short-answer objective tests, essay tests, and achievement rating scales. For the task of constructing effective objective tests, our review of representative standardized tests should have contributed several helpful concepts, techniques, and models.

Objective tests. Both standardized and teacher-made objective-test items often measure mastery of specific facts, terms, concepts, and procedures. As our review of some representative modern standardized tests has shown, however, with the exercise of ingenuity, they can be constructed to measure understanding of trends, relationships, syntheses of components, and generalizations or principles. They can also test analysis and interpretations of situations; applications of generalizations to concrete problem situations; and evaluations of materials, approaches, and solutions to problems. Although effective teacher-made tests for day-to-day use can justifiably mirror specific curriculum content more closely than is appropriate in the less frequently used standardized tests, they, like standardized tests, should be oriented toward appraisal of significant, generalized, and permanent objectives.

In writing good objective-test items, the teacher strives for clarity, precision, and conciseness of expression. He uses words of precise meaning and qualifies statements as necessary. He avoids nonfunctional words, nonessential specificity, distracting minor inaccuracies, and irrelevant cues such as pat verbalizations, overprecise or overlong correct alternatives in multiple-choice items, plural errors, and extrinsic sources of difficulty [11]. He adapts the form of the item to the requirements of the concept to be measured. In reviewing the common forms, let us illustrate them with some of the teacher-constructed items used to appraise understanding of the unit on "The Water Supply in Our Community" which we described in Chapter 1.

1. *Multiple choice.* This most popular type of objective test is adaptable to testing a wide variety of concepts involving reasoning, discriminating, and evaluating between right and wrong alternatives

or among problem solutions of variable quality. It is especially appropriate for testing understanding of definitions, purposes of things or skills, cause-and-effect relationships, discriminative associations or connections between concepts, evaluations of actions or processes, recognition and application of principles, and recognition of errors [33].

The stem should clearly express the problem, either as an incomplete statement or a direct question. All the alternatives should be appropriate to the stem, be comparable in form, and have some plausible relation to it. But only one of them should be clearly correct or be the best solution—unless, of course, the subject is directed to choose more than one alternative. For conciseness, the stem should include parts of the alternatives which would otherwise be needlessly repeated. Example [2, p. 48]:

> If borax softens magnesium hard water better than it does calcium hard water, it is because (1) magnesium borate is more soluble than calcium borate, (2) the borate and magnesium ions together produce suds, (3) calcium borate is more soluble than magnesium borate, (4) the sodium ions present in borax cause the difference in softening ability.

2. *Completion*. This form of the objective test is suitable only for questions which can be answered by a unique word, phrase, or number. As employed both in the *Stanford Achievement* and the *Gates* short reading tests, it will be remembered that the blank was completed from multiple-choice alternatives. Example [2, p. 49]:

> Assuming that you know that magnesium is the chief water hardness factor, you would use as the softening agent ————.

3. *True-false*. This often overused type of test frequently contains items inappropriately lifted from a specific context; it is suitable only for ideas which are true or false without qualification and without regard to a particular context. It is used in testing knowledge of the correct or appropriate choices or conclusions in significant dichotomous problem situations: Example [2, p. 48]:

> Hard water can be made as soft as distilled water by adding certain chemicals.

4. *Performance interpretation*. This work-sample type of the objective test appraises actual performance in the application of a principle or a skill. As our review of the standardized tests shows, it is often employed in tests of study skills to test students' proficiency in reading and interpreting a table, chart, map, or diagram. Example [2, p. 49]:

> Assuming that magnesium is the chief hardness factor in water, [the chart below shows that] one should use as the softening agent (1) Na_2CO_3, (2) Na_3PO_4, (3) Borax, (4) Any one of these agents.

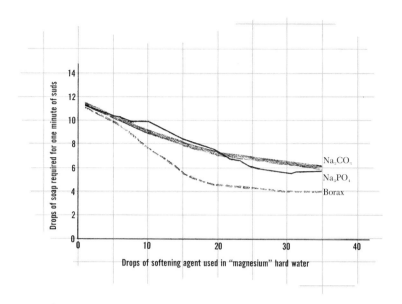

5. *Matching.* This form of the objective test is adaptable for test-ing understanding of complex multiple-faceted concepts or the ability to make discriminating applications of the coordinately related aspects of complex concepts. Matching items are especially suitable for test-ing understanding of associations between the elements in paired *systems* of things, such as events and dates, events and persons, events and places, terms and definitions, principles and specific applications, tools and their uses, causes and effects, conditions and results. Like the alternatives of a multiple-choice question, the parts of a matching question should all be interrelated and plausible. The introductory statement should clearly relate the primary statements to the alterna-tive responses. The primary statements should be brief and not too numerous, so that they can be easily remembered or rescanned as each response is matched with one of them. There may be an extra un-matched response, or a response may match more than one premise. Example (author's construction):

Match each of the following procedures for making water potable with the procedure's main function:

( ) Sand filter   1. Removes the color and odor
                                            2. Collects colloidally dispersed
( ) Charcoal absorption   solids
                                            3. Kills bacteria
( ) Alum precipitation   4. Softens the water
                                            5. Picks out the relatively large
( ) Chlorination   particles

Essay tests. Despite general recognition of the limitations of the essay test, this once most frequently used type of teacher-made test still has a role in the teacher's appraisal of learning. It is especially suited to appraising independent problem solving, where the child can draw upon functionally organized facts and concepts to relate, compare, contrast, discriminate, draw inferences, detect relationships, select pertinent information, state conclusions, or make interpretations. Example [2, p. 50]:

> Assuming the concentration of the calcium and magnesium ions to be equal, we see evidence that the hardness effect of these ions is not the same. What is this evidence?

Good test items are not easily or quickly produced. Efficient writing of teacher-constructed items is a long-range evolving process rather than a specific job to be done each time a test is needed. Whenever an idea for appraising a significant educational objective occurs to a teacher—when studying objectives, reading pupil texts and references, or observing learning activities, when a particular concept or skill is found to be especially needed, when an error occurs that needs correcting, and so on—an appropriate item on it should be written, or a plan should be determined for writing it.

Each item can be written on a 3- by 5-inch card, so that it can be filed conveniently in a box divided by labeled guide cards indicating the areas and subtopics of the course or curriculum. Whenever a test is needed, appropriate items are drawn from the file for effective arrangement and duplication. As items are used and critically evaluated and as better ideas for items occur, some items are discarded or revised. Thus, as a teacher grows in experience and in professional competency, his evolving file of test items is expanded and improved.

OBSERVATION OF PERFORMANCE AND PRODUCTS

As is suggested in Table 15.1, the teacher has numerous occasions for observing attainment of objectives in every area of the elementary and secondary curriculum. Observation is the teacher's most continuously employed evaluation procedure. The teacher observes his pupils in both individual and group learning activities—in the classroom, laboratory, auditorium, library, lunchroom, and on the playground.

For example, in oral reading, the teacher notes range, versatility, and effectiveness of the child's word-identification techniques. In mathematics, he notes the efficiency or inadequacy of modes of attack in problem solving, fertility and originality of hypotheses, or the precision and thoroughness of the pupil's deductive development of proof in geometry theorems. In the science laboratory, he observes the student's efficiency in setting up experiments, his accuracy in measuring and recording, the organization of his data, and his skill in locating sources of error. He notes the quality and effectiveness of expression

in English. In foreign language classes, he notes the accuracy of pronunciation. The orchestra teacher sees and evaluates his pupils' modes of approach in bowing or fingering their instruments and listens to the quality of intonation or time. Observation is especially appropriate for evaluating the attainment of certain uniquely achieved objectives—such as efficiency of mode of attack in problem solving, inventive or creative approaches to projects, development of short-cuts, exercise of initiative, assumption of social responsibilities, and complementary cooperation in group activities.

The attainment of many significant objectives is revealed by the teacher's examination of children's completed assignments and especially of their creative productions in writing, language, art, crafts, mathematics, science, social studies, home economics, and in technological courses.

One way to appraise attainment of ultimate objectives rather than mere memorization of curriculum content is to observe demonstrations of the *action patterns* which a course is intended to develop. For example, instead of asking high school students to *tell how* to plan, prepare, and serve a well-balanced meal for a family, Smith believes that they should be directed to actually plan, prepare, and serve a test meal to a simulated, student-comprised family. In such a test, each student is required to (1) write a plan (including the menu, recipes, market order, equipment, time-and-work schedule, and table setting), (2) share responsibilities in preparing and serving the meal, and (3) evaluate both the modes of production and the final product. By observation, the teacher and students evaluate the balance of the menu, the skill and efficiency of handling equipment (such as pulling just the right number or too many pots and pans from the cabinets), adherence to the time schedule, arrangement of the served meal, appropriateness of conduct during the meal, and the quality of the meal itself. The immediate feedback from such evaluative observations of performance and products effectively guides the learning. The students confirm correct performances, discover the causes of a poor product, and decide on ways to make the next meals better [35].

DEPENDABLE STANDARDIZED AND TEACHER-MADE TESTS

As we have already implied, teachers and counselors rely on test scores in making important decisions in many teaching and guidance functions. They use tests in placement, diagnosis, and guidance of learning, prediction of subsequent achievement, assessment of growth, and in the evaluation of student accomplishments. In order to justify our confidence in test-guided decisions, the tests themselves should be valid and reliable.

Validity. Tests are said to be valid to the extent that they measure what they are designed to measure. Since the primary purpose of achievement tests is to appraise the attainment of significant educational objectives, they are valid to the extent that they accomplish this purpose. Tests, however, have different kinds of validity. For dependability in their specific functions, achievement tests should have curricular, predictive, and construct validities.

In support of the *curricular validity* of the standardized tests we have described, their authors say that the test items sample the "common body" of concepts and skills "actually" or "most universally" taught and "agreed upon as desirable and of permanent worth [22, 28, 39]." To achieve curricular validity, the authors sampled the content of the most widely used modern textbooks, courses of study, teacher guides, and other materials suggested by the pertinent literature and authoritative yearbooks. Instead of simply reflecting the curriculum content, however, the more creative tests have been designed to appraise attainment of generalized, ultimate objectives. Such tests, for example, as the *ITED* and the *STEP* attempt to measure the student's ability "to use what [he] has learned [25]" or the application of "his school-learned skills in solving new problems [9]."

Guided by the criterion of curricular validity, the teacher—in selecting or constructing a test—attempts to match the objectives in the course or unit being appraised with an adequate and comprehensive sample of appropriate test items. A test whose items neatly cover the significant objectives of the course or unit has curricular validity. A test which fails to cover several of the objectives which should be appraised and which includes many items irrelevant to the course or unit is not likely to be valid.

The curricular validity of teacher-made tests of single units can sometimes be assured by systematically sampling *all* the objectives in the area covered by the test. For example, Harap and Mapes, in constructing a test to assess the understanding of fractions achieved by a fifth grade class in a project curriculum, analyzed the unit into 14 different concepts. The concepts ranged from "finding a fractional part of an integer, using unit fractions only [such as ¼ of 12]" to "dividing a mixed number by a mixed number [such as 30⅚ ÷ 3½]." They constructed items to cover all 14 concepts. In order to avoid any undue influence which computational errors might have on the final test scores, they formulated three problems for each concept. Success on two of the three problems was considered indicative of mastery of the concept [21].

Such a test, by validly assessing the extent to which a unit has been mastered, effectively guides pupil learning. For example, the pupil whose pretest and end-test scores on the fractions test are 4 and 12, respectively, learns that he has made progress. He discovers that he has mastered 12 of the 14 concepts. He sees that he has 2 more concepts to master, and the diagnostic arrangement of the test items also indicates which 2 concepts he needs to study further in order to complete his mastery of the unit.

The *predictive validity* of a test is indicated by its efficiency in forecasting subsequent achievement from indexes of present or earlier achievement. As was pointed out in Chapter 4, achievement tests are indicative both of how much a student has learned and, like aptitude tests, of his capacity for such learning. Several of the tests reviewed have demonstrated predictive validity. For example, the correlations between earlier-earned test scores and later-earned high school or college grades, both between composite test scores and average grades and between separate test scores and grades in specific corresponding courses, range from approximately .50 to .70 [9, 25, 31, 36]. The correlations between earlier- and later-earned test scores are often higher than between test scores and teacher grades. For example, the correlation between the composite score earned in the eighth grade on the *Iowa Tests of Basic Skills* and the composite score earned in the twelfth grade on the *Iowa Tests of Educational Development* is .80 [31, p. 76]. Between corresponding subtests of the *SRA* achievement series, given in the eighth grade, and the *ITED*, given in the ninth grade, the correlations range from .65 to .70 [36]. The test-test correlations are usually higher than the test-grades correlations—both because the tests have more in common with each other than with teacher marks and because the tests are often more reliable than teachers' marks.

The *construct validity* of a test is based on the confirmation of logical inferences about expected pupil performances on the test and

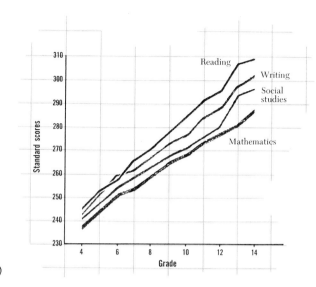

Fig. 15.3. *The continuous growth in achievement reflected in the mean scores of from 186 to 1,312 representative students at each level indicates the validity of STEP for assessing long-range educational growth. (After Sequential Tests of Educational Progress, Technical Report, Educ. Testing Serv., Princeton, N.J., 1958, pp. 23–24.)*

on its relations to other measures of learning ability or achievement. For example, as children mature and learn, we have found that they advance in school achievement. Since the developmental survey tests are designed to assess this growth, we should expect the mean scores of normative groups to increase with advancing grade placement. On this criterion, all the standardized tests reviewed have demonstrated construct validity. The growth in science knowledge shown in Figure 3.13, page 80, shows the typical growth revealed by the *Stanford Achievement Test*. The continuous growth from grade 4 through 14 in reading, writing, social studies, and mathematics, shown in Figure 15.3, confirms the validity of *STEP* for assessing long-range educational growth.

Using other criteria of construct validity, the authors of the *California Achievement Test* report correlations of from .49 to .83 between their test and the *California Test of Mental Maturity* and from .44 to .95 between their test and other corresponding achievement tests [39]. As an indication of the construct validity of teacher observations, Norton reports correlations between teacher ratings of study habits— on such factors as completion of assignments, promptness in beginning work, and extent of dallying—and ninth grade general science achievement of .30 and .37, for boys and girls, respectively [32].

Reliability. An index of a test's reliability is an estimate of the trustworthiness, accuracy, or freedom from error of the scores on it. There are three indexes of reliability, all obtained from statistical analyses of the relations between the pairs or other combinations of scores of a representative population. The correlations between the

Appraising learning 529

split halves of a test, or a Kuder-Richardson item analysis, yield an index of *internal consistency*, which shows the extent to which different parts of the same test appraise the person in the same way. The correlations between different forms of a test administered at nearly the same time yield an index of *equivalence*, which shows the consistency of performance on different, but equivalent samples of items administered at different times. If there is a distinct interval of time between the initial test and a retest, the correlation yields an index of *stability* of performance.

For most of the achievement tests reviewed in this chapter, the reliability correlations are based on the pairs of scores from split halves of the tests. The coefficients of internal consistency reported for the major subtests of the survey tests range from approximately .80 to .95, for relatively large, single-grade groups [9, 22, 25, 28, 31, 36, 39]. The within-subtest diagnostic scores of survey tests, however, are often much less reliable. For example, the eight subsidiary scores within the English part of the *EHSCB* range in split-half reliability from .36 to .78 [22]. Although always less reliable than the major subtest scores, the reliabilities of the diagnostic subscores of other tests are, however, sometimes higher than this. On the *Iowa Tests of Basic Skills*, they are reported to range from .76 to .90 for a sixth grade group [31].

The indexes of equivalence or correlations between alternate forms of the same test, taken at different times, are usually lower than the indexes of internal consistency. For example, the split-half correlations on *EHSCB* range from approximately .80 to .95; on the same groups, the alternate-form correlations range from approximately .70 to .92 [22]. Despite Gates's use of the more stringent alternate-form criterion rather than split-half reliability, his relatively long diagnostic reading tests yield reliable scores. For the primary tests, the coefficients of equivalence range—for words, sentences, and paragraphs—from .85 to .88 [17, 18]. For the three diagnostic scores of the *Reading Survey*, they range from .83 to .87 [19]. And for the five diagnostic scores of the *Basic Reading Tests*, they range from .83 to .87 [20].

The indexes of stability, which are like predictive validity, except that the same achievement test is *always* used both initially and for the retest, indicate that achievement tests measure relatively stable pupil characteristics. For example, the correlations between the fourth grade and sixth grade scores on the *Iowa Tests of Basic Skills* of 172 pupils range from .57 (for language) to .78 (for reading).[1]

Derived from the reliability coefficient and the standard deviation of the test scores, the standard error of measurement (SE meas. $= \text{SD} \sqrt{1-r}$) is a meaningful indication of a test score's unreliability. It indicates the extent to which an individual's "true" score

[1] Computed from data provided the author by Logan, Utah, schools.

(as estimated from many successive retests) may be expected to deviate from a single obtained score. The standard error of measurement may be expressed in varied units of measurement: raw score, standard score, grade equivalent, or percentile. Expressed in grade-equivalent units, on the *Iowa Tests of Basic Skills,* it ranges for sixth grade students from 2.4 months, for *Work-Study,* to 4.5 months, for *Vocabulary* [31, p. 74]. To guard against overprecise interpretations of test scores, the standard error of measurement is conveniently built into the profiles of some tests.

In Figure 15.1, the relatively short perpendicular lines crossing the horizontal line at grade equivalent 7.0 represent graphically the standard errors of measurement for each of the *Stanford Achievement* subtests. For the *Word Meaning* test, for example, it indicates that in about two-thirds of many immediate retests the grade equivalents can be expected to vary from 10.0 to 11.0, or that there are 68 chances in 100 that the child's true score lies somewhere between 10.0 and 11.0.

The reliabilities of the *differences* between pairs of scores, because they are affected by the unreliabilities of both of a pair of scores, are lower than the reliabilities of individual scores. For example, although the coefficients of internal consistency for the *Sequential Tests of Educational Progress* range from .83 to .91, most of the reliabilities of the *differences* between pairs of *STEP* tests range from .50 to .70. To ensure taking into account the reliabilities of the differences between pairs of *STEP* tests, the profiles of scores are plotted in "percentile bands that are one standard error wide [9, Suppl., p. 28]." For a difference reliability of .64 (as between *Science* and *Social Studies*) the chances are only 5 in 100 that a difference between nonoverlapping percentile bands reflects errors of measurement. Thus we can assume with considerable confidence that differences between nonoverlapping percentile bands represent significant differences in achievement rather than errors of measurement. Guided by the indexes of reliability built into the profile presented in Figure 15.3, we can confidently assume that Lawrence's achievement in mathematics, science, and listening exceeds his achievement in reading, social studies, and writing; and that he is higher in mathematics than in any other field except science. Between *Science* and *Listening,* however, or between *Social Studies* and *Writing,* the scores are not significantly different.

The matter of a test's reliability holds two important implications for teachers and counselors: (1) Since even relatively good tests are far from perfectly reliable, interpretations of every test score should take into account the standard error of measurement, and (2) in selecting or constructing tests, we need to be aware of the factors on which reliability depends. To achieve the reliabilities of the standardized tests we have reviewed, each test or diagnostic subdivision of it should be comprised of an adequate number of clear, unambiguous, and appropriate items. The items should represent thoroughly every significant aspect of the objectives in the field for which it is intended. All the items should faithfully reflect proficiency in the function measured. And the child's performance on the test and scoring of it should be freed from irrelevant factors. Since teacher-made tests are often deficient in these characteristics, they are usually less reliable than the more expertly constructed standardized tests. This is especially true of the essay form.

Unless essay tests are discriminately used, skillfully constructed, and carefully scored, they are notoriously prone to unreliability. On rescoring the same unmarked examination, the same teacher tends to assign a different grade the second time. And different teachers disagree markedly on the grades they assign to the same examination paper. For example, 142 teachers assigned percentage grades ranging from 50 to 98 to the same high school English paper [37]; 115 teachers assigned percentages ranging from 29 to 92 to the same high school geometry paper [38]; and 20 teachers assigned to the same history paper percentage grades ranging from 42 to 93 [12].

The frequent unreliability of the essay test results from several factors. Since so few questions can be answered within a reasonable time, the essay test is not likely to cover an adequate and representative sample of objectives. Consequently, it is possible that of two students whose total knowledge of a subject is equal, one may happen to know the answers to the few questions asked in a particular test, and the other may lack this particular segment of knowledge. Often ambiguously phrased essay questions elicit different interpretations from different students. And their scoring is subject to the influence of such irrelevant factors as variations in verbal fluency, composition skills, and speed and legibility of handwriting. For example, when the same English composition was graded first in "poor" and two months later in "good" handwriting, as measured by the Thorndike handwriting scale, 43 high school teachers raised the percentage grade an average of 9.15 points, or the equivalent of one letter grade [26].

Some of the common faults of the essay examination are avoidable. If essay questions are combined in tests with objective questions, more adequate and representative samplings of objectives can be achieved. Ambiguity of interpretation can be avoided by stating explicitly what is wanted and the sources of facts to use in answering the question. A well-defined scoring key indicating the points earned on each aspect of the answer lessens the influence of subjective, irrelevant factors. And by scoring each question separately, one at a time, for all students in a class, the teacher can maintain the same scoring standard from student to student. As Anderson and Traxler have shown, the essay test can be made to yield reliable scores when it is expertly constructed and scored [1].

SUMMARY

The appraisal of learning is intimately related to all the major functions of teaching. By enhancing the teacher's knowledge and understanding of her pupils, evaluation and measurement help the teacher to provide for the conditions of effective learning. Thus evaluation and measurement achieve their general purpose: the facilitation of learning. They achieve this general goal by aiding teachers specifically in (1) placement of pupils, (2) diagnosis of learning difficulties, (3) guidance of learning as a trial-and-check process, (4) assessment of progress, (5) prediction of subsequent learning, and (6) evaluation of curricula and methods. Evaluation and measurement also tend to define the particular objectives students come to think of as important and which they then strive most intensely to attain.

Since testing tends both to facilitate and to direct learning, it is important to encompass in our testing of school accomplishment *all* the important educational objectives. The broad scope of educational objectives—knowledge and understandings, skills and competencies, attitudes and interests, and action patterns in both the personal-social and the several academic areas of the curriculum—requires diverse testing procedures, each uniquely suited to appraisal of certain kinds of objectives.

For the complex and comprehensive task of appraising learning in the elementary and secondary schools, teachers and psychologists have developed a variety of procedures which test nonacademic and academic learning. The nonacademic procedures include interviewing, anecdotal records, rating scales, check lists, sociometry, participation charts, self-inventories, and projective methods. The tests of academic achievement include survey tests, unisubject tests, diagnostic tests, and teacher-made tests.[1]

To be effective in the facilitation of learning, all these procedures should be valid and reliable. They should yield scores and profiles which are meaningful and appropriate for achieving the specific functions of testing. In order to be able to use the modern tests available to them in a constructive way, teachers need to understand precisely

[1] Actually there is overlapping between the procedures we have classified as nonacademic and academic. The interview, for example, is used both for evaluating a child's mental health and for determining his work methods in such an activity as arithmetic-problem solving.

what the tests measure and how accurately they do it. An especially important contribution of modern testing concepts is that they can be applied in the improvement of teacher-made tests.

GUIDES FOR STUDY, REVIEW, AND APPLICATION

1. Achievement tests have other and more important uses than being a basis for assigning school marks. Explain and give examples of how appraisal of achievement facilitates learning in several ways. How effective is it?

2. Why is it important in evaluation of school accomplishment to encompass *all* the important educational objectives? Outline the scope of the objectives whose attainment we need to appraise. Describe the devices available for making these appraisals.

3. From the file of achievement tests available at your college—in the library, bureau of educational services, or elsewhere—examine a few survey tests of academic achievement. Consider—for the tests you examine—the scope covered, whether they measure mastery of curriculum content or the applications of the concepts and skills learned, how adequately they sample the objectives they are designed to appraise, and how the specific items are constructed. Do they have the features which should make them valid, reliable, and efficient aids in the facilitation of learning?

4. Referring to our classification of the functions of tests—placement, diagnosis, guidance, assessment, prediction, and evaluation—interpret as completely as you can the achievement profiles in Figures 15.1 and 15.2. Be sure that these interpretations take into account the standard errors of measurement of the tests.

5. What are the distinctive features and uses of diagnostic tests of achievement?

6. What are the specific uses, merits, and limitations of teacher-made tests of achievement? Describe as many effective types as you can find or invent. What are the distinctive uses of each type? As a test of your skill in test making, construct items for appraising understanding of a chapter in your text and try it out on your classmates.

REFERENCES

CHAPTER 1

1. Beck, R. H., Cook, W. W., and Kearney, N. C. *Curriculum in the Modern Elementary School.* Englewood Cliffs, N.J.: Prentice-Hall, 1953.
2. Bell, J. W. "Individualizing instruction at the high school level." *High Sch. J.,* 1959, 42, 232–240.
3. Birkmaier, Emma Marie (ed.) *Illustrative Learning Experiences.* The Modern School Practices Series, no. 2. Minneapolis, Minn.: Univ. Minn. Press, 1952. Copyright by the University of Minnesota.
4. Bloom, B. S. "The 1955 normative study of the tests of general educational development." *Sch. Rev.,* 1956, 64, 110–124.
5. Buswell, G. T. "Educational theory and the psychology of learning." *J. Educ. Psychol.,* 1956, 47, 175–184.
6. Buswell, G. T. "A comparison of achievement in arithmetic in England and Central California." *Arith. Teacher,* 1958, 5, 1–9.
7. Capehart, B. E., Hodges, A., and Roth, R. "Evaluating the core curriculum: a further look." *Sch. Rev.,* 1953, 61, 406–412.
8. Chase, F. S. "The response of the schools to the challenges of the twentieth century." *Sch. Rev.,* 1959, 67, 17–25.
9. Coladarci, A. P. "The relevancy of educational psychology." *Educ. Leadership,* 1956, 13, 489–492.
10. Conant, J. B. *The American High School Today.* New York: McGraw-Hill, 1959.

11. Cook, W. W. "Individual differences and curriculum practice." *J. Educ. Psychol.*, 1948, 39, 141–148.
12. Doremus, A. F. "A comparison of American with European-schooled youngsters–a challenge." *The Math. Teacher*, 1957, 50, 432–433.
13. Douglass, H. R. "The modern high school curriculum." *Sch. Rev.*, 1955, 63, 16–24.
14. Finch, F. H., and Gillenwater, V. W. "Reading achievement then and now." *Elem. Sch. J.*, 1949, 49, 446–454.
15. Findley, W. G. "The ultimate goals of education." *Sch. Rev.*, 1956, 64, 10–17.
16. Fischer, J. H. "Effective modern education as the educator sees it." *NEA J.*, 1959, 48, 15–18.
17. French, W., and Associates. *Behavioral Goals of General Education in High School.* New York: Russell Sage, 1957.
18. Haggard, E. A. "The proper concern of educational psychologists." *Amer. Psychologist*, 1954, 9, 539–543.
19. Horn, E. "A basic writing vocabulary." *Univ. of Iowa Monogr. in Educ.*, 1926, ser. 1, no. 4.
20. Jersild, A. T., and Tasch, R. J. *Children's Interests and What They Suggest for Education.* New York: Bur. of Publ., Teachers Coll., Col. Univ., 1949.
21. John Dewey Society, Shane, H. G. (ed.) *The American Elementary School.* Thirteenth Yearbook of the society. New York: Harper, 1953.
22. Kearney, N. C. *Elementary School Objectives.* New York: Russell Sage, 1953.
23. Ketcham, W. A. "The reading ability of high school students." *The Univ. of Mich. Sch. of Educ. Bull.*, 1959, 30, 73–76.
24. Kramer, K. "Arithmetic achievement in Iowa and The Netherlands." *Elem. Sch. J.*, 1959, 59, 258–263.
25. Kyte, G. C., and Neel, V. M. "A core vocabulary of spelling words." *Elem. Sch. J.*, 1953, 54, 29–34. Copyright by the University of Chicago.
26. Lee, J. M., and Lee, Dorris May. *The Child and His Curriculum.* New York: Appleton-Century-Crofts, 1940.
27. Leonard, J. P., and Eurich, A. C. *An Evaluation of Modern Education.* New York: Appleton-Century-Crofts, 1942.
28. Lund, F. H. "Spotlight on our schools." *Educ.*, 1958, 79, 115–125.
29. McLendon, J. C. "Are pupils learning the basic skills of English?" *Sch. Rev.*, 1953, 61, 226–231.
30. Ragan, W. B. *Modern Elementary Curriculum.* New York: Dryden, 1953.
31. Rinsland, H. D. *A Basic Vocabulary of Elementary School Children.* New York: Macmillan, 1945.
32. Rugg, H., and Shumaker, Ann. *The Child-centered School.* Yonkers-on-Hudson, N.Y.: World, 1928.
33. *The American School Curriculum*, Nat. Educ. Ass. Thirty-first Yearbook Amer. Ass. Sch. Administrators. Washington: Nat. Educ. Ass., Comm. of Amer. Sch. Curriculum, 1953.
34. *The Purposes of Education in American Democracy.* Washington: Nat. Educ. Ass., Educ. Policies Comm., 1938.
35. *The Pursuit of Excellence: Education and the Future of America*, Panel Report V of the Special Studies Project, Rockefeller Brothers Fund. New York: Doubleday, 1958.
36. Wilson, J. A. R. "Differences in achievement attributable to different educational environments." *J. Educ. Res.*, 1958, 52, 83–93.

CHAPTER 2

1. Azrin, N. H., and Lindsley, O. R. "The reinforcement of cooperation between children." *J. Abnorm. and Soc. Psychol.*, 1956, 52, 100–102.
2. Gates, A. I. "Connectionism: present concepts and interpretations." *The Psychology of Learning*, Forty-first Yearbook Nat. Soc. Study of Educ., part II, pp. 141–164, Chicago, 1942. Distributed by the Univ. of Chicago Press.
3. *Guilding the Growth of Children.* New York: McGraw-Hill, Text-Film Dept.
4. Guthrie, E. R. *The Psychology of Learning.* New York: Harper, 1935.
5. Guthrie, E. R. "Conditioning: a theory of learning in terms of stimulus response and association." *The Psychology of Learning*, Forty-first Yearbook

Nat. Soc. Study of Educ., part II, pp. 17–60, Chicago, 1942. Distributed by the Univ. of Chicago Press.

6. Guthrie, E. R. *The Psychology of Learning*, Rev. Ed. New York: Harper, 1952.

7. Guthrie, E. R., and Horton, G. P. *Cats in a Puzzle Box*. New York: Rinehart, 1946.

8. Harter, G. L. "Overt trial and error in problem solving of pre-school children." *J. Genet. Psychol.* 1930, 38, 361–372.

9. Hartmann, G. W. "The field theory of learning and its educational consequences." *The Psychology of Learning*, Forty-first Yearbook Nat. Soc. Study of Educ., part II, pp. 165–214, Chicago, 1942. Distributed by Univ. of Chicago Press.

10. Hilgard, E. R. *Theories of Learning*, 2d ed. New York: Appleton-Century-Crofts, 1956.

11. Hull, C. L. "Conditioning: outline of a systematic theory of learning." *The Psychology of Learning*, Forty-first Yearbook Nat. Soc. Study of Educ., part II, pp. 61–95, Chicago, 1942. Distributed by the Univ. of Chicago Press.

12. Jones, Mary C. "A laboratory study of fear: the case of Peter." *J. Genet. Psychol.*, 1924, 31, 308–315.

13. Keister, Mary E. "The behavior of young children in failure," in Barker, R. G., Kounin, J. S., and Wright, H. F. (eds.) *Child Behavior and Development*. New York: McGraw-Hill, 1943.

14. Lewin, K. "Field theory and learning." *The Psychology of Learning*, Forty-first Yearbook Nat. Soc. Study of Educ., part II, pp. 215-242, Chicago, 1942. Distributed by Univ. of Chicago Press.

15. MacCorquodale, K., and Meehl, P. E. "Edward C. Tolman," in Estes, W. K., Koch, S., Meehl, P. E., Mueller, Jr., C. G., Schoenfeld, W. N., and Verplanck, W. S. *Modern Learning Theory*. New York: Appleton-Century-Crofts, 1954. Pp. 177–266.

16. Melton, A. W. "Learning," in Monroe, W. S. *Encyclopedia of Educational Research*. New York: Macmillan, 1952. Pp. 668–690.

17. Miller, N. E., and Dollard, J. *Social Learning and Imitation*. New Haven, Conn.: Yale Univ. Press, 1941.

18. Mowrer, O. H. "On the dual nature of learning—a re-interpretation of 'conditioning' and 'problem-solving.'" *Harv. Educ. Rev.* 1947, 17, 102–148.

19. Mowrer, O. H. "Learning theory." *Rev. Educ. Res.*, 1952, 22, 475–495.

20. Mowrer, O. H. "Two-factor learning theory reconsidered, with special reference to secondary reinforcement and the concept of habit." *Psychol. Rev.*, 1956, 63, 114–128.

21. Munn, N. L. "Learning in children," in Carmichael, L. *Manual of Child Psychology*. New York: Wiley, 1954.

22. Pressey, S. L., and Robinson, F. P. *Psychology and the New Education*. New York: Harper, 1944.

23. Seward, J. P. "Reinforcement and expectancy: two theories in search of a controversy." *Psychol. Rev.*, 1956, 63, 105–113.

24. Skinner, B. F. "The science of learning and the art of teaching." *Harv. Educ. Rev.*, 1954, 24, 86–97.

25. Spence, K. W. *Behavior Theory and Conditioning*. New Haven, Conn.: Yale Univ. Press, 1956.

26. Strang, Ruth. *Helping Children Solve Problems*. Chicago: Science Research, 1953.

27. Thorndike, E. L. *Human Learning*. New York: Century, 1931.

28. Tolman, E. C. "Cognitive maps in rats and men." *Psychol. Rev.*, 1948, 55, 189–218.

29. Tolman, E. C. *Collected Papers in Psychology*. Berkeley, Calif.: Univ. of Calif. Press, 1951.

CHAPTER 3

1. Almy, Millie. "Are they too young for problem-solving?" *Progr. Educ.*, 1949–50, 27, 148–151.

2. Anderson, I. H., Hughes, B. O., and Dixon, W. R. "Age of learning to read and its relation to sex, intelligence, and reading achievement in the sixth grade." *J. Educ. Res.*, 1956, 49, 447–453.

3. Anderson, J. E. "The development of

social behavior." *Amer. J. Sociol.*, 1939, 44, 839–857.

4. Anderson, J. E., Harris, D. B., Werner, Emmy, and Gallistel, Elizabeth. *A Survey of Children's Adjustment over Time.* Minneapolis, Minn.: Inst. of Child Developm. and Welf., Univ. of Minn., 1959.

5. Ausubel, D. P., and Schiff, H. M. "The effect of incidental and experimentally induced experience on the learning of relevant and irrelevant causal relationships by children." *J. Genet. Psychol.*, 1954, 84, 109–123.

6. Bayley, Nancy. "Individual patterns of development." *Child Developm.*, 1956, 27, 45–74.

7. Bennett, G. K., Seashore, H. G., and Wesman, A. G. *A Manual for the Differential Aptitude Tests.* New York: The Psychological Corp., 1952.

8. Boney, C. D. "Shall beginning reading be delayed?" *Childh. Educ.*, 1949, 26, 168–172.

9. Brace, D. K. *Measuring Motor Ability, a Scale of Motor Ability Tests.* New York: A. S. Barnes, 1930.

10. Bradley, Beatrice C. "An experimental study of the readiness approach to reading." *Elem. Sch. J.*, 1956, 56, 262–267.

11. Britton, E. C., and Winans, J. M. *Growing from Infancy to Adulthood.* New York: Appleton-Century-Crofts, 1958.

12. Brooks, F. D. *Child Psychology.* Boston: Houghton Mifflin, 1937.

13. Brown, D. G. "Sex-role preference in young children." *Psychol. Monogr.*, 1956, 70, 1–19.

14. Brownell, W. A. "Readiness and the arithmetic curriculum." *Elem. Sch. J.*, 1938, 38, 344–354.

15. Brueckner, L. J. (chm.) *Educational Diagnosis,* Thirty-fourth Yearbook Nat. Soc. Study of Educ., Chicago, 1935. Distributed by the Univ. of Chicago Press.

16. Brueckner, L. J. "The development of readiness tests in arithmetic." *J. Educ. Res.*, 1940–41, 34, 15–20.

17. Burt, C. "The development of reasoning in school children." *J. Exp. Pedag.*, 1919–20, 5, 68–77, 121–127.

18. Carpenter, Aileen. "Tests of motor educability for the first three grades." *Child Developm.*, 1940, 11, 293–299.

19. Carter, L. B. "The effect of early school entrance on the scholastic achievement of elementary school children in the Austin public schools." *J. Educ. Res.*, 1956, 50, 91–103.

20. Clinton, R. J. "Nature. of mirror-drawing ability: norms on mirror-drawing for white children by age and sex." *J. Educ. Psychol.*, 1930, 21, 221–228.

21. Cole, Luella. *The Psychology of Adolescence.* New York: Rinehart, 1948.

22. Corey, S. M., and Herrick, V. E. "The developmental tasks of children and young people," in Seidman, J. M. *Readings in Educational Psychology.* Boston: Houghton Mifflin, 1955. Pp. 37–43.

23. Cuff, N. B. "Vocabulary tests." *J. Educ. Psychol.*, 1930, 21, 212–220.

24. Davis, R. A., and Taylor, H. E. "Significance of research on interests for the classroom teacher." *Educ. Adm. and Superv.*, 1943, 29, 357–369.

25. Dearborn, W. F., and Rothney, J. W. M. *Predicting the Child's Development.* Cambridge, Mass.: Science-Art Pubs., 1941.

26. Dennis, W. "Does culture appreciably affect patterns of infant behavior?" *J. Soc. Psychol.*, 1940, 12, 305–317.

27. Dennis, W. "On the possibility of advancing and retarding motor development of infants." *Psychol. Rev.*, 1943, 50, 203–218.

28. Doll, E. A. *Vineland Social Maturity Scale.* Vineland, N.J.: The Training School, 1936.

29. Dubin, Elizabeth R. "The effect of training on the tempo of development of graphic representation in pre-school children." *J. Exp. Educ.*, 1946, 15, 166–173.

30. Dusenberry, Lois. "A study of the effects of training in ball throwing by children ages three to seven." *Res. Quart.*, 1952, 23, 9–14.

31. Fast, Irene. "Kindergarten training and Grade I reading." *J. Educ. Psychol.*, 1957, 48, 52–57.

32. Fifer, G. "Grade placement of secondary school pupils in relation to age

and ability." *Calif. J. Educ. Res.*, 1952, 3, 31–36.

33. Finch, F. H., and Floyd, O. R. "The relation of chronological age to achievement in the study of French." *J. Educ. Psychol.*, 1935, 26, 52–58.

34. Fisher, M. B. "A comparison of the performance of freshmen and sophomores in a beginning course in psychology." *J. Exp. Educ.*, 1941, 10, 29–32.

35. Foster, Josephine C. "Verbal memory in the preschool child." *J. Genet. Psychol.*, 1928, 35, 26–44.

36. Freeman, F. N. "Survey of manuscript writing in public schools." *Elem. Sch. J.*, 1946, 46, 375–380.

37. Garr, J. M. *A Study of the Effects of Systematic and Meaningful Instruction upon a Complex Motor Skill.* Logan, Utah: Utah State Univ. Libr., 1954.

38. Gates, A. I. *Gates Reading Readiness Tests.* New York: Bur. of Publ., Teachers Coll., Col. Univ., 1939.

39. Gellerman, L. W. "The double alternation problem: II. The behavior of children and human adults in a double alternation temporal maze." *J. Genet. Psychol.*, 1931, 39, 197–226.

40. Goodenough, Florence L. *Measurement of Intelligence by Drawings.* Yonkers-on-Hudson, N.Y.: World, 1926.

41. Goodenough, Florence L. "The development of the reactive process from early childhood to maturity." *J. Exp. Psychol.*, 1935, 18, 431–450.

42. Goodenough, Florence L., and Smart, R. C. "Interrelations of motor abilities in young children." *Child Developm.*, 1935, 6, 141–153.

43. Gowan, J. C., and Seagoe, May. "The relation between interest and aptitude tests in art and music." *Calif. J. Educ. Res.*, 1957, 8, 43–45.

44. Greenberg, Pearl J. "Competition in children: an experimental study." *Amer. J. Psychol.*, 1932, 44, 221–248.

45. Guilford, J. P. "A system of psychomotor abilities." *Amer. J. Psychol.*, 1958, 71, 164–174.

46. Hale, C. J. "Physiological maturity of Little League baseball players." *Res. Quart.*, 1956, 27, 276–284.

47. Harrell, L. E., Jr. "A comparison of the development of oral and written language in school-age children." *Monogr. Soc. Res. in Child Developm.*, 1957, 22, serial no. 66 (3), 1–77.

48. Heidbreder, Edna F. "Problem-solving in children and adults." *J. Genet. Psychol.*, 1928, 35, 522–545.

49. Herr, Selma E. "The effect of pre-first-grade training upon reading readiness and reading achievement among Spanish-American children." *J. Educ. Psychol.*, 1946, 37, 87–102.

50. Hicks, J. A. "The acquisition of motor skill in young children: a study of the effects of practice in throwing at a moving target." *Child Developm.*, 1930–31, 1–2, 90–105.

51. Hildreth, Gertrude H., and Griffiths, Nellie L. *Metropolitan Readiness Tests.* Yonkers-on-Hudson, N.Y.: World, 1949.

52. Hodges, A. "Double alternation: a measure of intelligence." *J. Consult. Psychol.*, 1956, 20, 59–62.

53. Jenkins, Gladys G., Shacter, Helen, and Baurer, W. W. *These Are Your Children*, Expanded Ed. Chicago: copyright 1953 by Scott, Foresman.

54. Jenkins, Lulu Marie. "A comparative study of motor achievement of children five, six, and seven years of age." *Contr. to Educ.*, Teachers Coll., Col. Univ., 1930, no. 414.

55. Jersild, A. T. "Effects of delay on growth." *NEA J.*, 1948, 37, 150–151.

56. Jersild, A. T. *Child Psych.*, 4th Ed. Englewood Cliffs, N.J.: Prentice-Hall, 1954.

57. Jersild, A. T., and Bienstock, Sylvia F. "The influence of training on the vocal ability of three year old children." *Child Developm.*, 1931, 2, 272–291.

58. Jersild, A. T., and Bienstock, Sylvia F. "A study of the development of children's ability to sing." *J. Educ. Psychol.*, 1934, 25, 481–503.

59. Johnson, J. T. "An evaluation of research on gradation in the field of arithmetic." *J. Educ. Res.*, 1943, 37, 161–173.

60. Jones, H. E. *Development in Adolescence.* New York: Appleton-Century-Crofts, 1943.

61. Jones, H. E. "Physical ability as a factor in social adjustment in adoles-

cence." *J. Educ. Res.*, 1946, 40, 287–301.

62. Jones, Mary C. "The later careers of boys who were early- or late-maturing." *Child Developm.*, 1957, 28, 113–128.

63. Jones, Mary C., and Bayley, Nancy. "Physical maturing among boys as related to behavior." *J. Educ. Psychol.*, 1950, 41, 129–148.

64. Jones, R. H. "A comparison of intelligence of high school athletes with nonathletes." *Sch. and Soc.*, 1935, 42, 415–416.

65. Karlin, S. R. "Physical growth and success in undertaking beginning reading." *J. Educ. Res.*, 1957, 51, 191–201.

66. Kelley, T. L., Madden, R., Gardner, E. F., Terman, L. M., and Ruch, G. M. *Stanford Achievement Test* (Manual). Yonkers-on-Hudson, N.Y.: World, 1953.

67. Kendler, H. H., and Kendler, T. S. "Inferential behavior in preschool children." *J. Exp. Psychol.*, 1956, 51, 311–314.

68. Kinzer, J. R., and Fawcett, H. P. "The arithmetic deficiency of college chemistry students." *Educ. Res. Bull.*, 1946, 25, 113–114.

69. Koenker, R. H. "Arithmetic readiness at the kindergarten level." *J. Educ. Res.*, 1948, 42, 218–223.

70. Lantz, Beatrice. *Easel Age Scale*. Los Angeles, Calif.: Calif. Test Bur., 1955.

71. Lazarus, A. L. "Grouping based on high interest vs. general ability: a senior high school teacher's viewpoint." *Calif. J. Sec. Educ.*, 1955, 30, 38–41.

72. McCarthy, Dorothea. "Some possible explanations of sex differences in language development and disorders." *J. Psychol.*, 1953, 35, 155–160.

73. McCarthy, Dorothea. "Language development in children," in Carmichael, L. (ed.) *Manual of Child Psychology.* New York: Wiley, 1954.

74. McGraw, Myrtle B. *Growth, a Study of Johnny and Jimmy.* New York: Appleton-Century-Crofts, 1935.

75. Maier, N. R. "Reasoning in children." *J. Comp. Psychol.*, 1936, 21, 357–366.

76. Mattson, Marion Louise. "The relation between the complexity of the habit to be acquired and the form of the learning curve in young children."

Genet. Psychol. Monogr., 1933, 13, 299–398.

77. Meek, Lois H. "Patterns of growth during adolescence with implications for school procedures." *Progr. Educ.*, 1941, 18, 41–45.

78. Merrell, R. H. "The effects of travel, maturity, and essay tests upon the performance of college geography students." *J. Educ. Res.*, 1949, 43, 213–220.

79. Monroe, Marion. *Reading Aptitude Tests, Primary Form*. Boston: Houghton Mifflin, 1935.

80. Monroe, Marion. "Determining reading readiness." *Understanding the Child*, 1940, 9, 15–19.

81. Moore, T. V. "The reasoning ability of children in the first years of school life." *Stud. Psychol. and Psychiat.*, Catholic Univ. of Amer., 1929, 2 (2).

82. Morphett, Mabel V., and Washburne, C. "When should children begin to read?" *Elem. Sch. J.*, 1931, 31, 496–503.

83. Mussen, P. H., and Jones, Mary C. "Self-conceptions, motivation, and interpersonal attitudes of late- and early-maturing boys." *Child Developm.*, 1957, 28, 243–256.

84. Paterson, D. G., and others. *Minnesota Mechanical Ability Tests*. Minneapolis, Minn.: Univ. of Minn. Press, 1930.

85. Ragsdale, C. E., and Breckenfeld, I. J. "The organization of physical and motor traits in junior high school boys." *Res. Quart.*, 1934, 5, 47–55.

86. Rinsland, H. D. "Readiness for spelling." *Elem. Engl.*, 1950, 27, 189–191.

87. Roberts, Katherine E. "The ability of preschool children to solve problems in which a simple principle of relationship is kept constant." *J. Genet. Psychol.*, 1932, 40, 118–135.

88. Robinowitz, R. "Learning the relation of opposition as related to scores on the Wechsler Intelligence Scale for Children." *J. Genet. Psychol.*, 1956, 88, 25–30.

89. Robinson, Helen M. "Factors which affect success in reading." *Elem. Sch. J.*, 1955, 55, 263–269.

90. Seashore, H. G. "Some relationships of

fine and gross motor abilities." *Res. Quart.*, 1942, 13, 259–274.

91. Seils, L. "The relationship between measures of physical growth and gross motor performance of primary-grade school children." *Res. Quart.*, 1951, 22, 244–260.

92. Schonfield, D. "Special difficulties at reading age of 8+." *Br. J. Educ. Psychol.*, 1956, 26, 39–50.

93. Shuttleworth, F. K. "The physical and mental growth of girls and boys age six to nineteen in relation to age at maximum growth." *Monogr. Soc. Res. in Child Developm.*, 1939, 4 (3).

94. Sobel, B. "A study of the development of insight in preschool children." *J. Genet. Psychol.*, 1939, 55, 381–388.

95. Sommer, Agnes T. "The effect of group training upon the correction of articulatory defects in preschool children." *Child Developm.*, 1932, 3, 91–103.

96. Souder, H. C. "The construction and evaluation of certain readiness tests in common fractions." *J. Educ. Res.*, 1943, 37, 127–134.

97. Stendler, Celia B., and Young, N. "The impact of beginning first grade upon socialization as reported by mothers." *Child Developm.*, 1950, 21, 241–260.

98. Stolz, H. R., and Stolz, Lois M. "Adolescent problems related to somatic variations," in Henry, N. B. (ed.) *Adolescence*, Forty-third Yearbook Nat. Soc. Study of Educ., part I, Chicago, 1944. Distributed by the Univ. of Chicago Press.

99. Strayer, L. C. "Language and growth: the relative efficacy of early and deferred vocabulary training, studied by the method of Co-twin Control." *Genet. Psychol. Monogr.*, 1930, 8, 209–319.

100. Stroud, J. B., and Maul, Ruth. "The influence of age upon learning and retention of poetry and nonsense syllables." *J. Genet. Psychol.*, 1933, 42, 242–250.

101. Terman, L. M., and Merrill, Maud A. *Measuring Intelligence*. Boston: Houghton Mifflin, 1937.

102. Washburne, C. "The work of the Committee of Seven on grade-placement in arithmetic." *Child Development and the Curriculum*, Thirty-eighth Yearbook Nat. Soc. Study of Educ., part I, pp. 299–324, Chicago, 1939. Distributed by the Univ. of Chicago Press.

103. Washburne, C. *Child Development and the Curriculum*, Thirty-eighth Yearbook Nat. Soc. Study of Educ., part I, Chicago, 1939. Distributed by the Univ. of Chicago Press.

104. Wesley, S. M., Corey, D. Q., and Steward, Barbara M. "The Intraindividual relationship between interest and ability." *J. Appl. Psychol.*, 1950, 34, 193–197.

105. Wolfle, D. L., and Wolfle, H. M. "The development of cooperative behavior in monkeys and young children." *J. Genet. Psychol.*, 1939, 55, 137–175.

CHAPTER 4

1. "A question of IQ." *Time*, Dec. 9, 1957, pp. 52–54.

2. Alexander, Audrey M. "Teacher judgment of pupil intelligence and achievement is not enough." *Elem. Sch. J.*, 1952–53, 53, 396–401.

3. Bailey, Helen K. "A study of the correlations between group mental tests, Stanford-Binet, and Progressive Achievement Test used in the Colorado Springs elementary schools." *J. Educ. Res.*, 1949–50, 43, 93–100.

4. Barnes, P. J. "Prediction of achievement in grades one through four from Otis Quick-scoring Mental Ability Tests: Alpha Short Form." *Educ. Psychol. Measmt.*, 1955, 15, 493–494.

5. Barrett, H. O. "An examination of certain standardized art tests to determine their relation to classroom achievement and to intelligence." *J. Educ. Res.*, 1949, 42, 398–400.

6. Bayley, Nancy. "On growth of intelligence." *Amer. Psychologist*, 1955, 10, 805–818.

7. Bayley, Nancy. "Data on the growth of intelligence between 16 and 21 years as measured by the Wechsler-Bellevue Scale." *J. Genet. Psychol.*, 1957, 90, 3–15.

8. Bennett, G. K., Seashore, H. G., and Wesman, A. G. *Counseling from Pro-*

files, a Casebook for the Differential Aptitude Tests. New York: The Psychological Corp., 1951.

9. Bennett, G. K., Seashore, H. G., and Wesman, A. G. A Manual for the Differential Aptitude Tests. New York: The Psychological Corp., 1952.

10. Bennett, G. K., Seashore, H. G., and Wesman, A. G. "The differential aptitude tests: an overview." The Use of Multifactor Tests in Guidance, 1957. A Reprint Series from the Pers. and Guid. J.

11. Billhartz, W. H., and Hutson, P. "Determining college ability during junior high school years." Sch. and Soc., 1941, 53, 547–552.

12. Bradway, Katherine P. "IQ constancy on the Revised Stanford Binet from pre-school to the junior high school level." J. Genet. Psychol., 1944, 65, 197–217.

13. Burt, C. "The evidence for the concept of intelligence." Br. J. Educ. Psychol., 1955, 25, 158–177.

14. Buswell, Margaret M. "The relationship between the social structure of the classroom and the academic success of the pupils." J. Exp. Educ., 1953, 22, 37–52.

15. Byrns, Ruth, and Henmon, V. A. C. "Parental occupation and mental ability." J. Educ. Psychol., 1936, 27, 284–291.

16. Cohen, J. "The factorial structure of the WAIS between early adulthood and old age." J. Consult. Psychol., 1957, 21, 283–290.

17. Cohen, J. "A factor-analytically based rational for the Wechsler Adult Intelligence Scale." J. Consult. Psychol., 1957, 21, 451–457.

18. Coleman, W., and Cureton, E. E. "Intelligence and achievement: the 'Jangle Fallacy' again." Educ. and Psychol. Measmt., 1954, 14, 347–351.

19. Cornell, Ethel Letitia. "The variability of children of different ages and its relation to school classification and grouping." Educ. Res. Studies, no. 1. Albany, N.Y.: Univ. State of N.Y., 1937.

20. Crissey, O. L. "The mental development of children of the same IQ in differing institutional environments." Child Developm., 1937, 8, 217–220.

21. Cronbach, L. J. Essentials of Pscyhological Testing, 2d Ed. New York: Harper, 1960.

22. Davis, A., and Eells, K. Davis-Eells Tests of General Intelligence or Problem-solving (Manual). Yonkers-on-Hudson, N.Y.: World, 1953.

23. Dawe, Helen C. "A study of the effect of an educational program upon language development and related mental functions in young children." J. Exp. Educ., 1942, 11, 200–209.

24. Dolansky, M. P. "The essential high school content battery as a predictor of college success." J. Educ. Psychol., 1953, 44, 361–365.

25. Embree, R. B., and Floyd, O. R. "The predictive value of general science." J. Educ. Res., 1938, 31, 650–655.

26. Finch, F. H., and Nemzek, C. "The relationship of the Bernreuter Personality Inventory to scholastic achievement and intelligence." Sch. and Soc., 1932, 36, 594–596.

27. Flanagan, J. C. Flanagan Aptitude Classification Tests (Examiner's Manual, Administrator's Manual, student booklets, and "Gray" and "Blue" booklets). Chicago: Science Research, 1958.

28. Fracker, G. C., and Howard, V. M. "Correlation between intelligence and musical talent among university students." Psychol. Monogr., 1928, 39, 157–161.

29. Frandsen, A. N. "Mechanical ability of morons." J. Appl. Psychol., 1935, 19, 371–378.

30. Frandsen, A. N. "The Wechsler-Bellevue Intelligence Scale and high school achievement." J. Appl. Psychol., 1950, 34, 406–411.

31. Frandsen, A. N., and Barlow, Frances P. "Influence of the nursery school on mental growth." Intelligence: Its Nature and Nurture, Thirty-ninth Yearbook Nat. Soc. Study of Educ., part II, pp. 143–148, Chicago, 1940. Distributed by the Univ. of Chicago Press.

32. Frandsen, A. N., and Grimes, J. W. "Age discrimination in intelligence tests." J. Educ. Res., 1957, 51, 229–233.

33. Frandsen, A. N., and Higginson, J. B. "The Stanford-Binet and the Wechsler Intelligence Scale for Children." *J. Consult. Psychol.*, 1951, 15, 236–238.

34. Frederiksen, N., and Schrader, W. B. "The ACE Psychological Examination and high school standing as predictors of college success." *J. Appl. Psychol.*, 1952, 36, 261–265.

35. Freeman, F. N., et al. "The influence of environment on the intelligence, school achievement, and conduct of foster children." *Nature and Nurture: Their Influence upon Intelligence*, Twenty-seventh Yearbook Nat. Soc. Study of Educ., part I, pp. 103–217, Chicago, 1928. Distributed by the Univ. of Chicago Press.

36. Garrett, H. E. "A developmental theory of intelligence." *Amer. Psychologist*, 1946, 1, 372–378.

37. Gibbons, C. C. "A comparison of Kuhlmann-Anderson Test scores and teachers' estimates." *Sch. and Soc.*, 1938, 47, 710–712.

38. Graves, M. *Design Judgment Test* (Manual). New York: The Psychological Corp., 1948.

39. Gronlund, N. E., and Whitney, A. P. "The relation between teachers' judgments of pupils' sociometric status and intelligence." *Elem. Sch. J.*, 1958, 58, 264–268.

40. Guilford, J. P. "Three faces of intellect." *Amer. Psychologist*, 1959, 14, 469–479.

41. Gurnee, H. "An analysis of the perception of intelligence in the face." *J. Soc. Psychol.*, 1934, 5, 82–90.

42. Hildreth, Gertrude H. "Stanford-Binet retests of gifted children." *J. Educ. Res.*, 1943, 37, 297–302.

43. Hildreth, Gertrude H. "Three gifted children: a developmental study." *J. Genet. Psychol.*, 1954, 85, 239–262.

44. Hill, A. S. "Does special education result in improved intelligence for the slow learner?" *J. Exc. Child.*, 1948, 14, 207–213, 224.

45. Holzinger, K. J., and Crowder, N. A. *Holzinger-Crowder Unifactor Tests* (Manual). Yonkers-on-Hudson, N.Y.: World, 1955.

46. Hubbard, R. E., and Flesher, W. R. "Intelligent teachers and intelligence tests—do they agree?" *Educ. Res. Bull.*, 1953, 32, 113–122, 139–140.

47. Jackson, R. A. "Prediction of the academic success of college freshmen." *J. Educ. Psychol.*, 1955, 46, 296–301.

48. Janke, L. L., and Havighurst, R. J. "Relations between ability and social status in a mid-western community." *J. Educ. Psychol.*, 1945, 36, 499–509.

49. Jensen, V. H., and Clark, M. "A prediction study of Cooperative English Test scores." *Pers. and Guid. J.*, 1958, 36, 635–636.

50. Jones, R. H. "A comparison of intelligence of high school athletes with non-athletes." *Sch. and Soc.*, 1935, 42, 415–416.

51. Kinter, Madaline. *The Measurement of Artistic Abilities*. New York: The Psychological Corp., 1933.

52. Kirk, S. A. "An evaluation of the study by Bernardine G. Schmidt entitled: Changes in personal, social, and intellectual behavior of children originally classified as feebleminded." *Psychol. Bull.*, 1948, 45, 321–333.

53. Knauber, A. J. *The Knauber Art Ability Test*. Carnegie Corp. of N.Y. in cooperation with The Amer. Fed. of Arts, Conf. for Res. in Art, 1932.

54. Knauber, A. J. "The construction and standardization of the Knauber Art Tests." *Educ.*, 1935, 56, 165–170.

55. Koshuk, Ruth P. "Developmental records of 500 nursery school children." *J. Exp. Educ.*, 1947, 16, 134–148.

56. Krantz, Lavern L. "The relationship of reading abilities and basic skills of the elementary school to success in the interpretation of content materials in the high school." *J. Exp. Educ.*, 1957, 26, 97–114.

57. Kuhlmann, F. "The results of repeated mental re-examination of 639 feebleminded over a period of ten years." *J. Appl. Psychol.*, 1921, 5, 195–224.

58. Kuhlmann, F., and Finch, F. H. *Kuhlmann-Finch Tests for Elementary and High School Levels* (Manual). Minneapolis, Minn.: Amer. Guid. Serv., Inc., 1952.

59. Lamp, C. J., and Keys, N. "Can aptitude for specific musical instruments

be predicted?" *J. Educ. Psychol.*, 1935, 26, 587–596.

60. Lamson, Edna Emma. "High school achievement of fifty-six gifted children." *J. Genet. Psychol.*, 1935, 47, 233–238.

61. Lamson, Edna Emma. "To what extent are intelligence quotients increased by children who participate in a rich, vital school curriculum?" *J. Educ. Psychol.*, 1938, 29, 67–70.

62. Larson, Ruth C. "Studies on Seashore's 'Measures of Musical Talent.'" *Univ. of Iowa Studies*, 1927, 2, no. 6.

63. Lennon, R. T., and Schurtz, R. E. *A Summary of Correlations between Results of Certain Intelligence and Achievement Tests*, Test Serv. Notebook no. 18. Yonkers-on-Hudson, N.Y.: World, 1957.

64. Lewis, W. D. "Some characteristics of children designated as mentally retarded, as problems, and as geniuses by teachers." *J. Genet. Psychol.*, 1947, 70, 29–51.

65. Liddle, G. "The California Psychological Inventory and certain social and personal factors." *J. Educ. Psychol.*, 1958, 49, 144–149.

66. Lorge, I. "Schooling makes a difference." *Teachers Coll. Rec.*, 1945, 46, 483–492.

67. Lorge, I., and Thorndike, R. L. *The Lorge-Thorndike Intelligence Tests: General Manual.* Boston: Houghton Mifflin, 1955.

68. Louttit, C. M., and Browne, C. G. "The use of psychometric instruments in psychological clinics." *J. Consult. Psychol.*, 1947, 11, 49–54.

69. McCulloch, T. L. "The effect of glutamic acid feeding on the cognitive abilities of institutionalized mental defectives." *Amer. J. Ment. Def.*, 1950–51, 55, 117–122.

70. McHugh, Gelolo. "Changes in IQ at the public school, kindergarten level." *Psychol. Monogr.*, 1943, 55 (2) (whole no. 250).

71. McNemar, O. *The Revision of the Stanford-Binet Scale: an Analysis of the Standardization Data.* Boston: Houghton Mifflin, 1942.

72. Mason, C. F. "Pre-illness intelligence of mental hospital patients." *J. Consult. Psychol.*, 1956, 20, 297–300.

73. Meier, N. C. *The Meier Art Tests: I. Art Judgment.* Iowa City, Iowa: Bur. of Educ. Res. and Serv., Univ. of Iowa, 1942.

74. Merrill, Maud A. "The significance of IQ's on the Revised Stanford-Binet Scale." *J. Educ. Psychol.*, 1938, 29, 641–651.

75. Merrill, Maud A. *Problems of Child Delinquency.* Boston: Houghton Mifflin, 1947.

76. Minogue, B. M. "The constancy of the IQ of mental defectives." *Ment. Hyg.*, 1926, 10, 751–758.

77. Mitchell, Mildred Bessie. "The revised Stanford-Binet for university students." *J. Educ. Res.*, 1943, 36, 507–511.

78. Mohandessi, K., and Runkel, P. J. "Some socio-economic correlates of academic aptitude." *J. Educ. Psychol.*, 1958, 49, 47–52.

79. Moore, Grace Van Dyke. "Prognostic testing in music on the college level." *J. Educ. Res.*, 1932, 26, 199–212.

80. Olander, H. T., and Walker, B. S. "Can teachers estimate IQ?" *Sch. and Soc.*, 1936, 44, 744–746.

81. Otis, A. S. *Otis Quick-scoring Mental Ability Tests: New Edition* (Manuals for Alpha A–s, Grades 1–4 and Beta EM and FM). Yonkers-on-Hudson, N.Y.: World, 1954.

82. Paterson, D. G., and others. *Minnesota Mechanical Ability Tests.* Minneapolis, Minn.: Univ. of Minn. Press, 1930.

83. Pritchard, Miriam C., Horan, Kathryn M., and Hollingsworth, Leta S. "The course of mental development in slow learners under an experience curriculum." *Intelligence: Its Nature and Nurture*, Thirty-ninth Yearbook Nat. Soc. Study of Educ., part II, pp. 245–254, Chicago, 1940. Distributed by the Univ. of Chicago Press.

84. Proctor, W. M. "Psychological tests and guidance of high school pupils." *J. Educ. Res., Monogr.*, 1923, no. 1.

85. Quinn, K. V., and Durling, Dorothy I. "New experiment in glutamic acid therapy: 24 cases classified as mental deficiency, undifferentiated, treated with glutamic acid for six months."

Amer. J. Ment. Def., 1950–51, 55, 227–234.

86. Rogers, M. C. "Adenoids and diseased tonsils, their effect on general intelligence." *Arch. Psychol.*, 1922, no. 50, 1–70.

87. Sartain, A. O. "A comparison of the new Revised Stanford-Binet, the Bellevue Scale, and certain group tests of intelligence." *J. Soc. Psychol.*, 1946, 23, 237–239.

88. Schmidt, Bernardine G. "The rehabilitation of feeble-minded adolescents." *Sch. and Soc.*, 1945, 62, 409–412.

89. Schott, E. "IQ changes in foster home children." *J. Appl. Psychol.*, 1937, 21, 107–112.

90. Seashore, C. E., Lewis, D., and Saetbeit, J. G. *Manual of Instructions and Interpretations for the Seashore Measures of Musical Talent.* Camden, N.J.: Radio Corp. of Amer., RCA Victor Div., Educ. Dept., 1939.

91. Segel, D. "The multiple aptitude tests." *The Use of Multifactor Tests in Guidance*, 1957, pp. 56–66. A reprint series from the *Pers. and Guid. J.*

92. Segel, D. "Measurement index." *Guide Lines*, U.S. Office of Educ., Guid. and Student-pers. sec. Circ. 388, January, 1958.

93. Segel, D., and Raskin, Evelyn. *Multiple Aptitude Tests.* Los Angeles, Calif.: Calif. Test Bur., 1955.

94. Sloan, W., and Harmon, H. H. "Constancy of the IQ in mental defectives." *J. Genet. Psychol.*, 1947, 71, 177–185.

95. Sontag, L. W., Baker, C. T., and Nelson, Virginia L. "Personality as a determinant of performance." *Amer. J. Orthopsychiat.*, 1955, 25, 555–562.

96. Sontag, L. W., Baker, C. T., and Nelson, Virginia L. "Mental growth and personality development: a longitudinal study." *Monogr. Soc. for Res. in Child Developm.*, 1958, 23, serial no. 68, no. 2.

97. Stanton, H. M. *University of Iowa Studies in Psychology of Music.* Vol. II, *Measurement of Musical Talent.* Iowa City, Iowa: Univ. of Iowa, 1935.

98. Stoddard, G. D. (chm.) *Intelligence: Its Nature and Nurture,* part II, *Original Studies and Experiments,* Thirty-ninth Yearbook Nat. Soc. Study of Educ., Chicago, 1940. Distributed by Univ. of Chicago Press.

99. Stoddard, G. D. "On the meaning of intelligence." *Psychol. Rev.*, 1941, 48, 250–260.

100. Stroud, J. B., and Blommer, P. "Correlation analysis of WISC and achievement tests." *J. Educ. Psychol.*, 1957, 48, 18–26.

101. Sullivan, Elizabeth T., Clark, W. W., and Tiegs, E. W. *California Test of Mental Maturity—Elementary Series* (Grades 4–8) and *Manual.* Los Angeles, Calif.: Calif. Test Bur., 1951.

102. Super, D. E. "The multifactor tests: summing up." *Pers. and Guid. J.*, 1957, 36, 17–20.

103. Taylor, Elizabeth M. "A study in prognosis of musical talent." *J. Exp. Educ.*, 1941, 10, 1–28.

104. Terman, L. M. "The discovery and encouragement of exceptional talent." *Amer. Psychologist*, 1954, 9, 221–230.

105. Terman, L. M., and McNemar, Q. *Terman-McNemar Test of Mental Ability* (Manual of directions and test). Yonkers-on-Hudson, N.Y.: World, 1941.

106. Terman, L. M., and Merrill, Maud A. *Measuring Intelligence.* Boston: Houghton Mifflin, 1937.

107. Terman, L. M., and Merrill, Maud A. *Stanford-Binet Intelligence Scale, Manual for the Third Revision, Form L-M.* Boston: Houghton Mifflin, 1960.

108. Terman, L. M., and Oden, Melita H. *Genetic Studies of Genius,* vol. 5, *The Gifted Group at Midlife: Thirty-five Years' Followup of the Superior Child,* Stanford, Calif.: Stanford Univ. Press, 1959.

109. Thorndike, R. L. "Growth of intelligence during adolescence." *J. Genet. Psychol.*, 1948, 72, 11–15.

110. Thurstone, L. L. "A new conception of intelligence." *Educ. Rec.*, 1936, 17, 441–450.

111. Thurstone, L. L. "Primary abilities." *Occupations*, 1949, 27, 527–529.

112. Thurstone, Thelma G. "The tests of primary mental abilities." *The Use of Multifactor Tests in Guidance*, 1957, pp. 79–86. A reprint series from the *Pers. and Guid. J.*

113. *Using the Iowa Tests of Educational Development for College Planning.* Chicago: Science Research, 1957.
114. Wechsler, D. *Wechsler Intelligence Scale for Children.* New York: The Psychological Corp., 1949.
115. Wechsler, D. "Equivalent test and mental ages for the *WISC.*" *J. Consult. Psychol.,* 1951, 15, 381–384.
116. Wechsler, D. *Wechsler Adult Intelligence Scale* (Manual). New York: The Psychological Corp., 1955.
117. Wellman, Beth L. "Mental growth from pre-school to college." *J. Exp. Educ.,* 1937, 6, 127–138.
118. Whatley, Ruth G., and Plant, W. T. "The stability of *WISC* IQ's for selected children." *J. Psychol.,* 1957, 44, 165–167.
119. Wheeler, L. R. "A comparative study of the intelligence of East Tennessee mountain children." *J. Educ. Psychol.,* 1942, 33, 321–334.
120. Wingfield, A. H., and Sandiford, P. "Twins and orphans." *J. Educ. Psychol.,* 1928, 19, 410–423.
121. Wolfle, Dael. "Diversity of talent." *Amer. Psychologist,* 1960, 15, 535–545.
122. Woodworth, R. S. *Psychology,* 3d Ed. New York: Holt, 1934.

CHAPTER 5

1. Adams, J. E., and Ross, C. O. "Is skipping grades a satisfactory method of acceleration?" *Amer. Sch. Bd. J.,* 1932, 85, 24–25.
2. Adams, J. J. "Achievement and social adjustment of pupils in combination classes enrolling pupils of more than one grade level." *J. Educ. Res.,* 1953, 47, 151–155.
3. Anastasi, Anne. *Differential Psychology,* 3d Ed. New York: Macmillan, 1958.
4. Anderson, R. H. "Ungraded primary classes: an administrative contribution to mental health." *Understanding the Child,* 1955, 24, 66–72.
5. Anfinson, R. D. "School progress and pupil adjustment." *Elem. Sch. J.,* 1941, 41, 507–514.
6. Atwood, R. A. "Science self-taught." *Ill. Educ.,* 1958, 46, 348–349.

7. Baller, W. R. "A study of the present social status of adults who, when they were in elementary schools, were classified as mentally deficient." *Genet. Psychol. Monogr.,* 1936, 18 (3), 165–244.
8. Barthelmess, Harriet M., and Boyer, P. A. "An evaluation of ability grouping." *J. Educ. Res.,* 1932, 26, 284–294.
9. Bedoian, V. H. "Mental health analysis of socially overaccepted, socially underaccepted, overage and underage pupils in the sixth grade." *J. Educ. Psychol.,* 1953, 44, 366–371.
10. Bedoian, V. H. "Social acceptability and social rejection of underage, at age, and overage pupils in the sixth grade." *J. Educ. Res.,* 1954, 47, 513–520.
11. Benda, C. E. "Psychopathology of childhood," in Carmichael, L. *Manual of Child Psychology,* 2d Ed. New York: Wiley, 1954.
12. Bennett, Erma, Rowan, Norma, Kelly, Florence, Schuyler, Ruby, and Segar, W. B. "Schools can change grouping practices." *Childh. Educ.,* 1953, 30, 64–67.
13. Bishton, R. C. "A study of some factors related to achievement of intellectually superior eighth grade children." *J. Educ. Res.,* 1957, 51, 203–207.
14. Blessing, K. R. "An evaluation of special education services for educable retarded children with some suggested refinements." *Amer. J. Ment. Def.,* 1957, 61, 491–496.
15. Bobroff, A. "Economic adjustment of 121 adults, formerly students in classes for mental retardates." *Amer. J. Ment. Def.,* 1956, 60, 525–535.
16. Bond, G. L., and Fay, L. C. "A report of the Univ. of Minn. reading clinic." *J. Educ. Res.,* 1950, 43, 385–390.
17. Bray, G. "The use of projects in the teaching of physics." *Sch. Sci. and Math.,* 1956, 56, 237–239.
18. *Bridging the Gap between School and College, Evaluation Report No. 1.* New York: The Fund for the Advancement of Education, 1953.
19. Brown, Marion V. "Teaching an in-

tellectually gifted group." *Elem. Sch. J.,* 1949, 49, 380–388.

20. Brueckner, L. J., and Bond, G. L. *The Diagnosis and Treatment of Learning Difficulties.* New York: Appleton-Century-Crofts, 1955.
21. Brumbaugh, Florence. "A school for gifted children." *Childh. Educ.,* 1944, 20, 325–327.
22. Carroll, H. A. "Intellectually gifted children: their characteristics and problems." *Teachers Coll. Rec.,* 1940, 42, 212–227.
23. Charles, D. C. "Ability and accomplishment of persons earlier judged mentally deficient." *Genet. Psychol. Monogr.,* 1953, 47, 3–71.
24. Cole, Luella. *The Elementary School Subjects.* New York: Rinehart, 1946.
25. Cook, W. W. "Individual differences and curriculum practice." *J. Educ. Psychol.,* 1948, 39, 141–148.
26. Cooke, E. W. "Ability grouping." *Bull. of the Nat. Ass. of Sec.-sch. Principals,* 1952, 36, 79–83.
27. Cornelius, Ruth. "Reading with six-year-olds." *Childh. Educ.,* 1949, 26, 162–163.
28. Cummins, Evelyn W. "Grouping: homogeneous or heterogeneous." *Educ. Adm. and Superv.,* 1958, 44, 19–26.
29. Cutts, Norma Estelle, and Moseley, N. "Providing for the bright child in a heterogeneous group." *Educ. Adm. and Superv.,* 1953, 39, 225–230.
30. Dahlberg, C. C., Rosewell, Florence, and Chall, Jeanne. "Psychotherapeutic principles as applied to remedial reading." *Elem. Sch. J.,* 1952, 53, 211–217.
31. Davis, G. "Remedial work in spelling." *Elem. Sch. J.,* 1927, 27, 615–626.
32. Delong, V. R. "Primary promotion by reading levels." *Elem. Sch. J.,* 1938, 38, 663–671.
33. "Describe winning studies." *Sci. News Letter,* 1958, 73 (8), 116.
34. Dolch, E. W. "A remedial-reading specialist in every school." *Elem. Sch. J.,* 1940, 41, 206–209.
35. Dolch, E. W. "Success in remedial reading." *Elem. Engl.,* 1953, 30, 133–137.
36. Dressel, P. L., and Grabow, J. M. "The gifted evaluate their high school ex-

perience." *J. Exc. Child.,* 1958, 24, 394–396.
37. Eales, J., Reed, H., and Wilson, C. "Grouping practices in the secondary schools of Los Angeles County." *Calif. J. Sec. Educ.,* 1955, 30, 54–57.
38. Edmiston, R. W., and Benefer, J. G. "The relationship between group achievement and range of abilities within the groups." *J. Educ. Res.,* 1949, 42, 547–548.
39. Engel, Anna M. "The challenge of the slow learning child." *Educ. Leadership,* 1953, 11, 151–155.
40. Faust, C. H. "Why the new concerns for educating the gifted." *Sch. Rev.,* 1957, 65, 12–19.
41. Featherstone, W. B. "Realistic education of the mentally retarded." *Teachers Coll. Rec.,* 1951, 52, 471–480.
42. Fifer, G. "Grade placement of secondary pupils in relation to age and ability." *Calif. J. Educ. Res.,* 1952, 3, 31–36.
43. Fogler, S. "Remedial reading for selected retarded children." *Elem. Sch. J.,* 1950, 51, 22–30.
44. Gallagher, J. J. "Peer acceptance of highly gifted children in elementary school." *Elem. Sch. J.* 1958, 58, 465–470.
45. Gallagher, J. J., and Crowder, Thora. "The adjustment of gifted children in the regular classroom." *J. Exc. Child.,* 1957, 23, 306–312, 317–319.
46. Glad, D. D. "Grouping for development." *Childh. Educ.,* 1949, 25, 354–356.
47. Goodlad, J. I. "Research and theory regarding promotion and nonpromotion." *Elem. Sch. J.,* 1952, 53, 150–154. Copyright by the Univ. of Chicago.
48. Gowan, May S. "Why homogeneous grouping." *Calif. J. Sec. Educ.,* 1955, 30, 22–28.
49. Gray, W. S. "Education of the gifted child: with special reference to reading." *Elem. Sch. J.,* 1942, 42, 736–744.
50. Gray, H. A., and Hollingworth, Leta S. "The achievement of gifted children enrolled and not enrolled in special opportunity classes." *J. Educ. Res.,* 1931, 24, 255–261.

References   547

51. *Guiding the Growth of Children.* New York: McGraw-Hill, Text-Film Dept.

52. Guiler, W. S., and Edwards, V. "An experimental study of instruction in computational arithmetic." *Elem. Sch. J.,* 1943, 43, 353–360.

53. Gustad, J. W., and Fish, Janice P. "The use of the Cooperative Mechanics of Expression Test in classification at the college freshmen level." *Educ. and Psychol. Measmt.,* 1955, 15, 436–440.

54. Hahn, Julia L. "Hobby clubs for children with special gifts." *Educ. Method,* 1938, 18, 21–26.

55. Harris, A. J. "Motivating the poor reader." *Educ.,* 1953, 73, 566–574.

56. Harvey, Lois F. "Improving arithmetic skills by testing and reteaching." *Elem. Sch. J.,* 1953, 53, 402–409.

57. Havighurst, R. J. "Conditions favorable and detrimental to the development of talent." *Sch. Rev.,* 1957, 65, 20–26.

58. Heffernan, Helen. "Grouping pupils for well-rounded growth and development." *Calif. J. Elem. Educ.,* 1952, 21, 42–50.

59. "High school methods with superior students." *Res. Bull. of the Nat. Educ. Ass.,* 1941, 19, 155–197.

60. Hightower, H. W. "Individual differences." *Educ. Adm. and Superv.,* 1955, 41, 458–461.

61. Hildreth, Gertrude H. "Characteristics of young gifted children." *J. Genet. Psychol.,* 1938, 53, 287–311.

62. Hildreth, Gertrude H. "School-wide planning for the gifted." *Educ. Adm. and Superv.,* 1955, 41, 1–10.

63. Hittinger, Martha S. "A social studies program." *Childh. Educ.,* 1956, 33, 16–18.

64. Hollingworth, Leta S. "An enrichment curriculum for rapid learners at Public School 500: Speyer School." *Teachers Coll. Rec.,* 1938, 39, 296–306.

65. House, R. W. "A study of five pupils who needed help in reading." *J. Educ. Res.,* 1947, 41, 47–59.

66. Ingram, Christine P. *Education of the Slow-learning Child.* New York: Ronald, 1953.

67. Janes, H. P. "Is remedial reading effective with slow learners?" *Training Sch. Bull.,* 1953, 50, 51–53.

68. Jenkins, Marian. "Here's to success in reading." *Childh. Educ.,* 1955, 32, 124–131.

69. Johnson, C. E. "Grouping children for arithmetic instruction." *Arith. Teacher,* 1954, 1, 16–20.

70. Johnson, G. O. "A study of the social position of mentally handicapped children in the regular grades." *Amer. J. Ment. Def.,* 1950, 55, 60–89.

71. Johnson, G. R. "Educating bright children." *J. Exc. Child.,* 1943, 10, 41–44.

72. Johnson, W. H. "Program for conserving our superior elementary school students." *Educ. Adm. and Superv.,* 1943, 29, 77–86.

73. Johnston, J. W., Coleman, J. H., and Guiler, W. S. "Improving the reading ability of elementary school pupils." *Elem. Sch. J.,* 1941–42, 42, 105–115.

74. Jolles, I. "The importance of psychological diagnosis in the Illinois program for the educable mentally handicapped." *Amer. J. Ment. Def.,* 1950, 54, 512–515.

75. Jones, Daisy Marvel. "An experiment in adaptation to individual differences." *J. Educ. Psychol.,* 1948, 39, 257–272.

76. Justman, J. "Personal and social adjustment of intellectually gifted accelerants and non-accelerants in junior high school." *Sch. Rev.,* 1953, 61, 468–478.

77. Justman, J. "Academic achievement of intellectually gifted accelerants and non-accelerants in junior high school." *Sch. Rev.,* 1954, 62, 142–150.

78. Kellogg, Roberta M. "Skills instruction for the gifted child in regular classroom." *Nat. Elem. Prin.,* 1949, 29, 37–40.

79. Keys, N. *The Underage Student in High School and College: Educational and Social Adjustments.* Berkeley, Calif.: Univ. of Calif. Press, 1938.

80. Keys, N. "Should we accelerate the bright?" *J. Exc. Child.,* 1942, 8, 248–254, 269.

81. Kingston, A. J., Jr., and George, C. E. "The effects of special reading training upon the development of college students' reading skills." *J. Educ. Res.,* 1957, 50, 471–475.

82. Kirk, S. A. *Teaching Reading to Slow-*

learning Children. Boston: Houghton Mifflin, 1940.

83. Kirk, S. A., and Johnson, G. O. *Educating the Retarded Child.* Boston: Houghton Mifflin, 1951.

84. Kogan, N. "A study of young students in college." *J. Counseling Psychol.,* 1955, 2, 129–136.

85. Kottmeyer, W. "Improving reading instruction in the St. Louis Schools." *Elem. Sch. J.,* 1944, 45, 33-38.

86. Kyte, G. C., and Neel, V. M. "A core vocabulary of spelling words." *Elem. Sch. J.,* 1953, 54, 29-34.

87. Lally, Ann, and LaBrant, Lou. "Experiences with children talented in the arts," in Witty, P. *The Gifted Child.* Boston: Heath, 1951.

88. Lampman, Permilla. "Finding the correct reading group for each child in grade II." *Elem. Sch. J.,* 1944, 44, 358–360. Copyright by the Univ. of Chicago.

89. Lehman, Hilda, and Cole, Luella. "The effectiveness of drill in handwriting to remove specific illegibilities." *Sch. and Soc.,* 1928, 27, 546–548.

90. Levy, N. M., and Cuddy, J. M. "Concept learning in educationally retarded children of normal intelligence." *J. Consult. Psychol.,* 1956, 20, 445–448.

91. Lewis, W. D. "Some characteristics of children designated as mentally retarded, as problems, and as geniuses by teachers." *J. Genet. Psychol.,* 1947, 70, 29–51.

92. Lewry, Marion E. "Improving manuscript writing in primary grades." *Elem. Sch. J.,* 1947, 47, 508–515.

93. Long, A. "What makes a winning science project." *Sci. and Mech.,* 1958, 39, 95–99.

94. Lorge, I. "Superior intellectual ability: its selection, education, and implications." *J. Hered.,* 1941, 32, 205–208.

95. Luchins, A. S., and Luchins, Edith H. "Children's attitudes toward homogeneous groupings." *J. Genet. Psychol.,* 1948, 72, 3–9.

96. McElwee, Edna W. "A comparison of the personality traits of 300 accelerated, normal, and retarded children." *J. Educ. Res.,* 1932, 26, 31–34.

97. May, R. *Man's Search for Himself.* New York: Norton, 1953.

98. Miller, M. M., and Dresden, Katherine. "Kearny High studies evaporation and humidity." *Sch. Sci. and Math.,* 1952, 52, 549–555.

99. Morgan, Antonia Bell. "Critical factors in the academic acceleration of gifted children; hypothesis based on clinical data." *Psychol. Reps.,* 1957, 3, 71–77.

100. Morphett, Mabel V., and Washburne, C. "When should children begin to read?" *Elem. Sch. J.,* 1931, 31, 496–503. Copyright by the Univ. of Chicago.

101. "Name top young scientists." *Sci. News Letter,* 1958, 73 (5), 68.

102. Nelson, E. A., and Carlson, E. F. "Special education for gifted children: III. Evaluation at the end of three years." *J. Exc. Child.,* 1945, 12, 6–13, 24.

103. Nordlind, Margaret. "A contribution in the field of mental retardation by the Michigan Vocational Rehabilitation." *Amer. J. Ment. Def.,* 1950, 54, 543–546.

104. Passow, A. H., and others. "We must multiply our efforts to identify and develop our talent resources." *NEA J.,* 1958, 47, 470–477.

105. Postel, H. H. "Reading the entire book: an experiment in sustained reading." *Elem. Sch. J.,* 1958, 58, 389–390.

106. Pressey, S. L. "Acceleration and the college student." *The Annu. of the Amer. Acad. of Pol. Soc. Sci.,* 1944, 231–232; 34–41.

107. Pressey, S. L. "Concerning the nature and nurture of genius." *Sci. Mon.,* 1955, 81, 123–129.

108. Prewett, C. R. "The assignment as a technique of individualizing instruction." *High Sch. J.,* 1953, 36, 129–133.

109. Reed, H. B. *Psychology of Elementary School Subjects.* Boston: Ginn, 1938.

110. Reininger, Ruth E. "A curriculum for the educable mentally retarded preadolescent." *Elem. Sch. J.,* 1956, 56, 310–314.

111. Russell, R. W., and Cronbach, L. J. *Psychology, Education, and the National Welfare,* Test Serv. Bull., no. 90, Yonkers-on-Hudson, N.Y.: World, 1958.

112. Ryan, W. C., Strang, Ruth, and Witty, P. "The teacher of gifted children," in Witty, P. *The Gifted Child.* Boston: Heath, 1951. Pp. 106–130.

113. Sandin, A. A. "Social and emotional adjustments of regularly promoted and non-promoted pupils." *Child Developm. Monogr.,* 1944, no. 32, 1–142.

114. Sarason, S. B. "Mentally retarded and mentally defective children: major psycho-social problems," in Cruickshank, W. (ed.) *Psychology of Exceptional Children and Youth.* Englewood Cliffs, N.J.: Prentice-Hall, 1955. Pp. 438–474.

115. Sexon, J. A. "Teaching the gifted child." *Amer. Child.,* 1930, 16, 3–6.

116. Silverman, H. L. "Commentary on a slow-learner child: a brief case history." *Understanding the Child,* 1955, 24, 120–122.

117. Smith, Dora V. "Caring for individual differences in the literature class." *Educ.,* 1954, 74, 294–299.

118. Smith, Nila B. "Helpful books to use with retarded readers." *Elem. Sch. J.,* 1952, 53, 390–397.

119. Smith, R. R. "Provisions for individual differences." *The Learning of Mathematics: Its Theory and Practice,* Twenty-first Yearbook Nat. Council of Teachers of Math., Washington, 1953.

120. Sorenson, H. *Psychology in Education,* 2d Ed. New York: McGraw-Hill, 1948.

121. Stevens, G. D., and Stevens, H. A. "Providing for the education of the mentally handicapped child in the rural school." *Elem. Sch. J.,* 1948, 48, 442–446.

122. Sullivan, Helen B., and Tolman, Lorraine E. "High interest–low vocabulary reading materials, a selected booklist." *J. Educ.,* 1956, 139 (2), 1–132.

123. Sumption, M. R., Norris, Dorothy, and Terman, L. M. "Special education for the gifted child," in Henry, N. B. *The Education of Exceptional Children.* Forty-ninth Yearbook Nat. Soc. Study of Educ., part II, pp. 259–280, Chicago, 1950. Distributed by the Univ. of Chicago Press.

124. Terman, L. M. "The gifted student

and his academic environment." *Sch. and Soc.,* 1939, 49, 65–73.

125. Terman, L. M. "The discovery and encouragement of exceptional talent." *Amer. Psychologist,* 1954, 9, 221–230.

126. Terman, L. M., and Oden, Melita H. *Genetic Studies of Genius; vol. IV, The Gifted Child Grows Up.* Stanford, Calif.: Stanford Univ. Press, 1947.

127. Terman, L. M., and Oden, Melita H. "The Stanford studies of the gifted children," in Witty, P. (Ed.) *The Gifted Child.* Boston: Heath, 1951.

128. Traxler, A. E. "The use of tests in differentiated instruction." *Educ.,* 1954, 74, 272–278.

129. Turner, E., and Eyre, M. B. "A study of the emotional stability in elementary school students in grades four to eight." *Psychol. Bull.,* 1940, 37, 595.

130. Unzicker, Cecilia E., and Flemming, C. W. "Remedial instruction an aid to effective study." *Teachers Coll. Rec.,* 1933, 34, 398–413.

131. Washburne, C. W. "Adjusting the program to the child." *Educ. Leadership,* 1953, 11, 138–147.

132. Weaver, J. F. "Differentiated instruction in arithmetic: an overview and a promising trend." *Educ.,* 1954, 74, 300–305.

133. Wilkins, W. L. "High school achievement of accelerated pupils." *Sch. Rev.,* 1936, 44, 268–273.

134. Wilkins, W. L. "The social adjustment of accelerated pupils." *Sch. Rev.,* 1936, 44, 445–455.

135. Wilson, F. T. "Some special ability test scores of gifted children." *J. Genet. Psychol.,* 1953, 82, 59–68.

136. Witty, P. (ed.) *The Gifted Child.* Boston: Heath, 1951.

137. Witty, P. "Education for the talented and for leadership." *Teachers Coll. Rec.,* 1956, 57, 295–300.

138. Wolfson, I. N. "Follow up studies of 92 male and 131 female patients who were discharged from the Newark State School in 1946." *Amer. J. Ment. Def.,* 1956, 61, 224–238.

139. Worcester, D. A. *The Education of Children of Above-average Mentality.*

Lincoln, Neb.: Univ. of Neb. Press, 1956.

140. Worlton, J. T. "Individualized instruction in reading." *Elem. Sch. J.*, 1936, 36, 735–747.

CHAPTER 6

1. Allport, G. W. "The trend in motivational theory." *Amer. J. of Orthopsychiat.*, 1953, 23, 107–119.
2. Allport, G. W. *Becoming, Basic Considerations for a Psychology of Personality*. New Haven, Conn.: Yale Univ. Press, 1955.
3. Arnold, Magda B. "Motivation and desire to know." *Educ.*, 1956, 77, 220–226.
4. Berdie, R. F. "Aptitude, achievement, interest, and personality tests: a longitudinal comparison." *J. Appl. Psychol.*, 1955, 39, 103–114.
5. Briggs, T. H. "Praise and censure as incentives." *Sch. and Soc.*, 1927, 26, 596–598.
6. Brown, F. J. "Knowledge of results as an incentive in schoolroom practice." *J. Educ. Psychol.*, 1932, 23, 532–552.
7. Brubacher, John S. *A History of Problems of Education*. New York: McGraw-Hill, 1947.
8. Cannon, W. B. *The Wisdom of the Body*. New York: Norton, 1932.
9. Cantril, H. *The "Why" of Man's Experience*. New York: Macmillan, 1950.
10. Carlsen, G. R. "Behind reading interests." *Engl. J.*, 1954, 43, 7–12.
11. Chapman, J. C., and Feder, R. B. "The effect of external incentives on improvement." *J. Educ. Psychol.*, 1917, 8, 469–474.
12. Coombs, A. W. "The myth of competition." *Childh. Educ.*, 1957, 33, 264–269.
13. Cooper, I. . B. "Salute to a teacher." *Reader's Digest*, June, 1957, 70, 154–160.
14. Cronbach, L. J. *Essentials of Psychological Testing*, 2d Ed. New York: Harper, 1960.
15. Davids, A., and White, A. A. "Effects of success, failure and social facilitation on level of aspiration of emotionally disturbed and normal children." *J. Pers.*, 1958, 26, 77–93.
16. deGroat, A. F., and Thompson, G. G. "A study of the distribution of teacher approval and disapproval among sixth-grade pupils." *J. Exp. Educ.*, 1949, 18, 57–75.
17. Doby, J. T. "Some effects of bias on learning." *J. Soc. Psychol.*, 1960, 51, 199–209.
18. Douvan, Elizabeth. "Social status and success strivings." *J. Abnorm. Soc Psychol.*, 1956, 52, 219–223.
19. Elsbree, W. S. "School practices that help and hurt personality." *Teachers Coll. Rec.*, 1941, 43, 24–34.
20. Fay, P. J. "The effect of the knowledge of marks on subsequent achievement of college students." *J. Educ. Psychol.*, 1937, 28, 548–554.
21. Forlano, G., and Axelrod, H. C. "The effect of repeated praises or blame on the performance of introverts and extroverts." *J. Educ. Psychol.*, 1937, 28, 92–100.
22. Frandsen, A. "Appraisal of interests in guidance." *J. Educ. Res.*, 1945, 39, 1–12.
23. Frandsen, A. "Interests and general educational development." *J. Appl. Psychol.*, 1947, 31, 57–66.
24. Frandsen, A., and Darke, R. "An evaluation of personality ratings and intelligence in predicting scholarship." *Utah Educ. Rev.*, 1935, 29, 127–130.
25. Frandsen, A., and Sessions, A. D. "Interests and school achievement." *Educ. and Psychol. Measmt.*, 1953, 13, 94–101.
26. Fromm, E. *Escape from Freedom*. New York: Rinehart, 1941.
27. Gebhard, Mildred E. "The effect of success and failure upon the attractiveness of activities as a function of experience, expectation, and need." *J. Exp. Psychol.*, 1948, 38, 371–388.
28. Gordon, H. C., and Herkness, W. W. "Do vocational interest questionnaires yield consistent results?" *Occupations*, 1942, 20, 424–429.
29. Gorman, B. W. "How to get pupils to prepare assignments." *Sch. Rev.*, 1945, 53, 237–239.

30. Gough, H. G. "What determines academic achievement of high school students." *J. Educ. Res.*, 1953, 46, 321–331.

31. Gross, Sister Mary Mynette. "The effect of certain types of motivation on the honesty of children." *J. Educ. Res.*, 1946, 40, 133–140.

32. Grossack, M. M. "Some effects of cooperation and competition upon small group behavior." *J. Abnorm. and Soc. Psychol.*, 1954, 49, 341–348.

33. Gruen, Emily W. "Level of aspiration in relation to personality factors of adolescents." *Child Developm.*, 1945, 16, 181–188.

34. Hardman, Maud. "Art in elementary and secondary school." Lecture at Utah State Univ., 1956.

35. Harlow, H., Harlow, Margaret K., and Meyer, Donald. "Learning motivated by a manipulation drive." *J. Exp. Psychol.*, 1950, 40, 228–234.

36. Hartshorne, H., and May, M. A. *Studies in the Nature of Character*, vol. I, *Studies in Deceit*. New York: Macmillan, 1928.

37. Hartung, M. L. "Motivation for education in mathematics." *The Learning of Mathematics, Its Theory and Practice*, Twenty-first Yearbook Nat. Council of Teachers of Math., 1953. Pp. 42–68.

38. Havron, M. D., and Cofer, C. N. "On the learning of material congruent and incongruent with attitudes." *J. Soc. Psychol.*, 1957, 46, 91–98.

39. Henle, Mary. "Some effects of motivational processes on cognition." *Psychol. Rev.*, 1955, 62, 423–432.

40. "Henry J. in Hawaiian Playground." *Life*, Dec. 2, 1957, 43, 87–92.

41. Hilgard, E. R. "Success in relation to level of aspiration." *Sch. and Soc.*, 1942, 55, 423–428.

42. Hilgard, E. R. "Aspirations after learning." *Childh. Educ.*, 1946–47, 23, 115–118.

43. Hopkinson, Margaret. "Their own special butterfly." *NEA J.*, 1953, 42, 567.

44. Hurley, J. R. "Achievement imagery and motivational instructions as determinants of verbal learning." *J. Pers.*, 1957, 25, 274–282.

45. Hurlock, Elizabeth B. "An evaluation of certain incentives used in school work." *J. Educ. Psychol.*, 1925, 16, 145–159.

46. Hurlock, Elizabeth B. "The use of rivalry as an incentive." *J. Abnorm. and Soc. Psychol.*, 1927, 22, 278–290.

47. James, H. W. "Punishment recommended for school offenses." *Elem. Sch. J.*, 1928–29, 29, 129–131.

48. Janis, I. L., and Feshbach, S. "Effects of fear-arousing communications." *J. Abnorm and Soc. Psychol.*, 1953, 48, 78–92.

49. Jersild, A. T. *Child Psychology*, 5th Ed. Englewood Cliffs, N.J.: Prentice-Hall, 1960.

50. Johnston, R. A. "The effects of achievement imagery on maze-learning performance." *J. Pers.*, 1955, 24, 145–152.

51. Jones, E. E., and Aneshansel, Jane. "The learning and utilization of contravaluant material." *J. Abnorm. and Soc. Psychol.*, 1956, 53, 27–33.

52. Judson, A. J., and Cofer, C. N. "Reasoning as an associative process: I. 'Direction' in a simple verbal problem." *Psychol. Reps.*, 1956, 2, 469–476.

53. Keister, Mary Elizabeth, and Updegraff, Ruth. "A study of children's reactions to failure and an experimental attempt to modify them." *Child Developm.*, 1937, 8, 241–248.

54. Keys, A., Brozek, J., Henschel, A., Michelsen, O., and Taylor, H. L. *Experimental Starvation in Man, Laboratory of Physiological Hygiene*. Minneapolis, Minn.: Univ. of Minn. Press, 1945.

55. Kropotkin, A. "We all need praise." *Reader's Digest*, Dec., 1936, 29, 105.

56. Kuder, F. *Examiners Manual for the Kuder Preference Record, Vocational Form C*, 5th Ed. Chicago: Science Research, 1953.

57. Lantz, Beatrice. "Some dynamic aspects of success and failure." *Psychol. Mongr.*, 1945, 59 (1), 1–40.

58. Lazarus, A. L. "Grouping based on high interest vs general ability: a senior high school teacher's viewpoint." *Calif. J. Sec. Educ.*, 1955, 30, 38–41.

59. Leuba, C. "Toward some integration of learning theories: the concept of

optimal stimulation." *Psychol. Reps.,* 1955, 1, 27–33.

60. Levine, Phyllis B., and Wallen, R. "Adolescent vocational interests and later occupation." *J. Appl. Psychol.,* 1954, 38, 428–431.

61. Lowell, E. L. "The effect of need for achievement on learning and speed of performance." *J. Psychol.,* 1952, 33, 31–40.

62. McClelland, D., Atkinson, J. W., Clark, R. A., and Lowell, E. L. *The Achievement Motive.* New York: Appleton-Century-Crofts, 1953.

63. McReynolds, P. "A restricted conceptualization of human anxiety and motivation." *Psychol. Reps.,* 1956, 2, 293–312.

64. Magill, J. W. "Interest profiles of college activity groups, Kuder Preference validation." *J. Appl. Psychol.,* 1955, 39, 53–56.

65. Maller, J. B. "Cooperation and competition, an experimental study of motivation," in Crafts, L. W., et al. *Recent Experiments in Psychology.* New York. McGraw-Hill, 1938. Pp. 60–69.

66. Mantle, M. "Brave partisans boo Tony Kubek." *Salt Lake Tribune,* Oct. 6, 1957.

67. Maslow, A. H. "A theory of human motivation." *Psychol. Rev.,* 1943, 50, 370–396.

68. May, R. *Man's Search for Himself.* New York: Norton, 1953.

69. Mintz, A. "Non-adaptive group behavior." *J. Abnorm. and Soc. Psychol.,* 1951, 46, 150–159.

70. Morgan, C. T. "Physiological mechanisms of motivation," in Jones, M. R. (ed.) *Nebraska Symposium on Motivation.* Lincoln, Neb.: Univ. of Neb. Press, 1957. Pp. 1–35.

71. Murphy, G. "Toward a dynamic trace-theory." *Bull of Menninger Clinic,* 1956, 20, 124–134.

72. Nuttin, J. "Personality dynamics," in David, H. P., and Von Bracken, H. (eds.) *Perspectives in Personality Theory.* New York: Basic Books, 1957. Pp. 183–196.

73. O'Brien, Katherine. "Problem-solving." *The Math. Teacher,* 1956, 49, 79–86.

74. Otto, H. J. "An attempt to evaluate the threat of failure as a factor in achievement." *Elem. Sch. J.,* 1935, 35, 588–596.

75. Panlasigui, I., and Knight, F. B. "The effect of awareness of success or failure." *Research in Arithmetic,* Twenty-ninth Yearbook Nat. Soc. Study of Educ., part II, pp. 611–619, Chicago, 1930. Distributed by the Univ. of Chicago Press.

76. Park, J. "How they thought they were motivated." *J. Educ. Res.,* 1945, 39, 193–200.

77. Powers, Mabel K. "Permanence of measured vocational interests of adult males." *J. Appl. Psychol.,* 1956, 40, 69–72.

78. Putt, Dorothy. "Science experiences afford opportunity . . . for a realistic approach to problems." *Childh. Educ.,* 1952, 29, 78–79.

79. Rhine, R. J. "The effect on problem solving of success or failure as a function of cue specificity." *J. Exp. Psychol.,* 1957, 53, 121–125.

80. Rogers, C. R. "Some directions and end points in therapy," in Mowrer, O. H. *Psychotherapy: Theory and Research.* New York: Ronald, 1953.

81. Rosenberg, N. "Stability and maturation of Kuder Interest patterns during high school." *Educ. Psychol. Measmt.,* 1953, 13, 449–458.

82. Ross, C. C. "Influence upon achievement of knowledge of progress." *J. Educ. Psychol.,* 1933, 24, 609–619.

83. Schmidt, H. O. "The effects of praise and blame as incentives to learning." *Psychol. Monogr.,* 1941, 53 (240), 1–56.

84. Schoeppe, Aileen, Haggard, E. A., and Havighurst, R. J. "Some factors affecting sixteen-year-olds' success in five development tasks." *J. Abnorm. and Soc. Psychol.,* 1953, 48, 42–52.

85. Sears, Pauline S. "Levels of aspiration in academically successful and unsuccessful children." *J. Abnorm. and Soc. Psychol.,* 1940, 35, 498–536.

86. Sears, Pauline S. "Level of aspiration in relation to some variables of personality: clinical studies." *J. Soc. Psychol.,* 1941, 14, 311–336.

87. Shepler, W. D. "A study of scholastic

achievement in secondary school science in relation to pupils' relative preference for this subject." *Dissertation Abstr.*, 1956, 16, 1376–1377.

88. Shinn, E. O. "Interest and intelligence as related to achievement in tenth grade." *Calif. J. Educ. Res.*, 1956, 7, 217–220.

89. Solley, C. M., and Sommer, R. "Perceptual autism in children." *J. Gen. Psychol.*, 1957, 56, 3–11.

90. Stendler, Celia B., Damrin, Dora, and Haines, A. C. "Studies in cooperation and competition: I. The effects of working for group and individual rewards on the social climate of children's groups." *J. Genet. Psychol.*, 1951, 79, 173–197.

91. Symonds, P. M. "Human drives." *J. Educ. Psychol.*, 1934, 25, 681–694.

92. Symonds, P. M. "Classroom discipline." *Teachers Coll. Rec.*, 1949, 51, 147–158.

93. Symonds, P. M. "What education has to learn from psychology." *Teachers Coll. Rec.*, 1954–55, 56, 277–285.

94. Symonds, P. M. "What education has to learn from psychology: III. Punishment." *Teachers Coll. Rec.*, 1956, 57, 449–462.

95. Taft, Jessie. "The catch in praise." *Child Study*, 1930, 7, 133–135, 150.

96. Thompson, G. G., and Hunnicutt, C. W. "Effects of repeated praise or blame on the work achievement of introverts and extroverts." *J. Educ. Psychol.*, 1944, 35, 257–266.

97. "Top STS winners named." *Sci. News Letter*, 1958, 73 (11), 166.

98. Traxler, A. E., and McCall, W. C. "Some data on the Kuder Preference Record." *Educ. and Psychol. Measmt.*, 1941, 1, 253–268.

99. Turney, A. H. "Intelligence, motivation, and achievement." *J. Educ. Psychol.*, 1931, 22, 426–434.

100. Vaughn, J., and Diserens, C. M. "The experimental psychology of competition." *J. Exp. Educ.*, 1938, 7, 76–97.

101. Wesley, S. M., Corey, D. Q., and Stewart, Barbara. "The intra-individual relationship between interest and ability." *J. Appl. Psychol.*, 1950, 34, 193–197.

102. White, R. W. "Motivation reconsidered: the concept of competence." *Psychol. Rev.*, 1959, 66, 297–333.

CHAPTER 7

1. Anderson, Theresa. "A study of the use of visual aids in basket shooting." *Res. Quart.*, 1942, 13, 532–537.

2. Beauchamp, W. L. "Teaching a generalization of science." *Sci. Educ.*, 1939, 23, 9–10.

3. Bedell, R., and Nelson, E. S. "Word attack as a factor in reading achievement in the elementary school." *Educ. and Psychol. Measmt.*, 1954, 14, 168–175.

4. Bond, G. L., and Fay, L. C. "A report of the University of Minnesota reading clinic." *J. Educ. Res.*, 1950, 43, 385–390.

5. Bowers, Joan E. "Procedure to strengthen ability to solve arithmetic problems." *Sch. Sci. and Math.*, 1957, 57, 485–493.

6. Brownell, W. A., and Chazal, Charlotte B. "The effects of premature drill in third-grade arithmetic." *J. Educ. Res.*, 1935, 29, 17–28.

7. Brownell, W. A. "Rate, accuracy, and process in learning." *J. Educ. Psychol.*, 1944, 35, 321–337.

8. Cantril, H. *The "Why" of Man's Experience.* New York: Macmillan, 1950.

9. Cantril, H. "Perception and interpersonal relations." *Amer. J. Psychiat.*, 1957, 114, 119–126.

10. Connor, W. L., and Hawkins, Gertrude C. "What materials are most useful to children in learning to solve problems?" *Educ. Method*, 1936, 16, 21–29.

11. Corman, B. R. "The effect of varying amounts and kinds of information as guidance in problem solving." *Psychol. Monogr.*, 1957, 71 (2), 1–21 (whole no. 431).

12. Craig, R. C. *The Transfer Value of Guided Learning.* New York: Bur. of Publ., Teachers Coll., Col. Univ., 1953.

13. Cronbach, L. J. "The meaning of problems." *Suppl. Educ. Monogr.*, No. 66. Chicago: Univ. of Chicago Press, 1948. Pp. 32–43.

14. Davies, Dorothy R. "The effect of tuition upon the process of learning a complex motor skill." *J. Educ. Psychol.*, 1945, 36, 352–365.

15. Davis, R. A. "Helping the learner to help himself." *Educ. Digest*, 1951–52, 17, 39–41.

16. Dawson, D. T., and Ruddell, A. K. "An experimental approach to the division idea." *Arith. Teacher*, 1955, 2 (1), 6–9.

17. Douglass, H. R. "The modern high school curriculum." *Sch. Rev.*, 1955, 63, 16–24.

18. Duncker, K. "On problem-solving." *Psychol. Monogr.*, 1945, 58 (270), 1–112.

19. Fehr, H. F. "The role of insight in the learning of mathematics." *The Math. Teacher*, 1954, 47, 386–392.

20. Fehr, H. F. "A philosophy of arithmetic instruction." *Arith. Teacher*, 1955, 2 (2), 27–32.

21. Gates, A. I. "Implications of the psychology of perception for word study." *Educ.*, 1955, 75, 589–595.

22. Goodenough, Florence L., and Brian, C. R. "Certain factors underlying the acquisition of motor skill by pre-school children." *J. Exp. Psychol.*, 1929, 12, 127–155.

23. Goodson, M. R. "Problem-solving in elementary school." *Progr. Educ.*, 1950, 27, 143–147.

24. Harap, H., and Barrett, Ursula. "Experimenting with real situations in third grade arithmetic." *Educ. Method*, 1937, 16, 188–192.

25. Harding, L. W., and Bryant, Inez P. "An experimental comparison of drill and direct experience in arithmetical learning in a fourth grade." *J. Educ. Res.*, 1944, 37, 321–337.

26. Hartung, M. L. "Advances in teaching problem-solving." *Arithmetic*, *Supp. Educ. Monogr.*, No. 66. Chicago: Univ. of Chicago Press, 1948. Pp. 44–53.

27. Heffernan, Helen. "No mean hut." *Childh. Educ.*, 1957, 34, 112–117.

28. Heidbreder, Edna. "The attainment of concepts—a psychological interpretation." *Trans. N. Y. Acad. of Sci.*, 1945, (2) 7, 171–188.

29. Heidbreder, Edna. "The attainment of concepts: III. The process." *J. Psychol.*, 1947, 24, 93–138.

30. Heidbreder, Edna, Bensley, M., and Ivy, M. "The attainment of concepts: IV. Regularities and levels." *J. Psychol.*, 1948, 25, 299–329.

31. Heidbreder, Edna. "The attainment of concepts: VI. Exploratory experiments on conceptualization at perceptual levels." *J. Psychol.*, 1948, 26, 193–216.

32. Henderson, K. B., and Pingry, R. E. "Problem-solving in mathematics." *The Learning of Mathematics: Its Theory and Practice*, Twenty-first Yearbook Nat. Council of Teachers of Math., 1953. Pp. 228–270.

33. Hendrix, Gertrude. "A new clue to transfer of training." *Elem. Sch. J.*, 1947–48, 48, 197–208.

34. Hildreth, Gertrude H. "The difficulty reduction tendency in perception and problem-solving." *J. Educ. Psychol.*, 1941, 32, 305–313.

35. Hirschi, L. E. "An experiment in the teaching of elementary algebra." *Sch. Rev.*, 1958, 66, 185–194.

36. Hooper, Laura, and Staff. "The inner resources of children." *Childh. Educ.*, 1956, 33, 101–103.

37. Johnson, D. M. "A modern account of problem-solving." *Psychol. Bull.*, 1944, 41, 201–229.

38. Jones, P. S. "Discovery as a teaching tool." *Univ. of Mich. Sch. of Educ. Bull.*, 1955, 26, 87–92.

39. Keston, M. J. "An experimental evaluation of the efficacy of two methods of teaching music appreciation." *J. Exp. Educ.*, 1954, 22, 215–226.

40. Keister, Mary E. "The behavior of young children in failure," in Barker, R. G., Kounin, J. S., and Wright, H. F. (eds.) *Child Behavior and Development*. New York: McGraw-Hill, 1943.

41. Kittell, J. E. "An experimental study of the effect of external direction during learning on transfer and retention of principles." *J. Educ. Psychol.*, 1957, 48, 391–405.

42. Klein, G. S. "Cognitive control and motivation," in Lindzey, G. (ed.) *Assessment of Human Motives*. New York: Rinehart, 1958. Pp. 87–118.

43. Kogan, Z. *Essentials in Problem Solving*. New York: Arco Publ. Co., 1956.

44. Leeper, R. W. "What contributions might cognitive learning theory make to our understanding of personality?" *J. Pers.*, 1953–54, 22, 32–40.

45. Lewis, Eunice. "The role of sensory materials in meaningful learning." *The Math. Teacher*, 1956, 49, 274–277.

46. Lowry, W. C. "Pupil discovery in junior high school mathematics." *The Math. Teacher*, 1956, 49, 301–303.

47. Luchins, A. S. "Mechanization in problem-solving: the effect of 'Einstellung.'" *Psychol. Monogr.*, 1942, 54 (6), 1–95.

48. Luchins, A. S., and Luchins, Edith H. "A structural approach to the teaching of the concept of area in intuitive geometry." *J. Educ. Res.*, 1947, 40, 528–533.

49. Maier, N. R. F. "An aspect of human reasoning." *Br. J. Psychol.*, 1933, 24, 144–155.

50. Maier, N. R. F. "The behavior mechanisms concerned with problem-solving." *Psychol. Rev.*, 1940, 47, 43–58.

51. McConnell, T. R. "Discovery versus authoritative identification in the learning of children." *Univ. of Iowa, Studies in Educ.*, 1934, 9 (5), 13–62.

52. McCullough, Constance M. "Word analysis in the high school program." *Engl. J.*, 1952, 41, 15–23.

53. Miller, G. H. "How effective is the meaning method?" *Arith. Teacher*, 1957, 4, 45–49.

54. Mulholland, Vernie. "Fifth grade children discover fractions." *Sch. Sci. and Math.*, 1954, 54, 13–30.

55. Mutsfeld, H. "Science experiences afford opportunity for experimentation." *Childh. Educ.*, 1952, 29, 81.

56. O'Brien, Katherine. "Problem-solving." *The Math. Teacher*, 1956, 49, 79–86.

57. Parker, Elsie. "Teaching pupils the conscious use of a technique of thinking." *The Math. Teacher*, 1924, 17, 191–201.

58. Petty, O. "Requiring proof of understanding." *Arith. Teacher*, 1955, 2 (4), 121–123.

59. Reed, C. H. "Developing creative thinking in arithmetic." *Arith. Teacher*, 1957, 4 (1), 10–12.

60. Russell, D. H. *Children's Thinking*. Boston: Ginn, 1956.

61. Rutledge, J. A. "Some opportunities in chemistry for problem solving." *Sch. Sci. and Math.*, 1953, 53, 605–607.

62. Sauble, Irene. "Development of ability to estimate and to compute mentally." *Arith. Teacher*, 1955, 2 (2), 33–39.

63. Schafer-Simmern, Henry. *The Unfolding of Artistic Activity*. Berkeley, Calif.: Univ. of Calif. Press, 1950.

64. Sobel, M. A. "Concept learning in algebra." *The Math. Teacher*, 1956, 49, 425–430.

65. Stevenson, P. R. "Difficulties in problem-solving." *J. Educ. Res.*, 1925, 11, 95–103.

66. Stowe, L. "The amazing Crusoes of Lonesome Lake." *Reader's Digest*, 1957, 70, 82–86, 209–232.

67. Swenson, Esther. "The how and why of discovery in arithmetic." *Arith. Teacher*, 1954, 1 (2), 15–19.

68. Thiele, C. L. "The mathematical viewpoint applied to teaching of elementary school arithmetic." *Teaching of Arithmetic*, Tenth Yearbook Nat. Council of Teachers of Math., 1935. Pp. 212–232.

69. Thiele, C. L. "Fostering discovery with children." *Arith. Teacher*, 1954, 1, 6–11.

70. Thompson, L. M. "The role of verbalization in learning from demonstrations." Dissertation at Yale Univ., 1944, quoted by C. I. Hovland in Stevens, S. S. *Handbook of Experimental Psychology*. New York: Wiley, 1951.

71. Thorndike, R. L. "How children learn the principles and techniques of problem-solving." *Learning and Instruction*, Forty-ninth Yearbook Nat. Soc. Study of Educ., part I, pp. 192–216. Chicago, 1950. Distributed by the Univ. of Chicago Press.

72. Thorpe, Cleata B. "The equation: neglected ally of arithmetic processes." *Elem. Sch. J.*, 1960, 60, 320–324.

73. Tilton, J. W. "Individualized and meaningful instruction in arithmetic." *J. Educ. Psychol.*, 1947, 38, 83–88.

74. Wertheimer, Max. *Productive Thinking*, Enlarged Ed. New York: Harper, 1959.

75. Winch, W. H. "Immediate memory in school children." *Br. J. Psychol.*, 1906–08, 2, 52–57.

76. Wisely, Edna. "An approach to problem

solving." *Arith. Teacher,* 1957, 4 (3), 125–128.

77. Zuckerman, C. B., and Rock, I. "A reappraisal of the roles of past experience and innate organizing processes in visual perception." *Psychol. Bull.,* 1957, 54, 269–294.

CHAPTER 8

1. Aftreth, O. B. "Shall we expose our pupils to errors?" *Arith. Teacher,* 1957, 4, 129–131.
2. Angell, G. W. "Effect of immediate knowledge of quiz results on final examination scores in freshman chemistry." *J. Educ. Res.,* 1949, 42, 391–394.
3. Associated Press. "Pitching control the toughest to learn." *Salt Lake Tribune,* Mar. 3, 1958.
4. Beecroft, R. S. "Verbal learning and retention as a function of the number of competing associations." *J. Exp. Psychol.,* 1956, 51, 216–221.
5. Bijou, S. W. "Patterns of reinforcement and resistance to extinction in young children." *Child Developm.,* 1957, 28, 47–54.
6. Bourne, L. E., Jr. "Effects of delay of information feedback and task complexity on identification of concepts." *J. Exp. Psychol.,* 1957, 54, 201–207.
7. Bovyer, G. "Evaluation of group processes in a sixth grade social studies program." *Calif. J. Educ. Res.,* 1955, 6, 174–177.
8. Brownell, W. A. "Meaning and skill: maintaining the balance." *Arith. Teacher,* 1956, 3, 129–136.
9. Brownell, W. A., and Chazal, C. B. "The effects of premature drill in third grade arithmetic." *J. Educ. Res.,* 1935, 29, 17–28.
10. Connette, E. "The effect of practice with knowledge of results upon pitch discrimination." *J. Educ. Psychol.,* 1941, 32, 523–532.
11. Crandall, V. J., Soloman, D., and Kellaway, R. "The value of anticipated events as a determinant of probability learning and extinction." *J. Gen. Psychol.,* 1958, 58, 3–10.
12. Crosby, M. "Purposeful direction in speaking and writing." *Childh. Educ.,* 1954, 31, 22–29.
13. Della-Piana, G. M. "Two experimental feedback procedures: a comparison of their effects on the learning of concepts." *Dissertation Abstr.,* 1956, 16, 910–911.
14. Distad, H. W. "An analysis of the drill provisions in division of decimals in 10 arithmetic series." *J. Educ. Res.,* 1933–34, 27, 509–523.
15. Durkin, H. E. "Trial and error, gradual analysis, and sudden reorganization: an experiment in problem-solving." *Arch. Psychol.,* 1937, no. 210, 1–85.
16. Eisen, Agnes. "Economic education through a school store." *Elem. Sch. J.,* 1958, 58, 287–289.
17. Elwell, J. L., and Grindley, C. G. "The effects of knowledge of results on learning and performance: a coordinated movement of the two hands." *Br. J. Psychol.,* 1938, 29, 39–54.
18. Evans, N. D. "Homework." *Childh. Educ.,* 1957, 33, 218–220.
19. Frank, J. G. "Learning languages with the tape that talks back." *Mod. Lang. J.,* 1951, 35, 616–618.
20. Gates, A. I., Batchelder, Mildred R., and Betsner, Jean. "A modern systematic versus an opportunistic method of teaching." *Teachers Coll. Rec.,* 1925–26, 27, 678–700.
21. Grant, D. A., Hake, H. W., and Hornseth, J. P. "Acquisition and extinction of a verbal conditioned response with different percentages of reinforcement." *J. Exp. Psychol.,* 1951, 42, 1–5.
22. Greenspoon, J., and Foreman, Sally. "Effect of delay of knowledge of results on learning a motor task." *J. Exp. Psychol.,* 1956, 51, 226–228.
23. Harap, H., and Mapes, Charlotte E. "The learning of fundamentals in an arithmetic activity program." *Elem. Sch. J.,* 1934, 34, 515–525.
24. Harlow, H. F. "The formation of learning sets." *Psychol. Rev.,* 1949, 56, 51–65.
25. Harmon, J. M., and Miller, A. "Time patterns in motor learning." *Res. Quart.,* 1950, 21, 182–186.
26. Hildreth, Gertrude H. "An individual

study in word recognition." *Elem. Sch. J.*, 1935, 35, 606–619.

27. Hildreth, Gertrude H. *Learning the Three R's*. Minneapolis, Minn.: *Educ. Pubrs.*, 1947.

28. Hildreth, Gertrude H. "Skills develop with functioning." *Educ. Outl.*, 1949, 24, 13–19.

29. Hilgard, E. R. *Theories of Learning*, 2d Ed. New York: Appleton-Century-Crofts, 1956.

30. Holland, Henrietta. "Difficulties involved in long division and some suggestions for teaching the process." *Elem. Sch. J.*, 1941–42, 42, 585–596. Copyright by the Univ. of Chicago.

31. Holmes, Eleanor. "Vocabulary instruction in reading." *Elem. Engl. Rev.*, 1934, 11, 103–105, 110.

32. Holodnak, H. B. "The effect of positive and negative guidance upon maze learning in children." *J. Educ. Psychol.*, 1943, 34, 341–354.

33. Hook, J. N. "Suggestions for use of 'Ideaform.'" *Engl. J.*, 1956, 45, 33–34.

34. Hovland, C. I. "Human learning and retention," in Stevens, S. S. *Handbook of Experimental Psychology*. New York: Wiley, 1951. Pp. 619–689.

35. Jensen, B. T. "This thing called 'practice.'" *Peabody J. of Educ.*, 1955–56, 33, 221–226.

36. Keller, F. S. "Studies in International Morse Code: 4. A note on second-level training in code reception." *J. Appl. Psychol.*, 1945, 29, 161–163.

37. Knapp, C. G., and Dixon, W. R. "Learning to juggle: I. A study to determine the effect of two different distributions of practice on learning efficiency." *Res. Quart.*, 1950, 21, 331–336.

38. Knapp, C. G., Dixon, W. R., and Lazier, M. "Learning to juggle: III. A study of performance by two different age groups." *Res. Quart.*, 1958, 29, 32–36.

39. Lashley, K. S. "The acquisition of skill in archery." Papers from the Dept. of Marine Biol., Carnegie Inst. of Washington, 1915, 7, 105–128.

40. Leggitt, Dorothy. "Perceptual learning in penmanship." *Elem. Sch. J.*, 1940, 40, 764–770.

41. Little, J. K. "Results of use of machines for testing and for drill upon learning in educational psychology." *J. Exp. Educ.*, 1934, 3, 45–49.

42. Lorge, I., and Thorndike, E. L. "The influence of delay in the after-effect of a connection." *J. Exp. Psychol.*, 1935, 18, 187–194.

43. McIntosh, J. R. "Learning by exposure to wrong forms in grammar and spelling." *Teachers Coll. Contr. to Educ.*, 1944, no. 892.

44. Messick, S. J., and Solley, C. M. "Probability learning in children: some exploratory studies." *J. Genet. Psychol.*, 1957, 90, 23–32.

45. Mickelson, J. M. "What does research say about the effectiveness of the core curriculum?" *Sch. Rev.*, 1957, 65, 144–160.

46. Middlecoff, C. "Cut strokes off your score by using correct stance." *Salt Lake Tribune*, May 5, 1958.

47. Moyer, Haverly O. "Can ear-training improve English usage?" *Elem. Engl.*, 1956, 33, 216–219.

48. Oldfield, R. C., and Zangwill, O. L. "The acquisition of verbal repetition habits." *Br. J. Psychol.*, 1938–39, 29, 12–26.

49. Oseas, L., and Underwood, B. J. "Studies of distributed practice: V. Learning and retention of concepts." *J. Exp. Psychol.*, 1952, 43, 143–148.

50. Plowman, Letha F., and Stroud, J. B. "Effect of responses to informing pupils of the correctness of their objective test questions." *J. Educ. Res.*, 1942, 36, 16–20.

51. Raskin, Evelyn, and Cook, S. W. "The strength and direction of associations formed in the learning of nonsense syllables." *J. Exp. Psychol.*, 1937, 20, 381–395.

52. Reed, H. B. "Distributed practice in addition." *J. Educ. Psychol.*, 1924, 15, 248–249.

53. Reed, H. B. "An experiment on the law of effect in learning the maze by humans." *J. Educ. Psychol.*, 1935, 26, 695–700.

54. Reed, H. B. *Psychology of Elementary School Subjects*. Boston: Ginn, 1938.

55. Rosenblum, S. "The effects of differential reinforcement and motivation on

prediction of responses of children." *Child Developm.*, 1956, 27, 99–108.

56. *Salt Lake Tribune*, Feb. 2, 1958, p. 10.

57. Seashore, H. G., and Bavelas, A. "The functioning of knowledge of results in Thorndike's line-drawing experiment." *Psychol. Rev.*, 1941, 48, 155–164.

58. Seashore, H. G., and Bavelas, A. "A study of frustration in children." *J. Genet. Psychol.*, 1942, 61, 279–314.

59. Skinner, B. F. "The science of learning and the art of teaching." *Harv. Educ. Rev.*, 1954, 24, 86–97.

60. Symonds, P. M. "Practice versus grammar in the learning of correct English usage." *J. Educ. Psychol.*, 1931, 22, 81–95.

61. Symonds, P. M. "What education has to learn from psychology: II. Reward." *Teachers Coll. Rec.*, 1955–56, 57, 15–25.

62. Thorndike, E. L. "The law of effect." *Amer. J. Psychol.*, 1927, 39, 212–222.

63. Thorndike, E. L. *Human Learning.* New York: Century, 1931.

64. Thune, L. E. "Warm-up effect as a function of level of practice in verbal learning." *J. Exp. Psychol.*, 1951, 42, 250–256.

65. Tilton, J. W. *An Educational Psychology of Learning.* New York: Macmillan, 1951.

66. Torrance, E. P. "Methods of conducting critiques of group problem-solving performance." *J. Appl. Psychol.*, 1953, 37, 394–398.

67. Trowbridge, Margery H., and Cason, H. "An experimental study of Thorndike's theory of learning." *J. Gen. Psychol.*, 1932, 7, 245–260.

68. Twining, W. E. "Mental practice and physical practice in learning a motor skill." *Res. Quart.*, 1949, 20, 432–435.

69. Vandell, R. A., Davis, R. A., and Clugston, H. A. "The function of mental practice in the acquisition of motor skills." *J. Gen. Psychol.*, 1943, 29, 243–250.

70. Welch, L. "The relationship between conditioning and higher learning." *J. Gen. Psychol.*, 1955, 53, 221–229.

71. Wheat, H. G. "A theory of instruction for the middle grades." *Arithmetic in General Education,* Sixteenth Yearbook

Nat. Council of Teachers of Math., 1941. Pp. 80–118.

72. Wilman, J. "Keep accurate records to check weaknesses." *Salt Lake Tribune,* Oct. 21, 1957.

73. Woodworth, R. S. *Dynamics of Behavior.* New York: Holt, 1958.

74. Word, A. H., and Davis, R. A. "Acquisition and retention of factual information in seventh-grade general science, during a semester of eighteen weeks." *J. Educ. Psychol.*, 1939, 30, 116–125.

75. Wyatt, Ruth F. "Improvability of pitch discrimination." *Psychol. Monogr.*, 1945, 58, no. 2.

CHAPTER 9

1. Ausubel, D. P., Robbins, Lillian C., and Blake, E., Jr. "Retroactive inhibition and facilitation in the learning of school materials." *J. Educ. Psychol.*, 1957, 48, 334–343.

2. Blough, G. O., and Dodd, A. L. "Children are their own resources." *Childh. Educ.*, 1957, 34, 21–24.

3. Brownell, W. A. "A study of learning in one phase of arithmetic." *J. Gen. Psychol.*, 1941, 24, 457–465.

4. Brownell, W. A., and Moser, H. E. "Meaningful versus mechanical learning: a study in third grade subtraction." *Duke Univ. Res. Stud. in Educ.*, 1949, no. 8.

5. Calvin, A. D. "Configural learning in children." *J. Educ. Psychol.*, 1955, 46, 117–120.

6. Carey, Janice E., and Goss, A. E. "The role of mediating verbal responses in the conceptual sorting behavior of children." *J. Genet. Psychol.*, 1957, 90, 69–74.

7. Carpenter, F. "The effect of different learning methods on concept formation." *Sci. Educ.*, 1956, 40, 282–285.

8. Carpenter, W. W., and Fort, M. K. "What effect do visitors have on recitations?" *J. Educ. Res.*, 1930, 22, 50–53.

9. Cofer, C. N. "A comparison of logical and verbatim learning of prose passages of different length." *Amer. J. Psychol.*, 1941, 54, 1–20.

10. Cofer, C. N. "Reasoning as an associative process: III. The role of verbal responses in problem-solving." *J. Gen. Psychol.*, 1957, 57, 55–68.

11. Cole, Luella. "Instruction in penmanship for the left-handed child." *Elem. Sch. J.*, 1939, 39, 436–448.

12. Dietze, Doris. "The facilitating effect of words on discrimination and generalization." *J. Exp. Psychol.*, 1955, 50, 255–260.

13. Douglass, H. R., and Spitzer, H. F. "The importance of teaching for understanding." *The Measurement of Understanding*, Forty-fifth Yearbook Nat. Soc. Study of Educ., part I, pp. 7–26, Chicago, 1946. Distributed by the Univ. of Chicago Press.

14. Dynes, J. J. "Comparison of two methods of studying history." *J. Exp. Educ.*, 1932, 1, 42–45.

15. Erickson, L. H. "Color as an aid in teaching concepts." *Arith. Teacher*, 1958, 5, 10–14.

16. Evert, P. H., and Lambert, J. F. "Part II: The effect of verbal instructions upon the formation of a concept." *J. Gen. Psychol.*, 1932, 6, 401–413.

17. Fernald, Grace M. *Remedial Techniques in Basic School Subjects*. New York: McGraw-Hill, 1943.

18. Flanders, N. A. "Verbalization and learning in the classroom." *Elem. Sch. J.*, 1948, 48, 385–392.

19. Flournoy, Frances. "A consideration of the ways children think when performing higher-decade addition." *Elem. Sch. J.*, 1957, 57, 204–208. Copyright by the Univ. of Chicago.

20. Forlano, G. "School learning with various methods of practice and reward." *Teachers Coll. Contr. to Educ.*, 1936, no. 688.

21. Gates, A. I. "Recitation as a factor in memorizing." *Arch. Psychol.*, 1917, 6 (40), 1–104.

22. Germane, C. E. "The value of a controlled mental summary as a method of studying." *Sch. and Soc.*, 1920, 12, 591–593.

23. Germane, C. E. "The value of the corrected summary as compared with rereading the same article." *Elem. Sch. J.*, 1921, 21, 461–464.

24. Germane, C. E. "The value of the writ-

ten paragraph summary." *J. Educ. Res.*, 1921, 3, 116–123.

25. Guilford, J. P. "The role of form in learning." *J. Exp. Psychol.*, 1927, 10, 415–423.

26. Hafner, A. J. "Influence of verbalization on problem solving." *Psychol. Reps.*, 1957, 3, 360.

27. Hall, J. V. "Color clarified arithmetic processes." *Elem. Sch. J.*, 1950, 50, 96–98.

28. Hanna, P. R. *Arithmetic Problem: a Study of the Relative Effectiveness of Three Methods of Problem Solving*. New York: Bur. of Publ., Teachers Coll., Col. Univ., 1929.

29. *Helping children discover arithmetic*. New York: McGraw-Hill, Text-Film Dept.

30. Hertzberg, O. E. "A comparative study of different methods used in teaching beginners to write." *Teachers Coll. Contr. to Educ.*, 1926, no. 214.

31. Hildreth, Gertrude. "Puzzle-solving with and without understanding." *J. Educ. Psychol.*, 1942, 33, 595–604.

32. Hovland, C. I. "Human learning and retention," in Stevens, S. S. *Handbook of Experimental Psychology*. New York: Wiley, 1951. Pp. 613–689.

33. Howell, W. J. "Work-study skills of adolescents in grades VII–XIV." *Sch. Rev.*, 1953, 61, 277–282.

34. Hughes, Marie M. "Training pupils for successful group living." *Elem. Sch. J.*, 1950, 50, 453–459. Copyright by the Univ. of Chicago.

35. Husband, R. W. "Analysis of methods in human maze learning." *J. Genet. Psychol.*, 1931, 39, 258–278.

36. Jensen, M. B., and Lemaire, Agnes. "Ten experiments on whole and part learning." *J. Educ. Psychol.*, 1937, 28, 37–54.

37. Joyce, J. N. "The role of language as a cue in learning and extinction." *Dissertation Abstr.*, 1956, 16, 571.

38. Knapp, C. G., and Dixon, W. R. "Learning to juggle: II. A study of whole and part methods." *Res. Quart.*, 1952, 23, 398–401.

39. Koenker, R. H. "The 'crutch' in arithmetic." *Elem. Sch. J.*, 1958, 58, 232–233.

40. Krause, LaVern W. "A comparison of two methods of study." *Elem. Sch. J.*, 1943, 44, 45–48.

41. Kuenne, Margaret R. "Experimental investigation of the relation of language to transposition behavior in young children." *J. Exp. Psychol.*, 1946, 36, 471–490.

42. Kurtz, K. H., and Hovland, C. I. "The effect of verbalization during observation of stimulus objects upon accuracy of recognition and recall." *J. Exp. Psychol.*, 1953, 45, 157–164.

43. Kurtz, K. H., and Hovland, C. I. "Concept learning with differing sequences of instances." *J. Exp. Psychol.*, 1956, 51, 239–243.

44. Lambert, J. F., and Ewert, P. H. "The effect of verbal instructions upon stylus maze learning." *J. Gen. Psychol.*, 1932, 6, 377–399.

45. Lankford, Francis G., Jr. "Implications of the psychology of learning for the teaching of mathematics." *The Growth of Mathematical Ideas, Grades K–12*, Twenty-fourth Yearbook Nat. Council of Teachers of Math., 1959. Pp. 405–430.

46. Leggitt, Dorothy. "Measuring progress in working skills in ninth-grade civics." *Sch. Rev.*, 1934, 42, 676–687.

47. Lyon, D. O. "The relation of length of material to time taken for learning, and the optimum distribution of time." *J. Educ. Psychol.*, 1914, 5, 1–9, 85–91, 155–163.

48. McConnell, T. R. "Discovery versus authoritative identification in learning of children." *Univ. of Iowa Studies in Educ.*, 1934, 9 (5), 13–62.

49. Morgan, C. T., and Deese, J. *How to Study*. New York: McGraw-Hill, 1957.

50. Noble, C. E. "An analysis of meaning." *Psychol. Rev.*, 1952, 59, 421–430.

51. Noble, C. E. "The role of stimulus meaning (m) in serial verbal learning." *J. Exp. Psychol.*, 1952, 43, 437–446; 1952, 44, 465.

52. Noble, C. E., and McNeeley, D. A. "The role of meaningfulness (m) in paired associate verbal learning." *J. Exp. Psychol.*, 1957, 53, 16–22.

53. Norcross, Kathryn J., and Spiker, C. C. "The effects of type of stimulus pre-training on discrimination performance in preschool children." *Child Developm.*, 1957, 28, 79–84.

54. Perkins, M. J., Banks, H. P., and Calvin, A. D. "The effect of delay on simultaneous and successive discrimination in children." *J. Exp. Psychol.*, 1954, 48, 416–418.

55. Peterson, H. A. "Recitation or recall as a factor in learning of long prose selections." *J. Educ. Psychol.*, 1944, 35, 220–228.

56. Prentice, W. C. H., and Asch, S. E. "Paired association with related and unrelated pairs of nonsense figures." *Amer. J. Psychol.*, 1958, 71, 247–254.

57. Pressey, Luella C. "A class of probation students." *Research Adventures in University Teaching*, Bloomington, Ind.: Pub. Sch. Publ. Co., 1927.

58. Priebe, R. E., and Burton, W. Y. "The slow motion picture as a coaching device." *Sch. Rev.*, 1939, 47, 192–198.

59. Pyles (now Honzik), Marjorie K. "Verbalization as a factor in learning." *Child Developm.*, 1932, 3, 108–113.

60. Reed, H. B. "Factors influencing the learning and retention of concepts. I. The influence of set." *J. Exp. Psychol.*, 1946, 36, 71–87.

61. Shepard, Winifred O. "The effect of verbal training on initial generalization tendencies." *Child Developm.*, 1956, 27, 311–316.

62. Shepard, Winifred O., and Schaeffer, M. "The effect of concept knowledge on discrimination learning." *Child Developm.*, 1956, 27, 173–178.

63. Symonds, P. M. "What education has to learn from psychology: IV. Whole versus part learning." *Teachers Coll. Rec.*, 1957, 58, 329–339.

64. Thiele, C. L. "The mathematical viewpoint applied to teaching of elementary school arithmetic." *Teaching of Arithmetic*, Tenth Yearbook Nat. Council of Teachers of Math., 1935. Pp. 217–232.

65. Thiele, C. L. "Arithmetic in the early grades—from the point of view of interrelations in the number system." *Arithmetic in General Education*, Sixteenth Yearbook Nat. Council of Teachers of Math., 1941. Pp. 45–79.

66. Thompson, L. M. "The role of verbal-

ization in learning from demonstrations."
Dissertation at Yale Univ., 1944, quoted
by C. I. Hovland in Stevens, S. S.
Handbook of Experimental Psychology.
New York: Wiley, 1951.

67. Thorndike, E. L. *Human Learning.* New York: Century, 1931.

68. "Top 1957 science events." *Sci. News Letter,* 1957, 72 (25), 388.

69. Turner, Marion E. *The Child within the Group.* Stanford, Calif.: Stanford Univ. Press, 1957.

70. Vander Meer, A. W. "The economy of time in industrial training." *J. Educ. Psychol.,* 1945, 36, 65–90.

71. Warden, C. J. "The relative economy of various modes of attack in the mastering of the stylus maze." *J. Exp. Psychol.,* 1924, 7, 243–275.

72. Washburne, J. N. "The use of questions in social science material." *J. Educ. Psychol.,* 1929, 20, 321–359.

73. Wilburn, D. B. "Learning to use a ten in subtraction." *Elem. Sch. J.,* 1947, 47, 461–466.

74. Wolfle, D. L. "Military training and the useful parts of learning theory." *J. Consult. Psychol.,* 1946, 10, 73–75.

75. Wulff, J. J., and Stolurow, L. M. "The role of class-descriptive cues in paired-associates learning." *J. Exp. Psychol.,* 1957, 53, 199–206.

CHAPTER 10

1. Archer, C. P. "Transfer of training in spelling." *Univ. of Iowa Stud. in Educ.,* 1930, 5 (5), 1–62.

2. Artley, A. S. "Pattern versus principle in developing competence in word perception." *Elem. Sch. J.,* 1951, 51, 147–151.

3. Bagley, W. C. *Educational Values.* New York: Macmillan, 1911.

4. Bayles, E. E. "An unemphasized factor in current theories regarding the transfer of training." *J. Educ. Psychol.,* 1936, 27, 425–430.

5. Bensberg, G. J., Jr. "Concept learning in mental defectives as a function of appropriate and inappropriate 'attention sets.'" *J. Educ. Psychol.,* 1958, 49, 137–143.

6. Boeck, C. H. "The inductive-deductive

compared to the deductive-descriptive approach to laboratory instruction in high school chemistry." *J. Exp. Educ.,* 1951, 19, 247–254.

7. Brolyer, C. R., Thorndike, E. L., and Woodyard, Ella. "A second study of mental discipline in high school studies." *J. Educ. Psychol.,* 1927, 18, 377–404.

8. Buswell, G. T., and Kersh, B. Y. "Patterns of thinking in solving problems." *Univ. of Calif. Publ. Educ.,* 1956, 12 (2), 63–148.

9. Capoferi, A. "How can a junior high school mathematics teacher strengthen the science course?" *Sch. Sci. and Math.,* 1956, 56, 233–236.

10. Carroll, H. A. "Generalization of bright and dull children: a comparative study with special reference to spelling." *J. Educ. Psychol.,* 1930, 21, 489–499.

11. Dorsey, Mattie F., and Hopkins, L. T. "The influence of attitudes upon transfer." *J. Educ. Psychol.,* 1930, 21, 410–417.

12. Duncan, C. P. "Transfer in motor learning as a function of degree of first-task learning and inter-task similarity." *J. Exp. Psychol.,* 1953, 45, 1–11.

13. Forgus, R. H., and Schwartz, R. J. "Efficient retention and transfer as affected by learning method." *J. Psychol.,* 1957, 43, 135–139.

14. Garrett, H. E. "A developmental theory of intelligence." *Amer. Psychologist,* 1946, 1, 372–378.

15. Gates, A. I. "Functions of flash-card exercises in reading: an experimental study." *Teachers Coll. Rec.,* 1925, 27, 311–321.

16. Gates, A. I., and Taylor, G. "Acquisition of motor control in writing by preschool children." *Teachers Coll. Rec.,* 1923, 24, 459–469.

17. Glenn, W. H. "Think, David, think!" *The Math. Teacher,* 1957, 20, 440–441.

18. Grossnickle, F. E. "Transfer of knowledge of multiplication facts to their use in long division." *J. Educ. Res.,* 1936, 29, 677–685.

19. Hanna, P. R., and Moore, J. T. "Spelling—from spoken word to written symbol." *Elem. Sch. J.,* 1953, 53, 329–337.

20. Haslerud, G. M., and Meyers, Shirley. "The transfer value of given and individually derived principles." *J. Educ. Psychol.*, 1958, 49, 293–298.

21. Hendrickson, G., and Schroeder, W. H. "Transfer of training in learning to hit a submerged target." *J. Educ. Psychol.*, 1941, 32, 205–213.

22. Horn, E. "A basic writing vocabulary." *Univ. of Iowa Monogr. in Educ.*, 1926, ser. 1, no. 4.

23. Horn, E. "A source of confusion in spelling." *J. Educ. Res.*, 1929, 19, 47–55.

24. Horn, E. "Phonetics and spelling." *Elem. Sch. J.*, 1957, 57, 424–432.

25. Horrocks, J. E. "The relationship between knowledge of human development and ability to use such knowledge." *J. Appl. Psychol.*, 1946, 30, 501–508.

26. James, W. *Principles of Psychology.* New York: Holt, 1890.

27. Judd, C. H. "The relation of special training to general intelligence." *Educ. Rev.*, 1908, 36, 28–42.

28. Judd, C. H. *Psychology of High School Subjects.* Boston: Ginn, 1915.

29. Knight, F. B. "Transfer within a narrow mental function." *Elem. Sch. J.*, 1924, 24, 780–788. Copyright by the Univ. of Chicago.

30. Kong, W. *The Romance of Chinese Writing.* Los Angeles, Calif.: Quon-Quon Co., 1943.

31. Kuenne, Margaret R. "Experimental investigation of the relation of language to transposition behavior in young children." *J. Exp. Psychol.*, 1946, 36, 471–490.

32. Kyte, G. C., and Neel, V. M. "A core vocabulary of spelling words." *Elem. Sch. J.*, 1953, 54, 29–34.

33. Lewry, Marion E. "Improving manuscript writing in primary grades." *Elem. Sch. J.*, 1947, 47, 508–515.

34. Mandler, G., and Heinemann, Shirley H. "Effect of overlearning of a verbal response on transfer of training." *J. Exp. Psychol.*, 1956, 52, 39–46.

35. Olander, H. T. "Transfer of learning in simple addition and subtraction." *Elem. Sch. J.*, 1931, 31, 358–369, 427–437.

36. Orata, P. T. "The transfer of training and educational pseudo-science." *The Math. Teacher*, 1935, 28, 265–289.

37. Orata, P. T. "Recent research studies on transfer of training with implications for the curriculum, guidance, and personnel work." *J. Educ. Res.*, 1941, 35, 81–101.

38. Osburn, W. J. "Teaching spelling by teaching syllables and root words." *Elem. Sch. J.*, 1954, 55, 32–41.

39. Overman, J. R. "An experimental study of the effect of the method of instruction on transfer of training in arithmetic." *Elem. Sch. J.*, 1930–31, 31, 183–190.

40. Pratt, K. C. "Intelligence as a determinant of the 'functional' value of curricular content." *J. Educ. Psychol.*, 1938, 29, 44–49.

41. Ray, J. J. "The generalizing ability of dull, bright, and superior children." *Peabody Contr. Educ.*, 1936, no. 175.

42. "Revolution in language." *Time*, July 9, 1956, 68, part I, pp. 25–26.

43. Rinsland, H. D. *A Basic Vocabulary of Elementary School Children.* New York: Macmillan, 1945.

44. Roberts, Katherine E. "Learning in preschool and orphanage children; an experimental study of ability to solve different situations according to the same plan." *Univ. of Iowa Studies in Child Welf.*, 1933, 7 (3), 1–94.

45. Rosskopf, M. F. "Transfer of training." *The Learning of Mathematics: Its Theory and Practice*, Twenty-first Yearbook Nat. Council of Teachers of Math., 1953. Pp. 205–227.

46. Ruediger, W. C. "Indirect improvement of mental functions through ideals." *Educ. Rev.*, 1908, 36 (4), 364–371.

47. Saugstad, P. "An analysis of Maier's pendulum problem." *J. Exp. Psychol.*, 1957, 54, 168–179.

48. Schaaf, O. "Student discovery of algebraic principles as a means of developing ability to generalize." *The Math. Teacher*, 1955, 48, 324–327.

49. Sleight, W. "Memory and formal training." *Br. J. Psychol.*, 1911, 4, 386–457.

50. Spiker, C. C. "Experiments with children on the hypotheses of acquired distinctiveness and equivalence of cues." *Child Developm.*, 1956, 27, 253–263.

51. Thorndike, E. L. *Educational Psychology*, vol. II, *The Psychology of Learn-*

ing. New York: Teachers Coll., Col. Univ., 1914.

52. Thorndike, E. L. "Mental discipline in high school studies." *J. Educ. Psychol.*, 1924, 15, 1–22, 83–98.

53. Thorndike, E. L., and Woodworth, R. S. "The influence of improvement in one mental function upon the efficiency of other functions." *Psychol. Rev.*, 1901, 8 (I), 247–261.

54. Thorndike, E. L., and Woodworth, R. S. "The influence of improvement in one mental function upon efficiency of other functions." *Psychol. Rev.*, 1901, 8 (II), 384–395.

55. Thorndike, E. L., and Woodworth, R. S. "The influence of improvement in one mental function upon the efficiency of other functions." *Psychol. Rev.*, 1901, 8 (III), 553–564.

56. Webb, L. W. "Transfer of learning," in Skinner, C. E. (ed.) *Educational Psychology.* Englewood Cliffs, N.J.: Prentice-Hall, 1951.

57. Wesman, A. G. "A study of transfer of training from high school subjects to intelligence." *J. Educ. Res.*, 1945, 39, 254–264.

58. Winch, W. H. "Immediate memory in school children." *Br. J. Psychol.*, 1906–08, 2, 52–57.

59. Winch, W. H. "The transfer of improvement in memory of school children." *Br. J. Psychol.*, 1906–08, 2, 284–293.

60. Woodrow, H. "The effect of type of training upon transference." *J. Educ. Psychol.*, 1927, 18, 159–172.

61. Woodward, P. "An experimental study of transfer of training in motor learning." *J. Appl. Psychol.*, 1943, 27, 12–32.

CHAPTER 11

1. Allred, D. L. "Success as a determinant of attitudes," master's thesis, Utah State Univ. Lib., Logan, Utah, 1956.

2. Ashbaugh, E. J. "Variability of children in spelling." *Sch. and Soc.*, 1919, 9, 93–98.

3. Ausubel, D. P., Robbins, Lillian C., and Blake, E., Jr. "Retroactive inhibition and facilitation in the learning of school materials." *J. Educ. Psychol.*, 1957, 48, 334–343.

4. Ausubel, D. P., Schpoont, S., and Ceikier, Lillian. "Influence of intention on retention of school materials." *J. Educ. Psychol.*, 1957, 48, 87–92.

5. Ballard, P. B. "Obliviscence and reminiscence." *Br. J. Psychol.*, *Monogr. Suppl.*, 1911, 1–4, no. 2.

6. Bartlett, F. C. *Remembering.* London: Cambridge, 1932.

7. Bassett, Sarah J. "Factors influencing retention of history in sixth, seventh, and eighth grades." *J. Educ. Psychol.*, 1929, 20, 683–690.

8. Brueckner, L. J. "Certain arithmetic abilities of second grade pupils." *Elem. Sch. J.*, 1927, 27, 433–444.

9. Brueckner, L. J., and Distad, H. W. "The effect of summer vacation on the reading ability of first-grade children." *Elem. Sch. J.*, 1924, 24, 698–707.

10. Bruene, E. "Effect of summer vacation on the achievement of pupils in the fourth, fifth, and sixth grades." *J. Educ. Res.*, 1928, 18, 309–314.

11. Carmichael, L., Hogan, H. P., and Walter, A. A. "An experimental study of the effect of language on the reproduction of visually perceived form." *J. Exp. Psychol.*, 1932, 15, 73–86.

12. Carpenter, F. "The effect of different learning methods on concept formation." *Sci. Educ.*, 1956, 40, 282–285.

13. Carter, L. F., and Schooler, K. "Value, need, and other factors in perception." *Psychol. Rev.*, 1949, 56, 200–207.

14. Cartwright, D. S. "Self-consistency as a factor affecting immediate recall." *J. Abnorm. and Soc. Psychol.*, 1956, 52, 212–218.

15. Cohen, B. H., and Bousfield, W. A. "The effects of a dual-level stimulus-word list on the occurrence of clustering in recall." *J. Gen. Psychol.*, 1956, 55, 51–58.

16. Davis, R. A. *Psychology of Learning.* New York: McGraw-Hill, 1935.

17. Davis, R. A., and Moore, C. C. "Methods of measuring retention." *J. Gen. Psychol.*, 1935, 12, 144–155.

18. Davis, R. A., and Rood, E. J. "Remembering and forgetting arithmetic abil-

ities." *J. Educ. Psychol.*, 1947, 38, 216–222.

19. Deese, J. *The Psychology of Learning.* New York: McGraw-Hill, 1952.

20. Elder, H. E. "The effect of summer vacation on silent reading ability in the intermediate grades." *Elem. Sch. J.*, 1927, 27, 541–546.

21. Frutchey, F. P. "Retention in high school chemistry." *J. Higher Educ.*, 1937, 8, 217–218.

22. Garber, R. B. "Influence of cognitive and affective factors in learning and retaining materials." *J. Abnorm. and Soc. Psychol.*, 1955, 51, 384–389.

23. Gilliland, A. R. "The rate of forgetting." *J. Educ. Psychol.*, 1948, 39, 19–26.

24. Grossnickle, F. E. "Transfer of knowledge of multiplication facts to their use in long division." *J. Educ. Res.*, 1936, 29, 677–685.

25. Hall, J. F. "Retroactive inhibition of meaningful material." *J. Educ. Psychol.*, 1955, 46, 47–52.

26. Hildreth, Gertrude H. "An individual study in word recognition." *Elem. Sch. J.*, 1935, 35, 606–619.

27. Hovland, C. I. "Human learning and retention," in Stevens, S. S. *Handbook of Experimental Psychology.* New York: Wiley, 1951. Pp. 613–689.

28. Jenkins, J. G., and Dallenbach, K. M. "Obliviscence during sleep and waking." *Amer. J. Psychol.*, 1924, 35, 605–612.

29. Jenkins, J. G., and Sparks, W. M. "Retroactive inhibition in foreign language study." *Psychol. Bull.*, 1940, 37, 470.

30. Johnson, P. O. "The permanence of learning in elementary botany." *J. Educ. Psychol.*, 1930, 21, 37–47.

31. Karen, R. L. "Recognition as a function of meaningfulness and intention to learn." *Amer. J. Psychol.*, 1956, 69, 650–652.

32. Keys, N., and Lawson, J. V. "Summer vs. winter gains in school achievement." *Sch. and Soc.*, 1937, 46, 541–544.

33. Kolberg, O. W. "A study of summertime forgetting." *Elem. Sch. J.*, 1934, 35, 281–287.

34. Kramer, Grace A. "Do children forget during the vacation?" *Baltimore Bull. Educ.*, 1927, 56–60.

35. Krueger, W. C. F. "Further studies in overlearning." *J. Exper. Psychol.*, 1930, 13, 152–163.

36. Layton, E. T. "The persistence of learning in elementary algebra." *J. Educ. Psychol.*, 1932, 23, 46–55.

37. Levine, J. M., and Murphy, G. "The learning and forgetting of controversial material." *J. Abnorm. and Soc. Psychol.*, 1943, 38, 507–517.

38. McDougall, W. P. "Differential retention of course outcomes in educational psychology." *J. Educ. Psychol.*, 1958, 49, 53–60.

39. McKeachie, W. J., and Solomon, D. "Retention of general psychology." *J. Educ. Psychol.*, 1957, 48, 110–112.

40. Melton, A. W., and Irwin, J. M. "The influence of degree of interpolated learning on retroactive inhibition and the overt transfer of specific responses." *Amer. J. Psychol.*, 1940, 53, 173–203.

41. Morgan, L. D. "How effective is specific training in preventing loss due to summer vacation?" *J. Educ. Psychol.*, 1929, 20, 466–471.

42. Morris, W. W. "Story remembering among children." *J. Soc. Psychol.*, 1939, 10, 489–502.

43. Northway, M. L. "The influence of age and social groups on children's remembering." *Br. J. Psychol.*, 1936, 27, 11–29.

44. Patterson, M. V. W. "The effect of summer vacation on children's mental ability and on their retention of arithmetic and reading." *Educ.*, 1925–26, 46, 222–228.

45. Postman, L. "Learned principles of organization in memory." *Psychol. Monogr.*, 1954, 68 (3), 1–24 (whole no. 374).

46. Pressey, S. L., Robinson, F. P., and Horrocks, J. E. *Psychology in Education.* New York: Harper, 1959.

47. Redl, F., and Wattenburg, W. W. *Mental Hygiene in Teaching.* New York: Harcourt, Brace, 1951.

48. Sakoda, J. M. "Individual differences in correlation between clustering and recall of meaningful words." *J. Gen. Psychol.*, 1956, 54, 183–190.

49. Schrepel, Marie, and Laslett, H. R. "On the loss of knowledge by junior high school pupils over the summer vaca-

tion." *J. Educ. Psychol.*, 1936, 27, 299–303.

50. Spitzer, H. F. "Studies in retention." *J. Educ. Psychol.*, 1939, 30, 641–656.

51. Steele, D. C. "Teaching and testing the understanding of common fractions." *Univ. of Pittsburgh Bull.*, 1941, 37 (3), 317–328.

52. Stroud, J. B. "Experiments on learning in school situations." *Psychol. Bull.*, 1940, 37, 777–807.

53. Stroud, J. B., and Johnson, Ethel. "The temporal position of review." *J. Educ. Res.*, 1942, 35, 618–622.

54. Talland, G. A. "Cultural differences in serial reproduction." *J. Soc. Psychol.*, 1956, 43, 75–81.

55. Terman, L. M., and Merrill, Maud A. *Stanford-Binet Intelligence Scale, Manual for Third Edition.* Boston: Houghton Mifflin, 1960.

56. Tiedeman, H. R. "A study of retention of classroom learning." *J. Educ. Res.*, 1948, 41, 516–531.

57. Tiernan, J. J. "The principle of closure in terms of recall and recognition." *Amer. J. Psychol.*, 1938, 51, 97–108.

58. Twining, P. E. "The relative importance of intervening activity and lapse of time in the production of forgetting." *J. Exp. Psychol.*, 1940, 26, 483–501.

59. Tyler, R. W. "Permanence of learning." *J. Higher Educ.*, 1933, 4, 203–205.

60. Underwood, B. J. "Interference and forgetting." *Psychol. Rev.*, 1957, 64, 49–60.

61. Williams, R. D., and Knox, G. W. "A survey of dynamic principles governing memory." *J. Gen. Psychol.*, 1944, 30, 167–179.

62. Woodworth, R. S., and Schlossberg, H. *Experimental Psychology.* New York: Holt, 1954.

63. Word, A. H., and Davis, R. A. "Acquisition and retention of factual information in seventh-grade general science, during a semester of eighteen weeks." *J. Educ. Psychol.*, 1939, 30, 116–125.

CHAPTER 12

1. Anderson, J. E., and others. *A Survey of Children's Adjustment over Time.* Minneapolis, Minn.: Inst. of Child Developm. and Welf., Univ. of Minn., 1959.

2. Ausubel, D. P., Schiff, H. M., and Goldman, M. "Qualitative characteristics in the learning process associated with anxiety." *J. Abnorm. and Soc. Psychol.*, 1953, 48, 537–547.

3. Barker, R. G., Dembo, Tamara, and Levin, K. "Frustration and Regression," in Barker, R. G., Kounin, J. S., and Wright, H. F. (eds.) *Child Behavior and Development.* New York: McGraw-Hill, 1943.

4. Beier, E. G. "The effect of induced anxiety on flexibility of intellectual functioning." *Psychol. Monogr.*, 1951, 65 (365), 1–19.

5. Bennett, E. M. "A socio-cultural interpretation of maladjustive behavior." *J. Soc. Psychol.*, 1953, 37, 19–26.

6. Berkowitz, L. "The expression and reduction of hostility." *Psychol. Bull.*, 1958, 55, 257–283.

7. Bettelheim, B. *Love Is Not Enough: The Treatment of Emotionally Disturbed Children.* Glencoe, Ill.: Free Press, 1950.

8. Bird, Grace E. "Personality factors in learning." *Pers. J.*, 1927, 6, 56–59.

9. Blanchard, Phyllis. "Psychogenic factors in some cases of reading disability." *Amer. J. Orthopsychiat.*, 1935, 5, 361–374.

10. Bower, E. M. "The need for punishment." *Calif. J. Elem. Educ.*, 1953, 21, 41–48.

11. Castaneda, A., and McCandless, B. R. "The children's form of the manifest anxiety scale." *Child Developm.*, 1956, 27, 317–326.

12. Castaneda, A., Palermo, D. S., and McCandless, B. R. "Complex learning and performance as a function of anxiety in children and task difficulty." *Child Developm.*, 1956, 27, 327–332.

13. Christensen, C. M. "A note on Borow's college inventory of academic adjustment." *J. Educ. Res.*, 1956, 50, 55–58.

14. Cowen, E. L. "The influence of varying degrees of psychological stress on problem-solving rigidity." *J. Abnorm. and Soc. Psychol.*, 1952, 47, 512–519.

15. Davitz, J. R. "The effects of previous training on post frustration behavior."

J. Abnorm. Soc. Psychol., 1952, 47, 309–315.

16. Davitz, J. R. "Contributions of research with children to a theory of maladjustment." *Child Developm.*, 1958, 29, 3–7.

17. Edelston, H. "Educational failure with high intelligence quotient: a clinical study." *J. Genet. Psychol.*, 1950, 77, 85–116.

18. Erikson, E. H. *Childhood and Society.* New York: Norton, 1950.

19. Farber, I. E., and Spence, K. W. "Complex learning and conditioning as a function of anxiety." *J. Exp. Psychol.*, 1953, 45, 120–125.

20. Gaier, E. L. "Selected personality variables and the learning process." *Psychol. Monogr.*, 1952, 66 (17), 1–28 (whole no. 349).

21. Gochman, S. I. "Personality dynamics and learning: a study of individual differences in learning, retention, transfer of training, and speed of reaction as functions of personality." *Dissertation Abstr.*, 1956, 16, 1503.

22. Gowan, J. C. "Dynamics of the underachievement of gifted students." *J. Exc. Child.*, 1957, 24, 98–101, 122.

23. Gruen, Emily W. "Levels of aspiration in relation to personality factors in adolescents." *Child Developm.*, 1945, 16, 181–188.

24. *Guiding the growth of children.* New York: McGraw-Hill, Text-Film Dept.

25. Gynther, Ruth A. "The effects of anxiety and situational stress on communicative efficiency." *J. Abnorm. and Soc. Psychol.*, 1957, 54, 274–276.

26. Heffernan, Helen. "The organization of the elementary school and the development of a healthy personality." *Calif. J. Elem. Educ.*, 1952, 20, 129–153.

27. Hildreth, Gertrude H. "An individual study in word recognition." *Elem. Sch. J.*, 1935, 35, 606–619. Copyright by the Univ. of Chicago.

28. Hilgard, E. R. "Human motives and the concept of self." *Amer. Psychologist*, 1949, 4, 374–382.

29. Hoffman, M. L. "Conformity as a defense mechanism and a form of resistance to group influence." *J. Pers.*, 1957, 25, 412–424.

30. Horrall, B. M. "Academic performance and personality adjustment of highly intelligent college students." *Genet. Psychol. Monogr.*, 1957, 55, 3–83.

31. Hutt, M. L. "A clinical study of 'consecutive' and 'adaptive' testing with the Revised Stanford-Binet." *J. Consult. Psychol.*, 1947, 11, 93–103.

32. Jenkins, Gladys G., Shacter, Helen, and Bauer, W. W. *These Are Your Children.* Chicago: Scott, Foresman, 1953.

33. Jones, Mary C. "A study of socialization patterns at the high school level." *J. Genet. Psychol.*, 1958, 93, 87–111.

34. Kagan, J. "The concept of identification." *Psychol. Rev.*, 1958, 65, 296–305.

35. Kimball, Barbara. "The sentence-completion technique in a study of scholastic underachievement." *J. Consult. Psychol.*, 1952, 16, 353–358.

36. Korchin, S. J., and Seymour, L. "Anxiety and verbal learning." *J. Abnorm. and Soc. Psychol.*, 1957, 54, 234–240.

37. Landis, P. H. *Adolescence and Youth, The Process of Maturing.* New York: McGraw-Hill, 1945.

38. Lantz, Beatrice. "Some dynamic aspects of success and failure." *Psychol. Monogr.*, 1945, 59 (1), 1–40.

39. Lazarus, R. S., Deese, J., and Osler, Sonia F. "The effects of psychological stress upon performance." *Psychol. Bull.*, 1952, 49, 293–317.

40. Liss, E. "Learning difficulties: unresolved anxiety and resultant learning patterns." *Amer. J. Orthopsychiat.*, 1941, 11, 520–523.

41. Liss, E., and others. "Contemporary concepts of learning: round table." *Amer. J. Orthopsychiat.*, 1954, 24, 767–788.

42. McCandless, B. R., and Castaneda, A. "Anxiety in children, school achievement, and intelligence." *Child Developm.*, 1956, 27, 379–382.

43. Margaret, Ann. "Generalizations in successful psychotherapy." *J. Consult Psychol.*, 1950, 14, 64–70.

44. Montague, E. K. "The role of anxiety in serial rote learning." *J. Exp. Psychol.*, 1953, 45, 91–96.

45. Morgan, H. H. "A psychometric comparison of achieving and nonachieving college students of high ability." *J. Consult. Psychol.*, 1952, 16, 292–298.

46. Murphy, G. "What constitutes a well-integrated personality." *Menninger Quart.*, 1956, 10 (1), 1–9.
47. Murphy, Lois B. "Learning how children cope with problems." *Child.*, 1957, 4, 132–136.
48. Nicholson, W. M. "The influence of anxiety upon learning: interference or drive increment." *J. Pers.*, 1958, 26, 303–319.
49. Palermo, D. S., Castaneda, A., and McCandless, B. R. "The relationship of anxiety in children to performance in a complex learning task." *Child Developm.*, 1956, 27, 333–337.
50. Payne, D. E., and Mussen, P. H. "Parent-child relations and father identification among adolescent boys." *J. Abnorm. and Soc. Psychol.*, 1956, 52, 358–362.
51. Piekarz, Josephine A. "Getting meaning from reading." *Elem. Sch. J.*, 1956, 56, 303–309. Copyright by the Univ. of Chicago.
52. Redl, F., and Wattenburg, W. W. *Mental Hygiene in Teaching.* New York: Harcourt, Brace, 1951.
53. Redl, F., and Wineman, D. *Children Who Hate.* Glencoe, Ill.: Free Press, 1951.
54. Reynolds, G. S. "The effects of stress upon problem-solving." *J. Gen. Psychol.*, 1960, 62, 83–88.
55. Rosenstock, I. M. "Perceptual aspects of repression." *J. Abnorm. and Soc. Psychol.*, 1951, 46, 304–315.
56. Rosensweig, S. "An experimental study of 'repression' with special reference to need-persistive and ego-defensive reactions to frustration." *J. Exp. Psychol.*, 1943, 32, 64–74.
57. Sarason, I. G. "The effect of anxiety and two kinds of failure on serial learning." *J. Pers.*, 1957, 25, 383–392.
58. Sarason, I. G. "Effects on verbal learning of anxiety, reassurance, and meaningfulness of material." *J. Exp. Psychol.*, 1958, 56, 472–477.
59. Sarnoff, I. "Some psychological problems of the incipient artist." *Ment. Hyg.*, 1956, 40, 375–383.
60. Schroder, H. M., and Hunt, D. E. "Failure-avoidance in situational interpretation and problem solving." *Psychol.*

61. *Monogr.*, 1957, 71 (3), 1–22 (whole no. 432).
61. Sears, Pauline S. "Levels of aspiration in academically successful and unsuccessful children." *J. Abnorm. and Soc. Psychol.*, 1940, 35, 498–536.
62. Sears, R. R. "Experimental studies of projection: I. Attribution of traits." *J. Soc. Psychol.*, 1936, 7, 151–163.
63. Sherman, M. *Basic Problems of Behavior.* New York: Longmans, 1941.
64. Shoben, E. J., Jr. "A theoretical approach to psychotherapy as personality modification." *Harv. Educ. Rev.*, 1953, 23, 128–142.
65. Shoben, E. J., Jr. "Toward a concept of the normal personality." *Amer. Psychologist*, 1957, 12, 183–189.
66. Smith, Nila B. "Research on reading and the emotions." *Sch. and Soc.*, 1955, 81, 8–10.
67. Sperry, Bessie, and others. "Renunciation and denial in learning difficulties." *Amer. J. Orthopsychiat.*, 1958, 28, 98–111.
68. Stevenson, H. W., and Iscoe, I. "Anxiety and discriminative learning." *Amer. J. Psychol.*, 1956, 69, 113–114.
69. Strang, Ruth. "Inner world of gifted adolescents." *J. Exc. Child.*, 1950, 16, 97–101, 125.
70. Strang, Ruth. *Helping Children Solve Problems.* Chicago: Science Research, 1953.
71. Symonds, P. M. *The Dynamics of Human Adjustment.* New York: Appleton-Century-Crofts, 1946.
72. Talbot, Mira, and Henson, Isabelle. "Pupils psychologically absent from school." *Amer. J. Orthopsychiat.*, 1954, 24, 381–390.
73. Wedemeyer, C. A. "Gifted achievers and non-achievers." *J. Higher Educ.*, 1953, 24, 25–30.
74. Wenar, C. "The effects of a motor handicap on personality. I. The effect on level of aspiration." *Child Developm.*, 1953, 24, 123–130.
75. Williams, M. "Rate of learning as a function of ego-alien material." *J. of Pers.*, 1951, 19, 324–331.
76. Young, N., and Gaier, E. L. "Implications in emotionally caused reading

retardation." *Elem. Engl.*, 1951, 28, 271–275.

CHAPTER 13

1. Allen, R. M. *Personality Assessment Procedures.* New York: Harper, 1958.
2. Anastasi, Anne. *Psychological Testing.* New York: Macmillan, 1961.
3. Anderson, H. H., and Anderson, Gladys L. *An Introduction to Projective Techniques.* Englewood Cliffs, N.J.: Prentice-Hall, 1951.
4. Anderson, J. E. "Parents' attitudes on child behavior: a report of three studies." *Child Developm.*, 1946, 17, 91–97.
5. Arbuckle, D. S. *Teacher Counseling.* Reading, Mass.: Addison-Wesley, 1950.
6. Bell, H. M. *The Adjustment Inventory, Student Form.* Stanford, Calif.: Stanford Univ. Press, 1934.
7. Blanchard, Phyllis. "Reading disabilities in relation to difficulties of personality and emotional development." *Ment. Hyg.*, 1936, 20, 384–413.
8. Bullock, Burleen J., and Brown, W. H. "Screening a fourth grade class for emotional needs." *Understanding the Child*, 1953, 22, 116–120.
9. Buswell, Margaret Mary. "The relationship between the social structure of the classroom and academic success of the pupils." *J. Exp. Educ.*, 1953, 22, 37–52.
10. Capwell, Dora F. "Personality patterns of adolescent girls: II. Delinquents and nondelinquents." *J. Appl. Psychol.*, 1945, 29, 289–297.
11. Castaneda, A., and McCandless, B. R. "The children's form of the manifest anxiety scale." *Child Developm.*, 1956, 27, 317–326.
12. Channell, R. R. "Self inventories, teacher ratings, and interviews as a means of determining maladjustment," master's thesis, Utah State Univ. Lib., Logan, Utah, 1955.
13. Clancy, Nora, and Smitter, Faith. "A study of emotionally disturbed children in Santa Barbara County Schools." *Calif. J. Educ. Res.*, 1953, 4, 209–218, 222.
14. Clark, W. A., and Smith, L. F. "Further evidence on the validity of personality inventories." *J. Educ. Psychol.*, 1942, 33, 81–91.
15. Dreikurs, R. *Psychology in the Classroom.* New York: Harpers, 1957.
16. Eklund, G. L. "An experimental study of the effects of multiple counseling upon a group of underachieving seventh-grade students," master's thesis, Univ. of Utah, Salt Lake City, Utah, 1957.
17. Elliot, M. H. "Patterns of friendship in the classroom." *Progr. Educ.*, 1941, 18, 383–390.
18. "Everybody's mental health." *Time*, Dec. 10, 1956, p. 73.
19. Feinberg, H. "Achievement of children in orphan homes as revealed by Stanford Achievement Tests." *J. Genet. Psychol.*, 1954, 85, 217–229.
20. Frandsen, A., and Hunter, Marguerite. "The 'TAT' in school counseling." *Utah Guid. Monogr.*, 1952, no. 3, 1–12.
21. Goldfarb, W. "The effects of early institutional care on adolescent personality." *J. Exp. Educ.*, 1943, 12 (2), 106–129.
22. Gordon, I. J. *The Teacher as a Guidance Worker.* New York: Harpers, 1956.
23. *Guiding the growth of children.* New York: McGraw-Hill, Text-Film Dept.
24. Haan, Norma. "When the mentally ill child returns to school." *Elem. Sch. J.*, 1957, 57, 379–385.
25. Haggerty, M. E., Olson, W. C., and Wickman, E. K. *Haggerty-Olson-Wickman Behavior Rating Schedules.* Yonkers-on-Hudson, N.Y.: World, 1930.
26. Harmon, L. R., and Wiener, D. N. "Use of the Minnesota Multiphasic Personality Inventory in vocational advisement." *J. Appl. Psychol.*, 1945, 29, 132–141.
27. Harper, L. E., and Wright, B. D. "Dealing with emotional problems in the classroom." *Elem. Sch. J.*, 1958, 58, 316–325.
28. Hathaway, S. R., and Briggs, P. F. "Some normative data on new MMPI scales." *J. Clin. Psychol.*, 1957, 13, 364–368.
29. Hathaway, S. R., and McKinley, J. C. *Minnesota Multiphasic Personality In-*

ventory: Manual. New York: The Psychological Corp., 1951.

30. Hathaway, S. R., and Monachesi, E. D. "The Minnesota Multiphasic Personality Inventory in the study of juvenile delinquents." *Amer. Sociol. Rev.*, 1952, 17, 704–710.

31. Hattwick, LaBerta W., and Stowell, Margaret. "Relation of parental overattentiveness to children's work habits and social adjustments in kindergarten and the first six grades of school." *J. Educ. Res.*, 1936, 30, 169–176.

32. Hay, L. "How the classroom teacher can help the troubled child." *Nervous Child*, 1954, 10, 391–399.

33. Hirschberg, J. C. "The education of emotionally disturbed children: 4: The role of education in the treatment of emotionally disturbed children through planned ego development." *Amer. J. Orthopsychiat.*, 1953, 23, 684–690.

34. Jenkins, Gladys G., Shacter, Helen, and Bauer, W. W. *These Are Your Children,* Expanded Ed. Chicago: Scott, Foresman, 1953.

35. Jersild, A. T. *Child Psychology,* 5th Ed. Englewood Cliffs, N.J.: Prentice-Hall, 1960.

36. Johnson, O. G. "The teacher and the withdrawn child." *Educ. Digest,* 1957, 22, no. 8, 19–22.

37. Jones, H. E. *Development in Adolescence.* New York: Appleton-Century-Crofts, 1943.

38. Jones, R. S. "The emotional conditions of learning." *Progr. Educ.,* 1953, 30, 93–98.

39. Katz, B., and Lehner, G. F. J. *Mental Hygiene in Modern Living.* New York: Ronald, 1953.

40. Keys, N., and Guilford, M. S. "The validity of certain adjustment inventories in predicting problem behavior." *J. Educ. Psychol.,* 1937, 28, 641–655.

41. Layton, R. C. *Negative Attitudes of Students in Relation to Letter-Grading System of Reporting.* Salt Lake City, Utah: Lib., Univ. of Utah, 1956.

42. Lindgren, H. C. "The development of a scale of cultural idealization based on the California Test of Personality." *J. Educ. Psychol.,* 1952, 43, 81–91.

43. McCarthy, Dorothea A. "Personality and

learning." *Amer. Council Educ. Studies,* 1948, ser. 1, no. 35, 93–96.

44. Marsh, C. J. "The diagnostic value of the Bell Adjustment Inventory for college women." *J. Soc. Psychol.,* 1943, 17, 103–109.

45. Maslow, A. H. *The S-I Inventory* and *Manual.* Stanford, Calif.: Stanford Univ. Press, 1952.

46. Meek, Lois H. [reporting findings of Lois M. Jacks] "A child's relation to the group." *Progr. Educ.,* 1941, 18, 212.

47. Mehus, Hilda. "Learning and therapy." *Amer. J. Orthopsychiat.,* 1953, 23, 416–421.

48. Meyer, Charlene T. "The assertive behavior of children as related to parent behavior." *J. Home Econ.,* 1947, 39, 77–80.

49. Missildine, W. H. "The emotional background of thirty children with reading disabilities with emphasis on its coercive elements." *Nervous Child,* 1946, 5, 263–272.

50. Moran, T. F. "A brief study of the validity of a neurotic inventory." *J. Appl. Psychol.,* 1935, 19, 180–188.

51. Murray, H. A. *Thematic Apperception Test* (Manual). Cambridge, Mass.: Harv. Univ. Press, 1943.

52. Nimkoff, M. F. *The Child.* Philadelphia: Lippincott, 1934.

53. Olson, W. C., and Wattenberg, W. W. "The role of the school in mental health," in Nelson, H. B. *Mental Health in Education.* Fifty-fourth Yearbook Nat. Soc. Study of Educ., part II, pp. 99–124, Chicago, 1955. Distributed by the Univ. of Chicago Press.

54. Parker, Beatrice F. "The parent-teacher conference." *Elem. Sch. J.,* 1953, 53, 270–274.

55. Redl, F., and Wattenburg, W. W. *Mental Hygiene in Teaching.* New York: Harcourt, Brace, 1951.

56. Rogers, C. R. *A Test of Personality Adjustment.* New York: Association Press, 1931.

57. Rothman, Esther, and Berkowitz, Pearl. "The dynamics of need-acceptance relationships for the emotionally disturbed child in the classroom." *Nervous Child,* 1954, 10, 387–390.

58. Rotter, J. B. *Social Learning and Clin-*

ical Psychology. Englewood Cliffs, N.J.: Prentice-Hall, 1954.

59. Rush, B. H. "An investigation of parent-child relationships in broken homes and their relationship to school behavior." *Dissertation Abstr.,* 1956, 16, 1509.

60. Shaw, F. J. "Counseling from the standpoint of an inter-active conceptualist." *J. Counsel. Psychol.,* 1954, 1, 36–42.

61. Sherman, M. "The secret that will win you success." *Mag. Digest,* May, 1946, pp. 1–5.

62. Staver, Nancy. "The child's learning difficulty as related to the emotional problem of the mother." *Amer. J. Orthopsychiat.,* 1953, 23, 131–141.

63. Symonds, P. M., and Jensen, A. R. "The predictive significance of fantasy." *Amer. J. Orthopsychiat.,* 1958, 28, 73–84.

64. Tesseneer, R., and Tydlaska, Mary. "A cross-validation of a work attitude scale from the MMPI." *J. Educ. Psychol.,* 1956, 47, 1–7.

65. Tindall, R. H. "Relationships among indices of adjustment status." *Educ. and Psychol. Measmt.,* 1955, 15, 152–162.

66. Thorpe, L. P., Tiegs, E. W., and Clark, W. W. *California Test of Personality—Elementary, Form A, a Test of Personal and Social Adjustment* (Test and Manual). Los Angeles, Calif.: Calif. Test Bur., 1942.

67. Tomkins, S. S. "The present status of the Thematic Apperception Test." *Amer. J. Orthopsychiat.,* 1949, 19, 358–362.

68. Topp, R. F. "Preadolescent behavior patterns suggestive of emotional malfunctioning." *Elem. Sch. J.,* 1952, 52, 340–343. Copyright by the Univ. of Chicago.

69. Turney, A. H., and Fee, Mary. "An attempt to use the Bell Adjustment Inventory for high school guidance." *Sch. Rev.,* 1936, 44, 193–198.

70. Wattenburg, W. W. "Teachers can build emotional strength." *Educ.,* 1953, 74, 133–137.

CHAPTER 14

1. Amatora, Mary. "Validity in self-evaluation." *Educ. Psychol. Measmt.,* 1956, 16, 119–126.

2. Anderson, H. H., and Brandt, H. F. "Study of motivation involving self-announced goals of fifth grade children and the concept of level of aspiration." *J. Soc. Psychol.,* 1939, 10, 209–232.

3. Benjamins, J. "Changes in performance in relation to influences upon self-conceptualization." *J. Abnorm. and Soc. Psychol.,* 1950, 45, 473–480.

4. Benne, K. D., and Sheats, P. "Functional roles of group members." *J. Soc. Issues,* 1948, 4, 41–49.

5. Bills, R. E. "Personality changes during student-centered teaching." *J. Educ. Res.,* 1956, 50, 121–126.

6. Blue, J. T., Jr. "The effect of group study on grade achievement." *J. Educ. Psychol.,* 1958, 49, 118–123.

7. Brown, D. G. "Sex-role preference in young children." *Psychol. Monogr.,* 1956, 70, 1–19.

8. Brownfain, J. J. "Stability of the self-concept as a dimension of personality." *J. Abnorm. and Soc. Psychol.,* 1952, 47, 597–606.

9. Buswell, Margaret M. "The relationship between the social structure of the classroom and the academic success of the pupils." *J. Exp. Educ.,* 1953–54, 22, 37–52.

10. Cantoni, L. J. "A study in emotional adjustment: the correlation of student and adult forms of the Bell Adjustment Inventory over a period of thirteen years." *Educ. and Psychol. Measmt.,* 1955, 15, 137–143.

11. Capehart, B. E., et al. "An objective evaluation of a core program." *Sch. Rev.,* 1952, 60, 84–89.

12. Chittenden, G. E. "An experimental study in measuring and modifying assertive behavior in young children." *Monogr. Soc. Res. Child Developm.,* 1942, 7 (1), 1–81.

13. Cook, L. A. "An experimental sociographic study of a stratified 10th grade class." *Amer. Sociol. Rev.,* 1945, 10, 250–261.

14. Crane, Ora Mae, and Heaton, Margaret M. "Levels of discussion." *Childh. Educ.,* 1956, 33, 151–156.

15. Crawford, P. L., Malamud, D. I., and Dumpson, J. R. *Working with Teenage*

Gangs. New York: Welf. Council of N.Y.C., 1950.

16. Cronbach, L. J. *Educational Psychology.* New York: Harcourt, Brace, 1954.

17. Cunningham, Ruth, et al. *Understanding of Group Behavior of Boys and Girls.* New York: Bur. of Publ., Teachers Coll., Col. Univ., 1951.

18. Elliot, M. H. "Patterns of friendship in the classroom." *Progr. Educ.,* 1941, 18, 383–390.

19. Elsbree, W. S. "School practices that help and hurt personality." *Childh. Educ.,* 1941–42, 18, 197–204.

20. Flanders, N. A. "Personal-social anxiety as a factor in experimental learning situations." *J. Educ. Res.,* 1951, 45, 100–110.

21. Ford, N. A. "Literature as an aid to social development." *Teachers Coll. Rec.,* 1957, 58, 377–381.

22. Foshay, A. W. "Considerateness and aggression: an action research study." *Educ. Res. Bull.,* 1953, 32, 85–112.

23. Froehlich, C. P. "Does test taking change self ratings?" *Calif. J. Educ. Res.,* 1954, 5, 166–169, 175.

24. Fromm, E. *The Sane Society.* New York: Rinehart, 1955.

25. Gronlund, N. E. "Relationship between sociometric status of pupils and teachers' preferences for having them in class." *Sociometry,* 1953, 16, 142–150.

26. Gronlund, N. E. *Sociometry in the Classroom.* New York: Harper, 1959.

27. Gronlund, N. E., and Whitney, A. P. "Relation between pupils' social acceptability in the classroom, in the school, and in the neighborhood." *Sch. Rev.,* 1956, 64, 267–271.

28. Hall, C. S., and Lindzey, G. *Theories of Personality.* New York: Wiley, 1957.

29. Hartley, E. L., Rosenbaum, M., and Schwartz, S. "Children's perception of ethnic group membership." *J. Psychol.,* 1948, 26, 387–398.

30. Havighurst, R. J., Robinson, Myra J., and Dorr, Mildred. "The development of the ideal self in childhood and adolescence." *J. Educ. Res.,* 1946, 40, 241–257.

31. Haythorn, W. "Influence of individual members on the characteristics of small groups." *J. Abnorm. and Soc. Psychol.,* 1953, 48, 276–284.

32. Heimann, R. A., and Schenk, Q. F. "Relations of social class and sex differences to high school achievement." *Sch. Rev.,* 1954, 62, 213–221. Copyright by the Univ. of Chicago.

33. Helfant, K. "Parents' attitude versus adolescent hostility in the determination of adolescent sociopolitical attitudes." *Psychol. Monogr.,* 1952, 66, no. 345.

34. Henry, J. "Attitude organization in elementary school classrooms." *Amer. J. Orthopsychiat.,* 1957, 27, 117–133.

35. Hilgard, E. R., Sait, E. M., and Magaret, G. Ann. "Level of aspirations as affected by relative standing in an experimental social group." *J. Exp. Psychol.,* 1940, 27, 411–421.

36. Hill, D. S. "Personification of ideals by urban children." *J. Soc. Psychol.,* 1930, 1, 379–392.

37. Jenkins, Gladys G., Shacter, Helen, and Bauer, W. W. *These Are Your Children,* Expanded Ed. Chicago: Scott, Foresman, 1953.

38. Jensen, G. E. "The social structure of the classroom group: an observational framework." *J. Educ. Psychol.,* 1955, 46, 361–374.

39. Jersild, A. T. *Child Psychology,* 4th Ed. Englewood Cliffs, N.J.: Prentice-Hall, 1954.

40. Johnson, Lois V. "Socially useful learning." *Childh. Educ.,* 1955, 31, 311–315.

41. Keislar, E. R. "The validity of the Thurstone Temperament Schedule with adolescents." *Pers. and Guid. J.,* 1959, 38, 226–228.

42. Killian, L. M. "Ourselves and society." *J. Exc. Child.,* 1954, 20, 294–298.

43. Klugman, S. F. "Cooperative versus individual efficiency in problem solving." *J. Educ. Psychol.,* 1944, 35, 91–100.

44. LaBrant, Lou, and Willis, Margaret. "Some problems of adolescents," in Mental Health in the Classroom, Thirteenth Yearbook Nat. Soc. Study of Educ., Dept. Supervs. and Dirs. of Instr., 1940.

45. Lane, H., and Beauchamp, Mary. *Human Relations in Teaching.* Englewood Cliffs, N.J.: Prentice-Hall, 1955.

46. Lippitt, R., and White, R. K. "The social climate of children's groups," in Barker, R. G., Kounin, J. S., and Wright, H. F. *Child Behavior and Development.* New York: McGraw-Hill, 1943.

47. Lloyd, R. G., et al. "The relationship between academic achievement of pupils and the social structure of the classroom." *Rural Sociol.,* 1956, 21, 179–180.

48. Lorge, I., Fox, D., Davitz, J., and Brenner, M. "A survey of studies contrasting the quality of group performance and individual performance, 1920–1957." *Psychol. Bull.,* 1958, 55, 337–372.

49. McCarthy, Dorothea. "Guiding children's social development." *Childh. Educ.,* 1938, 15, 113–117.

50. Marinho, Héloise. "Social influence in the formation of enduring preferences." *J. Abnorm. and Soc. Psychol.,* 1942, 37, 448–468.

51. Marquart, Dorothy Irene. "Group problem solving." *J. Soc. Psychol.,* 1955, 41, 103–113.

52. Mead, G. H. *Mind, Self, and Society.* Chicago: Univ. of Chicago Press, 1934. Copyright by the Univ. of Chicago.

53. Mennes, A. H. "The effectiveness of multiple period curricular practices in high school English and social studies." *J. Educ. Res.,* 1956, 50, 59–69.

54. Miel, Alice. "Children in action." *Progr. Educ.,* 1949–50, 27, 155–158.

55. Moustakas, C. E. "Emotional adjustment and the play therapy process." *J. Genet. Psychol.,* 1955, 86, 79–99.

56. Murphy, G. "What constitutes a well-integrated personality." *Menninger Quart.,* 1956, 10 (1), 1–9.

57. Nance, Afton D. "A room full of learning." *Childh. Educ.,* 1956, 33, 12–15.

58. Olson, W. C. "The improvement of relations in the classroom." *Childh. Educ.,* 1946, 22, 317–325.

59. Perlmutter, V. H., and de Montmollin, G. "Group learning of nonsense syllables." *J. Abnorm. and Soc. Psychol.,* 1952, 47, 762–769.

60. Phillips, E. L. "Attitude toward self and others: a brief questionnaire report." *J. Consult. Psychol.,* 1951, 15, 79–81.

61. Raimy, V. C. "Self reference in counseling interviews." *J. Consult. Psychol.,* 1948, 12, 153–163.

62. Reese, Mary, and Oldendorf, Dorothy A. "Social living at Highcrest." *Mental Health in the Classroom,* Thirteenth Yearbook Nat. Educ. Ass., Dept. of Supervs. and Dirs. of Instr., 1940.

63. Rehage, K. J. "A comparison of pupil-teacher planning and teacher-directed procedures in eighth grade social studies classes." *J. Educ. Res.,* 1951, 45, 111–115.

64. Ryan, W. C., Strang, Ruth, and Witty, P. "The teacher of gifted children," in Witty, P. *The Gifted Child.* Boston: Heath, 1951. Pp. 106–130.

65. Sanford, R. N. "Dominance versus autocracy and the democratic character." *Childh. Educ.,* 1946, 23, 109–114.

66. Sarbin, T. R. "Role theory," in Lindzey, G. (ed.) *Handbook of Social Psychology,* vol. I, *Theory and Method.* Reading, Mass.: Addison-Wesley, 1954.

67. Shoben, E. J., Jr. "Toward a concept of the normal personality." *Amer. Psychologist,* 1957, 12, 183–189.

68. Simon, R., and Thompson, G. G. "A study of teacher actions desired by pupils in certain classroom situations: motivating children to overcome problem tendencies." *Quart. J. Child Behavior,* 1950, 2, 86–97.

69. Slavson, S. R. *Child Psychotherapy.* New York: Col. Univ. Press, 1952.

70. Smith, W. D., and Lebo, D. "Some changing aspects of the self-concept of pubescent males." *J. Genet. Psychol.,* 1956, 88, 61–75.

71. Spector, S. I. "Climate and social acceptability." *J. Educ. Sociol.,* 1953, 27, 108–114.

72. Stoughton, M. Louise, and Ray, Alice M. "A study of children's heroes and ideals." *J. Exp. Educ.,* 1946, 15, 156–160.

73. Strang, Ruth. "Characteristics of a classroom which promotes mental health." *Nervous Child,* 1954, 10, 363–367.

74. Taylor, D. W., and Faust, W. L. "Twenty questions: efficiency in problem solving as a function of size of

group." *J. Exp. Psychol.*, 1952, 44, 360–368.

75. Thelen, H. A. "The experimental method in classroom leadership." *Elem. Sch. J.*, 1952, 53, 76–85.

76. Thomas, R. M. *Judging Student Progress.* New York: Longmans, 1954.

77. Trow, W. C., and others. "Psychology of group behavior: the class group." *J. Educ. Psychol.*, 1950, 41, 322–338.

78. Wiles, K. "The fourth R." *Childh. Educ.*, 1957, 33, 203–208.

79. Winker, J. B. "Age trends and sex differences in the wishes, identifications, activities and fears of children." *Child Developm.*, 1949, 20, 191–200.

80. Wispe, L. G. "Evaluating section teaching methods in the introductory course." *J. Educ. Res.*, 1951, 45, 161–186.

81. Witty, P. A. "The teacher who has helped me most." *Elem. Engl.*, 1947, 24, 345–354.

82. Wright, H. F., Barber, R. G., Noll, J., and Schoggen, P. "Toward a psychological ecology of the classroom." *J. Educ. Res.*, 1951, 45, 187–200.

83. Wrightstone, J. W. "Evaluation of the experiment with the activity program in the New York City elementary schools." *J. Educ. Res.*, 1944, 38, 252–257.

84. Wrightstone, J. W. "Measuring the social climate of a classroom." *J. Educ. Res.*, 1951, 44, 341–351.

85. Yuker, H. E. "Group atmosphere and memory." *J. Abnorm. and Soc. Psychol.*, 1955, 51, 17–28.

CHAPTER 15

1. Anderson, H. A., and Traxler, A. E. "The reliability of the reading of an English essay test; a second study." *Sch. Rev.*, 1940, 48, 521–530.

2. Birkmaier, Emma Marie (ed.) *Illustrative Learning Experiences.* The Modern School Practices Series, no. 2, Univ. of Minn. Press, Minneapolis, Minn., 1952.

3. Bixler, H. H., Durost, W. N., Hildreth, Gertrude, Lund, K., and Wrightstone, J. W. *Metropolitan Achievement Tests* (Manual and Testbooks). Yonkers-on-Hudson, N.Y.: World, 1959.

4. Bloom, B. S. "Test reliability for what?" *J. Educ. Psychol.*, 1942, 33, 517–526.

5. Bloom, B. S. (ed.) *Taxonomy of Educational Objectives.* New York: Longmans, 1956.

6. Brueckner, L. J., and Bond, G. L. *The Diagnosis and Treatment of Learning Difficulties.* New York: Appleton-Century-Crofts, 1955.

7. Buros, O. K. *The Fifth Mental Measurements Yearbook.* Highland Park, N.J.: Gryphon Press, 1959.

8. Cook, W. W. "The functions of measurement in the facilitation of learning," in Lindquist, E. F. (ed.) *Educational Measurement.* Washington: Amer. Council on Educ., 1951.

9. *Cooperative Sequential Tests of Educational Progress* (Manual, Brief, Technical Rep., *SCAT–STEP* Suppl. and Test Booklets). Princeton, N.J.: Educ. Testing Serv., Co-op. Test Div., 1958.

10. *Cooperative Tests, Programs, Services for Elementary Schools, High Schools, Colleges* (1959–60 Catalog). Princeton, N.J.: Educ. Testing Serv., 1959.

11. Ebel, R. L. "Writing the test item," in Lindquist, E. F. (ed.) *Educational Measurement.* Washington: Amer. Council on Educ., 1951.

12. Eells, W. C. "Reliability of repeated grading of essay type examinations." *J. Educ. Psychol.*, 1930, 21, 48–52.

13. Fattu, N. A. "Testing as a teaching device." *High Sch. J.*, 1957–58, 41, 79–82.

14. Flanagan, J. C. "Can we measure what we teach?" *High Sch. J.*, 1957–58, 41, 93–96.

15. French, W. M., and Associates. *Behavioral Goals of General Education in High School.* New York: Russell Sage, 1957.

16. Gates, A. I. *The Improvement of Reading.* New York: Macmillan, 1947.

17. Gates, A. I. *Gates Primary Reading Test* (Manual and Test). New York: Bur. of Publ., Teachers Coll., Col. Univ., 1958.

18. Gates, A. I. *Gates Advanced Primary Reading Test* (Manual and Test). New York: Bur. of Publ., Teachers Coll., Col. Univ., 1958.

19. Gates, A. I. *Gates Reading Survey, for Grade 3 (Second Half) through Grade 10* (Manual and Test). New York: Bur.

of Publ., Teachers Coll., Col. Univ., 1958.

20. Gates, A. I. *Gates Basic Reading Tests* (Manual and Tests). New York: Bur. of Publ., Teachers Coll., Col. Univ., 1958.
21. Harap, H., and Mapes, Charlotte. "The learning of fundamentals in an arithmetic activity program." *Elem. Sch. J.*, 1934, 34, 515–525.
22. Harry, D. P., and Durost, W. N. *Essential High School Content Battery* (Manual and Testbook). Yonkers-on-Hudson, N.Y.: World, 1951.
23. Heffernan, Helen. "Evaluation more than testing." *NEA J.*, 1958, 47, 227–229.
24. Henmon, V. A. C. "Improvement in school subjects throughout the school year." *J. Educ. Res.*, 1920, 1, 81–95.
25. *Iowa Tests of Educational Development* (Manual and Testbook). Chicago: Science Research, 1952.
26. James, H. W. "The effect of handwriting on grading." *Engl. J.*, 1927, 16, 180–185.
27. Kearney, N. C. *Elementary School Objectives.* New York: Russell Sage, 1953.
28. Kelley, T. L., Madden, R., Gardner, E. F., Terman, L. M., and Ruch, G. M. *Stanford Achievement Test* (Manual and Testbooks). Yonkers-on-Hudson, N.Y.: World, 1953.
29. Keys, N. "The influence on learning and retention of weekly as opposed to monthly tests." *J. Educ. Psychol.*, 1934, 25, 427–436.
30. Lindquist, E. F. (ed.) *Educational Measurement.* Washington: Amer. Council on Educ., 1951.
31. Lindquist, E. F., and Hieronymous, A. N. *Iowa Tests of Basic Skills* (Manual and Testbook). Boston: Houghton Mifflin, 1955.
32. Norton, D. P. "The relationship of study habits and other measures to achievement in ninth grade general science." *J. Exp. Educ.*, 1959, 27, 211–217.
33. Ross, C. C., and Stanley, J. C. *Measurement in Today's Schools*, 3d Ed. Englewood Cliffs, N.J.: Prentice-Hall, 1954.
34. *Selecting an Achievement Test: Principles and Procedures.* Evaluation and Advisory Service, ser. no. 3. Princeton, N.J.: Educ. Testing Serv., 1958.
35. Smith, Eugenia. "Testing can be teaching." *Practical Home Econ.*, 1955, 34, 10–11.
36. *SRA Achievement Series* (Manual and Testbooks). Chicago: Science Research, 1955.
37. Starch, D., and Elliot, E. C. "Reliability of grading high school work in English." *Sch. Rev.*, 1912, 20, 442–457.
38. Starch, D., and Elliot, E. C. "Reliability of grading work in mathematics." *Sch. Rev.*, 1913, 12, 254–257.
39. Tiegs, E. W., and Clark, W. W. *California Achievement Tests* (Manual and Test Booklets). Calif. Test Bur., 1957.
40. Wood, H. B. "Testing used as part of the learning process." *Clearing House*, 1953, 27, 454–456.

GLOSSARY

This glossary includes definitions of nearly all the technical terms and many common words used in this textbook. It should be a convenient alternative when a dictionary happens not to be at hand.

Abasement. Depreciation, humiliation.

Abstract. Symbolic of the general, common features of a class of things or events rather than of a particular thing or event.

Academic. Designates the intellectual aspects of education, particularly the formal school subjects which deal with organized knowledge.

Academic-social learning. The association of academic subjects with students' interests in personal and community problems, as in the study of arithmetic and economics in connection with conducting a children's school-supplies store.

Acceleration. Advancement more rapid than the average. Applied to rate of grade progress in school, it refers to skipping grades or to completing more than one grade in a year.

Acceptance. An attitude or relationship in which an individual feels a sense of personal worth.

Action patterns. Relatively stable ways of behaving; habits.

Adaptable. Capable of adjusting behavior to meet varied situations effectively.

Adjustment. The quality of an individual's behavior (its efficiency and satisfyingness) in relation to his environment, especially in his interpersonal relations.

Adventitious. Extrinsic; accidental; not essentially related to other events.

Affective. Pertaining to the pleasant or unpleasant qualities of emotional experience.

Ambivalence. Having opposing traits or tendencies, such as both loving and hating, dominating and submitting, or advancing and retreating.

Analogy. A relationship, similarity, or congruence between things or events.

Anecdotal records. Recorded observations of significant incidents of child behavior.

Ancillary. Subservient; auxiliary; a preliminary help to another process.

Anxiety. A persisting fear of threat to oneself, arising from severe insecurity or from difficult-to-inhibit, dangerous impulses, and involving feelings of apprehension, dread, and uneasiness.

Aperture. An opening.

Appraise. To estimate, measure, or evaluate the quality or excellence of performance or results.

Approach. A way of beginning; a tentative mode of attack.

Aptitude. Potential capacity for learning and becoming proficient in some particular area, such as music, art, or mathematics.

Articulate. To fit; to bring things or ideas into functional relationship; to utter a pattern of sounds distinctly.

Aspiration (level of). The level of performance in a succession of learning tasks with established possibilities for improvement which an individual sets for himself and aspires toward in a next trial.

Assessment. Appraisal of individual traits or accomplishments; more specifically, evaluation of *progress* or *change* in school achievement, abilities, interests, or personality traits.

Attitude. A predisposition to act, believe, or feel favorably or unfavorably toward objects, persons, situations, or ideas.

Augmented. Increased in amount, size, or degree.

Autistic. Distorting of perception and thinking by one's personal desires and needs.

Automatization of responses. Reduction to internal, response-produced stimuli of cues needed for guiding behavior.

Autonomy. Independence; self-direction.

Basic skills. The skills in language, reading, and arithmetic required for further academic accomplishment.

Battery (of tests). A group of several tests of aptitude and/or achievement standardized to yield comparable scores.

Behavior pattern. An organization or configuration of specific responses adapted to a particular purpose.

Belongingness [Thorndike]. The logical appropriateness or fittingness of learned stimulus-response connections.

Bifactor test. A test yielding two scores, such as from the verbal and nonverbal parts of an intelligence test.

Capacity. The innate basis of potential abilities.

Check list. An appraisal device; a list of traits or behavior patterns which a rater checks to indicate those characteristic of an individual.

Coefficient. A numerical index of magnitude, as of *degree* of correlation between two variables.

Coefficient of determination. An index of the proportion of variation in one trait related to the variation in another with which it is correlated; the square of the coefficient of correlation (r^2).

Coercive. Pertaining to restraining or compelling certain behavior in another person by force or punishment.

Cognitive. Pertaining to the mental processes of perceiving and conceiving, of knowing or comprehending.

Cognitive map. Figuratively, a brain-produced mental map or schema which guides behavior, and which is continually being organized and reorganized during learning.

Cohesive. Holding together; feeling of belonging and striving for mutually satisfying interaction among the members of a group.

Compensatory. Referring to defensive overemphasis on a particular pattern of behavior because of frustration and threatened loss of self-esteem in another area.

Complementary. Refers to the different factors completing a whole; as, each person contributing according to his unique talent and mutually making up for the lacks of others in the group.

Components. The elements, constituents, or parts of a whole.

Compulsive. Impelled to irrational, anxiety-motivated patterns of behavior.

Concept. An idea or generalization which

represents a class of things or events, such as carbohydrates as a class of foods.

Conceptualize. To interpret, understand, or conceive things or events in terms of concepts or generalizations.

Concomitant. Accompanying, joined, associated events or conditions.

Concrete. Pertaining to direct experience with real, actual, specific things.

Concurrently. Going on at the same time; together.

Conditioned response. An acquired response which an individual has learned to make to stimuli which originally did not elicit it.

Conditioning. Learning by association; the attaching or shifting of responses to new (conditioned) stimuli.

Configuration. The pattern or arrangement of parts constituting a whole.

Congruent. Fitting; coinciding; appropriate.

Connectionist [Thorndike]. One who accepts the general theory that learning consists of establishing specific stimulus-response connections, and that complex behavior can be analyzed into such stimulus-response components.

Consonant substitution. The phonetic principle according to which several different words of the same form can be written (or read) merely by substituting a different initial consonant, such as in *bat, mat,* and *sat.*

Constancy (of IQ). The tendency of IQs not to fluctuate beyond minimal limits (as indicated by a test's standard error of measurement).

Construct. A set of assumed or scientifically established relationships among several facts or concepts.

Context cues. Clues for identifying a word from the meaning suggested by a phrase or the sentence as a whole.

Contiguity. Position or occurrence of things or events close together in place or time.

Control group. A group of subjects, in an experimental design, used for comparison with an experimental group on whom the effect of some special treatment is being tested. The special treatment given the experimental group is withheld from the control group.

Correlation. A numerical index of the degree of relationship between two variables or measures on the same population, such

as intelligence and reading achievement for a group of school children. Coefficients of correlation range from +1.00 (perfect relationship) through .00 (no relationship) to −1.00 (perfect inverse relationship).

Counteraggression. Reciprocated hostility; counterattack.

Counterbalanced order. An order of presentation of learning tasks or tests being compared in an experiment to equalize the practice effects from one activity to another. For example, in comparing mastery of learning tasks A and B, half the subjects (randomly chosen) would learn A first and B second, while the other half would learn B first and A second.

Creative productivity. The degree of full constructive use of one's talents.

Criterion. Guide; standard; the level of achievement or performance considered indicative of mastery or adequate for the purpose of an experiment.

Crutch. An auxiliary device sometimes helpful in the initial stages in learning a process, usually abandoned for a more efficient mode of attack as the learner becomes more proficient and confident.

Cue. A discriminated stimulus which signals or guides behavior.

Cultural bias. A tendency of some tests intended for general use to give an experience advantage to particular groups or segments of a culture.

Cultural heritage. Society's store of accumulating knowledge which each generation both uses and extends.

Cumulative records. Expanding records on significant aspects of a child's progress throughout his school years, including data on physical growth and health, abilities, interests, emotional and social adjustment, and achievement.

Curriculum. All the subjects and other learning experiences from which the school objectives are to be attained.

Decrement. A decrease or loss.

Deductive. Inferring from general principles specific applications or implications.

Defense mechanism. Any of several irrational patterns of behavior (denial, rationalization, projection, etc.) which individuals develop unconsciously to allay anxiety and to protect the self-concept from threat.

Denial. A mode of self-defense in which the individual resists recognition of anxiety-producing impulses and threats to his self-concept.

Determinant. A cause, a determiner of an event or action.

Developmental (sequences, levels). Orderly successions of stages—in motor, intellectual, social, and other phases of development—which children go through as a result of both maturation and learning.

Developmental tasks. The major personal accomplishments required of children in achieving each new level of social maturity. Some of the common developmental tasks of adolescents, for example, are becoming more independent, achieving appropriate and comfortable heterosexual relationships, and preliminary identification with a vocational role.

Deviate. One who differs considerably from the average; a deviant.

Deviation IQs. A device for interpretation of certain intelligence-test scores, in which deviations above or below a mean IQ of 100 are computed in terms of the standard deviation (often set at 15) of the distribution of scores.

Diagnostic test. A test, usually an achievement test, for which items are constructed and arranged to yield scores indicative of an individual's specific strengths and weaknesses.

Dichotomous. Pertaining to the division of a group into two classes.

Differential abilities. Relatively independent factors or specialized abilities, such as verbal reasoning, number facility, spatial visualization, and perceptual speed.

Differentiation. Subdividing a general homogeneous pattern or function into one of more discriminated specific parts or functions.

Discipline. To establish personal or social control appropriate to the social activity of one's group; to train for general intellectual effectiveness. Also an academic field of study.

Displaced aggression. Misdirected aggression; attacks on innocent persons or objects rather than on the real cause of the anger-producing frustration.

Distributed practice. Division of the total time required for mastering a learning task into several short periods with rest intervals between them.

Diverse. Different; separate; distinct.

Drill. Repetitive practice intended to improve the proficiency of skills.

Dynamic. Active, energizing, effective as a determiner of action; changing.

Eclectic. Pertaining to choosing and combining ideas from diverse sources and theories.

Ego. The conscious, directing, self-controlling, and self-evaluating aspect of personality; the self.

Elective. Designates the subjects or courses among which students may choose.

Elicit. To draw out, to bring forth, or to stimulate a response.

Emit. To make a response without a specific stimulus, as distinguished from "elicit" (where the stimulus responded to is usually identified).

Empirical. Based on facts, experience, observation or experimentation rather than on speculation.

Emulate. To strive to imitate or equal.

Engender. To cause, produce, or generate.

Episode. A unitary segment of behavior; a separate incident.

Equate. To make equal, as to select experimental and control groups so that they will be equal with respect to sex, age, intelligence, or other relevant factors.

Evaluate. To judge or appraise the efficiency or quality of performance or results.

Explicit. Openly, directly, and unambiguously expressed; not merely implied.

Extinction. The stopping or discontinuing of an unrewarded conditioned response.

Extrinsic (associations, motivation). Outside; unrelated; rewards external to satisfaction in the behavior itself.

Facet. Any of several views, aspects, or phases of a subject, personality, or object.

Factor analysis. A procedure for analyzing the intercorrelations among a set of variables or scores on different tests, (1) to reveal the underlying factors accounting for the several performances and (2) to determine the extent to which each test measures each factor.

Factors. The parts making a whole, such as maturation and learning as determinants of development or the differential abilities comprising intelligence.

Father figure. A person who symbolizes one's real father; a mature person who functions as a father in requiring obedience or giving advice, for example.

Feedback. The perceptual reactions of a person to his own responses; a process by which goal-directed responses are checked and corrected.

Frustration. Experience of emotional tension from being blocked in motive satisfaction or goal-directed striving.

Functional. Pertains to the ready availability for use of the knowledge and skills we learn.

Generalization. The derivation of a general concept or principle from observation of varied specific instances and the extended application of this concept or principle to different new situations.

Generate. To produce or originate.

Genetic. Pertaining to the hereditary determiners (the genes) of development. (Synonymous with "genotypical.")

Gifted children. Usually the highest 1 or 2 per cent of the population in verbal-abstract abilities, those having IQs above 130 or 140. With a broader connotation, a larger number of children with special talents in specific fields such as art, music, or mathematics.

Goal-directed. Oriented toward a goal; as the hypothesis-guided provisional trials of the learner.

Grade equivalents. The grade levels which correspond to the mean scores on standardized achievement tests of representative children at each grade level at each of the nine months of the usual school year. For example, a grade equivalent of 4.2 means achievement equal to the average of children in the second month of the fourth grade.

Grade placement. The grade levels at which curriculum content or students are placed so as to match children's abilities with the levels of difficulty of the learning tasks.

Hierarchical. Referring to ordered arrangement of processes or things according to degrees of importance or dominance.

Homeostatic needs. Physiological processes which regulate and maintain optimum body states with respect to such conditions as temperature, air, sugar, and salt.

Homogeneous. Pertaining to the relative similarity or uniformity among the members of a group in intelligence or reading proficiency, for example.

Hypothesis. A tentative explanation of certain observations, a provisional assumption or supposition, or a predicted solution to a problem.

Identical elements. The specific parts or components which two or more larger patterns of behavior have in common.

Identifiable. Pertains to the recognition of things, to distinguishing them from others or from the background.

Identification (act of). Effort toward self-enhancement, or self-defense, by taking the role of an admired and/or loved other person.

Impede. To hinder or obstruct action.

Impel. To incite, drive, or urge to action.

Implement. A tool. Also, to provide the means for accomplishing a purpose or plan.

Implication. An inference; a probable consequence or result.

Implicit. Implied; not directly given or observable. Thought processes, for example, are implicit responses, inferred from explicitly observed behavior.

Impotent. Without power, strength, or effect.

Impulse. A tendency to motive-satisfying action.

Impulsion. A sudden, forced, thrusting movement of the body or a limb.

Incentive. The object, goal, or situation which an individual has learned will satisfy a motive; as, food is an incentive for a person motivated by hunger.

Incidence. Frequency of occurrence.

Increment. An added unit; gain; increase.

Individual difference. The deviation of one individual from another or from the average in abilities, proficiencies, interests, physique, or any other trait.

Individualize. To adjust curricula and instruction to each student's abilities, interests, and needs.

Inductive. Generalizing; discovering among different things or from varied experiences a common feature or principle.

Inherent. Belonging to an object or process as an integral part of it.

Inhibition (proactive, retroactive, interactive). Preventing, stopping, or interfering with a process. In *proactive* inhibition, earlier-learned content intrudes to interfere with recall of later-learned content. In *retroactive* inhibition, later-learned content interferes with recall of earlier-learned content. In *interactive* inhibition, there is mutual interference at recall between earlier- and later-learned content.

Innate. Inborn; inherited.

Insight. Understanding; seeing through a problem so that the organization and interrelations of the significant parts are comprehended.

Instinctive. Pertaining to the innate factors in certain behavior patterns characteristic of a species, to which the structure of the animal predisposes it.

Integration. A combination of parts organized to achieve a unified, coherent whole.

Intellectual efficiency. The quality of the individual's working and problem-solving methods; the efficiency with which an individual uses his intelligence.

Intelligence. General (verbal-abstract) capacity for learning and problem solving; more specifically, capacity for comprehending and dealing effectively with symbols in abstract relationships.

Interest. A conditioned response of pleasure or satisfaction which accompanies intellectual consideration of some thing or idea, or participation in some activity.

Interim. The time between.

Interindividual difference. Any of trait differences between individuals. (See *Individual difference.*)

Intermittent. Alternating; coming now and then; discontinuous.

Internal consistency. The degree to which all the items of a scale or test measure the same function.

Interpersonal relations. Relations between people.

Interpolated. Inserted or placed between other parts or events.

Intervening (processes, events). Response-shaping processes which are inferred to go on within the organism between the stimulus and the response; events between the beginning and the end of a series.

Intra-. Within. For example, *intraindividual* differences are trait variations within the individual; *intragroup* refers to conditions within rather than between groups; and

intraclass grouping is subdivision into small groups within a class.

Intrinsic. Inherent, belonging. *Intrinsic interest*, for example, is motive satisfaction in an activity itself, apart from ulterior or extrinsic rewards.

Introject. To take as one's own (into oneself) the attitudes or behavior patterns of others.

Inventory (personality, interests, study methods). A comprehensive list of questions on attitudes and personal characteristics, likes and dislikes, or study habits, from which a classified arrangement of the individual's answers yields a profile of personality characteristics, interests, or study skills.

IQ (intelligence quotient). The ratio of a child's mental age to his chronological age, indicative of his rate of mental development and relative brightness (IQ = MA/CA).

Job analysis. Analysis of a learning process or problem-solving approach to find the most efficient mode of attack.

Laissez-faire. Designates a kind of leadership which provides a minimum of control and guidance.

Latent learning. Hidden but potentially observable learning which is assumed to occur without obvious reinforcement, and is manifest later in performance when reinforcement is provided.

Learning curve. A graphical representation of progress from successive practice trials.

Locomote. To move about; to crawl or walk.

MA (mental age). An index of mental maturity. The age equivalent of the mean score of representative children of a given age on a developmental intelligence scale. For example, the child who earns the mean score of representative ten-year-olds is assigned a mental age of 10–0.

Madrigal. Unaccompanied, several-part singing which makes use of counterpoint and imitation.

Maladjustment. Lack of harmony with one's environment, especially with respect to interpersonal relations; failure to achieve personal and social efficiency and happiness.

Maturation. Development resulting from growth of the nervous system and other anatomical structures upon which capacity for increasingly complex learning and performance are dependent.

Maturation curve. A graphical representation of development produced by growth rather than learning.

Mean. The measure of central tendency of a distribution of scores obtained by summing the scores and dividing by the total number.

Meaning. The relationships to other things and events, the generalizations, the significance, or the understanding things or symbols bring to mind in a given person.

Median. The measure of central tendency in a distribution of scores representing the point above and below which there are equal numbers of scores.

Mediation. Going between—bridging—two events or ideas.

Mental health. Being personally and socially efficient, well adjusted, enjoying living, and achieving self-realization.

Mental map. An imagined plan or guide to behavior.

Mentally retarded children. Children whose mental growth is so slow that even minimal attainment in reading and other basic skills requires highly individualized or special class instruction; those with IQs below 70 to 75.

Metabolic. Pertaining to the biological processes of building up and destroying protoplasm incidental to growing and deteriorating and to assimilating and discharging energy.

Metamorphosis. Change or transformation of form or structure.

Minimum essentials. The fewest carefully selected concepts and skills in language, reading, arithmetic, social studies, and science which every adult needs for functioning in the simple, nonprofessional life activities.

Modes of attack. Specific approaches or defined methods of accomplishing learning tasks or of finding solutions to problems.

Motive. An internal condition of the individual which arouses, sustains, directs, determines the intensity of effort, as well as defining the consequences of goal-directed behavior. (Roughly synonymous with "drive," "need," and "desire.")

Motor (development, skills). Emergence of abilities and acquisition of skills involving body movements and coordinated manipulations of body parts.

Negativism. Persistent resistance to complying with requests and directions of other people, especially of parents and teachers.

Neurotic. Emotionally maladjusted; characterized by personally and socially ineffective reactions to frustration.

Nonsense syllable. A pronounceable but meaningless combination of letters; used in learning experiments where control of amount of prior experience is desired.

Norm. Any of various mean or median scores of representative populations on standardized tests, by comparison with which individual test scores can be interpreted.

Novel. New; encountered for the first time.

Nurture. The influences of the home, school, and other environmental factors on the development of individuals.

Objective (tests). Unaffected by subjective, personal bias or other irrelevant factors.

Objectives (of the school). The concepts, skills, attitudes, and interests which the school aims to achieve.

Optimum. The best for a given purpose and set of conditions.

Orientation. A direction, point of view, or mental set toward a situation or problem.

Overachiever. A student whose level of school achievement significantly exceeds that of typical students of the same intelligence or aptitude.

Overconformity. Anxious, excessive compliance with authority, to the extent of inhibiting spontaneity.

Overlearning. Practicing something beyond the point of initial mastery.

Overprotection. Pampering, indulging, and shielding beyond an individual's needs.

Overt. Unconcealed; apparent; observable.

Overview. A scanning or survey of a whole.

Paired associates. The presentation for memorizing of pairs of items, such as "antelope-21" with the expectation that in subsequent presentations of the first member of a pair the second will be recalled.

Paradox. Apparently contradictory facts or concepts.

Participation chart. A chart expressing the quantity and quality of each individual's contributions to a group discussion.

Pattern. Organization, the showing of variations; as in a profile of differential abilities.

Pedagogy. Study of the principles and methods of teaching.

Peer. An equal. Peer groups or peer friendships refer to a child's associates of his own age.

Percentile scores. Test scores rendered comparable by ranking them from 0 to 100, in which ordered system any percentile score indicates the percentage of individuals in the distribution below this score.

Perception. Awareness, attachment of meaning to, or interpretation of a stimulus (which perception makes a percept).

Perception of effects. Perceiving the consequences of goal-directed, provisional trials in learning to ascertain their correctness.

Perceptual-motor. Pertains to overt actions made in response to nonverbal (usually visual) cues.

Perceptual organization. Refers to aptitude for organizing, achieving meaning in, and reasoning with spatial and pictorial patterns.

Performance scale. An intelligence scale comprised largely of nonlanguage items, such as assembling puzzles or making designs with blocks.

Perfunctory. Done indifferently, mechanically, without care or close attention.

Permissiveness. That attribute of a secure teacher-child or parent-child relationship in which the child feels free to express both negative and positive feelings without guilt or expectation of criticism.

Perseveration. Persistence in naïvely giving as a solution to a new problem one found acceptable in a previous problem, rather than attacking the new problem by creative problem solving.

Personality. The dynamic organization of *all* the traits that determine an individual's unique adjustments to his environment.

Pervade. To spread through; to be diffused throughout.

Phonetic analysis. Analysis of words into the sounds which the letters and letter combinations represent.

Plateau. A flat segment in a learning or maturation curve indicating a temporary period of no apparent progress.

Potentialities. Talents and proficiencies which, though not yet manifest, may emerge with maturation and education or other stimulating experience.

Practice. Repeated and checked goal-directed attempts to improve performance.

Pragmatic. Pertaining to judging a process in terms of practical values, consequences, or outcomes.

Precipitating. Pertaining to the situation or stimulus which elicits a response or act which the individual is already set or predisposed to make.

Principle. A unifying generalization, an underlying explanation, or a rule applicable in a variety of specific instances.

Problem solving. A goal-directed, multiple, trial-and-check approach to new situations and learning tasks, in which the individual discovers new modes of response.

Proficiency. Acquired skill, understanding, or expertness in some performance.

Profile. A graphic representation of the variations in comparable scores of a single person on multiple-factor tests of abilities, achievement, interests, or personality.

Prognosis. The predicted outcome for an individual in a given course of study or other specified experience.

Project. A comprehensive learning activity in which often several school subjects and certain social learning activities of the school are organized about children's current interest in a community problem.

Projection. A self-defensive mode of adjustment in which the individual attributes to others his own undesirable traits or impulses.

Projective methods. Procedures in which the individual unwittingly reveals his attitudes, motives, and self-concept in such unstructured situations as telling stories about pictures, completing sentences, interpreting ink blots, or drawing human figures.

Propensity. Inclination toward certain behavior patterns.

Provisional trial. A way of testing a tentative hypothesis by trying it; a try-and-see mode of responding to a learning task.

Psychosomatic symptoms. Physiological symptoms of mental illness, such as gastric ulcer as a possible sign of anxiety.

Psychotic symptoms. Signs of severe mental

disorder or personality disorganization, such as loss of contact with reality.

Puberty. Attainment of sexual maturity (pubescence).

Punitive. Punishing. Such distinctions as *extrapunitive* (punishment of others) and *intropunitive* (self-punishment) are sometimes made.

Quintile. Any of five points or ranges into which the 100 percentile scores are divisible: 20th, 40th, 60th, 80th, and 100th, or the ranges from zero to 20th and between these points.

Range. The difference between the lowest and highest scores obtained on a test by some group.

Rating scale. An appraisal device in which a rater is guided in judging the degree to which an individual exhibits certain defined traits, such as work habits, which may range from "very effective" to "very ineffective."

Rationalizing. Defending oneself by irrational excuse making; finding face-saving reasons for guilt-producing actions.

Reaction formation. A defense mechanism in which the individual develops a behavior pattern which contradicts an unconscious impulse or disposition, such as overconformity in a child subject to aggressive impulses.

Readiness (for learning). Relative mental and experience maturity needed for successfully beginning or taking a next step in some learning activity.

Reasoning. The employment of symbols in problem solving; the inductive generalization of principles and their application to new problems.

Reciprocal. Mutual, interacting, complementary.

Refraction. The deflection from a straight path of a ray of light as it passes from one medium into another, as from air into water.

Regression. Reversion to a simpler and developmentally earlier level of behavior when threatened with failure on a more mature level.

Reinforcement. The motive-satisfaction or reward which attends, and presumably strengthens, a stimulus-response connection being learned.

Reliability. The degree to which measuring instruments yield self-consistent scores on repeated applications, usually indicated by intercorrelations between scores on different forms, parts, or retests of the same test.

Remedial teaching. Teaching directed toward overcoming diagnosed, specific difficulties.

Reminiscence. The phenomenon of recalling, with the passage of time, more rather than less of something memorized.

Repression. A defense mechanism of unconsciously keeping out of mind or inhibiting anxiety- and guilt-provoking impulses and ideas.

Residual. A remainder.

Response. A reaction such as manipulating something, talking, thinking, or feeling. The action may result from external or internal stimulation or be emitted as a result of central-nervous-system activity.

Retardation. Failure to keep pace with one's age mates in mental growth, school achievement, or grade progress.

Retention (in learning). The remembering (retaining) of something once learned.

Reward. Any motive-satisfying object or event, such as food, approval, security, or the intrinsic satisfaction of learning effort and accomplishment.

Rigidity. Relative inflexibility or inability to change one's attitude, way of perceiving, or mode of attack.

Role. The behavior pattern expected of the occupant of a defined position in a group, such as the teacher, the pupil, or the chairman.

Sagacity. Keenness of discernment and judgment; seeing what is relevant.

Satiate. To satisfy a motive completely so that no more of the incentive is wanted.

Saving method. Measurement of retention by determining the decrease in time or trials required for relearning as compared to original learning.

Schemata (or schema). An outline, formulation, or classification for guiding behavior or interpreting experience.

Search model. The general criteria which any specific solution of a given problem must meet, thus a functional guide in solving a problem.

Secondary (in education). The second level

of education, the junior and senior high school level between elementary and collegiate.

Segment. Any of the parts into which an object or process can be readily divided.

Self-actualization. Satisfying full development and use of one's talents.

Self-concept. An individual's full view and appraisal of himself—his physique, abilities, social roles, and worth.

Self-defeating. Pertaining to anxiety-motivated behavior which handicaps the individual in attaining more important motive-satisfactions and goals, such as being overcritical of other people whose esteem is needed or not trying at all because of fear of failing.

Self-discovery (in learning). The learning of concepts, skills, or solutions to problems from one's self-initiated (and teacher-encouraged) exploratory, trial-and-check problem-solving efforts.

Self-enhancement. A raised sense of personal worth; an increment to evaluation of self, often from development or more constructive use of one's talents.

Self-perspective. An adequate, unambiguous, and sufficiently distant view of oneself.

Self-realization. Full development of one's potentialities; use of one's talents and other resources for personal satisfaction and social contributions.

Self-recitation. A memorizing and study technique in which the learner leaves the copy in advance of complete mastery and actively and creatively strives for independent performance of the task (contrasted with passive reading and rereading, or "absorption" of the material).

Self-recrimination. Accusing, blaming oneself.

Sequential. Pertaining to following an ordered series of events, as in successive stages of growth or school achievement.

Serial anticipation method. Memorizing in order the members of a list (such as words or nonsense syllables) in which the measure of learning is the number of promptings required to bring the list to an errorless reproduction.

Set (mental, learning). A preparatory, goal-directed orientation or expectation.

Skill. Developed ability to perform complex mental and/or motor acts easily, adaptably, and proficiently.

Slow learner. Not "mentally retarded," but below average in verbal-abstract intelligence to the extent that normal academic progress is frustrated; children whose IQs range from 70 or 75 to 85 or 90.

Socialization. The social learning processes by which a child acquires his social roles.

Socioeconomic status. One's rank in a given society as determined by the level of his occupation, income, and social class.

Sociogram. A diagrammatic representation of the friendship or other interpersonal relationships among the members of a group.

Sociometric. Pertaining to measurement of interpersonal relations, such as the pattern of friendship relationships within a group of school children.

Solipsistic. Pertaining to the individual's intimate personal experiences which only he can know.

Spatial visualization. Picturing in one's mind the assembled parts or disassembled whole of two- or three-dimensional patterns.

Special class. A class with a modified curriculum and methods of teaching; adapted especially to the needs of mentally retarded or gifted children.

Spontaneous activity. Intrinsically motivated behavior; behavior or accomplishment which in itself is satisfying.

Spurious. Deceptively distorted. A correlation between intelligence and achievement, for example, may be spuriously high because of irrelevant factors such as marked age differences in the population on which the correlation is based.

Standard deviation (SD, σ). A measure of the spread or deviations of scores about the mean of a distribution. It is the root of the average of the sum of the squared deviations. In a normal distribution about two-thirds of the cases fall within the limits of one SD above and below the mean.

Standard error of measurement. The extent of variation in test scores expected on retests because of the unreliability of the measuring instrument, estimated by the formula, σ meas. $= \sigma y \sqrt{1 - r_{11}}$.

Standardization. The establishment of uniform methods of administering, scoring, and interpreting tests and the collection of representative norms with which individual scores can be compared for interpretation.

Standard score. A derived score (z) in standard-deviation (SD) units for making the raw scores (X) from different tests comparable. By the formula $z = (X\text{-}Mean)/SD$ raw scores are expressed as deviations (in SD units) from the mean. The z scores can be translated to any desired frame, such as with a mean of 100 and an SD of 15. In such a frame (standard score $= 100 + 15z$), a standard score of 115 is, of course, one standard deviation above the mean.

Statistical significance. Referring to estimates of the probability that experimental results from samples of a population can be trusted to be representative of the entire population. The ratio of an obtained experimental difference on some measure to the variations to be expected from errors of sampling and measurement. For large samples, the z-ratio should be 1.96 and 2.58 to indicate significance at the 5 and 1 per cent levels, respectively. For small samples, the T ratios indicative of statistical significance must exceed these values.

Stereoscope. An instrument which presents two pictures taken from slightly separated points of view, which the viewer fuses into a single image with solidity or depth.

Stereotype. An undiscriminating and oversimplified conception of an object, person, or group.

Stereotyping. Implies making the behavior of individuals uniform, routine, and fixed.

Stimulus. Any object, event, or energy change either outside or within the individual which excites a response.

Structure. The pattern, arrangement, or organization of the parts in a whole; used in a figurative sense when referring to mental processes.

Structuring. Discovering, defining, and planning an approach to mastery of a learning task or problem.

Subsume. To classify under, as classifying *maple* under *trees*.

Survey course. A course which combines several related subjects, such as a social studies course which includes history, geography, economics, sociology, and political science.

Survey tests of achievement. Tests which measure and yield comparable scores for several curriculum areas, such as in reading, language, arithmetic, social studies, and science.

Symbol. A word, number, diagram, or mental representation of something from an individual's experience, such as a picture or image which may stand for an object or a concept.

Symbolize. To use words, ideas, images, or other symbols for representing things and events in memory and imagination.

Systematic (practice, teacher guidance). Organized; scheduled; methodically conducted.

Talent. Relatively high degree of aptitude or specialized ability.

Teacher guidance. Guidance of children in approaching learning problems by explaining, demonstrating, correcting provisional trials, or leading questions and arrangements for self-discovery learning.

Telescope. To shorten and simplify by combining discrete elements so as to create a smoothly functioning pattern.

Temperament. A biologically determined disposition or tendency affecting the individual's emotional responsiveness.

Tendency. A set, inclination, or propensity for a certain direction of behavior.

Tentative. Holding an hypothesis provisionally, subject to change.

Trace (memory). A hypothetical residual pattern left in the nervous system as a result of learning or experience and because of which behavior is subsequently altered.

Trait. A differentiated and relatively enduring characteristic of personality, such as verbal reasoning, interest in art, emotional control, or love of other people, which can be appraised in degree and compared from one individual to another.

Transfer of training. The application to new learning tasks or problems of principles, concepts, or skills learned previously in different situations.

Trial. One of a series of attempts to solve

a problem or to improve an individual's skill in a learning task.

Trial-and-check process. An approach in the learning of concepts, skills, or solutions to problems by a sequence of goal-directed, provisional trials, each of which is checked to see whether or how nearly the goal is attained.

Trial and error. Referring to the sequence of varied attempts (trials) a learner makes in trying to discover a solution to a problem-solving task.

T score. A standard score in which the mean is arbitrarily set at 50 and the standard deviation at 10.

Underachiever. A student whose academic achievement is significantly below that of the typical student of the same intelligence or aptitude.

Unit. A segment or distinctive part of a whole, as of a subject or curriculum; a project in an integrated curriculum.

Validity. The extent to which a test actually measures the traits for which it was designed; usually indicated by correlations between scores on the test and other accepted criteria of validity, such as school achievement in the case of intelligence tests.

Verbal. Expressed in words.

Verbal-abstract (intelligence). Designates a restricted connotation of general intelligence, based on the verbal and other abstract symbols frequently found in tests of general intelligence.

Verbatim. Following the original exactly, word for word.

Vicarious. Taking the place of; as substituting imagination for real action.

Warm-up. The forepart of a practice session or performance in which the individual accomplishes the set and adjustments for efficient performance.

Word identification. The process in reading of determining the meaning of an unfamiliar word—from the context, pronouncing it phonetically, visual analysis, or other clues.

Word recognition. The process in reading of recognizing a word for which the pronunciation and meaning have been previously identified.

Work methods. Habitual ways of doing a job, which vary in efficiency.

Work sample. An actual sample of performance in an activity, as in appraising a child's drawing or handwriting proficiency.

CREDITS FOR PICTURE GALLERIES

CHAPTER 1

Counterclockwise from top left: The Play Schools Association; School for the Deaf, Board of Education, City of New York; Queens College, New York; Board of Education, City of New York; same; Hays from Monkmeyer; Board of Education, City of New York.

CHAPTER 3

Counterclockwise from top left: Elizabeth Hibbs from Monkmeyer; Bank Street College of Education; The Play Schools Association; National Recreation Association; The Play Schools Association; Meisel from Monkmeyer; Hays from Monkmeyer; Max Tharpe from Monkmeyer.

CHAPTER 5

Left page: top, Burk Uzzle from Black Star; *bottom left,* Board of Education, City of New York; *bottom right,* Hunter College. *Right page: top,* Childcraft Equipment Co.; *bottom left,* Merrim from Monkmeyer.

CHAPTER 6

Top, left to right: Queens College, New York; Board of Education, City of New York; National Recreation Association; Board of Higher Education, City of New York. *Bottom, left to right:* National Recreation Association; Board of Education, City of New York; Courtesy of The Metropolitan Museum of Art.

CHAPTER 7

Left side of page: Chas. Pfizer & Co., Inc. *Right side, top to bottom:* Board of Higher Education, City of New York; The Psychological Corporation; Hunter College; Socony Mobil Oil Co., Inc.

CHAPTER 8

Left page: top left, National Recreation Association; *middle left,* Hunter College; *middle right,* Swiss National Tourist Office; *bottom,* Carroll Seghers II from Black Star. *Right page:* Swiss National Tourist Office.

CHAPTER 10

Left page: left, National Hospital for Speech Disorders; *right,* Hunter College. *Right page: top,* Hays from Monkmeyer; *lower left,* Hunter College Elementary School; *lower right,* Post-Dispatch pictures from Black Star.

CHAPTER 11

Top to bottom: Queens College, New York; Leonard Kamsler; Max Tharpe from Monkmeyer.

CHAPTER 12

Left page: left, Queens College Early Childhood Center; *right,* The Play Schools Association. *Right page: top to bottom,* Robert J. Smith from Black Star; courtesy of The Metropolitan Museum of Art; National Recreation Association.

CHAPTER 13

Left page: left, Brooklyn College; *right,* The Play Schools Association. *Right page: top to bottom,* Joe Pazen from Black Star; Mental Health Film Board; National Recreation Association.

CHAPTER 14

Counterclockwise from top left: Robert J. Smith from Black Star; Dick Checani; Standard Oil Co. (N.J.); The Play Schools Association, copyright Roy Pinney; Arden N. Frandsen; Burk Uzzle from Black Star.

NAME INDEX

Adams, J. E., 177, 546
Adams, J. J., 180, 546
Aftreth, O. B., 282, 557
Alexander, Audrey M., 156, 541
Allen, R. M., 438–440, 569
Allport, G. W., 235, 551
Allred, D. L., 374, 564
Almy, Millie, 77, 537
Amatora, Mary, 476–477, 571
Anastasi, Anne, 163, 440, 546, 569
Anderson, Gladys L., 445, 569
Anderson, H. A., 533, 574
Anderson, H. H., 445, 472, 569, 571
Anderson, I. H., 91, 537
Anderson, J. E., 81–82, 412–413, 450, 537–538, 566, 569
Anderson, R. H., 179, 546
Anderson, Theresa, 248–251, 554
Aneshansel, Jane, 214, 552
Anfinson, R. D., 176, 546
Angell, G. W., 281, 557
Arbuckle, D. S., 459–460, 569

Archer, C. P., 338, 346–347, 562
Arnold, Magda B., 232, 551
Artley, A. S., 254–255, 562
Asch, S. E., 323–324, 561
Ashbaugh, E. J., 382, 564
Atkinson, J. W., 213, 553
Atwood, R. A., 186, 546
Ausubel, D. P., 91, 324, 386–387, 409, 538, 559, 564, 566
Axelrod, H. C., 221, 551
Azrin, N. H., 40–41, 536

Bagley, W. C., 350, 562
Bailey, Helen K., 150, 541
Baker, C. T., 138–140, 545
Ballard, P. B., 370–371, 564
Baller, W. R., 196, 546
Banks, H. P., 310, 561
Barber, R. G., 464, 574
Barker, R. G., 405–406, 566
Barlow, Frances P., 137, 142, 542

Ingram, Christine P., 192–193, 548
Irwin, J. M., 382, 565
Iscoe, I., 410, 568
Ivy, M., 258, 555

Jackson, R. A., 158, 543
James, H. W., 552, 575
James, W., 355–356, 563
Janes, H. P., 196, 548
Janis, I. L., 218, 552
Janke, L. L., 137, 543
Jenkins, Gladys G., 66, 82–83, 402, 414–415, 419, 446–448, 539, 567, 570, 572
Jenkins, J. G., 372–374, 382, 565
Jenkins, Lulu M., 71, 93, 539
Jenkins, Marian, 167, 548
Jensen, A. R., 445, 571
Jensen, B. T., 276, 558
Jensen, G. E., 484, 572
Jensen, M. B., 321, 560
Jensen, V. H., 158, 543
Jersild, A. T., 17, 65, 93, 103, 434, 460, 472, 536, 539, 552, 570, 572
Johnson, C. E., 168–169, 548
Johnson, D. M., 256, 555
Johnson, Ethel, 383–384, 566
Johnson, G. O., 189–195, 548, 549
Johnson, G. R., 188, 548
Johnson, J. T., 96, 539
Johnson, Lois V., 466–467, 572
Johnson, O. G., 456–457, 570
Johnson, P. O., 369–370, 565
Johnson, W. H., 178, 548
Johnston, J. W., 197, 548
Johnston, R. A., 213, 552
Jolles, I., 178, 193, 548
Jones, Daisy M., 170, 548
Jones, E. E., 214, 552
Jones, H. E., 86–87, 435–438, 442, 539–540, 570
Jones, Mary C., 33, 41, 86, 89, 537, 540, 567
Jones, P. S., 255, 555
Jones, R. H., 151, 540, 543
Jones, R. S., 454, 570
Joyce, J. N., 315, 560
Judd, C. H., 342–343, 361, 563
Judson, A. J., 214, 552
Justman, J., 178, 548

Kagan, J., 416, 567
Karen, R. L., 387, 565
Karlin, S. R., 86, 540
Katz, B., 446, 570
Kearney, N. C., 8–9, 15, 508, 535–536, 575
Keislar, E. R., 477, 481, 572
Keister, Mary Elizabeth, 46, 223, 537, 552, 555
Kellaway, R., 284, 557

Keller, F. S., 288, 558
Kelley, T. L., 80, 509–513, 527, 530, 540, 575
Kellogg, Roberta M., 186–187, 548
Kelly, Florence, 179, 546
Kendler, H. H., 78, 540
Kendler, T. S., 78, 540
Kersh, B. Y., 339–340, 344, 562
Keston, M. J., 248–251, 555
Ketcham, W. A., 20, 536
Keys, A., 213, 552
Keys, N., 151, 154, 178, 369, 442, 506, 543–544, 548, 565, 570, 575
Killian, L. M., 473, 572
Kimball, Barbara, 399–400, 567
Kingston, A. J., Jr., 197, 548
Kinter, Madaline, 129, 135, 154, 543
Kinzer, J. R., 78, 94, 540
Kirk, S. A., 142, 189–195, 543, 548–549
Kittell, J. E., 249, 555
Klein, G. S., 244, 555
Klugman, S. F., 468, 572
Knapp, C. G., 298, 320, 558, 560
Knauber, A. J., 129, 135, 543
Knight, F. B., 224–225, 338, 344, 553, 563
Knox, G. W., 390–391, 566
Koenker, R. H., 94, 330, 540, 560
Kogan, N., 178, 549
Kogan, Z., 267, 555
Kolberg, O. W., 382, 565
Kong, W., 336, 563
Korchin, S. J., 410, 567
Koshuk, Ruth P., 142, 543
Kottmeyer, W., 170, 549
Kramer, Grace A., 370, 565
Kramer, K., 19, 536
Krantz, Lavern L., 157, 543
Krause, LaVern W., 309, 561
Kropotkin, A., 221, 552
Krueger, W. C. F., 381–382, 565
Kuder, F., 228–230, 552
Kuenne, Margaret R., 315, 561, 563
Kuhlmann, F., 121–122, 133, 543
Kurtz, K. H., 313, 323, 561
Kyte, G. C., 16, 193, 354, 536, 549, 563

LaBrant, Lou, 185, 475–477, 549, 572
Lally, Ann, 185, 549
Lambert, J. F., 312, 560, 561
Lamp, C. J., 151, 154, 543–544
Lampman, Permilla, 168–169, 549
Lamson, Edna E., 138, 142, 544
Landis, P. H., 416–417, 567
Lane, H., 482–486, 572
Lankford, F. G., Jr., 319, 561
Lantz, Beatrice, 77, 222, 406–407, 540, 552, 567
Larson, Ruth C., 154, 544
Lashley, K. S., 271–272, 558

Rock, I., 242, 557
Rogers, C. R., 442, 553, 570
Rogers, M. C., 144, 545
Rood, E. J., 384–386, 564–565
Rosenbaum, M., 474, 572
Rosenberg, N., 230, 553
Rosenblum, S., 285, 558–559
Rosenstock, I. M., 415, 568
Rosensweig, S., 415, 568
Rosewell, F., 201, 547
Ross, C. C., 225, 505, 523, 553, 575
Ross, C. O., 177, 546
Rosskopf, M. F., 336, 563
Roth, R., 21, 483, 535
Rothman, Esther, 459, 570
Rothney, J. W. M., 86, 538
Rotter, J. B., 453, 570–571
Rowan, Norma, 179, 546
Ruch, G. M., 80, 509–513, 527, 530, 540, 575
Ruddell, A. K., 255, 555
Ruediger, W. C., 350, 563
Rugg, H., 21, 536
Runkel, P. J., 143, 544
Rush, B. H., 450, 571
Russell, D. H., 256, 556
Russell, R. W., 183, 549
Rutledge, J. A., 257–260, 556
Ryan, W. C., 471, 550, 573

Saetbeit, J. G., 130–131, 135, 545
Sait, E. M., 472, 572
Sakoda, J. M., 379, 565
Sandiford, P., 145, 546
Sandin, A. A., 176, 550
Sanford, R. N., 485, 573
Sarason, I. G., 410, 568
Sarason, S. B., 191–193, 550
Sarbin, T. R., 474, 573
Sarnoff, I., 399, 568
Sartain, A. O., 150, 545
Sauble, Irene, 267, 556
Saugstad, P., 351, 563
Schaaf, O., 351, 563
Schaefer-Simmern, H., 265, 556
Schaeffer, M., 314, 561
Schenk, Q. F., 479, 572
Schiff, H. M., 91, 409, 538, 566
Schlossberg, H., 371, 376, 381, 566
Schmidt, Bernardine G., 142, 545
Schmidt, H. O., 221, 553
Schoeppe, Aileen, 234–235, 553
Schoggen, P., 464, 574
Schonfield, D., 94, 541
Schooler, K., 390, 564
Schott, E., 144, 545
Schpoont, S., 387, 564
Schrader, W. B., 158, 543

Schrepel, Marie, 378, 565–566
Schroder, H. M., 419, 568
Schroeder, W. H., 343, 563
Schutz, R. E., 150, 544
Schuyler, Ruby, 179, 546
Schwartz, R. J., 346, 562
Schwartz, S., 474, 572
Seagoe, May, 103, 539
Sears, Pauline S., 223, 407, 553, 568
Sears, R. R., 416, 568
Seashore, C. E., 130–131, 135, 545
Seashore, H. G., 73, 86, 125–128, 134, 152–154, 272–273, 279, 538, 540–542, 559
Segar, W. B., 179, 546
Segel, D., 128, 545
Seils, L., 71, 541
Sessions, A. D., 230, 551
Seward, J. P., 33, 537
Sexon, J. A., 186, 550
Seymour, L., 410, 567
Shacter, Helen, 66, 82–83, 402, 414–415, 419, 446–448, 539, 567, 570, 572
Shaffer, F., 71, 538
Shane, H. G., 17–18, 21, 536
Shaw, F. J., 461, 571
Sheats, P., 471, 571
Shepard, Winifred O., 313–314, 561
Shepler, W. D., 230, 553–554
Sherman, M., 409, 412, 568, 571
Shinn, E. O., 230, 554
Shoben, E. F., Jr., 398, 422–424, 489, 568, 573
Shumaker, Ann, 21, 536
Shuttleworth, F. K., 70, 93, 541
Silverman, H. L., 189, 550
Simon, R., 489, 573
Skinner, B. F., 39–40, 288, 537, 559
Slavson, S. R., 472, 573
Sleight, W., 355, 563
Sloan, W., 143, 545
Smart, R. C., 73, 539
Smith, Dora V., 170, 550
Smith, Eugenia, 527, 575
Smith, L. F., 442, 569
Smith, Nila B., 198, 404, 550, 568
Smith, R. R., 167, 550
Smith, W. D., 478, 573
Smitter, Faith, 434, 569
Sobel, B., 94, 541
Sobel, M. A., 255–256, 556
Solly, C. M., 214, 284, 554, 558
Soloman, D., 284, 378, 557, 565
Sommer, Agnes T., 94, 541
Sommer, R., 214, 554
Sontag, L. W., 138–140, 545
Sorenson, H., 172, 550
Souder, H. C., 100, 541
Sparks, W. M., 373, 382, 565
Spector, S. I., 486, 573
Spence, K. W., 33, 39, 410, 537, 567

SUBJECT INDEX

Attitudes, and mental health, 412–413
  in remembering, 388–389
Automatization of responses, 292–293
Avoidance of learning, 419–420

Behavioral classifications of objectives, 8–11
Belongingness in learning, 38, 274

California Test of Mental Maturity, 123–124
California Test of Personality, 440–444
Check list in appraising adjustment, 436–437
Checking of provisional trials, 276–277, 285–290
Classmates' opinions in appraising adjustment, 437–438
Cognitive learning theory, 41–47
  applications, 44–46
  emotional control in, 46–47
  experiments supporting, 42–44, 284, 301–302
Cognitive structure, 44–45
  role, in forgetting and remembering, 373–374
  in problem solving, 242–243
Cognitive structuring of tasks, implicit practice in, 301–302
Competition, 218–220
Concomitant learnings, 48–52, 201
Concrete-to-abstract approach, 325–326
Conditioning, explanation, 34
  experiments supporting, 34–35
  illustrations, 33
  in teaching, 35
Constancy of IQ, 137–139
Construct validity, 528–529
Constructiveness, effect of frustration on, 406
Contiguity in learning, 34–35, 47, 280–281
Cooperation, 218–220
Counseling, 458–460
Creative self, 478–480
Crutches as aids in learning, 330–332
Cues, identifiability and learning, 38–39, 309–311
  responding to variations in, 292, 338–340
Curricular validity, 527–528
Curriculum, courses, 4, 12–14
  definition, 12
  historical background, 4
  and mental health, 451–453
  of modern school, 5, 12–14
    elementary school subjects in, 12
    personal-social experiences in, 14
    secondary school subjects in, 12–14
Curriculum guides, children's interests and needs, 17
  cultural heritage, 15
  individual differences, 20
  local resources, 18

Curriculum guides, organization, types, 20
  readiness, 19
  social utility, 16
  society's changing needs, 16
  transfer of training, 17

Davis-Eells Test of General Intelligence, 119–121
Defense mechanisms, classification, 414–420
  effect on learning, 46–47, 419–420, 423
  learning of, 413–414
Democratic teacher guidance, 484–486
Denial as defense mechanism, 415
Developmental sequence, in achieving efficiency, 330–332
  as sign of readiness, 97–98
Developmental tasks, 81–84
Diagnostic and remedial teaching, 197–201
Diagnostic tests, 100, 518–522
Differential abilities, 124–128, 183
Differential aptitude tests, 125–128
Differentiated curricula, 174
Discipline, classroom management, 488–493
  as self-discipline, 489–490
Discriminations in learning, 292
Displaced hostility, 417–418
Distributed practice, effectiveness, 298–300
Disuse in forgetting, 376
Drill in learning, 298

Educational psychology, 3–6
Effective learning, conditions, 53–54, 56–57
  in diagnostic and remedial teaching, 198–201
  in guidance of social learning, 466–468, 490–493
  in mental health guidance, 454–455
  methods, 308–333
  in teaching science, 54–55
Emotional disturbances, of learning, 46–47, 201, 401–403
  explanation, 403–404
  of problem solving, 401–403
Environment, effect on intellectual development, 140–144, 183–184
Evaluation, of *all* learning objectives, 507–508
  of modern education, 25–27
Exceptional children, education of, 180–196
Experience, effect on development, 93–95

Failure, effect, on aspiration, 223
  on mental health, 201, 222
  as motivation, 198, 222–224
Feedback in learning, 276–277
Flanagan Aptitude Classification Tests, 128

Interpretations of stimuli, extended beyond the given, 243–245
Interviewing in appraising mental health, 443–444
Intraclass grouping, criteria for, 167–168
variations, 165–169
Intraindividual differences, 84–85, 127, 162–163, 228–229, 512–514

Job analyses in efficient learning, 326–330

Knauber Art-Ability Test, 129
Knowledge of progress, 224–225
Kuder Preference Record, 228–230
Kuhlman-Finch tests (of intelligence), 121–122

Language, development, 75–76
experience in, 93–94
maturation in, 89–92
Latent learning, 42–43
Learning, definition, 52–53
efficiency of, factors affecting, 308–330
essential conditions, 53–54, 56–57
in diagnostic and remedial teaching, 198–201
in guidance of social learning, 466–468
in mental health guidance, 454–455
in teaching, of science, 53–55
of self-discipline, 490–493
improvement, 307–308
as problem solving, 48–49
role of cognitive maps, 41–42, 45–47, 242–243
Learning curves, 37–38, 40, 249, 251, 253, 271, 278, 281, 282, 301
Learning difficulties of able children, 196–197
diagnostic and remedial teaching for, 197–201
Learning how to learn, 253, 307–308, 347–350, 355–357
Learning theories, basic concepts, 47–48
classification, 32–33
cognitive-processes theory, 41–47, 242–246
conditioned-response theory, 33–36, 49
trial-and-error, reinforcement theory, 36–41
Lewerenz Tests in Fundamental Abilities of Visual Art, 129
Lorge-Thorndike intelligence test, 122–123

Maladjustment, characteristics, 403–404
correction and prevention, 451–462
effects on learning, 46–47, 404, 409–412

Maladjustment, factors affecting, 401, 422
parent-child relations, 447–450
and frustration tolerance, 409–412
incidence, 434
theory, 403–404, 420–424
Mastery role, in motivation, 222–224
in retention, 381–383
in transfer, 357–358
Maturation, 88–93
Meaningfulness, in learning, 316–319
in retention, 377–379
Meier Art Judgment Test, 129–130
Memorizing, 293, 308–309, 316–318
improvement, 355–357
Memory traces, 376, 391–393
Mental age, meaning, 112–114, 135–136
as sign of readiness, 90–91
Mental development, constancy of rate, 137–139
factors affecting, 139–146
biological determinants, 144–146
educational stimulation, 140–142
home care, 143–144
institutionalization, 143–144
medical treatment, 144
personality, 139–140
socioeconomic status, 142–143
Mental health, appraisals, 434–446
characteristics, 399
as condition of effective learning, 398–400
development, 420–422, 446–447
provisions for, in teaching, 201, 453–457
role in, of home, 446–450
of school, 450–462
and school accomplishment, 398–400
Mental health consultants, 461–462
Mental health guidance, conditions of learning in, 454–455
example, 427–433
individualization, 455–457
procedures, 431–433, 451–462
role in, of curriculum, 451–453
of parent-teacher cooperation, 460–461
of peer relations, 457–458
of professional consultants, 461–462
of teacher counseling, 458–460
of teaching procedures, 453–457
Mental immaturity, effects on learning, 61–62
Mental set, in forgetting, 375–376
in remembering, 387–388
in transfer, 350–351
Mentally retarded children, 188–196
attainments, 195–196
characteristics, 189–191
curriculum and methods for, 194–195
goals for, 193–194
in heterogeneous classes, 191–192
identification, 193
special class for, 192–193

Methods of learning, effect, on retention, 383
    on transfer, 343, 355–357
    improvement, 307–308
Minnesota Mechanical Ability Tests, 131
Minnesota Multiphasic Personality Inventory, 439–440
Mistakes in learning, 281–282
Modern school, accomplishments, 19, 26
    challenge, 26–27
    criticisms, 25–26
    curriculum, 4–11
    example, 22–25
    objectives, 7–11
Motivation, classroom illustrations, 207–211
    defined, 206–207
    effects, on learning, 211–213, 232–233
        on perception, 213–214, 243–246
        on retention, 387–389
    teaching provisions for, 235
    theory, 234–235
        illustrated, 235–238
Motive-incentive conditions, classification, 216–217
    evaluation, 217–233
Motives, development, 215
    kinds, 215–216
Motor abilities and skills, 70–73
    emergence, 71
    improvements in, 71–72
    organization of, 72–73
    role in development, of experience, 93
        of maturation, 88–89

Need to achieve, 212–213
Nonpromotion, 175–176
Norms for tests, 114, 116–117, 119, 121–122, 127, 130–131, 146, 512, 514, 520

Objective tests, 522–524
Objectives, educational psychology, 3
    elementary school, 8–9
    general, 7, 241
    secondary school, 9–11
Observation in appraising, of academic achievement, 525–527
    of mental health, 435
Organization of concepts, effects, on curriculum, 20–22
    in learning, 322–325
    in retention, 379–381, 386–387
    in transfer, 346–347
    patterns, 322–325
    role of practice in, 293
Otis Quick-Scoring Mental Ability Tests, 118–119
Overachiever, mental health of, 399
Over-all view in learning, 319–321

Overlearning, effects, on retention, 381–383
    on transfer, 357–358

Parent-child relations, effect, on mental health, 446–450
    on self-concept, 474–475
Parent-teacher conference, in appraising achievement, 508
    in mental health guidance, 460–461
Participation chart, 495–497
Peer relations, in mental health guidance, 457–458
    and self-concept, 476–478
Percentile scores, 127, 512–514
Perception, of effects, factors affecting efficiency of, 279–281
    role in learning, 276–279
    teaching provisions for, 285–290
        self-checking, 285–286
        special devices, 288–290
        teacher checking, 286–288
        tests, 290
    of things, factors affecting, 243–246
    in infancy, 242
Personal-social learning, 14, 466–468
Personality, organization of traits in, 84–87
Personality questionnaires, 438–442
Personality tests, 438–446
Phonetics in reading and spelling, 345–347, 354–355
Physical growth, individual differences in, 66–70
    predictability, 70
    rates, 66–69
    trends, 66–67
Physiological drives, 215
Practice, definition, 270–271, 273–276
    factors affecting efficiency of, 276, 295–302
    processes requiring, 291–295, 303
        automatizing responses, 292–293
        discovering solutions, 294–295
        generalizing responses, 291–292
        imitating complex patterns, 294
        making discriminative responses, 292
        refining skills, 293
    as repetition, 273–275
    role of discovery in, 275–276
Practice opportunities, efficient use, by distribution of time, 298–300
    by drill, 298
    by functional practice, 295–298
    by implicit and explicit practice, 301–302
    by systematic practice, 297–298
    by warm-up, 300–301
Praise as motivation, 221–222
Predictive validity, 148–154, 528–529

Transfer of training, role, in teaching, 360–
  362
  spelling, 354–355
Trial-and-check process in learning, 270–276,
  282
Trial-and-error learning, illustrations, 36–38,
  271–272
  reinforcement in explanation, 38–41
Two-factor explanation of learning, 48–52,
  424

Underachiever, mental health of, 399–400

Validity of tests, of academic achievement,
  157–158, 527–529
  of differential abilities, 152–154

Validity of tests, of intelligence, 148–152
  of "practical" aptitudes, 154
Verbalization, in discriminating, 313
  effectiveness in learning, 311–312, 314–
  316
  in generalizing, 313–314
  in perceptual-motor learning, 312
  in remembering, 312–313
Vocabulary, growth, 75
  and intelligence, 113, 115 .

Warm-up role in practice, 300–301
Wechsler Adult Intelligence Scale, 114–116
Wechsler Intelligence Scale for Children,
  114–118
Whole versus part methods, 321–322